AN INTRODUCTION TO
THE THEOLOGY OF THE NEW TESTAMENT

AN INTRODUCTION TO
THE THEOLOGY OF THE
NEW TESTAMENT

ALAN RICHARDSON

SCM PRESS LTD

334 00709 7

First published 1958
by SCM Press Ltd
58 Bloomsbury Street, London WC1
Eighth impression 1979

Printed in Great Britain by
Fletcher & Son Ltd, Norwich

CONTENTS

PREFACE

PERHAPS it is desirable to explain what is implied in the title of this book, since the propriety of writing 'theologies' of the Old and New Testaments is called in question in some quarters today. There are those who deny that there can be such a thing as a theology of the New Testament; yet the leading British New Testament scholar can use as the sub-title of one of his most influential books, 'The sub-structure of New Testament theology'.[1] Is it right to assume that the apostolic Church possessed a common theology and that it can be reconstructed from the New Testament literature? The only way to show that this question can be answered in the affirmative is to frame an hypothesis concerning the underlying theology of the New Testament documents and then to test the hypothesis by reference to the text of those documents in the light of all available critical and historical knowledge. If this task is one of the systematic exegesis of all the books of the New Testament at once, it may be said to transcend what is usually understood by exegesis by reason of the all-inclusive character of its induction or hypothesis; if it is thought of as a task which falls within the scope of descriptive (history-of-religion) science, then it is one which supremely illustrates the truth that there can be no history (whether of religion or of anything else) which does not depend upon a principle of interpretation, which the historian must necessarily bring to his study.[2]

This, then, is what is meant by New Testament theology in the title of this book: the framing of an hypothesis concerning the content and character of the faith of the apostolic Church, and the testing of this hypothesis in the light of all available techniques of New Testament scholarship, historical, critical, literary, philological, archaeological, and so on. Once this definition of New Testament theology has been understood, the objections most commonly levelled against it cannot be sustained. It is objected, for instance, that biblical theology reads into the scriptural text certain dogmatic affirmations and then ignores all inconvenient literary and historical facts; or again it is objected that

---

[1] C. H. Dodd, *According to the Scriptures*, 1953.

[2] See Alan Richardson, *Christian Apologetics*, 1947, Chap. IV; also a suggestive article, 'The Problem of Old Testament Theology and the History of Religion', by James Barr in *The Canadian Journal of Theology*, Vol. III, 1957, No. 3. The terms of its discussion are relevant to the issues involved in the consideration of New Testament theology.

it replaces the spirit of impartial scientific enquiry by the temper of the dogmatic theologian, so that the study is precluded because the conclusions are prescribed. Such objections are based upon a misconception of the nature of scientific method. New Testament theology is 'scientific' in just the same way as any other science is scientific: the scientist never starts with an empty mind; he gets a 'hunch', frames an hypothesis, and then devises experiments to see whether the observable data can be 'seen' better in this new way. A Newton or an Einstein has a 'hunch' about a wider uniformity in the behaviour of falling apples and revolving planets; but the nub of the matter, namely, the all-important business of verification, lies in devising means of testing the hypothesis. Here the natural scientist's task is much easier than that of the historian, who cannot 'repeat the experiment'. But the scientific procedure is essentially the same. New Testament theology likewise begins with an hypothesis which, it is claimed, makes 'sense' (i.e. in this context, 'history') of all the historical data of the New Testament and its period; it devises tests based upon the rigorous methods of modern theological science—philological, critical, historical, etc.—whereby the hypothesis can be evaluated and by which it can be weighed against alternative hypotheses. So specialized nowadays has biblical scholarship become that the New Testament theologian must rely upon the expert studies of scholars in many fields, the scholars who themselves are not immediately concerned with ultimate hypotheses and meanings, but who (in Lord Acton's phrase) 'get their meals in the kitchen'; he must take the conclusions of all the manifold and detailed investigations in every relevant field of scholarship and evaluate 'hypotheses'—his own and those of others—in the light of them. The task, of course, lies beyond the competence of one man; and yet it must be attempted. We must all have *some* notion at the back of our minds about the meaning of the New Testament as a whole, and it is just as well that some people should try to say what it is. We can hardly decide whether we will hold a New Testament theology; we can decide only whether it is to be one which has been carefully pondered and criticized or one which we have acquired more or less uncritically and subconsciously and which is now kept in the ideological lumber-room of our minds which we never visit. Even the sternest critics of 'New Testament theology' possess such a room, although they may have lost the key to it.

Those who have reflected little upon the nature of scientific method usually subscribe to the illusion that the scientist collects a lot of facts and that, when he has discovered enough of them, he will find that they are arranged in or conform to an orderly pattern or law. Actually, of course, the reverse is the truth: the scientist, with a flash of insight (some such word is unavoidable here), lights upon his new hypothesis, and *then* he discovers facts which corroborate it. He *sees* them because now he is looking for them: without the hypothesis—the hunch, the flash, the intuition—he would never have seen them because he would not have known what he was looking for. The mind of the historian works in just the same way as that of the natural scientist; after all, it is the same human instrument, but it is directed to a different range of human experience. He thinks of (or accepts from others) his principle of interpretation first, and it suggests to him his 'hypothesis' (if we may so continue to speak); then he spends hours of research elucidating the 'facts' which it illuminates and which in turn support it. This does not mean that one principle of interpretation in history is as good as another, any more than it means that one scientific hypothesis is no 'truer' than another. It means that what facts are *seen* will depend upon the principle of interpretation from which we start. That is why New Testament theology, when written by Christians, will necessarily begin with apostolic faith, but when written by liberal humanists, will begin with (not merely conclude with) the conviction that the achievement of Jesus and his Church must be explained in terms of what great and good men can accomplish. There is no 'objective' historical ground from which the two positions can be 'scientifically' evaluated; there is no neutral territory from which the philosopher or historian can pronounce upon their 'truth'. As Professor Barr remarks, historical investigation can tell us that Jeremiah maintained that God had given Jerusalem into the hands of Nebuchadnezzar; but it cannot tell us whether in fact God acted in history or not. Similarly historical theology can perhaps tell us whether the apostles believed that God had raised Christ from the dead; but it cannot tell us whether he did in fact do so. No human science can investigate God or his action in history. Science (including historical science) cannot evaluate the principles of interpretation by which it itself proceeds. The statement 'The apostles mistakenly believed that Christ rose from the dead' is neither more nor less scientific than the statement 'Christ rose from the dead'. Neither statement is capable of scientific verification. It would, however, be preposterous to argue that therefore both statements are meaningless: otherwise how could they be recognized to contradict each other? If, then, New Testament theology cannot demonstrate ultimate theological propositions scientifically, what is the use of it?

New Testament theology, in the sense in which this book employs the term, cannot 'prove' historical (or theological) hypotheses, but it can test them. It can shew that some hypotheses are better than others, because they enable more facts to be 'seen' in a coherent way. It is, in fact, constantly devising tests for hypotheses, even if it is not always putting forward new hypotheses. (It may be doubted whether any really *new* hypotheses can ever now be put forward; in this matter we may ask, in the words of the Preacher, 'Is there a thing whereof men say, See, this is new?'). And it is always modifying hypotheses in the light of new knowledge and of changing perspectives; for the ultimate solutions are never finally formulated, and each hypothesis must be stated afresh in each new age of history. The task of making 'the theology of the New Testament' is one which has to be done over and over again, not only by reason of the accumulation of new knowledge but also because of the changed spirit or temper of each period of history. No generation looks at history from the same perspective as its predecessor, and this is why no final history is ever written and why every generation must re-write history. Because Christianity is an *historical* faith, there can never be a final theology of the New Testament. Even the attitudes of purely literary criticism change from one generation to another. It is a mistake to suppose that it is the accumulation of scientific data which is chiefly responsible for the constant need of the restatement of man's apprehensions of ultimate truth.

From the point of view of the committed Christian, New Testament theology involves the unrelenting effort at restatement of the faith of the Church of Jesus Christ in the light of changing attitudes and of new knowledge. It is a perennial necessity in the matter of what St Paul calls ἡ ἀπολογία καὶ βεβαίωσις τοῦ εὐαγγελίου. It cannot prove an hypothesis to be true; but it is always possible to shew that one hypothesis is better than another. In this book, for instance, the hypothesis is defended that Jesus himself is the author of the brilliant re-interpretation of the Old Testament scheme of salvation ('Old Testament theology') which is found in the New Testament, and that the events of the life, 'signs', passion and resurrection of Jesus, as attested by the apostolic witness, can account for the 'data' of the New Testament better than any other hypothesis current today. It makes better 'sense', or better history, than, for instance, the hypothesis that St Paul (or someone else) transformed the simple ethical monotheism of a young Jewish carpenter-rabbi into a new mystery-religion of the dying-and-rising-god pattern with the crucified rabbi as its cult-hero. In this book an attempt is made to articulate clearly the principle of interpretation which gives rise to the hypothesis here defended; that is why in the first chapter the basic conception of *faith* is discussed. No pretence is made of remaining within the limits of purely descriptive science, as in those theologies of the New Testament which conceal their real principle of interpretation, and profess as a matter of 'objective' history to trace the evolution ('history-of-religion') of Christianity from its beginnings as a simple Jewish ethical pietism through its obscuration under layers of apocalyptic fanaticism and Hellenistic mysticism to its final emergence into the full-blown 'Gnostic Catholicism' of the second-century Church. In other words, the principle of interpretation here employed is that of historic Christian faith, and the thesis is defended that it enables us to present a more coherently and rationally satisfying 'history' than do the liberal-humanist or existentialist principles of interpretation which have latterly been used in the construction of other 'theologies' of the New Testament.

Those who have reflected little upon what may be called the methodology of theological science, whether they be hard-working scholars engaged in the pursuit of the regular theological disciplines or (as they would call themselves) 'simple' preachers and teachers of the Gospel, may wonder what all this talk of 'hypotheses' and 'ultimate meanings' is about. Let them be reassured. We are only re-stating in terms of the contemporary discussion of scientific methodology a truth which has long been known to be true of both science and theology. It has long been recognized that the physicist's or historian's insight is what enables him to perceive not merely the significance of certain facts, but even the facts themselves, and that apart from such insight the meaning of what is seen will entirely disappear. This recognition, which underlies all scientific investigation, is crucial for theology. It was clearly enunciated by St Augustine in his famous formula, *Nisi credideritis, non intelligetis.*[1] A proper understanding of Christian origins or of New Testament history is possible only through the insight of Christian faith. If unfaith can provide a reasonable, coherent and intellectually satisfying account of the New Testament data, the Christian faith is otiose; but until we are confronted with a more credible 'theology of the New Testament' based on humanist or existentialist insights than anything which has so far appeared, we shall continue to believe that acceptance of the apostolic witness to Christ's Lordship and to his resurrection makes better sense of the historical evidence than any other hypothesis. The relation, then, of New Testament theology to faith is this: that it provides the means by which we may always be ready with an ἀπολογία whenever we are asked what is the λόγος of our Christian hope. In an age of confusion and uncertainty it is the instrument whereby we can know the ἀσφάλεια of the things in which we were instructed. Therefore New Testament theology is not something which can be left by the preachers and teachers of the churches to specialists

[1] E.g. *In Joan. Evang.* XXIX, 6; *Serm. de Script. NT*, CXXVI, 1.1. See Richardson, *Christian Apologetics*, Chap. X, and also footnote on p. 19 *infra*.

in universities and seminaries: it concerns the Sunday sermon, the Bible class, the catechism, and indeed the whole of the life of the local church. If this book does not help in the task of preaching the faith of Jesus Christ in the second half of the twentieth century, it will have failed in its purpose; it was not written as an academic exercise.

Perhaps one further word might be added to help those who may be puzzled by the direction taken by New Testament scholarship in the last decade or two, when it has seemed as if the 'assured results' of more than half a century's New Testament research have come unstuck. If what we have said about the nature of New Testament theology has been assimilated, and if we see that it partakes of the character of *fides quaerens intellectum*, then we shall be in a better position to understand, or at least to appreciate, a rather curious paradox in the realm of recent New Testament interpretation. Confidence in the historian's ability to trace 'objectively', or in a presupposition-less manner, the development of the theology of the Church in the New Testament period has often gone hand-in-hand with scepticism concerning the apostolic testimony: the witness of the apostles (which is, after all, the only first-hand evidence we possess) is explained away as 'first-century mythology' or 'mere *Gemeindetheologie*' or something of the kind, in order that a modern 'scientific' explanation may be put in its place. Belief in 'scientific history' has tended to lead to the repudiation of the apostolic witness. On the other hand, scepticism about the historian's ability to reconstruct 'what happened', or about his ability to perceive any 'facts' at all except through the spectacles of his own presuppositions, often goes hand-in-hand with the whole-hearted acceptance of the apostolic testimony. Thus, we are confronted by the paradox of contemporary New Testament studies, that those who deeply scandalize the older 'liberal' scholars by their readiness to detect symbols and images in what until recently seemed to be purely 'factual' narrative, and thus seem to reduce the historical factor in the New Testament to shadowy proportions, nevertheless seem to have no difficulty in believing the *kerugma* of Jesus's divine Sonship, of his resurrection and his return in Judgment. The 'conclusions' of the liberal or 'historicizing' critics have been stood upon their head: what the liberals deemed to be mythology has become history and their history has become mythology. No wonder the conservatives are bewildered nowadays—and the conservatives are, of course, the liberals. Time has made ancient good uncouth. It has become apparent that we cannot build a theology of the New Testament—whether an orthodox one, like Gore's, or an heretical one, like Bultmann's—upon an imaginary bed-rock of objective historical 'fact'. No wonder that a discussion of the methodology of theological science is being called for. No wonder that the layman or the hard-pressed parochial clergyman (who, of course, has 'no time to keep up with his reading', other things being so much more important than the ministry of the Word) is perplexed when he hears that, for example, St Luke 'the historian' has turned out to be a highly allusive and symbolical rabbinic theologian who stylizes history in order to convey his profound insight into the meaning and truth of the Gospel. Perhaps St Luke realized (better than we have done) that the re-presentation of historical truth is required in every generation of Church history, if Theophilus is to know the ἀσφάλεια of the catechism which he has learned. Perhaps St Luke knew (better than we have known) that Theophilus needs to be given instruction in New Testament theology. It is hoped that this book will do something to explain to those who are perplexed by the revolution in theological method which has taken place during the last decade or two how it comes about that the things in which we have been instructed, though they have lost one kind of ἀσφάλεια, have gained another.

It remains only for the author to acknowledge his indebtedness to many teachers. It is obvious that such a work as this must rely upon the labours of scholars in many branches of biblical research. In the nature of the case it has been practicable to mention by name only those to whom a specific debt is owed, or those in whose writings the student will find especial help upon particular topics. A debt of gratitude is owed to many others besides those mentioned in the Index of Authors. Acknowledgment is also gladly made of the generous help in the arduous task of proof-reading which has been received from Mrs C. J. Fordyce and my colleague Dr R. P. C. Hanson. Finally the author wishes to express his deep appreciation of the assistance which has been given to him by the staff of the Student Christian Movement Press at every stage of the production of this book, and in particular by Miss Kathleen Downham, the Assistant Editor, without whose practical encouragement there might have appeared a decidedly inferior product at a much later date.

ALAN RICHARDSON

Nottingham,
All Saints' Day,
1957

ABBREVIATIONS

Acc. Scrip.		C. H. Dodd, *According to the Scriptures*, 1953.
Aq.	.	Aquila's version of the Greek OT (2nd cent. A.D.).
ARSV	.	American Revised Standard Version of the Holy Bible, 1952.
Auct. Heb.		The writer of the Epistle to the Hebrews.
AV .	.	The Authorized Version of Holy Scripture, 1611; known in America as the King James Version.
BCP	.	The Book of Common Prayer and Administration of the Sacraments . . . according to the Use of the Church of England, 1662.
CD .	.	The Damascus Document (trans. in R. H. Charles, *Apocrypha and Pseudepigrapha of the Old Testament*, II, 1913; see also C. Rabin, *The Zadokite Documents*, 1954; also Gaster, *SDSS* [below], 71-94).
Cl. lit.	.	Classical literature.
DCG	.	Hastings' *Dictionary of Christ and the Gospels*, 2 vols., 1906, 1908.
ET .	.	English translation.
EVV	.	English Versions of Holy Scripture (AV and RV).
GSJ	.	C. K. Barrett, *The Gospel according to St John*, 1955.
HDB	.	Hastings' *Dictionary of the Bible*, 5 vols., 1898-1904.
ICC	.	International Critical Commentary.
IFG	.	C. H. Dodd, *The Interpretation of the Fourth Gospel*, 1953.
Joh. lit.	.	Johannine literature.
JTS	.	*Journal of Theological Studies.*
L .	.	Material peculiar to St Luke's Gospel.
LXX	.	The Septuagint Version of the Old Testament (edition used, A. Rahlfs, *Septuaginta*, 2 vols., Stuttgart, 1935).
M .	.	Material peculiar to St Matthew's Gospel.
NS .	.	New Series.
NT .	.	New Testament.
OL .	.	Old Latin versions of the Holy Scriptures (*c.* A.D. 150-200).
OT .	.	Old Testament.
PRJ	.	W. D. Davies, *Paul and Rabbinic Judaism*, 1948.
Q .	.	Material common to St Matthew's and St Luke's Gospels but not found in St Mark's; nothing is implied concerning a documentary 'source' by the use of this symbol.

1 QS   .   *The Manual of Discipline* (of the Dead Sea Sect); see Millar Burrows, *The Dead Sea Scrolls*, 1956 (New York, 1955); also next item below.

SDSS   .   T. H. Gaster, *The Scriptures of the Dead Sea Sect*, 1957 (*The Dead Sea Scriptures*, Doubleday Anchor Books, Garden City, N.Y., 1956).

SJT   .   *Scottish Journal of Theology.*

SNT   .   K. Stendahl, *The Scrolls and the New Testament*, 1958 (New York, 1957).

Symm.   .   Symmachus' Greek version of the OT (late 2nd cent. A.D.).

Strack-Bill.   H. L. Strack and P. Billerbeck, *Kommentar zum Neuen Testament aus Talmud und Midrasch*, 4 vols., Munich, 1922-28.

Th. .   .   Theodotion's Greek version of the OT (*c.* A.D. 180-190).

TWBB   .   Alan Richardson (ed.), *A Theological Word Book of the Bible*, 1950.

TWNT   .   G. Kittel (ed.), *Theologisches Wörterbuch zum Neuen Testament*, Stuttgart, 1933—.

Vulg.   .   The Vulgate, St Jerome's Latin version of the Holy Scriptures.

WH   .   *The New Testament in the Original Greek;* the text revised by B. F. Westcott and F. J. A. Hort, 1896.

I

FAITH AND HEARING

IT is fitting to begin a consideration of the theology of the New Testament with a study of the fundamental concept of faith, since apart from faith the inward meaning of the NT is unintelligible. 'If you will not believe, you shall not understand.'[1] There is nothing in the OT which exactly corresponds to the NT concept of faith (πίστις); πίστις and πιστεύειν are rare in LXX. In the OT God is the faithful one, unchanging and ever loyal to his covenant and promise. This truth is, of course, reaffirmed in the NT: 'He is faithful (πιστός) that promised' (Heb. 10.23; cf. Rom. 3.3; I Thess. 5.24; II Thess. 3.3). The OT insists that man on his side must be faithful to God, i.e. trustful, obedient, steadfast, and confidently relying upon God's faithfulness as upon a rock in a turbulent sea (e.g. Isa. 26.3f.), or as a wife who is faithful to her husband (e.g. Hos. 2.20). 'The righteous will live by his steadfast trust' (Hab. 2.4)—a text which St Paul will use in a free (non-LXX) translation for his own purposes (Rom. 1.17; Gal. 3.11; cp. Heb. 10.38).[2] This OT sense of confident and steadfast reliance upon the faithful promises of God is frequently found in the NT, especially in Hebrews, where faith is defined as the giving of substance to things hoped for and the proving of things not (yet) seen (Heb. 11.1): we prove for ourselves the reality of the unseen only by trusting ourselves to God's faithfulness. Then we understand the truth, and only then (11.3). It was by faith of this kind that all the heroes of the OT had accomplished their mighty and heroic feats (Heb. 11 *passim*). Jesus himself is the great exemplar of faithfulness in this sense ('the captain and perfecter of faith', 12.2), for he had endured the cross and every infirmity and temptation known to us (4.15; cf. 2.17f.). St Paul prefers to call hope (ἐλπίς) what Hebrews speaks of as faith: 'we hope for that which we see not' (Rom. 8.25); nevertheless Paul too can use πίστις and πιστός in the OT sense (Rom. 3.3; I Cor. 1.9; 10.13; Gal. 3.9),

---

[1] *Nisi credideritis, non intelligetis*, the sentence which St Augustine was so fond of quoting from the OL of Isa. 7.9. The OL follows the LXX, but Vulg. and EVV follow the Hebrew: 'If ye will not believe, surely ye shall not be established.' St Augustine enunciates a profound principle of biblical theology, but the Heb. text illustrates the rôle of 'believing' in OT usage (cf. Isa. 26.3f.; Hab. 2.4).

[2] See *infra*, 235.

and it is quite impossible to discover any single meaning for all of Paul's varied uses of πίστις. But in general the NT, and Paul in particular, go far beyond the OT conception of faith. The lament of the OT prophets had been that, though God had remained faithful to his covenant, Israel had again and again proved faithless; and they despaired of Israel's ability to recover herself unless God intervened and gave to Israel a new heart and a new spirit and made a new covenant with a new creation (Jer. 31.31-4; Ezek. 37.14, 26, etc.). God must himself give or create the faith which he demands. According to the NT this was precisely what had happened through the establishing of the new covenant of the Lord Jesus Christ. Therefore in the NT faith becomes primarily faith in Jesus Christ, who is himself both the object and the giver of the faith of his disciples. It was Jesus himself who taught his disciples the cardinal necessity of faith.

THE TEACHING OF JESUS ABOUT FAITH

St Mark's summary of the Galilean preaching of Jesus represents it as a demand for repentance and faith in view of the drawing nigh of the reign of God (Mark 1.15). The Synoptic accounts of the teaching of Jesus indicate that he constantly appealed for faith—faith in the good news that God's reign had drawn nigh, or faith in himself as being in some way the sign that God's reign was at hand. Such faith was, of course, faith in God, but not merely in the sense that every Jew confessed his faith in God every time he recited the *Shema'*. It was believing that God was *even now* accomplishing his purpose, the καιρός having been fulfilled, and that he was, in spite of all opposition and of all appearances to the contrary, bringing in his reign (Mark 11.22). Jesus did not publicly proclaim himself to be the Messiah, and (if St Mark is to be accepted as historical in this matter) his own disciples did not recognize him as the Messiah until his public ministry was drawing to its close (Mark 8.27-30); even then they were bidden to keep silence. Yet from the beginning of his preaching Jesus had looked for faith in his own person. In what sense, then, did he expect people to believe in him? His own self-designation, 'Son of Man', provides us with the clue. The Son of Man was the *sign* vouchsafed to that generation that the New Age was dawning.[1] Jesus selected the title for this very reason; he took it from the Book of Ezekiel, in which the prophet had used it some 90 times of himself. It is rare in the rest of the OT, and it seems not to have been in general use in our Lord's day as a title of the Messiah.[2]

[1] See a suggestive and instructive art. by E. J. Tinsley in *SJT*, Vol. 8, No. 3 September, 1955, 297-306.
[2] See *infra*, 130-2.

Ezekiel had regarded himself as a sign vouchsafed to his generation (as indeed other prophets had regarded themselves; cf. Isa. 8.18; see esp. Ezek. 12.6; 24.24). The son of man, Ezekiel, had been sent to speak God's word to the house of Israel, whether they would hear or whether they would forbear (3.4, 11, etc.): 'He that heareth let him hear' (3.27). The Son of Man, Jesus, is also sent to proclaim God's word to the house of Israel (Matt. 10.6), and he cries, 'He that hath ears to hear, let him hear' (Mark 4.9, etc.; esp. Matt. 11.15—John the Baptist as a sign).

Jesus's conception of himself as a sign must be understood against the general biblical teaching about signs. In the OT signs both confirm faith and test it. Men are tempted to reject the sign which God gives and to demand signs of their own devising and thus to provoke or 'tempt' God by their unbelief (Ex. 17.7; Num. 14.11; Deut. 9.22; Pss. 78 *passim*; 95.8-10; 106 *passim*). Jesus himself is tempted in the Wilderness to ask for signs of his own choosing, but, unlike the Old Israel, he overcomes the temptation (Matt. 4.1-11; Luke 4.1-13). Jesus upbraids the contemporary generation of Pharisees and Sadducees, who ought to have been able to discern the signs of the times ($\kappa\alpha\iota\rho o\iota$), because they do not understand; even the pagan Ninevites had repented at the sign of the prophet Jonah, and the Queen of the South had recognized the sign of Solomon (Matt. 16.1-4; Luke 11.29-32). No sign other than that which was given—himself—would be vouchsafed to this generation (Mark 8.11f.). His mighty works were not the signs for which disobedient Israel was looking, but even heathen Tyre and Sidon would have understood and repented if they had seen the acts of power which had been done in Chorazin and Bethsaida (Matt. 11.20-24; Luke 10.13). Jesus did not perform his miracles in order to compel men to believe against their will, but he nevertheless regarded his miracles as signs to those who had eyes to see: men without faith would find them not signs ($\sigma\eta\mu\epsilon\hat{\iota}\alpha$) but mere wonders ($\tau\acute{\epsilon}\rho\alpha\tau\alpha$), and he himself, the true Sign, would be for them a stumbling-block ($\sigma\kappa\acute{\alpha}\nu\delta\alpha\lambda o\nu$) (Matt. 11.2-6; Luke 7.19-23). It seems clear that Jesus regarded John the Baptist as well as himself as one of 'the signs of the times' (Matt. 11.7-19; Luke 7.24-35). As God had given to the Old Israel signs of his redemptive activity when he led his people forth from Egypt, across the Red Sea and through the Wilderness, so now he was setting forth the signs of his still mightier redemption at the drawing nigh of the Kingdom of God. Many of the recorded acts of Jesus in the Synoptic Gospels are set forth as fulfilments of the story of redemption told in the Law (i.e. the Pentateuch), which the prophets had declared must be fulfilled. 'The Son of Man goeth even as it is written of him' (Mark 14.21);

the Scriptures were fulfilled (Mark 14.49). Each of the Synoptists under-
lines this truth in his own way. Jesus is baptized in the Jordan as Israel
had been in the Red Sea (cf. I Cor. 10.2); he sojourns in the Wilderness
forty days, being tempted, as Israel was tempted (or tempted God)
forty years long; on a mountain he calls a New Israel and appoints the
Twelve (Mark 3.13-19) and gives a New Law (Matt. 5.1; Luke 6.12-49);
on a mountain he stands transfigured with Moses and Elijah, who each
had of old time encountered God on Horeb; he gives the signs of the
Bread from Heaven, as Moses and Elisha once had done. Finally he
goes up to take his Kingdom, passing as the old Joshua (Gk., Jesus)
had done through Jericho; and before he departs he ratifies a new
covenant in his blood and institutes a new passover which his disciples
shall keep until his return in glory.

Such in briefest outline is the way in which the Gospels (and the NT
as a whole) set forth the course of the historical life of Jesus. Many
other details, as will be noted in the following pages, elaborate this
basic conception of Jesus as himself the New Israel who accomplishes
and brings to its triumphant conclusion the rôle which the Old Israel
essayed but did not complete. Where the Old Israel had failed, the New
Israel conquered. The Scriptures were fulfilled; the story of redemption
was concluded. Since the rise of modern biblical scholarship the question has been asked, Who first thought of this way of setting forth the
significance of the historical life of Jesus? Every conceivable kind of
answer has been given. It could not have been the Evangelists who first
thought of it, because St Paul knew it long before St Mark's Gospel
was written. It could hardly have been St Paul, if we may trust the
evidence which he himself supplies, including, of course, his own pro-
testations of loyalty to the Gospel which he had received. Could it,
then, have been the community at large, the Church into which St
Paul was baptized? Some scholars have assumed that the early Christian
community collectively worked out the theology of Christ as the fulfilment of the Scriptures. Such a conclusion, however, is not convincing,
because communities do not think out such brilliant reconstructions
as this uniquely original reinterpretation of the OT plan of salvation.
There must have been some profoundly original mind which started
the whole development on its course. Are we to assume that some creative thinker, whose name and whose memory have perished, is the
genius behind the NT theology? Such a conclusion would indeed be an
argumentum ex silentio. There remains only one other possibility: the
mind behind the NT reinterpretation of the OT theology of redemption
was that of Jesus himself. Could any solution be more probable? It was
the Lord himself who first suggested, as much by his deeds (signs) as

by his words, the fundamental lines of the theology of the NT. One gains the impression from reading the Gospels that the disciples were slow to understand what Jesus was trying to teach them during his historical ministry (e.g. Mark 4.40f.; 6.51f.; 8.16-21; 9.32, etc.; cf. Luke 24.25; John 14.9, etc.), and that it was not until after the crucifixion and resurrection that the clues which he had left with them began to shape in their minds a coherent pattern. After the resurrection of Jesus they themselves were conscious that they were being guided by the Spirit of the living Lord into all the truth concerning him (John 16.12-15); the things which the historical Jesus had said to them were now brought vividly to their remembrance through the activity of the Holy Spirit in their midst, and now they understood their inner meaning (John 14.26). This is the hypothesis upon which the argument of this volume is based, and it is our contention that it makes better sense of the NT evidence than does any other; its validity will be tested by its success or failure as a foundation for a coherent and soundly historical account of the theology of the apostolic Church.

THE FAITH OF THE APOSTOLIC CHURCH

Jesus during his ministry had offered himself as a sign of the drawing nigh of God's reign. By their refusal of the sign, Israel was judged and was found wanting, like those who of old had tempted God in the Wilderness. But a remnant of disciples, though they had left him to stand alone when his 'hour' (Mark 14.41)—the hour of the glorification of the Son of Man (John 12.23)—at last came, had their faith reconstituted by the overwhelming events of his resurrection. Henceforward the content of faith was more sharply defined than it could have been during the days of Jesus's ministry. Jesus had challenged men to see in his preaching and his δυνάμεις the evidence of the coming of God's reign: he had demanded faith in himself as the divinely given Sign. Such faith, he had said, enabled a man to see that he was living amidst the convulsions of the End of the Age: the Messiah's feet were even now standing upon the mount of Olives (Zech. 14.4), and by faith the mountain was being cast into the sea (Mark 11.22f.; Rev. 8.8; I Cor. 13.2; cf. Ps. 46.2). The expected Messianic Woes were to fall first upon the Messiah himself, then upon his disciples, and, after a time of unprecedented tribulation for the whole world, the End would come (Mark 13). The crucifixion of Jesus was the fulfilment of the first part of this prophecy; then came his glorious resurrection, which his apostles preached with joy amidst persecutions and sufferings, knowing that upon them had been poured out the Holy Spirit, which the prophets had foretold as the sign of the dawning of the Day of the Lord (Mark

13.9-11; Acts 2.16-21; Joel 2.28-32, etc.). The resurrection of Jesus had become the supreme sign vouchsafed by God that his purpose of the ages had been accomplished in Christ: it was that vindicating sign for which Jesus had refused to ask in the Wilderness or in Gethsemane (Matt. 26.53f.) or on Golgotha (Mark 15.32). Therefore the apostles 'preached Jesus and the resurrection' (Acts 17.18) and everywhere the preachers' word was confirmed by 'consequent signs' (Mark 16.17, 20).

After the events of Easter and Pentecost it was inevitable that faith should now be centred wholly upon Jesus, whom God had clearly and decisively made Lord and Christ, as his resurrection showed (Acts 2.36). Faith is henceforward 'the faith which is through him' (Acts 3.16); it is 'faith in the working of God who raised him from the dead' (Col. 2.12), or, more simply still, 'faith in Jesus Christ' (Gal. 3.22; cf. Acts 16.31, etc.), or 'the faith of Jesus' (Rev. 14.12). To repent and believe the good news is still in the apostolic Church, as it was in the days of Jesus's ministry in Galilee, the condition of salvation: it was necessary to take up an attitude of obedient trustfulness towards the signs which God had given that he was now fulfilling those last days which had been foretold by the prophets of old. It is St Paul who, more explicitly than any other NT writer, stresses the truth that salvation is obtained only by means of the obedient response of faith to the proclamation of God's action in Jesus Christ; faith is for him, in the deepest of the many senses in which he uses the word, the 'yes' of the whole personality to the fact of Christ. Faith in Christ achieves a right relationship with God, a relationship in which all hostility is done away; this relationship is expressed in terms of δικαίωσις (justification), since for Paul salvation means primarily the attainment of δικαιοσύνη (righteousness), which Christians possess through faith in Jesus Christ (Rom. 3.22). The divine righteousness and salvation go forth from God amongst men (cf. Isa. 45.21-25; 46.13; 51.5f.; 54.17), and they are now appropriated through faith in Christ: this is for Paul the heart of the gospel (Rom. 1.16f.).[1]

The object of faith is thus Christ himself, but before men could believe in him, they had first to be told about him, and sometimes the word πίστις is used in the sense of the content of the preaching about Christ, the belief in Christ (e.g. Acts 6.7; 13.8; 14.22; 24.24; Gal. 1.23; Eph. 4.5, 13; I Tim. 4.1; 5.8; Jude 3, 20; Rev. 2.13). The faith, in the sense of the message which the apostles and evangelists proclaimed, was an affirmation of what God had done in Christ. Since the publication of C. H. Dodd's *The Apostolic Preaching* (1936), it has been customary to refer to the original Christian preaching as the *kerugma* and to

[1] See *infra*, 232f.

distinguish it from the Church's doctrinal and ethical teaching (διδαχή) and exhortation (παράκλησις). The first Christian preachers went to the world with a *kerugma*, not with an ethical appeal ('the Sermon on the Mount', etc.). The word κήρυγμα is used six times in the Paulines and Pastorals, and not elsewhere in NT (except Matt. 12.41=Luke 11.32, where however we read of the κήρυγμα of Jonah). 'It was God's good pleasure', writes St Paul, 'through the foolishness of the κήρυγμα to save them that believe' (I Cor. 1.21). The distinction between κήρυγμα and διδαχή is useful provided that we do not think of the Church's preaching as being addressed solely to those who were outside; the Church's most urgent preaching of the faith was and must always be addressed to herself (I Cor. 9.27). The NT makes it abundantly clear that the earliest Christian proclamation was a preaching of the cross and resurrection of Jesus. C. H. Dodd in the book mentioned has shewn that it is possible to discover the apostolic κήρυγμα, dating from the earliest days of the Church, which underlies the whole NT. Its form can be most readily reconstructed from the sermons which St Luke has put into the mouth of St Peter in the early chapters of Acts—sermons which, if they are not the *ipsissima verba* used by St Peter on the occasions specified, nevertheless seem to be sermon-headings used by the preachers of the original Aramaic-speaking Church. The content of the early κήρυγμα as contained in St Peter's speeches has been summarized by Professor Dodd thus: (1) The Age of Fulfilment has dawned, the 'latter days' foretold by the prophets (Acts 2.16; 3.18, 24). (2) This has taken place through the ministry, death and resurrection of Jesus Christ; the Scriptures are cited to shew that the prophets foretold these events. (3) By virtue of the resurrection Jesus has been exalted at the right hand of God as Messianic head of the new Israel (Acts 2.33-6; 3.13; 4.11; 5.31). (4) The Holy Spirit in the Church is the sign of Christ's present power and glory (Acts 2.17-21, 33; 5.32). (5) The Messianic Age will shortly reach its consummation in the return of Christ (Acts 3.20; 10.42). (6) The κήρυγμα closes with an appeal for repentance, the offer of forgiveness and of the Holy Spirit, and the promise of salvation, i.e. the life of the Age to Come (Acts 2.38f.; 3.19, 25f.; 4.12; 5.31; 10.43).[1] In different forms and words this basic 'faith' of the earliest preachers reappears throughout the NT.

THE PREACHING OF THE GOSPEL

The preaching of the Church is regarded in the NT as itself one of the signs of the arrival of the Age of Fulfilment. In the OT we hear little about preaching; Jonah had preached to the Ninevites (Jonah 3.2) and

[1] See Dodd, *The Apostolic Preaching*, new ed., 1944, 21-4.

they had repented (Matt. 12.41). He became a sign (σημεῖον) to the
Ninevites, as the Son of Man became a sign to his own generation
(Luke 11.30). The preaching of the Church is still the offering to the
world of the true sign from heaven. The inner meaning of preaching is
eschatological. There can be little doubt that Jesus himself deliberately
adopted the conception of 'preaching the gospel' in the sense of proclaiming the arrival of the day of salvation from (the Second) Isaiah;
at least, the NT use of εὐαγγελίζεσθαι, 'to preach good tidings', is based
on the use of the word in Isaiah, where it refers to the proclaiming of
the day of salvation, whether from Babylonian captivity or in a deeper
Messianic sense (Isa. 40.9; 41.27; 52.7, quoted in Rom. 10.15; cf.
Nahum 1.15; Luke 2.10). According to St Mark and the evangelists
generally, the εὐαγγέλιον of Jesus consisted in the announcement of the
arrival of the promised salvation (the Kingdom of God) at the fulfilment
of the καιρός (Mark 1.15). In his sermon at Nazareth, as recorded by
St Luke, Jesus pointedly refers to himself the words of Isa. 61.1 to the
effect that God has anointed (ἔχρισεν, 'Christed') him to preach the gospel
to the poor (εὐαγγελίσασθαι πτωχοῖς, LXX) (Luke 4.18). Elsewhere he
sees in his preaching of the gospel to the poor the Messianic fulfilment
of the Scriptures (Matt. 11.5; Luke 7.22); the preaching, whether of
Jesus or of his disciples, along with the miracles, was the sign that the
Kingdom of God was at hand (Matt. 10.7; Luke 10.9). Jesus understood his own mission in terms of the proclamation of the day of salvation; and the evidence of the NT indicates that he trained and commissioned a band of disciples to undertake a world-wide enterprise of
preaching along the lines of the Isaianic eschatological conception of
the mission of the Servant (Mark 8.35; 10.29; 13.8-10). It was because
of Jesus's adoption of the Isaianic interpretation of the Messianic
office in terms of the Servant of the Lord that the word εὐαγγέλιον
became a *terminus technicus* in the vocabulary of the NT and the Church
became a preaching Church.

In Mark 13.4, after Jesus has spoken of the approaching destruction
of the Temple, the disciples ask the question, 'When shall these things
be? and what shall be the sign (τὸ σημεῖον) when these things are all
about to be accomplished?' Jesus replies that certain things must
happen first, 'for the end (τὸ τέλος) is not yet': there will be wars—
nation shall rise against nation—earthquakes, famines and persecutions
of the disciples. The latter will stand before rulers and kings for his
name's sake (13.7-9). To these signs he adds another: 'the gospel must
first be preached to all the nations (Gentiles)' (13.10). St Matthew's
version is even more explicit: 'This gospel of the Kingdom shall be
preached in the whole world for a testimony unto all nations; and then

shall the end (τέλος) come' (Matt. 24.14). This is the standpoint of the apostolic Church, and there is no reason to suppose that the Church had misunderstood her Master on this important theme: the missionary activity of the Church is itself one of the signs of the End.[1] The signs of the End reappear in the Apocalypse in the vision of the Four Horsemen (Rev. 6.1-8). The rider on the Red Horse represents War: he has a sword in his hand. The rider on the Black Horse represents Famine: he holds the scales in his hand and cries, 'A measure of wheat for a penny.' The rider on the Pale Horse, whose name is Death, represents Persecution. These are three of the signs spoken of by the Lord, and they are deeply impressed upon the Church's consciousness. But there is also the rider on the White Horse; in contrast with the other three, he is not a sinister figure: he wears a crown, the symbol of victory, and he goes forth 'conquering and to conquer'. He reappears in Rev. 19.11-16, where he is called 'the faithful and true', and his name is 'the word of God' (ὁ λόγος τοῦ Θεοῦ). He represents, of course, the fourth eschatological sign, the missionary preaching of the Church: 'out of his mouth proceedeth a sharp sword, that with it he should smite the nations' (Rev. 19.15; cf. Heb. 4.12; Eph. 6.17). The apostolic Church held a high view of the power of the preached word of God; it was not only a word of salvation but, to those who resisted, it was a word of judgment: 'in righteousness he doth judge and make war' (Rev. 19.11). Jesus himself had declared that he had come not to cast peace on the earth but a sword (Matt. 10.34); the 'sword of his mouth', the preached word, is the instrument of Messianic decision (cf. Isa. 11.4; 49.2; Hos. 6.5; Rev. 1.16). During the period of the 'woes', before the coming of the End, the Church must be a witnessing Church, bringing despite all persecutions the opportunity of repentance and belief to all the nations. Again, the figure of the Isaianic Servant underlies the whole conception, the suffering herald of salvation who lightens the Gentiles. The NT stresses the fact that the Church had received from her risen Lord a renewed command to be his witnesses 'unto the uttermost part of the earth' (Acts 1.8) and to 'make disciples of all nations' (Matt. 28.19; cf. Mark 16.15). The missionary preaching of the Church was to continue until the consummation of the Age (ἕως τῆς συντελείας τοῦ αἰῶνος, Matt. 28.20). Jesus did not say that all the nations must (or will) accept the gospel before the End comes; indeed, he does not encourage an easy-going optimism about this possibility: 'Narrow is the gate and

---

[1] By something of an exegetical *tour de force* G. D. Kilpatrick reaches the strange conclusion that 'universalism is absent from Mark. There is no preaching the Gospel to Gentiles in this world and there is no interest in their fate in the world to come'; see his essay in *Studies in the Gospels*, ed. D. E. Nineham, 1955: 'The Gentile Mission in Mark and Mark 13.9-11' 145-58. See also J. Jeremias, *Jesus' Promise to the Nations*, ET, 1958.

straitened is the way that leadeth unto life, and few there be that find it'
(Matt. 7.14; Luke 13.24). The task of the missionaries is to preach to the
whole inhabited world (οἰκουμένη, Matt. 24.14; πᾶσα κτίσις, Mark 16.15),
whether they will hear or whether they will forbear. It is a thought-
provoking reflection that we are today living in the first age in which
this command of the Lord may fairly be said to have been fulfilled, and
that the other 'signs of the end' of which he spoke are also likely to be
spectacularly fulfilled in the century of world-wars, of atomic explosions
and of world food shortage; but we shall be wise to heed his warning
not to speculate on the date of the End (Mark 13.32; Acts 1.7) but to be
ever watchful and ready, as servants who await their lord's return
(Mark 13.33-37). In every period of history between the first coming of
Christ 'in great humility' and his final coming 'in his glorious majesty'
the signs are always present—the wars, convulsions, famines, persecutions and the witnessing Church—and there is a true sense in which no
age is nearer to the συντέλεια (consummation) than any other. The signs
of the End are present in every age. A study of the NT should, however,
deliver us from thinking that Church history is bound to be a 'success
story', or from disillusionment and unbelief when the preaching of the
gospel meets with failure or opposition. As has been wisely said, the
only surprising thing about persecution is that Christians should be
surprised when they encounter it, in view of the plain warnings of their
Lord (Matt. 5.11f.; 10.16-39; John 15.18-21).

It was St Paul who understood the commandment of the Lord to
preach the gospel to all the nations as being specially addressed to
himself. Like Jeremiah of old, he thinks of himself as divinely predestined from his birth to accomplish this task: 'Paul, a slave of Jesus
Christ, called to be an apostle, separated unto the gospel of God. . . .'
(Rom. 1.1). He had received his commission and his gospel not from
men but from God (Gal. 1.1, 11f.). Christ had sent him not to baptize—
others who followed after him would do that—but to preach the gospel
(I Cor. 1.17). Necessity was laid upon him: 'woe is me if I preach not
the gospel' (I Cor. 9.16; cf. Rom. 15.15f.). When Paul speaks of 'my
gospel' (Rom. 2.16; 16.25), he does not mean that his gospel is other
than that of the whole Church. There cannot be 'another gospel'
(Gal. 1.6-9), and Paul emphasizes that his preaching is faithful to the
Church's παράδοσις (tradition, catechism) which he has handed on to
his converts (I Cor. 11.2, 23-25; 15.1-3). By 'my gospel' he means 'my
personal apprehension of the truth of Christ', for he knows well that
the gospel is a mystery which can be laid hold of only by personal faith
(Rom. 16.25; Eph. 6.19), since it is veiled except to the eye of faith
(II Cor. 4.3). He laid 'the gospel which I preach among the Gentiles'

before the 'pillars' of the Church in Jerusalem, who apparently gave their approval of it, since they recognized his 'apostleship of the Gentiles' (Gal. 2.1-10). It would seem that Paul loyally accepted and handed on the general παράδοσις of the Church, and that he preached among the Gentiles his own apprehension of the εὐαγγέλιον, that Jew and Gentile alike are justified by faith and not by works of the Law. He thoroughly understands the teaching of the Lord, that the divine plan of salvation cannot be consummated until all nations have heard the news. He accordingly sets out on his incredible enterprise of preaching the gospel to all nations; he journeys tirelessly through Asia Minor, through Greece, and on to Rome; he hopes to go even to Spain (Rom. 15.28). To the disappointment of his earlier hopes he must have come to realize that he would not live to witness the completion of his great work and that the evangelization of the whole *oikoumene* would be a long and gradual process. But he has fulfilled the words of the Lord; he has borne his testimony before kings and rulers, courts and councils; he has suffered in his own person the Messianic woes, a theme to which he frequently alludes (II Cor. 1.5-7; 4.10; Phil. 3.10; Col. 1.24, etc.). He thoroughly understands that because the Church is a 'fellowship of the gospel' (Phil. 1.5) it is therefore a fellowship of Christ's sufferings (Phil. 3.10; cf. 1.29), since the gospel is itself 'the word of the cross' (I Cor. 1.18).

HEARING AND OBEDIENCE

Faith in its NT sense is never mere intellectual assent to an hypothesis or dogma, except perhaps in Ep. James where it is accordingly estimated as inadequate as a means of justification: even the demons believe propositions such as that God is one (James 2.19).[1] Salvation by faith alone must inevitably be rejected if faith is defined as intellectual assent (James 2.14-26). In the NT generally, however, faith is closely associated with hearing, and in biblical language hearing is almost synonymous with obeying. The whole biblical theology is a theology of the word: God speaks his word, man must hear and obey. Hence the Christian faith is disseminated by the characteristic activity of preaching. God has offered his salvation to all who call upon his name. 'But how shall they call on him in whom they have not believed? and how shall they believe in him whom they have not heard? and how shall they hear without a preacher? and how shall they preach unless they be sent?' (Rom. 10.14f.). 'Belief (πίστις) cometh by hearing (ἀκοή)'— and hearing is the result of the preaching of the word of Christ (Rom. 10.17). Πίστις ἐξ ἀκοῆς—this is what is meant by 'faith' in the writings

---

[1] See *infra*, 240f.

of St Paul and in the NT generally; faith is response to the preached word of Christ; it is obedience to God's call to salvation. In the OT *shama'*, 'to hear', has the sense of 'to obey', by which it is frequently translated in EVV. (In ancient Israel the ear of a slave was pierced to emphasize his duty of obedience.) In LXX the word is often rendered by ὑπακούω ('to hearken'), a verb often used in NT in the sense of 'to obey'. Faith is an obedient, personal response to the personal address of God, which is conveyed by the words of the preachers. Thus Jesus himself had spoken about hearing (obeying) his words. 'Everyone which heareth these words of mine *and doeth them* shall be likened unto a wise man, which built his house upon the rock . . .' (Matt. 7.24; Luke 6.47); 'my mother and brethren are these which hear the word of God *and do it*' (Luke 8.21); 'blessed are they that hear the word of God *and keep it*' (Luke 11.28; cf. John 12.47). The Parable of the Sower is especially a parable about hearing: 'he that was sown upon the good ground, this is he that heareth the word, and understandeth it . . .' (Mark 4.20; Matt. 13.23; Luke 8.15); indeed, all the parables have an inner sense which only the inward, responsive ear can hear: 'with many such parables spake he the word unto them, as they were able to hear it' (Mark 4.33, etc.); 'take heed what ye hear' (Mark 4.24); 'hear and understand' (Mark 7.14). The enacted parables of the healing of the deaf convey the same sense of the opening of the inward ears of those who are deaf to God's address (cf. esp. Mark 7.32-37, Ἐφφαθά). 'To hear' in its full biblical meaning includes both to understand and to obey. Without such understanding and obedience there is no faith. Faith therefore involves personal decision, trust, commitment and obedience; it is a wholehearted acceptance of the claim of God upon a man, in the situation in which he exists, with the appropriate response in life and action. Thus it is that in the NT obedience becomes virtually a technical expression for the acceptance of the Christian faith (e.g. Acts 6.7; Rom. 1.5; 6.17; 16.19; Gal. 5.7; II Thess. 1.8; I Pet. 1.2; 3.1; 4.17). In I Pet. 1.14 τέκνα ὑπακοῆς simply means 'Christians'. The example of Christ's own obedience is not far removed from the thought underlying this usage. St Paul contrasts Adam's disobedience with the obedience of Christ (Rom. 5.19), and Christ's supreme act of obedience was the death on the cross (Phil. 2.8; cf. Mark 14.36; Heb. 5.8f.). The Christian disciple must bring every thought into captivity to the obedience of Christ; his whole thinking must be done in the light of the Christian faith (II Cor. 10.5).

But, though faith necessarily involves decision and response, the NT none the less thinks of it as a gift from God. It is God who calls and converts, who opens the blind eyes and unstops the deaf ears, who gives what he demands. 'By grace have ye been saved through faith; and that not of yourselves; it is the gift of God' (Eph. 2.8); it is God's action in Christ which has made faith possible, so that faith can be understood only as a gift of grace. But this does not minimize the importance of human decision. God treats man as a responsible being, a person who can freely accept or reject his gracious call to salvation. Because man is not a puppet in the hand of God, or because God *speaks* to man, addresses him by his name, therefore the response of faith is a real decision on man's part; but because man is aware that the whole initiative in the matter is God's, that it is God who has created the possibility of faith, therefore the Christian believer readily uses the language of predestination and thinks of faith as wholly God's gift. Yet it is a gift which could have been refused, since God does not force himself upon us (cf. Mark 10.17-22). Christian obedience is an obedience rendered possible only by divine aid, but it is an obedience which man could at any moment refuse. Hence faith is not something accomplished or attained once for all at one specific moment; it is a relationship which must be maintained by constant striving, since man is never free from the temptation to unbelief and disobedience (I Cor. 9.26f.). The Christian life is a constant striving for faith (Phil. 1.27). Because faith is a virtue, unbelief is sin; it is disobedience. 'The god of this age has blinded the minds of the unbelieving' (II Cor. 4.4); 'the prince of the power of the air' is the spirit who now works in 'the sons of disobedience' (Eph. 2.2). Before their conversion to the faith, those who are now Christians were 'dead through their trespasses and sins' (Eph. 2.1). To many in the modern world the statement that unbelief is sin seems a hard saying, but it is the consistent biblical point of view. Men who are concerned wholly with this world, its values and pleasures, resist the Christian gospel because it makes a demand upon them; atheism is often the rationalization of the refusal to face the challenge of obedience. 'It is so hard to believe,' said Kierkegaard, 'because it is so hard to obey.'

FAITH AND REPENTANCE

The association of faith with repentance in the Gospels emphasizes the moral aspect of the act of turning to God in faith; nevertheless repentance is a strongly eschatological notion. The fundamental idea in the biblical conception of repentance is that of turning or returning to one's due obedience, as of rebels returning to serve their lawful king, or of a faithless wife coming back to her husband. It represents a fundamental reorientation of the whole personality. The burden of the preaching of the OT prophets was that Israel should 'turn again' unto the Lord; God would accept the person of the penitent. He does not desire cultus or sacrifice (Amos 5.21-25; Hos. 5.6; 6.6; Micah 6.6-8; Isa. 1.11-17; Jer. 6.20; 7.21-23; 14.12; Pss. 40.6; 51.16); indeed, the sacrificial system was available only for sins of inadvertence (Num. 15.27-31). God forgives the penitent not because of any restitution they may make, but because it is his nature to do so (Isa. 43.25; Ps. 103.3, 8-18). Some of the prophets speak as if 'turning again' and walking humbly with God (Micah 6.8) were a simple possibility; man can turn to God if he tries hard enough. But at its profoundest level the OT recognizes that this is just what men cannot do: man can bring to God, not his righteousness, but only his penitence, 'a broken and a contrite heart' (Ps. 51.17; Isa. 64.6); God must create a 'clean heart' or a 'new heart' (Ps. 51.10; Jer. 31.31-34; Ezek. 36.25-29). 'Turn thou me, and I shall be turned' (Jer. 31.18). The prophets of the Return from the Exile (Deutero-Isaiah, Haggai, Zechariah) had hoped that it would prove a return to the Lord in a spiritual sense; but with the disappointment of such a hope, the eschatological character of Israel's repentance became more marked. God would pour out a new Spirit upon Israel at the end of the age, when he brought in his reign. In the expectation of the dawning of the reign of God, when God would pour out his Spirit, John the Baptist, the last of the prophets, called again for repentance and symbolized it by his prophetic 'sign' of baptism ($\beta \acute{\alpha} \pi \tau \iota \sigma \mu \alpha$ $\mu \epsilon \tau \alpha \nu o \acute{\iota} \alpha s$, Mark 1.4) in anticipation of the coming baptism in Holy Spirit (Mark 1.8). Jesus himself preached repentance along with the necessity of belief in God's action in bringing in his reign (Mark 1.15).

After the resurrection of Christ the Church proclaimed that God had in fact offered to the world repentance as a gift, both to Jews and Greeks. 'Him did God exalt . . . a Prince and a Saviour, for to give repentance to Israel and remission of sins' (Acts 5.31); 'to the Gentiles also hath God granted repentance unto life'—i.e. the life of the Age to Come (Acts 11.18). It is the goodness of God which leads men to repentance (Rom. 2.4); through the pastoral ministry of the Church God gives men 'repentance unto the knowledge of the truth' (II Tim. 2.25). It is hardly surprising that the gift of repentance, being associated with the outpouring of the Spirit (cf. esp. Acts 11.18), should be closely connected with baptism. It had, moreover, been associated with baptism ever since the preaching of John's 'baptism of returning'. St Luke doubtless had in mind Peter's future baptism in Holy Spirit at Pentecost when he recorded Jesus's words to Peter, 'When once thou hast turned again ($\epsilon \pi \iota \sigma \tau \rho \acute{\epsilon} \psi \alpha s$), strengthen thy brethren' (Luke 22.32). By their own 'turning again' men can prepare the way for the coming of the Spirit, but it is God who gives repentance and faith. As we have seen in the matter of faith, there is something which men can and must do: they must recognize their need of a saviour, or else they cannot receive the gift of salvation. A veil lies over their hearts, and they do not know the truth, but 'whensoever a man shall turn (ἐπιστρέψῃ) to the Lord, the veil is taken away' (II Cor. 3.16, RV mg.). Those who are 'turned aside' from the Lord do not know their need for a saviour; with all such the preaching of Jesus fell on stony ground. They were the 'righteous' (i.e. self-righteous) who had no need of repentance (Luke 15.7; cf. Mark 2.13-17). They are typified in the picture of the Elder Brother in Luke 15.25-32 or the Pharisees who objected to the friendship of Jesus with 'sinners'. Repentance is thus a *sine qua non* of the Christian life, not only in its beginning but at every stage; it involves a constant awareness of the fact that all our faith and all our virtues are God's gift and not our achievement. But it is inevitably specially associated with the beginning of the Christian life. Probably from the earliest times an acknowledgment of repentance—turning from the world, the flesh and the devil, and turning towards truth and righteousness and Christ—was required of catechumens at their baptism, just as was a confession of faith. This act of baptismal repentance can never be repeated if a man has once become apostate, for baptism cannot be received a second time; this is perhaps the meaning of the difficult words of Heb. 6.6.[1] This, however, does not imply that the whole Christian life is not one long process of 'turning again', just as faith is in need of constant re-appropriation. 'To repent' and 'to believe' are both verbs which can be used especially of the catechumen's initial act of 'conversion' and of faith; thus, in Rom. 13.11 we read, 'Now is salvation nearer than when we *first* believed' (RV)—ἦ ὅτε ἐπιστεύσαμεν (cf. also I Cor. 15.11). The emphasis on 'conversion' as a definite and all-important date in the Christian's life, characteristic of certain sect-types of Christianity, finds little support in the NT teaching as a whole; the latter does not regard turning to God as a process that can be completed once for all on a particular date; and furthermore such an emphasis tends to disparage the faith of children brought up from infancy in Christian households, by which the NT would seem to set considerable store. Indeed, the word 'convert' is rare in EVV; RV usually prefers 'turn again'; the word 'conversion' is hardly a biblical word at all, occurring in EVV only at Acts 15.3. It should perhaps be added that the OT often uses 'repent' in the morally neutral sense of 'change one's mind' (e.g. 'The LORD repented that he had made Saul king', I Sam. 15.35; cf. also 15.29; Num. 23.19; Pss. 106.45; 110.4); in this sense Judas 'repented himself', i.e. changed his mind (Matt. 27.3). The NT words μετανοεῖν and μεταμέλεσθαι, though they need not

---

[1] See *infra*, 348f.

mean more than 'change one's mind', in fact carry with them the biblical overtones of ἐπιστρέφειν, to turn (back) to, or to turn towards. In their NT context (apart from Matt. 27.3) they should be read in the sense of the biblical eschatological giving of repentance through the pouring out of the Spirit in the latter days.

REGENERATION

The Fourth Gospel nowhere mentions repentance, but it stresses the kindred notion of the new birth (John 3.3-8; cf. 1.12f.). The idea of regeneration (παλιγγενεσία) was 'in the air' in both Jewish and Greek environs. The metaphor of being 're-born' is a natural one, which would occur to thoughtful men in any time or place, and no elaborate theories of borrowing from one culture to another are necessary. As E. G. Selwyn suggests, it arises from the experience expressed in such a phrase as 'I have become quite a different person', while the analogous concept of 'new creation' is a throwing into theological metaphor of the truth suggested in such a phrase as 'The world has become quite a different place'. 'We are justified,' he concludes, 'in view of the variety of context in which ἀναγέννησις and παλιγγενεσία occur, in saying that the words were used in Graeco-Jewish circles to signify any decisively new stage in nature, history or personal life.'[1] The idea of regeneration is found also in the Mystery Religions, being used (like *metamorphosis*) to describe the change through which the initiate passed.[2] Rabbinic Judaism, however, despite the common saying that 'the proselyte is like a new-born child', had no real doctrine of individual regeneration;[3] but in later Judaism there had arisen a strong expectation of a second or new birth for Israel as a nation (Ezek. 37; Isa. 65.17; 66.22), which would be bound up with the creation of a new heaven and a new earth in a vast scene of cosmic regeneration (cf. also Enoch 25.6; 50.1; Baruch 5.1-9; II Pet. 3.13; Rev. 20.11; 21.1). It may be added that neither παλιγγενεσία nor ἀναγεννάω is found in LXX (or, for that matter, in classical Gk. literature).

The NT claims that this mighty act of new creation, or of cosmic regeneration, has been accomplished by God in Jesus Christ, though this truth is perceived as yet only by the eye of faith; the time was shortly coming when it would be revealed to all men, at the parousia or

---

[1] *The First Epistle of St Peter*, 1946, 122. See also C. E. B. Cranfield, in *TWBB*, 31(a). C. H. Dodd in *IFG*, 49f., cites instances from the *Corpus Hermeticum* (esp. the hymn Περὶ Παλιγγενεσίας, C.H.XIII) to shew that, as in Johannine thought, the knowledge of God, which confers eternal life, is possessed by those who have passed through rebirth from the realm of σῶμα or σάρξ into the realm of πνεῦμα or νοῦς; but this Hermetic material is, of course, post-NT in date.

[2] See refs. given by F. Büchsel in Kittel, *TWNT*, I, 671-4.

[3] So Dodd, *IFG*, 304, referring to Strack-Bill., II, 420-3.

apocalypse of Christ. The coming of Christ at his birth in the flesh was
the inauguration of the new creation, and his death was potentially the
dying of the whole human race, just as his resurrection was potentially
the re-creation of all mankind. The eschatological Spirit is the breath
which God breathes into his new creation and which gives it life (cf.
John 20.22; Ezek. 37.5-10, 14; Wisd. 15.11). The verb ἐνεφύσησε in
John 20.22 echoes Gen. 2.7; cf. Gen. 1.2; and the idea of the new creation is thus clearly implied;[1] cf. also the 'rushing mighty wind' at Pentecost, St Luke's baptism of the apostles in Holy Spirit (Acts 2.2). The
verb ἀναγεννάω occurs in NT only at I Pet. 1.3 ('begat us again unto a
living hope') and 1.23 ('having been begotten again not of corruptible
seed but of incorruptible, through the λόγος of God'). But the sense of
having been re-made in Christ pervades the NT writings. The Christian
is a new creation (II Cor. 5.17; Gal. 6.15); he walks in newness of life
(Rom. 6.4) and serves in newness of spirit (Rom. 7.6); his 'inward man'
is renewed day by day (II Cor. 4.16); his mind is renewed (Rom. 12.2):
in short, he is re-created in the original image of the Creator (Col.
3.10). Jew and Gentile have become one new man in Christ (Eph. 2.15;
Gal. 3.28). The day of the creation of the new heavens and new earth
has dawned, and the Christians are the firstfruits of the New Age: 'of
his own will he brought us forth by the word of truth, that we should
be a kind of firstfruits of his creatures' (James 1.18; cf. Rom. 8.23;
Rev. 14.4). The earliest Christians knew that they were living in the
expected day of regeneration because they had received the gifts of the
Spirit. Jesus himself had promised his disciples, who for his sake had
left all and followed him, that in the Messianic community of the
missionary dispensation, when the gospel was being preached in all the
world, they would receive 'a hundred fold now in this time (νῦν ἐν τῷ
καιρῷ τούτῳ) houses and brethren and sisters and mothers and children
and lands, with persecutions, and in the age to come (ἐν τῷ αἰῶνι τῷ
ἐρχομένῳ) the   fe of the (new) age' (ζωὴν αἰώνιον) (Mark 10.30). Many a
Christian, os acized by his own family because of his profession of the
faith of Chris , would by St Mark's day have experienced the gaining of
a new family in the fellowship of the Church. Into the Marcan context
of this saying St Matthew has very significantly introduced another:
'And Jesus said unto them, Verily I say unto you, that ye which have
followed me, in the regeneration (παλιγγενεσία) when the Son of Man
shall sit on the throne of his glory, ye also shall sit upon twelve thrones
judging the twelve tribes of Israel' (Matt. 19.28). From St Matthew's
standpoint, Christ had taken all authority in heaven and earth after his
resurrection from the dead (28.18), a truth symbolized in the NT

[1] So E. C. Hoskyns, *The Fourth Gospel*, 2nd ed. revised, 1947, 547.

generally by the picture of Christ's sitting at the right hand of God (Mark 16.19; Acts 2.33; Rom. 8.34; Eph. 1.20; Col. 3.1; Heb. 1.3, 13; I Pet. 3.22), or in the Apocalypse by his sitting down with the Father in his throne (Rev. 3.21). The saying would thus be understood by St Matthew to mean that the apostles had been appointed by Christ to rule the Church—i.e. the twelve tribes of the new Israel—regarded as the sphere of 'the regeneration' now proleptically accomplished.

It is perhaps, however, in his sayings about the necessity of becoming as little children that Jesus most clearly teaches the meaning of regeneration. 'Verily I say unto you, whosoever will not receive the Kingdom of God as a little child, he shall not enter into it' (Mark 10.15); 'Verily I say unto you, Except ye turn and become as little children, ye shall in no wise enter into the Kingdom of Heaven' (Matt. 18.3). To become a child over again means to be made anew, to be born a second time; so the Fourth Evangelist interprets the matter: 'Except a man be born anew (or from above) he cannot see the Kingdom of God' (John 3.3). Entering the New Age means becoming a new person, entering the sphere of the Messianic regeneration. Perhaps here we have a clue to the difficult saying of Matt. 11.11f.: 'Verily I say unto you, among them that are born of women there hath not arisen a greater than John the Baptist; yet he that is little (Gk. 'lesser') in the Kingdom of Heaven is greater than he.' That is to say, those who are once-born (born of women only) are 'unregenerate' in the eschatological (not the moral) sense; those who have been born a second time into the Kingdom of God are 'greater' even than the greatest of them.[1] The basic reality about being a Christian is not a moral but an eschatological truth. It concerns one's relationship to the sphere of regeneration. So Christians pray, 'Grant that we being regenerate and made thy children by adoption and grace may daily be renewed by thy Holy Spirit.'[2]

The connection between the eschatological conception of regeneration and Christian baptism is obvious, since baptism is the sacrament of the 'birth from above', of entry into the Kingdom of God and into the sphere of the operation of the Holy Spirit. It is noteworthy that the only other occurrence of παλιγγενεσία (besides Matt. 19.28) in the NT is to be found in a context relating to baptism: 'According to his mercy he saved us, through the washing (RV mg., 'laver') of regeneration (διὰ λουτροῦ παλιγγενεσίας) and renewing (ἀνακαινώσεως) of the Holy Spirit, which he poured out upon us richly through Jesus Christ our Saviour; that being justified by his grace, we might be made heirs, according to hope, of the life of the Age to Come' (Titus 3.5-7). Faith,

---

[1] I owe this suggestion to Dr R. P. C. Hanson.
[2] BCP, Collect of Christmas Day.

repentance and regeneration are themes associated with the beginning of the Christian life and therefore inevitably with baptism. The order of events was first the acceptance by the hearer of the word preached, the λόγος Χριστοῦ, the εὐαγγέλιον or κήρυγμα, then his instruction in the πίστις or the παράδοσις by the Church's teachers; next came his baptism at which he made his personal confession of faith (ὁμολογία), and finally his admission to the Eucharist and to full membership of the Church.

From the earliest days of the Church there was a tradition (παράδοσις) of teaching (διδαχή) to which the Church's preachers were loyal. It contained an exposition of the κήρυγμα as set forth in the actual historical facts of the life, ministry, death and resurrection of Jesus, along with such words of the Lord himself as were of importance in interpreting those facts and had decisive significance for the life and witness of the primitive communities of disciples (ἐκκλησίαι). This is the tradition which finally took literary shape in our Synoptic Gospels and upon which the Fourth Gospel is a profound meditation. St Paul, as we have already pointed out, was most anxious to hand on this παράδοσις faithfully and urged his converts to adhere to it strictly. From him we may learn that there is not only no conflict between the παράδοσις κατὰ Χριστόν (Col. 2.8) and πίστις in its most inward sense, but also that the latter requires and rests upon the former, since faith is not a mere subjective state of mind or belief in a 'spiritual principle' or the acceptance of a magical 'name', but is faith in an actual historical person, who really lived and taught and died and rose again. In I Cor. 11.23-25 we find St Paul reminding the Corinthians how he had taught them the tradition of the Lord's Supper and in I Cor. 15.3-7 the tradition of the Lord's resurrection: the Corinthians must hold fast to the very words of the gospel-tradition which he had taught them (15.1f.). He exhorts the Thessalonians to 'stand fast and hold the traditions (παραδόσεις) which ye were taught, whether by word or epistle of ours' (II Thess. 2.15), and he commands them in the name of the Lord Jesus Christ to withdraw from those who walk not after the παράδοσις received from himself and his fellow-workers (II Thess. 3.6). He warns the Colossians against accepting a man-made tradition (παράδοσις τῶν ἀνθρώπων) (Col. 2.8), for he himself had experienced the futility of following that same man-made tradition which the Lord Jesus had denounced (Gal. 1.14; Mark 7.8). He gives thanks to God that the Roman Christians had become 'obedient from the heart to that form of teaching (τύπος διδαχῆς) whereunto ye were traditioned' (παρεδόθητε) (Rom. 6.17); we may note that in this instance he is assuming that a church which he has not founded has been instructed in the one universal τύπος διδαχῆς or catechism.

After St Paul's time, when the great authorities upon the oral tradition had disappeared from the scene, and when all kinds of strange teachings were being put about by heretical innovators, it was all the more necessary to lay stress upon holding fast the original apostolic 'deposit' (παραθήκη). The word occurs three times in the Pastorals (I Tim. 6.20; II Tim. 1.12, 14) and nowhere else in NT. The duty of the apostles' successors in the oversight of the Church is above all things to guard 'the good deposit' (καλὴν παραθήκην) through the power of the indwelling Holy Spirit (II Tim. 1.14). It is hardly surprising that the surviving literature of the sub-apostolic age should be preoccupied with the urgency of contending for 'the faith once for all delivered to the saints' (τῇ ἅπαξ παραδοθείσῃ τοῖς ἁγίοις πίστει) (Jude 3). In those difficult days it would be an encouragement to Christians to be reminded that they had once made their baptismal profession of the faith, as Timothy is reminded that he had confessed the good confession (ὡμολόγησας τὴν καλὴν ὁμολογίαν) in the sight of many witnesses: so Christ himself had witnessed (μαρτυρήσαντος) the good confession before Pontius Pilate at his baptism of death (I Tim. 6.12f.).[1] In the earliest days of the Church it is probable that the 'creed' which the candidate for baptism was required to profess 'in the sight of many witnesses' (i.e. the whole local church) was some short and simple formula, such as 'Jesus is Lord' or 'Jesus Messiah is Son of God' (cf. Acts 8.37, Western Text, RV mg.; 16.31; Rom. 10.9f.; I Cor. 12.3; Heb. 4.14, which seems to quote a baptismal ὁμολογία, 'Jesus the Son of God'; I John 4.15). Perhaps a definite trace of a baptismal credal-hymn survives in I Tim. 3.16. With the disconcerting multiplication of heretical teachers and sects that denied or contradicted some element in the universal catechism or tradition of the Church, such elementary credal formulae would be expanded with the express object of excluding false teaching, and in this way more elaborate baptismal creeds would come into being. Thus during the second century and afterwards there were stabilized such forms as the Old Roman Creed or the confession which we know as the Apostles' Creed.[2]

[1] See also *infra*, 337n.

[2] Since this chapter was written, there has appeared H. Riesenfeld's *The Gospel Tradition and its Beginnings*, 1957, which deals admirably with the importance of tradition in the NT period. For the earliest credal forms see O. Cullmann, *The Earliest Christian Confessions*, ET, 1949.

2

KNOWLEDGE AND REVELATION

THE Hebrew mind did not share the optimism of the Greeks of the classical period concerning the possibility of man's knowledge of ultimate reality. The Greek philosophers did not doubt the ability of those who devoted themselves to the βίος θεωρητικός to comprehend truth (ἀλήθεια) or ultimate being (τὸ ὄντως ὄν) in its pure and changeless essence. To know what is constitutes man's highest achievement; through such knowing he partakes of the nature of that which he contemplates and thus shares the quality of the eternal. This knowledge is thought of as a form of seeing (θεωρία), and it constitutes man's highest good. This sanguine view of the possibility of man's knowledge of reality is utterly foreign to the Hebrew mind. To the latter the knowledge of God comes not by contemplating his being and attributes but by obeying his commandments, and the OT knows nothing of a 'theoretical' or even mystical vision of God. The contemplation of a changeless and eternal form of the Good or of Being as such is as far removed as possible from the biblical understanding of the knowledge of God; this knowledge comes only through actual obedience to God's concrete, particular will in the living moment of decision which is called 'now'. The prophets of Israel had indeed a knowledge of God, but it was not attained either by mystic vision or by philosophical speculation; it had been won through their obedience to his will at the crises of their nation's history. It came by 'hearing' rather than by 'seeing'.

THE OLD TESTAMENT BACKGROUND

It is doubtless because of this *moral* basis of the knowledge of God that the OT writers are reticent in claiming that men can possess it.[1] God is high and holy, and beyond the reach of base and sinful men. 'Canst thou by searching find out God?' asks Job, expecting the answer No (Job 11.7; cf. 38-41). The pagans might claim to find a revelation of God in the wonders of nature, but the standpoint of the Bible is that of Job 26.14: 'Lo, these are but the outskirts of his ways, and how small a whisper do we hear of him.' God *ought* to be known, especially

[1] C. H. Dodd (*IFG*, 163) says that he cannot discover in the OT a passage in which a prophet expressly claims that he knows God.

to Israel, who possess the knowledge of his Law; but the writings of the prophets are full of laments that Israel does not know God because she is disobedient to his will: 'The ox knoweth his owner, and the ass his master's crib, but Israel doth not know, my people doth not consider' (Isa. 1.3); 'there is no knowledge of God in the land' (Hos. 4.1; cf. Jer. 4.22). Ignorance of God is culpable; even the Gentiles ought to have known God (Jer. 10.25) and his moral law (Amos 2.1). Israel's disobedience is a deliberate refusal to know Yahweh (Jer. 9.6). The denial of God is 'folly' in the moral sense which this word carries in the Bible (Pss. 14; 53). Conversely the doing of God's will is to know God; the knowledge of God comes through obeying his commandments. This fundamental biblical truth is well brought out in the words which Jeremiah spoke to the son of good King Josiah: 'Did not thy father eat and drink (i.e. prosper), and do judgment and justice? then it was well with him. He judged the cause of the poor and needy; then it was well. Was not this to know me? saith the LORD' (Jer. 22.15f.). In the OT 'knowledge of God' is virtually a synonym for obedience to God's will (e.g. Hos. 6.6), and to know God means to exercise lovingkindness, judgment and righteousness, as Yahweh himself does (Jer. 9.24). The knowledge of God is a fourfold strand binding together obedience to God's will, worship of his name, social righteousness and national prosperity; ignorance of God *per contra* spells disobedience, idolatry, social injustice and national disaster. The prophets perceived that it was these latter melancholy features, rather than the former, which characterized the life of Israel as a nation; and hence they came to look upon the knowledge of God not as a present attainment but as a future gift. They thought of it as an eschatological possibility, to be realized in the day when God would make a new covenant with the house of Israel: 'They shall teach no more every man his neighbour . . . saying, Know the LORD: for they shall all know me, from the least of them unto the greatest of them, saith the LORD' (Jer. 31.34). In the day of the Lord, but not till then, 'the earth shall be full of the know-ledge of the LORD, as the waters cover the sea' (Isa. 11.9; cf. 33.6; 52.6; 54.13, etc.).

Thus, knowledge in the biblical sense of the word is not theoretical contemplation but an entering into subjective relations as between person and person—relations of trust, obedience, respect, worship, love, fear and so on. It is knowledge in the sense of our knowledge of other persons rather than of our knowledge of objects, 'existential' rather than 'scientific' knowledge. I cannot know a person with whom I refuse to enter into personal relations. To disobey God is to refuse to enter into the relation which he has so graciously made possible and hence is to remain ignorant of him. It is of the profoundest significance that the Hebrew word 'know' (*yadha‘*) is used of sexual intercourse (e.g. Gen. 4.1, 17, 25; Num. 31.18, 35; Judg. 21.12; cf. Matt. 1.25; Luke 1.34), for the husband-wife relationship is the most intimate personal relation in human life, the most active and satisfying knowing that exists. This is the biblical truth which Freud has distorted in representing all knowledge as sexual. When the OT says that God knows Israel, as it does frequently and emphatically (e.g. Amos 3.2; Hos. 5.3), it implies that God has entered into the fullest and closest personal relations with Israel, as a husband with a wife; he has done so with no other nation. God has concerned himself personally and intimately with Israel—called her, loved her, cherished her, chastened her, forgiven her. Israel's knowledge of God may be feeble and fleeting, but God's knowledge of Israel is sure and strong. Evil men may fondly imagine that God is too exalted to take knowledge of their deeds and intents, but there is nothing in human life which eludes God's perception (Ps. 10); the wicked have lost all knowledge of God and even have come to deny his existence. But God knows every human heart, even its most secret thoughts (Ps. 139). Though man's knowledge of God may be a fugitive and tentative thing, nothing more indeed than an eschatological possibility, God's knowledge of man is the one great certainty in the minds of the biblical writers.

THE HELLENISTIC WORLD: GNOSTICISM

The word *yadha‘* is translated into Greek in the LXX by γινώσκειν or εἰδέναι. The question arises whether it loses something of its Hebrew meaning and acquires new overtones. According to some leading scholars today, the terms γινώσκειν and γνῶσις had by the first century A.D. become important technical terms in the vocabulary of the higher pagan religion. On the continent of Europe this higher pagan religion is often called by scholars 'Gnosticism', because it was essentially a religion of salvation by knowledge; until recently English scholars usually reserved this term for certain second-century Christian heresies, like those of Basilides and Valentinus. The objection to speaking of Gnosticism in the first century A.D. is that we are in danger of hypostatizing certain rather ill-defined tendencies of thought and then speaking as if there were a religion or religious philosophy, called Gnosticism, which could be contrasted with Judaism or Christianity. There was, of course, no such thing; a thoughtful person could not have been converted to Gnosticism in the same way as he could have been to Judaism or Christianity: what he might have done would have been to become an initiate in one of the many mystery cults. It will be noted that when scholars like Bultmann describe a Gnostic doctrine they take their first-century 'evidence' from the NT itself. But this is a question-begging proceeding, since the NT is susceptible of a very different interpretation; if there is no real evidence for a developed 'Gnosticism' in the first century outside the NT, then the NT can hardly be used as evidence for its existence. The most that could be said is that certain notions were 'in the air' in the later part of the first century, such as subsequently crystallized into the doctrines of the Gnostic sects about which we learn from such writers as Irenaeus in the second century.

By NT times the ancient world had certainly suffered a failure of nerve. Gone was the optimism of the classical philosophers about the power of the human mind to contemplate eternal truth and to hold communion with the Ideal Realm; the scepticism and relativism of later philosophy, combined with the insidious spread of certain types of oriental belief, notably the mystery cults and magic, had dethroned the philosophical intellect and exalted credulity. The 'established' religion of the old gods of Mount Olympus was now no longer a living reality in the minds of the people, but was only an outward ceremonialism for state occasions; the flourishing 'evangelical nonconformity' of the mystery cults offered to their initiates the secret learning necessary to salvation and endowment with supernatural powers.[1] Though ultimate truth was now held to be inaccessible to the unaided reason of man, the mystery-cults claimed to reveal it to their adherents; the god imparts *gnosis* in ecstatic or mystical vision, and the initiate is born again through the magical operation of the regenerating word ($\lambda \acute{o} \gamma o s$ $\pi a \lambda \iota \gamma \gamma \epsilon \nu \epsilon \sigma \acute{\iota} a s$). This divinely communicated *gnosis* seems in fact to have been a farrago of cosmological and mythological speculation (cf. the $\psi \epsilon \upsilon \delta \acute{\omega} \nu \upsilon \mu o s$ $\gamma \nu \hat{\omega} \sigma \iota s$ of I Tim. 6.20). The possession of such *gnosis* is power, for it is the divine $\delta \acute{\upsilon} \nu a \mu \iota s$ which makes a man $\pi \nu \epsilon \upsilon \mu a \tau \iota \kappa \acute{o} s$, a partaker of the divine nature, and so immortal. A more intellectual version of this mystery-pattern in the form of a religio-philosophical belief became the standard expression of the higher paganism of the second and third centuries; its literary deposit is the *Corpus Hermeticum*[2] which was produced in Egypt for the most part in the second and third centuries A.D.[3] Those scholars who readily find Gnostic influences

[1] Cf. N. P. Williams's essay in *Essays Catholic and Critical*, ed. E. G. Selwyn, 1926, 3rd ed. 1929, 385-423; see also R. Bultmann, art. 'Gnosis' in Kittel, *TWNT*, ET by J. R. Coates (Bible Key Words), 1953; *Theology of the New Testament*, I, ET, 1952, 164-83 and 294-303; R. Reitzenstein, *Die Hellenistischen Mysterienreligionen*, 3rd ed., Leipzig and Berlin, 1927; C. H. Dodd, *The Bible and the Greeks*, 1935, 99-248; *IFG*, 151-69; W. D. Davies, *PRJ*, 191-200; F. C. Burkitt, *Church and Gnosis*, 1932.
[2] A clear account of this will be found in C. H. Dodd, *IFG*, 10-53; the literature on the subject is referred to in the footnotes on p. 11.
[3] Dodd, *IFG*, 11.

at work in the NT argue that the beginnings of this type of thought must have been fairly well defined in the first century; they then set out to look for evidences of it in the NT, and are thus in peril of interpreting the earlier by means of the later writings.

THE KNOWLEDGE OF GOD IN THE NEW TESTAMENT

There is little in the Synoptic Gospels which bears directly on the theme of man's knowledge of God; but there is one saying, attributed to Jesus, which is of the very greatest importance. Everything else in the NT that deals with this subject might be regarded as commentary upon it. It is the saying of Matt. 11.27 (=Luke 10.22), which has been well described as a Johannine thunderbolt in the Synoptic sky: 'All things have been delivered unto me of my Father: and no one knoweth the Son, save the Father; neither doth any know the Father, save the Son, and he to whomsoever the Son willeth to reveal him.' Bultmann feels that 'the verse presents us with Gnostic language' and that therefore nothing of the kind could have been spoken by Jesus.[1] But the saying is eminently capable of being interpreted according to the Hebrew understanding of 'knowledge', and when so interpreted it makes perfectly good sense and is supported by the whole of the rest of the NT teaching. It is an excellent example of the way in which one can find Gnostic *motifs* if one is looking for them, though a biblical interpretation is readily available. Whether the actual saying (in an Aramaic original) was spoken by Jesus in precisely this form is a problem which can hardly be settled; the important point is that the verse epitomizes what the apostolic Church understood him to have taught about his own relation to God and its consequences for the relationships of mankind in general to God.[2] If, as we shall later maintain,[3] Jesus thinks of himself as the Messianic Son of God along the lines of traditional Hebrew thought upon this subject (e.g. Ps. 2.7; II Sam. 7.14; Exod. 4.22f., etc.), it is in his capacity as Messianic Son that all things have been delivered to him. Jesus himself takes the place of the old Israel as God's son. No one knows the Son save the Father, just as no one 'knew' Israel except Yahweh (Amos 3.2, etc.); the relation of God and Jesus is unique, just as the relation of God and Israel was unique. But Israel had refused the obedience of a son, so that now the Messianic Son, foretold by Israel's prophets, must render that perfect obedience

---

[1] *Gnosis* (ET), 50; cf. R. Bultmann, *Die Geschichte der Synoptischen Tradition*, 2nd ed. 1931, 171f.; there is no reference to this verse in the indexes of his *Theology of the New Testament*, I and II, 1952 and 1955.

[2] Attention may be called to the excellent exposition of this verse in R. H. Fuller, *The Mission and Achievement of Jesus*, 1954, 89-95.

[3] See *infra*, 147-53.

by which the true knowledge of God is to be consummated in the last days. So now the Father knows the (Messianic) Son in the distinctive biblical (non-Gnostic) sense of 'know': he commissions him, sends him, works through him, and holds the closest possible personal relationship with him. The Son alone knows the Father, as no other man does, since no one else has offered the perfect obedience of a son to the Father. Thus the Son is the divinely appointed means of bringing the knowledge of God to the world ('and he to whomsoever the Son willeth to reveal him'), and he has become the light of the Gentiles, as disobedient Israel never did. The saying implies that, apart from Christ's revelation of God, there is no true knowledge of God in the world. This is the teaching of the whole NT, hard though it may be for a 'broadminded' generation to understand it. Its truth, however, is more readily seen if we bear in mind the biblical sense of the word 'knowledge'. It does not mean the possession of certain philosophical truths about the nature and attributes of God, but knowledge-by-personal-relations with God. It is through Jesus Christ, the Messianic Son, and through him alone, that mankind can have knowledge of God in this biblical sense.

It is the Fourth Evangelist who most searchingly investigates the implications of the doctrine of the revealing work of the Messianic Son of God. Bultmann holds that Johannine thought starts from the Hellenistic Gnostic conception of knowledge, not that of the OT,[1] apparently largely on the ground that sometimes 'knowing' is equated in Greek fashion with 'seeing' (e.g. John 14.7-9; I John 3.6; 4.14). He disregards the fact that the vocabulary of 'seeing' is part of a universal human religious language, a basic metaphor of all ages and places; it may be found everywhere from ancient Egypt or Babylonia to modern Japan or Peru. Men have spoken of 'seeing' that a thing is true ever since the birth of language. The OT abounds in such imagery. To claim that because St John occasionally (and how very occasionally!) uses language about 'seeing' he therefore 'starts from the Gnostic conception of knowledge' is to admit the necessity of manufacturing evidence out of nothing. Even to say that St John 'speaks the language of Hellenistic mysticism'[2] is surely an exaggeration in respect of a writer whose vocabulary excludes all technical religious and philosophical expressions except Hebraic ones (such as Messiah, Son of God, Son of Man, Word, Glory) and limits himself to words of everyday human discourse (such as light, life, know, truth, see). Can it be entirely by chance that the Fourth Evangelist has avoided altogether the magic-words of the Hellenistic ψευδώνυμος γνῶσις (I Tim. 6.20) or φιλοσοφία (i.e. Gnostic

---

[1] *Gnosis* (ET), 48.   [2] C. H. Dodd, *IFG*, 201.

speculation, Col. 2.8)—such words as γνῶσις itself, πίστις and σοφία?

In St John's teaching the knowledge of God starts with an act of faith in Christ. Such belief means trustful obedience to Christ's words. Those who will not 'hear' Christ's λόγος cannot know (the inner meaning of) his speech (λαλιά) (8.43). There is an inward hearing, as there is an inward seeing, which comes from the trustful and obedient reception of his word. Such believing reception does not depend upon the actual physical seeing and hearing of the Jesus of history. Indeed, believing in the full sense is possible only after the 'lifting up' (i.e. the crucifixion and resurrection) of the Son of Man (8.28); many who saw Jesus in the flesh did not believe and the fullest blessing is reserved for those who have not seen and yet have believed (20.29). Seeing, then, is not necessarily believing, for many saw and did not believe (6.64, 66, etc.); but, on the other hand, believing involves a new seeing, as is implied in the story of the Man Born Blind and its conclusion about the opening of the inner eyes of faith in the man who was healed, as contrasted with the blindness of the unbelieving Pharisees (9.1-41). Such belief is not a human achievement at all; it is the gift of God (6.65). It means primarily a personal trust in and commitment to Christ, but it can be expressed in the form of a ὅτι clause, for example, belief *that* God sent Christ (17.8). The distinctively Johannine use of πιστεύειν followed by εἰς (not found in LXX and perhaps eight times in the rest of NT) emphasizes the strongly personal character of faith, a trustful relationship with a person (e.g. πιστεύετε εἰς τὸν Θεόν, καὶ εἰς ἐμὲ πιστεύετε, 14.1). The peculiarly Johannine πιστεύειν εἰς τὸ ὄνομα (1.12; 2.23; 3.18) is probably a reference to the baptismal confession of faith in Christ's name.[1]

St John's use of πιστεύειν indicates the sense in which he uses γινώσκειν, 'to know', a word found in John and I John more often than in all the rest of the NT. The frequent association of 'believe' and 'know' is particularly instructive: believing is the act by which we come to know that Christ is come forth from the Father, so that the two words, if they are not synonymous, are fully complementary. Believing (hearing and obeying) results in knowing (personally experiencing), and one cannot know if one will not believe. Thus, for instance, the Johannine version of St Peter's Confession runs, 'We have believed and know that thou art the Holy One of God' (6.69), though this has happened only because Christ has first chosen them (6.70). 'To know' in the Johannine usage, as generally in the Bible, means to enter into relations with someone and thus to have personal experience of him, as distinct from mere knowledge by description; it is first-hand or 'I-thou' know-

[1] Cf. C. H. Dodd, *IFG*, 184.

ledge, not scientific-objective knowledge. The relation of Christ with
the Father is the perfect example of this kind of knowledge, which, as
we have seen, on its manward side involves obedience; the Son knows
the Father because of his perfect obedience and identity of will (4.34;
5.30; 6.38; 14.31, etc.). To know God means to obey his commandments, and the criterion of our knowledge of God can be only whether
we obey his will: 'Hereby we know that we know him, if we keep his
commandments' (I John 2.3; cf. 2.5; 5.18-20). The commands of
Christ, which may be summed up in the 'new commandment' of love
(John 13.34; cf. 15.12, 17; I John 2.7f.; 3.11; II John 5), are the commands of God himself, because the Son speaks and does only that which
he has received from the Father. Therefore by obeying the commands
of Christ, or the love-commandment, his disciples are brought into the
same relation to Christ as Christ bears to the Father (John 10.14f.);
but this knowledge-relation is based upon the prior action of Christ in
choosing his disciples (John 15.16; cf. 13.18; 5.21; I John 4.10, 19). To
know Christ is to know God, because of the hypostatic union of Christ
with the Father; it is to enter into the closest possible relationship, one
which can be spoken of as 'abiding in' (John 15.4-10), or simply as
being 'in' Christ or God (17.21-23). Although γινώσκειν thus primarily
represents the personal, subjective experience of relation with another, it
may be used with a ὅτι clause, since knowledge, however inward, must
be capable of being to some extent objectified, i.e. expressed in words.
The usual form of words by which St John thus indicates the content
of the knowledge of God is the affirmation that Christ is come forth
from the Father, or that the Father sent the Son (16.27, 30; 17.3, 8, 21,
23, 25; cf. 3.2), statements which are equally the content of πιστεύειν ὅτι.
'The Jews' think that they know all about Christ, since they know that
he comes from Galilee (7.41), but they do not possess the deeper knowledge that Christ comes forth from God (7.27-29). To know that Christ
comes from God is possible only to those who know Christ personally
in the subjective relation of loving trust and obedience. Such knowing
is even now a partaking by faith of the life of the Age to Come (ζωὴ
αἰώνιος) (17.3); this participation in the life of the Age is a relationship
with the Father through the keeping of the words of Christ and therefore is an abiding in love, such as shall characterize the coming Age
(14.19-21). It is consequently an anticipation of the vision of the glory
(δόξα) which shall be at the End, and which the disciples had seen in the
incarnate Son (1.14; 2.11), but which had not been manifested to 'the
world' (cf. 14.22). The disciples of Christ see the truth and the glory that
are in him by the eye of faith; they 'see', but not with the vision
(θεωρία) of Gnostic speculation or mystic contemplation; in this life all

'seeing' is faith-seeing and all knowledge of God is faith-knowledge. That is why in the Fourth Gospel the words 'see', 'hear', 'believe', and 'know' are in certain contexts more or less interchangeable. Knowing is indeed occasionally equated with seeing, but not in any Gnostic or mystical sense; knowing is 'seeing with the eye of faith', and this is a position which is fully biblical and is the common teaching of the NT.

St Paul, unlike St John, does not seek to avoid such words as γνῶσις, ἐπίγνωσις (which is indistinguishable in meaning from γνῶσις), σοφία, πίστις, μυστήριον, etc. This may be because he is a missionary and deliberately uses words already present in the religious vocabulary of his converts. The latter would know all about the mystery-cults with their claim to impart saving *gnosis*. It would be natural for Paul to speak to such converts about 'the excellency of the γνῶσις of Christ Jesus my Lord' (Phil. 3.8) or about 'the μυστήριον of God, namely Christ, in whom all the treasures of σοφία and γνῶσις are hidden' (Col. 2.2). The fact, if such it be, that Paul tries to express the truth about Christ in terms familiar to those for whom 'religion' had always meant the mysteries, does not mean that he accepted any of the tenets of a supposed Gnostic religious philosophy; still less do the allegedly 'Gnostic' language and outlook of Colossians-Ephesians imply that we must (with Bultmann) consider those writings to be non-Pauline. We know so little about the mystery religions (and nothing at all about any first-century 'Gnosticism' except what may be deduced from the NT) that all such theories are precarious. We are on surer ground if we recognize that in the Paulines there are two kinds of knowledge. There is first a 'puffed up' knowledge, a worldly wisdom, which is vehemently repudiated (e.g. I Cor. 1.20; 2.5, 13; 8.2; 13.2, 8), and which doubtless represents the pretended γνῶσις and σοφία of the mystery-cults and the preachers of philosophy (Col. 2.8). But there is also a knowledge of God through Christ, a true wisdom which Paul claims to be superior to all pagan substitutes. The test by which the false knowledge and wisdom can be distinguished from the true is the test of love (ἀγάπη)—a test strikingly similar to that proposed in I John (e.g. esp. 4.8). The false *gnosis* puffs up in pride, instead of promoting *agape*. Therefore, says Paul, even if I know the secrets of all the mystery religions and all their vaunted *gnosis*, I am still nothing if I have not *agape* (I Cor. 13.2). *Gnosis*, whether Greek intellect or Hellenistic revelation, is valueless apart from love. The Corinthians may think that they know all about idols—the Christian revelation has 'debunked' them, of course; but that does not solve the practical problem of εἰδωλόθυτα and the weaker brother's conscience: 'Now concerning εἰδωλόθυτα, we know that we all have *gnosis*. *Gnosis* puffeth up, but *agape* builds up; if anyone thinks that he knows anything, he knows not yet as he ought to know; but if anyone loves God, the same is known by him' (I Cor. 8.1-3). That is to say, it is not *gnosis* that is the saving power, but love. It is love which tells us the real meaning of knowledge; knowledge is not something that we have a right to be conceited about, for the true knowledge is not our knowledge of God at all, but God's knowledge of us. In the matter of true knowledge, or saving knowledge, all is of God and nothing of ourselves; beside this kind of knowledge, which Paul would prefer to call *agape*, since it is a personal relation with God, all the *gnosis* of the academies and the sects amounts to nothing. Even the Jew has no occasion to boast of his possession of 'the form of *gnosis* and truth in the Law' (Rom. 2.20), because this knowledge, so far from saving him, is actually his condemnation (Rom. 2.17-29).

St Paul sets the whole question of *gnosis* in its true perspective by his wholly biblical emphasis upon the fact that our knowledge of God is not the important thing, not something on which we dare stake our salvation, but God's knowledge of us. We love God only because God 'knows' us (I Cor. 8.3), that is, in biblical language, calls us, enters into personal relations with us, commissions us to his service, and so on. It is not our cleverness or merit which has led us to the knowledge of God; thus he writes to the Galatians, 'At that time, not knowing God, you were slaves to those which by nature are no gods (i.e. the demons or pagan deities); but now that you have come to know God ($\nu\hat{v}\nu$ $\delta\grave{\epsilon}$ $\gamma\nu\acute{o}\nu\tau\epsilon\varsigma$ $\Theta\epsilon\acute{o}\nu$), or rather to be known by God ($\mu\hat{a}\lambda\lambda o\nu$ $\delta\grave{\epsilon}$ $\gamma\nu\omega\sigma\theta\acute{\epsilon}\nu$-$\tau\epsilon\varsigma$ $\acute{v}\pi\grave{o}$ $\Theta\epsilon o\hat{v}$), how turn ye back again . . . ?' (Gal. 4.8f.). It was by the preaching of the word of Christ that the converts from paganism had come to the knowledge of the true God, but this had taken place only because God in his outgoing love had first 'known' them. Thus for those who have responded to the word of God in Christ there is indeed a real knowledge of God, and it suffices us; but it is not yet final or perfect knowledge. In this life it can but be partial knowledge (I Cor. 13.9); it is knowledge by faith, not yet by sight. Our knowledge of the mind of Christ, through faith in him, is sufficient for our daily guidance (I Cor. 2.16). Even now we have light enough, 'a spirit of wisdom and revelation in the knowledge of him, having the eyes of your heart enlightened, that ye may know. . . .' (Eph. 1.17f.).[1] Here again the NT metaphor occurs also—knowledge is a seeing by means of the eyes of the heart, that is, by faith; it is the only kind of knowledge which we can have in this present age. It is partial knowledge, *per speculum*, and it must vanish away in that final day of revelation when 'I shall

---

[1] Cf. the prayer of I Clem. Rom. 59: 'Open the eyes of our hearts that we may know thee.'

know even as also I have been known' (I Cor. 13.12). This picture of the day of the Lord as a day of perfect knowledge is common to the OT and the NT.

A GENERAL REVELATION TO ALL MANKIND

It is clear from such a passage as Gal. 4.8f. that St Paul did not think that the Gentiles had any real knowledge of God until they received the Gospel of Christ. Yet, like the OT prophets, he holds that the Gentiles are blameworthy for their ignorance. They ought to have known God, but their knowledge was obscured by their sinfulness, especially their idolatry (Rom. 1.18-32). St Paul seems to have accepted the view of contemporary rabbinic Judaism that certain ethical demands were binding upon all men, including the Gentiles. Rabbinic thought had assimilated certain Greek ideas which were 'in the air', such as the Stoic notion of a universal moral law, or law of nature. Such a notion is already found, for instance, in Wisd. 13.1-9, a passage which clearly underlies Paul's thought in Rom. 1.18-32. There is no Hebrew word for 'nature', and the idea of nature is totally foreign to the OT; yet in the first century A.D. a pupil of Gamaliel's can write such a sentence as 'Does not even nature herself ($\phi\acute{\upsilon}\sigma\iota\varsigma$ $\alpha\mathring{\upsilon}\tau\acute{\eta}$) teach you that if a man has long hair it is a disgrace to him?' (I Cor. 11.14).[1] The rabbis, in fact, had formulated a doctrine of the universal knowledge of God under their own characteristic forms.[2] There had been a revelation since the days of Adam, or, as Paul says in Rom. 1.20, 'since the creation of the world', and this revelation had been renewed in the days of Noah, when history began again after the Flood (Gen. 9.1-7). It was held that the 'Noachic commandments', then enjoined upon all mankind, included such injunctions as not to worship idols, not to blaspheme, to establish justice, not to kill, not to commit adultery, not to steal, and so on—there was no single fixed version. It is possible that the 'apostolic decrees' issued by the Council of Jerusalem (Acts 15.20, 29) were intended as a Christian version of this Noachic Code: Gentile Christians are dispensed from the meticulous observance of the Law of Moses, but they must keep the universal moral law; at least this suggestion makes sense of a very difficult passage, but it too has its own difficulties. The Jewish rabbis were well aware that the Gentiles recognized certain ethical standards, even if they did not frequently live up to them; and they instinctively perceived that such moral awareness could ultimately have come only from the God of righteousness, whose *special* revelation of himself had been given in the Torah of Moses. Thus, St Paul in

---

[1] Note also the use of $\phi\acute{\upsilon}\sigma\iota\varsigma$ and $\phi\upsilon\sigma\iota\kappa\acute{o}\varsigma$ in Rom. 1.26f. and in Rom. 2.14.

[2] See W. D. Davies, *PRJ*, 115-17.

Rom. 2.14f. recognizes that the Gentiles, who have no Torah such as the Jews have, nevertheless sometimes do by nature (φύσει) the things of the moral law; they are therefore, he says, a law to themselves, that is, they are their own legislators; they prove that the content of the moral law is written on their hearts, their conscience (συνείδησις) bearing witness to it, their own moral judgments accusing or excusing them in the light of it.

The idea of conscience, thus introduced by Paul the rabbi into Christianity with far-reaching results, is found in Acts, the Pastorals, Hebrews and I Peter, as well as more than a dozen times in the Paulines. It seems to have been an ethical commonplace of the Greek world, just the kind of notion which a missionary religion could adapt for its own purposes.[1] It had already been accepted by Greek-speaking Jews, for we find the word in the LXX at Eccles. 10.20, Ecclus. 42.18 and Wisd. 17.11, though it is only in the last of these passages (where it is equated with 'a witness within') that it bears its technical ethical meaning. The word συνείδησις (lit. 'co-knowledge', *con-scientia*) implies a second consciousness, i.e. the reflective judgment which a man has alongside of his consciousness of what he is doing; this second consciousness is personified and projected as confronting and passing judgment upon the first, accusing or excusing. This universal awareness of right and wrong, together with the sense of obligation to do the right, which is called conscience, is taken by Paul as evidence of a universal human knowledge of the moral law, and therefore, however dimly, of the Author of the moral law. In this matter St Paul is following current rabbinic teaching, such as he had learnt from Gamaliel, even if the concepts of 'conscience' and 'nature' are Greek rather than Hebrew ways of stating it. Of course, as Paul goes on to argue strongly, this knowledge of God's law among the Gentiles is not a saving knowledge, any more than the Jews' knowledge of the Torah is for them saving knowledge. In both cases the law condemns: conscience is always the guilty conscience. Nevertheless the very existence of conscience among the Gentiles is evidence that they possess the knowledge of God. God has revealed himself since the creation of the world through the things which he has made, and his invisible attributes of everlasting power and divinity are clearly visible to the eye unclouded by sin (Rom. 1.20).

This teaching is not strictly a doctrine of a 'natural knowledge' of God, because in the previous verse Paul says that God revealed (ἐφανέρωσε) to mankind that which may be known about him (1.19). The rabbinic background here is still that of the myth of the Covenant

---

[1] For a full discussion of the subject see C. A. Pierce, *Conscience in the New Testament*, 1955.

with Noah and the renewal by its means of the original Covenant that God had intended to make with the whole human race through the first man, Adam. Therefore, it is better to speak of a 'general revelation' than of a 'natural knowledge' of God. But Paul the rabbi goes on to shew how this general revelation of God was disregarded and abused by mankind. Having come to know God (γνόντες τὸν Θεόν, Rom. 1.21; cf. Gal. 4.9), men nevertheless refused to worship him as God, desiring rather to glorify themselves, a process which leads to the darkening of reason and to the irrational worship of human deities and even of birds and cows and snakes. Superstition gives rise to immorality, for when men worship something other than God they cease to respect his moral law. As the Jews had always known, idolatry is the parent of fornication and of every kind of abomination. In typical rabbinic fashion Paul in Rom. 1.21-32 traces the superstitions and vices of the pagan world to their roots in idolatry, the worship of the creature instead of the Creator. Thus God's general revelation of his power and divinity through the works of creation is obscured by sin, and the truth is suppressed by unrighteousness (Rom. 1.18); nevertheless conscience remains among the Gentiles to testify to the original revelation of God to all mankind.

According to Acts 17.22-31 St Paul on suitable occasions based his preaching of the Gospel upon his rabbinic conception of a general revelation. He attempted to lead the Athenians on the Areopagus from the doctrines of Stoic philosophy to the revelation in Jesus Christ. He takes the existence of an altar inscribed Ἀγνώστῳ Θεῷ as evidence of their awareness of the God who made the world and does not inhabit temples made with human hands. He refers to 'some of your own poets' and quotes Aratus, the Cilician Stoic, to the effect that men are God's offspring. Paul, of course, would not have agreed with this view without qualification, since he does not think that all men are φύσει sons of God, but only that they are capable of becoming sons of God by adoption and grace; nevertheless taking the poet's words to mean that men have been made by God, he points out how such an insight is totally incompatible with popular idolatrous religious beliefs. He then goes on to speak of a coming judgment of the world by the Appointed Man, whose resurrection from the dead is the assurance of his future rôle as judge. There is no reason to suppose that St Luke has fabricated the content of Paul's preaching to the Athenians; Jewish apologists, trained in the rabbinic-Stoic anthropology of universal human conscience, must often have used this kind of argument in their discussions with Gentile 'God-fearers'. It was not the familiar Stoic-rabbinic approach which scandalized Paul's hearers, but the preaching of

judgment and resurrection. Some commentators have suggested that it
was the failure of his philosophical apologetic on the Areopagus that
made Paul resolve that henceforward he would preach nothing but Christ
crucified and never again start from 'the wisdom of this world' (I Cor.
1.18-31). Such a suggestion is altogether unlikely. It is much more
probable that Paul meant what he actually wrote to the Corinthians,
namely, that his preaching of Christ was not a new mystery religion, a
man-made σοφία (I Cor. 2.1, 5f., 13), but a *kerugma* which, however
foolish it might sound, was attested by the Holy Spirit of God. He is
certainly not confessing that he had ever preached a man-made σοφία,
at Athens or anywhere else; he is protesting that this is the one thing he
could never do. Furthermore it was not the rabbinic apologetic which
had scandalized the Athenians; it was the idea of judgment and of a
resurrection from the dead which they had mocked (Acts 17.32); it
was the preaching of Christ crucified which appeared foolishness to the
Greeks (I Cor. 1.23). Paul knew well enough that there would have been
no scandal in Christianity as a new σοφία. It was the kerugmatic element
in the faith, not the philosophical, which was resented by the 'disputers
of this age'. There is no reason to doubt that in his summary of Paul's
preaching on the Areopagus St Luke has given us a faithful account of
the kind of approach which St Paul was accustomed to make to an
audience of educated Greeks, whenever he had an opportunity to
preach to them.

We need not doubt, despite Karl Barth,[1] that St Paul adhered to the
rabbinic teaching that a general revelation of God had been vouchsafed
to the world before ever the Torah was given through Moses. God had
made a covenant with mankind before he made his covenant with
Abraham, of which circumcision was the sign (Gen. 17.1-14). Had it not
been so, mankind generally would have had no knowledge that one way
of behaving was better than another, and could not have recognized
certain kinds of conduct as good; there would have been no point in
the exhortation, so frequently addressed to the Christian communities,
to seek to convince the Gentiles by their example (Rom. 12.17; I Tim.
6.1; Titus 2.5; cf. Rom. 2.24). It is because of the grace of God in general
revelation that the moral life of the good pagan can put the lax Jew to
shame and may be reckoned unto him for circumcision (Rom. 2.26f.).
For this reason also the office-bearers of the State are performing a
divine service (λειτουργοὶ Θεοῦ), and Christians should therefore be
subject to them not only for fear of their displeasure but also for conscience' sake (Rom. 13.4-6; I Pet. 2.13f.; Titus 3.1). It is by reason of
this truth, which is mythologically expressed in the story of God's

_____
[1] *The Epistle to the Romans*, ET, Hoskyns, 1930, 46f.

covenant with Noah, that the State itself—even the government of Nero—has its divinely appointed rôle in the providential ordering of the world.[1]

REVELATION AND PAROUSIA

The biblical teaching is that God revealed himself to all mankind through the works of creation, especially through man, since man was made in God's own image (Gen. 1.26f.). But man's character of *imago Dei* was sadly defaced though not obliterated by his fall into sin. There remained in man traces of his 'original righteousness' in his reason and conscience, however feeble and distorted these have been rendered by sin. God, however, in his mercy vouchsafed to mankind a 'special revelation' of himself, whereby man in the midst of his sinfulness might through faith in God's promise come to a saving knowledge of God as his creator and redeemer. Man could not have rediscovered God for himself or known him as he is, had not God revealed himself through the veils of ignorance and superstition which are the consequences of man's attempt to put himself into the place of God. But the full revelation of God will not be made until the final 'day of the Lord', when faith shall be swallowed up in sight; in the meantime God has granted a revelation to the eye of faith which even now assures us of our ultimate salvation. Thus, though 'revelation' is primarily an eschatological conception, there is, as we shall see, a sense in which it is right to speak of a revelation in history.

Two verbs are chiefly used in the NT to convey the idea of revealing. The first, ἀποκαλύπτειν (with its cognate noun, ἀποκάλυψις) means to unveil, to take the cover off something and let it be seen. It is used with an everyday, secular meaning in classical Greek writers and in the LXX. But in the NT it is never used in the everyday, literal sense, but only as a technical theological term;[2] thus at I Cor. 11.5f., where Paul is speaking about removing a woman's head-covering, or at II Cor. 3.13f., where he is speaking about removing the veil from Moses's face, he employs different compound forms of the verb: ἀκατακάλυπτος, uncovered, and ἀνακαλύπτειν, to unveil, respectively. In the NT ἀποκαλύπτειν is always used of God's act of revealing and is never used in a human, secular sense. (The OT has, of course, used the words in the sense of divine revelation, e.g. LXX, I Sam. 2.27; Ps. 97 (98).2; Dan. 2.19). In the NT Mark, John (except in an OT quotation at 12.38), Acts and Heb. never use ἀποκαλύπτειν. But it is found in Matt. 10.26 (=Luke 12.2), Matt. 11.25, 27 (=Luke 10.21f.), Matt. 16.17 and

---

[1] For a fuller consideration of the idea of 'general revelation' see Alan Richardson, *Christian Apologetics*, Chap. V. For the covenant with Noah see the same author's *Genesis I-XI* (Torch Commentaries), 1953, 105-12.

[2] So G. S. Hendry, *TWBB*, 195f.

Luke 17.30, all in words attributed to Jesus. Along with the OT quotation in Luke 2.32 these are the only uses of the word in the Gospels. The second verb, φανεροῦν (with its derived noun, φανέρωσις) means to make manifest something formerly hidden or unknown. This word can be used in its ordinary, everyday sense (e.g. Mark 3.12; 6.14) or with the deeper meaning of divine revelation by which hidden, mysterious truth is disclosed. The noun occurs in NT only at I Cor. 12.7 and II Cor. 4.2.

When we today use the word 'revelation' in theological discussion, we nearly always mean 'historical revelation', through Israel or through Christ. But when the NT speaks of revelation, it nearly always means the final unveiling at the end of the age, i.e. at the parousia. The word ἀποκάλυψις, used simply and without qualification, means the parousia, the revealing of Jesus Christ at his coming at the end of the age. The OT 'day of the Lord' now takes on the sense of 'the day of (the coming of) the Lord Jesus'; thus St Paul describes the Corinthians as 'waiting for the ἀποκάλυψις of our Lord Jesus Christ, who shall also confirm you unto the end, unreprovable in the day of our Lord Jesus Christ' (I Cor. 1.7). The Messiah will return to deliver the creation from its ills, and he will not come alone, for the sons of God shall appear with him in glory—'the ἀποκάλυψις of the sons of God' (Rom. 8.18f.; cf. II (4) Esd. 13.26, 29, 39). Rest will come to those who are afflicted in this age 'at the ἀποκάλυψις of the Lord Jesus from heaven with the angels of his power' (II Thess. 1.7: we may ask whether the angels here are to be identified with the 'sons of God' of Rom. 8.19; cf. Job 1.6; 2.1; 38.7; Pss. 29.1; 89.6 RV mg.). Tribulations must be endured by the faithful until the Man of Sin is revealed, the son of perdition, who is described in Danielic language as 'exalting himself against all that is called God' and sitting in the sanctuary (ναός) of God; then the Restrainer will be revealed in his own season (καιρός): 'then shall be revealed the lawless one, whom the Lord Jesus shall slay with the breath of his mouth and bring to nought by the manifestation (ἐπιφάνεια) of his coming (παρουσία)' (II Thess. 2.3-8). The word ἐπιφάνεια, an appearing, manifestation, usually in the sense of a supernatural appearing, is used in NT only here (II Thess. 2.8) and in the Pastorals (five times), always (except at II Tim. 1.10) in the sense of the final appearing of Christ in glory at the end of the age. The word παρουσία (from πάρειμι, to be at hand, to have arrived, to be present) can be used in a secular everyday sense for someone's arrival or presence (e.g. I Cor. 16.17; II Cor. 10.10); but its significant use in the NT is as a technical term for the visible coming of Christ at the end of the age, the Christian 'day of the Lord', the day of revelation, when Christ will raise the dead, hold the last judgment and set up the kingdom of God in power and glory (Matt. 24.3, 27, 37, 39; I Cor. 15.23; I Thess. 2.19; 3.13; 4.15; 5.23; II Thess. 2.1, 8f.; James 5.7f.; II Pet. 1.16; 3.4, 12; I John 2.28). It is this event of the parousia of Christ which is referred to quite simply as ἡ ἀποκάλυψις, *the* revelation. Thus, I Peter speaks of 'a salvation ready to be revealed (ἀποκαλυφθῆναι) at the last time (ἐν καιρῷ ἐσχάτῳ)' (1.5), a time which is also referred to as ἐν ἀποκαλύψει 'Ιησοῦ Χριστοῦ (1.7 and 1.13), or ἐν τῇ ἀποκαλύψει τῆς δόξης αὐτοῦ (4.13; cf. 5.1).

The NT itself does not speak of a 'second coming' of Christ; the nearest approach to that expression is to be found in Heb. 9.28, where it is said that 'Christ shall appear a second time (ἐκ δευτέρου), apart from sin, to them that wait for him, unto salvation'. The technical term ἡ δευτέρα παρουσία is at least as old as Justin Martyr (*Apol.* 1.52, etc.) and is contrasted with ἡ πρώτη παρουσία (*Dial. c. Tr.* cc. 40, 110, 121; cf. Ignatius, *Phil.* 9), i.e. the incarnation, birth and ministry of Christ. The word ἔλευσις (cf. ἐλεύσομαι), a coming, advent, is found in NT only at Acts 7.52, where it refers to Christ's first coming; but it is later used in the plural, αἱ ἐλεύσεις, to refer to the first and second comings of Christ (Irenaeus, *Adv. Haer.* I.10). Some theologians disapprove of the traditional expression, 'the second coming of Christ', on the ground that it implies that Christ, once present on earth, is now absent, but will come again. But the phrase was never intended to suggest a doctrine of the 'real absence' of Christ; it was used to convey what the NT certainly teaches: that Christ is not now present in the same way as he was present in the days of his flesh, and that he is not yet present in the way in which he will be present in the day of his 'appearing'. Christ is truly present to his Church today, but he is present not in his earthly body, nor yet in his visible 'glory'; he is present in the reality of the Holy Spirit.

There is also a difference between the revelation that will be made at Christ's parousia and the revelation that has been given in history. At the parousia the revelation will be a 'sight' revelation as contrasted with the 'faith' revelation that is given in history. The revelation in the historical Jesus could be received only by the eye of faith—and this is equally true of his original disciples in the days of his flesh and of his disciples in every subsequent century who have accepted their testimony. At the 'apocalypse' of Christ in the 'last time' it will be impossible for anyone, with or without faith, to avoid beholding him as he is, in his glorious majesty. During his incarnate life, a veil, impenetrable to eyes without faith, concealed beneath the form of a servant the royal dignity of the King of kings, so that Annas and Caiaphas, Herod and Pilate, those who crucified him, did not perceive that Jesus was indeed a King.

But at his coming at the end of the age he will be manifest in all his majesty not only to the eyes of faith but to every eye: 'Behold, he cometh with the clouds; and every eye shall see him, and they which pierced him' (Rev. 1.7). No longer in that day shall we see 'darkly'— ἐν αἰνίγματι—but 'face to face' (I Cor. 13.12): tongues and prophecies and *gnosis* shall vanish away in the day when faith is swallowed up in sight. 'We shall see him even as he is' (I John 3.2).

How then does the NT regard what we call 'historical revelation'? It thinks of it as a foretaste of the fulness of the grace and truth (cf. John 1.14) which shall be hereafter, at the end of the age—a foretaste mercifully vouchsafed here and now to those who have responded in faith to the word of salvation in Christ, a tasting of the powers of the Age to Come (Heb. 6.5). Thus, St Peter speaks (or is made to speak) of himself as 'a partaker of the glory that *shall be* revealed' (I Pet. 5.1). The goal of world-process, namely Christ (I Cor. 15.27f.; Eph. 1.10; Col. 1.20), has already appeared in history, but in such a lowly form that only those who possessed the gift of faith could see in him 'the Man ordained to judge the world in righteousness' (Acts 17.31). The glory was present indeed in the incarnate Son, but it was veiled in such a way that only those who believed his word could see it (John 1.14; 2.11; 14.22). In past times God had spoken to the ear of obedient faith through the prophets, and his culminating address—his 'last word'— had now been spoken in Jesus Christ his Son, the agent of creation by whom the worlds also were sustained (Heb. 1.1-3; cf. John 1.1-5). Those who do not disregard so great an act of salvation, spoken of by the Lord himself, confirmed by those who heard him, now await his second appearing 'unto salvation' (Heb. 2.3; 9.28). Faith itself is thus an eschatological participation in things hoped for but not yet seen (Heb. 11.1). The NT understanding of the economy of salvation can be seen in such a passage as I Pet. 1.10-12: the Spirit of Christ in the OT prophets testified beforehand both the sufferings and triumphs (δόξαι) of Christ, and the revelation was made to them not so much for the sake of their own generation, but so that those to whom the Gospel would be preached in the age of the Holy Spirit would properly comprehend things long hidden, that even the angels desire to look into. The suggestion of this passage is that the prophets in their own age did not fully understand the things which they wrote; the latter could be understood only by those who possess in Jesus Christ the key to the Scriptures (so also John 5.39; II Cor. 3.14-16; Gal. 3.8; Luke 24.25-27, 44-48, etc.). But the words uttered by the prophets, when understood in the light of Christ, may be spoken of as revelation; and in I Pet. 1.12 there is a positive instance of ἀποκαλύπτειν being used of what we would call 'historical' revelation although the same passage makes it clear that revelation in the absolute sense is still a future event that will take place 'at the last time' (1.5; cf. 1.7, 13). Similar teaching is found in Rom. 16.25f., where Paul equates his own gospel, the *kerugma* of Jesus Christ, with the revelation of a mystery which had been kept in silence through age-long times, but now is manifested. Revelation here again is 'historical' revelation. The function of 'the scriptures of the prophets' is to make known to all nations this revelation 'unto obedience of faith'. Thus historical revelation is essentially 'faith-revelation'. The Church makes use of the Jewish Scriptures to prove to the Gentiles the truth of the Gospel of Christ, in which the ancient prophecies are fulfilled. As later Christian apologists were to argue, it was part of the providential divine plan that the Jews in their dispersion should have carried their Scriptures into every Gentile land, so that the preachers of the Gospel, when they arrived, should have confirmatory evidence of their message already awaiting them there.[1]

If now we ask whence apostolic Christianity derived this conception of revelation, the answer would seem to be: from the Lord Jesus himself. He had called upon men to have faith in the eschatological event which his own preaching and mighty works inaugurated; he had led them to discern beneath the lowly form of the Son of Man, who had not where to lay his head (Luke 9.58), the royal person of the Son of Man who would sit 'on the throne of his glory' in judgment upon the nations (Matt. 25.31f.). If, as seems likely, Jesus conceived of his own Messianic vocation along the lines of the Suffering Servant of Isaiah's prophecy, we have in Isa. 53 the prototype of the despised and rejected Son of Man who was not recognized by his contemporaries as the Lord's Anointed, but who nevertheless is vindicated and shewn to be the bringer of righteousness and salvation. If, further, Jesus had identified the Isaianic Servant with the Danielic 'one like unto a son of man' who should come with the clouds of heaven (Dan. 7.13; Matt. 16.27; 24.30; 26.64; Mark 14.62), then it would seem that the NT conception of revelation as the unveiling of the Son of Man, begun now by faith, to be completed at the parousia, is directly traceable to the authority of Jesus himself. The further elaboration and vindication of this suggestion must await our exposition of Jesus' conception of his own person and work. It should, however, be noted here that some recorded words of Jesus in the Gospels speak of a future revelation which (it is reasonable to suppose) is the same event as the coming of the Son of Man in his power and glory: 'there is nothing covered that shall not be revealed. . . .' (Matt. 10.26=Luke 12.2). More explicitly in another

[1] E.g. St Augustine, *Ep.* CXXXVII, iv.16.

passage Jesus speaks of the parousia of the Son of Man as being like a lightning-flash, sudden and visible to all; there will be no need to peer 'here' and 'there', for the flash will be seen from east to west (Matt. 24.27=Luke 17.24; cf. Luke 17.30). The Gospels represent Jesus himself as teaching that 'the day of the Son of Man' will be a sudden unveiling of the truth which is now hidden and visible only to the eye of faith, but which will then be made manifest in all its blinding splendour to every human eye.

REVELATION AND MYSTERY

In the NT revelation and mystery are concepts inseparable from each other.[1] God's existence is not a problem which we can solve by intellectual effort; it is a mystery which we can perceive by faith. In this age every act of unveiling must at the same time be an act of veiling; not until the final day of revelation will there be an unveiling in which there will be no veiling at all. Revelation in this age is always the disclosure of the *hidden* God; the Bible expresses its sense of the mystery of the divine being by means of its insistence upon the hiddenness of God and of all his ways (cf. Isa. 45.15; also Deut. 29.29; Job 11.7; 15.8; 36.22f.; Rom. 11.33f.). The Hebrew tongue is rich in synonyms for 'hide' and 'hidden', and nothing could more clearly indicate the profoundly religious quality of the biblical mind than its deep sense of the hidden mystery of God.[2] God's being is inaccessible to man's understanding, and even in revealing himself in his saving acts God remains hidden from us; he does not thereby lay his nature open to the inspection of philosophers, since his saving and revealing acts are also mysterious. Jesus himself actually thanks God that the divine truth is hidden from the clever and sophisticated but is revealed to 'babes' (Matt. 11.25= Luke 10.21). He speaks of God's reign as a 'mystery', i.e. as a hidden reality, in this age (Mark 4.11 and pars.). So, too, St Paul speaks of the Christian knowledge of God in this age as a 'hidden wisdom': 'we speak God's wisdom in a mystery, even the wisdom that hath been hidden' (I Cor. 2.7). The mysterious truth of the Gospel cannot be made known through ordinary publicity channels but only through 'the hearing of faith'—a truth constantly overlooked by busy, untheological clergymen who imagine that they can bring home the message of the Gospel by modern advertising techniques and business methods.

[1] Cf. J. B. Lightfoot on Col. 1.27 (*St Paul's Epistles to the Colossians and Philemon*, 3rd ed., 1879, 168): 'μυστήριον is almost universally found in connection with words denoting revelation or publication; e.g. ἀποκαλύπτειν, ἀποκάλυψις, Rom. 16.25; Eph. 3.3, 5; II Thess. 2.7; γνωρίζειν, Rom. 16.26; Eph. 1.9; 3.3, 10; 6.19; φανεροῦν, Col. 4.3; Rom. 16.26; I Tim. 3.16; λαλεῖν, Col. 4.3; I Cor. 2.7; 14.2; λέγειν, I Cor. 15.51.'

[2] See W. Stählin, *The Mystery of God*, ET, 1937, 14; G. S. Hendry, *TWBB*, 108.

Thus they convert the mystery of evangelization into a 'problem of communication'. At the same level of misunderstanding untheological scholars have imagined that the mystery of God, the hiddenness of his being and his ways, about which the NT speaks, is something akin to the 'mysteries' of Graeco-oriental religion. It is, of course, on the contrary, the continuation and working out in the NT of the ancient Hebrew awareness of the utter mystery of God's being and its inaccessibility to the finite capacities of all created intelligences.

The NT writers—certainly a Hellenistic Jew like St Paul—could hardly have been unaware of the meaning of 'mystery' in the pagan religion of their day, yet they do not set forth 'the mystery of the Gospel' (Eph. 6.19) in the guise of a new mystery-cult. Like the author of Wisdom, they would have dismissed such 'mysteries' with contempt (Wisd. 14.15, 23). The Gospel of Jesus Christ was proclaimed in the market-place to all who would listen: it was not a hotch-potch of magical catchwords whispered to the initiates amidst superstitious ceremonies behind locked doors. It was clearly a different kind of 'mystery' from the pagan 'mysteries'. The mystery about which St Paul writes is not a secret *gnosis* magically conferring immortality upon the few: it is the hidden plan of salvation for the whole world, Jew and Gentile alike, which had been kept hidden through all the ages until now, when in these last times it has been disclosed in Jesus Christ and is now proclaimed by those who preach him—i.e. the ministers of Christ and stewards of the mysteries of God (I Cor. 4.1)—and it stands, an open secret, for all who will believe the good news (Rom. 11.25; 16.25f.; I Cor. 2.7; Eph. 1.9; 3.3-6; Col. 2.2; 4.3). But Paul can use the word in other senses—e.g. of unintelligible things spoken in a 'tongue' (I Cor. 14.2), of the mystery of how we shall all be changed at the last trump (I Cor. 15.51), of the mystery of lawlessness (II Thess. 2.7), or of the 'mystic sense' or hidden meaning of an OT passage (Eph. 5.32). Outside the Paulines the word is used in the NT in I Tim. 3.9, 16, somewhat colourlessly, and also in Revelation, where it usually bears the sense of a mystic image seen in a vision (Rev. 1.20; 17.5, 7); but at Rev. 10.7 the μυστήριον τοῦ Θεοῦ is clearly the whole divine plan for the creation, now reaching its consummation, according to the good tidings proclaimed by the prophets of old (cf. Rom. 16.25f.). The only use of μυστήριον outside the Paulines, I Tim. and Rev. is at Mark 4.11 (and pars. Matt. 13.11, Luke 8.10), which will be discussed below.[1]

The NT conveys the sense of the deep mystery of revelation in many ways, even when the word μυστήριον is not used. The hiddenness of the truth and its inaccessibility apart from faith are everywhere implied,

---

[1] See *infra*, 92-5.

Thus, there is a mystery of the person of Christ, a mystery of the Kingdom of God, a mystery of the divine plan of salvation. A mystery in this biblical sense is something quite different from a secret. It does not cease to be a mystery when it has been revealed, whereas, of course, a secret ceases to be a secret. As we have noted, the verb 'reveal' could not appropriately be used in the sense of making known an ordinary, everyday piece of information (cf. the current newspaper jargon: 'A spokesman of the Foreign Office revealed that . . .'). When the mystery of the person of Christ is revealed to his disciples (cf. Matt. 16.17), it is not less mysterious than before. A secret, though concealed at present, may at any time be 'made public', and then it ceases to be a secret. But a mystery cannot be made public in this way; it cannot be laid open to public inspection even when it is preached from the house-tops. To take an illustration: Judas may have 'revealed' (in the newspaper sense of the word) to the high priest the secret of Jesus's Messiahship; but he did not and could not reveal the mystery of it, and the high priest remained in total ignorance of it. Or again, Pilate's superscription may have made public the news that Jesus was the king of the Jews; but the inward mystery of the Kingship of Jesus can never be disclosed by means of a public notice-board. The mystery of the person of Christ is not at all the same thing as the so-called 'Messianic secret'. The NT writers, as we have noted, whether consciously or not, reserve ἀποκαλύπτειν for the disclosure of mystery and never use it of the making public of a piece of information after the manner of a 'press-release'.

The paradox of revelation, as the Bible understands it, is that God can reveal himself to sinful man only by veiling the brightness of his true glory. This veiling of his brightness is a gracious act of the divine condescension: the true light, appearing amongst men, was veiled in order that they might see. Otherwise they would have been blinded by excess of light. Thus, the incarnation itself was necessarily a veiling as well as a revealing of the light; if it had not been the former, it could not have been the latter. Spiritual truth, if we may use the language of St Thomas Aquinas, must be mediated through corporeal images; *in statu viatoris* there is no direct vision of God, for the sight would sear our eyes; the light can reach us, in the phrase which St Thomas is fond of quoting from Dionysius, only when 'wrapped in a maze of sacred veils'. Hence the necessity of the incarnation: the divine truth must veil its brightness in the robe of human nature, and so God reveals himself by the paradoxical act of hiding himself in our humanity.[1] The divine splendour is at once veiled and revealed in the flesh which Christ took from the Virgin Mary his mother. The divine Son wears his

[1] See A. L. Lilley, *Religion and Revelation*, 1932, 49.

human robe so perfectly that men in every generation since his own (cf. Mark 6.2f.) have looked upon him as merely one of themselves and have failed to penetrate the *incognito* which he had assumed. So, too, the divine life of the Church, his continuing body on the earth, necessarily involves a veiling of the inner mystery of its existence: 'your life is hid with Christ in God' (Col. 3.3); but it will be fully revealed in its glorious reality at the manifestation of Christ (Col. 3.4). Similarly the Church's sacraments are veils penetrable only by faith ('Beneath these signs are hidden Glorious things to sight forbidden'[1]). Even the words of the Scriptures themselves are veils; in Luther's metaphor, they are the human swaddling-clothes in which the Christ is laid. All forms of revelation are necessarily veilings of the truth and are signs of the infinite condescension of God, who accommodates his divine majesty to the capacity of our human weakness.

[1] St Thomas Aquinas, *Lauda, Sion, Salvatorem.*

3

THE POWER OF GOD UNTO SALVATION

CHRIST'S gospel of the reign of God is 'the power of God unto salvation to every one who believes' (Rom. 1.16). It is the proclamation that God's purpose of salvation, adumbrated by the divine activity in Israel's history to which the prophets of the old dispensation had pointed, is now being fulfilled through the exaltation of the crucified Messiah, who will presently return and consummate all things. In this divine activity God has revealed his character of righteousness and his purpose of salvation. In the biblical view God cannot be known as he exists in himself, but only in so far as by his activity he discloses himself. His being is beyond our scrutiny and we can know him only because he has revealed himself in human history. The divine activity, by which God has made himself known, is expressed in the NT by a number of words which denote the outgoing, spontaneous action of God: δύναμις, ἐξουσία, ἐνέργεια, κράτος, βασιλεία, δόξα, φῶς, ζωή, λόγος, σοφία, πνεῦμα, χάρις, ἀγάπη, ὀργή, θυμός, δικαιοσύνη, σωτηρία—and many more. From an early date such 'attributes' were ascribed to God and to Christ in the Church's worship (e.g. Rev. 4.11; 5.12f.; 7.12; Matt. 6.13, RV mg. only). In such doxologies God is praised for his creative and redemptive activity, through which alone we have knowledge of him and of his will to save us. Many of these active manifestations of God are more or less synonymous with one another, since it is the same divine δύναμις which is operative under different forms. For example, Christ may be said to have been raised from the dead by means of God's δύναμις (I Cor. 6.14), or by his δόξα (Rom. 6.4), or by his ἐνέργεια (Col. 2.12); yet it is much more frequently asserted in Acts, in Paul and in the sub-Pauline books, that *God* raised him from the dead.

CHRIST THE POWER OF GOD

The desire to avoid anthropomorphism led the rabbis to speak of something as having been done by such attributes as the power, or the wisdom, or the spirit (of God), although they meant that God had done it.[1] Hence to speak of God's δύναμις is simply to speak of God acting. The God of the Bible is pure δύνασθαι, the source of all δύναμις and ἐξουσία, of whom alone it may be said, πάντα δυνατά (Mark 10.27; cf. Gen. 18.14; Job 42.2; Jer. 32.17, 27; Zech. 8.6; Luke 1.37). The NT nowhere says *tout court* that Christ is God (Rom. 9.5 may be punctuated in several ways: see RV mg.), but it does say that he is the δύναμις of God (I Cor. 1.24), i.e. he is *the* activity of God *par excellence*. Christ is God's most characteristic, most revealing, action. In the earthly life of Jesus the δύναμις Θεοῦ was veiled; yet it expressed itself in those δυνάμεις which manifested to the eyes of faith the impending destruction of Satan's counter-kingdom. After his resurrection Christ received all ἐξουσία in heaven and on earth (Matt. 28.18; I Cor. 15.27f.; Eph. 1.20-22; Phil. 2.9f.; Heb. 2.8; I Pet. 3.22; Rev. 11.15-17; 17.14); before it the NT speaks of the reign *of God*, but after it *Christ* reigns, and the phrase βασιλεία τοῦ Χριστοῦ is permissible (Eph. 5.5; Col. 1.13; II Pet. 1.11; Rev. 11.15). The *Christus regnans* from his exalted place at God's right hand pours down his gifts—the gift and the gifts of the Spirit (Eph. 4.8; I Cor. 12.4-11, etc.), whose workings here and now are the empirical evidence of the exaltation of Christ (Acts 2.33). The βασιλεία τοῦ Θεοῦ is made visible to faith in the operation of the Holy Spirit (Rom. 5.5; Eph. 4.8, etc.); the βασιλεία of God or of Christ is present and active in a new way, ἐν δυνάμει, 'with power', i.e. with the power of the Holy Spirit (Rom. 15.13; Mark 9.1). The power which the missionary Church experienced was in fact the power of the Spirit (Rom. 15.13, 19; I Cor. 2.4; Eph. 3.16, 20; Col. 1.11, 29; II Tim. 1.7, etc.); and indeed in many contexts δύναμις and πνεῦμα are virtually synonymous terms (e.g. Luke 1.17, 35; 4.14; 5.17; 6.19; cf. Mark 5.30). Christ himself was conceived by the power of the Holy Spirit (Matt. 1.18, 20; Luke 1.35) and he was anointed in Holy Spirit at his baptism (Mark 1.10 and pars.); but it is not until after his resurrection that the power of the Spirit is imparted to his disciples (John 7.39): 'Tarry ye here in the city until ye be clothed with δύναμις from on high' (Luke 24.49); 'Ye shall receive δύναμις when the Holy Spirit is come upon you' (Acts 1.8).

The association and even identification of δύναμις and Holy Spirit in the NT gives us the clue to the much discussed saying of Jesus in Mark 9.1: 'Verily, I say unto you, There be some here of them that stand by, which shall in no wise taste of death, till they see the reign of God come ἐν δυνάμει.' Jesus conceives of his own Messianic mission as

[1] 'The Power' was a rabbinic periphrasis for the divine name (G. Dalman, *Words of Jesus*, ET, 1902, 200f.) and it is thus used at Mark 14.62; Matt. 26.64; cf. Luke 22.69. There is good OT precedent for speaking of God as δύναμις, e.g. Pss. 45.2 (LXX; EVV, 46.1), 58.17 (LXX; EVV, 59.16).

that of bringing in the New Age foretold by the prophets, in which the Holy Spirit would be poured out upon all flesh (Joel 2.28, etc.).[1] His own death was to be the means of bringing in the Age of the Spirit. Jesus was declaring that God's βασιλεία, whose advent he had proclaimed, would shortly be manifested in the activity (δύναμις) of the outpoured Spirit of God. The βασιλεία during Christ's ministry on earth is, as it were, an irresistible δύναμις silently at work in the world (Mark 4.26-32); shortly, however, as some of those standing by would discover, this βασιλεία τοῦ Θεοῦ would be 'demonstrated' in the Spirit and in δύναμις (cf. I Cor. 2.4). As Paul, who rejoiced in the distribution of the Spirit's gifts, was able to declare, the reign of God is not now merely a matter of preaching, of words only, but is present in the Church in all its dynamic reality—οὐ γὰρ ἐν λόγῳ ἡ βασιλεία τοῦ Θεοῦ ἀλλ' ἐν δυνάμει (I Cor. 4.20); the phrase ἐν δυνάμει well characterized the quality of the Church's life in the Spirit. We may sum up the matter thus: during his earthly ministry Jesus preached the reign of God ἐν λόγῳ, and his word possessed its own self-realizing power (e.g. Matt. 8.16): but after his death and exaltation the reign of God was present in a new way, ἐν δυνάμει, i.e. in the power of the Holy Spirit. St John, as is his custom, makes very clear the standpoint of the apostolic Church in this matter (John 7.39; 14.16f., 26; 15.26; 16.7-14; 20.22).[2] But neither St John nor any other NT writer regards the coming of Christ in the Holy Spirit's δύναμις as his final parousia. The Age of the Spirit of Power will endure until what St John calls 'the last day' (John 6.39f., 54). The δυνάμεις of the historical Jesus, like the Spirit-empowered triumphs of the Church of Christ on earth, are, as it were, an eschatological anticipation or ἀρραβών of that day when Christ shall have abolished all (alien) ἀρχή, ἐξουσία and δύναμις and will deliver up the βασιλεία to God, namely, the Father, who shall then be 'all in all' (I Cor. 15.24, 28). This final consummation of all things is referred to quite simply by St Paul as 'the end' (εἶτα τὸ τέλος, I Cor. 15.24). All δύναμις will have returned to God, from whom it came.

THE GLORY OF THE LORD

'Glory' (δόξα) in the NT is an eschatological conception closely associated with βασιλεία and δύναμις (e.g. Matt. 6.13, RV mg.; Mark 13.26, etc.) and with πνεῦμα (e.g. I Pet. 4.14). The word δόξα is taken over from the LXX, where it is used to translate Heb. *kabhod*, which

---

[1] See further *infra*, 107-9.

[2] The words δύναμις, δυνάμεις, do not occur in the Gospel or Epp. of John, possibly because of their associations in pagan religion and Gnostic speculation; cf. Acts 8.10, where Simon Magus is popularly acclaimed 'that δύναμις of God which is called Great'. Δύναμις is, however, frequent in Rev., esp. in the doxologies (4.11; 5.12; 7.12; etc.).

originally meant 'weight' and came to mean 'substance', 'wealth', 'honour', 'reputation' (e.g. Ps. 49.16f.; Isa. 66.11f.); its significant use, however, is in the sense of the visible brightness of the divine presence, a sense found in the P traditions concerning the Law-giving and the Tabernacle (e.g. Ex. 16.10; 24.16; 40.34f.; cf. II Cor. 3.7).[1] This visible 'glory' is also seen in prophetic vision. (e.g. Isa. 6.3; Ezek. 8.4, etc.). After OT times the rabbis spoke of the glory or 'visible brightness of the presence' of God as the *shekhinah* (Heb. 'that which dwells', 'dwelling'); this word does not appear in the OT but is frequent in the Targums as a periphrasis for 'God', like *memra* ('word') or *yekara* (another word for 'glory'). The kind of play on words that is beloved of the Semitic mind can be reproduced in biblical Greek by the rough assonance of the words *shekhinah*, ἐπισκιάζειν (to overshadow) and σκηνή (a tabernacle, tent) or σκηνεῖν (to dwell in a tent, encamp). Thus, in the Transfiguration story the cloud (Mark 9.7; Luke 9.34; in Matt. 17.5, significantly, a *bright* cloud) represents the cloud which overshadowed the 'tent of meeting' when the glory of Yahweh filled the tabernacle (Ex. 40.34f.), and the same verb, ἐπισκιάζειν, is used. Peter's suggestion about making three σκηναί belongs to the same cycle of ideas (Mark 9.5 and pars.). It is significant that in II Pet. 1.17 the Synoptists' 'voice out of the cloud' becomes 'a voice from the excellent glory', and Jesus is said to have received τιμή and δόξα from the Father.[2]

This later Jewish conception of the *shekhinah* as God's visible, glorious presence dwelling in Israel doubtless influences the language and thought of the NT on the subject of δόξα at several points, e.g. Luke 2.9; Acts 7.2, 55; 9.3; Rom. 9.4; Heb. 9.5. Striking use of it is made by the Fourth Evangelist. He records no scene of Transfiguration, as do the three Synoptists; he regards the whole of Christ's incarnate life as an embodiment of the δόξα of God, though the glory is revealed only to believing disciples and not unto 'the world' (John 2.11, etc.): the incarnation of the Logos necessarily involves the transfiguration of the human Jesus. The Christ of the Fourth Gospel is the locus, so to speak, of the tabernacling presence or δόξα of God; cf. John 1.14, 'The word ... tabernacled (ἐσκήνωσεν) among us and we beheld his δόξα' (cf. Ex. 40.34f.; Lev. 26.11f.; Ezek. 37.26-28; Rev. 21.3).[3] The whole NT regards the incarnate Lord as the first instalment, as it were, of the unveiling of the δόξα in the latter days (Isa. 60.3, 19; 66.10f., 18f.;

[1] In cl. Gk. δόξα meant 'opinion' (cf. 'orthodoxy'), a meaning found in the bib. lit. only at IV Macc. 5.18; also 'appearance' (so at LXX Isa. 11.3, but quoted in John 7.24 as 'judge not according to ὄψις'); hence 'reputation', 'honour', 'substance' (thus John 12.43, 'They loved the δόξα of men more than the δόξα of God'; also Rom. 2.7, 10).

[2] The Transfiguration story is treated at length *infra*, 181-5.

[3] See further *infra*, 163-5.

Hag. 2.7, 9). During his earthly life the δόξα was indeed present, but eschatologically; it was veiled from men without faith (II Cor. 3.7–4.6). The incarnate Lord must enter into his δόξα by suffering and death (Luke 24.26), as Jesus himself had with such difficulty taught his disciples (Mark 8.31; 9.12; 10.32-45, esp. v. 37; Luke 12.50, etc.). All four Gospels present the passion-story, not as a martyrdom, as if inviting us to pity the sad fate of a helpless victim, but rather as the story of a conqueror's triumphal progress: 'Weep not for me; weep rather for yourselves. . . .' (Luke 23.28); the *gloria in excelsis* sung by the angels at Christ's birth (Luke 2.14) is taken up by the chorus at the Triumphal Entry into Jerusalem (Luke 19.38). The Fourth Evangelist especially stresses that the hour of Christ's crucifixion is the 'hour' of his glorification (John 7.30; 12.16, 23, 27f.; 13.31f.; 17.1, 5): Christ goes to his cross like a king to his crowning. 'Worthy is the Lamb that hath been slain to receive. . . .' (Rev. 5.12). But it is only by the gift of faith that we may discern the divine presence and glory in the figure of the Crucified; unbelievers, blinded by the god of this age, do not see the glory of God shining in the face of Jesus Christ (II Cor. 4.4, 6); and as for the demonic rulers of this age, had they known who Jesus was, they would not have crucified the Lord of glory (I Cor. 2.8). Christ is the effulgence (ἀπαύγασμα) of that Wisdom-glory of God, which was present at the first creation of all things (Heb. 1.3; Wisd. 7.26) and which shall be revealed again in the latter days. In the meanwhile his followers participate even now, as it were proleptically, in the glory that shall be hereafter, for Christ imparts it to them (John 17.10, 23; Rom. 8.30); there is a growth in δόξα that is very like growth in holiness (sanctification) (II Cor. 3.18). This is due to the participation by Christians in the eschatological Spirit, the Spirit of glory (I Pet. 4.14; II Cor. 3.8, 18), through whose ministration they already know the δόξα that shall be revealed (Rom. 8.18). Those who have suffered and died with Christ, receiving his baptism of death and of Holy Spirit, are also glorified with Christ (Rom. 8.17, 30).

A consequence of this glorification is that there is restored to man in the new creation the δόξα which according to the teaching of the rabbis Adam had lost at the Fall; for man had been created by God a little lower than the angels to be crowned with δόξα and τιμή (Ps. 8.6, LXX [EVV, 8.5]; cf. Heb. 2.7)—the very δόξα and τιμή which the disciples on the Mount of Transfiguration had seen Jesus receive from the Father (II Pet. 1.17). The δόξα which was originally a part of the natural endowment of Adam is possessed by the Last Adam and imparted by him to his disciples; clearly St Paul is thinking of the restoration of man's lost δόξα through the work of the life-giving Spirit. The reflection of the divine glory with which the face of Adam (man) once was radiant, God's εἰκών (Gen. 1.26f.), is now visible again in Christ (II Cor. 4.4; Col. 1.15), and 'we all, with unveiled face reflecting as a mirror the δόξα of the Lord, are transformed into the same εἰκών from δόξα to δόξα, even as from the Lord the Spirit (ἀπὸ κυρίου πνεύματος)' (II Cor. 3.18). Foreordained to be conformed to the εἰκών of God's Son (Rom. 8.29), Christians must bear the heavenly εἰκών (I Cor. 15.49), for in the new creation of the latter days the lost image of God is to be renewed. The mystery which is now made known even among the Gentiles is therefore this: 'Christ in you, the hope of δόξα' (Col. 1.27; cf. Eph. 1.18; 3.16). If we ask whether our transformation (μετα-μόρφωσις, cf. II Cor. 3.18) in δόξα is a physical or merely ethical process, the answer doubtless is that it is both: moral goodness (or holiness) has its numinous manifestation in δόξα. But the δόξα is veiled except at certain specific moments, as when Moses's face shone (Ex. 34.29-35; II Cor. 3.7), or at the Transfiguration of Jesus (Mark 9.2f. and pars.), or possibly on such rare occasions as when Stephen's face was as the face of an angel (Acts 6.15). The final and complete unveiling of the δόξα must await the parousia. Jesus himself had spoken of his coming 'in the δόξα of his Father' (Mark 8.38), or of his 'coming in clouds with great δύναμις and δόξα' (Mark 13.26): he is using the traditional language of Jewish apocalyptic to express the ultimate truth about his own person and mission in relation to God's purpose for this world (cf. Dan. 7.13f.; Zech. 14.5f.; Matt. 24.30; 25.31; 26.64; John 1.51; Acts 1.11; I Thess. 4.16; Rev. 1.7, etc.). The parousia will be *the* revelation of Christ's δόξα (I Pet. 1.7; 4.13).

THE LIGHT OF THE WORLD

'Light' is one of those 'archetypal images' by means of which the universal religious consciousness of mankind in every age articulates itself; evidence is plentifully forthcoming from ancient Stonehenge to modern Japan. It is therefore not surprising that we should meet with the symbolism of light in the Bible, which speaks the language of humanity: if it tells of unique, divine events, it must do so in the universal speech of human religious aspiration everywhere. The divine word must be clothed in human words, since otherwise it would be unintelligible to us. Thus, light in the OT is a frequent metaphor for God's truth, holiness and goodness, and is conspicuous in the language of devotion (e.g. Pss. 4.6; 27.1; 36.9; 37.6; 43.3; 97.11; 112.4; 118.27; 119.105, cf. Prov. 6.23). Profound truth is symbolized in the OT conception of God as the creator of light (Gen. 1.3; Ps. 74.16; Isa. 42.16; 45.7) and as clothed in it (Ps. 104.2). By a natural extension of the metaphor darkness is conversely a symbol of evil, misfortune, judgment, ignorance, oppression and separation from God; Sheol is described as a place of darkness (e.g. Pss. 49.19; 88.12). (It should also be remembered that 'thick darkness' is a symbol of the mysterious and inaccessible character of the hidden God; e.g. Ex. 20.21; Deut. 4.11; II Sam. 22.10; I Kings 8.12; Pss. 18.9; 97.2. God's utter transcendence is portrayed by the fact that he is Lord of the darkness as well as of the light: Ps. 139.12; Isa. 45.7.)

It is not surprising that the NT also should make use of the metaphor of light, and we need hardly look to Persian influences for an explanation. A NT writer like St John may conceivably have had in mind the significance attributed to light in 'the higher paganism' of the Hellenistic world, and it is possible that his language is chosen so as to appeal to the interested pagan; but at the deeper level St John's τὸ φῶς τὸ ἀληθινόν owes nothing to such concepts as Philo's φῶς φωτὸς ἀρχέτυπον.[1] St John's thought, as we shall see, is biblical and eschatological, removed *toto caelo* from all *religionsgeschichtliche* generalizations; in any case the OT supplies a parallel to every Johannine use of φῶς. As good missionaries, the NT teachers would doubtless adapt the half-seeing gropings of pagan religion into a means of communicating the final truth, as when in a later century the Catholic Church made use of the Roman celebration of *Sol Invictus* (25th December) as the yearly festival of the coming of the True Light into the world. But the NT is no mere republication of the truths of natural religion; it is not merely a step or two higher up the ladder of philosophical truth than Platonism, Stoicism and Gnosticism, even at their highest. Christ is not an expression of truth: he is *the* truth. This is what is meant when the NT (more particularly St John) speaks of him as the light (John 1.9; 8.12; 9.5; 12.35, 46; I John 2.8; cf. Luke 1.78f.; II Cor. 4.6; Eph. 5.14; Heb. 1.3), for truth, like light, is its own criterion and cannot be judged by anything beyond itself (Matt. 6.22f.; Luke 8.16; John 8.12-18). When the NT writers say that God is light (I John 1.5; cf. James 1.17; I Tim. 6.16; Rev. 21.23), they are not affirming the Stoic-materialist conception of light as divine. 'Light is God' is metaphysics: 'God is light' is metaphor; and if the view that God is light is 'the basic assumption of most gnostic systems and of the oriental religions which form their base',[2] it is none the less true that gnostic and oriental notions are not in the minds of the NT writers, who are occupied with biblical-eschatological concepts quite alien to non-historical religious systems. The

---

[1] Philo, *de Somn*. 1.75. Philo says that God is not only light, but is the archetype of every other light. See C. H. Dodd, *IFG*, 203; C. K. Barrett, *GSJ*, 278.

[2] Barrett, *GSJ*, 277.

apostolic Church did not worship light as an emanation or even a manifestation of God; there is a world of difference between saying that Christ is a reflection of God[1] or a light from God and saying that light is an aspect of God; and this is, in a word, the difference between apostolic Christianity and 'the higher paganism'. The NT writers are declaring a gospel about Christ, not teaching a metaphysical religion about light.

The fact is that the NT conception of light is basically eschatological, and it may perhaps best be summed up in the words of St John: 'The darkness is passing away, and the true light already shineth' (I John 2.8; cf. Rom. 13.12). The later OT prophets had taught that the end should be like the beginning; the light which had been made on the first day of creation (Gen. 1.3) should shine forth in all its pristine splendour as the last things were fulfilled. The original of this apocalyptic conception would seem to be Zech. 14.6f.: 'in that day' there will be no more day-and-night, as we know them; it will be all one day, as Yahweh himself knows endless day: 'at evening time there shall be light'. Similar conceptions may be found in Isa. 24.23; 30.26; 58.8, 10; 60.1-3. It is, however, in Isa. 60.19 that we find the clearest reference in the canonical Hebrew Scriptures to the archetypal light of the new creation in the latter days: as in the beginning, before the creation of the sun and moon, the light of the divine presence gives all the brightness that is required: 'The sun shall be no more thy light by day, neither for brightness shall the moon give light unto thee; but Yahweh shall be unto thee an everlasting light, and thy God thy glory.' The way in which this conception passed into later Judaism may be seen in II (4) Esd. 7.39-42: 'This is a day that hath neither sun nor moon nor stars . . . neither darkness nor evening nor morning . . . neither noon nor night nor dawn, neither shining nor brightness nor light, save only the splendour of the glory of the Most High' (*nisi solummodo splendorem claritatis Altissimi*—perhaps, as it has been conjectured, ἀπαύγασμα δόξης ὑψίστου).

The NT sayings about light should be read against this background. The opening phases of the last divine act of history have begun with the coming of Jesus Christ and his Church: 'the darkness is passing away, and the true light already shineth' (I John 2.8). The true light (τὸ φῶς τὸ ἀληθινόν, John 1.9) has already come into the world with the coming of

---

[1] Cf. Heb. 1.3, ὃς ὢν ἀπαύγασμα τῆς δόξης . . . αὐτοῦ. The word ἀπαύγασμα, a *hapax legomenon* in NT, does not occur in LXX translations from the canonical Heb. Scriptures, but is found in Wisd. 7.26, which *Auct. Heb.* is quoting; σοφία is there declared to be ἀπαύγασμα φωτὸς ἀιδίου. The quotation shews that *Auct. Heb.* accepts the identification of Christ with the pre-existent Wisdom of God, though he (like the Fourth Evangelist) never uses σοφία.

Christ: he is the true light, i.e. the archetypal light of the first creation that lightens every mortal man (πάντα ἄνθρωπον ἐρχόμενον εἰς τὸν κόσμον, John 1.9);[1] and for a little while (μικρὸν χρόνον, John 12.35) the light was in the world (cf. John 9.5, 'When I am in the world, I am the light of the world'), shining in the darkness, which could neither extinguish nor understand it (John 1.5).[2] The incarnation of the Word was the initial stage of the realization of the divine plan, which will shortly culminate in the dawning of the day of light. St Paul teaches the same doctrine: God, who originally said 'Let there be light', has now shone in our hearts to give the illumination (φωτισμός) of the knowledge of the δόξα of God in the face of Jesus Christ (II Cor. 4.6). The Christian Church, the eschatological community of the last days, consists of those who have been called out of darkness into God's marvellous light (I Pet. 2.9), having been delivered out of the power of darkness (Col. 1.13), and who already walk in the light of the End-time (Eph. 5.8f.; cf. John 11.9; 12.35f.; I Thess. 5.4f.; I John 1.7). At their baptism they had cast away the works of darkness and put on the armour of light (Rom. 13.12) and had had 'the eyes of their heart enlightened' (Eph. 1.18). Having thus been made meet to be partakers with the saints in light (Col. 1.12), and being by faith already 'in the light' (I John 2.10), they look forward to the day of revelation, when the Lord will come and will bring to light the hidden things of darkness (I Cor. 4.5). Their appointed task until that day is one of eschatological witness, of bringing the nations into the light (Acts 13.47; 26.17f.). The eschatological reality of Christ as the 'light for revelation to the Gentiles' (Luke 2.32; cf. Isa. 42.6; 49.6; 52.10; 60.3) and as τὸ φῶς τοῦ κόσμου (John 8.12; cf. 9.5; 11.9; 12.46) becomes a task laid upon the missionary Church: the new Israel must undertake the work which the old Israel had refused. 'The day' is at hand, and the evidences of the fulfilment of scriptural prophecy are even now before us, 'whereunto ye do well to take heed, as unto a lamp shining in a squalid place, until the day dawn and the daystar arise in your hearts' (II Pet. 1.19; cf. Mal. 4.2; Luke 1.78; Rev. 2.28; 22.16).

Thus, the NT use of the metaphor of light is thoroughly Jewish and eschatological, and this is especially true of the Johannine writings. The OT had taught that God's word is light or gives light (Ps. 119.105; cf. Gen. 1.3), and the rabbis had identified Torah with light (basing themselves on Prov. 6.23, 'The commandment is a lamp and the Torah is light'; cf. Test. Levi 14.4). Not Torah, says St John, is the world's

---

[1] See Dodd, *IFG*, 204n.

[2] The verb καταλαμβάνειν (in John 1.5, ἡ σκοτία αὐτὸ οὐ κατέλαβεν), meaning 'to seize', includes the meanings 'to overcome' and 'to understand'; both meanings are intended here. See Barrett, *GSJ*, 132.

light, as the rabbis claimed, but Christ, for he is the λόγος-σοφία of God (and cf. Heb. 1.3; Wisd. 7.26). The true light, the creation-light and end-light, is already shining: the bright, the morning star, the herald of the dawning day of the Lord, has already been seen in the coming of Jesus (cf. Rev. 22.16). The Scriptures of the prophets concerning the last days are being fulfilled: the sun of righteousness has arisen with healing in his wings (Mal. 4.2). The seer in his vision sees that the last things are like the first, and the new creation is suffused with the archetypal light of God's presence: 'The city hath no need of the sun, neither of the moon, to shine upon it; for the glory of God did lighten it, and the lamp thereof is the Lamb' (Rev. 21.23); and again, 'There shall be no more night; and they need no light of lamp, neither light of sun, for the Lord God shall give them light' (Rev. 22.5). The universal plan of God is accomplished, and the nations walk in the paradisal light (Rev. 21.24).

THE LIFE OF THE AGE TO COME

In the Bible God is the sole source of life; as contrasted with the dead and impotent gods of heathendom he is 'the living God' (e.g. Deut. 5.26; I Sam. 17.26, 36; Pss. 42.2; 84.2, etc.; cf. Matt. 16.16; 26.63, etc.—the phrase occurs some fourteen times in NT). He is the fountain of life (Ps. 36.9), and the metaphor of a 'living well' or 'living waters' (Jer. 2.13; 17.13; John 4.10) is one that springs readily to mind in a hot, dry climate (Cant. 4.15; Ps. 42.1f.). In later Judaism the conception of 'life' had acquired a markedly eschatological character as a quality of the Age to Come, and in the later writings of the OT we find the picture of the healing river, or living waters, which will flow out from Jerusalem in the Messianic Age (Ezek. 47.1-12; Zech. 14.8; Joel 3.18; cf. Isa. 12.3; 33.21), bringing life to the world. St John, in whose writings Jewish eschatology is adapted to Christian ends with consummate skill, fastens on the idea and represents Christ as the fulfilment of the promise of 'living waters' (John 4.10) in the latter days: 'The water that I shall give him shall become in him a well of water springing up unto the life of the (new) Age' (John 4.14). The rabbis claimed that the Torah, or the Scriptures which contained it, were the channel of life; 'Ye search the Scriptures, because ye think that in them ye have ζωὴ αἰώνιος' (John 5.39); 'The Torah is great, because it gives to those that practise it life in this age and in the Age to Come' (*Pirqe Aboth* 6.7). But life is in the Word (John 1.4), made flesh in Christ, not in Scripture, not in Torah—the superabundant life of God, the life of the Age to Come (ζωὴ αἰώνιος), brought to us by Christ, who is ζωή (John 3.16; 10.10; 20.31), and whose life is the life of God: 'As the

Father hath life in himself, even so gave he to the Son also to have life in himself' (John 5.26). He is the bread of life (John 6.48): 'if any man eat of this bread, he shall live εἰς τὸν αἰῶνα' (6.51). He is the life-giver, giving resurrection-life to the dead (5.21; 6.33; 11.25f.), who is identified with the quickening Spirit (John 6.63; cf. I Cor. 15.22, 45; II Cor. 3.6; Rom. 8.2, 11; Gal. 3.21; I Pet. 3.18).[1] In Christ the scriptural prophecies of the healing rivers of living waters are fulfilled: 'Jesus stood and cried, saying, If any man thirst, let him come unto me and drink. He that believeth on me, as the Scripture hath said, out of his belly shall flow rivers of living water. But this he spake of the Spirit, which they that believed on him were to receive' (John 7.37-39). These cryptic words mean that out of the Church, the new Jerusalem, the Spirit-filled body of believers in Christ, the healing rivers of living waters flow. So, too, in the seer's vision in Rev. 22.1f., when all is fulfilled in the new Jerusalem, a river of water of life, bright as crystal, flows out of the throne of God and out of the Lamb, in the midst of the street of the heavenly city. The tree of life stands again, as once it stood by the river which flowed through Eden (Gen. 2.9f.), beside the paradisal river, bearing its twelve fruits and its leaves 'for the healing of the nations', as Ezekiel also had long before seen it in his vision (Ezek. 47.12; cf. also Rev. 2.7; 22.14, 19). Man, who was excluded from the divine source of life by reason of his sin (Gen. 3.24, the flaming sword that kept the way of the tree of life), is now, through the action of the life-giving Spirit (of) Christ, restored to that archetypal state of fellowship with the living God for which he was first created and now is created anew.

Thus, the conception of life, which the NT takes over from later Judaism, is thoroughly eschatological. The Spirit of God will breathe life into the new creation of the latter days, as he did at the first creation (Gen. 2.7; cf. Ps. 104.29f.; Job 33.4); cf. Ezek. 37.9f. and esp. v. 14: 'I will put my Spirit in you and ye shall live.' Pharisaic Judaism understood the outpouring of the Spirit of life in the latter days to imply a resurrection of the dead, as in John 5.29: 'those that have done good unto the resurrection of life (εἰς ἀνάστασιν ζωῆς), and those who have practised evil things unto the resurrection of judgment.' This conception of a general resurrection makes its first definite appearance

[1] We shall see in Chapter 5 that the NT does not carefully distinguish between the Risen Christ and the Holy Spirit (*infra* 121). It is a firm tenet of biblical religion that only God can give life to the dead, and whether Christ or the Spirit is described as ὁ ζωοποιῶν hardly matters, since in any case the work is that of God himself. In John 5.21, Rom. 4.17, Heb. 11.19, etc., it is God who gives life to the dead; in John 5.21 (cf. 6.33, 51, etc.), I Cor. 15.22, 45, Christ is the life-giver; and in John 6.63 (τὸ πνεῦμά ἐστιν τὸ ζωοποιοῦν), Rom. 8.2, 10f., II Cor. 3.6 (τὸ πνεῦμα ζωοποιεῖ) the Spirit is the life-giver. The one thing which NT Christianity denies is the claim of rabbinic Judaism (e.g. John 5.39) that Torah is the life-giver: νόμος ὁ δυνάμενος ζωοποιῆσαι (Gal. 3.21).

in Jewish literature in Dan. 12.2: 'Many of them that sleep in the dust of the earth shall awake (ἀναστήσονται), some to ζωὴ αἰώνιος, and some to shame and everlasting contempt (αἰσχύνη αἰώνιος).' This is the only occurrence of the expression ζωὴ αἰώνιος in Greek translations of the OT, but it gives us a reliable indication of what Greek-speaking Jews meant by it. The phrase is entirely Jewish: it occurs once in Philo (*de Fuga* 78) but is not found in pagan religious and philosophical writers until long after the NT period.[1] It is perhaps worth noting that the writer to the Hebrews, who is often thought to have come under Alexandrian and Platonic influences more than any other NT author, never uses ζωὴ αἰώνιος (the nearest he comes to it is in 7.16, δύναμις ζωῆς ἀκαταλύτου). It would therefore be clearly improper to read Platonic notions about eternity into the phrase: αἰώνιος in this context cannot mean 'eternal' in the Platonic sense of being outside time, in the way in which the truths of geometry are strictly timeless. It is doubtful whether any of the biblical writers conceived even of God himself as being outside time in this sense.[2] The Fourth Evangelist is the NT writer who is most commonly interpreted in a Platonic manner; but whether he intended his frequent use of ζωή or ζωὴ αἰώνιος to be understood in this way by the Hellenistic intelligentsia (for whom it is suggested that he wrote) is highly dubious. First, there is no difference at all between his use of the words and that of other NT writers, such as St Mark; and there is nothing which cannot be more simply explained in a Hebraic rather than in a Greek way. Secondly, the essential continuity of his meaning, despite all differences of expression, with that of the Apocalypse of St John should suggest caution in this matter. And thirdly, he himself explicitly tells us that to have ζωὴ αἰώνιος means to be raised up by Christ at the last day (John 6.40, 54), an idea which he takes very seriously indeed (John 6.39f., 44, 54; 11.24; 12.48), but one which would have little attraction for Greek philosophers, if we may judge by the evidence of Acts 17.31f.

The fact is that in the NT ζωή, or more fully ζωὴ αἰώνιος, is an eschatological conception; it is one of the characteristic marks of the Age to Come, like glory, light, etc. In the contemporary rabbinic conception, the Age to Come (cf. Mark 10.30, ὁ ἐρχόμενος αἰών; Heb. 6.5, ὁ μέλλων αἰών), as distinct from this age (ὁ νῦν αἰών or ὁ αἰὼν οὗτος), was to be characterized by ζωή, that is, ζωὴ αἰώνιος, the life of the (coming) αἰών. Thus, what appears in EVV as 'eternal life' or 'life everlasting' really means 'the life of the Age to Come'. The phrase ζωὴ αἰώνιος need

---

[1] So C. H. Dodd, *IFG*, 146.

[2] See O. Cullmann, *Christ and Time*, ET, 1951; also John Marsh, *The Fulness of Time* (1952) and art. 'Time' in *TWBB*.

not necessarily imply *ever*-lasting life (e.g. Enoch 10.10), but the usual meaning is life after death indefinitely prolonged in the World to Come (Dan. 12.2; Test. Asher 5.2; Ps. Sol. 3.16; II (4) Esd. 7.12f.; 8.52-54). Throughout the NT ζωὴ αἰώνιος means 'the life of the World to Come'. It is synonymous with ἡ βασιλεία τοῦ Θεοῦ. Thus, in the discussion about conditions of entry into the reign of God, the Rich Man in Mark 10.17 asks, 'Good Master, what shall I do that I may inherit ζωὴ αἰώνιος?' Or again, if we examine the parallelism of Mark 9. 43-47, we shall see that to enter into ζωή and to enter into the βασιλεία τοῦ Θεοῦ are one and the same thing. The Fourth Evangelist prefers ζωή or ζωὴ αἰώνιος (there is no difference of meaning between the two forms) to ἡ βασιλεία τοῦ Θεοῦ, which is found only in the Nicodemus conversation (John 3.3 and 5). We may compare 3.3, 'Except a man be born again, he cannot see the βασιλεία τοῦ Θεοῦ', which is explained in 3.5 as meaning 'he cannot enter the βασιλεία τοῦ Θεοῦ', with 3.36: 'He that believeth on the Son of Man hath ζωὴ αἰώνιος, but he that obeyeth not the Son shall not see ζωή', i.e. enter into the life of the Age to Come. Both St Mark and St John contrast 'this age' with the life of the Age to Come in exactly the same way: in Mark 10.30 Jesus says that those who have left all and followed him shall 'receive a hundredfold νῦν ἐν τῷ καιρῷ τούτῳ houses and brethren... and ἐν τῷ αἰῶνι τῷ ἐρχομένῳ ζωὴν αἰώνιον'; in John 12.25 we find a characteristically Johannine rendering of a Synoptic saying (cf. Matt. 10.39; 16.25; Mark 8.35; Luke 9.24; 17.33): 'He that hateth his soul (ψυχή) ἐν τῷ κόσμῳ τούτῳ shall keep it εἰς ζωὴν αἰώνιον.' There seems to be little difference amongst the Evangelists in their understanding of the matter. St Matthew generally prefers ζωή (without the adjective), as at 7.14: 'Straitened the way that leadeth unto ζωή' (but cf. Matt. 19.29: Mark 10.30). At Matt. 25.46 we find ζωὴ αἰώνιος contrasted with κόλασις αἰώνιος; but if we reflect that αἰώνιος in this context probably does not mean 'everlasting', we shall be spared the moral anxieties raised by the translations, 'eternal punishment' (RV) or 'everlasting punishment' (AV). The real issue concerns the character of the punishment as that of the order of the Age to Come as contrasted with any earthly penalties.

The tension between the 'now' and the 'not yet', which characterizes NT eschatology, is particularly evident in respect of ζωή. As the writer of I Tim. says, Christian piety holds the promise of life now as well as in the Age to Come (4.8). Even now Christians, through their possession of the earnest of the Spirit, are already living in the Age to Come, i.e. they possess ζωή here and now; but their possession of it is 'hidden', like all the eschatological realities. 'For ye died (in your baptism in which you received the Spirit of life), and your (gift of new) ζωή is hid with Christ in God' (Col. 3.3). Thus, the Christian life implies bearing in our bodies the putting-to-death of Jesus, in order that ἡ ζωὴ τοῦ Ἰησοῦ may be manifested in our mortal flesh (II Cor. 4.10f.). Both in the sacraments and in daily sacrificial living Christians lay hold on ἡ αἰώνιος ζωή, or ἡ ὄντως ζωή (I Tim. 6.12, 19). But they know that they have not won it or earned it for themselves; it is the free gift of God (Rom. 6.23), the gift of Christ which is contrasted with Adam's legacy of death (Rom. 5.17, 21; I Cor. 15.22). In the new creation of the latter days, to which Christians already by faith belong, they have put away the old man—the Adam in us all, alienating us from the ζωή of God—and have put on (in their baptism) the 'new man' (Eph. 4.18-23; cf. Acts 11.18), and even now they live the life of the Spirit, manifesting the Spirit's fruit, knowing that 'he that soweth unto the Spirit shall of the Spirit reap ζωὴ αἰώνιος' (Gal. 6.8; cf. James 3.17f.). By the eschatological quality of love in the Church Christians know that they have already passed from death to ζωή (I John 3.14). They look forward to the manifestation of their hidden ζωή at the parousia: 'when Christ our ζωή shall be manifested, then shall ye also with him be manifested in glory' (Col. 3.4). Christians are 'co-heirs of the grace of ζωή' (I Pet. 3.7; cf. Titus 3.7); they will receive the crown of ζωή (James 1.12; Rev. 2.10); and their names are written in the book of ζωή (Rev. 3.5; 17.8; 20.12, 15; 21.27; cf. Ex. 32.32f.).

THE WRATH OF GOD

The conception of the ὀργή or wrath of God in the NT is eschatological in the same sense as are the conceptions of (e.g.) βασιλεία, δόξα and ζωή; that is to say, they refer properly to the End-time, but, since the opening scenes of the last act of the drama of world history are now being staged, their preliminary manifestations are already apparent to the eyes of faith. The OT had long ago demythologized the notion of a god or gods whose anger was manifested in thunderstorms and other natural phenomena, and had reached a conception of the wrath of Yahweh closely related to the idea of the Covenant. God's wrath is visited upon Israelites who had violated the Covenant (e.g. Lev. 10.6; Num. 16.46; 25.3; I Chron. 27.24; Ps. 78.31, 49, 59, etc.) and upon the Gentiles who afflicted the covenant-people (e.g. Ps. 79.6f.; Jer. 50. 11-18; Ezek. 38.18f.). As time went by and God's judgment upon Israel's oppressors seemed to be indefinitely delayed, the awaited infliction of the divine wrath was gradually focussed upon the Day of the Lord, the Day of Judgment (Isa. 2.10-22; Jer. 30.7f.; Joel 3.12-17; Obad. 8-11; Zeph. 3.8). By the time of our Lord the rabbis could use

the expression 'the wrath' as a synonym for the last judgment of the
Gentiles and of apostate Jews (cf. II (4) Esd. 7.36f., 'the furnace of
Gehenna').[1] And John the Baptist, reviving the old prophetic teaching
that it was Israel rather than the Gentiles who had reason to fear the
Day of the Lord (cf. Amos 3.2; 5.18; Joel 2.1f.), scornfully asks, 'Who
warned you to flee from the wrath to come?' (Matt. 3.7=Luke 3.7).
In the NT ὀργή is essentially ὀργὴ μέλλουσα or ὀργὴ ἐρχομένη (I Thess.
1.10), but its hidden workings are already present and active in the
world. In this sense it is entirely true to say that the NT conception of
ὀργή is thoroughly eschatological.[2]

It is St Paul who in Romans gives us the most careful and considered
teaching on the subject of the divine wrath. As a good Jew he thoroughly
understands the consistent OT doctrine that God's wrath is an inevitable consequence of his righteousness. The coming of Christ did not
mean that God was no longer a God of wrath; on the contrary, it
clearly revealed God's wrath against all human ungodliness and unrighteousness (Rom. 1.18). Because of the universality of sin, the whole
race of mankind is the object of God's wrath (Rom. 3.9-18); unredeemed mankind are by nature (φύσει) 'children of wrath' (Eph. 2.3;
cf. 5.6). The Gentiles are without excuse, because they ought to have
known and obeyed God's moral law, but have become utterly corrupted (Rom. 1.18-32); the Jews likewise are without excuse, because
they are condemned by the very Law of which they boast (Rom. 2).
The Law cannot avert wrath; on the contrary the Law engenders wrath
(Rom. 4.15). Every man through the hardness of his heart treasures up
for himself 'wrath in the day of wrath and revelation of the righteous
judgment (δικαιοκρισία) of God' and there is no distinction between
Jew and non-Jew (Rom. 2.8f.). In Paul, as in the NT generally, though
the expression ἡ ὀργή is used absolutely, it always means 'the wrath *of
God*' and not a kind of impersonal 'inevitable process of cause and
effect in a moral universe';[3] we can rationalize the idea in that way,
if we like, but it would be a mistake to suppose that the NT writers did
so.[4] Nor is it possible to find a distinction between Paul (or the NT
writers generally) and Jesus in this matter.[5] It is true that the actual
word ὀργή is placed in the mouth of Jesus only in Luke 21.23 (but not

---

[1] Strack-Bill., I, 115f.

[2] Sanday and Headlam, *Romans* (ICC), 1895, Rom. 1.18, *ad loc.*; G. Stählin,
TWNT, V, 430f.

[3] C. H. Dodd, *Romans* (The Moffatt New Testament Commentary), 1932, 23.

[4] However, since this chapter was written, there has appeared the fine study of
this subject by A. T. Hanson, *The Wrath of the Lamb* (1957), which strongly advo-
cates the 'impersonal' view. On the other hand, C. K. Barrett in his recent Commentary on *Romans* (1957) says that 'it is doubtful whether this view can stand'
(33).

[5] Dodd, *ibid.*

in pars., Mark 13.19; Matt. 24.21, which have θλῦψις), but he frequently speaks of the judgment which is to come, using the current apocalyptic figure of ἡ ἡμέρα κρίσεως (Matt. 10.15; 11.22, 24; 12.36, 41f.) and the rabbinic expression, ἡ κρίσις τῆς γεέννης (Matt. 23.33).

There can be no doubt at all that Jesus taught the dread reality of the last judgment (e.g. Matt. 5.21f.; Mark 9.43-48, etc.), however we may explain the meaning of his parabolic and pictorial language. He clearly regards himself as related to ὀργή and κρίσις as he is related to βασιλεία, ζωή or δόξα. He is the bearer of the divine wrath, as when, for example, he is constrained to pronounce the doom of Jerusalem and the divine judgment upon Judaism, the barren fig-tree (Mark 11.14, 20; Luke 13.34f.; 19.41-44; cf. Mark 12.9f.). He is the bringer of the 'woes' of the Messiah, because these things must be before the End can come (Mark 13.5-27). The Messiah must inevitably exercise God's judgment (Matt. 25.31f.; John 5.22, 30; 8.16; 9.39; Rom. 14.10; II Cor. 5.10; II Tim. 4.1, 8; I Pet. 4.5; Rev. 6.10; 19.11), and it is thus impossible to distinguish between God's wrath and the character and work of Jesus Messiah. God and Christ are one, even in judgment, as the NT and Catholic theology consistently affirm; only a certain kind of degenerate Protestant theology has attempted to contrast the wrath of God with the mercy of Christ. But it is only in Rev. 6.16 that the NT explicitly attributes ὀργή in the full eschatological sense to Christ; in his graphic vision of the 'woes' of the End the seer uses the terrible expression, 'the wrath of the Lamb'.[1] It must, however, be remembered that the NT teaches that in the miracle of the divine mercy it is Christ himself who is the actual bearer of the divine ὀργή in another sense also: upon him the Messianic woes have fallen[2] and he has borne on behalf of mankind the full weight of the judgment of God, so that God remains righteous though he acquits sinners (Rom. 3.24-26). The cross of Christ is the visible, historical manifestation of the ὀργὴ τοῦ Θεοῦ: it is the supreme revelation of the wrath of God against all ungodliness and unrighteousness of men (Rom. 1.18; cf. II Cor. 5.21; Mark 15.34). The Johannine writer emphasizes this truth in his own distinctive way. In his visions of the End he sees those who had served the counter-kingdom of the Beast and worshipped his image as being given to drink of 'the cup of the wine of the anger of the wrath of God' (Rev. 16.19; cf. 14.10); but in the vision of the Faithful and True, the Word of God, the King of kings and Lord of lords, who wears many diadems and rules the nations with a rod of iron, the seer notices that his

[1] St Mark did not hesitate to ascribe the human emotion of ὀργή to Jesus (3.5), and, though Matt. and Luke omit the expression, all four gospels represent Jesus as moved with righteous indignation at the hardness of men's hearts.
[2] See *supra*, 23.

garment is sprinkled with blood—his own blood: 'and he treadeth the winepress of the wine of the wrath of God' (Rev. 19.11-16). The metaphor of the treading of the winepress ('the grapes of wrath') (cf. 14.20) is derived from Isa. 63.3, which depicts a conqueror trampling in his enemies' blood; the meaning of Rev. 19.15 is that Christ has conquered through *his own* blood, and the last reference in the NT to the divine ὀργή shews us the Christian picture of God as himself providing the means of the propitiation of his wrath (cf. I John 4.10).

Though God's wrath will be fully revealed only in the 'last time' (Rom. 2.5), it is nevertheless at work here and now in the present age, accomplishing God's purpose. The ὀργή works through the State to achieve this purpose (Rom. 13.4f.), and Caesar's power is one of the chief instruments of the divine wrath; the destructive fury of Rome and of the nations is one of the signal effects of the operation of the divine ὀργή as the end approaches (Rev. 11.18; 14.10; cf. Mark 13.7f.). More particularly the destruction of Jerusalem in A.D. 70 is regarded as a manifestation of the judgment of God upon faithless Jewry (Luke 21.23f.), and Jerusalem is identified in the mind of the seer with 'the great city'—now Babylon, now Sodom, now Jerusalem, now Rome—which typifies lust, domination, sensual pleasure and self-pride and which is the special object of the wrath of God (Rev. 11.8; 14.8, 10; 16.19; 17.1-18.24). Not only in the spectacular events of world history, however, is the judgment of God now being manifested. It is a process that is going on wherever the word of God is being proclaimed; men are judging themselves, as it were, according to their acceptance or rejection of the Gospel (Heb. 4.12f.). Evil-doers will hate the light, and they are judged already (John 3.18-20); to reject the preaching of Christ's name is to reject ζωή, which is the same thing as to incur the wrath of God (John 3.36). By our acceptance of Christ in this day of opportunity we anticipate the verdict of 'the last day' (John 3.18; 12.48). We still must await that verdict with fear and trembling (Rom. 2.6), not presuming upon the long-suffering goodness of God, putting our trust not in our own merits but in Jesus who delivers us from the wrath to come (I Thess. 1.10). Judgment is indeed in progress here and now, as St John affirms (John 3.18f.); St Paul points to an instance of the ὀργή coming upon certain Jews who had opposed the preaching of the Gospel to the Gentiles in Thessalonica (I Thess. 2.16). The divine judgment is mysteriously operative also in the sacraments of the Church;[1] the Church is the starting-place on earth of the divine

[1] See C. F. D. Moule, 'The Judgment Theme in the Sacraments' in *The Background of the New Testament and its Eschatology* (ed. W. D. Davies and D. Daube), 1956.

judgment (I Pet. 4.17). The fact that the eschatological ὀργή of God is thus operating is the result of the drawing nigh of the last things with the coming of Jesus Messiah; as St John puts it succinctly, '*νῦν κρίσις ἐστὶ τοῦ κόσμου τούτου*: *now* shall the prince of this world be cast out' (John 12.31; cf. 16.11). Judgment, like ὀργή of which it is the expression, is a future reality manifesting its power in the present. Christians must therefore humbly accept the evidences of the divine κρίσις at work in the world and amongst themselves (I Pet. 5.6), confident that God has not appointed them for ὀργή (I Thess. 5.9) and that in the final reckoning there is no condemnation (κατάκριμα) to them that are in Christ Jesus (Rom. 8.1). Or, as St John puts it, 'Herein is love made perfect with us, that we may have boldness in the day of judgment' (I John 4.17).

RIGHTEOUSNESS AND SALVATION

If in the biblical view judgment is an inevitable consequence of God's righteousness, so also is salvation. Righteousness (Heb. *zedheq*, LXX usually δικαιοσύνη) is for the Hebrews the fundamental character of God, whereas in the Greek mind it is essentially a natural human virtue (cf. the 'justice' of Plato's *Republic*, which arises out of man's innate δικαιοσύνη).[1] For the Hebrews righteousness did not consist in living in accordance with our higher nature, but in doing the will of God, made known to Israel in the Torah. God must do right because by definition whatever he wills is that which is right (cf. Gen. 18.25), and therefore also he must demand righteousness from his people. The δίκαιος, the righteous man, lives (i.e. prospers) by his faithfulness (to God's commandment) (Hab. 2.4). But even sinful and rebellious Israel shall be restored and saved because God is δίκαιος. However faithless Israel may have been to her covenant and promise, God remains faithful; because he is righteous, he will not abandon his people but will find a way to blot out their iniquities and to justify them, so that they may stand in his presence as righteous. 'Thou hast wearied me with thine iniquities. I, even I, am he that blotteth out thy transgressions for mine own sake; and I will not remember thy sins. Put me in remembrance (of the Covenant); let us plead together: set thou forth the cause, that thou mayest be justified' (Isa. 43.24-26). It is 'for his own sake' (that is, because he cannot deny his own nature by breaking the Covenant) that God will justify Israel and his chosen servant Jacob, and he will

---

[1] Cf. G. Schrenk, *TWNT*, ET, *Righteousness* (Bible Key Words), 1951, p. 14, who refers to *Rep.* iv. 433c.ff. Though in Greek mythology Δίκη was a goddess (avenging Justice), δικαιοσύνη came to be regarded as a part of the natural order, like every other human virtue. The Greek Bible hardly uses δίκη; it occurs three times in NT (Acts 28.4; II Thess. 1.9; Jude 7), the sense of avenging justice being present in each case.

pour his Spirit on Jacob's seed (Isa. 44.2f.; cf. Deut. 9.5; Ezek. 36.22, 32). Thus, it is because God is righteous, not because of any righteousness of her own, that Israel may hope for salvation: Yahweh is 'a just God and a saviour' (Isa. 45.21).

This association of righteousness and salvation is especially characteristic of Isa. 40-55. In the earlier strata of the OT salvation meant simply deliverance from national disaster and physical perils (e.g. Judg. 15.18; I Sam. 11.9, 13, etc.). But the word came more and more to be specially appropriated for the great deliverance from Egypt at the Red Sea (Ex. 14.13; 15.2), and, by analogy with it, for the deliverance from Babylon and the return from the Exile (Isa. 45.17; 46.13; 52.10). As in ancient Hebrew mythology the original act of creation was regarded as a great divine act of salvation (cf. Ps. 74.12-14), so the salvation-act of the exodus from Egypt (or of the return of the exiles from Babylon) was likewise thought of as a great divine act of new creation (Isa. 43.15-19; Wisd. 19.6-8).[1] This grand conception of creation-salvation, as we find it especially in Deutero-Isaiah, develops an eschatological character, because the pattern of the exodus-deliverance (and of the deliverance from Babylon) is regarded as the type of the deliverance that will be effected by God in the latter days, when he brings in his new creation—the new heavens and the new earth (cf. Isa. 65.17; 66.22). The 'day' on which this new creation takes place will be pre-eminently the day of salvation. In that day 'all flesh' shall come to worship before the Lord (Isa. 66.23). This OT scheme of a coming salvation, of which the original creation of the world (considered as an act of salvation from the Dragon) and the deliverance at the Red Sea are the types, supplies the framework of the NT scheme of salvation. The NT claims that the expected great act of salvation and new creation has already taken place in the death and resurrection of Jesus Christ and that its final consummation will be revealed at the parousia of Christ. In the meanwhile, between the first and the second comings of Christ, the Church is the eschatological community of salvation (οἱ σωζόμενοι, those who are in the state of being saved, Acts 2.47; I Cor. 1.18; II Cor. 2.15; cf. I Cor. 15.2); it is even now by faith the new creation, eschatologically appearing in this present age, though its true character is known only to faith (II Cor. 5.17; Gal. 6.15). It is for this reason also that 'salvation' in the later OT and in the NT becomes synonymous with 'redemption'. God's act of deliverance from Egypt was referred to as his act of redeeming Israel, as one redeems a slave from his bondage; this would be the duty of the go'el (redeemer, next-of-kin) towards a man who had fallen into bondage. Of course, there is no suggestion here that God paid a

___

[1] See further on this subject *infra*, 203-7.

ransom-price to anyone for Israel's redemption; the conception is only a vivid metaphorical way of emphasizing God's mighty act of salvation in history. The salvation of the new people of God by the Messiah is the chief theme of the NT, and the redemption metaphor naturally reappears in many forms, though again without any suggestion that a ransom-price has been paid to anyone.[1]

It may be said, then, that OT prophecy at its highest and best has enunciated a doctrine of salvation through the operation of the righteousness of God, despite the sinfulness and utter unworthiness of Israel. It is, in fact, a doctrine of justification, not by works, but by the faithfulness of God alone. This means that, though Israel has proved faithless to her covenant promise, God cannot be faithless, and, because of his righteousness, will find a way of justifying sinful Israel. Such a high conception of God's salvation proved too lofty for later Judaism to sustain, and there developed the system of legalism which converted religion into a matter of keeping a balance-sheet, a statement of debits and credits in our dealings with the righteous God. In rabbinic Judaism a man was δίκαιος (counted righteous) if his merits outweighed his transgressions; if he had tried hard, he could eke out his barely adequate merits by drawing upon the superfluity of merit piled up by Abraham, Isaac and Jacob and other heroes of Israel, especially the Maccabean martyrs. It was against this whole conception of 'the merits of the Fathers' that John the Baptist protested: 'Think not to say within yourselves, We have Abraham to our father' (Matt. 3.9; Luke 3.8). According to the rabbinic doctrine a man would be saved by his works; every act of charity, almsgiving and piety had its credit-value, and if the total of his good deeds exceeded that of his bad ones, he would be acquitted at the Last Judgment. The revival by Jesus of the whole Isaianic conception of salvation as the result not of man's righteousness but of the outgoing, saving righteousness of God, involved a complete break with the distinctive doctrines of Pharisaic Judaism and a consequent series of clashes with the Pharisees: the Pharisees' exalting of 'the precepts of men' had in fact been prophesied by Isaiah himself (Mark 7.6f., quoting Isa. 29.13). Instead of a doctrine of salvation by one's own merits and works, Jesus himself taught a doctrine of the justification of sinners by the outgoing righteousness of God. It is the theme of such parables as the Prodigal Son (Luke 15.11-32; note the Pharisaic doctrine of merit upheld by the elder son, vv. 25-30), the Pharisee and the Publican (Luke 18.9-14; note esp. δεδικαιωμένος, v. 14); the Labourers in the Vineyard (Matt. 20.1-16), or the Great Supper (Luke 14.16-24). It is implicit in his conception of himself as the instrument of God's

[1] See further on redemption *infra*, 218-23.

salvation of penitent sinners: 'I came not to call the righteous, but sinners' (Mark 2.17). It is demonstrated in his acts of healing (the Leper, Mark 1.40-45; the Paralytic, Mark 2.1-12, etc.) and in his relations with sinful men and women (Zacchaeus, Luke 19.1-10; the Sinner Woman, Luke 7.36-49). In his words and in his works Jesus proclaims himself to be the Servant-Messiah of whom Isaiah had prophesied, 'By his knowledge (i.e. obedience) shall my righteous servant justify many; and he shall bear their iniquities' (Isa. 53.11).[1]

It is St Paul, alone amongst the NT writers, who revives and develops the Isaianic concept of the divine righteousness, which works salvation, and who thus gives forceful expression to the teaching of Jesus himself about the justifying righteousness of God. Paul uses δικαιοσύνη more often than all the rest of the NT writers together. The other NT writers take over the general LXX and Jewish usage, viz. δικαιοσύνη is conduct pleasing to God and in harmony with his will, although of course God's will is interpreted in the light of the teaching and work of Jesus (e.g. Matt. 5.6, 10, 20; 6.1, 33; Luke 1.75; Acts 10.35; 24.25; I Tim. 6.11; James 1.20; 3.18; I Pet. 3.14; I John 3.7, 10; Rev. 22.11). A writer like the Fourth Evangelist hardly uses the concept at all (only at John 16.8, 10); but in I John 2.29 it is implied that δικαιοσύνη is a quality of life conferred at baptism. It is Christ himself who is ὁ δίκαιος (I John 2.1, 29; Acts 3.14; 7.52; 22.14—perhaps a Messianic title). Outside the Paulines I Pet. 2.24 is almost unique in its association of the life of righteousness with the death of Christ, but (as Paul never does) this verse quotes Isa. 53 as applicable to Christ's passion.

St Paul conceives of the δικαιοσύνη Θεοῦ, after the fashion of Deutero-Isaiah, as an outgoing, energizing δύναμις of God, comparable with (say) the divine σοφία or ἀγάπη. The conception is thoroughly eschatological. The divine righteousness, which was to appear at the end of the age, has already been manifested in history. The judgment and salvation which that righteousness would accomplish in the latter days have already been achieved in the life, death and resurrection of Jesus Christ. By it those who believe and are baptized into Christ are 'justified' or accounted righteous by God. Thus, the prophecies of the old dispensation are fulfilled. 'Yahweh hath made known his salvation; his righteousness hath he openly shewed in the sight of the nations' (Ps. 98.2; cf. Pss. 24.5; 71.15f.). 'In Yahweh shall all the seed of Israel be justified, and shall glory' (Isa. 45.25). 'Thus saith Yahweh, Keep ye judgment and do righteousness: for my salvation is near to come, and my righteousness to be revealed' (Isa. 56.1; cf. also 46.12f.; 51.5f.). Such prophecies as these are fulfilled for St Paul in the gospel of Jesus Christ, in

[1] See further on justification *infra*, 232-40.

which, he says, is revealed δικαιοσύνη Θεοῦ, though in this age it is known and communicated only by faith (ἐκ πίστεως εἰς πίστιν) (Rom. 1.17; cf. Phil. 3.9); this gospel is δύναμις Θεοῦ εἰς σωτηρίαν (Rom. 1.16). Righteousness and salvation have gone forth from God in the coming of Jesus Christ.

For St Paul the righteousness of God (and therefore his salvation) are especially revealed in the death of Christ. In Rom. 3.25f. he says that God's purpose in setting forth Christ as expiating by his sacrificial death ('blood') the sins of those who believe in him was to demonstrate his righteousness. It was necessary to demonstrate the divine righteousness at this present καιρός in case wrong conclusions should be drawn from God's forbearance and passing over of sins in past ages. Thus God may now be seen to be δίκαιος, the righteous God, who (in accordance with scriptural prophecy) justifies the remnant of faithful Israel, that is, those who have faith in Jesus. Because of his own righteousness God, who cannot go back on his covenant and promise, freely justifies those who had broken the covenant and were utterly powerless to achieve righteousness and salvation for themselves. Thus, God has shewn forth his saving righteousness in the sacrificial death of Christ, and the sole requirement of those who would avail themselves of this salvation is that they should believe and be baptized in the faith of Jesus Messiah.[1]

---

[1] LXX renders different Heb. words for 'save' by σώζειν, a verb found more than 100 times in NT. In the Gospels it is used some 14 times in the sense of 'make whole' at cures of the sick and the demon-possessed, and some 20 times in the technical theological sense (e.g. Matt. 1.21; 10.22; 19.25). The double meaning of 'save' and 'heal' is essential in the healing miracles; compare Mark 5.34 or Luke 17.19 with Luke 7.50. The promised salvation has come (e.g. Luke 19.9; Acts 13.23); the Isaianic prophecies are fulfilled; the gospel is God's saving power (Rom. 1.16). The word σωτηρία (salvation) occurs 46 times in NT, the form τὸ σωτήριον four times (Luke 2.30; 3.6; Acts 28.28; Eph. 6.17); the adj. σωτήριος only once (Tit. 2.11). Σωτήρ (Saviour) appears in the Gospels only at Luke 1.47, 2.11 and John 4.42; in Acts only at 5.31 and 13.23; in the Paulines only at Eph. 5.23 and Phil. 3.20; but no less than ten times in the Pastorals. Out of 24 NT occurrences eight refer to 'God our Saviour' (all except two in the Pastorals); the other instances relate to Christ. Isaianic influence is determinative of the NT use of 'save'. In LXX 'saviour' is σωτήρ (e.g. Isa. 45.15, 21); 'redeemer' is λυτρωτής (see *infra*, 219), ὁ λυτρούμενος (e.g. Isa. 41.14; 43.14; 44.24), ὁ ῥυσάμενος (e.g. Isa. 44.6; 48.17); cf. ὁ ῥυόμενος (Isa. 59.20 cited in Rom. 11.26).

4

THE KINGDOM OF GOD

THE phrase 'Kingdom of God' in EVV is not a good translation of ἡ βασιλεία τοῦ Θεοῦ, since βασιλεία (like its Aramaic equivalent *malkuth*) means strictly 'reign', 'sovereignty'—'kingship' rather than 'kingdom'. It is not so much a place over which God rules as God's reign itself. The Hebrews had been familiar with the concept of God as King, ever since the earliest teachers of prophetic religion had demythologized the ancient cultic notion of the king as god.[1] The NT conception of 'the Kingdom of God' has in fact a very long history behind it, stretching far back into the earliest strata of primitive mythology.[2] Its more immediate antecedents, however, were in Jewish Messianic belief and apocalyptic imagery. It was a commonplace of Jewish religion that God was King of the whole earth; the problem which had to be explained was why, since he was King *de jure*, he did not succour his people and set himself up as King *de facto*. It came to be held by many that it was the wickedness of his own people which caused God to delay the active taking up of his reign over all the earth; the day, however, would come when, either directly or through a Messianic Prince, God would intervene upon the earth and set up his *de facto* reign. The apocalyptists, despairing of a salvation from within history, looked forward to the end of this world-age (αἰών), when amidst spectacular irruptions of divine power God would establish his reign, bringing salvation to his elect and judgment to their oppressors. By the time of our Lord many devout Jews were earnestly 'looking for the consolation (παράκλησις) of Israel' (Luke 2.25). Expectation was rife, but only the Zealots thought that God's reign could be hastened by political action. The Pharisees believed that the day of the Lord would dawn when the Law was perfectly obeyed by God's chosen people. Suddenly John the Baptist startled the country by his dramatic appearance in the rôle of the Elijah, the expected precursor of 'the great

---

[1] See Alan Richardson, *Genesis I-XI*, 32-4.

[2] See, e.g., A. Bentzen, *King and Messiah*, ET, 1955; S. Mowinckel, *He that Cometh*, ET, 1956, Part I.

and terrible day of the LORD' (Mal. 3.1; 4.5f.; Matt. 11.14; Mark 9.11-13; Luke 1.17), proclaiming that the Messianic judgment was about to begin (Matt. 3.10-12). The day of the Lord, or 'the great day' (Joel 2.11, 31; Zeph. 1.14; Jude 6; Rev. 6.17), or 'the day of wrath' (Zeph. 1.15, 18; 2.3; Rom. 2.5; Rev. 6.17) was near. Another way of saying the same thing was to declare that the reign of God was imminent, and this in fact is how St Matthew summarizes the proclamation of John: ἤγγικεν ἡ βασιλεία τῶν οὐρανῶν (Matt. 3.2). (It should be noted that the Matthaean 'Kingdom of heaven' is synonymous with 'Kingdom of God'; the phrase is a reverential avoidance of the use of the word 'God'.) 'The day of Yahweh' in Jewish thought meant the day in which God would set up his *de facto* reign, the day of judgment for his adversaries and of salvation for his people. John the Baptist revived the old prophetic insight that the day of the Lord would be a day of judgment not merely for the Gentiles but for the Jews themselves and for their religious leaders: therefore repent, and bring forth fruit worthy of repentance (Matt. 3.2, 8, 11).

THE KINGDOM OF GOD IN THE TEACHING OF JESUS

The Gospels represent Jesus as taking up the proclamation of the imminence of the reign of God as soon as the Baptist was silenced by Herod (Mark 1.14). He continues where John leaves off. 'The καιρός is fulfilled: the reign of God is at hand' (Mark 1.15). He regards John as being in his very person a prophetic 'sign', a calendar-point marking the end of the καιρός which is now fulfilled and heralding the advent of the reign of God, the dawning of the promised 'day of the Lord' (Matt. 11.13; Luke 16.16). Jesus is represented in the Gospels as teaching that the days of his own ministry were *the days of the preaching of the reign of God* (Luke 16.16), and that the reign of God thus proclaimed would shortly come 'with power' (ἐν δυνάμει)—within the lifetime of those who had actually listened to his preaching. Even now, in the days of his preaching, men could accept or reject God's reign; they could, as it were, anticipate for their own personal existence the day of the Lord; they could in an eschatological sense even now pass through judgment and find salvation. But the fact that the great decision could be taken by those who heard Jesus proclaiming the drawing nigh of God's reign must not mislead us into supposing that the reign of God had already arrived in any other sense than that the preaching is an eschatological anticipation of it. In the light of recent discussion of such texts as Mark 1.15 (cf. Matt. 10.7; Luke 10.9) it would seem that we must conclude that ἤγγικεν ἡ βασιλεία τοῦ Θεοῦ must be translated (with RV) 'the kingdom of God is at hand' and not (with C. H.

Dodd) 'the kingdom of God has come'.[1] Nor must we allow the Hebraic manner of speaking of a future event in the past tense to mislead us into an interpretation of certain texts which would be at variance with the whole NT eschatological programme: ἔφθασεν ἐφ᾽ ὑμᾶς ἡ βασιλεία τοῦ Θεοῦ (Matt. 12.28=Luke 11.20; cf. Luke 10.18 and I Thess. 2.16) must mean in its context that the exorcisms wrought by Jesus are the signs of the coming victory of the Kingdom of God over the counter-kingdom of Satan.

Two OT texts appear to be of the utmost significance for the conception of the reign of God as it appears in the teaching of Jesus and in the NT generally, viz. Ex. 19.6 and Dan. 7.22. The former occurs in the account of the covenant-making at Sinai, when Israel became a holy nation and a 'kingdom of priests' (LXX, βασίλειον ἱεράτευμα, Aq. βασιλεία ἱερέων, Symm., Th. βασιλεία ἱερεῖς, Vulg. *regnum sacerdotale*). Jesus conceived of himself as establishing by his self-oblation a new covenant between God and a new Israel (Mark 14.24; I Cor. 11.25), i.e. as inaugurating a new priestly kingdom to fulfil the task which the old Israel had failed to accomplish. He thought of himself as the new Moses (cf. Deut. 18.15, 18) leading a new people of God by a greater redemption than that of the exodus from Egypt into the Promised Land of the Age to Come. The Gospels represent him not merely as proclaiming the reign of God but as actually setting up the community of the reign of God, the fellowship of the Messianic rule. In this reign those who were called were to be not merely passive subjects, ruled over; they were to be co-rulers in the Messianic reign which God had appointed to Jesus himself: 'I appoint unto you a βασιλεία, even as my Father appointed unto me . . . and ye shall sit on thrones judging the twelve tribes of Israel' (Luke 22.29f.; cf. Matt. 19.28). But the reign of the elect was to be of an utterly different character from that of the kings and so-called 'benefactors' of the Gentiles, since in the divine realm royalty is measured in terms of service (Mark 10.42-45; Luke 22.24-28); the apostolic Church had learnt from the Lord himself that it is through tribulations that we must enter into the kingly rule of God (Acts 14.22). The expression εἰσελθεῖν εἰς τὴν βασιλείαν τοῦ Θεοῦ means much more than to become a subject of God's Kingdom; it means to receive a share in God's Kingship, to be one of those appointed to reign. Jesus himself speaks of 'the poor in spirit', i.e. the

---

[1] C. H. Dodd, *The Parables of the Kingdom*, 1935, 43f. For a convincing criticism of the theory of 'realized eschatology' in the Gospels, see R. H. Fuller, *The Mission and Achievement of Jesus*, 20-35. We would prefer to speak of 'an eschatology that is in process of realization' (J. Jeremias, *The Parables of Jesus*, ET 1954, 159; cf. Dodd, *IFG*, 447n., where Dodd speaks of 'the not altogether felicitous term "realized eschatology" ').

Christian *ḥasidhim*, as those to whom the heavenly Kingship belongs;
they are the meek who, according to the prophecy of Ps. 37.11, shall
inherit the earth. As the old Israel obtained the inheritance of the
Promised Land, so the new Israel shall possess the earth as its inheritance. It may have been sayings of this kind which led later Christian
apocalyptists to think in terms of a literal reign of the saints upon the
earth, if this is the correct interpretation of Rev. 20.4-6. Whether or
not Jesus himself thought in terms of a literal earthly reign, he is
recorded as having spoken of his fellowship of disciples as the little
flock to whom it was the Father's good pleasure to give the reign
(Luke 12.32).

This last citation brings us to the second of the OT passages which
have powerfully affected the thought of Jesus and his followers upon
the theme of the reign of God. In his vision Daniel saw the figure of
one like unto a son of man who came with the clouds of heaven and to
whom were given 'dominion and glory and a kingdom' (Dan. 7.13f.);
this vision is subsequently explained by another in which, after 'the
horn of the beast' had prevailed in war against the saints, 'judgment was
given to the saints of the Most High; and the time came that the
saints possessed the *malkuth* (βασιλεία)' (7.21f.); the final triumph is
recorded thus: 'And the kingdom and the dominion, and the greatness
of the kingdoms under the whole heaven, shall be given to the people
of the saints of the Most High . . .' (7.27). Jesus's 'little flock' of the
disciples constitutes the nucleus of 'the people of the saints of the Most
High', Daniel's corporate Son-of-Man figure, to whom the βασιλεία
τοῦ Θεοῦ is to be given. The whole passage, as we shall see subsequently,
has exercised a profound influence (humanly speaking) upon Jesus's
understanding of his own mission and destiny. He conceives his task
as that of setting up 'the people of the saints of the Most High', so that
they may receive the βασιλεία and the dominion whose advent he proclaims. The greatness of the kingdoms under the whole heaven shall be
given to the people of the saints of the Most High: the meek shall inherit
the earth. Christ announces the imminent fulfilment of the expectation
of the triumph of the righteous, to which Daniel's vision gives poignant
expression (Matt. 5.5; cf. also Wisd. 3.8; Ecclus. 4.15).

THE REIGN OF THE SAINTS

Taught by our Lord himself, the NT writers develop a conception of
the Church as 'the people of the saints' to whom God is giving his
βασιλεία, which is even now evident in the operation of the outpoured
Spirit of power. St Paul teaches that those who have received grace and
righteousness (i.e. 'the saints') shall reign in ζωή (i.e. in the life of the

Age to Come) through Jesus Christ (Rom. 5.17). This reign of God in
which Christians participate is, however, not only a future reality.
Like all the eschatological realities of the NT it exhibits the tension of
'even now' and 'not yet': so much at least may be inferred from Paul's
rebuking of the self-sufficient pride of the Corinthians, who had not
realized that the reign in which Christians share is a genuinely corporate
activity and not the privilege of any 'holier-than-thou' sect within the
total body of Christ (I Cor. 4.8). In dissuading the Corinthians from
resorting to the secular courts for judgment in disputes between
Christians Paul writes, 'Know ye not that the saints shall judge the
world? . . . Know ye not that we shall judge angels?' (I Cor. 6.2f.).
Daniel's vision is fulfilled; judgment is given to the saints of the Most
High. Similarly the writer of I Peter sees the Church of Jesus Christ as
the fulfilment of the promise made at Sinai that the people of God
should be made a βασίλειον ἱεράτευμα (I Pet. 2.9f.), a kingdom of priests
unto God. The writer of the Apocalypse reaffirms that Christians have
been made a βασιλεία, priests unto God (Rev. 1.6; 5.10; 20.6); he is
emphatic that the saints reign upon the earth (5.10). As the old Israel,
having been redeemed from Egypt, was made a nation subject only
to its divine King, and to no earthly power, so the Church of Christ,
the new Israel, redeemed from bondage to the hostile powers of this
age, has become a nation under God as King (λαὸς Θεοῦ, I Pet. 2.10),
owing no other loyalty, whether to Caesar or to any of the rulers of this
world-age. The idea of the royal status and priestly calling of the
individual Christian was inherent in the baptismal ceremony by which
he had been initiated into the Church; and if I Peter is (as many suppose) a kind of baptismal instruction, the thought must have been
present explicitly to the writer's mind. For baptism was essentially
an anointing in Holy Spirit, and anointing was the rite by which both
kings and priests were traditionally consecrated in the old Israel; thus
baptism is, as it were, both the 'coronation' of the saints at their entry
into the kingly rule of God and their 'ordination' to the priestly ministry
which was to be set up in the Messianic Age (cf. Isa. 61.6; 66.21).

Let us try to summarize the biblical view of the history of the
βασιλεία τοῦ Θεοῦ. At the first appearance in the Bible of the idea
of a divine kingdom, God appoints Israel as his priestly ruler in
relation to all the other nations, not in order that Israel should
dominate the rest of the world in Gentile fashion, but that the nation
over which God alone was King should serve the other nations as
priest-king to bring them also into the obedience of Yahweh (Ex.
19.4-6). Israel fails to carry out her divinely appointed task, to which
her prophets recall her again and again. Finally, so impotent is Israel

among the nations, that the belief arises that God must give again the βασιλεία to the faithful remnant of his people and that he will do so in the latter days (Dan. 7). John the Baptist arises and proclaims that the βασιλεία of God, thus foreshadowed and promised, is at hand, and Jesus shews the signs by which men of faith may discern the time of its arriving. He believes (Mark 9.1) that after his death the outpouring of the Holy Spirit will take place and then the βασιλεία τοῦ Θεοῦ will have come 'with power'; the βασιλεία is thus given as an eschatological reality to the saints. This is the fundamental conception of the Church in the NT. The Church is the Messianic community, the 'little flock', those to whom the divine βασιλεία is covenanted; the 'power' of the Spirit is evidence of their true status as the elect, the saints of God, even though now in this age it is veiled. The true status of the elect will not be publicly manifested until the parousia of Christ at the end of the present age; but then the 'sons of God' will be revealed (Rom. 8.19; I Pet. 4.13). In that day Christ will be glorified in his saints (II Thess. 1.10), for he shall come with all his saints (I Thess. 3.13; cf. Deut. 33.2f.; II (4) Esd. 6.3; Dan. 7.10; Mark 8.38; II Thess. 1.7; Jude 14). At the parousia Christ will visibly take up his reign over the nations (cf. Rom. 15.12; Isa. 11.10) which will be judged by him (Matt. 25.31f.; cf. Joel 3.12), for all judgment is given to the Son of Man (John 5.22, 27; Dan. 7.13f., 22, 26), i.e. the Messianic Lord surrounded by the court of his angels and his saints. At the parousia, i.e. the coming of Christ to judgment and to establish his βασιλεία, there will take place the resurrection of the dead (Dan. 12.2; John 5.25-29; I Cor. 15.23; I Thess. 4.13-17; Rev. 20.12f.), and the manifested reign of the saints will begin. St Paul does not tell us how long this reign of the saints upon the earth after the return of Christ will last; he mentions the resurrection of 'those that are Christ's' at his parousia, and he continues immediately, 'Then cometh the End (εἶτα τὸ τέλος), when he shall deliver up the βασιλεία to God, even the Father' (I Cor. 15.23f.); Christ shall be subjected to the Father, and God will be all in all (15.28). It would seem that Paul expects the handing over of the βασιλεία by Christ to the Father to take place almost immediately after the parousia, but he does not say so explicitly.

The writer of the Apocalypse is more definite. He tells us (Rev. 20.4-6) that there will be a 'first resurrection' consisting only of the martyrs who had been beheaded for their refusal to worship the Roman Emperor; they will live and reign with Christ for a thousand years. Not until the thousand years are ended does the resurrection of the rest of the dead take place. The martyrs who rise at the first resurrection are the saints to whom judgment is given according to Daniel's

vision; they sit on thrones and exercise judgment. In them is fulfilled
also the prophecy inherent in the call of Israel as a nation of priest-
kings: 'they shall be priests of God and of Christ, and shall reign with
him the thousand years' (20.6). One who has part ($\mu\acute{\epsilon}\rho os$, cf. John 13.8;
Rev. 22.19; contrast 21.8) in the first resurrection is not merely blessed
(cf. Rev. 1.3; 14.13; 16.15; 19.9; 22.7) but also $\ddot{a}\gamma\iota os$—worthy indeed
of the title 'saint'; over such 'the second death' has no power ($\dot{\epsilon}\xi ov\sigma\acute{\iota}a$)—
a 'second death' is, of course, implied in the idea of a general resurrec-
tion (as at Dan. 12.2; cf. John 5.29, $\epsilon\dot{\iota}s\ \dot{a}v\acute{a}\sigma\tau a\sigma\iota v\ \kappa\rho\acute{\iota}\sigma\epsilon\omega s$): all those
whose names are not found in the book of life are cast into 'the lake of
fire', which is 'the second death' (20.14f.). (The $\delta\epsilon\acute{v}\tau\epsilon\rho os\ \theta\acute{a}v a\tau os$,
therefore, has nothing to do with $\dot{\eta}\ \dot{a}v\acute{a}\sigma\tau a\sigma\iota s\ \dot{\eta}\ \pi\rho\acute{\omega}\tau\eta$ and does not
follow from it; it is a corollary of the idea of a *general* resurrection,
not of that of a limited resurrection of the 'saints'.) The seer's vision
seems to imply that after the parousia (though this word actually occurs
in Joh. lit. only at I John 2.28) the martyr-saints will reign over all those
who are alive on the earth at the time, since the dead have not yet been
raised for judgment; but it should be noted that Rev. 20.4-6 (the only
NT passage concerning the Millennium with the possible exception of
II Pet. 3.8) does *not* say that the thousand years' reign will be on the
earth (but cf. 5.10 and 20.9). When the thousand years are completed,
Satan is loosed for the final struggle, in which the devil is cast into the
lake of fire and brimstone; and the general resurrection of the dead and
the ensuing judgment begin (20.7-15).

The Apocalyptist's picture of the reign of the saints is entirely in line
with the current Jewish apocalyptic speculation of his time. The
expectation of a reign of the saints was widespread but took different
forms. In Daniel the rule of the saints is to be of everlasting duration
(Dan. 2.44; 4.3, 34; 6.26; 7.14, 27; cf. Micah 4.7 and John 12.34). In the
pseudepigraphic writings and amongst the rabbis very different periods
of time were suggested for the duration of the rule of the saints—from
40 years (R. Aqiba) to 7,000 years. In II (4) Esd. 7.28f., the Messianic
rejoicing at the revelation of 'my son (Jesus)' is to last 400 years, after
which it is declared that 'my son Christ' will die and all living men with
him.[1] We can but conjecture whence St John derives his 'thousand
years'. It is probable that the figure is based upon Ps. 90.4: the parousia
is to take place at 'the day of Jesus Christ' (Phil. 1.6; cf. I Cor. 1.8;
Phil. 2.16), or 'the day of the Lord' (I Thess. 5.2; II Thess. 2.2), or more
simply still, 'that day' or 'the day' (I Cor. 3.13; II Thess. 1.10; II Tim.
1.12; 4.8; Heb. 10.25; II Pet. 1.19). This 'day' will be like one of the

---

[1] This passage (cf. Zech. 12.10) has no connection with a doctrine of a suffering
Messiah along the lines of Isa. 53. See S. Mowinckel, *He that Cometh*, 290f., 410-15.

'days' of the creation (Gen. 1.1–2.4), about which the rabbis conjectured that each represented a thousand years on the reckoning of Ps. 90.4; indeed, the day of the Lord will be the day of the calling into being of the new creation, when he that sitteth on the throne shall say, 'Behold, I make all things new' (Rev. 21.5; cf. II Cor. 5.17).[1]

It is fitting that the last book of the Bible should concern itself with the question of the true βασιλεία. The saints, elected by God to share his reign, were being persecuted even to death by Rome, the new Babylon (Rev. 16.19; 17.5; 18.10, 21; cf. I Pet. 5.13), the monstrous caricature of God's kingdom, with its false *Deus et Dominus noster, Imperator, Divi Filius*, whom the court poets worshipped as *Princeps principum*, King of kings and Lord of lords, the guardian of the *imperium aeternum*.[2] Against this show of overwhelming 'power and riches and wisdom and might and honour and glory and adulation' (Rev. 5.12), the seer presents his vision of the figure of the one who alone is worthy to sit upon the throne and receive the tribute of heaven and earth; and he sees the coming fulfilment of Daniel's prophecy that the βασιλεία τοῦ κόσμου shall become the kingdom of our *Kurios*, not of *Kurios Kaisar*, and he hears the voices of the heavenly rulers of the old and of the new Israel joining in the hymn: 'We give thee thanks, O Lord God, the Almighty ... because thou hast taken thy great power and didst reign' (Rev. 11.15-17). In A.D. 91 Domitian's great bronze statue of the *Equus Maximus* was dedicated in Rome; St John sees the vision of another horseman, the rider on the white horse, Λόγος Θεοῦ, going forth conquering and to conquer (Rev. 6.2; 19.11-16, 19-21). Much misunderstanding has been caused during the Christian centuries by failure to appreciate the character of the poetic images in the visions of St John and by treating them as if they were literal predictions which form an almanac of future events. It is futile to ask such questions as whether the thousand-year reign of the saints will take place on the earth or in some future world; St John did not consider himself to be imparting information of this kind. He is asserting the coming victory of Christ and his saints, despite the apparent universal triumph of Satan's counter-kingdom and the empire-wide adoration of his εἰκών, the Emperor, 'the image of the Beast', i.e. of Satan himself (Rev. 13.1-18, esp. v. 15; 14.9, 11; 15.2; 16.2; 19.20; 20.4; cf. 13.1 with Dan. 7.3 and II (4) Esd. 11.1). In a series of great apocalyptic images St John discloses the truth of the fulfilment of God's purpose. As God in the beginning had created man to be lord of the creation and high-priest of nature (Gen. 1.26; 2.19f.; Ps. 8.4-8),

[1] That this kind of calculation is not foreign to the ancient church may be seen from *Ep. Barnabas* 15; cf. also II Pet. 3.8, where it is just possible that 'the day of the Lord' may last for a thousand years in the light of v. 10.
[2] Cf. E. Stauffer, *Christ and the Caesars* (ET, 1955), esp. Chap. XI.

as he had by an act of re-creation at the exodus called and constituted a nation of kings and priests to be the servant of his great design (Ex. 19.4-6); so through the work of Christ, the Lamb slain from the foundation of the world (Rev. 13.8; cf. John 17.24), this great divine purpose is being achieved even amidst the terrible events of the reigns of Nero and Domitian; and the final triumph is not in doubt. The New Jerusalem comes down from heaven, a kingdom of priests whose white robes are washed in the blood of the Lamb; and God's reign is for ever established through Christ and his saints. The new creation completes and fulfils the old. But it is only through suffering that the βασιλεία τοῦ Κυρίου ἡμῶν is established; the Lamb is slain, and the martyr-saints have followed the Lamb and are the first-fruits unto God (Rev. 14.4). The seer has learnt the lesson which Jesus taught both in word and in life, that true βασιλεία is service, even costly self-sacrifice; God's servants are priests, but they have no need of a temple (Rev. 21.22; cf. John 4.23); they are kings, but this means that they are servants of him of whom alone it may be said, *cui servire regnare est.*

'THE MYSTERY OF THE KINGDOM OF GOD'

Jesus regarded the imminent reign of God as a mystery in the biblical sense of the term. That is to say, even though the news of the near approach of the reign of God were proclaimed throughout the land, it would still remain an incomprehensible mystery apart from personal faith in God's purpose of salvation. Jesus remarks that, although the crowds flock to hear him, the number of those who believe and understand is very small. There are few, he says, who find the narrow gate and strait way that lead to life (ζωή), a synonym for ἡ βασιλεία τοῦ Θεοῦ (Matt. 7.14; cf. Luke 13.23f.). In the Parable of the Sower (Mark 4.3-9 and pars.) much of the good seed of the preached word falls where birds devour it, drought parches it and thorns choke it; only a proportion of it brings forth fruit.[1] So it is with the preaching of the reign of God; yet just as the farmer, in spite of the inevitable failures, reaps a good harvest, so the harvest of the gospel-preaching at the consummation of the Age will be found to have yielded its thirty-fold, sixty-fold and hundred-fold. We need not be discouraged because only a minority responds. It is a 'little flock' to which the Father is pleased to give the βασιλεία (Luke 12.32). There is a 'mystery of election' implicit in the gospel-story; this man sees, but that one does not; to one is given faith, while from another the gift is withheld. And even as it is at the preaching of the Son of Man, so shall it be at his parousia:

[1] We shall continue to hold that in this parable 'the seed is the word of God' (Luke 8.11) in spite of Dodd, *Parables of the Kingdom*, 13ff. and Jeremias, *The Parables of Jesus*, 61ff.

'Then shall two men be in the field; one is taken and one is left; two women grinding at the mill; one is taken and one is left' (Matt. 24.40f.; cf. Luke 17.34f.). This mystery cannot be explained on rational lines; it will always remain a mystery why 'this one' sees the truth as it is in Christ while 'that one'—no less intelligent, moral, 'decent'—remains entirely unmoved by the gospel-preaching.

It is the consideration of this mystery of election which leads Jesus himself to distinguish between those who are 'inside' and those who are 'outside', those to whom it is given to know the mystery of the reign of God and those to whom all things are done in riddles (Mark 4.11f.; cf. Matt. 13.11-15; Luke 8.10). Since the days of Jülicher[1] it has been fashionable to assume that Mark at this place has misunderstood the intention of Jesus in teaching by parables. Jesus taught in parables, it is said, not to prevent men from seeing ('that seeing they may see, and not perceive'), but in order to make them see; he told stories because this was the best way of making simple folk perceive religious truth. Of course, Jesus taught in parables for this reason, and Mark has no wish to deny it. Mark is concerned with a much more profound question—the mystery of election, the mystery of the blind eyes and deaf ears; it is the same question as that of the hardening of Israel which St Paul discusses in Rom. 9-11. There is no reason to suppose that Mark is not in fact giving us a summary of the teaching of Jesus himself upon this matter. As we shall frequently have occasion to notice, Jesus thought of the figure of the Isaianic Servant as a prophecy of his own ministry, suffering and vindication. (We must constantly bear in mind that in the thinking of Jesus and his contemporaries the figure of the historical Isaiah and that of the Servant of our 'Deutero-Isaiah' are one and the same person prefiguring the Messiah who is to come.) As in the days of Isaiah, so shall it be now. Isaiah had seen the glory of God in the Temple at Jerusalem and had known the whole earth to be full of it (Isa. 6.1-4), but Israel remained utterly blind to the divine glory. In Isa. 6.9f. the mystery of the blind eyes is stated in a characteristically Hebrew poetic form—a form in which a result is expressed, as here, by means of a command: 'Go and tell this people, Hear ye indeed, but understand not; and see ye indeed and perceive not. Make the heart of this people fat, and make their ears heavy, and shut their eyes; lest they see with their eyes, and hear with their ears, and understand with their heart, and turn again and be healed.' Israel's heart is gross, her ears heavy, her eyes shut, *with the result that* she cannot repent and be healed; but the Hebraic way of saying this is to use the final form

---

[1] A. Jülicher, *Die Gleichnisreden Jesu*, Freiburg, 1899. See A. Nygren, *Agape and Eros*, ET by P. S. Watson, 1953, 81-91.

('lest'), thereby evincing a deeply religious awareness that in some sense the hardening of Israel's heart and the failure of her understanding is due to the sovereign will of God: her blindness, perhaps, is a punishment for her failure to obey God's righteous will.[1] 'A sentence of judicial blindness' has been passed upon Israel.[2]

It would seem reasonable to suppose that Jesus found in the failure of Israel to respond to the preaching of the Servant-Prophet (Isaiah of Jerusalem) a precedent for the failure of Israel to respond to the preaching of the Servant-Messiah. As in Isaiah's day, when only a remnant 'returned', so in his own time the majority saw but did not perceive, heard but did not understand. All things were indeed done, as far as they were concerned, 'in parables' (Mark 4.11). The deeply significant meaning of this word ($\pi\alpha\rho\alpha\beta o\lambda\dot{\eta}$), like its Hebrew original (*mashal*; Aramaic *mathla*), cannot be rendered by any English word, since it signifies not only 'parable' in our English sense of story-with-a-deeper-meaning but also 'riddle', 'dark saying', 'obscurity'. The whole life, death and resurrection of Christ are a 'parable' in the deep double meaning of the word: they enable those to whom the mystery is 'given' to understand the truth of God's salvation, but to those who are 'outside' they are riddles and obscurities. So much is involved in Jesus's own conception of himself as a 'sign' to his generation. It seems by no means improbable that Jesus should have used the word 'parable' (in its Aramaic form) in a deliberately equivocal way, as Mark reports him as doing. It seems more than probable that he should have meditated deeply upon Isa. 6.9f., which Mark reports him as quoting in this context: 'Unto you (disciples) is given the mystery of the reign of God, but unto them that are without ($\tau o\hat{i}s$ $\check{\epsilon}\xi\omega$) all things are done $\dot{\epsilon}\nu$ $\pi\alpha\rho\alpha\beta o\lambda\alpha\hat{i}s$: that ($\dot{\iota}\nu\alpha$) seeing they may see, and not perceive, and hearing they may hear and not understand; lest haply ($\mu\dot{\eta}\pi o\tau\epsilon$) they should turn again and it should be forgiven them' (Mark 4.11f.). Mark here quotes Isa. 6.9f. from a Palestinian Targum; as we have noted, in accordance with Semitic usage a command expresses a result, and the final construction ($\dot{\iota}\nu\alpha$) is used where we would use a consecutive, 'with the result that'. Mark thinks in a Semitic way, and he does not in the least intend to suggest that Jesus taught in parables *in order that*

---

[1] An illustration of the use of a final construction when nothing more than a result is intended may be found in Ps. 51.4: the Psalmist does not mean that he committed evil in order to give God the opportunity of pronouncing just judgment, but that his transgressions result in the exercise of the righteous judgment of God. Cf. V. Taylor, *The Gospel According to St Mark*, 1952, 256: 'The saying (Mark 4.12) is based on Isa. 6.9f., which in the form of a command ironically describes what in fact would be *the result* of Isaiah's ministry: "Go, and tell this people. . . ." This use of a command to express a result is typically Semitic.'

[2] The quotation is from B. W. Bacon, Hastings's *DCG*, II, 213b.

his hearers should not understand. What Mark sees very clearly is that because the true character of Jesus as Messiah can be perceived only by the eyes of faith, all his words and works are riddles to those who stand outside the community of faith. It would not, of course, occur to St Mark that by his Semitic use of ἵνα he was creating grave difficulties for non-Semitic minds; but Matthew, who appreciates such linguistic differences, alters ἵνα to ὅτι, thus removing an adventitious stumbling-block, but losing in the process something of the deep Hebraic sense that in some mysterious way the closing of the blind eyes and the hardening of the heart do not occur apart from the will of God. Matthew quotes Isa. 6.9f. almost verbatim from the LXX and turns the whole matter into a straight fulfilment of OT prophecy: 'Unto them is fulfilled the prophecy of Isaiah . . .' (Matt. 13.14).[1]

THE MIRACLES OF THE KINGDOM OF GOD

It has been traditional in Christian theology down the centuries to regard the miracles of Christ as proofs of his divine nature. It is anachronistic to read back such an attitude into the NT records. Miracles were everyday events in an age which knew nothing about the fixity of natural law, and every village had its wonder-worker. To cast out a demon or to work some other kind of miracle was no proof of divinity: one might be in league with Beelzebub or some other spirit (Mark 3.22). A good man, particularly a teacher of the Law, could reasonably be expected to have the power to heal and to cast out evil spirits (cf. Matt. 12.27). The Synoptists stress the fact that the mighty works performed by Jesus created astonishment amongst those who witnessed them and caused his fame to spread throughout the whole country (Mark 3.7-12, etc.); but, as St Mark points out, they were susceptible of more than one explanation (Mark 6.14-16). The first-century question was not whether Jesus could perform miracles but by what authority he performed them (Mark 11.28). To perceive the ἐξουσία behind the miracles of Christ was to penetrate the mystery of his person; to fail to perceive it was equivalent to hearing the parables only as enigmas, without understanding their meaning. The response which Jesus wanted from those who witnessed his mighty works was

---

[1] Luke retains the ἵνα but omits the μήποτε clause; he abbreviates and compresses the passage to a single verse, and consequently his treatment of it is of little interest from our present viewpoint. Both Matthew and Luke alter Mark's singular μυστήριον τῆς βασιλείας to the plural, τὰ μυστήρια τῆς β. (Indeed Matt. 13.11 and Luke 8.10 are a striking example of an agreement of Matt. and Luke against Mark.) Perhaps by the time Matt. and Luke were written 'the mysteries' had come to mean 'the sacraments', a usage common in the second century and onwards, and Matt. and Luke may have wished this meaning to be understood here. The Vulgate translates μυστήριον by *sacramentum* in Dan. 2.18; 4.6; Tob. 12.7; Wisd. 2.22; Eph. 1.9; 3.3, 9; 5.32; I Tim. 3.16; Rev. 1.20; but here the word used is *mysterium*.

not astonishment, but repentance and faith: 'Woe unto thee, Chorazin! . . . Bethsaida! for if the mighty works had been done in Tyre and Sidon which were done in you, *they would have repented* long ago in sackcloth and ashes' (Matt. 11.21; Luke 10.13). Jesus refused to work miracles with the object of dazzling people into accepting him or of compelling them to believe against their will (Matt. 4.1-11; Luke 4.1-13). He refused to give a sign (i.e. to work a miracle) to the Pharisees when they tried to test (tempt) him (Mark 8.11f.; Matt. 16.1-4; Luke 11.16); men must read by faith the signs which are given to them; they must not demand signs of their own devising, 'that we may see and believe' (Mark 15.32). Christ was himself the true Sign from Heaven, and his miracles were signs (σημεῖα) to those who recognized him; to those who were 'outside' the community of faith he was a stumbling-block and his miracles were only τέρατα, 'wonders' which aroused astonishment and perhaps even admiration, but which were essentially inexplicable enigmas: τοῖς ἔξω ἐν παραβολαῖς τὰ πάντα.

We need therefore feel no surprise at the paradox that, while Jesus refused to give a sign to those who demanded one, he nevertheless regarded his miracles as signs which would be understood by those who had responded to the proclamation of the drawing nigh of the reign of God. We may roughly divide the Gospel miracles into three groups: the Isaianic signs, the exorcisms, and the more elaborately theological parable-miracles. These groups to some extent overlap, because an Isaianic-sign type of miracle may be elaborated into a profound theological parable-miracle (e.g. the Blind Man of Bethsaida, Mark 8.22-26, the 'type' of St Peter in the following verses; or the Man Born Blind in John 9); exorcisms, too, are capable of considerable theological elaboration (e.g. Legion, Mark 5.1-20). It is, of course, the two former groups, the Isaianic signs and the exorcisms, which constitute the oldest and firmest strata in the Gospel tradition of the miraculous works of Jesus; and about both these types of miracle words of the Lord have been preserved in the oldest strata of the written Gospels.

First, to John the Baptist's question, 'Art thou he that should come?' Jesus replies to the effect that John's messengers could see for themselves that the things prophesied concerning the days of the Messiah were being fulfilled: 'The blind receive their sight (τυφλοὶ ἀναβλέπουσι), the lame walk, the lepers are cleansed, the deaf hear, the dead are raised up, and the poor have the good news preached to them' (Matt. 11.4f.= Luke 7.22). The words are a rough conflation of two passages from Isaiah: 'Then the eyes of the blind shall be opened and the ears of the deaf shall be unstopped; then shall the lame man leap as an hart, and the tongue of the dumb shall sing' (Isa. 35.5f.); and 'The Spirit of the

Lord God is upon me, because the LORD hath anointed me to preach good tidings to the poor (LXX, πτωχοῖς); he hath sent me to bind up the broken-hearted, to proclaim liberty (LXX, ἄφεσιν) to the captives, and the opening of the eyes (RV mg.; LXX, τυφλοῖς ἀνάβλεψιν) to them that are bound; to proclaim the year of the LORD's good pleasure (RV mg.) and the day of vengeance of our God. . . .' (Isa. 61.1f.). Our Lord's words leave us in no possible doubt that he himself regarded his miracles as evidences or σημεῖα of the dawning of the day of the Lord which had been predicted by Isaiah. His own relationship to that day or reign of God, now dawning, is made clear by his reading of Isa. 61.1f. in the synagogue at Nazareth (Luke 4.16-30) and declaring, 'Today this scripture is fulfilled in your ears' (4.21). Jesus had been anointed in Holy Spirit (πνεῦμα Κυρίου ἐπ' ἐμέ, οὗ εἵνεκεν ἔχρισέν με— 'he hath made me Christ') to proclaim the good news of the reign of God to the 'poor' (i.e. in biblical language the humble and devout) and to demonstrate the arrival of God's reign by his δυνάμεις—especially the enacted parable or σημεῖον of the opening of the eyes of the blind. It is worth noting that Luke (4.18) quotes the LXX version with its τυφλοῖς ἀνάβλεψιν ('recovering of sight to the blind', RV). The Isaianic prophecies specially stress the opening of the blind eyes, and in one very important passage this work is ascribed directly to the Servant of the Lord, with whom Jesus identified himself as Son of Man:[1] in Isa. 42.1-7 (the first 'Servant Song', 42.1-4, with the following verses) it is said that the Servant of the Lord, his chosen in whom he delights, will be given for a covenant of the people and a light of the Gentiles, 'to open the blind eyes, to bring out the prisoners from the dungeon, and them that sit in darkness out of the prison house'. This is the passage (Isa. 42.1) which along with Ps. 2.7 is generally agreed to underlie the words heard by Jesus at his baptism (Mark 1.11);[2] we may therefore infer how deeply significant it was for Jesus as he reflected upon his mission. It is hardly surprising that the opening of the blind eyes plays such a prominent part amongst the recorded miracles of Jesus in the Gospels. Other δυνάμεις, however, play a similar rôle. For instance, in Isa. 32.3f. we read, 'The eyes of them that see shall not be dim (RV mg., 'closed'), and the ears of them that hear shall hearken; the heart of the rash shall understand knowledge, and the tongue of the stammerers (LXX, αἱ γλῶσσαι αἱ ψελλίζουσαι) shall be ready to speak plainly.' St Mark, who does not wish the significance of his story of the Deaf-Mute ('Ephphatha') to be missed, carefully describes the deaf man as μογιλάλος (RV, 'one that had an impediment in his speech') (Mark 7.32-37); the significance of his use of this particular word lies

---

[1] See *infra*, 135.   [2] See *infra*, 179.

in its rarity: Isa. 35.6 and Mark 7.32 are in fact the only occurrences in LXX and NT. The exclamation of the bystanders, καλῶς πάντα πεποίηκε (7.37), is reminiscent of Gen. 1.31, πάντα ὅσα ἐποίησε, καλὰ λίαν: Christ's work is the *new* creation, and it is very good. All Christ's healing miracles may be regarded as fulfilments of the Isaianic signs, but especially the healings of the blind and the deaf; Jesus himself says to his disciples, 'Blessed are your eyes for they see, and your ears for they hear; for verily I say unto you that many prophets and righteous men (Luke, 'kings') desired to see the things which ye see and saw them not, and to hear the things which ye hear and heard them not' (Matt. 13.16f.; Luke 10.23f.). The significance of Christ's miracles is not that they prove that he is a divine being, or that he has access to supernatural power; still less do they demonstrate the power of mind over matter or illustrate the wonderful possibilities of faith-healing. Their significance is precisely that they are the *gesta Christi*, τὰ ἔργα τοῦ Χριστοῦ (Matt. 11.2), the acts of the Messiah, 'the works which none other did' (John 15.24). Because they are the fulfilments of OT prophecy, not because they are stupendous or astonishing, they bear witness to the fact that Christ is sent by the Father (John 5.36; cf. 9.4, 10.37f.). Because they are the works *of Christ*, those who have witnessed them have already tasted the δυνάμεις of the Age to Come (Heb. 6.5).

The Synoptists record words of Jesus which indicate his attitude towards the second group of his δυνάμεις, namely, the exorcisms. These also he regards as evidences of the drawing nigh of the reign of God. He says to the Pharisees, 'If I by the Spirit (Luke 'finger') of God cast out demons, then is the reign of God come upon you' (ἔφθασεν ἐφ' ὑμᾶς ἡ βασιλεία τοῦ Θεοῦ) (Matt. 12.28; Luke 11.20). He is replying to the charge that he casts out demons by the power of Beelzebub; such a notion is absurd, because it presupposes civil war in Satan's kingdom. The truth is rather that the counter-kingdom of Satan is being invaded: the 'strong man' is no longer able to guard his palace; a stronger than he has come upon him and is spoiling his goods; the exorcisms demonstrate that the reign of God is putting to an end the reign of Satan (Mark 3.27; Matt. 12.29; Luke 11.21f.). Jesus, in fact, conceives of his own mission as the beginning of the onslaught upon the powers of evil, which will end in the complete overthrow of Satan. Thus, the success of the mission of the seventy, who had subjugated the demons in Christ's name, is the occasion of his vision of Satan fallen like a flash of lightning from heaven (Luke 10.17f.). Unlike the miracle-stories of the Isaianic type, the exorcism-stories are not significant as fulfilments of OT prophecies concerning the latter days. It was not until after the close of the OT period proper that there developed the apocalyptic conception of the world as being subjected to the rule of Satan and his demonic hosts. By the time of our Lord this conception was prevalent, and not only the usual cases of demon-possession, but also other forms of infirmity, were attributed to the power of Satan and his minions to enslave human beings. For example, the crippled woman who is healed in the synagogue on the Sabbath day (Luke 13.10-17) and who is described as having a πνεῦμα ἀσθενείας,[1] is referred to by Jesus as 'a daughter of Abraham whom Satan had bound'. Release from Satan's bondage was a sign of the drawing nigh of the reign of God.

The group of miraculous raisings of the dead has a rather different significance from both the Isaianic signs and the exorcisms. The OT does not prophesy the raising of the dead in the Messianic Age until we come to its very latest strata, e.g. Isa. 25.8; Dan. 12.2; and so, as with the exorcisms, the significance of the raisings of the dead does not lie in the fulfilment of specific OT prophecies. They are significant rather as anticipations of Christ's own resurrection and of the resurrection of believers in him. As St John shews us in the case of Lazarus, they are demonstrations of the truth that Christ is himself 'the resurrection and the life' (John 11.25). Jesus himself claims to have raised the dead, for his reply to John the Baptist's question includes the words, 'The dead are raised up' (Matt. 11.5; Luke 7.22), although the Isaianic passages do not contain such a prediction. When he sends out the Twelve, he bids them 'raise the dead' (Matt. 10.8): this, too, is clearly one of the signs that the reign of God has drawn nigh. The imminence of the reign of God is demonstrated by the advent of the divine δύναμις which, after certain anticipatory signs, is manifested decisively in the raising up of Jesus from the dead; it will be manifested again in the coming of the βασιλεία ἐν δυνάμει (Mark 9.1), and will be finally revealed at the apocalypse or parousia of the Son of Man in great power and glory.

The three accounts in the Gospels of specific individuals being raised by Jesus from the dead are all weighted with deep theological significance. The Raising of Jairus's Daughter (Mark 5.22-43) is the most 'factual' of the three, but even here it seems as if theological motives are at work, especially in relation to St Mark's structural plan for his Gospel. The Raising of the Widow's Son at Nain (Luke 7.11-17), peculiar to St Luke, reflects the evangelist's interest in the Elijah theme: Christ, the new Elijah, re-enacts in the Shunem locality the great deeds of Elijah and Elisha, each of whom restored a dead son to a widowed mother (I Kings 17.17-24; II Kings 4.21-37).[2] In the Fourth Gospel

---

[1] I.e., a spirit which caused weakness (J. M. Creed, *The Gospel According to St Luke*, 1930, *ad loc.*).

[2] Cf. Alan Richardson, *Miracle Stories of the Gospels*, 1941, 113.

the Raising of Lazarus (John 11) is probably not intended by the evangelist to be taken literally; he is teaching in his own allusive way the truth that Jesus was put to death because he claimed to be 'the resurrection and the life' and demonstrated his claim by his mighty works, including the raising of the dead: the story is not a literally true story but it nevertheless contains the truth of history. 'This man doeth many σημεῖα; if we let him alone, all men will believe on him . . .' (John 11.47f.). The realistic rulers of the Sanhedrin knew well enough that preaching is harmless and ineffective, and they would hardly have taken the trouble to have had Jesus put out of the way if he had confined his activities to preaching. The truth of history is that Jesus was put to death because by his miracles he shewed himself to be the Messiah; the Jewish rulers could see well enough what was implied in Jesus's deeds, and they did not want that kind of a Messiah. St John has apparently constructed his Lazarus-parable out of the Lucan parable known as 'Dives and Lazarus' (Luke 16.19-31); that parable deals with a specific refusal to shew the sign of resurrection to the unbelieving, self-satisfied 'rich'. Such crass materialists are not converted by 'signs'; they have the Scriptures, but they do not 'repent': 'neither will they be persuaded, if one rise from the dead'. St John dramatizes the truth of Jesus's parable: the miracles of Jesus did not convert the rulers of the Jews, nor were they converted by the resurrection of Christ himself.

THE NATURE MIRACLES OF THE GOSPELS

The so-called 'nature miracles' in the Gospels are of a highly elaborated theological character. It is worth noting that what may appear to us to be a 'nature miracle' may be an exorcism in first-century belief: Jesus casts out the demon of the storm in Mark 4.35-41 just as he casts the unclean spirits out of demoniacs (cf. ἐπετίμησε and πεφίμωσο in 4.39 with Mark 1.25). The two Sea Miracles, the Casting out of the Demon of the Storm (Mark 4.35-41) and the Walking on the Sea (Mark 6.45-52), illustrate the unity of Christ with the Lord whose power is dramatically set forth in the OT by reference to his control of the deep, of the storms and winds and waves (e.g. Pss. 65.7;[1] 89.9; 93; 107.23-30). The symbolical significance of Christ's Sea-Miracles rests in the last resort upon the imagery of the ancient mythology in which the high God smites 'the deep' (*Tiamat*; *Tehom*, Gen. 1.2; Rahab, Isa. 51.9f.; Ps. 89.9f.; Leviathan, Ps. 104.26; Job 41.1); of course, the old religion has been 'demythologized', but the suggestive power of the myth remains; and to shew forth Christ as lord of the winds and waves is a striking way of emphasizing his oneness with the 'I AM' of the OT revelation

---

[1] Cf. Hoskyns and Davey, *The Riddle of the New Testament*, 1931, 169 and 172.

(cf. Mark 6.50 and John 6.20 with Ex. 3.14, 'I AM hath sent me unto you').

The two Feeding Miracles (Mark 6.32-44 and 8.1-10 and pars.) doubtless embody a number of theological themes, some of which are developed more explicitly in John 6: Christ as the new Moses who gives the Bread from Heaven (cf. the manna, Ex. 16; Ps. 78.23-29, esp. v. 29, LXX 77.29), the new Elijah-Elisha (cf. II Kings 4.42-44, esp. v. 44, and note the *barley*-loaves of John 6.9), the True Bread, the Giver of the Bread of Life to the Jews (the 5,000 and the twelve κόφινοι) and the Giver of the Bread of Life to the Gentiles also (the 4,000 and the seven σφυρίδες: Mark 8.19f.), the Host at the Messianic Banquet in the Kingdom of Heaven, the Host at the eschatological anticipation of the latter in the Church's Eucharist (cf. esp. Mark 6.41 and 8.6).[1] Theological motives of this kind dominate the narratives as our Evangelists have recorded them for us, and it is hardly possible to discover from them 'what really happened' as a matter of strict historical fact. Our view of 'what happened' will depend in the last resort upon what we think of Christ—who he was and what he achieved. Broadly speaking, three views of the Feeding Miracles are possible. The old rationalizing view was that the 'miracle' consisted in Jesus's persuading the crowd to share its provisions by means of his own and his disciples' example of unselfishness in sharing their loaves and fishes. Or with Schweitzer it might be held that what really took place was a sacramental meal in which Christ gave to everyone present a morsel of bread in token that those who had shared his table in his obscurity would share it in his glory.[2] Or thirdly we may hold that Jesus, being the Christ, the Son of God, did actually perform the σημεῖα of the Bread of Life, as the apostolic witness attests; whether or not the miraculous nature of his action was perceived only by his disciples, we may hold that the stories of the Feeding Miracles reveal Jesus in his glory as the eschatological Son of Man, bringing in by a miracle of new creation the dawning day of the Lord.[3] In his teaching Jesus occasionally made use of the picture of the Messianic Banquet (Luke 14.15-24; Matt. 8.11). The rabbis believed that the heavenly manna would be restored again to the faithful in the days of the Messiah, and this idea probably underlies the reference to the 'hidden manna' in Rev. 2.17.[4] We may therefore conclude

[1] For the case against a eucharistic interpretation of the Feeding Miracles see G. H. Boobyer, *JTS*, NS, Vol. III, Pt. 2 (October, 1952); for the case in favour of it see Alan Richardson, 'The Feeding of the Five Thousand' in *Interpretation* (Richmond, Va.), April, 1952, 144-9; also *Miracle Stories*, 94-8.

[2] A. Schweitzer, *The Quest of the Historical Jesus* (ET, 1911), 374.

[3] Cf. E. Lohmeyer, *Das Evangelium des Markus*, Göttingen, 1937, 128-30.

[4] See R. H. Charles, *Revelation* (ICC), 1920, *ad loc.*

that the early Church saw in the stories of the desert Feedings deep eschatological significance; they were signs given to those who had eyes to see which demonstrated the truth of who Jesus really was. It is clear that St Mark himself looked upon them in this way (Mark 6.52; 8.14-21). There is much in the symbolism of the stories which remains to be explained. In particular, we would like to know more about the symbolism of fish in the early Church: bread and fish appear frequently in the frescoes of the catacombs as a symbol of the Eucharist (and cf. Luke 24.41-43; John 21.9-13). The letters of the Greek word ἰχθύς (fish) came early to stand for Ἰησοῦς Χριστός, Θεοῦ υἱός, σωτήρ, and thus the likeness of a fish became a secret sign of a Christian household, meeting-place or burial-place. It is often urged that bread and wine, rather than bread and fish, would have been the appropriate elements of the feedings if they had been thought of as possessing eucharistic significance; to this it can only be replied that because Jesus actually used bread *and fish* in the desert meals, therefore fish came to have a significance in the early tradition which no later developments could obscure. The fact of the fish is a kind of guarantee of the historicity of the Feeding stories; it roots them in Galilee, in the tradition of the fishermen-disciples who (in a homely metaphor) were made fishers of men (Mark 1.16-20; cf. Luke 5.10). The long continuance of the symbolism of fish and fishing in the παράδοσις is a seal of the historicity of the Galilean gospel. Perhaps, as Dr Austin Farrer suggests,[1] the early Church, which saw in the multiplied bread an analogy with the manna which fell from heaven, saw also in the fish an analogy with the quails that came up from the sea. 'Whence should I have flesh,' asks Moses, 'to give to all this people? . . . shall all the fish of the sea be gathered together for them, to suffice them?' (Num. 11.13, 22). At least, it is clear to us that in the Feeding stories, even in St Mark's version, we do not have simple straightforward historical accounts of 'what happened', but elaborately theological interpretations which have turned the historical facts into profound parables of the significance of the person of Christ and of the Eucharist in his Church.[2]

[1] *A Study in St Mark*, 1951, 291.

[2] For a more detailed consideration of the miracles of the Gospels it may be permissible to refer to the present writer's *Miracle Stories of the Gospels*, 1941; fifth reprint, 1956. A fuller consideration of the Raising of Lazarus (John 11.1-44) will be found in his Commentary on St. John's Gospel (Torch series), *ad loc.*, to be published in 1959.

5

THE HOLY SPIRIT

THE word 'spirit' (*ruach*, πνεῦμα, also 'wind', 'breath') is used in the Bible in several different ways—the Spirit of God, the spirit of man, and the whole realm of 'spirits', good and evil. Our chief concern is with the Spirit as one of the most distinctively biblical means of expressing the outgoing activity of God. In the OT 'Spirit of God' is one of the ways in which God's action may be mentioned without actually making the anthropomorphic statement that God *did* this or that. Thus, 'the Spirit of God', like the Word and the Wisdom of God, becomes a periphrastic description of God's initiative and action in the creation, providential ordering, redemption and eschatological deliverance of the world as a whole and of Israel in particular. God's Spirit is a reverential way of speaking of his presence (e.g. Pss. 51.11; 139.7; note the parallelism in each case; in the LXX 'presence' is πρόσωπον) or of his δύναμις in action (cf. Luke 1.35; and cf. Matt. 12.28 with Luke 11.20 and the latter with Ex. 8.19). As such the Spirit of God cannot be rigidly distinguished from his creative Word; cf. Gen. 1.2; Judith 16.14 and especially Ps. 33.6, 'By the word of the LORD were the heavens made, and all the host of them by the breath (*ruach*; LXX, πνεῦμα) of his mouth.' Similarly the functions of the Spirit and of the Wisdom of God are interchangeable (Wisd. 7.22); the Spirit is *par excellence* 'the Spirit of prophecy', yet it may be said that it is the Wisdom of God which makes men prophets (Wisd. 7.27; cf. 9.17). Spirit, Word and Wisdom are three ways of reverently speaking about the activity of the transcendent God.

Our modern difficulties about the relation of the Spirit to God arise because we hold a conception of personality unknown to the biblical writers. We think of separate and distinct personalities, hard and impermeable, each sharply distinguished from the others: hence our 'problem' of the doctrine of the Trinity. In the Bible persons are not thus separate and distinct; they flow into one another. A man lives in his sons, who may thus collectively be called by his name (e.g. Israel). A man may receive a portion of another man's 'spirit' and thus may in some sense *become* that other man. A man may reappear in history as another person, who, though he is not the same person, is nevertheless in some way identified with him. A good example is that of Elijah who in the biblical tradition becomes almost the same person as Elisha; the biblical way of expressing this is to say that a double portion of Elijah's spirit is upon Elisha (II Kings 2.9; cf. Deut. 21.17) or that 'the spirit of Elijah doth rest on Elisha' (II Kings 2.15; cf. Ecclus. 48.12). Elijah acts through Elisha.[1] In a similar way God acts through those upon whom his Spirit comes. The $\pi\nu\epsilon\hat{\upsilon}\mu\alpha$ of a man is his $\delta\acute{\upsilon}\nu\alpha\mu\iota\varsigma$, his person in action; and the same is true of God's $\pi\nu\epsilon\hat{\upsilon}\mu\alpha$. It is his $\delta\acute{\upsilon}\nu\alpha\mu\iota\varsigma$, i.e. it is God acting. Thus, when the $\pi\nu\epsilon\hat{\upsilon}\mu\alpha$ of God is said to come upon a man he behaves in a manner consistent with the particular view of God which the narrator holds. When the Spirit of Yahweh comes upon Saul, he prophesies after the manner of the ecstatic prophets and —very significantly—is 'turned into another man' (I Sam. 10.6, 10; cf. 19.23f.); but prophecy in its more developed biblical sense is also the result of the operation of God's Spirit (e.g. Ecclus. 48.24). Micah is contrasted with the false prophets because he is genuinely 'full of power by the Spirit of the LORD' (Micah 3.8). The characteristic sphere of the operation of the Spirit is that of prophecy (II Sam. 23.2; Neh. 9.30; II (4) Esd. 14.22; Wisd. 9.17; Mart. Isa. 1.7); the biblical position is stated thus by a NT writer, 'No prophecy ever came by the will of man, but men spake from God, being moved by the Holy Spirit' (II Pet. 1.21; cf. I Pet. 1.12; II Tim. 3.16, $\pi\hat{\alpha}\sigma\alpha$ $\gamma\rho\alpha\phi\grave{\eta}$ $\theta\epsilon\acute{o}\pi\nu\epsilon\upsilon\sigma\tau\sigma\varsigma$: cf. also Luke 1.70; Acts 1.16, etc.). Jesus himself is recorded as attributing the prophetic words of David (i.e. Ps. 110.1) to the activity of the Holy Spirit (Mark 12.36). God gives his word to his prophets through the operation of his Spirit. But the working of the Spirit amongst men is by no means confined to the sphere of prophecy: the OT attributes to the Spirit such things as Joseph's skill as a ruler (Gen. 41.38); Joshua's military genius (Num. 27.18); the craftsmanship of Bezalel and Oholiab (Ex. 31.2-6); moral excellence (Pss. 51.10f.; 143.10; Neh. 9.20; Isa. 30.1). It may be noted that the OT never uses the expression 'the Holy Spirit' absolutely, but it speaks twice of *God's* Holy Spirit (Ps. 51.11; Isa. 63.10); the Spirit of God has no existence apart from God

---

[1] In the NT Elijah lives again in John the Baptist, just as in the OT conception he lives again in Elisha; thus Malachi's prophecy concerning the Forerunner is fulfilled (Mal. 3.1-3; 4.4-6; cf. Matt. 11.7-14, etc.). Herod and Herodias play the rôles of Ahab and Jezebel in the re-enacted drama (Mark 6.14-29). Cf. Luke 1.17, 'He (John) shall go in the $\pi\nu\epsilon\hat{\upsilon}\mu\alpha$ and $\delta\acute{\upsilon}\nu\alpha\mu\iota\varsigma$ of Elijah, to turn the hearts of the fathers to the children . . .', etc. (quoting Mal. 4.6); but in the Lucan account of the *ministry* of Christ all references to John as the Elijah are dropped, because St Luke wishes to present Christ himself as the one whom Elijah prefigured. Perhaps a similar motive lies behind the denial that the Baptist is the *Elijah redivivus* in John 1.21.

any more than the spirit of Elijah can exist apart from Elijah. God's Spirit is God acting.

THE ESCHATOLOGICAL CHARACTER OF THE SPIRIT

We might reasonably ask, if Spirit is, like Wisdom and Word, a way of indicating the divine activity, why in the NT Christ is not identified with Spirit as he is with the Wisdom and the Word of God. Various answers may be suggested. In the first place it may be pointed out that the statement is only partly true, since the Risen Christ is, as we shall see, not sharply distinguished from the Spirit of God. Secondly, the identification is soft-pedalled because it would lead to a reduced conception of the person of Christ in the Hellenistic world; it was at all costs necessary to avoid the suggestion that Jesus was merely a 'pneumatic man', someone who exercised 'spiritual gifts'. If the Christology of the Church had been reduced to a 'pneumatology', the Gospel would have been no different from the commotion associated with the names of other 'spirit-filled' teachers and miracle-workers of the Hellenistic world; we meet several such in Acts—Simon Magus (8.9-24), Elymas (13.6-12), and the seven sons of Sceva (19.14). But there is another and even more profound reason, viz. the eschatological character of the Holy Spirit in the NT conception. The incarnate Jesus could not be identified with the Spirit before his death and resurrection, because it was those very events which were to bring about the shedding abroad of the Holy Spirit in the latter days. St John with his characteristic penetration sums up the New Testament position in this matter. The prophecies of the Scriptures concerning 'rivers of living water' (Isa. 12.3; Ezek. 47.1) were shortly to be fulfilled in the pouring forth of the Holy Spirit: Jesus, when he spoke metaphorically of the living water, was really speaking of the 'Holy Spirit, which they that believed on him were to receive, for the Spirit was not yet (given), because Jesus was not yet glorified', i.e. in Johannine language, crucified, risen and ascended (John 7.38f.). In order to understand the background of this NT position it is necessary to consider what had happened to the doctrine of the Spirit in later Judaism.

Towards and after the close of the OT period Torah was magnified at the expense of prophecy. 'In the third century B.C. the Law had come to be conceived as the final and supreme revelation of God. When once this idea of an inspired Law—adequate, infallible and valid for all time—had become an accepted dogma of Judaism, as it became in the post-Exilic period, there was no longer room for independent representatives of God appearing before men, such as the pre-Exilic prophets, God had, according to the official teachers of the Church, spoken his last and final word through the Law.'[1] Hence prophecy was held to be in abeyance (I Macc. 4.46; 14.41); it was indeed unnecessary. 'The Law has not only assumed the functions of the ancient pre-Exilic prophets, but it has also, so far as lay in its power, made the revival of such prophecy an impossibility.'[2] To claim to be a prophet was made a capital offence; according to Zech. 13.1-5, if a man declared himself to be a prophet, his father and mother were to put him to death! A writer who had something to say must therefore express himself pseudonymously; and hence from 200 B.C. onwards all the works of the apocalyptists, who succeeded the prophets, are pseudonymous: an ancient worthy like Daniel, or, better still, patriarchs like Enoch or the Twelve, would gain a hearing when prophecy was silenced and the canon virtually closed. Some apocalyptic writings managed to secure inclusion in the corpus of an earlier prophet (e.g. Isa. 24-27; Zech. 9-14); in Charles's view Joel is the latest OT apocalyptist whose work is not pseudonymous. It is clear that during this period the Spirit, who was pre-eminently the spirit of prophecy, would no longer be regarded as a present reality; and indeed we even find it widely taught that the revelation given in the Torah was communicated not by the Spirit but by the mediation of angels (Jubilees 1.27; Test. Dan 6; cf. Deut. 33.2; Acts 7.38, 53; Gal. 3.19; Heb. 2.2). But the doctrine of the Spirit was not entirely forgotten or suppressed: the Spirit was projected into the future. Had not the canonical prophets taught that the Spirit of God would be active in the new creation of the latter days, that he would rest upon every member of a renewed Israel, and that through him all would have direct access to God (Ezek. 11.19; 36.26f.; 37.14; Isa. 32.15; Zech. 12.10; Jer. 31.34 and especially Joel 2.28f.)? In this way there develops the thoroughly eschatological conception of the Holy Spirit which is found everywhere in the NT.[3]

---

[1] R. H. Charles, *Apocrypha and Pseudepigrapha*, II, p. viii.

[2] Charles, *ibid*.

[3] The eschatological character of the Spirit is not prominent in the Qumran literature, and the 'spirit of truth' is not integrally connected either with the Messiah(s) or with the Messianic Age. Throughout history the two spirits in man (of truth and of error) are engaged in ceaseless strife, and the spirit of truth will not conquer until the final age, when God will make all things new (1 QS iv. 21; Gaster, *SDSS*, 55f.). According to W. D. Davies (in Stendahl, *SNT*, 171-82) there is only one passage in the Scrolls where an eschatological character is unambiguously ascribed to the spirit of truth (viz. 1 QS iv. 20f., where it is said that the spirit of truth will be 'sprinkled' on men in the final age). This is surprising in view of the Qumran community's lively expectation of the End. But the concept of the Spirit in the Scrolls has, in W. D. Davies's apt phrase, 'been domiciled within a legalistic community', and there is hardly any point of contact between it and the dynamic Holy Spirit of the apostolic Church. The Essenes, however, are still looking for the coming of the final age, whereas the Christian Church, in which the Spirit is already given, is itself a sign that the End-time has already begun.

THE HOLY SPIRIT IN THE GOSPELS

The apostolic Church considered itself to be living in the latter days, the age of the fulfilment of the prophecies concerning the pouring forth of God's Spirit upon all flesh (Acts 2.16-18; 10.45; Rom. 5.5; Gal. 4.6; Titus 3.6, etc.). This pouring forth of the Holy Spirit in accordance with prophecy took place through the death, resurrection and ascension of Jesus Christ (John 16.7; 20.22; Acts 2.33; Eph. 4.8). Before the death of Christ the Holy Spirit was *incognito*, unknown to the disciples, although the Spirit was present to and active in Christ himself, again in accordance with prophecy (Isa. 11.2; 61.1, etc.). The Spirit is particularly active in the circumstances of Christ's birth of the Virgin[1] (Matt. 1.18, 20; Luke 1.15, 35, 41, 67; 2.25, 27), and the Spirit descends upon Christ at his baptism[2] (Mark 1.10; Matt. 3.16; Luke 3.22; cf. John 1.32f.). Thereafter Jesus lived under the inspiration and in the power of the Spirit (e.g. Mark 1.12; Matt. 4.1; Luke 4.1, 14, 18; Matt. 12.18, 28), but the Spirit was not manifest even to his chosen disciples. As St John explains, 'the Spirit was not yet' (7.39). We need not therefore be surprised that there are comparatively few references to the Holy Spirit in the Gospels, save in connection with the birth or the baptism of Jesus. In Matt. 12.28 Jesus claims that he casts out demons 'by the Spirit of God' but this means nothing more than 'by divine power'; St Luke, doubtless in the interests of his typology, alters the expression to 'by the finger of God', which means the same thing (Luke 11.20; cf. Ex. 8.19; 31.18; Deut. 9.10; Ps. 8.3). It is St John who records that Jesus gave to his disciples formal teaching about the future sending of the Holy Spirit (John 14.16-18, 26; 15.26; 16.7-14), and there is nothing improbable about the suggestion that he did so, since he thought of his own death as inaugurating the age of the new covenant with the New Israel of the latter days. Indeed, the Synoptists themselves indicate that Jesus spoke about the coming of the Spirit. We have already noted that St Mark records that he foretold the imminent coming of God's reign with power (Mark 9.1); and St Mark must have understood God's βασιλεία ἐν δυνάμει to mean the Spirit-filled Church of Christ.[3]

Again, Jesus speaks of blasphemy against the Holy Spirit. In the Marcan version of the Beelzebub controversy Jesus concludes his parable of the Strong Man by adding that all men's sins and blasphemies may be forgiven, 'but whosoever shall blaspheme against the Holy Spirit hath never forgiveness but is guilty of an eternal sin (οὐκ ἔχει ἄφεσιν εἰς τὸν αἰῶνα, ἀλλ' ἔνοχός ἐστιν αἰωνίου ἁμαρτήματος), because

---

[1] See *infra*, 174f.   [2] See *infra*, 178-81.   [3] *Supra*, 63f.

they said, He hath an unclean spirit' (Mark 3.29f.; cf. Matt. 12.31). The context makes it clear that Jesus means that to reject the inbreaking Aeon (the Kingdom of God) and to dismiss the signs of its arrival—such as the exorcisms which demonstrate the overthrow of Satan's counter-kingdom—as the work of Beelzebub, is to reject the salvation which God is bringing and is in fact to be guilty of unforgivable sin against the New Age: τὸ αἰώνιον ἁμάρτημα must mean 'sin against the Aeon of Salvation', which inevitably excludes one from the forgiveness offered to those who repent and believe. The chief implication of αἰώνιος is not 'eternal' or 'everlasting', but rather 'pertaining to the Age to Come'; and similarly it is doubtful if we ought to translate οὐκ ἔχει ἄφεσιν εἰς τὸν αἰῶνα as 'hath never forgiveness' but rather as 'hath not forgiveness in the Age to Come', i.e. shall not enter into the βασιλεία τοῦ Θεοῦ. In Matt. 12.32 and Luke 12.10 we find a slightly different version of the saying: Jesus declares that blasphemy against the Son of Man shall be forgiven, 'but whosoever shall blaspheme against the Holy Spirit, it shall not be forgiven him, neither in this aeon nor in that which is to come' (Matthew's version). Perhaps it is meant that it is pardonable not to recognize in the humiliation of the Servant Messiah the royal person of the Son of God (cf. Isa. 53.4f.; Luke 23.34) and that therefore blasphemy against the Son of Man may be forgiven; but that to reject the demonstration of the reign of God in the power of the Spirit, as it is experienced in the life of the Church, is to put oneself outside the sphere of forgiveness altogether. Blasphemy against the Holy Spirit would thus have meant apostasy, the sin of those 'who were once enlightened and tasted of the heavenly gift, and were made partakers of the Holy Spirit, and tasted the good word of God and the powers of the Age to Come, and then fell away' (Heb. 6.4-6). It is impossible that such should be forgiven (*ibid.*, and cf. also Heb. 10.26-31; 12.14-17). To apostatize from the faith is to 'do despite unto the Spirit of grace' (Heb. 10.29). To speak against the Son of Man is not an unforgivable sin in one who has not yet been 'enlightened' (i.e. believed and been baptized); there is always open to such a man the possibility of repentance and belief. But for the baptized Christian to depart from the Church is the ultimate and unforgivable sin, blasphemy against the Holy Spirit. Whatever the words used by our Lord—and the difficulty is to see what meaning could have been attached to the saying about blasphemy against the Holy Spirit in advance of the pouring out of the Spirit—the apostolic Church would seem to have understood him as teaching that apostasy is mortal sin. A distinction is drawn between 'mortal' and 'venial' sins in I John 5.16f.; sin which is 'not unto death' may be forgiven by God; but there is also ἁμαρτία πρὸς θάνατον, and it is pointless to pray for such as have committed it. The general tone of the Johannine epistles would suggest that 'sin unto death' is apostasy (cf. I John 2.19; cf. John 13.30; 17.2). But we should probably be wrong if we assumed that all sin against the Holy Spirit is apostasy. 'Resisting' or 'grieving' the Holy Spirit are sins of which the NT writers are keenly aware (Acts 7.51; I Thess. 4.8; Eph. 4.30; cf. Isa. 63.10). Ananias and Sapphira 'lied to the Holy Spirit' and 'tempted the Spirit of the Lord' (Acts 5.1-11), and they suffered the extreme penalty. It has often been remarked that in the Gospels it is St Peter who is pre-eminently the one who blasphemes against the Son of Man (the Denial, Mark 14.66-72 and pars.); he is forgiven (cf. Mark 16.7) and thereafter serves and obeys the Holy Spirit.

Lastly, it should be noted that St Mark's Gospel records that Jesus taught his disciples that they would be empowered by the Holy Spirit in their work of preaching the Gospel to all the nations: 'When they deliver you up, be not anxious beforehand what ye shall speak, but whatsoever shall be given you in that hour, that speak ye: for it is not ye that speak but the Holy Spirit' (Mark 13.11). St Luke's version of this saying is very interesting: 'Settle it therefore in your hearts not to meditate beforehand how to answer, for I will give you a mouth and wisdom which all your adversaries shall not be able to gainsay' (Luke 21.14f.). Clearly St Luke, who in Acts dramatically describes the fulfilment of this prophecy through the coming of the Spirit, does not distinguish between the activity of the Spirit and the operation of the Risen Christ ('*I* will give you a mouth'—cf. Ex. 4.12—'and wisdom'—cf. Acts 6.10: 'They were not able to withstand the wisdom *and the Spirit* by which he [Stephen] spake'). This is, moreover, the teaching which St John ascribes to Jesus: the Spirit, the Paraclete whom Jesus will send from the Father, will bear witness in and through the witness of the disciples (John 15.26f.), and the action of the Spirit is the action of the Risen Christ himself, who comes to his disciples in the coming of the Paraclete (cf. John 14.18, 'I come unto you'). As we have already suggested, there is no reason at all to doubt that Jesus expected the imminent fulfilment of the prophecy of the pouring out of the Spirit in the latter days; nothing indeed is more probable than that he should have done so. The Gospels give us sufficient evidence for holding that he did in fact teach his apostles to expect the gift of the Spirit.

THE HOLY SPIRIT IN THE APOSTOLIC CHURCH

The Christian religion owes its existence to the intensity of the conviction of the apostolic Church that the outpouring of the Holy Spirit had taken place; the Church's experience of the Spirit was proof that the Messianic Age had arrived and that the prophecies of the Scriptures were fulfilled in Jesus Christ. Church membership was a participation in Holy Spirit, κοινωνία τοῦ ʿΑγίου Πνεύματος (II Cor. 13.14; Phil. 2.1); the Spirit of unity (cf. Ezek. 11.19) worked so mightily that 'the multitude of them that believed were of one heart and soul' (Acts 4.32); under the unifying power of the Spirit the earliest Christians 'had all things common' (Acts 2.44-47). There is one body of the believers because there is one Spirit (Eph. 4.3f.); all the individual Christians have been made to drink of the one Spirit (I Cor. 12.13; Eph. 2.18). The individual's baptism was the moment of his personal initiation into the sphere of the operation of the Holy Spirit, the act by which he was 'sealed unto the day of redemption' (Eph. 4.30). It was also the occasion of his endowment with the Spirit, who in assigning to him his particular task or ministry within the total ministry of the Church also imparted to him the gift or grace (χάρισμα) that enabled him to perform it (I Cor. 12.12-31). There were many different gifts, for the individual members of the body of Christ performed many different functions (I Cor. 12.4-11; cf. Heb. 2.4). All Christians were regarded as possessing the Spirit, which was not the exclusive privilege of any particular 'order' or 'orders' within the Church. It was a mark of the spiritual immaturity of many within the Gentile churches that they tended to admire the more spectacular χαρίσματα—the extraordinary, the ecstatic and the excitable manifestations of the Spirit's workings, such as glossolalia or 'speaking with tongues'. Paul is at pains to moderate the zeal of the Corinthians for such 'revivalist' emotionalism; we obtain a somewhat startling impression of early Christian worship from his remarks upon this subject in I Cor. 14. He does not wish to deny that glossolalia is genuinely a sign of the Spirit's activity, but it should not be allowed to distract attention from more important things: 'I thank God I speak with tongues more than you all; howbeit in the congregation (ἐν ἐκκλησίᾳ) I had rather speak five words with my understanding, that I might instruct others, than ten thousand words in a tongue' (I Cor. 14.18f.). It is clear from this chapter that 'speaking with tongues' is the phenomenon which has often reappeared since Paul's time, especially in revivalist meetings. Under the impulse of religious excitement the critical faculties of the mind are in abeyance, while the devotee utters nonsense syllables, which, though devoid of intelligible meaning, possess a strange power of communicating the religious emotion to others. St Paul tries to direct the attention of the Corinthians towards what he calls 'the greater gifts' and 'the more excellent way' (I Cor. 12.31). The greatest gifts are faith, hope and love, especially love (13.13). Even if one could speak with angelic tongues but had not love, the result would be merely a brassy noise (13.1). The true fruit of the Spirit is 'love, joy, peace, long-suffering, kindness, goodness, belief, meekness, self-control' (Gal. 5.22). Such virtues are not natural possibilities which we can attain if we try hard enough; they are the Spirit's choicest gifts; they are supernatural, not natural, virtues. The Christian life is a constant apprehension of the supernatural power of the Spirit; it may be described as walking by the Spirit, being led by the Spirit, or living by the Spirit (Gal. 5.16, 18, 25; Rom. 8.4, 14; etc).

The Spirit is the Spirit of power (II Tim. 1.7; cf. Acts 1.8; 10.38; Rom. 15.13; I Cor. 2.4; Eph. 3.16), enabling Christians to perform deeds beyond their own strength. This power is compulsive but not coercive; the Spirit guides, leads and directs (e.g. Acts 8.29; 10.19; 11.12; 13.2; 20.23, 28; 21.11, etc.), but does not override the personality of those who are thus directed. The Spirit, in fact, is the Spirit of liberty, releasing men from bondage to the Law (Gal. 5.13-18; Rom. 8.2; II Cor. 3.6, 17; cf. John 8.31-36). In the power of the Spirit Christians freely and gladly choose to do the will of God. At every point the Spirit helps them, even in their deepest prayer-life, at the very centre of their personalities; even in their most inarticulate prayers the Spirit prays within them, making intercession for the saints (Rom. 8.26f.). He is the Spirit of life (John 6.63; I Cor. 15.45), who breathes life into the new creation, the Church, as originally he breathed life into the first creation (Gen. 1.2; 2.7, etc.); or alternatively he is the life (the *ruach*, the πνεῦμα) thus breathed into the new creation (John 20.22; Rev. 11.11). Hence after their baptism in the Holy Spirit Christians walk in newness of life, the life of the new creation, the life of the Age to Come (Rom. 6.4; 7.6, etc.). The Spirit is the Spirit of adoption, since he is the Spirit received in baptism, whereby Christians are adopted into the household of God as joint-heirs with Christ; the Spirit bears his inward testimony, reassuring the baptized that they are indeed sons of God and thus enabling them to cry 'Abba', Father (Rom. 8.12-17; Gal. 4.6). This inward testimony of the Spirit is given to all Christians, whereas the gift of prophecy is given as a special χάρισμα only to the particular ministry of 'prophets' within the Church (Rom. 12.6; I Cor. 12.10, 29; Eph. 4.11); all prophecy within the new dispensation, as in the old, is due to the operation of the Spirit of prophecy (II Pet. 1.21; cf. I Pet. 1.10f.; Rev. 1.10; 19.10; and e.g. Acts 21.11). In I Cor. 12.8-10 St Paul mentions nine gifts or activities of the Spirit amongst church members; they range from 'wisdom' to the interpretation of tongues. Under the influence of Isa. 11.2 in the LXX version a sevenfold conception of the Spirit and of his activities grew up in the Church and became traditional, particularly in the *Spiritus septiformis* of Latin devotional theology.[1] In the Johannine Apocalypse a sevenfold representation of the Spirit is found; the 'seven spirits' in Rev. 1.4 obviously denote the Holy Spirit, occurring as they do in a Trinitarian context (cf. also Rev. 3.1; 4.5; 5.6). But probably the influence of Zech. 3.9 and 4.10 (combined with the fact that the Seer is thinking of *seven* churches) is determinative rather than Isa. 11.2, since the LXX text is not of much importance in the Apocalypse generally. The seven spirits of the Apocalypse are best understood as an imaginative way of referring to the sevenfold operation of the one Holy Spirit. St John does not characterize his seven spirits individually; such literalism is no part of his poetic design. In Rev. 5.6 the seven spirits are said to be the eyes of the Lamb, and they are sent forth into all the earth. Here the 'mission' of the Spirit, who is the Spirit of Christ, is poetically represented and is declared to be universal in scope ('into all the earth') (cf. Luke 24.49; John 14.26; 15.26; 16.7; Gal. 4.6).

THE TESTIMONY OF THE SPIRIT

The Holy Spirit's testimony to the world at large is not borne directly, but through the Spirit-endowed church members. There was apparently an order of evangelists in the apostolic Church which was specially endowed by the Spirit to preach the Gospel of Christ (Eph. 4.11; II Tim. 4.5; Acts 21.8), though all the evidence suggests that every Christian, whatever his individual 'ministry', was expected to bear his testimony to Christ whenever he could do so. The disciples of Christ bear joint witness with the Holy Spirit (John 15.26f.). It is because of the presence of the Spirit within them that they testify so freely and so boldly to the truth of Christ—the words $\pi\alpha\rho\rho\eta\sigma\acute{\iota}\alpha$ and $\pi\alpha\rho\rho\eta\sigma\iota\acute{\alpha}\zeta o\mu\alpha\iota$ are of frequent occurrence in this connection in the NT (e.g. Acts 4.29, 31; Eph. 6.19; cf. Mark 13.11).

Above all things the Spirit in the NT is the Spirit of testimony; his chief function is to bear witness to Christ (John 15.26; 16.13-15) or alternatively to the truth ($\dot{\alpha}\lambda\acute{\eta}\theta\epsilon\iota\alpha$), for Christ is truth (John 14.6). Thus, the Spirit may be called the Spirit of truth (John 16.13), and his function is to guide the disciples of the Risen Christ into all the truth (*ibid.*); indeed, it may be said that the Spirit *is* the truth (I John 5.7), just as it is said that Christ is truth. The Spirit is the Spirit of Christ and therefore must be the Spirit of truth, because Christ is truth, i.e. ultimate reality manifested in action: truth is something to be *done*, not merely thought or 'believed' (cf. John 7.17). When St John speaks of the Spirit's guiding the disciples into all the truth (16.13), he does not mean truth in our

---

[1] The LXX adds the spirit of godliness ($\epsilon\dot{\nu}\sigma\acute{\epsilon}\beta\epsilon\iota\alpha$) to the six attributes in the Heb. of Isa. 11.2, 'The spirit of wisdom and understanding, the spirit of counsel and might, the spirit of knowledge and of the fear of the Lord'.

wide modern sense—e.g. all the truths of modern science, medicine, technology, etc. He is speaking of the actual experience through which the disciples had gone. The Gospels make it clear that up to the point of the crucifixion of their Lord the disciples had only a fitful and insecure grasp of his deeper teaching, but after the resurrection they understood in the light of the Spirit's leading the things which Jesus during his ministry had been trying to explain to them: 'he shall teach you all things, and bring to your remembrance all that I said unto you' (14.26). This is precisely what in fact happened to the apostles: it was only after the resurrection that they came to understand the truth which Jesus had taught them and had enacted before their eyes. In every age the Holy Spirit takes of the things of Christ and manifests them to the understanding of believing hearts; he testifies not of himself, but of Christ. This is the Spirit as the interpreter of Scripture; without the inward testimony of the Holy Spirit at the reading or the preaching of the Scriptures their message would remain locked up in the written or spoken words. Or, in the metaphor which St Paul uses in II Cor. 3.14-18, the meaning of Scripture remains 'veiled' until the Spirit of Christ does away with the veil that lies over men's hearts. The letter of the Torah—the written Scriptures—merely deadens; it is the Spirit which gives life to the words (II Cor. 3.6). The same conception of the Spirit as breathing life into the words—the 'dead letter'—of Scripture appears in II Tim. 3.16. St Luke's story of the Walk to Emmaus carries the same meaning in the form of a parable, for the Risen Christ and the Holy Spirit are not differentiated, so far at least as their operations are concerned, in the New Testament.[1] The (Spirit of) the Risen Christ interprets in all the Scriptures the things concerning himself (Luke 24.27). This is the experience of the early Church and indeed of Christians in every age: 'Was not our heart burning within us . . . while he opened to us the Scriptures?' (24.32). The Risen Christ in the apostolic Church is the true interpreter of Holy Scripture; apart from his presence and inspiration the Scriptures are a mysterious enigma, as they remain to this day for the unbelieving Jews (II Cor. 3.13f.). St Luke is at pains to emphasize how the Risen Christ is active in the exposition of the Scriptures in the Church: 'He opened their mind that they might understand the Scriptures' (Luke 24.45). Of course, the Scriptures which St Luke and St Paul have in mind in these passages are the Scriptures of the OT (II Cor. 3.14, ἐπὶ τῇ ἀναγνώσει τῆς παλαιᾶς διαθήκης), which constituted the only Scripture of the apostolic Church; but what they imply concerning the *testimonium Sancti Spiritus internum* (or, as we might say, *testimonium internum Christi resurrecti*) has been found by

---

[1] See further, *infra*, 121f.

Christians in every age of the Church to be true of the Scriptures of the NT.[1]

The Spirit of testimony thus brings home to our hearts the significance of the fact of Christ (John 14.26); but he remains the Spirit of prophecy, guiding the Church into all truth (John 16.13), shewing the things which shall come to pass hereafter (Rev. 1.19; 4.2; cf. 1.1; 22.6), i.e. such 'revelations' of the parousia as are disclosed in the Apocalypse. The Book of Revelation must be taken as the only adequate commentary upon the words, 'When he, the Spirit of truth, is come, he shall guide you into all the truth . . . he shall declare unto you the things that are to come' (John 16.13). The eschatological character of the Holy Spirit in the thought of the Johannine writer is clearly apparent also in the insistence that the revealing work of the Spirit is a 'hidden' disclosure of the truth in the biblical sense. The Spirit, even now, judges the world, convicting it of the sin of unbelief, and bearing testimony to the righteousness of God which has been manifested in the exaltation of Christ to the Father's abode (cf. Rom. 1.17), and to the reality of judgment, by testifying that the prince of this world has already been judged (John 16.8-11). But the world cannot receive the Spirit or know anything about him; it is only the disciples of Christ to whom the testimony of the Spirit can come (John 14.17); there is a hiddenness about the Spirit, as there is about Christ himself, for Christ manifests himself to his disciples, but not to the world (John 14.22).

Furthermore it should be noted that the peculiarly Johannine title for the Spirit, i.e. the 'Paraclete', bears a markedly eschatological sense. In secular Greek usage ὁ παράκλητος means 'advocate', one who defends in a court of law, or in a more general sense 'helper'. But the words παράκλησις, παρακαλεῖν in the LXX and in the NT carry a distinctive biblical meaning. Faithful Jews in the days when Jesus was born were looking for the παράκλησις of Israel (Luke 2.25), i.e. the fulfilment of the Isaianic prophecies concerning the 'comforting' or 'consolation' of the remnant which trusted in God's promise of redemption (cf. Isa. 40.1; 51.12; 66.13). The Book of Isaiah closes with an eschatological picture of the consolation of faithful Israel 'as one whom his mother comforteth' (66.13), when Yahweh shall come in fire and whirlwind for redemption and judgment (66.15, cf. the coming of the Spirit at Pentecost with tongues of fire and the rushing of a mighty wind, Acts 2.2f.), for the gathering of the nations who shall see his δόξα (66.18) and from whom priests and Levites shall be taken (66.21; cf. Rev. 1.6; 5.10; 20.6), at the making of the new creation, 'the new heavens and the new earth' (66.22; cf. Isa. 65.17; Rev. 21.1; II Pet. 3.13).

[1] See on this subject Alan Richardson, *Christian Apologetics*, 211-20.

The coming of the Spirit, 'the Comforter', represents a fulfilment of these prophecies, though known only to the disciples to whom the Spirit is given and not yet to 'the world'. The consolation of Israel is fulfilled in the Church and hence the Spirit is appropriately styled 'the Comforter'. Those who had grieved over the wretchedness of Israel's fate in the vicissitudes of worldly history were consoled by the knowledge of the eschatological splendour, revealed by the Holy Spirit, which was even now being ushered in: there was consolation in Christ (Phil. 2.1), for God had anointed him with the Spirit 'to comfort all that mourn, to appoint unto them that mourn in Zion . . . the oil of joy for mourning' (Isa. 61.1-3). Jesus himself announced the fulfilment of these prophecies: 'Blessed are they that mourn, for they shall be comforted' (Matt. 5.4; cf. Luke 4.17-21; John 16.20-22; II Cor. 1.7; Rev. 7.17; 21.4).

It is to be noted that παράκλησις in the sense of exhortation or encouragement with a view to endurance until the parousia is one of the specific gifts of the Spirit (Rom. 12.8; cf. I Cor. 14.3); such consolation or patient hope is to be derived especially from the study of the Scriptures (Rom. 15.4f.). St Luke understands the meaning of the name Barnabas to be 'son of παράκλησις' (Acts 4.36); however such a translation was reached, it would seem that in Luke's view the apostle Barnabas was endowed with the especial χάρισμα of exhortation. The comforting of those that mourn in the light of the Christian eschatological hope is one of the ministries for which the Church is endowed by 'singular gifts of the Holy Ghost'.[1]

One final indication of the eschatological character of the Spirit in the NT remains to be mentioned, i.e. the conception of the Spirit as an 'earnest' (ἀρραβών) of the final salvation which Christians will one day possess. An ἀρραβών is something given on account, a 'deposit' or first instalment, a pledge that full payment will be made. The Holy Spirit, in which Christians were 'sealed' at their baptism, is an 'earnest' or pledge of their inheritance (ἀρραβὼν τῆς κληρονομίας ἡμῶν) in the sphere of ultimate redemption (Eph. 1.14). God has 'bought back' (redeemed) his own possession, and the proof of this is to be found in the 'deposit' which he has given. The Spirit is an assurance vouchsafed to those who are anointed and sealed (i.e. baptized); to them God has given 'the earnest of the Spirit in our hearts' (II Cor. 1.22; 5.5). In this life, i.e. in the Age of the Spirit, we do not yet enjoy the fulness of our inheritance as sons of God and joint-heirs with Christ; we possess, however, the guarantee of the Spirit, who witnesses in our hearts to the truth of our sonship and inheritance (Rom. 8.16f.). Or, as St John puts

[1] BCP, Collect of St Barnabas.

the truth of the matter, we know that God 'abides' in us by the Spirit which he gave us (I John 3.24), and likewise we know that we abide in him (I John 4.13). The Holy Spirit is the gift of God's presence and power within us in this life and the pledge of the fulness of the divine life that will be ours in the Age to Come.

THE GIVING OF THE SPIRIT: PENTECOST

The NT writers agree that the giving of the Holy Spirit was withheld until after the resurrection and exaltation of Christ, with which events it is intimately connected. But there is no agreement about the manner and the time of the coming of the Spirit. Only two writers describe the original imparting of the Spirit, St Luke and St John; and their accounts differ in every particular except that the event took place in Jerusalem. According to St John the ascension of the Lord seems to have taken place between the appearance to Mary Magdalene in the early morning (20.17) and the appearance to the disciples the same evening when the doors were shut (20.19); at this evening appearance the Risen Jesus imparted the Holy Spirit to the disciples by 'insufflation' (ἐνεφύσησε καὶ λέγει αὐτοῖς, Λάβετε Πνεῦμα ῞Αγιον) (20.22). Thus, in St John's view the resurrection, the ascension and the giving of the Spirit all seem to have occurred on the same day; this is certainly what we would have inferred from the Fourth Gospel if our minds had not been so familiar with the Lucan version of the events. The evidence of St Paul, so far as it goes, would seem to agree with the Johannine rather than the Lucan view: Paul does not sharply distinguish between the resurrection or ascension of Christ as separate events, and he certainly regards the appearance of Christ to himself on the Damascus road as being entirely parallel to the appearances to Peter and the other apostles and brethren (I Cor. 15.5-7), as if they were all (like that to himself) post-ascension appearances of the Lord.

St Luke, however, gives an entirely different and much more detailed account of the events of the ascension and the coming of the Spirit; and one for which there is no corroboration of any kind by other NT writers. Moreover, it would seem that St Luke is fitting his history into a very elaborate theological scheme. He lays stress on a period of 'waiting' between the resurrection and the coming of the Spirit (Luke 24.49, 53). In Acts 1.3 he says that Jesus appeared to the apostles 'by the space of forty days', after which there is further waiting (1.4); it would seem that the ascension takes place at the end of the forty days (1.9-11) and the apostles return to Jerusalem (1.12; cf. Luke 24.52). Then on the day of Pentecost, seven weeks after the day of Christ's resurrection, the Spirit descended on the apostles; the house in which they were assembled was filled with a 'rushing, mighty wind'[1] and 'tongues as of fire' sat upon each of the apostles (Acts 2.1-3). 'And they were all filled with Holy Spirit, and began to speak with other tongues, as the Spirit gave them utterance' (2.4).

St Luke thus alone amongst the NT writers itemizes and dates the resurrection and ascension of Christ, and the coming of the Spirit, as separate historical events. The Church has constructed her Calendar upon his model, and for the purposes of the due liturgical observance of the truths of our salvation it has proved valuable beyond estimation. But the Lucan scheme would appear to be based upon theological reflection rather than upon historical reminiscence, and it is probable that the Johannine account preserves the more primitive apostolic teaching in this matter. Recent scholarship has tended to show that St Luke's Gospel is as deeply concerned with theological interpretation as St Mark's or St John's; and Luke-Acts would seem to present the truth of the Gospel by means of a brilliantly stylized presentation of history which brings out profound theological truth in story form. In other words, Luke uses the historical in the same sort of way as does the author of the Fourth Gospel—to convey the truth of history by means of an imaginative reconstruction of historical happenings. Some people will doubtless find such a conclusion disturbing on first encountering it, but further reflection will lead them to perceive that it could not be otherwise. Christ's resurrection and ascension and the coming of the Holy Ghost are not historical events of the same order as, say, Julius Caesar's embarcation from Gaul and arrival in Britain in 55 B.C.; that is to say, they are not events which can be described in matter-of-fact eye-witness reports. Only their effects within history can be studied, not the events themselves. A deep insight of the religious mind, found beyond biblical religion as well as within it, insists that human eyes cannot perceive the means by which the miraculous acts of deity are performed. This does not mean that there is any uncertainty for Christian faith about the historicity of the resurrection and exaltation of Christ or about the coming of the Spirit; it means that we must not expect to find in the Bible accounts of these events which may be read as wholly literal descriptions of 'what happened'. The mode of the divine operation of these wonders is concealed from us even in the accounts which convey to us their meaning and their truth. We misunderstand the nature of historical testimony if we insist on a literalist

---

[1] The word used here for 'wind' is πνοή, which, though it can mean 'wind', 'breeze' (as here and at Job 37.9, LXX) primarily means 'breath'; St Luke doubtless intends a reference to Gen. 2.7, LXX: ὁ θεὸς . . . ἐνεφύσησεν εἰς τὸ πρόσωπον αὐτοῦ πνοὴν ζωῆς (cf. John 20.22). God breathes the breath of life into his new creation. At Acts 17.25 πνοή appears again in the sense of 'breath'.

interpretation of the brilliant Lucan or Johannine presentations of the truth of history.

The theological scheme which underlies St Luke's itemizing of the original threefold unity of resurrection, ascension and outpouring of the Spirit is based upon current rabbinic patterns. Rabbinic Judaism regarded the Feast of Pentecost as the anniversary of the giving of the Law on Sinai, which was reckoned as having taken place on the fiftieth day after the exodus. It was on the day of Pentecost that the Old Covenant was sealed and 'the Church in the Wilderness' (Acts 7.38) was constituted. These things are a foreshadowing of the New Covenant of Jesus Christ and the foundation of his Church. It is on the day of Pentecost, the fiftieth day after 'the exodus' which Christ accomplished in Jerusalem (Luke 9.31), that the Spirit is poured out from on high, the apostles receive the seal of the Spirit and the Church of Christ is constituted. The Pentecostal Law is fulfilled in the Pentecostal Spirit; the fires of Sinai are replaced by the fire of the Spirit's presence. As John Keble correctly interpreted the Lucan typology,

> The fires that rushed on Sinai down
> In sudden torrents dread,
> Now gently light, a glorious crown,
> On every sainted head.[1]

Moses is the type of Christ; his work foreshadows Christ's, and the Covenant with Israel is the prefiguring of the New Covenant now made with a new Israel. The type of the events from the death of Jesus to the coming of the Spirit is summarized by St Stephen in Acts 7.34-38. Moses, who had heard the affliction of his people in Egypt, came down to deliver them. Israel, however, rejected Moses, whom God sent to be both a ruler and a deliverer or judge ($\delta\iota\kappa\alpha\sigma\tau\dot{\eta}s$). Yet, having wrought wonders and signs, he led them forth through the Red Sea (cf. Luke 9.31) and through the forty years' wanderings in the wilderness. This was the very Moses who himself had predicted that God would raise up a prophet like himself (Deut. 18.15, 18), that is, Jesus Christ. Christ had wrought his exodus-wonder at his resurrection from the dead, and he had shown the signs of his living presence to his apostles during forty days. When the forty years are accomplished in the Wilderness, Moses was taken up ('assumed') into heaven, according to rabbinic theology; after the forty days of his appearings are accomplished, Jesus ascends into heaven (cf. Luke 9.51, his $\dot{\alpha}\nu\dot{\alpha}\lambda\eta\mu\psi\iota s$, *assumptio*). The new Moses has completed the work which was prefigured by the old. We find in Heb. 12.18-29 a comparing and contrasting of the

---

[1] 'When God of old came down from heaven', *English Hymnal*, 158.

Covenant made amidst the fearful fires and convulsions of Sinai with the making of the New Covenant and the constituting of 'the general assembly and Church of the firstborn who are enrolled in heaven'; but the coming of the Law is not in this passage contrasted with the coming of the Spirit. Indeed, *Auct. Heb.* differs from St Luke perhaps most markedly in the fact that he rarely employs language about the Holy Spirit.[1]

It would therefore seem that a good deal of 'theologizing' lies behind the Lucan Pentecost story; the latter conveys profound Christian truth under the form of a straightforward historical narrative. But the truth behind the story, namely, that after the exaltation of Christ the pouring out of the Spirit from on high took place, is the plain historical truth, although the Lucan account in Acts 2 is not a literally true story; the literal truth of 'what happened' is not recoverable by us, because the biblical writers, even St Luke, are not chroniclers of the literal. The events as they took place so utterly transcended the normal, everyday happenings which human language is capable of describing that they could not adequately be recounted in human words at all, and yet they are communicable in the wordless language of the Christian experience of the Holy Spirit. It is as if St Luke himself is trying to tell us this in his account of the speaking with tongues on the day of Pentecost (Acts 2.5-11). The sounds uttered by the apostles, upon whom the Spirit had come, were not rational syllables and words at all, and yet the effect was as if every man of whatever language heard in his own tongue the declaration of the mighty works of God. The truth of the coming of the Spirit is too utterly transcendent to be described in human words; yet the Spirit's coming is the very reality which renders human words unnecessary. There are no language barriers which can thwart the revealing power of the Spirit, and there is no 'problem of communication' that the Spirit cannot solve. St Luke regards 'speaking with tongues' (glossolalia) as an unmistakable sign of the gift of the Spirit (Acts 2.4; 10.46; 19.6) and as a symbol of the reversal of that confounding of speech which is the result of human sin. Pentecost is Babel in reverse: the parable of the Tower of Babel in Gen. 11.1-9 tells of how, because of pride, men had lost their ability to speak with one another; they had no common language because they were not bound together in common obedience to God's will. St Luke seeks to show how

---

[1] Apart from three references to the Holy Spirit's speaking through the Scriptures (3.7; 9.8; 10.15), there are in the whole of the Epistle to the Hebrews only four references to the (Holy) Spirit (2.4; 6.4; 9.14; 10.29)—just enough to shew that the author is familiar with this way of speaking about the activity of God, yet few enough to shew that a very profound presentation of Christian truth can be adequately made with a different vocabulary.

God wills to re-create mankind in one great family, united in one covenant of love through Jesus Christ, speaking one universal language of
the Holy Spirit of God. The audience which listened to St Peter on the
day of Pentecost was, of course, entirely Jewish (with some proselytes),
but they were Jews of the Dispersion who spoke the languages of their
countries of sojourn. Later in Acts, St Luke will show that there is an
outpouring of the Spirit upon Gentiles as well as upon Jews; the
Cornelius episode (Acts 10) represents the Gentile Pentecost. The Holy
Spirit falls upon those who hear the word preached by St Peter, and they
receive the Spirit and speak with tongues *before* they are baptized:
this means that the Holy Spirit, taking the initiative, clearly indicates
God's intention that the Gentiles should be members on equal terms
with Jews of the new divine community (10.44-48; 11.17f.). The
Messiah's baptism of Holy Spirit was universal (Acts 11.16 in its context), and thus the prophecy of Joel 2.28 was fulfilled: God had poured
out his Spirit upon *all* flesh.

THE 'PERSONALITY' OF THE HOLY SPIRIT

To ask whether in the NT the Spirit is a person in the modern sense
of the word would be like asking whether the spirit of Elijah is a person.
The Spirit of God, is, of course, personal; it is God's δύναμις in action.
But the Holy Spirit is not a person existing independently of God; it
is a way of speaking about God's personally acting in history, or of the
Risen Christ's personally acting in the life and witness of the Church.
The NT (and indeed patristic thought generally)[1] nowhere represents
the Spirit, any more than the δύναμις or σοφία of God, as having
independent personality. This does not mean that the Spirit is only a
temporary mode of God's self-revelation or activity; on the contrary,
the Spirit is one of God's permanent ways of being God. Πνεῦμα is the
form of the activity of the transcendent God within history from the
creation to the consummation. It is no arbitrary choice of words which
is made by St Luke when he equates πνεῦμα and δύναμις (e.g. Luke
1.17, 35; 24.49; in the last reference πνεῦμα is virtually defined as
'power from on high'). Even St Luke's most 'personified' ways of
speaking of the Spirit must be understood as a biblical contrivance
for avoiding having to say that God did this or said that. For instance,
when he writes, 'The Holy Spirit said, Separate me Barnabas and Saul'
(Acts 13.2), he means nothing other than that God revealed his will to
a prophet or prophets (cf. 13.1). We may recollect that St Luke could

---

[1] The ancient Church, including the Nicene Fathers themselves, 'did not attribute
to the Spirit (as the Arians did) a personality separate from the personal life of
God' (H. B. Swete, *The Holy Spirit in the Ancient Church*, 1912, 376).

also write, 'Therefore also the σοφία of God said, I will send unto them prophets and apostles . . .' (Luke 11.49).

What is the relation between Christ and the Holy Spirit? As we have noted, Christ is not identified with πνεῦμα Θεοῦ as he is with σοφία Θεοῦ, λόγος Θεοῦ and δύναμις Θεοῦ, although in the Old Testament πνεῦμα is a personification of the divine activity of the same order as σοφία, λόγος and δύναμις. With the doubtful exception of II Cor. 3.17 the NT never says that Christ *is* the Spirit of God. Apart from the reasons suggested above there is also the fact that the Gospels represent the Spirit as operating upon Jesus and Jesus as working by the Spirit. It was necessary therefore to draw a distinction between Christ and the Spirit, particularly during the days of his flesh. But after the resurrection this distinction becomes blurred, and the NT writers do not attempt to distinguish between the operation of the Risen Christ and the operation of the Holy Spirit. Christ himself comes in the coming of the Spirit. St John can write, 'He (the Paraclete) will come to you' and 'I will come to you' as if both sentences mean the same thing (cf. John 16.7, etc., with 14.18, 28). The Spirit who interprets the Scriptures is none other than the Risen Lord himself (Luke 24.13-35; John 14.26; 16.13f.; II Cor. 3.17f.); the παράδοσις (tradition) of the Church is actually shaped and guided by the Spirit of the Risen Christ—that apostolic παράδοσις which was even now being written down in what eventually became known in the Church as the Scriptures of the New Testament. Christ was speaking through the Spirit the 'many things' which his disciples could not bear (understand, receive) in the days of his flesh (John 16.12-15; 14.26). The Spirit of Christ, who is the Lord of the Church's παράδοσις, is also the *Spiritus Interpres Scripturae* of the Old Covenant. The Jews, though they diligently read their Scriptures in all their synagogues, do not understand what they read (II Cor. 3.12-18; cf. Mark 12.24; John 5.37-47; Acts 8.30f.); it is as though a veil has been thrown over the scriptural truth, like the veil worn in their synagogues when the Scriptures are read. It performs the same function as the veil which Moses had to put over his face when he came forth from God's presence to speak with Israel (Ex. 34). In the Jewish synagogue this veil remains unlifted to this day; but in the Christian Church it is done away in Christ. Just as Moses took off the veil when he returned into the presence of Yahweh (Ex. 34.34), so the veil is removed from the Scriptures when a man turns to Christ (II Cor. 3.16). Christ is the interpreting Spirit—ὁ δὲ Κύριος τὸ Πνεῦμά ἐστιν· οὗ δὲ τὸ Πνεῦμα Κυρίου, ἐλευθερία (3.17). Paul is not here concerned with the niceties of Trinitarian definition but with the problem of the interpretation of Scripture; and therefore we cannot use the verse as if it were a considered pronouncement about the relation of Christ and the Spirit. What Paul is saying is that the Spirit (of Christ) is Lord of the Scriptures, and where the Spirit reigns there is full liberty of interpretation; we are no longer fettered by 'the letter' (cf. 3.6), i.e. the literalism which deadens. Now Christians are metamorphosed in the image of the Lord (Jesus) himself from one level of glory to another by the operation of the Κύριος Πνεῦμα (3.18)— a unique phrase which can only mean 'the Spirit of the *Christus regnans*'.

The Spirit is declared to be both the Spirit of God and also the Spirit of his Son (Gal. 4.6), or of Jesus (Acts 16.7), or of Jesus Christ (Phil. 1.19). In I Pet. 1.11 the Spirit of Christ is said to have testified before-hand to the sufferings of (the historical) Christ. In a passage like Rom. 8.9-11 St Paul can speak alternatively of the Spirit of God and the Spirit of Christ, obviously meaning the same thing. There are not two Spirits, a Spirit of God and a Spirit of Christ; there is only one Spirit. This is because of the unity of Christ and the Father (John 10.30; 17.11, 22, etc.), not, of course, the abstract unity of mathematical identity, but the personal unity of mind, attitude and intention which is presupposed by the conception of God's incarnation of himself in Christ. It is not merely that the Spirit of God was in the human Jesus, for God's Spirit is in all those to whom he testifies that they are the adopted sons of the Father (Rom. 8.14-17); the Spirit is the Spirit *of* Christ, not merely the Spirit *in* Christ. Christ sends the Spirit (John 15.26; 16.7), or is associated with the Father's sending of the Spirit (John 14.16, 26): the Spirit proceeds (ἐκπορεύεται) from the Father (John 15.26), and although no *filioque* clause is found, it is clear that the 'double procession' (from the Father *and* the Son) is intended by the Fourth Evangelist. The Spirit has no independent existence apart from the Father and the Son, whereas the Son is the Son of the Father. Thus the Father may be said to be (in the language of the patristic age) the principle or source of deity: *Pater est fons totius Trinitatis*.

The New Testament formulates no doctrine of the Trinity, but its threefold doxological and liturgical formulae (e.g. Matt. 28.19; II Cor. 1.21f.; 13.14; I Pet. 1.2; Jude 20f.; Rev. 1.4-6) sufficiently demonstrate that the apostolic Church worshipped one God in Trinity and Trinity in unity. The one true God of the old Jewish faith, the God of Abraham, Isaac and Jacob, had now acted in a new way: what was involved was not (so to speak) an enlargement of God, but an enlargement of man's revealed knowledge of God—not the taking of two other 'persons' into the divine society, but the revelation of God's different ways of being God, now understood (but only within the mystery of faith) for the first time. There is in the NT no hint of a δεύτερος Θεός, or δημιουργός distinct from the God of the OT revelation, nor is there any problem at all of 'reconciling' the divinity of Christ and of the Spirit with Jewish monotheism. Christ and the Spirit are equally God in his self-determined modes of operation in the creation, redemption and sanctification of the world. They are co-equally God, yet at the same time the Father (as we have learned through Christ to call the very principle and source of deity) is the primary way of God's being God, to which the other ways are subordinate (John 14.28; I Cor. 15.24-28): Christ receives his authority and co-equal divinity from the source of deity, i.e. from the Father (Matt. 28.18; John 3.35; 13.3; 17.2; Acts 2.36; I Cor. 15.27; Eph. 1.10, 20-22; Phil. 2.9f.; Heb. 1.2; 2.8; I Pet. 3.22; Rev. 5.12f., etc.). The very word 'Son' implies derivation, subordination and dependence; and yet it also asserts identity of substance and therefore co-equal divinity. Though it is a metaphor drawn from human existence, it is the most adequate word to express the relation of Christ to the Father, not only in his incarnate life but in his essential being. The God of the NT revelation is Father, Son and Holy Spirit, one God, now made known to us through his historical and personal self-disclosure in the three permanent and essential ways of his being God. In every activity of each of the three 'persons' of the Godhead it is always the one-and-the-same God who acts; this NT principle was subsequently formulated in Catholic theology by means of the formula: *opera Trinitatis ad extra sunt indivisa.* That is to say, the *personae* must not be rigidly separated from one another and identified with particular divine functions (e.g. creating, redeeming, sanctifying), for all the *personae* act in every divine work. The later Catholic doctrine of co-inherence (*perichoresis*) is in full accord with NT statements about the activities of the 'persons' of the Godhead. Thus, for instance, St Paul does not distinguish between the Exalted Christ as Intercessor and the Spirit as Intercessor: compare Rom. 8.26 with Rom. 8.34. If there is a difference here, it is chiefly one of emphasis: the Spirit intercedes within us, even in our most inarticulate groanings, while Christ intercedes for us 'at the right hand of God'. Similarly in the Fourth Gospel the Son has returned to his Father's dwelling-place, while the Spirit continues his work here below in the Church. Christ intercedes for his disciples (14.16; 17.9, 15, 20), though he does not need to do so, because the Father loves them already (16.26f.); and it is said in I John 2.1 that 'we have an advocate (παράκλητος) with the Father, Jesus Christ the righteous'. But in the Fourth Gospel the Holy Spirit is distinctively called the Paraclete, and it must therefore be supposed that the activity of intercession is considered to be a function of the Spirit, although the intercession of the Spirit is not mentioned specifically in the Fourth Gospel. In such ways as these the NT clearly regards the work of the ascended Christ and the work of the Holy Spirit as inseparably and indivisibly the activity of the one God, whose age-long plan for man's redemption and restoration is now made known, as in a mystery, to the enlightened eyes of those who believe in Christ.

6

THE REINTERPRETED MESSIAHSHIP

WHEN once we have shaken off the liberal presuppositions which have dominated so much New Testament research from Harnack to Bultmann, we recognize that the assumption that Jesus himself thought out (humanly speaking) the problem of his own existence and taught the answer to his disciples makes far better sense of the historical evidence than all the attempts of the liberal critics to explain the evidence away. As we shall see, our Lord's brilliant reinterpretation of the old Jewish images of the Messiah makes it quite clear that he understood his mission to be that of gathering the new Israel into the Church of the Messiah.

'CHRIST'

The word $\chi\rho\iota\sigma\tau\delta s$ is the verbal adjective used in LXX to translate Heb. *meshiah* ('anointed'). The latter is applied in the OT to anyone specially appointed by God to a theocratic function, e.g. kings and priests. Even a Gentile prince like Cyrus could be so described (Isa. 45.1). The high priest is 'the anointed priest' (Lev. 4.3, 5, 16; 6.22). It is, however, the king of Israel who is *par excellence* 'the Lord's Anointed', and David in particular is regarded as the type-ideal. When the historical kingship came to an end, the liturgical use of the Psalms kept the idea fresh and perhaps even suggested the coming in the future of a Messianic King in whom the ideal should be perfectly embodied; but the term is never used technically in this sense in the OT.[1] We find descriptions of the Ideal Ruler who is to come (e.g. Isa. 9.6f.; 11.1-10; Jer. 23.5f.; Ezek. 34.23f.), but we do not find him spoken of as 'the Messiah'. According to Charles[2] the word is first found in this technical sense in the Similitudes of Enoch (48.10; 52.4), which he dates *c.* 94-79 B.C. It appears again in Pss. Sol. (*c.* 40 B.C.) at 17.36 and 18.6, 8; also in II (4) Esd. 7.29 and 12.32, and in Apoc. Baruch 29.3; 30.1; 39.7; 40.1; 70.9; 72.2. The NT bears plentiful evidence of its general use in this sense in our Lord's day (Mark 8.29; 12.35; 13.21; Luke 2.26; John 1.20, 25, etc.).

The expectation of a Messiah from the house of Judah is firmly

[1] Cf. R. H. Charles, *The Book of Enoch*, 1893, 136.   [2] *Ibid.*

grounded in the OT; it rests upon promises made to David by God (II Sam. 7, esp. v. 16: 'Thy throne shall be established for ever'; cf. in Ps. 89 the reference to God's covenant with David, vv. 28, 34, 39). God's fidelity to his promise to David is a common theme among the prophets (Amos 9.11; Hos. 3.5; Micah 5.2; Isa. 9.7; 11.10; 16.5; 37.35; Jer. 23.5f.; 33.15ff.; Ezek. 34.23f.; 37.24f.; Zech. 12.7ff.). The expectation of the advent of a Davidic figure in fulfilment of these very clear prophecies is continued beyond the OT period; cf. Ecclus. 47.11; I Macc. 2.57, and especially Ps. Sol. 17—a remarkable prophecy of a Messianic King who shall be David's son. The NT provides evidence that the coming of a Davidic Messiah was normal rabbinic teaching in the first century A.D.: 'How say the scribes that the Christ is the son of David?' (Mark 12.35). It is clear from St Mark's narrative that when blind Bartimaeus hails Jesus as 'Son of David' a Messianic salutation is intended (Mark 10.47f.).

It is truly astonishing, in view of the weight of OT prophecy concerning the Davidic Messiah, how little the NT makes of the matter. The evangelists represent Jesus as the new Moses, the new Joshua, the new Elijah, and so on; but there is perhaps only one *pericope* in the tradition which sets forth Jesus as the new David, viz. the Walking through the Cornfields on the Sabbath (Mark 2.23-28). Jesus defends the behaviour of his disciples by reference to David's precedent in I Sam. 21.1-6; perhaps the story is intended as a type-fulfilment of 'what David did'. The Johannine mention of Jesus's crossing of the brook Kidron (John 18.1) is altogether too obscure to be understood as a fulfilment of II Sam. 15.23. The NT writers lay no stress upon the Davidic kingship as a type of Christ's. In this they are doubtless following the teaching of their Lord, who must have been embarrassed by the nationalistic sentiments attached to the notion of a Davidic Messiah. In his teaching in the Temple Jesus seems to repudiate the idea altogether, quoting Ps. 110.1 to prove that David's son could not be David's Lord (i.e. the Messiah) (Mark 12.35-37). The Messiah is incomparably greater than any earthly king, and the Messianic kingdom is not to be reduced to the dimensions of a merely Davidic empire (cf. John 6.15; 18.36). Jesus claims indeed to be King of the Jews (Mark 15.2), but he has rejected every worldly notion of kingship and seeks no earthly crown; and when David's son came to David's city (Mark 11.10) to claim his rightful rule, the promised 'throne of David' (Luke 1.32) turned out to be a cross outside the city's wall. The new David was no conqueror come to restore the kingdom to Israel (Acts 1.6) but the righteous lowly one, riding upon an ass (Zech. 9.9; Mark 11.7). Thus it comes about that almost the only detail of the scriptural prophecies in which the New Testament writers are interested is the question of the *descent* of Jesus from the royal line of David. Whatever Jesus himself may have implied about this in the saying behind Mark 12.35-37, the apostolic Church unquestionably held the Davidic descent to be an article of faith (perhaps Rom. 1.3 is part of an early credal hymn); cf. especially Matt. 1.1, 20; Luke 2.4, 11; John 7.42; Rom. 1.3; II Tim. 2.8; Rev. 5.5; 22.16. The actual title 'Son of David' is used several times by Matthew (9.27; 12.23; 15.22; 20.30f.; 21.9 and 15) but is found in Mark and Luke only at Mark 10.47f.=Luke 18.38f. and nowhere in John. It is particularly important for Matthew's Jewish apologetic that Jesus was born in Bethlehem (Matt. 2.1) of the lineage of David (Matt. 1.20).

For a brief time, in certain quarters at least, the expectation of a Messiah from the house of Judah gave place to that of one from the house of Levi. We find it most clearly enunciated in the Testaments of the Twelve Patriarchs, which R. H. Charles considered to have been written after the accession of John Hyrcanus and before his breach with the Pharisees (i.e. between 137 and 107 B.C.).[1] According to the Pharisaic author, the Messiah is an impressive figure and he will be priest, king and prophet; cf. Test. Reub. 6.7-12; Test. Levi 8.14; Test. Jud. 24.1-3; Test. Dan 5.10f.; Test. Jos. 19.8-12. After the breach with the Pharisees this expectation perished, and in the first century B.C. additions were made expressing the hope of a Messiah from Judah.[2] The expectation of a Messiah from Levi was extinct by NT times and has left no traces in the NT, though other influences from the Testaments of the Twelve Patriarchs are strong. In the canonical literature Ps. 110 is perhaps the only passage which looks for a non-Davidic Messiah, although we cannot be sure of its original form or date. If Maccabean, it may refer to an actual ruler, such as Simon, or to an ideal prince of the Hasmonean dynasty as yet unborn. This ruler, described as 'my lord', is seated at God's right hand and rules from Zion in the midst of his enemies; he is to be 'a priest for ever, after the order of Melchizedek'

---

[1] R. H. Charles, *Apocrypha and Pseudepigrapha*, II, 289.

[2] Charles, *op. cit.*, 294. It should, however, be noted that scholarly opinion is increasingly of the opinion that Charles has misinterpreted the evidence of Test. XII Pat. and that the Testaments in fact assert a doctrine of two Messiahs, one from the priestly tribe of Levi and one from the royal line of Judah. The Essene doctrine (for such it appears to be) of Two Messiahs develops a tendency which was as old as the recognition of 'the two sons of oil' (i.e. anointed ones) of Zech. 4.14, viz. Joshua the prince and Zerubbabel the high priest (cf. Haggai 1.14; 2.4f.). The Qumran sect held the doctrine of two Messiahs ('the anointed ones of Aaron and Israel', 1 QS ix. 10f.; Gaster, *SDSS*, 15, 67, 108); and the Damascus Document attests the same expectation, if K. G. Kuhn is right in thinking that two Messiahs are in fact implied in the phrase 'the coming of the Messiah of Aaron and Israel' (CD xii. 23; xiv. 10; xix. 10; cf. xx. 1) in its original form. But the doctrine of Two Messiahs has left no trace on the NT, and the latter reflects the normal expectation of the Jews of our Lord's day. On the whole question see K. G. Kuhn, 'The Two Messiahs of Aaron and Israel' (reprinted from *NT Studies* I, 1954-5, in Stendahl, *SNT*, 54-64).

(cf. Gen. 14.18)—i.e. he is no more a Levitical Messiah than he is a Davidic one; he will strike down many kings and judge among the nations. Whatever the original meaning of the Psalm, it is one of the scriptural *testimonia* most frequently alluded to in the NT[1] and it is understood to prefigure a kingship and a priesthood of Jesus Christ which utterly transcend anything contained in the current Jewish expectation of a Davidic Messiah. This is, of course, precisely the point of Jesus's own employment of it in Mark 12.35-37. The writer to the Hebrews fashions out of it his elaborate argument concerning the derivation of Christ's high priesthood (Heb. 5-7).

THE SON OF MAN: EZEKIEL AND DANIEL

In the Gospels 'Son of Man' is the favourite designation of Jesus for himself; the phrase occurs eighty-one times in the Gospels and is found in all the principal 'sources' (Mark, Q, M, L and John). In every instance it is used by Jesus of himself (John 12.34 is hardly a true exception). Outside the Gospels it occurs only once in the NT, viz. Acts 7.56 (apart from the Old Testament quotations in Heb. 2.6; Rev. 1.13; and 14.14). We have no clear evidence that the title was in use as a synonym for the Messiah when Jesus began to use it of himself.[2] The interpretation of 'Son of Man' is therefore of the first importance for our understanding of our Lord's teaching concerning his own person and mission.

In the Old Testament 'son of man' (Heb. *ben adam* or, synonymously, *ben 'enosh*) is a Semitism for 'man'; e.g. Ps. 8.4, 'What is man that thou art mindful of him, and the son of man that thou visitest him?' The expression, however, does not appear frequently, except in Ezekiel, where the prophet uses it (*ben 'enosh*) more than ninety times as a designation of himself. No explanation of its meaning is vouchsafed, but it seems to indicate the dignity of the otherwise insignificant person whom God has condescended to address: 'Son of man, stand upon thy feet, and I will speak with thee' (Ezek. 2.1). The Aramaic form *bar 'enash* occurs in Dan. 7.13; in late Aramaic (second century A.D.) the form *bar nash* simply means 'man' or 'one' (as in '*on dit*', '*man sagt*', 'one feels'). If this usage may be presumed to belong to the first century also, then it might be argued that Jesus used the phrase to refer modestly to himself; e.g. Luke 9.58, 'I have nowhere to lay my head'. This suggestion may be dismissed for two good reasons. First, it is incredible that the bi-lingual Mark (and other translators) should have perpetrated the howler of translating the phrase by ὁ υἱὸς τοῦ ἀνθρώπου, as much a

[1] C. H. Dodd, *Acc. Scrip.* 34f., 120f.
[2] The expression 'son of man' has not thus far been found in the Qumran literature.

barbarism in Greek as 'son of man' is in English. St Mark and the others must have understood the phrase to be a *terminus technicus,* and they rendered it literally because there was no Greek equivalent. Secondly, there are grave theological difficulties in the way of supposing that Jesus meant, for example, that man as such has power on earth to forgive sins (Mark 2.10) or is Lord of the divine institution of the Sabbath (Mark 2.28); if Mark had thought that Jesus meant this, he could have made him say so quite easily. It may well be, however, that the expression contains an overtone of the meaning of Man as such, man *par excellence,* as in the Johannine sense of Ἴδε, ὁ ἄνθρωπος (John 19.5): *bar nasha* might mean 'the Man', and as such it *might* have been a name for the Messiah. But we are on uncertain ground here.

Apart from Ezekiel the only other OT passage which is of great importance in this regard is Dan. 7.13f.: 'I saw in the night visions, and behold, there came with the clouds of heaven one like unto a son of man, and he came even to the Ancient of Days, and they brought him near before him. And there was given him dominion, and glory, and a kingdom, that all the peoples, nations and languages should serve him: his dominion is an everlasting dominion, which shall not pass away, and his kingdom that which shall not be destroyed.' The human figure ('one like unto a son of man') contrasts strongly with the 'four great beasts' which preceded it, a lion, a bear, a leopard and the strong and terrible unnamed beast with ten horns. Each beast represents one of the successive pagan empires which had oppressed the Jews, and the fourth is the Greek Seleucid Empire. Antiochus Epiphanes is the persecutor who arises after the ten kings (the ten horns): 'he shall speak words against the Most High, and shall wear out the saints of the Most High: and he shall think to change the times and the law' (7.25). After he has been judged and disposed of (7.26), 'the kingdom, and the dominion, and the greatness of the kingdoms under the whole heaven, shall be given to the people of the saints of the Most High: his kingdom is an everlasting kingdom, and all dominions shall serve and obey him' (7.27). The human figure represents Israel, which, after the oppression of the pagan empires that culminated in Antiochus's attempt to abolish the Torah, now receives from God ('the Ancient of Days') the rule over all the other nations of the world in perpetuity. There is no suggestion here of an actually existing Messianic Son of Man, for the figure of 'one like unto a son of man' is only a symbol representing Israel in the imagery of the seer's dream, just as the beasts had symbolized the pagan empires. There is no Messiah, unless we say that Israel is the Messianic community. All that we have—and it is of the utmost importance in the development of NT theology—is a striking piece of visual symbolism foretelling the downfall of the last and most terrible of the oppressors and the giving of world dominion to the suffering nation of Israel ('the people of the saints of the Most High'). As we saw in Chapter 4, it lies behind Jesus's conception of God's giving the kingdom to the 'little flock' of those whom he was calling to become the new people of the saints of the Most High.

THE SON OF MAN: ENOCH AND II (4) ESDRAS

In the Similitudes of Enoch[1] 'the Anointed' is identified with the Son of Man. But scholarly opinion is divided whether the work provides evidence that in the days of our Lord the title 'Son of Man' was an accepted designation of the Messiah, indicating a particular type of Messiah (heavenly or supernatural). R. H. Charles held that 'the influence of Enoch has been greater than that of all the other apocryphal and pseudepigraphical books taken together' on the New Testament writers,[2] and on the continent of Europe it is still widely assumed that the concepts found in Enoch formed the religious background of the Jews of Palestine in the time of our Lord. On the other hand, J. Y. Campbell has argued that 'the evidence of the Book of Enoch is quite inadequate to prove anything at all about Jewish Messianic expectations, or Messianic titles, in the time of Jesus.'[3]

The Similitudes proclaim the coming of a new heaven and a new earth and the establishment of the Kingdom of God through the agency of the Anointed, who is the heavenly Son of Man, a supernatural being, not of human descent at all, Davidic or other. He sits on God's throne (I Enoch 51.3; 62.3, 5; 69.27, 29) and possesses universal dominion (62.6); all judgment is committed to him (61.9; 69.27; cf. John 5.22, 27). Charles thought that Jesus took over both the conception and the expression 'Son of Man' from this source but transformed it by reconciling it to its apparent antithesis, the Isaianic Servant of Yahweh, with some influence from Dan. 7, which in Charles's view is the ultimate source of the designation 'Son of Man'.[4] It is true that reigning, judging, revealing and succouring the righteous are all elements in the Gospel picture of the Son of Man; and yet it is equally true that the latter

---

[1] The Similitudes constitute chh. 37-71 of I Enoch (to be distinguished from II Enoch, or Book of the Secrets of Enoch), or the Ethiopian Enoch as it is sometimes called, since it survives (except for Greek and Latin fragments) only in an Ethiopic translation of a Greek version of a Hebrew or Aramaic original.

[2] *The Book of Enoch*, 41.

[3] *JTS*, Vol. XLVIII, 1947, 146-8; see also Campbell's art. 'Son of Man' in *TWBB*, 230ff., and E. Sjöberg, *Der Menschensohn im Äthiopischen Henochbuch*, Lund, 1946, esp. *Kap*. II, 40ff. C. H. Dodd endorses Campbell's judgment, *Acc. Scrip.*, 116f.

[4] *The Book of Enoch*, Appendix B, 312-17.

picture is a long way removed from the fantasies of Enoch. There is no saying of Jesus in the Gospels which echoes any phrase from that compilation, and there is no reason at all to think that Jesus had ever read the work, whether or not we think that Paul or the Johannine writer may have done. On the other hand it seems highly probable that Jesus was much influenced by the Danielic vision of the giving of the kingdom to the people of the saints of the Most High, a vision which itself is far removed from the fully developed Enochian conception of the heavenly Son of Man. Charles thought that the latter was developed out of the Daniel passage, while Mowinckel thinks that Dan. 7.13f. and the Similitudes have a common background.[1] There is a considerable difference between 'one like unto a son of man' as a poetic symbol of the people of Israel and the pre-existent heavenly Messiah of Enoch; but it may be that one or both conceptions can be traced back to the ancient myth of the Primal Man.[2]

It is possible that the same ancient, non-biblical myth of a Primal Man lies behind II (4) Esd. 13 (in the Apocrypha), in which 'Ezra' dreams that he sees 'as it were the likeness of a man' come up from the sea (13.3); all the nations of the earth assemble to make war upon him (13.5), but he graved himself a great mountain and flew up upon it (13.6); a 'flood of fire and flaming breath' came out of his mouth and annihilated the assembled armies (13.10f.). The man then came down from the mountain and assembled another multitude, a peaceable one (13.13). The interpretation of the vision is given in 13.20ff.: the man from the sea is 'he whom the Most High hath kept a great season' for the deliverance of his creation (13.26): 'the days shall come when the Most High will begin to deliver them that dwell upon the earth. . . . And one shall think to war against another, city against city, place against place, people against people and kingdom against kingdom. And it shall be, when these things shall come to pass, and the signs shall happen which I shewed thee before, then shall my son be revealed, whom thou sawest as a man ascending' (13.29-32). The nations shall gather against him, but he shall stand on Mount Zion, 'the mountain graven without hands' (13.36). 'And this my Son shall rebuke the nations . . . and he shall destroy them without labour (i.e. effortlessly) by the law, which is likened unto fire' (13.37f.). The 'peaceable multitude' turns out to be the ten tribes of Israel which had been deported by Shalmaneser in 722 B.C., whom the Most High had preserved miraculously in 'another land' (13.39-50).

[1] See Gösta Lindeskog in *The Root of the Vine*, ed. A. Fridrichsen (1953), 15n.; S. Mowinckel, *He that Cometh*, Chap. X.

[2] See J. M. Creed, art. 'The Heavenly Man', *JTS*, Vol. XXVI, 1925, 113-36.

Again, nothing more than the most general parallels can be discerned between this fanciful conception and the idea of the Son of Man in the Gospels; it is of little help in determining what Jesus could have meant by the title and it has had little influence upon the development of NT thought (its date cannot be much before A.D. 70 at the earliest). It is generally agreed that the so-called 'Ezra Apocalypse' (or 4 Esdras), i.e. II Esd. 3-14 in the Apocrypha, was originally written in Hebrew and therefore records an aspect of Palestinian thought; but it would be highly conjectural to assume that its distinctive ideas were congenial or even familiar to Jesus and his disciples. It supplies no evidence for the view that 'Son of Man' was a usual appellation for the Messiah amongst the Jews, although 'the Anointed' who will come as Judge (12.32) is doubtless the same figure as the Man from the Sea who is called 'my Son' (13.37, 52; cf. 7.28; 14.9). Some degree of 'Christianizing' must have taken place in the transcription of the work as we now have it (e.g. 7.28f.); but the vision of the Man from the Sea owes nothing to Christian sources. The sea is a symbol of mystery (13.52), long familiar in legend (*Tiamat, Tehom*), and the figure who comes from it is simply called 'the Man': it is this Man who effects the deliverance of the lost tribes of Israel. He is nowhere actually called 'Son of Man'. His gathering together of scattered Israel is perhaps the closest parallel to the work of the Son of Man in the Gospels (cf. Luke 19.10; 15.4; Matt. 10.6; 15.24; John 11.52). It would seem that neither the Similitudes of Enoch nor the Ezra Apocalypse is of much help in the attempt to discover the 'sources' of the conception of the Son of Man in the Gospels, and that therefore we must fall back upon the teaching of the canonical prophets (including Daniel); as we shall see, it is not necessary to look beyond these for the raw materials out of which the Gospel figure of the Son of Man is constructed—provided, of course, that there is a highly original mind which is capable of selecting and re-interpreting what is there to hand.

SON OF MAN IN THE GOSPELS

There are three kinds of Son-of-Man sayings attributed to Jesus in the Synoptic Gospels.[1] First, there are the sayings in which he seems to be referring to himself as Son of Man at the time of speaking; e.g. Mark 2.10, 28 (the sayings about the Son of Man's power to forgive sins and lordship over the Sabbath); Mark 14.41; Matt. 8.20=Luke 9.58 ('not where to lay his head'); Matt. 11.19=Luke 7.34 ('The Son of Man came eating and drinking'); Matt. 12.32=Luke 12.10 ('speak a

[1] See the admirable analysis in R. H. Fuller, *The Mission and Achievement of Jesus*, 95ff., which has been followed here; and cf. R. Bultmann, *Theology of the New Testament*, I, 30.

word against the Son of Man'); Matt. 13.37 ('He that soweth the good seed is the Son of Man': cf. 13.41); Luke 19.10 ('The Son of Man came to seek and to save'). (It will be noted that all Streeter's four 'sources' are involved.) There is thus plentiful evidence that Jesus referred to himself during his ministry as the Son of Man: perhaps those hearers who had not penetrated the mystery of his person took *bar nasha* to be a modest reference to himself, and nothing more; others, more understanding, would realize that something deeper was implied. Bultmann explains away this whole class of sayings as a simple mistranslation of *bar nasha*; the difficulty of such a view is that the author of St Mark's Gospel spoke Aramaic as his mother tongue.

The second class of sayings refers to the coming sufferings and resurrection of the Son of Man. It consists of the Marcan predictions of the passion (Mark 8.31; 9.12, 31; 10.33, 45; 14.21) together with Luke 17.25 (which identifies the glorious Son of Man of the parousia with the suffering Son of Man of the passion; see the preceding verses), Luke 22.22 and 24.7. Again Bultmann dismisses the whole class, this time on the grounds that they are prophecies after the event. We may admit that the form in which St Mark has written his group of predictions of the passion is affected by his knowledge of the way in which they were fulfilled (especially the details of 10.33f.); we may also admit that Jesus did not have a superhuman pre-view of the future events in detail. But we may nevertheless hold that his study of the OT prophets had (humanly speaking) led him to perceive that the Servant of the Lord would have to suffer before he triumphed, and from the moment of his own acceptance of the rôle of the Servant-Messiah at his baptism he knew that he must die. His study of the OT combined with his experience of preaching the Kingdom of God had led him to the knowledge that before the Son of Man could be glorified he must first suffer many things and be rejected of his generation (Luke 17.24f.). There is no ground for dismissing (with Bultmann) the predictions of the passion as the subsequent invention of the Hellenistic Church. There are several strongly 'Semitic' passages which shew that Jesus himself expected to be rejected, to suffer and to die, before he could bring his work to its triumphant conclusion, e.g. Luke 9.31; 12.50; 13.32f.; a Hellenistic community could have invented such passages only if it had been deliberately fabricating Aramaic 'antiques'. As we shall see, the idea of suffering is an essential ingredient in Jesus's conception of the Son of Man, and it is therefore most probable that he taught his disciples that the Son of Man must suffer, and furthermore that he himself must suffer because he was the Son of Man. The report of the dismay which the disciples felt when they first encountered this revolutionary doctrine is very good evidence of the historicity of the matter: why should the Hellenistic community have gone to the length of fabricating the story of Peter's rebuke (Mark 8.32f.), if Jesus had in fact never provoked it? The episode is poor *Gemeindetheologie*, but it has the authentic historical ring.

The third group of Son-of-Man sayings is the eschatological one in which the future glory of the exalted and triumphant Son of Man is affirmed. Again all four 'sources' of the Synoptic Gospels are involved: Mark 8.38; 9.9; 13.26; 14.62; Matt. 12.40=Luke 11.30; Matt. 24.27= Luke 17.24; Matt. 24.37=Luke 17.26; Matt. 24.44=Luke 12.40; Matt. 10.23; 13.41; 19.28; 24.39; 25.31; Luke 17.22, 30; 18.8. (R. H. Fuller regards as editorial Matt. 16.28; 24.30; Luke 12.8).[1] Bultmann allows that this group of sayings emanates from Jesus himself, but argues that he did not identify himself with the eschatological Son of Man, who is always referred to in the third person; the identification was made by the Church at a later date. Even the sure-footed Fuller stumbles here and concedes that Jesus did not think of himself as Son of Man during his earthly life-time but only as 'Son of Man designate'—the one who must first suffer and then, and only then, will be the Son of Man coming in glory.[2] This view is unacceptable because, as we shall see, Jesus used the self-designation 'Son of Man' to mean precisely 'a Messiah who suffers according to the Scriptures'; the distinctive feature about the Christian, as over against the Jewish, doctrine of the Messiah was that the Christ must suffer, and it was precisely this conception of Messiahship that the term 'Son of Man' was used by Jesus to connote. 'The Son of Man must suffer', said Jesus as he taught his disciples: 'the Christ must suffer', said the Christian preachers as they proclaimed the scriptural doctrine of the Messiah, now fulfilled in Jesus's death and resurrection (Acts 3.18). Moreover, as Fuller has pointed out previously,[3] there was no ready-made conception of the Son of Man current in the days of our Lord, as so many continental scholars are still uncritically apt to assume;[4] and therefore the term 'Son of Man' must have meant whatever Jesus taught his disciples that it meant. They had ready-made ideas about the Messiah, which needed radical correction; that is why Jesus seems somewhat to set aside the title 'Messiah' and use instead the designation 'Son of Man', into which he could pour a more scriptural content (Mark 8.29-31). Bultmann's view that Jesus never thought of himself as being in any way identified with the eschatological Son of Man follows

[1] *Op. cit.*, 97.   [2] *Op. cit.*, 103-8.   [3] *Op. cit.*, 98.
[4] E.g., E. Stauffer, *New Testament Theology*, ET, 1955, Chap. 24 and note 317 on p. 280; also Bultmann, *op. cit.*, I, 53, and H. Riesenfeld in *The Background of the New Testament and its Eschatology*, ed. W. D. Davies and D. Daube, 84.

naturally from his desire to shew that Jesus had no Messianic consciousness at all, in order that faith in Christ might be liberated from all
historical questions, such as whether Jesus considered himself to be
the Messiah.[1] It is based on modern existentialist philosophy rather
than on a scholarly consideration of historical evidence, and we need
not pursue it here. The difficulty about Jesus's references to the coming
Son of Man in the third person is an artificial one, and the sense of his
words is not at all obscure. Thus, the meaning of Jesus's reply to the
high priest's direct question whether he was the Messiah (Mark 14.61f.)
would have been: 'Yes, I am the Messiah, as you will realize when you
see the Son of Man sitting at the right hand of power, and coming with
the clouds of heaven'; or, possibly, 'Call me "Messiah", if you like that
term—I don't think it very suitable; you will realize who I am when you
see. . . .' This at least is what St Mark had understood to be the tenor
of Jesus's confession at the trial, and no adequate reasons have been
adduced by Bultmann or other critics to lead us to think that they have
better information on the point.

A radical re-interpretation of current Jewish notions about the
Messiah is involved in the Son-of-Man conception in the Gospels, and
it was made necessary by the deep spiritual insight expressed in the
phrase 'the Son of Man must suffer'. It can hardly be doubted that
the scriptural basis of this insight was Isa. 53 and the recognition that
the suffering Servant of the Lord there depicted is a prophecy of the
Messiah. Once this insight has been attained, other scriptural passages
would also be adduced, especially Pss. 22 and 69. The whole passage
Isa. 52.13–53.12, including almost every phrase of it, echoes through
the New Testament—the Synoptists, John, Acts, Paul, Heb. and I
Peter.[2] 'Son of Man' is a title which the NT writers regarded as inter-
changeable with 'Servant' (cf. the use of $\delta o \xi \acute{a} \zeta \epsilon \iota \nu$ in John 12.23 with
Isa. 52.13 (LXX); cf. Acts 3.13, etc.).[3] 'The Son of Man goeth [to
suffering] even as it is written of him' (Mark 14.21), because the Son
of Man is the Servant of the Lord.[4] A brilliant new synthesis of OT
themes had been effected, not merely as a new theological teaching,
but as the programme of action for the ministry of Jesus. According to
Bultmann, however, Jesus himself was entirely unaware of it, and the
credit for this profoundly original reinterpretation of OT theology
must go to some unnamed theological teacher of the Hellenistic Church

---

[1] *Op. cit.*, 26.

[2] C. H. Dodd, *Acc. Scrip.*, 94; see list of passages quoted in NT on pp. 92-4; also
for Ps. 22, pp. 97f.; Pss. 31 and 34, pp. 98f.; Ps. 69, pp. 57-9, 96f.; Ps. 119, pp. 99f.

[3] Cf. Dodd, *op. cit.*, 92n.

[4] That the Marcan suffering-rising Son-of-Man sayings are influenced by Isa. 53
is well argued by R. H. Fuller, *The Mission and Achievement of Jesus*, 56-8.

before St Paul was converted. Jesus held only the conventional 'Enochian' notions about the Son of Man, current in his day, and the real originator of the Christian doctrine of the Christ is some anonymous genius who explained the new theology to the Church after the latter had already spread to the Hellenistic world. Bultmann, in fact, does not even trouble to look for a theological innovator of genius; he is content to say vaguely that 'the reinterpretation of the (Jewish Messiah-Son-of-Man) concept was done not by Jesus himself but by the Church *ex eventu*'.[1] But the brilliant theological interpretation which we find in the NT is not the work of a 'community'. The bold new teaching about the Son of Man, i.e. a Messiah who should suffer, was the original work of Jesus himself, and no other plausible suggestion has ever been put forward.

THE CORPORATE SON OF MAN

In his notable book *The Teaching of Jesus*, T. W. Manson suggested that in the mind of our Lord the Son of Man was primarily a corporate personality rather than an individual. Jesus conceived it to be his mission to create the people of the saints of the Most High, to whom the kingdom should be given (cf. Luke 12.32). Thus, as in the Danielic simile of 'one like unto a son of man', a group or remnant of the righteous would be implied. Jesus expected his disciples to endure the sufferings of the Son of Man, but in the end he was crucified, not between James and John, who had begged the positions of privilege on his right hand and on his left in his glory (Mark 10.37), but between two thieves; and thus in the end Jesus was left alone to bear the part of the Son of Man.[2] The suggestion is by no means implausible, as Jesus might well have understood the figure of the Isaianic Servant to represent the righteous remnant rather than an individual. The difficulty would be to prove that Jesus ever thought this way, in view of the fact that the Gospel-tradition was formed by those who had come to see in Jesus alone the true lineaments of the Son of Man. There is, however, as we shall see, a profound New Testament truth embodied in the conception of the corporate Son of Man, and it arises out of the life and teaching of Jesus himself.

The grandeur and originality of Jesus's doctrine of the Son of Man lies in the way in which the present lowly person, who has not where to lay his head, and who is about to be rejected and to suffer a shameful death, is nevertheless not a different person from the Son of Man who will be seen sitting at the right hand of God—the 'my lord' of Ps.

[1] *Op. cit.*, 31.

[2] T. W. Manson, *The Teaching of Jesus*, 1931, 232. See also his article 'The Son of Man in Daniel, Enoch and the Gospels' in *Bulletin of the John Rylands Library*, Vol. XXXII, 1950, 171-93.

110.1—and coming with the clouds of heaven (Mark 14.62) in the glory
of his Father with his angels, rendering to every man according to his
deeds (Matt. 16.27). The Son of Man, who is come to seek and to save
that which is lost, the Shepherd-Redeemer of the Israel of God (Luke
19.10; 15.3-7; Ezek. 34.16), is none other than the Judge who presides
at the last great controversy of Yahweh with rebellious humanity,
sitting on the throne of his glory for the judgment of the nations, the
Shepherd-Ruler who separates the sheep from the goats (Matt. 25.31f.;
Ezek. 34.17) and gives the kingdom to the saints, the blessed of the
Father, for whom it was prepared from the foundation of the world
(Matt. 25.34; cf. Dan. 7.13f.; Luke 12.32; 22.28-30). Small wonder
that un-faith cannot grasp the depth of the paradox of almighty love
and should seek to separate the lowly from the triumphant Son of
Man. But the depth of the paradox is not yet exhausted. The Son of
Man in glory, the judge of all the nations, is not cut off by virtue of his
triumphant reign from the sufferings and sorrows of the world below;
he is still the one of whom the Scriptures declared that 'in all their
affliction he was afflicted' (Isa. 63.9). Nor is it only in the sufferings of
the elect that he suffers; he is identified with the whole of suffering
humanity—the hungry, thirsty, outcast, naked, sick and imprisoned,
wherever they are, for he is not simply the Saviour of the Church but
the Saviour of the world. It is not that he is identified Stoic-fashion
with 'humanity' in the abstract, but with every single man in his utter
individuality.[1] It is in *this* man or *this* child, whom I can *now* succour
or refuse, that I encounter my judge, the Son of Man; we meet Christ in
the poor wretch who in all his repulsiveness claims our help and pity
(Matt. 25.35-46). We usually think of the Good Samaritan in the
parable (Luke 10.25-37) as the Christ-like figure; and indeed, so he is,
for Jesus 'went about doing good' (Acts 10.38). But in a profounder
sense the man who fell among thieves is the representative of Christ—
the 'neighbour' who needs my help. It is Christ, the one who is stripped
and beaten and left half dead, that the Samaritan succoured and took
care of. This is the heart of Christian ἀγάπη: 'ye did it unto me'. There
is no merit in our service, for our best is unworthy of him who did so
much for us. The poor sufferer whom I help confers a favour on me,
not I on him, because he shews me Christ, makes Christ real to me,
enables me to touch, handle, tend and serve Christ.

Because Christ is the representative of all mankind and is present
to every living person, therefore persons can be his representatives,
whether they know it or not, and to receive them means to receive
Christ himself. This is an application of the very Jewish idea of personal

[1] Cf. Théo Preiss, *Life in Christ*, ET, 1954, 55.

representation, which was later to develop into the institution of the *shaliach*, whereby one person could legally represent and act for another person or for a society.[1] But Jesus is not using the conception in any legal sense when he names certain classes of persons, who specially need his protection, as his representatives, viz. little children and his apostles, the former because of their weakness and innocence, the latter because of the sufferings and perils which attend the faithful preaching of the Gospel (Mark 9.37 and Matt. 18.5; Matt. 10.40-42; Luke 10.16; John 13.20; cf. Gal. 4.14; Philemon 17). Every helpless sufferer is a *shaliach* of Christ; the apostles are *sheluchim* (plural of *shaliach*) not because of any legal appointment to an 'apostolic succession' but because they stand helpless 'as sheep in the midst of wolves . . . hated of all men for my name's sake' (Matt. 10.16-22). Thus it was that Saul on the Damascus road heard the voice of the Lord saying, 'Saul, Saul, why persecutest thou *me*?' (Acts 9.4): it has been plausibly argued that what is involved in these words is the very essence of the Pauline conception of the Church as the body of Christ, the number of those baptized into Christ, the corporate personality of the Son of Man.[2]

St Paul takes seriously the idea that Christ's disciples must share the sufferings of the Son of Man, with whom they have become united through baptism into his death (Rom. 6.4f.), and he rejoices to fill up those sufferings of Christ which are still required for the sake of his body, the Church (Col. 1.24); he conceives of the Church itself as participating in the sufferings of Christ (Phil. 3.10) and of Christ's sufferings as overflowing into the Church's life (II Cor. 1.5-7; cf. Phil. 1.29; Rom. 8.17; Gal. 6.17). Christ and his Church are one body in which, if one member suffers all members suffer with it (I Cor. 12.26f.). All this is implicit in Jesus's conception of the suffering Son of Man who has gathered to himself the faithful remnant of Israel. As has often been pointed out,[3] Paul dispenses with the Semitism 'Son of Man' but retains the idea; his doctrine that 'we being many are one body in Christ' (Rom. 12.5; cf. I Cor. 12.12) is only a development of what is implied in the Gospel teaching about the Son of Man, and likewise his doctrine of Christ as 'the last Adam' or 'man from heaven' (I Cor.

---

[1] See further *infra*, 324f.

[2] Cf. J. A. T. Robinson, *The Body*, 1952, 58. See also *infra*, 250f.

[3] E.g. C. H. Dodd, *IFG*, 243; K. Lake and Foakes Jackson, *Beginnings of Christianity*, I, 1920, 380: 'All the essentials of the eschatological doctrine connoted by the apocalyptic Son of Man are found in Paul, but not the phrase itself. Is not this because he was too good a Grecian to translate *Bar-nasha* by so impossible a phrase as ὁ υἱὸς τοῦ ἀνθρώπου, and rendered it idiomatically by ὁ ἄνθρωπος? When for instance he speaks in I Cor. 14.47 of the second "man" as the Lord from Heaven, is he not thinking of the *Bar-nasha* of Enoch?' On this last point we prefer to reserve judgment.

15.45-47) is only another way of presenting the Christian conception of the Son of Man. Christ is the 'new man' into whose representative personality all 'the saints of the Most High' are incorporated; Paul's Christology and his doctrine of the Church meet in the conception of Christ as *Ben Adam*. The new humanity of the ἔσχατος ᾿Αδάμ is as it were the robe which the convert 'puts on' when he is baptized into the Church (Col. 3.10f.), just as Christ is the 'perfect man' ('completed humanity') into which the Church corporately grows up (Eph. 4.13). Thus, Paul's conception of the Christian as being ἐν Χριστῷ is grounded in the basic conception of the Son of Man as taught by Jesus and apprehended by primitive Christianity. It is very significant that in I Cor. 15.21 Paul uses the simple ἄνθρωπος of Christ in connection with *testimonia* which elsewhere are associated with the expression 'Son of Man';[1] this ἄνθρωπος, by whom came the resurrection of the dead, is the Christ in whom, in contrast with the old ἄνθρωπος (Adam), all shall be made alive (I Cor. 15.21f.); as the triumphant Son of Man, the κύριος of Ps. 110.1, 'he must reign till he hath put all his enemies under his feet' (15.25). For Christ is not only the 'inclusive representative'[2] of the new humanity; he is also the Lord who sits at God's right hand. But Paul is also quoting here another *testimonium,* viz. Ps. 8.6, where it is said of the Son of Man: 'Thou hast put all things in subjection under his feet', and where it is the *animal* creation that is thus subdued: we are reminded that in the vision of Dan. 7 it is the empires of the *beasts* which give way to the reign of the saints of the Most High represented by the figure of 'one like unto a son of man'. It is perhaps worth recalling that all the three OT *testimonia* concerning the Son of Man which are known to have been used by the apostolic Church[3] (Pss. 8.4-8; 80.17; Dan. 7.13f.) are references to a corporate figure; they thus fit naturally into the New Testament conception of the Son of Man who gathers up the new humanity into himself and becomes the climax and culmination of the whole long process of creation and re-creation, the last Adam, not the man who was formed of the dust of the earth, but the Son of Man from heaven (I Cor. 15.45-47).[4]

A not wholly dissimilar conception of the corporate Son of Man is found in Hebrews. In Heb. 2.6 we find Ps. 8.4 quoted and the expression 'son of man' is taken as referring to Christ. The context shews that the writer is concerned with the truth that the saints (οἱ ἁγιαζόμενοι) are made one with Christ, the sanctifier, through his suffering, death and

---

[1] So C. H. Dodd, *IFG*, 243; cf. *Acc. Scrip.*, 121.

[2] C. H. Dodd's phrase, *Acc. Scrip.*, 119.

[3] C. H. Dodd, *Acc. Scrip.*, 117.

[4] On the Pauline conception of the Church, see *infra*, 242-58.

exaltation (esp. 2.11). The Son of Man, for a little while made lower than the angels, is exalted and all things are made subject to him by means of those very sufferings through which he brings 'many sons' to glory (2.10): the author of our salvation is made perfect through sufferings (. . . τὸν ἀρχηγὸν τῆς σωτηρίας αὐτῶν διὰ παθημάτων τελειῶσαι, 2.10). 'To make perfect' here does not mean to make *morally* perfect one who was formerly lacking moral perfection (though the verb can mean this, e.g. Phil. 3.12), for such a meaning would be repugnant to *Auct. Heb.* with his strong sense of the moral perfection of Christ (e.g. 4.15; 7.26f.). In the whole context of Heb. 2.5-18 the conception of τελείωσις must primarily mean 'wholeness' and 'unity', as at John 17.23: ἵνα ὦσι τετελειωμένοι εἰς ἕν—'that they may be perfected into one', i.e. completely united. This is proved by the words which immediately follow, 'Both he that sanctifieth and they that are sanctified are all of one' (ἐξ ἑνὸς πάντες) (2.11). The saints are Christ's brethren (2.12), related to him in a flesh-and-blood union—that very flesh-and-blood which Christ shared with them (2.14). The same conception of the τελείωσις of the Son [of Man] reappears in Heb. 5.9 and 7.28: the perfecting of the Son consists in the gathering to himself of those who are being sanctified. Thus, in a non-Pauline type of primitive Christianity we find a conception of a corporate Son of Man whose perfection consists in bringing 'many sons' to glory in the unity of the Sanctifier and the sanctified.

The doctrine of the Son of Man, as we have found it in the Synoptists, St Paul and Hebrews, is developed and expounded by the author of the Fourth Gospel in his own characteristic way. He thoroughly understands the Synoptic teaching concerning Christ's representation in and by his disciples, and he gives us his own version of certain Synoptic sayings: 'He that receiveth whomsoever I send receiveth me, and he that receiveth me receiveth him that sent me' (John 13.20; cf. Matt. 10.40; Luke 10.16); 'a slave is not greater than his master; if they persecuted me, they will also persecute you' (John 15.20; cf. Matt. 10.24f.; also John 13.16). Unlike Paul, St John does not avoid the expression 'Son of Man', using it some thirteen times. C. H. Dodd says that 'the term "Son of Man" throughout this Gospel retains the sense of one who incorporates in himself the people of God'.[1] The influence of Dan. 7.13f. is clear in John 5.25-28: 'he (the Father) gave him authority to execute judgment, because he is the Son of Man'; it may be noted that the two following verses (5.28f.) shew the influence of Dan. 12.2. Again, there are many echoes of the Isaianic Servant of the Lord.[2] The Servant's mission is to gather Israel to the Lord (Isa. 49.5; cf.

---

[1] *IFG*, 248.   [2] Cf. C. H. Dodd, *IFG*, 246f.

John 11.52), to be a light of the Gentiles (Isa. 49.6; cf. John 8.12; 12.46). The great Johannine themes of exaltation and glorification are brought together in Isa. 52.13: LXX, Ἰδού, συνήσει ὁ παῖς μου, καὶ ὑψωθήσεται καὶ δοξασθήσεται σφόδρα. In the NT ὑψόω is the technical term for the exaltation of Christ (e.g. Acts 5.31; Phil. 2.9); in the Fourth Gospel it strikingly becomes a synonym for Christ's crucifixion: 'I, if I be *lifted up* (ὑψωθῶ) from the earth, will draw all men unto myself. But this he said, signifying by what manner of death he should die' (John 12.32f.; cf. 3.14; 8.28; 18.31f.). For St John Christ's crucifixion is his exaltation and glorification (12.23; 13.31f.). But the lifting up of the Son of Man is the means of drawing all men to him (πρὸς ἐμαυτόν, 12.32), the means by which the children of God that are scattered abroad are gathered into one (11.52), and by which the disciples are perfected into one (17.23). In the death, resurrection and ascension of Christ, the Servant of the Lord is indeed exalted and glorified, and Dodd is surely right in saying that 'it would appear that the evangelist found in the Servant of the Lord an embodiment of the people of God, and applied what is said of him to the Son of Man, conceived as embodying collectively in himself redeemed humanity'.[1] In other words, the Johannine presentation of the concept 'Son of Man' is substantially the same as we have found it to be in other parts of the NT and, as we saw grounds for thinking, as it was originally taught by Jesus himself to his apostles. In this as in other matters the suggestion, frequently made, that St John elaborately develops primitive Christian doctrine to a degree never contemplated by our Lord and his first disciples is a misleading exaggeration. St John clarifies the doctrine and re-states it in his own individual way, but he neither adds to it nor subtracts from it; he is not an innovator or a maker of doctrine, but a faithful and illuminating expositor of the tradition which he has received.

THE GNOSTIC MYTH OF THE HEAVENLY MAN

We have not thus far mentioned the Gnostic myth of the Man from heaven, because we have been able to account for the New Testament doctrine of the Son of Man by reference to purely biblical sources. Others, notably Bultmann,[2] have held that the New Testament teaching

[1] *IFG*, 247. The corporate aspect of the Son of Man is stressed in John 1.51 ('Ye shall see the heaven opened, and the angels of God ascending and descending upon the Son of Man'), if Dodd is right in seeing here a reference to the angels ascending and descending upon Jacob (=Israel) in Gen. 28.12. He quotes C. F. Burney (*The Aramaic Origin of the Fourth Gospel*, 1922, 115): 'Jacob, as the ancestor of the nation of Israel, summarizes in his person the ideal Israel *in posse*, just as our Lord, at the other end of the line, summarizes it *in esse* as the Son of man' (*IFG*, 246).

[2] See especially *Theology of the New Testament*, I, 166f.; also S. Mowinckel, *He that Cometh*, 426-32.

has been infected by Gnostic speculations concerning the 'heavenly Man'. According to this widespread oriental myth a heavenly light-being has been cast out of the celestial realm, either because he was vanquished in combat or because of his folly. He fell down to earth and the original unity of his personality was shattered into a myriad fragments (i.e. human selves) and the fragments are now imprisoned in the lower regions (i.e. this world) in evil matter (i.e. human bodies). Subjected to the demonic rulers of this world-age, from which they could be liberated only by the destruction of the demonic Kingdom, men (the fragmented Man) forget their heavenly origin and home. The Gnostic redeemer, however, who is another light-being sent by the highest God, comes down from heaven to set men free by imparting *gnosis*. He is sometimes described as the 'son' or 'image' of the most high god in heaven. He dispenses the sacraments by which men are purified and their forgotten knowledge of the world of light is revived; he communicates the secret pass-words by means of which the soul at death on its journey towards the realms of light may safely elude the hostile planetary guardians of the heavenly spheres, who are agents of the demonic powers. During his earthly sojourn the heavenly Man disguises himself in human form, so as to escape recognition by the hostile demonic rulers of this world, but, of course, he does not really endure privation or suffering. Often the myth is syncretistically absorbed into local mystery-cults, as when the Gnostic redeemer is identified with Attis, the Phrygian cult-deity. In much the same way Bultmann considers that Hellenistic Christianity has been invaded by Gnostic motifs, which are noticeable in Paul, but much more powerfully influential in the writer of Colossians-Ephesians and in the author of the Fourth Gospel. Paul's 'second man from heaven' (ὁ δεύτερος ἄνθρωπος ἐξ οὐρανοῦ, I Cor. 15.47) or ὁ ἐπουράνιος (15.48); the νέος ἄνθρωπος of Col. 3.10 or the ἀνὴρ τέλειος of Eph. 4.13; and the Johannine Son of Man who descends from and ascends into heaven (John 3.13; 6.62, etc.), are all NT versions of the Gnostic myth of the heavenly Man. C. H. Dodd agrees as regards the Johannine Son of Man, at least to the extent of thinking that the Fourth Evangelist is attempting to convey Christian truth in a form which the higher paganism would find congenial and comprehensible.[1]

Against all such contentions the following points may be advanced. First, the literature to which Bultmann and Dodd appeal for their reconstruction of the Gnostic myth of the heavenly *Anthropos* or of the

---

[1] Cf. *IFG*, 244: 'The φῶς ἀληθινόν is what Philo calls ἀρχέτυπον φωτός. It is, in other words, the Platonic idea of light. It is no long step from that to say that for John the Son of Man is the ἀληθινὸς ἄνθρωπος, the real or archetypal Man, or the Platonic Idea of Man.' (See *supra*, 68.)

'higher paganism' (i.e. the *Corpus Hermeticum*) is a century or more later in date than the Fourth Gospel and is itself likely to have borrowed from Christian sources; the only first-century literature to which Bultmann appeals is the NT itself, and this is capable of a simpler explanation. There is no real evidence for the existence of 'the Gnostic myth' in the first century A.D. Secondly, the Pauline (including Colossians-Ephesians) and Johannine conceptions of the Son of Man as the body of Christ or the perfected unity of the disciples of Christ are, as we have seen, legitimate expositions of what the original teaching of Jesus had already contained, while the teaching of Jesus concerning the Son of Man is derived (humanly speaking) from his profound meditation upon OT themes. The doctrine of the NT can be explained without recourse to an hypothesis, for which no independent evidence exists, about the Gnostic myth; Occam's razor here applies: *entia non sunt multiplicanda*. Thirdly, we have no reason to question that Paul and John, like other Christian thinkers and teachers in a missionary situation, would strive to solve 'the problem of communication' by using language and thought-forms which their audience or readers would understand; some of the formal expression of their teaching may doubtless be accounted for in this way. Opinions are likely to differ on the question of degree. But there is a difference *toto caelo* between using the language of Hellenism and syncretistically enlarging or adulterating the *kerugma* with it. There remains all the difference in the world between the Gnostic redeemer of the *Poimandres* and the historical Son of Man of the Gospels, who had not where to lay his head; and if it should appear that Daniel, Enoch, Philo and Poimandres all have a common ancestor in the primitive myth of the *Urmensch* or Primal Man of Iranian religion, the difference would not be diminished in the slightest degree. Indeed, there is no cause for surprise, if we take seriously the truth of the Incarnation, in the discovery that the incarnate Son should wear his human clothes with natural ease, as though they had been made for him—as indeed in the age-long purpose of God they had been prepared for the day of his coming. But a long process of 'demythologizing' the ancient legends had been going on in the history of Israel, and that is why the biblical picture of the Son of Man is so far removed from the Gnostic myth of the *Anthropos*—as far as eschatology and justification are removed from the cosmology of the planetary spheres and the *abracadabra* of secret pass-words. No syncretism is possible between such opposites, as the Catholic Church discovered in the long struggle with Gnostic heresy after the close of the NT period. 'The difference can be summed up very briefly: in the Gnostic myth Man is the divine principle substantially and eternally identical with the sum of the souls of men scattered but predetermined to salvation. In the thought of Jesus the Son of Man freely identifies himself with each of the wretched ones by an act of substitution and identification, and he will gather them together at the last day. . . . It is essential that the Son of Man, that is, Man, is *not* identified with humanity as a whole— Jesus is unfamiliar with this Stoic concept—but with each man. Thus it is not at all a question of an identity of substance between the primal Man and the totality of his scattered members but of a sovereign act of self-identification.'[1]

THE SIGN OF THE SON OF MAN

It remains only to piece together the answer to the question of the source materials out of which the conception of the Son of Man was fashioned in the mind of our Lord. Here we must exercise the utmost restraint, because it is above all things necessary to avoid giving the impression that we are classifying Jesus as 'a religious genius' or a 'prophet' or something of the kind. Anything in the nature of a 'psychological approach' is to be strongly deprecated. We are only asking what the evidence of the Gospels shews us about the sources used by our Lord in the fashioning of his doctrine of the Son of Man, that is, his conception of his own ministry and mission. If we reject the view that he adopted the current notions of speculative apocalyptic or that he was influenced by oriental-Gnostic mythology, we must give reasons for preferring an alternative explanation, viz. that it was out of biblical materials that Jesus fashioned his interpretation of his own person and work. There is nothing incongruous with belief in the divinity of the Son of God if we think that, because our Lord was truly incarnate, his mind worked as a human mind, thinking human thoughts and working with the ideas of other human minds, although we do not presume to give a psychological account of his mental processes. We do not think of him as a kind of biblical critic of the first century, analysing the OT into elements which could be regarded as 'acceptable' and then synthesizing them into a reconstructed theology. A better, though still imperfect, analogy would be that of a painter holding his palette, full of rich colours of every clashing shade; out of them all, the mind of the artist creates a new and beautiful combination of shades: the colours were all present on the palette, so that in a sense the picture was there too. Yet it was not there; it did not exist until the creative imagination of the artist took the colours—but not all of them, and not in equal quantities— and blended them into a pattern of meaning. So Jesus fashioned the theology of the NT out of the many-coloured insights and mysteries of the OT.

[1] Théo Preiss, *Life in Christ*, 53. See also *infra*, 247.

The evidence would seem to shew that Jesus preferred 'Son of Man' to 'Messiah' as a designation for himself, not because he did not regard himself as fulfilling the prophecies of the Scriptures concerning the Lord's Anointed, but because the title was so open to misconception. 'Son of Man', on the other hand, was a term which could be made to carry the meaning which Jesus wanted to pour into it. It had been Ezekiel's title for himself as the Lord's servant, to whom he had condescended to speak and to reveal his truth, as indeed he spoke to all 'his servants the prophets' (Amos 3.7). Our Lord thought of the OT prophets as themselves personally representing and foreshadowing that Messianic Servant of the Lord whose coming they foretold: Isaiah was himself the type of the '*ebed Yahweh* whose glory and humility he foretold (Isa. 9.6f.; 11.1-9; 53, etc.; nothing was known of a 'second' or a 'third' Isaiah); Jeremiah in his faithful witness and steadfast endurance under persecution was a type of the Righteous King of whom he wrote (Jer. 23.5); Ezekiel was the sign given by God to his generation, and he spoke of the Shepherd-Servant who would save the flock of God (Ezek. 34.23); Daniel, who suffered for righteousness' sake, had foretold the giving of the Kingdom to 'one like unto a son of man' who had suffered much tribulation but was to be exalted (Dan. 7.13f.).[1] It was from the general picture of the Lord's Servant, whom the OT prophets had delineated and represented in their person and work, that our Lord derived his conception of the Son of Man, that is, his understanding of his own character, call and destiny. The alternation between the Lord's servant as an individual and as a community is present in the thought of Jesus, exactly as it is in the OT writings; it was easier for the Hebrew mind than it is for us to understand how Israel could be an individual patriarch and also a nation that was like the sand of the sea in number; the Hebrew doctrine of personality allows for the truth that all men are 'in Adam' or 'in Christ', while yet they remain themselves, in a way in which we, with our modern notion of rigidly separated selves, find difficult to understand.

The choice of the actual term 'Son of Man' is not hard to explain. Jesus regarded himself, as Ezekiel had regarded himself (Ezek. 12.6; 24.24), as a sign to his generation. The sign of the Son of Man indicated to those who would 'hear' that God's purpose of salvation was about to be accomplished. The Book of Ezekiel was accepted as canonical by

---

[1] Cf. C. H. Dodd, *Acc. Scrip.*, 117n.: 'To say, as is often said, that the OT knows nothing of a suffering Son of Man is inaccurate.' He is referring to Dan. 7.13f. Nor should we forget Daniel himself (in Dan. 2 and 6, etc.) as a type of Christ: he suffers and is vindicated, and Isa. 53 could fittingly be applied to him. We must put aside all modern critical notions when we try to understand how Jesus would have read the OT.

Judaism from about 200 B.C. (cf. Ecclus. 49.8); and Ezekiel came to be regarded, along with Moses, Elijah and Elisha, as in a special sense a *shaliach* of God as no other prophet was. All four were held to have done things (notably raising the dead: Ezekiel appears to be credited with the working of a resurrection on the evidence of Ezek. 37.1-14) which in the normal course of events are the work of God himself.[1] But, because of the deviations of the Book from the Mosaic Law, it was later forbidden to be read by any Jew under thirty years of age,[2] and it only narrowly escaped the fate of being classed as an apocryphal book. But it nevertheless had a great influence upon many Jews, especially of the apocalyptic school; its influence upon the author of the Revelation of St John is considerable. Jesus himself was deeply influenced by it; his parables of shepherding are clearly inspired by his meditation upon Ezek. 34. The 'son of man' who was 'set for a sign unto the house of Israel' (Ezek. 12.6) becomes merged in true Hebrew fashion with the Isaianic Servant of the Lord and with the other prophetic types of the Messiah who was to come; he corporately gathers and represents the Israel of God; indeed, he *is* the Israel of God, the recreated humanity of the new Adam, the Man in whom the image of God is perfectly restored. The work of the Good Shepherd, the gathering together of the scattered flock (Ezek. 34.12-16), the congregation of the Lord, the people of the saints of the Most High, has now begun and is the real meaning of the existence and mission of the Church of Jesus Messiah; but it cannot come to its fruition until that day when the Son of Man in glory sits in judgment on the nations and the Shepherd-Ruler separates the sheep from the goats (Matt. 25.31f.; Ezek. 34.17).

[1] Cf. Strack-Bill., III, 5f.   [2] Jerome, *Praefatio ad Ezech.*

7

THE CHRISTOLOGY OF THE
APOSTOLIC CHURCH

'**M**ESSIAH**'** and 'Son of Man' are titles which would carry
no meaning outside Jewish circles: Paul the missionary,
writing to his Gentile converts, uses 'Christ' almost as a
proper name, and never uses 'Son of Man' at all. There were, however,
other designations of Jesus which would sound perfectly intelligible
in Gentile ears, especially 'Son of God' and 'Lord'. Indeed, Bousset
held that the title 'Son of God' was first given to Jesus by the Hellenistic community, and Bultmann thinks that, though it was used by the
original Jewish-Christian Church, it was 'simply a royal title', meaning
nothing more than 'Messiah' in the undeveloped sense of the expected
Son of David.[1] The evidence, however, hardly admits of such simple
conclusions.

'SON OF GOD'

In the Hellenistic world, where the distinction between the divine and
the human was generally blurred, 'son of God' could mean little more
than a very good man (cf. Mark 15.39 with Luke 23.47: 'a son of God'
means simply 'a righteous man'). The world was full of 'divine men'
($\theta\epsilon\hat{\iota}o\iota$ $\check{\alpha}\nu\delta\rho\epsilon\varsigma$) who claimed to be sons of God and who sometimes were
actually worshipped as manifestations of deity (cf. Acts 8.10; 12.22;
14.11f.; 28.6). And, of course, the Emperor was *divi filius*. The basis of
such language is the old Greek belief in men's physical descent from the
gods; kings, philosophers, priests and righteous men were what they
were in virtue of their divine ancestry (cf. Acts 17.28). It need hardly be
stressed how wide a gulf separates all such thinking from the biblical
belief in man's *creation* by God. It is exceedingly unlikely that any
Christians, even Hellenistic ones, would have begun to call Jesus 'the
Son of God' because they had mistaken him for one of the Greek
'sons of God' of the type of Simon Magus or Elymas, still less of the

[1] See W. Bousset, *Kyrios Christos*, 1913, ET, 1921, 52ff.; R. Bultmann, *Theology
of the New Testament*, I, 50; for a critical refutation of such views see R. H. Fuller,
The Mission and Achievement of Jesus, 80-95; V. Taylor, *The Names of Jesus*, 1953,
59-65.

type of Caligula or Herod Agrippa (cf. Acts 12.22), or of the wandering Stoic philosophers. The *kerugma* of the NT documents is evidence that no such misconceptions had arisen. But it may well be that the title 'Son of God' was widely employed in the Gentile churches because it was intelligible to a Gentile congregation; sound instruction about its Christian meaning would have been given. It is prominent in the Fourth Gospel, Paul, Heb. and the Epistles of John. It does not occur in the Pastorals, James, I and II Pet. (except in the quotation at II Pet. 1.17), II John, Jude; in Rev. only at 2.18 and in Acts only at 9.20 (Paul preached that Jesus is the Son of God) and in the quotation from Ps. 2.7 at 13.33. V. Taylor rightly points out that in John, Paul and Heb. it occurs in passages of a strongly doctrinal character and seems to be associated with teaching rather than with worship: 'the first Christians fervently believed in "the Son", but they invoked "the Lord".'[1]

The meaning of 'Son of God' in the NT is based, as we shall see, on its distinctive use in the OT. Four types of usage are found there, though the phrase is not at all frequent. In the old mythological conception angels are 'sons of God' (Gen. 6.2; Job 1.6; 38.7): the question of their obedience is of cardinal importance. Secondly, the king is occasionally called God's son, e.g. II Sam. 7.14, 'I will be his father, and he shall be my son.' The most important example of this class, judging by the frequency of the allusions to it in the NT, is Ps. 2.7, 'Thou art my son; this day have I begotten thee.' This is doubtless a Hebrew adaptation of a Babylonian hymn for the enthronement of the king; the latter re-enacts the part of the Primal Man who was the first ruler of the world (cf. Gen. 1.26-28; Ps. 8); but in the Hebrew version the king is king by adoption and not by procreation.[2] In this Psalm the Lord's Anointed, the king set upon the holy hill of Zion, is declared to be God's son (cf. also Ps. 89.26f.). It need hardly be added that the obedience of the king to the divine law was the criterion by which the reality of his kingship was to be measured: a disobedient king was not a king at all. Thirdly, in the later literature righteous men are called sons of God (e.g. Ecclus. 4.10; Wisd. 2.18; Pss. Sol. 13.8; 17.30; 18.4; cf. Luke 6.35; Matt. 27.43), because they render the obedience of sons. Lastly, but by no means of least importance, Israel is spoken of as God's son: 'Israel is my son, my first-born' (Ex. 4.22); 'When Israel was a child, then I loved him, and called my son out of Egypt' (Hos. 11.1). As throughout the OT the characteristic excellence of a son consists in obedience to his father's will, so at the very call (or adoption) of Israel, the promise of obedience is made (Ex. 24.7); so Pharaoh had been told, 'Let my son go, *that he may serve me*' (Ex. 4.23). The prophets lament Israel's

---

[1] *Op. cit.*, 57.   [2] See A. Bentzen, *King and Messiah*, 16-20.

disobedience and consequent failure to fulfil this vocation to divine sonship. An interesting illustration of the biblical conception of sonship is to be found in Jesus's parable of the Two Sons in Matt. 21.28-31. It follows from this Hebraic view of sonship as obedience—so strongly emphasized in the Wisdom books—that the basic definition of a son of God, whatever it might have been before the prophetic work of demythologizing the old cult-legends had begun, becomes 'one who does the righteous will of God'. It is this Hebraic doctrine which reappears in the NT teaching concerning the Sonship of Christ, and which is hardly likely to have been the invention of 'the Hellenistic community'.

The idea of the Fatherhood of God is not prominent in the OT, though it is not entirely absent (e.g. Deut. 32.6; Ps. 103.13; Isa. 63.16; 64.8; Mal. 3.17); it is rather that Yahweh is the Father of Israel as a nation than that the individual Israelite was in the habit of thinking of God as *his* Father. There is therefore something original and distinctive in the teaching of Jesus about God as the Father of each individual disciple. Jesus did not, of course, teach the liberal protestant notion that God is Father of all men *qua* men and that all men are therefore brothers (Harnack's 'essence of Christianity'); God is Father only of those who have by faith and repentance entered into his reign and accepted the obedience of sons.[1] Men may become sons of God in virtue of the unique Sonship of Christ, not through any moral endowments or exertions of their own. The distinctive teaching of Jesus about God as the Father of individual believers arises out of his own unique consciousness of sonship. He himself was wont to address God as *'abba* ('Father') in the same way as a son would address his earthly father. This was not the practice within Judaism in the days of Christ; the Jew would address God liturgically as *'abbi* ('my father'), but would not use the familiar *'abba*.[2] But the use by Jesus of the intimate *'abba* (Mark 14.36; cf. Luke 11.2, RV) left such an indelible impression on the minds of his disciples that it even survived translation into Greek (Rom. 8.15; Gal. 4.6). Though the Gospels are reticent upon the subject of the inner life of Jesus, they leave us in no doubt about his consciousness of his own special relation to the Father. The use of *'abba* makes it difficult to deny that Jesus thought of himself as uniquely God's Son or to suppose that the Church derived the idea of his Sonship from any other source than Jesus himself. He is conscious of having been assigned a special mission and task by God; he conceives of his own response in biblical terms, viz. sonship and obedience. Israel had

[1] See H. F. D. Sparks, 'The Doctrine of the Divine Fatherhood in the Gospels' in *Studies in the Gospels*, ed. D. E. Nineham, 241-62.

[2] See G. Kittel in *TWNT*, I, 4ff.

been disobedient to the vocation of sonship: Christ becomes the sole Israel of God by virtue of his unique obedience—'not what I will, but what thou wilt' (Mark 14.36). He is therefore uniquely the Son of God.

It is as the New Israel that Jesus is to be understood as Son of God, not in any Hellenistic sense of θεῖοι ἄνδρες. It was Jesus himself who first thought of himself in this way; it was he who first related the experience of his baptism and of his temptation in the Wilderness and taught their meaning to his disciples. Both are expositions of what it means to say that Jesus is Son of God. The beloved Son in whom God is well pleased (Mark 1.11; cf. Matt. 3.17; Luke 3.22) is presented not only in terms of Ps. 2.7 but also of Isa. 42.1: 'Behold, my servant whom I uphold, my chosen in whom my soul delighteth.'[1] Jesus clearly conceived his Sonship as the perfect obedience of the Servant of the Lord. The reiterated 'If thou art the Son of God' in the Temptation Story (Matt. 4.3, 6; Luke 4.3, 9) emphasizes the fact that the Sonship of Christ is the same thing as the obedience of the Servant. The very shape of the Gospel narrative brings out the meaning of Christ's Sonship as the obedience of the New Israel. As Israel of old, the 'son' whom God called out of Egypt, was baptized in the Red Sea and tempted in the Wilderness, so also God's Son the Messiah is baptized and tempted; Matthew's quotation of Hos. 11.1 (Matt. 2.15) contains profound theological truth, whatever we may think of the historicity of the Flight into Egypt (Matt. 2.13-15). A new Israel is called out of 'Egypt' in order that a new and better covenant may be made, and one which will not be invalidated by inability on the human side to fulfil the essential condition of obedience. Throughout the ministry of Jesus his Sonship is recognized (in St Mark's telling) only by the demons with their supernatural insight (Mark 3.11; 5.7), but it is affirmed in the presence of the three chosen witnesses by the voice from the cloud at the Transfiguration, 'This is my beloved Son' (Mark 9.7), in the very words which Jesus later uses in his parable of the Wicked Husbandmen, ὁ υἱός μου ὁ ἀγαπητός (Mark 12.6). The old Israel is rejected and is no longer God's beloved 'son'; the final act of disobedience is the killing of him of whom it might surely have been said, 'They will reverence my son' (Mark 12.6). In two synoptic passages which record the teaching of Jesus, he speaks of himself as the Son of God. There is the 'Q' saying of Matt. 11.27=Luke 10.22 ('no one knoweth the Son save the Father'), which, as we have already seen,[2] is a characteristically Hebraic affirma-

---

[1] The reference of Mark 1.11 to Isa. 42.1 rests upon a non-LXX translation in which for παῖς we have υἱός and for ἐκλεκτός we have ἀγαπητός; see C. H. Dodd, *Acc. Scrip.*, 89; O. Cullmann, *Baptism in the New Testament*, ET, 1950, 16-18.
[2] *Supra*, 43f.

tion that the true knowledge of God is possessed only by the Son of God, because knowledge comes by obedience and only the Son renders perfect obedience to the Father. There is also Mark 13.32, 'Of that day or that hour knoweth no one, not even the angels in heaven, neither the Son but the Father'—one of Schmiedel's 'pillar' passages, since no one would have put such a confession of ignorance into the mouth of Jesus.[1] The absolute use of 'the Son' in a passage which is certainly not a literary production of 'the Hellenistic community' is evidence that Jesus used the term of himself. It is not improbable that he should have done so, if he thought of himself as in any sense the Lord's Anointed, because such slight evidence as exists points to the fact that 'Son of God' was a Messianic title in his day; cf. Mark 14.61, 'Art thou the Christ, the Son of the Blessed?' and Matt. 16.16, 'Thou art the Christ, the Son of the living God.' Apart from the NT itself the earliest evidence is II (4) Esd. 7.28f. (where 'my son, the Messiah' may not be original), 13.32, 37, 52; 14.9; but the work belongs to the latter part of the first century A.D.[2]

It is in doctrinal passages that St Paul uses the expression 'Son' or 'Son of God', and it has been remarked that from these passages a full credal statement could be constructed. The Gospel concerns God's Son (Rom. 1.3f., 9), and this is what Paul had preached (II Cor. 1.19); God had sent forth his Son, born of a Jewish woman, that we might become God's adopted sons (Gal. 4.4f.); though he was the object of his love (Col. 1.13), God had not spared him (Rom. 8.32), in order that we might be reconciled through him (Rom. 5.10) and be conformed to his image (Rom. 8.29), until we attain to the unity of the faith through the knowledge of the Son (Eph. 4.13). In the fellowship of God's Son (I Cor. 1.9) we await his parousia (I Thess. 1.10) and the day when all things have been subjected to the Son and the Son himself is subjected, that God may be all in all (I Cor. 15.28). Here is the *kerugma* of apostolic Christianity presented with the help of a term which, though familiar to Gentiles in the context of popular Hellenistic religious beliefs, has been made to serve as an instrument of missionary instruction.

In Ep. Heb. the expression 'Son' or 'Son of God' occurs some twelve times—four times as frequently as κύριος titles, in contradistinction from Pauline usage. The biblical emphasis upon Sonship as obedience is strong. The Christology of Hebrews is erected upon Ps. 2.7 (cf. Heb. 1.5; 5.5), and the whole work is an exhortation to 'hold fast our confession, Jesus the Son of God' (4.14). As Son of God the place of

[1] Cf. P. W. Schmiedel's article 'Gospels', *Enc. Bib.* II, col. 1881: 'Absolutely credible passages' . . . 'the foundation pillars for a truly scientific life of Jesus.'

[2] Cf. Strack-Bill., III, 15-22.

Jesus is higher than that of Moses or the angels, yet this Sonship is not anything possessed by him as over against God, but is the expression of utter obedience to the divine will: 'though he was Son, yet he learned obedience by the things which he suffered; and having been made perfect, he became unto all them that obey him the effective instrument of salvation in the (new) Age' (5.8f.; cf. 2.9f.; Phil. 2.8, 'obedient unto death').

In the Fourth Gospel the biblical character of Sonship as obedience is strongly in evidence. The category of 'Son of God' is one by which the evangelist obviously sets great store; the whole Gospel, he tells us, was written in order that it might be believed that Jesus is the Christ, the Son of God (John 20.31; cf. 11.27). The deepest theological teaching of the book is expressed in terms of the Father-Son relationship. In his mission of bringing life and judgment the Son is in complete unity with the Father, and the meaning of Christ's person and work is set forth in terms of the divine Sonship. Sonship connotes the perfect unity of Christ with the Father which is established upon the basis of the perfect obedience of the Son, whose meat and drink is to do the Father's will (John 4.34): 'I do always the things that are pleasing to him' (8.29; cf. 10.36-38): 'I seek not mine own will, but the will of him that sent me' (5.30; cf. 6.38; 17.4). The Johannine conception of Sonship is biblical in a way which has nothing in common with pagan myths about 'sons of God'.

The peculiarly Johannine expression ὁ μονογενὴς υἱός is used of Christ in the NT only at John 1.14, 18; 3.16, 18; I John 4.9 (the expression is found in a non-theological sense in Luke 7.12; 8.42; 9.38; also, of Isaac, in Heb. 11.17). It is a synonym for the Synoptic ἀγαπητός (Mark 1.11; Matt. 3.17; Luke 3.22, and Mark 9.7; cf. 12.6), as both μονογενής and ἀγαπητός are used in LXX to translate the same Hebrew word meaning 'only'. The fact that ἀγαπητός is used of Abraham's only son is doubtless the reason why it is applied to Christ, the Lamb of God (LXX, Gen. 22.2, 12; John 1.29, 36), and also why it is prominent in the Synoptic narratives of the baptism of Jesus,[1] where it will bear the meaning of 'my only son'.[2] Similarly for John μονογενής will mean 'beloved', for he lays particular stress upon the truth that 'the Father loveth the Son' (John 3.35; 5.20; 10.17; 15.9; 17.23-26). But he emphasizes that Christ's Sonship is unique by reason of his unique relation to the Father, whereas we are sons by the ἐξουσία which Christ gives to us

---

[1] See *infra*, 180.

[2] Cf. C. H. Turner, *JTS*, Vol. XXVII, 1926, 113ff. On ἀγαπητός as a distinct title, 'the Beloved', e.g. Eph. 1.6; *Ep. Barn.* 3.6; 4.3, 8; cf. Col. 1.13, see J. Armitage Robinson, *St Paul's Epistle to the Ephesians*, 1903, Additional Note, 229: ' "The Beloved" as a Messianic Title.'

(John 1.12). In the Greek versions of the OT ὁ ἀγαπητός is used as a designation of Israel (cf. ὁ ἐκλεκτός) and also of the Servant of the Lord (Isa. 42.1, quoted explicitly in Matt. 12.18); the implications for the NT conception of Christ as himself the New Israel are obvious.

'THE LORD'

In secular Greek κύριος might be simply an indication of respect ('Sir'), or it might mean the 'master' or 'owner' of workmen, slaves, etc. There are several examples of such secular use in the Gospels, e.g. Matt. 21.30; 27.63; Mark 7.28 (what shall we say of 11.3?); Luke 16.3-8; John 20.15 (cf. with v. 13). Κύριος would be a natural equivalent of *rabbi* or διδάσκαλος. But throughout the Hellenistic world κύριος was used also in a religious sense to denote the divinities of the mystery-cults (cf. I Cor. 8.5f., θεοὶ πολλοὶ καὶ κύριοι πολλοί) and, of course, it had become a title for the divine emperor or even for a petty tyrant like Herod. Before the close of the first century the emperor was accorded the official title, *Dominus et Deus noster*. In the course of an excellent summary of the *data*, V. Taylor[1] quotes A. Deissmann: 'It may be said with certainty that at the time when Christianity originated "Lord" was a divine predicate intelligible to the whole Eastern world.'[2] The word was thus universally available to the preachers of the Gentile mission, whose main task would be to make their converts see why it was that for Christians there was only one Lord, Jesus Christ (I Cor. 8.6). Throughout Acts, Paul and the NT generally[3] there is abundant evidence of the widespread use of Κύριος in the first-century Church: it is used by itself or in combinations with 'Jesus' and 'Christ'—'our Lord', 'the Lord Jesus', 'our Lord Jesus Christ', 'Christ Jesus our Lord', 'the Lord Christ', etc. We must conclude that in both liturgy and catechesis the word was in universal use. For Greek-speaking Christians a mysterious depth of meaning must have been added by the fact that Κύριος was the word used to represent Yahweh and Adonai in the LXX.

Nevertheless we must not suppose (with W. Bousset) that Κύριος as a title for Jesus originated in the Gentile Church, e.g. at Antioch. Decisive evidence to the contrary is supplied by I Cor. 16.22, where Paul inserts the Aramaic liturgical formula, *Maran atha*, 'the Lord cometh'—the formula which is presumably translated in Rev. 22.20 as Ἀμήν, ἔρχου, Κύριε. This verse alone is sufficient to prove that the title 'Lord' was not an invention of the Hellenistic community. Possibly also the phrase

---

[1] *The Names of Jesus*, 40.

[2] *Light from the Ancient East* (ET, 2nd ed., revised, 1927), 350.

[3] The only books in which κύριος is not found are Titus and the Johannine epistles; for details and statistics see V. Taylor, *op. cit.*, 41-5.

῎Οντως ἠγέρθη ὁ Κύριος (Luke 24.34) is another such Aramaic liturgical formula. The Aramaic *Mar* (lord) can be used only with a pronominal suffix, as in such forms as *Mari* (my lord), *Maran* (our lord); it may be conjectured from the Talmuds that a rabbi could be greeted respectfully as *Mari*.[1] Thus, even if we were to conclude that Jesus was addressed by his disciples as *Mari*, it would not necessarily mean that the title was being used in its developed Christological sense. It is only Luke among the Synoptists who suggests that Κύριος was in regular use during the ministry of Jesus (cf. his frequent, 'And the Lord said . . .'). On the other hand, Jesus was understood by his disciples to have quoted Ps. 110.1 in relation to himself and to have spoken of the Messiah as 'Lord' (Mark 12.35-37); and this *testimonium* exercised a considerable influence upon the development of the Christology of the early Church.[2] Moreover, the Gospels record that Jesus taught his disciples that there existed a κύριος-δοῦλος relationship between himself and them (Matt. 10.24f.; Luke 17.5-10; John 13.13f.; 15.15, 20), so that during the days of his ministry they had come to look upon him as their Lord. Nevertheless the true meaning of the Lordship of Christ could not have fully come home to them until after the resurrection, for it was by this event that they came to know assuredly that God had made him both Κύριος and Χριστός, this Jesus who was crucified (Acts 2.36). Even so, this does not mean that their faith in Christ's Lordship was not grounded upon their actual dealings with him in the days of his flesh, as he exercised his Lordship over their lives, when he had chosen them and they had responded, when he led and they followed, commanded and they obeyed. Had they not witnessed his Lordship over evil spirits and noted his authority over men and over multitudes? There is no reason to deny that the apostolic testimony to the Lordship of Christ is based upon an historical reality, upon the actual historical experience of the apostles who had surrendered their lives to his obedience and found in him their Lord. Apart from such an historical reality it is difficult to see how the Lordship of Christ became in the early Church the central —perhaps for a time the sole—article of the confession of faith. The earliest baptismal creed may have been the simple formula 'Jesus is Lord' (cf. Rom. 10.9; I Cor. 12.3; Phil. 2.11).[3] Even if *Maran* and Κύριος are a purely post-resurrection usage, they are based upon the experienced Lordship of the Jesus of history.

---

[1] See A. E. J. Rawlinson, *The New Testament Doctrine of the Christ*, Bampton Lectures for 1926, Appended Note I, 231-7; also pp. 37 and 76-9 of the text.

[2] Cf. C. H. Dodd, *Acc. Scrip.*, 34f.

[3] Cf. O. Cullmann, *The Earliest Christian Confessions*, ET, 1949, 41 and 55-62.

THE WISDOM OF GOD

None of the titles thus far considered (Messiah, Son of Man, Son of God, Lord) necessarily implies the pre-existence of Christ, if we reject the view that Jesus's conception of the Son of Man is 'Enochian' in character. But as soon as the Church found itself worshipping Jesus Christ as Son of God and Lord, the recognition of his pre-existence must have followed immediately. If Christ were one with God, if he were himself divine, he could not have had an origin in time; the Son of God could have undergone a human birth and lived a human life, but he could not have begun to exist only at a particular moment during the reign of Herod the Great. His message, his person and his work alike compelled belief in his pre-existence. He could not be what the Christian experience of salvation declared him to be, if he had not as God *chosen* to become man; and the Christian Gospel would lose its originality, wonder and meaning if the divine Son did not voluntarily choose to take the form of a slave and become obedient even to death by crucifixion (Phil. 2.5-8; II Cor. 8.9). 'Unlike us, he *chose* the oblivion of birth and the humiliation of life. He consented not only to die but to be born. . . . His sacrifice began before he came into the world, and his cross was that of a lamb slain before the world's foundation' (Rev. 13.8; cf. I Pet. 1.19f.).[1]

It would not be difficult for those brought up under rabbinic Judaism to think of something as pre-existent; such a conception was only a poetic way of emphasizing the religious importance of the thing; and the Torah, the Temple and the Messiah were already thought of in this manner.[2] There was, however, one pre-existent reality which was taken very seriously, namely, the Wisdom of God; and to identify something with the pre-existent Wisdom was to attribute to it the highest possible divine reality under God himself. It was by NT times a rabbinic commonplace that the Torah was identical with the Wisdom of God, and therefore all the things which the Wisdom writers had said about Wisdom were applicable to the Law itself. Hence, for NT writers like Paul and John, to identify Christ with the Wisdom of God was to make the highest possible claim for Christ, since no higher category than the pre-existent Wisdom was known to rabbinic Judaism. It meant that Christ had superseded Torah as the source of righteousness, sanctification and redemption, as Paul declares in I Cor. 1.30; or, as St John puts it, Christ and not Torah is the $\pi\lambda\acute{\eta}\rho\omega\mu\alpha$ of all grace: 'Torah was given by Moses, but grace and reality came by Jesus Christ' (John 1.16f.;

[1] The quotation is from P. T. Forsyth, *Person and Place of Jesus Christ*, 1909; sixth ed., 1948, 271.
[2] See W. D. Davies, *PRJ*, 162; W. L. Knox, *St Paul and the Church of the Gentiles*, 1939, 112f.

cf. 1.14). The πλήρωμα χάριτος καὶ ἀληθείας is not the Law of Moses as rabbinic Judaism taught, but Jesus Christ.

It was natural that the apostolic Church should have used the σοφία-λόγος conception as its highest category of interpretation of the person of Christ. The primitive Church drew its categories not from Hellenistic religious speculation, but from the Scriptures of the OT, as these were understood by rabbinic Judaism; the latter itself had been considerably influenced by its contact with Hellenistic thought, and the Pauline-Johannine σοφία-λόγος teaching is a characteristic example of Christianized rabbinic theology of the Hellenistic period, i.e. of the thought of Palestinian Judaism made captive to the obedience of Christ (II Cor. 10.5). The development of the Wisdom Christology in the OT, which prepared the categories of thought by means of which the apostolic doctrine of the person of Jesus Christ received its fullest expression in the NT, is a familiar story and may be briefly summarized as follows.

The earliest personification of Wisdom (ḥokmah, σοφία) which is found in the Wisdom Literature occurs in Job 28.12-27, where it amounts to little more than a poetic emphasis upon the divine quality of wisdom in the operation of the universe and the conduct of human life. But in Prov. 8.22-31 Wisdom is personified and hypostatized as God's instrument and architect ('master-workman', LXX: ἁρμόζουσα, from ἁρμόζω, 'I fit together', especially of a joiner's work) in the creation and also as delighting in the habitable earth (οἰκουμένη) and bringing life and salvation to mankind. In Ecclus. 24.1-34 this conception is elaborated, and it is said that he who created Wisdom before the beginning of the world made her tabernacle to rest in Israel and established her in Zion (vv. 8-10). In v. 23 is found the evidence that by the beginning of the second century B.C. Wisdom had already been identified with Torah, 'the law which Moses commanded us for a heritage'. Henceforward it became a commonplace of rabbinic Judaism that Wisdom and Torah were one and the same, and therefore Torah was the pre-existent instrument of creation, without which nothing was made that was made; indeed, all that was made was created for the sake of the Torah.[1] To the above passages should be added Wisd. 7.15-8.1, where Wisdom is called the 'artificer of all things' (πάντων τεχνῖτις) (7.22), 'an effulgence from everlasting light' (ἀπαύγασμά ἐστιν φωτὸς ἀιδίου) (7.26). Wisdom, moreover, has also her part to play in the sphere of salvation: 'From generation to generation passing into holy souls she maketh men friends of God and prophets' (7.27).

---

[1] For the rabbinic teaching concerning Wisdom and Torah see W. D. Davies, *PRJ*, chap. 7; C. H. Dodd, *IFG*, 75-86.

Thus, by the first century A.D. Judaism had developed a doctrine of Wisdom which had much in common with the Stoic conception of the λόγος, or immanent reason of things. The Jewish doctrine had arisen after Yahweh had come to be thought of in post-exilic Judaism as the utterly transcendent, holy and all-powerful Creator of the universe, and it served the necessary purpose of supplying Judaism with a doctrine of the divine immanence, albeit expressed in a poetical rather than a metaphysical way. As a doctrine it was invaluable because on the one hand it gave expression to the Jewish conviction that morality was of cosmic significance at a time when the concept of divine transcendence might have led to the belief that God was beyond good and evil (cf. Ps. 73.11; Job 22.12f.), and on the other hand it rendered unnecessary such extravagances concerning aeons and emanations, intermediaries and 'light-beings', as were spawned in profusion by Hellenistic religious teachers in their efforts to fill the gap between this world and the divine realm. Thus, while the Wisdom-conception of rabbinic Judaism had nothing in common with Gnostic mythologies concerning emanations (even if one of these might be called Σοφία), it could easily have been understood by a philosophical 'God-fearer' as a poetic description of the part played by the immanent Reason (λόγος) of the Stoic world-view: 'Unique yet many-sided, rarified yet mobile, clear in expression, unpolluted, distinct, unharmed, loving what is good, penetrating, unimpeded, beneficent, philanthropic, reliable, regular, unanxious, omnipotent and all-seeing, piercing even through the most highly intelligible of spirits, most subtle, more volatile than motion itself, Wisdom pervades and penetrates all things by reason of her pureness' (Wisd. 7.22-24). Jewish σοφία and Stoic λόγος obviously had much in common, and they met one another in the Judaism of the Dispersion. How far the author of the Book of Wisdom (*c.* 50 B.C.) is indebted to Greek thought it is not our purpose to investigate, but it is clear that an educated Jew of Alexandria could hardly remain uninfluenced by Greek philosophical ideas. And we must not imagine that Hellenistic and Palestinian Judaism were completely separate and distinct from each other; on the contrary, they met continually, and the rabbis of Palestine had every opportunity of learning about the Stoic or Philonian Logos. There was much coming and going; a Greek-speaking student from, say, Tarsus would come and study in Jerusalem under a teacher like Gamaliel, and the traffic in ideas would not be entirely one-way.[1]

[1] Cf. D. Daube, *The New Testament and Rabbinic Judaism* (1956), ix: 'The sharp distinction between a Hellenistic and a Rabbinic Judaism in the NT period is being abandoned as it is found that many Hellenistic ideas had crept into, or been consciously taken over by, Rabbinism long before, and that the process, though slowed down, was not halted.' Cf. also p. 86.

Thus it happened that the Church's teachers had a convenient scriptural and rabbinic conception ready to hand when they needed to articulate the doctrine of the pre-existent divinity of Christ. It is interesting to note that it is not the NT figures whom scholars have associated with Alexandria, viz. Stephen (Acts 7.1-53) and the writer to the Hebrews, who identify Christ with the σοφία Θεοῦ. The word σοφία does not occur in Ep. Heb., although its author is generally agreed to have been a Hellenistic Jew. It is Paul and the Fourth Evangelist, both trained in Palestinian rabbinism, who make use of the category of the σοφία Θεοῦ. In one place St Paul explicitly states that Christ is the power of God and the Wisdom of God (I Cor. 1.24), i.e. he is God in action, the σοφία Θεοῦ of the Wisdom writers, what one of the latter called 'a breath (vapour, ἀτμίς) of the δύναμις Θεοῦ' (Wisd. 7.25). Paul is anxious to explain that he is not talking about any mythological Gnostic σοφία; he is not concerned with any such worldly wisdom, any Hellenistic speculation: such wisdom of men is foolishness with God. The 'word of the cross' has demonstrated the foolishness of worldly wisdom, and Christ has been revealed as the σοφία Θεοῦ (I Cor. 1.18-31). Christ Jesus was made unto us Wisdom from God, and therefore righteousness and sanctification and redemption (1.30). In all this Paul's interest is not at all metaphysical or speculative; his concern is rather to convince the Corinthians that now that the true σοφία Θεοῦ has come, they need no longer puzzle their minds with problems raised by mythology and speculation, the 'wisdom of this world'. In Colossians he finds it necessary to speak much more strongly about Gnostic speculations, and he uses the language of the Wisdom literature to put an end to it. He is aiming, perhaps unconsciously, at letting the Wisdom theology drive out from the Gentile churches all such speculations and fantasies, as it had already excluded them from the Judaism in which he had been brought up. Christ is 'the image of the invisible God, the firstborn of all creation; for in him were all things created . . . all things have been created through him and unto him' (Col. 1.15-17). The language is that of the passages of the Wisdom literature which we have quoted above, and it is significant that Paul in one of his two great affirmations of the pre-existence of Christ (the other is Phil. 2.5-11) should have used it so readily and so naturally, without quoting precisely, but none the less clearly indicating that this was the language which had become the vehicle of his thinking. The πλήρωμα of the Godhead dwelt in Christ, as formerly the Wisdom writers had conceived it to dwell in Wisdom; it dwelt in Christ σωματικῶς, 'in bodily form' (Col. 2.9). Whereas formerly Wisdom had taken up her abode in Israel and had tabernacled there (Ecclus. 24.8), so now σοφία was embodied in Christ, who was corporately the true Israel of God (Gal. 6.16). In Christ all the treasures of σοφία are hidden (Col. 2.3).

THE WORD OF GOD

St John is the only NT writer to describe Christ as the Word of God (λόγος Θεοῦ), and even in John the description is found explicitly only in the preface to the Gospel, or 'Prologue' as John 1.1-18 is often called. The tendency of much recent criticism of the Fourth Gospel to regard the Prologue as a Hellenization of the *kerugma*, or at least as an attempt to commend the gospel to philosophical pagans of the Hellenistic world, has had two unfortunate results: first, to obscure the unity and the biblical character of the Johannine σοφία-λόγος teaching; and secondly, to lead to the widespread assumption of (at least) two Johns of widely differing mentality. These two results are, of course, intimately connected. The mysterious unity of 'Johannine' thought is obscured by the supposition that there are two Johns—one a Hellenizing, philosophically-minded Jew, who disliked apocalyptic and millenarian notions and was desirous of setting forth the Christian gospel in a form acceptable to the 'higher pagans'; the other, the author of Revelation, a fanatically apocalypticist Jew, who could hardly even write the Greek language, and who indulged in millenarian fantasies of a Jewish kind, giving them a Christian veneer. With the literary problem we are not here concerned: there may have been a whole school of different 'Johns' behind the Johannine literature of the NT. We are, however, concerned to point out that there is a certain unity of theological outlook in that literature, and that this is decidedly true of the doctrine of the Word of God.[1] When we use the word 'John' we mean the common mind behind the Johannine literature, and we make no assumptions about whether it was that of an individual (the son of Zebedee, John of Ephesus, etc.) or of a school of teachers.

In the New Testament generally λόγος (when used technically) means the message or good news—either that proclaimed by Jesus (e.g. Mark 2.2; 4.14; Matt. 13.19; Luke 5.1; 8.11) or that preached by the apostles concerning Christ (e.g. Acts 6.2; 13.5; I Cor. 1.18; II Tim. 2.9; Rev. 1.9). Since Christ is himself the word or message preached by the Church, it is but a short step to the Johannine identification of Christ with the Word of God as such, a conception which the New Testament inherits from OT theology. The Word (Heb. *dabhar*) was (like Wisdom or Spirit) in the OT theology one of the ways of speaking of the creative activity of God; God created the world by his Word.

---

[1] Cf. E. Stauffer, *New Testament Theology*, 39-43, 58; Austin Farrer, *A Rebirth of Images*, 1949, chap. I.

Originally this statement does not involve the hypostatization of 'word' and there is no need to use a capital letter: God created the world simply by speaking: 'God said, Let there be . . . and there was' (Gen. 1.3, 6f., 9, 14, 20, 24—the 'six words' of Creation). No more striking or less anthropomorphic way of describing God's sovereign power of creation could be imagined; the conception of God making things with his hands is utterly transcended; he needs only to utter his will and it is done: 'he commanded and they were created' (Ps. 148.5; cf. Ps. 147.15-19; also Ps. 107.20; Isa. 55.11). 'By the word of Yahweh were the heavens made, and all the host of them by the breath of his mouth. . . . For he spake, and it was done; he commanded, and it stood fast' (Ps. 33.6, 9). But not only is the Word of the LORD thus active in the creation and providential ordering of the world; it is also the means by which God makes known his saving will to Israel: 'The word of the LORD came unto . . .'[1] Thus, λόγος Θεοῦ, like σοφία Θεοῦ, had become in Judaism a way of speaking about God's activity in creation, providence, revelation and redemption. Rabbinic Judaism had no need for two such conceptions, yet, since both were found in the Scriptures, neither could be abandoned. The obvious identification of λόγος with σοφία had taken place long before NT times, and indeed it had been made by the Wisdom writers themselves: 'I came forth from the mouth of the Most High' (Ecclus. 24.3); 'she is a breath of the power of God' (Wisd. 7.25); 'the LORD giveth Wisdom; out of his mouth cometh knowledge and understanding' (Prov. 2.6). To say that Yahweh created heaven and earth by 'the breath of of his mouth' (i.e. word) (Ps. 33.6) means that the creative Wisdom is itself the Word of God.

We can only conjecture why St John avoids σοφία and chooses λόγος, though we may be emphatic that the λόγος of his prologue is both the λόγος Θεοῦ and the σοφία Θεοῦ of the OT Scriptures. Probably he eschews σοφία because of the misuse of that term in the Hellenistic world: he does not wish it to be thought that Christ and his gospel are just one more competing human σοφία of the type against which St Paul finds it necessary to warn his converts. The word σοφία (or for that matter σοφός) never occurs in the Johannine writings, except in the doxologies of Rev. 5.12 and 7.12 (which may be quotations from a Christian hymn or even ultimately from a hymn to the 'divine' Emperor) and in the problematical Rev. 13.18 and 17.9. Similarly the writer to the Hebrews avoids the word, although he is not averse to using Greek

---

[1] In the prophetical books λόγος is invariably used in LXX to translate the familiar phrase 'The word of the LORD came'; but in the historical books λόγος and ῥῆμα are used indiscriminately. Perhaps it is significant that at Luke 3.2, 'the word of the Lord came unto John', ῥῆμα is used; St Luke may have refrained from using λόγος because it had become a Christian *terminus technicus*.

philosophical conceptions in his interpretation of Christ's person and work, and although he unquestionably thinks of Christ in terms of the Wisdom of God: the language of Heb. 1.1-3 is decisive, with its distinct reminiscences of Wisd. 7.26. Even St Paul uses the language of the σοφία Θεοῦ sparingly, although it is the key-conception of his Christology. We might well ask how it is that St Paul does not use the concept of the λόγος Θεοῦ, in view of the fact that he had thought out the doctrine of the new creation in Christ. We can but guess. Perhaps Apollos had warned him about Philo's speculative attempt to reconcile Moses and Plato by means of his doctrine of the λόγος as the divine principle of reason about which the Scriptures spoke, when interpreted by the right allegories! Perhaps he avoided the term for the same reason that John avoids σοφία, namely because of its Gnostic associations. But the fact that John uses λόγος does not mean that he had ever heard of Philo; and attempts to exhibit verbal parallels merely serve to emphasize that all the *close* parallels to the Johannine usage are to be found in the OT. It is *possible* that John chose the word λόγος for apologetic reasons; it would be comprehensible to the intellectuals of the Hellenistic world, and rabbinic Judaism itself had been influenced by and had exercised influence upon Stoic thought in several directions. But nothing is said in St John about the λόγος Θεοῦ, or indeed about any point of Christology, which requires elucidation in Greek categories; there is no need to look beyond OT and rabbinic materials in the interpretation of any of the Johannine writings, which are Palestinian-Hebraic through and through.[1]

St John follows the rabbinic line of thought: λόγος—σοφία—Torah. In the beginning was the Word, the instrument of God's activity in the creation of the world (John 1.1; Gen. 1.1ff.; Ps. 33.6, etc.). The operation of the Word is described in the Prologue in terms which recall the language used by the Wisdom writers to express the part of σοφία in the creation and providential ordering of the world.[2] The conception reappears in Rev. 3.14, where Christ is called ἡ ἀρχὴ τῆς κτίσεως τοῦ Θεοῦ, a title based upon Prov. 8.22 (cf. Col. 1.15, 18, πρωτότοκος

[1] C. H. Dodd has made the most thorough-going attempt to find affinities between the language of the Fourth Gospel and that of Philo and of the *Corpus Hermeticum* and to trace similarities of thought (*IFG*, especially 276f.; also 10-73). He is probably inclined to exaggerate the resemblances and at the same time to overlook the far more striking parallels with Jewish and Jewish-Christian apocalyptic thinking. It is a curious feature of his great book that there are only fifteen references to the Revelation of St John in his index, and ten of these are dealt with on one half-page (231). Note, *per contra*, the affinities between the Fourth Gospel and the Tests. of the XII Patriarchs listed by E. Stauffer, *New Testament Theology*, Appendix II, 334-7. The Qumran discoveries have illustrated the Jewish character of the Fourth Gospel (see W. F. Albright in *The Background of the New Testament and its Eschatology*, ed. W. D. Davies and D. Daube, 153-71; also R. E. Brown in Stendahl, *SNT*, 183-207).

[2] See the list of parallels cited by C. H. Dodd, *IFG*, 274f.

πάσης κτίσεως . . . ὅς ἐστιν ἀρχή), where ἀρχή should be understood as the principle of creation, not, of course, as the first created thing. The designation ἀρχή is used again in Rev. 21.6 and 22.13, verses which stress the Johannine conception of Christ as the first principle and goal of the creation, the beginning and the end (τὸ τέλος). The Prologue of the Gospel stresses the activity of the σοφία-λόγος in the creation of the world, while the Johannine Apocalypse emphasizes that Christ is not only the ἀρχή, but also the τέλος of world-process. It is important that we should not isolate the Prologue from the rest of the Johannine writings, for if we do so, we shall miss the unity of Johannine thought as a whole.

Of course, the startling originality of the Johannine λόγος doctrine, differentiating it from the σοφία teaching of the Wisdom writers (to say nothing of the impersonal λόγος of Philo and the Stoics) is contained in the simple yet astounding assertion that ὁ λόγος σὰρξ ἐγένετο (John 1.14). The pure λόγος of Philo and the Greek philosophers, being divine, could have had no dealings with evil matter, corrupt flesh; and nothing more clearly shews the Hebraic and biblical character of Johannine thought than its insistence upon the *incarnation* of the λόγος, which was not only with God but actually was God (or divine) (John 1.1). The λόγος was *embodied*. Philo and the Stoics could not have conceived this, but, even if they had been able to conceive it abstractly, they could not have known it. Nor could anyone, says St John, had it not been that certain men had actually seen the living λόγος with their eyes, heard him and handled him with their hands, and that others had believed their testimony (I John 1.1-3). (How misleading it is to say, as is often said, that the term λόγος only appears in the full Christological sense in the Prologue to the Gospel; cf. also Rev. 19.13.) The truth about the incarnation of the λόγος is not something that can be known by pure reason, but only by historical encounter (ἐγένετο). The Christian faith is therefore not a philosophy but a *kerugma*.

The context of the declaration concerning the incarnation of the λόγος reminds us of various themes of the Wisdom writers: σοφία pitched her tabernacle in Jacob and found her inheritance in Israel (Ecclus. 24.8). Israel, that is to say, possessed the Torah (i.e. σοφία). But Israel rejected the Torah: the λόγος came to his inheritance (τὰ ἴδια), but his own people (οἱ ἴδιοι) would not receive him (John 1.11). We are reminded of another Wisdom poet, whose song is now incorporated in Enoch 42.1f., who sang of how Wisdom found no dwelling on earth: 'Wisdom found no place where she might dwell; then a dwelling-place was assigned to her in the heavens. Wisdom went forth to make her dwelling among the children of men, and found no dwelling place; Wisdom returned to her place and took her seat among the

angels.' So St John thinks of Christ the Word, rejected on earth, returning to the Father's house in heaven, there to prepare a place for such as
had received him (John 14.2f.). For there had been *some* who had
received him, those who were 'born of God' (i.e. baptized; cf. John 3.3,
5), and who had been given the right to become children of God (i.e.
those who by baptism had become members of the Church, the family
of God) (John 1.12). Behind these thoughts lies the persistent Johannine
theme of the true and the false Israel. There were 'the Jews' who claimed
to possess the Torah, the heavenly Wisdom which, they thought,
tabernacled in Israel; but they were not Abraham's children at all
(John 8.39-44); cf. Rev. 2.9, 'the blasphemy of them which say they are
Jews, and they are not, but a synagogue of Satan' (also Rev. 3.9).
It is in Christ alone, the true Israel, that the σοφία Θεοῦ dwells. The
claims made by the rabbis for Torah were true only of Christ, the
embodied σοφία of God. Torah, said the rabbis, was life in this age and
in the Age to Come; like water, Torah is life for the world. Again,
Torah was the bread which, like manna from heaven, is given by God
to sustain the world; Torah was also wine. The words of the Torah
were life for the world.[1] St John contrasts the truth of Christ with the
claims made for the Torah when he declares that Christ is the Life,
the Living Water, the True Bread, the Vine (cf. also the miracle of
Cana, 2.1-11), and the Light of the world. As he puts it succinctly in the
Prologue, Torah was given through Moses; the reality of grace came
through Jesus Christ (1.17). Many of the statements in the Prologue are
counterparts of the rabbinic theology of Torah, conceived as God's
agent in the creation and governance of the world.[2] But whereas Torah
in this rôle is merely a poetical conception, which was taken only half-
seriously, St John's assertion that the creative λόγος became incarnate
in Jesus Christ for the salvation of the world is not mythical at all and
was not intended as a myth (like Plato's myth of the Demiurge in the
Timaeus): ὁ λόγος σάρξ ἐγένετο. Wisdom, i.e. God himself in action,
became flesh-and-blood, became a piece of human history—for that is
what σάρξ means in this Johannine sense.

The old Wisdom writer had sung of Wisdom as tabernacling in
Israel—

> καὶ ὁ κτίσας με κατέπαυσεν τὴν σκηνήν μου
> καὶ εἶπεν Ἐν Ιακωβ κατασκήνωσον,
> καὶ ἐν Ισραηλ κατακληρονομήθητι, . . .
> ἐν σκηνῇ ἁγίᾳ ἐνώπιον αὐτοῦ ἐλειτούργησα
> καὶ οὕτως ἐν Σιων ἐστηρίχθην.

> (Ecclus. 24.8, 10).

[1] For references see C. H. Dodd, *IFG*, 82-4.   [2] See C. H. Dodd, *IFG*, 85

As we read in Baruch 3.29-37, no one needs to go up to heaven to bring down the commandment (Torah) (cf. Deut. 30.12f.), because Wisdom has appeared on earth and is conversant with men: God has 'given it unto Jacob his servant, and to Israel that is beloved of him'. The metaphor of Wisdom 'tabernacling' in Israel is, of course, based upon the Pentateuchal stories of the Tabernacle in the Wilderness, where the glory of God dwelt amongst men: 'the cloud covered the tent of meeting and the glory of Yahweh filled the tabernacle' (Ex. 40.34-38). God had made his promise to Israel, 'I will set my tabernacle among you . . . and I will walk among you, and will be your God, and ye shall be my people' (Lev. 26.11f.). We thus see the sources of the Johannine conception of the tabernacling of God with men; σκηνοῦν, lit. 'to dwell as in a tent', 'encamp', or (in biblical English) 'tabernacle', which in LXX represents the Hebrew *shakhan*, to dwell (e.g. Judg. 5.17), is found in the NT only in the Fourth Gospel and in Revelation (John 1.14; Rev. 7.15; 12.12; 13.6; 21.3). It is based on the promise of God that he would 'dwell' or 'walk' in Israel (Lev. 26.11f.; Ezek. 37.27; Zech. 2.10; 8.3, 8), a promise which the Wisdom writers had found fulfilled in the tabernacling Wisdom of God and which was understood by the rabbis to mean the tabernacling Torah, the glory of Israel. Thus we understand John 1.14: it was in the person of Jesus Christ that the promise of God was fulfilled; the words of the Wisdom writer (Ecclus. 24.8) were a prophecy of him: 'the λόγος-σοφία became flesh and tabernacled among us (ἐσκήνωσεν ἐν ἡμῖν) and we beheld his glory.' St John insists that the δόξα of God was manifested in Christ to the eyes of his disciples (e.g. John 1.14; 2.11; 17.5), just as the glory of Yahweh filled the Tabernacle of old (Ex. 40.34). The conception of the shekhinah[1] is not far away: the assonance of σκηνοῦν, *shakhan* and *shekhinah* makes the words suggestive of one another. When in Rev. 7.15 St John writes that 'he that sitteth on the throne shall spread his tabernacle over them' (σκηνώσει ἐπ' αὐτούς) he is probably alluding to Isa. 4.5f., where the Pillar of the Exodus suggests the overshadowing of Israel by the shekhinah.

The 'going away' and 'glorification' of Christ do not mean that the divine presence and glory have been withdrawn from the world; Christ is present in the Paraclete (cf. John 14.18), and he is present in the hearts of his faithful disciples (14.23). He is present as the conquering Word proclaimed by the missionary Church; this truth is symbolized by the picture in the Apocalypse of the horseman upon the white horse, who came forth 'conquering and to conquer', and whose name is ὁ λόγος τοῦ Θεοῦ (Rev. 6.2; 19.13).[2] In the final visions of the Apocalypse

[1] See *supra*, p. 65.   [2] See *supra*, p. 27.

the Johannine doctrine of the λόγος is consummated; the λόγος who was the ἀρχή of the first Creation (Rev. 3.14; Prov. 8.22) meets us again as the τέλος (Rev. 21.6; 22.13): he is not only the Alpha, he is also the Omega. He is the agent of the new creation, as he had been the agent of the old creation in the beginning; so now, when the first heaven and the first earth are passed away, and the new heaven and new earth are brought into being, it is he who makes all things new, just as in the old creation there was not made without him anything that was made (Rev. 21.1-7). And the metaphor of the tabernacling presence appears in words which are a loose quotation of Lev. 26.11f.; the voice out of the throne says, 'Behold, the Tabernacle of God (ἡ σκηνὴ τοῦ Θεοῦ) is with men, and he shall tabernacle (σκηνώσει) with them, and they shall be his peoples (λαοί—a very significant plural), and God himself shall be with them (and be their God)' (Rev. 21.3). And still the σοφία-Χριστός gives freely to him that is athirst of the water of life (Rev. 21.6; cf. John 4.10; 7.37; Rev. 22.17). In the Fourth Gospel and in the Apocalypse alike, the Wisdom-Word of God is the controlling theological conception; he takes flesh in Christ and tabernacles with men, in accordance with the ancient promises of the Scriptures; and the goal or τέλος of the whole cosmic process will be the creation of a new heaven and a new earth in which the Word will tabernacle, not with a few disciples chosen out of the world, but with 'the nations' (λαοί). Christ will then be seen to be τέλος as well as ἀρχή, the Omega as well as the Alpha (Rev. 1.8, 17, etc.), the Amen (Rev. 3.14) to the whole long liturgy of world-history. In the meanwhile, however, the judgment of the world is going forward in preparation for that consummation. The judgment inevitably issues from the fact that the light is come into the world (John 3.18f.); meanwhile the sword of the gospel is dividing the nations by their response to the preached Word (Rev. 19.11-16). The apocalyptic picture of the Son of Man coming in judgment, destroying the wicked with 'the breath of his mouth' (a synonym for 'word', cf. Ps. 33.6, etc.), is one which is usually applied to the parousia or the final judgment (cf. II (4) Esd. 13.10f.; II Thess. 2.8); it is ultimately based upon the metaphor of Isa. 11.4, 'With righteousness shall he judge the poor, and reprove with equity for the meek of the earth: and he shall smite the earth with the rod of his mouth, and with the breath of his lips shall he slay the wicked.' The metaphor is a favourite one with St John (cf. Rev. 1.16; 2.12, 16; 19.15, 21) but seems to have been in general use in the early Church (cf. Eph. 6.17; Heb. 4.12; Wisd. 18.16). As a metaphor of the judgment of the world by the Word of God it seems rather startling to us; but it merely illustrates in a vivid way the reality and the finality of judgment by the Word, a theme strongly emphasized by St John (John 3.16-21; 5.22-28; I John 4.17; Rev. 20.12f., etc.). 'The dead shall hear the voice (φωνή) of the Son of God' (John 5.25; cf. 11.43). 'The voice of the Son of God' is another way of speaking about the judgment of the Word. We shall fail to understand the utterly biblical and eschatological character of the Fourth Evangelist's doctrine of Christ as the Word of God, if we ignore the very obvious parallels in the Johannine literature itself.[1]

THE NEW TORAH

In identifying Christ with the creative Wisdom-Word of rabbinic Judaism the NT writers are virtually claiming that he is a new Torah, though they do not explicitly so call him.[2] The archetypal Light, which had come into existence on the first day of creation, was to be found not in the Torah of Moses but shining in the face of Jesus Christ (II Cor. 4.6; cf. Gen. 1.3; Prov. 6.23; Ps. 119.105, etc.). Christ took the place which had been occupied in Judaism by Torah and indeed overflowed it altogether. To have achieved this in the hearts of devout Jews requires an adequate explanation, for such a transformation of the very centre of a living and vigorous religion must have a cause equal to the greatness of the effect. That cause must surely be found in the person of the historical Jesus himself. Indeed, the Gospels indicate that he thought of himself as completing and fulfilling the work of Moses. His authoritative way of handling the Torah of Moses is clear evidence of this. He spoke with authority, not like the scribal interpreters of the old Torah; and his hearers were astonished at what they themselves recognized as καινὴ διδαχή, new Torah (Mark 1.22, 27). 'Ye have heard that it was said to them of old time . . . but I say unto you . . .' (Matt. 5.21f., 27f., 33f., 38f., 43f.). The roots of the Christian doctrine of Christ as the Wisdom of God are planted firmly in the person and words of the historical Jesus. He did not think of himself as setting aside the Mosaic Torah; it was not the Torah but the scribal evasions of it ('the tradition of the elders') which he attacked (Mark 7.13). He calls the Torah 'the word of God' (ὁ λόγος τοῦ Θεοῦ) (Mark 7.13). His own 'new teaching' was designed to correct the accommodations which had had to be made in the Torah because of the hardness of men's hearts (Mark 10.5); he was concerned to restore its original intention and to fulfil it (Matt. 5.17). 'Till heaven and earth pass away, one jot or one

---

[1] Perhaps a note should be added to the effect that it is unlikely that St John's doctrine of the λόγος is a hypostatization of *memra* (Aramaic='word'), frequent in the Targums of the OT as a rabbinic device for avoiding the name of God. The rabbinic *memra* is only a literary devotional usage, not a principle of philosophical explanation. Cf. C. K. Barrett, *GSJ*, 128: '*Memra* is a blind alley in the study of the biblical background of John's logos doctrine.'

[2] See W. D. Davies, *PRJ*, chap. 7, esp. 148-50.

tittle shall in no wise pass away from the Torah' (Matt. 5.18). It is not surprising that his disciples came to look upon him as the expected 'prophet like unto Moses' (Deut. 18.15, 18). When in the Gospels Jesus is referred to as 'a prophet' or 'the prophet', we must understand that Moses, or the new Moses, is usually implied; the word does not mean that Jesus is just one of the series of OT prophets, but that he is specifically the Moses who was to come (cf. Matt. 21.11, 46; Luke 7.16; 13.33; 24.19; John 4.19; 6.14; 7.40; 9.17). Moreover, Jesus himself had given 'signs' to demonstrate this truth to those who had eyes to see (the feeding miracles).

It is St Matthew's Gospel which makes the most thorough attempt to present Jesus's teaching as the new Torah, given by 'the prophet, Jesus, from Nazareth of Galilee' (Matt. 21.11). Though written in Greek, its Judaism is that of the Talmud, not that of Alexandria; it is akin to the rabbinism of Jamnia which came to dominate subsequent Judaism.[1] B. W. Bacon long ago pointed out that Matthew has collected the teaching of the Lord into five 'books' or discourses on the analogy of the Five Books of the Law,[2] viz. Matt. 5–7; 9.36–11.1; 13.1–53; 18.1–19.1; 24–25; each of these five sections ends with the formula, 'It came to pass that when Jesus had made an end of all these sayings,' and therefore the arrangement is probably not accidental.[3] St Matthew, it may be argued, has so arranged the materials of his Gospel as to suggest that the promulgation of the New Law was accompanied by the same signs and wonders as were wrought by Yahweh when he delivered his people from Egypt.[4] St Luke would seem to have adopted a quite different arrangement of the materials, but he also in his own way sets forth Jesus as the deliverer of a new 'Protonomy' and a new Deuteronomy.[5] The fact is that the whole Gospel tradition, as we have already noted, is cast into a Pentateuchal shape, because the Exodus-deliverance of Israel from Egypt was the only pattern of redemption which the NT writers knew.[6] Jesus is the new law-giver, the prophet-deliverer like unto Moses, and the mediator of a new covenant. But he was these things, not because some learned rabbi imagined him, after long and

---

[1] See G. D. Kilpatrick, *The Origins of the Gospel According to St Matthew*, 1946, 106.

[2] *Studies in Matthew*, 1930.

[3] This arrangement into five 'books' is not less significant if we think that the Gospel as a whole is designed in the form of a new Hexateuch (see Austin Farrer in *Studies in the Gospels*, ed. D. E. Nineham, 75-7). The fact that a NT writer thinks of Christ as a new Moses does not at all prevent him from thinking of him also as a new Joshua.

[4] F. W. Green, *St Matthew*, Clarendon Bible, 1936, 5.

[5] See C. F. Evans in *Studies in the Gospels*, 37-53.

[6] See *supra*, 21f.

sustained meditation upon OT theology, but because he was just what he was, the one who compelled his followers to think out the meaning of what he had done and said, in terms which had once been applicable to Moses and the Torah, but which must for ever afterwards be appropriate only to him.

The 'Pentateuchal shape' of all four Gospels is a sufficient answer to all theories about the Hellenization of the faith of the apostolic Church. If we may briefly sum up the course of the development of NT Christology, as we have noted it in this chapter and the one which preceded it, we may observe three stages of its growth. First, there is the appearance of Jesus as 'the Prophet' who startled the Jewish people and their rabbis by claiming authority to perfect and fulfil the Torah of Moses, and by demonstrating through word and sign that the Prophet whom Moses had bidden them to hear had indeed arrived among them. Secondly, there is the Messiah-Servant Christology, which Jesus had taught to his disciples in the later stages of his earthly ministry, and which was based upon the scriptural insight that the Prophet, when he came, would be rejected by those who should have hearkened. And thirdly, there is the developed Wisdom-Word Christology of the apostolic Church, which after the resurrection went on through the illumination of the Holy Spirit to work out the conclusions that had been inevitably involved in the life, teaching, work, death and resurrection of Jesus. This developed apostolic Christology, by identifying Christ with the creative Wisdom-Word of God, had far overflowed the bounds of a Moses-Prophet Christology, though its categories remained not one whit less Jewish. As the writer to the Hebrews clearly saw, a 'new-Moses' Christology was inadequate to express the truth about the Apostle and High Priest of the Christian confession: Moses, after all, was only a servant in the household of Israel, even though he was the greatest of its servants; he had charge over the house only until Christ, the Son and heir, should come. Or, in a different metaphor, Christ was not merely a part of the house, as Moses was; he was the builder of the whole house (Heb. 3.1-6).

8

THE LIFE OF CHRIST

IT is widely recognized nowadays that the Four Gospels do not
supply the materials necessary for the writing of a 'life' of Christ
after the manner of a modern biography. No sooner had the view
that St John's Gospel is 'theological' attained widespread acceptance
than the rise of form-criticism led to a similar conclusion concerning
St Mark's Gospel. The former generation of scholars, as represented,
for example, by F. C. Burkitt's *Gospel History and its Transmission*
(1906), had argued strongly for the reliability of the Marcan outline of
the life of Jesus; but the form-critics, as represented by Karl Ludwig
Schmidt's *Der Rahmen der Geschichte Jesu* (1919), brought forward
reasons for holding that the framework of narrative in which Mark
had set the various *pericopae* that he had found floating loose in the
tradition was only a convenient literary invention of the Evangelist's
and could not be regarded as historical. A position mid-way between
the extremes of Burkitt and K. L. Schmidt was taken up by C. H. Dodd
in a very influential article entitled 'The Framework of the Gospel
Narrative', published in 1932,[1] in which he maintained that a skeleton
outline of the history of Jesus's ministry was preserved in the primitive
Christian tradition and was used by St Mark in the writing of his Gospel. A similar position is adopted by Vincent Taylor in *The Life and
Ministry of Jesus* (1954) and by a number of British and American
scholars.[2]

At the present time a change seems to be taking place in the attitude
of many scholars towards the question of the historical framework of
the Gospel narrative. Whereas it was formerly considered to be essential
that we should be able to construct an outline of the life of Jesus, at
least in principle, today it is being asked whether the matter is of any
real importance for Christians at all. The changed attitude is largely due
to the influence of the late R. H. Lightfoot, who raised the fundamental

---

[1] In the *Expository Times*, June, 1932; reprinted in his book of essays, *New
Testament Studies*, 1953.

[2] D. E. Nineham has submitted Dodd's argument to rigorous criticism in *Studies
in the Gospels* (ed. Nineham, 223-39) and Taylor's arguments to similar scrutiny in
Theology, LIX, No. 429, March, 1956, 97-103.

question of what a Gospel (e.g. St Mark's) really is.[1] The older critics, including the form-critics, never asked this question, because they thought the answer was obvious. To one whose mind is still uncritical of the liberal conception of history as objective and ascertainable by impartial investigation, the validity of a Gospel will depend primarily upon its demonstrable historicity; hence the dismay of the conservative (i.e. 'liberal') mind at the conclusions drawn by many of the colleagues and disciples of Lightfoot concerning the typological and theological character of documents which, not so long ago, were considered valuable in Christian apologetic primarily because they were historically reliable.[2] To those who do not share the liberal outlook it is not a matter of the standing or falling of Christian truth that we should be able to construct, even in principle, an historical outline of the life of Christ. They are not disconcerted to find that St Luke 'the historian' is turning out to be a more elaborately rabbinical typologist even than St Mark or St John! They have come to entertain a rather different conception of the nature of historical testimony or apostolic witness from that which dominated the minds of so many NT scholars from the nineteenth-century pioneers to the late B. H. Streeter on the one hand or the form-critics on the other.

Thus, there is developing today a radical Gospel criticism by the side of which the liberal orthodoxy of the recent past (including that of the form-critics) appears decidedly conservative. Yet, paradoxically enough, it is this contemporary radical criticism which is prepared to take seriously the apostolic witness to those very things which liberal criticism felt itself obliged to explain away out of respect for its conception of 'scientific' history—such things as the Virgin Birth, the miracles, the Messianic consciousness of Jesus, the Transfiguration and even (in extreme cases!) the Resurrection itself. Such matters were, according to the canons of liberal criticism, devotional embroideries, which, if one wished, one might, as a believing Christian, accept, as it were privately, but which had nothing to do with history; a liberal theology was essentially one which dispensed with such legendary accretions and built itself squarely upon the rock of 'objective' historical fact. Thus, the life of Christ in which the Evangelists were interested was not at all the 'life' sought after by those who so diligently pursued

---

[1] The question implicitly underlies, for instance, the whole of Dr Lightfoot's *The Gospel Message of St Mark*, 1950.

[2] For a further consideration of this important problem see the two articles of D. E. Nineham cited in the penultimate footnote above. There is, of course, no reason to suppose that the question (about whether it is in fact possible to reconstruct from the Gospel sources a reliable outline of the life of Jesus) will be settled for a long time to come; all that is being pointed out is that the Christian faith does not depend for its validity upon the changing opinions of scholars on such a matter.

'the quest of the historical Jesus'. The radical criticism of today, however, is prepared to take seriously the apostolic testimony to the action in history of the God of miracle, the living God, who is not bound to reveal himself within the rigid limits which pre-quantum physics and nineteenth-century historical method had prescribed for him. The 'life' of Jesus, the only *historical* life, is the one to which the apostolic testimony bears witness, and there can be no other.

THE BIRTH OF CHRIST

The NT writers are concerned to emphasize the fact that Jesus was a real person, not a docetic apparition or pagan theophany (cf. 'come in the flesh', I John 4.2; II John 7). He was born of a Jewish woman (Gal. 4.4), of a certain family and descent (Rom. 1.3), and belonged to a particular district (Mark 6.1—Mark does not think it necessary to mention its name; but cf. Luke 4.16; John 7.41f.); his mother's name was Mary and his brothers' names were James, Joses, Judas and Simon; the names of his sisters are not recorded (Mark 6.3; cf. 3.31f.). But, while the Gospel writers make it clear that Jesus was a real man like other men, they have no interest whatever in the biographical details; they tell us nothing about his home life, education, appearance, etc.; they see no significance at all in the fact that he was a τέκτων ('craftsman', perhaps 'carpenter', Mark 6.3).[1] Two NT writers, and only two, relate the circumstances of the birth of Jesus (Matt. 1-2; Luke 1-2), but it is not out of biographical interest that they do so. Their purpose is, on the one hand, to stress the actuality of the human birth of Jesus, in opposition to all docetism; and, on the other hand, to affirm his divine origin and eschatological mission.

St Matthew's and St Luke's accounts of the birth of Christ have almost nothing in common except the names of Joseph and Mary and the fact that Jesus was born at Bethlehem. Even on this latter point Matt. says that Joseph and Mary lived at Bethlehem whereas Luke says that Jesus was born there because of the census. Christian tradition conflates the two accounts quite happily, as for instance in the picture of the Magi offering their gifts in a stable. There is, however, one statement which both accounts, despite their many dissimilarities, have in common, viz. that Joseph had not had sexual intercourse with Mary (Matt. 1.18; Luke 1.34) and that Jesus was born without human fatherhood through the Holy Spirit (Matt. 1.18; Luke 1.35).[2] It is most

---

[1] See Alan Richardson, *The Biblical Doctrine of Work*, 1952, 30-2.

[2] There is no probability of textual corruption in Luke 1.34, since the single OL MS *b* can hardly stand against every other authority (see J. M. Creed, *Gospel according to St Luke*, 13f.). St Luke equates the Holy Spirit with the δύναμις of the Most High. In an interesting study of ἐπισκιάζω, 'to overshadow', D. Daube suggests that

important to recognize that both Matt. and Luke state the fact of Christ's birth of a virgin in a straightforward and unargumentative way; they offer no hints as to why it should have happened thus and they draw no conclusions from it. So-called 'theological' objections to the historicity of the Virgin Birth are based upon a reading into the narratives of motives which are not present in them. Thus, E. Brunner objects that the Virgin Birth attempts to explain the primary miracle of the Incarnation by means of a secondary 'biological' miracle, and therefore belief in the Virgin Birth is really a form of little faith.[1] But the Gospel accounts show no desire to 'explain' anything at all; they simply relate an historical happening and leave the matter without any form of explanation: 'Now the birth of Jesus Christ was on this wise' (Matt. 1.18). Brunner also objects that the Virgin Birth is an attempt to defend the sinlessness of Jesus against the doctrine of Original Sin (presumed to infect sexual intercourse). But this is to read later Manichaean notions into the Gospels: it was deemed necessary to assert an immaculate conception for the Virgin Mary herself and also a doctrine of her perpetual virginity. But there is no hint in the Gospels of such notions, which are quite alien to the healthy biblical attitude towards sex.

The truth is that it is very difficult to suggest any motives which prompted the invention of the story of the Virgin Birth, if it is not an historical fact. For instance, it is often said that the Church in its Hellenistic environment would naturally desire to claim a divine birth for Christ, because such a birth was conventionally ascribed to all great men—Hercules, Pythagoras, Plato, and of course, the Emperor; the story of Christ's birth followed the accepted conventions of popular Hellenistic religion. Passing over the fact that the birth stories of Matt. and Luke are as *Jewish* as anything in the NT, it is necessary only to point out one obvious fact in order to dispose of this kind of superficial argument: there is not one single parallel in all Hellenistic religion and mythology to the story of the Virgin Birth of Christ. All the alleged parallels turn out upon examination not to be parallels at all. There is no instance of a *virgin* birth amongst them, since they all fall into the class of legends of a woman's becoming pregnant through intercourse with a divine being—a notion utterly repellent to the biblical mind (cf. Gen.

the Lucan story of the Annunciation points the parallel between Mary and Ruth; cf. Luke 1.38, 'Behold the handmaid of the Lord', with Ruth 3.9, 'I am Ruth thine handmaid: spread therefore thy skirt over thine handmaid. . . .' 'In Rabbinic literature Ruth is celebrated both as representative of the true proselyte and as an ancestress of David and the Messiah. Her life is often interpreted as prefiguring Messianic events, and where this is done, Boaz sometimes stands for God himself' (D. Daube, *The New Testament and Rabbinic Judaism*, 33). This would explain the 'overshadowing' of Mary by the Holy Spirit.

[1] *The Mediator*, ET, 1934, 322-7.

6.1-4). The source of the Gospel birth stories is not Hellenistic mythology.[1]

Equally clearly the story of the Virgin Birth was not invented to fulfil OT prophecies or types. There are stories of miraculous births in the OT (Isaac: Gen. 17.15-22; 18.9-15; 21.1-7; Samson: Judg. 13.2-25; Samuel: I Sam. 1), but again they are not *virgin* births, since in every case there is a human father. Matthew is hard put to it to find a scriptural 'prophecy' of Christ's miraculous birth, and he can find one only because he reads Isa. 7.14 in a Greek Bible, which has παρθένος where the Heb. simply has 'young woman' (Matt. 1.22f.). Of course, there is deep spiritual truth in the likening of Christ's birth to the sign which Isaiah had given to King Ahaz, when the Kings of Israel and Syria were invading his realm—a young woman would conceive and call her child Immanuel, 'God is with us': Christ is a sign from God that the invading powers of evil are about to be defeated. So, too, Matthew adduces other fulfilments of scriptural prophecy—for instance, Micah's foretelling of the coming forth of the Shepherd of Israel from Bethlehem of Judah (Matt. 2.5f.; Micah 5.2). In Herod's massacre of the male children he sees the fulfilment of Jeremiah's prophecy of Rachel weeping in Ramah (Matt. 2.17f.; Jer. 31.15): Christ was to be the fulfilment of the promise of the home-coming of the lost tribes of Israel (cf. John 11.52). In the story of the Flight into Egypt he sees the fulfilment of Hosea 11.1 (Matt. 2.15).[2] In the dwelling at Nazareth he sees the fulfilment of a prophecy that Christ should be called a Nazarene, but what scriptural text he alludes to has never been explained (Matt. 2.23). The Massacre of the Innocents and the Flight into Egypt could be accounted for as legends invented to fulfil OT prophecies, but in the case of the former at least the 'prophecy' is so far-fetched as to make such a theory highly improbable; but the birth at Bethlehem and the dwelling at Nazareth are both corroborated by St Luke and therefore are not to be explained away as Matthaean fulfilments of OT prediction. The story of the Wise Men (Matt. 2.1-12) fulfils no scriptural prophecy; indeed, it seems rather to be itself a prophecy that awaits fulfilment (the in-gathering of the Gentiles). But we must be careful not to let traditional Christian interpretations of the story affect our judgment of it: for instance, tradition has regarded the episode as 'the Manifestation of Christ to the Gentiles', but there is nothing in the story to suggest that Matthew did not intend the Wise Men to be thought of as Jews of the Dispersion. (Nor does he tell us that they were *three* in number!) To preserve a reverent agnosticism concerning the foundation in fact of these richly devotional tales would seem to be the way of wisdom.

[1] See C. K. Barrett, *The Holy Spirit and the Gospel Tradition*, 1947, 6-10.
[2] See *supra*, 150.

The fact that no NT writer other than Matthew and Luke mentions the Virgin Birth of Christ[1] proves nothing more than that it was no part of the original *kerugma*, a truth which is surely sufficiently obvious. At what date the clause about the Virgin Birth of Christ found its way into the baptismal confessions of faith cannot be determined. But its appropriateness in that context would surely have quickly become apparent: Christ was born, as Christians are born, 'not of blood, nor of the will of the flesh, nor of the will of an husband (ἀνήρ), but of God' (John 1.13): at their baptism Christians who confess belief in his name receive the right to become children of God (John 1.12). In baptism they are born 'of the Spirit', and the birth of Christ is the result of the operation of the Spirit. This, indeed, is the chief significance of the Virgin Birth for both Matthew and Luke: it is the sign of the inauguration of the Last Things, the first result of the outpouring of the Holy Spirit in the latter days, when the new creation was being inaugurated in the day of Israel's redemption (Isa. 32.15; Ezek. 36.26f.; 37.14; Ps. 51.10f.; Joel 2.28f.; Zech. 12.10, etc.). The birth of Christ was for mankind what the baptism of a Christian is for the individual, viz. the inauguration of the Last Things, and both are the result of the operation of the Holy Spirit. The Creator-Spirit (Gen. 1.2; Pss. 33.6; 104.30; Wisd. 7.21f., 25; Judith 16.14) is bringing in the new creation; the life-giving Spirit is being breathed into the new humanity (cf. Gen. 2.7; John 20.22). The Spirit, the power of the Most High (Luke 1.35), is the life-giving agent in the birth of the new man, Jesus Christ (cf. I Cor. 15.45). In both Matt.'s and Luke's birth narratives stress is laid upon the inauguration of the New Age. The significance of Matt.'s repeated use of the word γένεσις (1.1; 1.18) should not be overlooked; he is writing a new Book of Genesis, which describes the γένεσις of Jesus Christ, the new Adam, the new creation. His five fulfilments of that 'which was spoken by the Lord through the prophets', discussed in the penultimate paragraph above, emphasize the truth that the things to which the prophets had looked forward are now beginning to come to pass: 'Mary . . . was found with child of the Holy Spirit' (1.18). 'That which is begotten in her is of the Holy Spirit' (1.20). His name is Jesus, Joshua, the Deliverer, who shall lead the New Israel to the Land of Promise.[2]

---

[1] The reading in John 1.13, *qui . . . natus est*, for οἰ . . . ἐγεννήθησαν cannot be regarded as original, though it is found in several Western authorities; but it *could* be held that St John is teaching that the birth of Christians ('of water and the Spirit', John 3.5) is, like the human birth of Jesus, of divine and not human volition; see C. K. Barrett, *GSJ*, 137f.

[2] The name *Jesus* is the Latin form of Ἰησοῦς, which is the Greek transliteration of Joshua (late Heb. and Aramaic, Jeshua); cf. Acts 7.45 and Heb. 4.8. The name was not uncommon amongst Jews (Luke 3.29; Col. 4.11). The Heb. word means 'Yahweh will save' (cf. Matt. 1.21).

St Luke lays great stress upon the part played by the Holy Spirit in all the circumstances attending the birth of Jesus. John the Baptist's birth is miraculous, as Isaac's had been; he is none other than the new Elijah foretold by Malachi (4.5f.; cf. Ecclus. 48.10), and he is 'filled with Holy Spirit from his mother's womb' (Luke 1.15); his mother Elizabeth and his father Zacharias are filled with Holy Spirit (Luke 1.41, 67). At the presentation in the Temple the Holy Spirit is upon Simeon (2.25-27) and presumably (though we are not explicitly told so) upon Anna the prophetess (2.36-38). As in Matt.'s entirely different stories, angels play their part as bearers of divine revelation (Matt. 1.20; 2.13—though the angel appears to Joseph in a dream; Luke 1.11-20; 1.26-37, the Annunciation; 2.9-15, the Shepherds), yet it is not the angels but the Holy Spirit who is the agent of God in the event of Christ's birth. The dawning of the New Age is proclaimed in the three hymns, Mary's *Magnificat* (Luke 1.46-55), Zacharias's *Benedictus* (1.68-79) and Simeon's *Nunc Dimittis* (2.29-32): ἡ ἀνατολὴ ἐξ ὕψους (Luke 1.78; cf. Mal. 4.2)—the new dawn—has already broken; God has 'visited and wrought redemption for his people' (1.68); he has holpen Israel his servant (1.54); and human eyes have actually seen his salvation (2.30). The three hymns are as Jewish as any of the Psalms of the OT, but they are as Christian as anything in the NT in their conviction that the Age of Promise was inaugurated in the hour of Christ's conception by the Holy Spirit.

The doctrine of the Virgin Birth of Christ is an integral part of the theology of the NT. It expresses the truth that God has set in motion the train of events which will culminate in the final judgment of the world and the salvation of his elect; it is as biblical and as Jewish a doctrine as any belief that can be found in the NT. The birth of Christ is an eschatological event ushering in the New Age, and is itself a manifestation of the expected outgoing activity of the Spirit in the latter days. It is a unique event, and there are no parallels to it either in the OT or in the pagan world; St Matthew and St Luke present it in its proper eschatological setting and clearly do not regard it as merely demonstrating that Christ is one of the θεῖοι ἄνδρες of Graeco-oriental religiosity. It is unique because it holds the once-only place reserved for the coming of the Saviour in the divine economy of salvation, of which the OT is the advance proclamation and the NT is the evidence of fulfilment. It is a unique event because Christ is unique and does not fit into any pattern of 'religious geniuses' or 'divine men'; it is an ineradicable element in the total apostolic witness to Christ which has been given through the guidance of the Holy Spirit to the Church. Reluctance on the part of some modern Christians to believe in the Virgin

Birth of Christ has been due to a failure to understand the Bible and the nature of its testimony; ignorance of scriptural meaning always results in failure to perceive the wonderful activity of God (cf. Matt 22.29).

THE BLESSED VIRGIN MARY

When St Luke calls Jesus Mary's firstborn son (τὸν υἱὸν αὐτῆς τὸν πρωτότοκον, 2.7), he doubtless intends it to be understood that Jesus is the eldest of several sons (cf. Luke 8.19f.). Probably (though we cannot be certain, since Luke is such a very subtle theologian) he did not perceive that Christ's brethren, of whom he is πρωτότοκος, i.e. all baptized Christians, are in a true sense sons of Mary, the Second Eve. St Paul had spoken of Christ as the πρωτότοκος among many brethren, but the expression relates to the fatherhood of God (Rom. 8.29); upon the same analogy it would have been possible to speak of Mary as the 'mother' of all Christians, just as Eve was 'the mother of all living' (Gen. 3.20). The NT, however, does not explicitly develop the parallel between Mary and Eve as it does that between Christ and Adam; John 16.21 and I Tim. 2.15 would be very far-fetched references by which to support such a parallel. It may be that a parallel is implied in Rev. 12.1-6 and 13-17, where, in a highly allusive passage, St John describes his vision of the 'woman arrayed with the sun' who gives birth to 'a son, a male child'. The latter is clearly Christ, for he is to 'rule all the nations with a rod of iron' (cf. Ps. 2.9; Rev. 2.27; 19.15). In the symbolism of the vision the 'woman' is probably the Jewish Church, which gives birth to Christ, and becomes the Jewish Christian community; the flight of the woman to the wilderness (vv. 6, 14) may be an allusion to the flight of the Jerusalem Christians to Pella in the desert at the outbreak of the war with Rome in A.D. 66. But there may be a reference to Mary as the mother of the man child (ἄρρην or ἄρσην), as contrasted with Eve, for the reference in 12.17 to the war of the dragon, or *serpent*, against the seed of the woman is an unmistakable allusion to Gen. 3.15. Such double symbolism is frequent in the Apocalypse, and the woman may well represent both the Jewish Church and Eve-Mary, whose seed 'keep the commandments of God and hold the testimony of Jesus'. But it can hardly be said that the parallel between Eve and Mary is clear beyond doubt; we find a hint rather than an assertion of it.

Yet the parallel is real enough. As Christ is 'Adam in reverse' (Phil. 2.6; I Cor. 15.22, 45), so Mary is 'Eve in reverse'. Eve's disobedience is the starting point of the sinful rebellion of the human race against God's holy will; Mary's humble acceptance of the divine will is the starting point of the story of the redemption of the human race from sin: 'And Mary said, Behold the handmaid of the Lord; be it unto me according to thy word' (Luke 1.38). Eve's pride, which generated the fatal ambition to be 'as God' (Gen. 3.5), is contrasted with 'the lowliness of his handmaiden' (Luke 1.48). As Eve was 'sent empty away' from Paradise (Gen. 3.23f.), so Mary is as the hungry who are filled with good things (Luke 1.53). The *Protevangelium* (Gen. 3.15) is fulfilled: the seed of the woman crushes the serpent's head; the Son of Mary delivers from the power of sin the fallen sons of Eve. The sorrow of Eve in conception (Gen. 3.16) is contrasted with the joy of Mary: 'My spirit hath rejoiced in God my Saviour' (Luke 1.47). The child-bearing of women, says the writer of I Tim. 2.15 mysteriously, is a sharing of the redemptive burden; he is speaking of women in general, not of Mary in particular. Yet how truly this insight is relevant to her who was the highly favoured one, or the one endued with grace (Luke 1.28 and RV mg.), in that the one who was born of her was to be called holy, the Son of God (Luke 1.35). Mary's *Magnificat* is her expression of gratitude for her unique privilege in bearing the burden of redemption and of her joy that THE MAN is born into the world (cf. John 16.21). The whole Church has rejoiced with her to sing *Magnificat*; all generations of Christians have called her 'Blessed' (Luke 1.48). How far St Luke himself, who records Mary's song, was aware of all its biblical implications, especially the parallelism with Eve, is a matter insusceptible of definite assertion; but recent scholarship has brought forward good reasons for supposing that he was a theologian of deep and subtle biblical insight, so that we must hesitate to say that he was unmindful of considerations such as these.[1]

Thus, while the NT accords to Mary a position of honour, there is no suggestion that she is to be worshipped or placed alongside Christ as 'co-mediatrix'. Christ is not set forth as a Hellenistic 'divine man',

---

[1] J. M. Creed (*Gospel according to St Luke*, 22f.) thinks that in Luke 1.46 'Elizabeth' should be read for 'Mary' as in some OL texts, since it is hard to see why 'Mary' should have been altered to 'Elizabeth'. Moreover Elizabeth's situation was much more like that of Hannah, on whose song in I Sam. 2.1-10 the *Magnificat* is obviously modelled. The ταπείνωσις (humiliation, not humility) is that of childlessness; cf. I Sam. 1.11, ἐὰν ἐπιβλέπων ἐπιβλέψῃς ἐπὶ τὴν ταπείνωσιν τῆς δούλης σου. . . . Against this view two strong arguments may be adduced. First, all Greek MSS. read καὶ εἶπε Μαριάμ. Secondly, the theological considerations noted above in the text would seem to show that the *Magnificat* holds its place in Luke's narrative precisely because of its significance as *Mary's* song. The alternative view, that it is Elizabeth's song, involves a reversion to the prejudice of a former generation of critics, who tended to think that the Evangelists were rather stupid scissors-and-paste editors, quite capable of including hymns of the Baptist sect in their Gospels without any clear notion of what they were doing. Perhaps Harnack was right in suggesting that the original reading in Luke 1.46 was simply καὶ εἶπεν. This would explain the OL variant as the work of a scribe who had noted the parallel with Hannah's song and was impressed with the Elizabeth story as a fulfilment of prophecy.

and Mary is not a pagan mother-goddess. Her part in the drama of salvation is limited solely to her historical rôle of having borne the Christ. Outside the birth narratives of Matt. and Luke there are only scant references to her in the Gospels: the Synoptists record how 'his mother and brethren' came to seek Jesus during his public ministry (Mark 3.31-35; Matt. 12.46-50; Luke 8.19-21); John represents her as present at the miracle of Cana (John 2.1-5) and also tells us that she was one of the women who stood by the cross at the crucifixion and that Jesus commended her to the care of the Beloved Disciple (19.25-27). There are no other references to her in the Gospels apart from Mark 6.3 (=Matt. 13.55) and the oblique Luke 11.27. Outside the Gospels the only reference is Acts 1.14, where we read that Mary was one of the women who 'continued stedfast in prayer' with the disciples after the Ascension. The attempts of the Apocryphal Gospels to compensate for the almost complete lack of interest of the canonical Evangelists add nothing to our knowledge of the historical Mary. The fact is that no attitude of *hyperdulia*[1] had arisen in the Church in NT times, and the only NT reference to the subject is a word of the Lord which deprecates any excessive veneration for a physical relationship and commends a moral relationship as more blessed: 'A certain woman out of the multitude lifted up her voice, and said unto him, Blessed is the womb that bare thee, and the breasts which thou didst suck. But he said, Yea, rather, blessed are they that hear the word of God, and keep it' (Luke 11.27f.).

THE BAPTISM OF JESUS

In the recent past it has been widely assumed that the significance of the baptism of Jesus by John in the river Jordan lay in the fact that Jesus then underwent a deep religious experience which convinced him of his divine mission and powers. All such psychologizing is entirely repugnant to the outlook of the Synoptic Evangelists, who do not presume to speak about any 'experiences' of Jesus. In their eyes the significance of the baptism is that it represents the anointing of Jesus with the Holy Spirit to the office and work of the Messianic Servant of the Lord. As the kings of Israel were anointed and so became *meshiaḥ Yahweh*, the Lord's Anointed (e.g. I Sam. 16.13; Ps. 89.20; II Kings 9.3); as also at a later time priests were anointed for their sacred office (Ex. 29.7; 40.13-15; Lev. 8.12; Ps. 133.2, etc.); and, above all, as the figure of the Isaianic Prophet was anointed with the Spirit of the Lord (Isa. 11.2; 42.1; 44.3; 61.1), so Jesus, the Messianic Prophet, Priest

---

[1] *Hyperdulia* ('veneration', not a NT word) is distinguished by Roman Catholic theologians from *latria* (cf. λατρεία, John 16.2; Rom. 9.4; 12.1; Heb. 9.1, 6), the supreme adoration which is properly offered to the Godhead alone.

and King, is anointed with the Spirit of the Lord.[1] Even the Fourth
Evangelist, who omits all reference to the baptism of Jesus, nevertheless makes the Baptist bear testimony to the descent of the Spirit as a
dove upon Jesus (John 1.32f.) and insists upon his abundant endowment with the Spirit (John 3.34).

The Synoptic record of the baptism of Jesus uses the rabbinic device
of the *Bath-qol* to express the divine significance of the event. The
words uttered by 'the voice which came out of the heavens' (Mark 1.11)
identify Jesus with the Servant of the Lord of the Isaianic Servant
Songs: 'Thou art my Son, the Beloved; in thee I am well pleased'
(Mark 1.11; cf. Matt. 3.17; Luke 3.22). The reference is to Isa. 42.1,
'Behold, my servant whom I uphold; my chosen, in whom my soul
delighteth; I have put my Spirit upon him.' In the non-LXX version
of Isaiah read by Mark (cf. Matt. 12.18-21) υἱός was used instead of
παῖς and ἀγαπητός instead of ἐκλεκτός.[2] The words spoken by the voice
are also reminiscent of Ps. 2.7, 'The Lord said unto me, Thou art my
son; this day have I begotten thee.' Mark does not in fact add the
second part of the quotation from the Psalm, and there is, of course, no
suggestion here of an adoptionist Christology. The day of baptism, as
Christians well knew, was a day of 'begetting anew', and Christ at his
baptism was, as it were, sacramentally 'begotten' of the Father as his
beloved or unique Son.

Mark's account would lead us to suppose that Jesus alone saw the
heavens rent asunder and the dove descending, as in a vision, and that
likewise he alone hears the voice (cf. Mark 1.10, εἶδε); Matthew scarcely
alters this impression, saying that it was Jesus who saw the dove
descending (Matt. 3.16); but Luke suggests that the events happened
for all to see (cf. σωματικῷ εἴδει, 3.22). We cannot in fact reconstruct
'what happened' at the baptism because the Gospel writers themselves
were not concerned to impart this kind of information; nor does our
ignorance in any way affect our understanding of the significance of the
event. We may be sure that its meaning was taught to the disciples by
Jesus himself, and it is a reasonable inference that he had already
accepted his vocation as the Servant-Messiah when he went with the
crowds to be baptized by John. He had already accepted the rôle of the
Suffering Servant who 'was stricken for the transgression of his people,
although he had done no violence, neither was any deceit in his mouth'
(Isa. 53.8f.). He was the Servant (cf. ὁ διακονῶν, Luke 22.27) who would
justify many and bear their iniquities (Isa. 53.11), and this is why he

---

[1] Prophets are not anointed in the OT; the only exception is Elisha (I Kings 19.16).
The Isaianic Prophet-figure is, of course, an altogether special or ideal case, who
takes on the character both of king (Isa. 9.6f., etc.) and priest (Isa. 53.12).
[2] On ἀγαπητός see *supra*, 150 and 152f.

was baptized. The sinless one is baptized with John's 'baptism of repentance unto remission of sins' (Mark 1.4) for the same reason that he died: 'the Lord hath laid on him the iniquity of us all' (Isa. 53.6). As the Representative Man he bears the sins of the world to the baptism of repentance, as later he would bear them to the baptism of the cross. There is the deepest significance in Jesus's conception of his death as a baptism, and one that could and must be shared by his disciples (Mark 10.38f.; Luke 12.50), a bearing of God's people from Egyptian slavery by way of baptism in the sea of death (cf. I Cor. 10.1f.) through a mighty exodus (cf. Luke 9.31) to the Land of Promise.

The baptism of Jesus is, then, a foreshadowing of his death. The objection that the sinless one needs no baptism of repentance is the same objection as that which was made against the doctrine that the Messiah must suffer (cf. Mark 8.31-33, etc.; I Cor. 1.23). In the early Church the difficulty about why the sinless Christ was baptized seems to have been felt in certain quarters; Matthew inserts two verses into the Marcan narrative of the baptism: 'But John would have hindered him, saying, I have need to be baptized of thee, and comest thou to me? But Jesus answering said unto him, Suffer it now, for thus it becometh us to fulfil all righteousness ($\pi\lambda\eta\rho\hat{\omega}\sigma\alpha\iota$ $\pi\hat{\alpha}\sigma\alpha\nu$ $\delta\iota\kappa\alpha\iota\sigma\sigma\acute{\nu}\nu\eta\nu$). Then he suffereth him' (Matt. 3.14f.). Matthew has fundamentally the right answer to the problem: Jesus is baptized, Jesus dies, for the sake of $\delta\iota\kappa\alpha\iota\sigma\sigma\acute{\nu}\nu\eta$, for the justification of the people of God (cf. Isa. 53.11, 'My righteous servant shall justify many').

The Fourth Evangelist emphasizes the same truth (though he has not mentioned the baptism of Jesus) by making John the Baptist testify to Jesus as the 'Lamb of God, that taketh away the sin of the world' (John 1.29; cf. 1.36). The reference here may be to Gen. 22.8, 'God will provide the lamb for the burnt offering'. The story of the sacrifice of Isaac is one of the OT themes which underlie the Synoptic account of the baptism, for the phrase in Mark 1.11, $\Sigma\grave{\upsilon}$ $\epsilon\hat{\iota}$ $\acute{o}$ $\upsilon\acute{\iota}\acute{o}\varsigma$ $\mu o\upsilon$ $\acute{o}$ $\mathring{\alpha}\gamma\alpha\pi\eta\tau\acute{o}\varsigma$, is a clear echo of Gen. 22.12 (LXX, $\tau o\hat{\upsilon}$ $\upsilon\acute{\iota}o\hat{\upsilon}$ $\sigma o\upsilon$ $\tau o\hat{\upsilon}$ $\mathring{\alpha}\gamma\alpha\pi\eta\tau o\hat{\upsilon}$). Probably the Synoptic account is influenced by the remarkable prophecy of Test. XII Pat., Levi 18.2-12 (dated by R. H. Charles, *c.* 109-106 B.C.) to the effect that God would raise up a new priest, in whose priesthood sin should come to an end (cf. John 1.29, $\acute{o}$ $\alpha\mathring{\iota}\rho\omega\nu$ $\tau\grave{\eta}\nu$ $\mathring{\alpha}\mu\alpha\rho\tau\acute{\iota}\alpha\nu$ $\tau o\hat{\upsilon}$ $\kappa\acute{o}\sigma\mu o\upsilon$). In v. 6 we read: 'The heavens shall be opened (cf. Mark 1.10), and from the temple of glory shall come upon him sanctification with the Father's voice (cf. the *Bath-qol*) from Abraham to Isaac'—and what Abraham says to Isaac is, 'God will provide a lamb for the burnt offering', and nothing else (Gen. 22.8). The reference in Test. Levi 18.7 to the Spirit's resting upon this 'new priest' is further evidence that this passage has influenced the form which the Synoptic story of the baptism has taken and has also had some bearing upon the Fourth Evangelist's use of the title 'Lamb of God' at this point in his narrative. The whole question of the meaning of that title is, however, very complicated, but at least we are probably on the right lines if we think of Jesus at his baptism as already offering himself as the sacrificial Lamb provided by God for the taking away of the sin of the world.[1] The whole NT theology of sacrifice is already implicit in the action of Jesus in going to be baptized 'unto the remission of sins'. There is no reason at all to suppose that Jesus did not have a clear conception of what he was doing; it is surely more probable that Jesus should have thought out this profound re-interpretation of the OT plan of salvation than that the Church should have done so a decade or two later.

The symbolism of the dove in the narrative of the baptism (Mark 1.10; Matt. 3.16; Luke 3.22) is not immediately apparent, since there seem to be no very close analogies in rabbinic writings.[2] The most probable explanation is that which connects the dove with Gen. 1.2, where the Spirit 'broods' over the old creation: so here, at the New Creation, on its 'first day', so to speak, the Spirit again broods over the waters (of Jordan). Jesus is made 'the Lord's Anointed', the first-born of those 'many brethren' who shall through their baptism in Holy Spirit themselves become χριστοί, anointed, and shall be made corporately into the new Adam, the New Creation. But, as is so often the case in biblical symbolism, a symbol may have a double reference, and we must always refuse to accept an either-or: possibly there is some reference to Gen. 8.8-12 (Noah's dove), since the early Church thought of the deliverance of Noah in his ark as a baptism of the human race (I Pet. 3.20f.). Other biblical references to doves shed no light on the matter. The doves which so often appear on or over the fonts of Christian churches remind us that our baptism is efficacious only because Christ was baptized and that in our baptism, as in his, the inward reality of the action is the descent of the Holy Spirit.

THE TRANSFIGURATION OF CHRIST

A rich complexity of theological motives is discernible in the Synoptic accounts of the Transfiguration (Mark 9.2-8; Matt. 17.1-8; Luke 9.28-36). We are far removed, even in Mark, from simple eye-witness accounts of 'what happened'. All that we can say about the historical happening is that the three chosen witnesses underwent an experience which was beyond the power of human language to express, but which

[1] See further *infra*, 225-9.
[2] See C. K. Barrett, *The Holy Spirit and the Gospel Tradition*, 35-9.

they understood as a divine ratification of their conviction that Jesus
was the Messiah of God. They articulated this conviction in a manner
natural to Jews of the first century: it had been revealed to them that
Jesus was indeed the prophet like unto Moses (Deut. 18.15, 18), who
was to accomplish a redemption greater than that of the historical
exodus and deliverance from Egypt. The mount of the Transfiguration
is, of course, the new Sinai; it is futile to try to identify it geographically,
because the Evangelists had no interest in geography for its own sake.
The new Moses, like the old, hears the voice of God on the 'holy mount'
(II Pet. 1.18). In Ex. 24.16 we read, 'And the glory of Yahweh abode
upon Mount Sinai and the cloud covered it six days; and the seventh
day he called unto Moses out of the midst of the cloud.' 'After six days
Jesus taketh with him Peter and James and John' (Mark 9.2); St Mark
does not tell us *what* it was six days after, for the reason that he is not
giving a chronological account but a theological one: on the seventh
day God called to the new Moses out of the midst of the cloud (Mark
9.7). When Moses came down from Sinai the skin of his face shone,
because he had spoken with God, and the children of Israel were afraid
to come near him (Ex. 34.29f.); so, too, when Jesus came down from
the Mount where he had been transfigured, the multitude which ran to
salute him was 'greatly amazed' (Mark 9.15): St Mark leaves it to the
Church's teachers, who are to use his compact notes of lessons, to explain to the catechumens the significance of the crowd's amazement.
St Luke, noting that it was Moses's *face* that shone (Ex. 34.29, LXX:
δεδόξασται ἡ ὄψις τοῦ χρώματος τοῦ προσώπου αὐτοῦ), adds to the Marcan
stress upon the whiteness of Jesus's garments the detail that 'the fashion
of his countenance was altered' (τὸ εἶδος τοῦ προσώπου αὐτοῦ ἕτερον,
Luke 9.29). The voice out of the cloud (*Bath-qol*) repeats (with minor
variations) in all three Synoptists the words of the heavenly voice at the
baptism of Jesus, 'This is my beloved Son'; but there is a very significant
addition—'hear ye him' (ἀκούετε αὐτοῦ), a virtual quotation of Deut.
18.15, αὐτοῦ ἀκούσεσθε, 'to him shall ye hearken'. The voice from the
cloud testifies that this is the promised prophet like unto Moses, to
whom God's people must hearken.

The introduction of Elijah into the scene, along with Moses, does
not alter the character of the Synoptic Transfiguration narrative as a
notable specimen of genuinely primitive Jewish-Christian Christological
teaching of the Moses-Prophet type. For in rabbinic thought Elijah
is himself a second Moses, who contended for the Torah and who also
was vouchsafed an encounter with God on 'the holy mount' (Horeb-
Sinai: I Kings 19.8); he is 'Moses-over-again', just as Elisha is 'Elijah-
over-again', according to the biblical doctrine of personalities as

overflowing into one another. Both Moses and Elijah (in the rabbinic view) had not died, but had been translated to heaven—a point which is seized upon by St Luke. Thus, it is not strictly correct to say that in the Transfiguration story Moses represents the Law and Elijah the Prophets, which alike bear testimony to Jesus, because Moses is essentially 'the Prophet' and Elijah is simply another Moses. The two figures had been assimilated in Jewish thought at least since the writing of Mal. 4.4f. In the story Moses and Elijah represent the old order as contrasted with the new, in which it is fulfilled. After the voice from heaven has testified, they vanish away, and the disciples see no one any more save Jesus only with themselves (Mark 9.8).

It is hardly surprising that the liberal critics, who failed to see that profound biblical truth is conveyed in the form of pictures and symbols, should have been at a loss to attach any meaning to the story of the Transfiguration. For a long time it was customary to regard it as a 'misplaced Resurrection story' (J. Wellhausen, A. Loisy, R. Bultmann, etc.); more recently it has become usual to emphasize its eschatological character.[1] There can be little doubt that Moses and Elijah figure in the story because of the expectation of the 'prophet like unto Moses' and of the Elijah, who should appear in the last days (Mal. 4.4f.; Mark 9.11, etc.), and Lohmeyer is doubtless near the mark when he conjectures that the three disciples are the *Keim und Kern*, the foundation members, of the eschatological community, to whom is revealed the mystery of the heavenly Son of Man in the glory of his parousia. In St Mark's view Peter, James and John are given a glimpse of the future glory of the Messiah, whom they had confessed, as the *incognito* of his person is for a brief moment unveiled. It is, however, only St Luke who specifically mentions the δόξα and says that it was seen by the disciples (9.31f.); but the idea of the eschatological δόξα is not far away from the Marcan account. St Peter's suggestion about building three tabernacles is not, of course, a *gauche* remark, as it used so often to be said to be: it is a natural part of the eschatological symbolism of the story. The Jews had come to look forward to the tabernacling presence of the Messiah with his righteous elect ones (represented here by Moses and Elijah) (cf. Ezek. 37.27; 43.7, 9; Zech. 2.10f.; 8.3, 8; Tob. 13.10; John 1.14; Rev. 21.3, etc.), and Peter was dimly aware that the days were nigh when the tabernacle of God was to be with men. But the time was not yet fulfilled; the work of Christ was not yet completed—Peter did not yet fully understand; he did not yet realize that the Christ must suffer:

---

[1] See E. Lohmeyer, *Das Evangelium des Markus*, G. H. Boobyer, *St Mark and the Transfiguration Story*, 1942, and esp. A. M. Ramsey, *The Glory of God and the Transfiguration of Christ*, 1949, 101-11.

'he wist not what to answer' (Mark 9.6). It is St Luke who brings out the poignancy of the situation: Moses and Elijah spoke with Jesus about the very matter which the disciples could not yet understand, namely, 'his exodus which he was about to accomplish at Jerusalem' (Luke 9.31). The new Moses must accomplish his exodus deliverance before his *assumptio*, his being received up (Luke 9.51) into the glory of his heavenly reign. But the glory is already his, even though now it is veiled; and on the Mount of Transfiguration the chosen witnesses are given a proleptic glimpse of it. The Transfiguration experience was for the apostles a means of assurance concerning the fulfilment of those things for which Christians hope; it was a momentary revelation of glory in the darkness, like a lamp shining in a squalid place, which must suffice until the day dawn and the day-star of the unveiled parousia-glory arise (II Pet. 1.16-19). By faith the δόξα of God was even now seen by Christians shining in the face (πρόσωπον) of Jesus Christ, even as it had shone upon the face of Moses (II Cor. 4.6; Ex. 34.29-35). The visible shining of the δόξα in the face of Jesus Christ in the sight of the three witnesses was a testimony vouchsafed by God to his chosen apostles, like the δόξα-light which had shone upon Paul himself on the Damascus road (Acts 22.11). The Transfiguration was a sign to those who would believe the apostles' testimony that the faith and hope of the Gospel of Christ were not illusory.

St Luke in particular thinks of Jesus as the new Moses who re-enacts the drama of salvation of which the Torah was the classical and original *kerugma*; like Moses of old, Jesus accomplishes an exodus and goes forward to his 'assumption'.[1] Of course, the historical events of the life of Jesus do not fit neatly into the Pentateuchal pattern, and it is an indication of the canonical Evangelists' respect for history that they do not attempt to force them into it. For instance, Moses on the holy Mount has made with God the sacred Covenant and ratified it with the blood of the animal victims (Ex. 24); but there is no suggestion of a covenant-making on the Mount of Transfiguration, because the Evangelists have no wish to pursue a typological fulfilment, however striking, which would detract from the historical scene of covenant-making on the night on which Jesus was betrayed (Mark 14.24; cf. Ex. 24.8). But, being Jews, they seize upon the typological parallels wherever they can, because the Pentateuchal scheme of salvation was the only kerugmatic pattern they knew: God's act of salvation proclaimed in the OT was inevitably taken as the type of which the apostolic *kerugma* was the fulfilment. The story of Moses foreshadows that of

---

[1] For the elaboration of this theme see C. F. Evans, 'The Central Section of St Luke's Gospel' in *Studies in the Gospels*, ed. D. E. Nineham, 37-53.

Jesus. The desert sojourning, the ascent of the holy Mount, the feeding with bread from heaven and the 'exodus' in Jerusalem are obvious fulfilments of the Mosaic pattern; but it would have been difficult to find any parallel for the resurrection in the Pentateuch; indeed, the NT writers are hard pressed to find OT parallels at all.[1] For St Luke, however, with his schematized Ascension after forty days, there was the widely current rabbinic belief in the Assumption of Moses. In the OT only Enoch (Gen. 5.24; Ecclus. 44.16; 49.14; Heb. 11.5) and Elijah (II Kings 2.11) are translated or 'assumed' to heaven without dying; hence their prominence in apocalyptic literature as revealers of secrets. But by the first century A.D. Moses also is accorded a similar honour.[2] The ἀνάλημψις Μωυσέως was thus a foreshadowing of Christ's ascension, and in Luke 9.51f. we read, 'It came to pass, when the days were being fulfilled that he should be assumed (ἐγένετο δὲ ἐν τῷ συμπλη-ροῦσθαι τὰς ἡμέρας τῆς ἀναλήμψεως αὐτοῦ), he stedfastly set his face to go to Jerusalem, and sent messengers before his face. . . .' The noun ἀνάλημψις here is a *hapax* in the NT, but of course the verb ἀναλαμβάνειν is used of the ascending of Christ to heaven (Acts 1.2, 11, 22; I Tim. 3.16; Mark 16.19). In the LXX and other Jewish writings ἀνάλημψις is used of miraculous translations. C. F. Evans is doubtless moving along right lines when he calls attention to the careful working out in St Luke's Gospel of the theme of Jesus as the new Moses and also—a distinctively Lucan idea—as the new Elijah.[3]

THE PASSION STORY

All the NT writers believe that the OT foretells the Gospel story, at east in figure. The Jewish Scriptures constituted in apostolic days the only written record of God's revelation; and therefore this revelation must contain, albeit in hidden types and symbols, an account of the events that were to be fulfilled in the days of the Messianic salvation. The NT view is stated concisely in I Pet. 1.10-12: 'Concerning which salvation the prophets sought and searched diligently, who prophesied of the grace that should come unto you: searching what time or what manner of time the Spirit of Christ which was in them did point unto,

[1] See *infra*, 190-2.

[2] The work known as *The Assumption of Moses*, now extant only in a single Latin MS., was originally written in Heb. or Aramaic by a quietist Pharisee shortly after the death of Herod the Great. It is in a lost appendix to this work, quoted by Greek patristic writers, that there appear references to the dispute between Michael and Satan over the body of Moses, which was followed by the triumphant 'assumption' of Moses into heaven. (An allusion to this legend, or a quotation from this work, is found in the canonical Jude 9.) See the edition of R. H. Charles (1897); also F. C. Burkitt, art. 'Moses, Assumption of' in *HDB* III, 448-50; also C. F. Evans, *op. cit.*

[3] *Op. cit.*; see also *supra*, 118.

when it testified beforehand the sufferings of Christ, and the glories that should follow them. To whom it was revealed, that not unto themselves, but unto you, did they minister these things, which now have been announced unto you through them that preached the Gospel unto you in the Holy Spirit sent forth from heaven.' The mysteries of salvation, which lie veiled in the OT even from the understanding of the prophets themselves, are now made manifest through the Spirit's activity when the good news of God's action in Christ is proclaimed by the Church's preachers. Christ is the key to the Scriptures.

This view of the fulfilment of the Scriptures is very clearly apparent in the Passion story. If the Christian preachers had indeed something scandalous to proclaim (cf. I Cor. 1.23; Gal. 5.11; I Pet. 2.8; Deut. 21.23), then it was above all things necessary to demonstrate that Christ died according to the Scriptures (I Cor. 15.3). There are good reasons for thinking that the Passion story is the oldest part of the Gospel tradition to receive definite shape,[1] and it is not difficult to see why. It was necessary from the earliest days of the preaching to meet the obvious objection that Jesus could not be the Messiah, not only because of the scriptural difficulty (Deut. 21.23), but also because Roman justice had tried him and condemned him to death as a malefactor. The sufficient answer to this objection was to let the facts speak for themselves, to tell quite simply and without adornment the story of how Jesus died. The Passion story was from the beginning an essential part of the Gospel preaching; and from the beginning it was found to have a wonderful power to convince men's hearts.

The belief having arisen that the Isaianic picture of the Servant of the Lord was a prophecy of Christ (Matt. 12.18-21; Acts 3.13, 26; 4.27, 30; 8.32-35; I Pet. 2.21-25), it would naturally be assumed by the Gospel-writers that all the details of the oracle in Isa. 52.13–53.12 must have been fulfilled; so also with Ps. 22 and certain other passages. Thus, Mark 15.29f. ('. . . railed on him, wagging their heads, and saying, Ah, thou that destroyest the Temple and buildest it in three days, save thyself and come down from the cross') is clearly reminiscent of Ps. 22.7f. ('All they that see me laugh me to scorn; they shoot out the lip and shake the head, saying, Commit thyself unto the Lord; let him deliver him, seeing he delighteth in him'). Matthew, in order that the parallel with Ps. 22 should not be missed, puts into the mouths of the railing chief priests a definite quotation from the Psalm: 'He trusteth on God; let him deliver him now, if he desireth him' (Matt.

---

[1] Cf. V. Taylor, *The Formation of the Gospel Tradition*, 1933, 44ff.; R. H. Lightfoot, *History and Interpretation in the Gospels*, 1934, 126ff.; M. Dibelius, *From Tradition to Gospel*, ET, 1934, 23; R. Bultmann, *Form-Criticism*, ET, 1934, 65.

27.43). Possibly the story about the soldiers' parting Jesus's garments and casting lots for them (Mark 15.24) is an inference from Ps. 22.18: 'They part my garments among them, and upon my vesture do they cast lots.' Certain MSS. of Mark add a verse (Mark 15.28, AV; RV mg. only) to underline the significance of the crucifixion between two robbers: 'And the scripture was fulfilled which saith, And he was reckoned with the transgressors' (Isa. 53.12); in Luke the quotation is made by Jesus himself in his address to the disciples after the Last Supper (Luke 22.37). The offering of vinegar on a sponge (Mark 15.36) fulfils Ps. 69.21, 'They gave me also gall for my meat, and in my thirst they gave me vinegar to drink.' Matthew doubtless had this verse in mind when he converted the statement of Mark 15.23 that, as soon as they arrived at Golgotha, Jesus was given some wine mingled with myrrh (the ordinary *posca* or soldiers' drink), which he refused, into the statement that the wine was mingled with gall (Matt. 27.34), which Jesus tasted before refusing. Again, it may be that the tradition recorded in certain MSS. of Matt. 27.49 (see RV mg.) that water flowed from the pierced side of Jesus (as explicitly stated in John 19.34) was based upon Ps. 22.14, 'I am poured out like water.'

These examples must suffice to shew how the evangelists wrote their stories of the Passion in such a way as to illustrate the early Church's conviction that the Scriptures concerning Christ had a τέλος (Luke 22.37). The Passion story was foretold by the prophets: 'the Son of Man goeth even as it is written of him' (Mark 14.21; cf. Luke 24.25-27, 44; Acts 3.18, 24). Everything that had happened, including the minutest details of the Passion drama, was according to 'the determinate counsel and foreknowledge of God' (Acts 2.23). In Matt. 26.53f. Jesus himself is made to say, 'Thinkest thou that I cannot beseech my Father, and he shall even now send me more than twelve legions of angels? How then should the Scriptures be fulfilled, that thus it must be?' Or again, he says to those who had come with swords and staves to arrest him, 'All this is come to pass that the Scriptures of the prophets might be fulfilled' (Matt. 26.56). The vivid details of the Passion narratives, such as the casting lots by the soldiers or the vinegar on the sponge, are not recorded by the Evangelists because they were good story-tellers with an eye for pictorial effect, but because these incidents demonstrated the principle, τοῦτο τὸ γεγραμμένον δεῖ τελεσθῆναι (Luke 22.37). The scandal of the cross (Gal. 5.11) was pre-determined in all its details by the will of God. It is in the life and death of Jesus Christ that the problem of free will and predestination finds its most poignant expression, and here, too, if anywhere, it must find its solution. The predetermined one freely chooses his appointed destiny: 'not what I will, but what thou wilt' (Mark 14.36). In Christ, the elect of God, perfect freedom and absolute determination intersect; human freedom and divine omnipotence meet and are one. The problem of free will and determination can be solved only in the new humanity of Jesus Christ.[1]

The Passion-story cannot, of course, be considered apart from the preaching of the resurrection to which it is the prelude. Taken together the passion and resurrection narratives fulfil the vindication-*motif* which occurs frequently in the OT. 'The stone which the builders rejected, the same was made the head of the corner' (Mark 12.10, quoting Ps. 118.22; cf. also Acts 4.11; I Pet. 2.7; compare Isa. 28.16 and Eph. 2.20). It is natural that Israel, having suffered much in the course of her history, should look to God for her vindication (ἐκδίκησις); the theme is a common one, especially in apocalyptic passages (e.g. Zech. 3; Dan. 7, and cf. the Revelation of St John *passim*). But the longing for vindication is often scarcely distinguishable from the desire for vengeance upon the oppressors, and it is significant that the word ἐκδίκησις means not only vindication but also vengeance. The prayer that God will speedily avenge injustice can easily pass over into a lust for revenge. The OT teaches that vengeance belongs to God (Deut. 32.35, cited in Rom. 12.19 and Heb. 10.30; Ps. 94.1; Isa. 1.24; 59.18; Nahum 1.2; Ecclus. 28.1), and this principle is strongly re-asserted by our Lord in Luke 18.7f., etc. He absolutely forbids all revenge or retaliation on the part of his followers (Matt. 5.38-48; 6.14f.; Luke 9.51-55; 17.3f.; cf. 23.34), and St Paul understands his teaching precisely (Rom. 12.17-21; I Thess. 4.6). On the other hand, the Apostle can paint a lurid and terrifying picture of the ἐκδίκησις which will be visited at the parousia upon those who now afflict the Church and disobey the Gospel of our Lord Jesus (II Thess. 1.6-9), to which there are equally lurid parallels elsewhere in the NT (e.g. Mark 9.43-48; Jude 7; Rev. 21.8). Perhaps these are best taken as graphic ways of insisting upon God's character of avenging righteousness, which must nevertheless not be dwelt upon to the exclusion of his character of willing the conversion and redemption of the sinner. It is not entirely true to say that in the OT Isa. 52.13–53.12 is the only passage in which the suffering one, having been vindicated, actually saves his persecutors and makes intercession for the transgressors: the Joseph-saga (Gen. 37–50) is a superb setting-forth of the biblical doctrine of vicarious suffering, for Joseph, when triumphant, saves his brethren who had done him cruel wrong. But the NT nowhere refers explicitly to the example of Joseph and does not explicitly set

[1] For a valuable consideration of the problem here raised see D. M. Baillie, *God Was in Christ*, 1948, esp. 106-32.

forth Joseph as a type of Christ;[1] this, however, does not prevent us from recognizing in the 'primitive' Joseph-stories a deep biblical insight into the nature of vicarious suffering which is fulfilled in the story of Christ in the Gospels: 'And Israel said unto Joseph, Do not thy brethren feed the flock in Shechem? Come and I will send thee unto them. And he answered, Here am I' (Gen. 37.13). The whole Gospel story of how God overrides men's evil purposes and out of their misdeeds works their salvation is implicit in the children's story of Joseph and his brethren. It is, however, to Isa. 53 that the apostolic Church looks for guidance on the subject of ἐκδίκησις in the sense both of vindication and of vengeance, and its practical application is perhaps most clearly set forth in I Pet. 2.18-25: '. . . Hereunto were ye called, because Christ also suffered for you, leaving you an example. . . .' The most evil deed that men have ever committed, the nailing of God's Messiah to the cross, is made by God the means of the salvation of sinners: God's vengeance is, in the final shewing of the NT, a heaping of the fiery coals of his love upon the head of his enemy (cf. Rom. 12.20).[2]

[1] Dr Austin Farrer, however, has presented a strong case for the view that a Joseph-typology is to be found in the Marcan Passion story: as Joseph (the Patriarch) begged permission to bury the old Israel (Gen. 50.4-6), so Joseph (of Arimathaea) begs permission to bury the new Israel (Mark 15.42-46), etc. See *The Glass of Vision*, 1948, 144f.; *A Study in St Mark*, 141, 174, 333f. See also Helen Gardner, *The Limits of Literary Criticism*, 1956, 25-39.

[2] On ἐκδικέω and ἐκδίκησις see also footnote 3 on p. 198 *infra*.

9

THE RESURRECTION, ASCENSION
AND VICTORY OF CHRIST

THE principal argument for the truth of Christ's resurrection
does not consist in a skilful piecing together of the documentary
evidence of the Gospels, or even of the NT as a whole, but in
what the Church does every Sunday and in the quality of her life on
every day of the week. When the Church meets to break the bread in
accordance with her Lord's command, she not only proclaims his death
(I Cor. 11.26), but also witnesses to his resurrection. The weekly
celebration of the death of a dead leader would be no occasion of joy
and thanksgiving, and the fact that from the earliest days the disciples
met to make joyful memorial of his death, re-enacting the solemn scene
in the upper room on the night on which he was betrayed, is the strong-
est possible evidence of the certainty of their knowledge of his resurrection. 'He was known of them in the breaking of the bread' (Luke
24.35). The coming together again of the disciples, who had 'all left
him and fled' (Mark 14.50), is proof enough that something miraculous
had occurred; and the existence of the Church at all, if we have regard
to the circumstances in which Jesus's mission had apparently ended in
total failure and disaster, should be sufficient to convince us that the
explanation given by the apostles themselves, is the only one which
can command rational assent. It alone can account for their courageous
witness before the very tribunal which had condemned their Master
(Acts 4.5-22). Henceforth they were witnesses of his resurrection
(Acts 1.22; 2.32; 4.33).

'ACCORDING TO THE SCRIPTURES'
The apostolic Church believed that Christ was 'raised on the third
day according to the Scriptures' (I Cor. 15.4). 'Thus it is written, that
Christ should suffer and rise again from the dead the third day' (Luke
24.46; cf. 24.25f.). Yet it is difficult to find specific OT passages which
can be regarded as definite prophecies of Christ's resurrection on the
third day. Isa. 53.10-12 predicts a triumphant vindication of the righteous Servant, but is not quoted as a resurrection proof-text in the NT;

also Ps. 22, taken as a whole, speaks of triumph after suffering, since the NT writers did not know the critical view that vv. 22-31 belong to a separate composition. Prophecies of the resurrection were found in the Psalms, e.g. Ps. 2.1f. (quoted in Acts 4.25f.), Ps. 16.8-11 (Acts 2.25-28), Ps. 110.1 (Acts 2.34f.), Ps. 118.22 (Acts 4.11, etc.). But none of these passages can be held to foretell a resurrection *on the third day*; yet this is what St Luke and St Paul declare to be written in the Scriptures. Three OT passages might perhaps have been in their minds.

The first is Hos. 6.2: 'After two days he will revive us; on the third day he will raise us up, and we shall live before him.' To our modern minds this may seem far-fetched, but to the NT writers it would appear entirely apposite. Hosea is predicting the restoration of Israel after her punishment for her infidelity is over: the NT thinks of Christ as the new Israel, chastened for our sins and raised for our justification (Rom. 4.25). The new Israel recapitulates and fulfils the history of the old. The OT was written, as St Paul says, τυπικῶς—'by way of figure'; the form of Christ is discernible in the whole and in the parts. The things which happened to Israel 'happened to them by way of example (τυπικῶς), and they are written for our admonition, upon whom the ends of the ages are come' (I Cor. 10.11). Thus, Christ is the Christian passover-lamb and Easter is the Christian *Pascha* (cf. I Cor. 5.7f.): the Church reads Ex. 12.1-14 as the OT lection on Easter Sunday morning. At Eastertide we sing St John Damascene's Αἴσωμεν πάντες λαοί (*c*. A.D. 750):

> 'Come, ye faithful, raise the strain
>   Of triumphant gladness;
> God hath brought his Israel
>   Into joy from sadness;
> Loosed from Pharaoh's bitter yoke
>   Jacob's sons and daughters;
> Led them with unmoistened foot
>   Through the Red Sea waters.'
>   (Trans. J. M. Neale)

The second passage is Jonah 1.17: 'Jonah was in the belly of the fish three days and three nights.' We have definite evidence in Matt. 12.40 that some at least in the Church of NT times understood it as a prophecy of the burial and resurrection of Christ: 'As Jonah was three days and three nights in the belly of the sea-monster, so shall the Son of Man be three days and three nights in the heart of the earth.' (St Luke does not interpret the σημεῖον of Jonah in this way; Luke 11.29-32.) Again, if the references seem to us far-fetched, we must remember that Jonah's adventure was a parable of Israel's 'burial' in the land of Exile and subsequent resurrection (cf. Ezek. 37.1-14), and that in NT thought the Messiah must recapitulate the history of Israel.

The third passage, which is more conjectural, is Ex. 19.10f.: 'The LORD said unto Moses, Go unto the people, and sanctify them today and tomorrow . . . and be ready against the third day: for the third day the LORD will come down in the sight of all the people upon Mount Sinai.' It is perhaps just conceivable that the otherwise somewhat inexplicable introduction of 'the *mountain* where Jesus had appointed them' in Matt. 28.16 is an allusion to the coming down of the Lord upon the mount on the third day in the story of the making of the Old Covenant. But the matter must remain very doubtful, and it is noteworthy chiefly as indicating how difficult it is to find clear prophecies in Scripture of a resurrection on the third day. Indeed, it may be said with emphasis that the resurrection-story could not have been constructed out of OT precedents (as the Passion story can be constructed in a measure out of Ps. 22 and Isa. 53), and it is clear that the NT writers did not find it easy to accumulate any very substantial body of *testimonia* concerning the resurrection. The Gospel story would hardly have contained a resurrection-episode if it had been composed by learned rabbis out of OT prophecies concerning a Messiah, even if they could have constructed a Passion narrative of such a kind. The story would have concluded with something rather more like the 'assumption of Moses'. The events of the life, death and resurrection of Jesus do not fit exactly into the Pentateuchal pattern; the canonical Evangelists are content to do their best with the historical material in their hand, and, where it cannot be poured into the Pentateuchal mould, they are not at all embarrassed at having to leave so many of its intractable elements sticking out of the framework of the OT pre-view of the Messianic salvation.

THE DOCUMENTARY EVIDENCE OF THE RESURRECTION

There is sufficient evidence in the NT that from the earliest times the apostolic παράδοσις contained a definite account of the appearances of the Lord after his resurrection. The tradition of Christ's resurrection was taught to the catechumens along with the rest of the material concerning the life and words of Jesus. The preachers had, of course, proclaimed the resurrection of Christ as part of the Church's κήρυγμα, and we may confidently regard the speeches put into the mouth of St Peter by St Luke (Acts 2.14-36; 3.12-26; 4.8-12; 5.29-32; 10.34-43) as examples of the earliest Christian preaching.[1] Those who had been attracted into the Church's fellowship by the message of the preachers were handed over to the teachers for instruction in the παράδοσις concerning the Lord Jesus which formed the basis of the Church's teaching upon all aspects of faith and morals. Two specimens of the παράδοσις of the resurrection of Christ have been preserved in summary form in the NT.

The first is found in I Cor. 15.1-9, where Paul reminds his Corinthian converts of the words in which he preached the Gospel to them. He thinks of it as the common παράδοσις of the Church, not as a private teaching of his own; it is 'that which also I received' (v. 3). It carries us back to a time before the earliest written Gospel. It recounts how Christ had been raised on the third day according to the Scriptures, that he had appeared to Cephas (i.e. Peter), then to the Twelve (? the Eleven), then to above five hundred brethren at once, then to James, then to all the apostles, and last to Paul himself. Certain points remain obscure in this summary statement. The appearance to Peter is not described in the Gospels but is mentioned in Luke 24.34 and is doubtless foreshadowed in Mark 16.7. Nor is the appearance to James recorded in the canonical Gospels; and we have no other reference to the appearance to the five hundred brethren. Nevertheless such is the tradition which Paul had received and which he delivered to his churches; and there were alive in his day many who could have challenged his teaching, if it had departed from the generally accepted tradition.

The second example of the Church's παράδοσις, similarly summarized, is found in Mark 16.9-15. It has been the tendency of many NT scholars in recent years to assume that the whole of Mark 16.9-20 ('the Longer Ending') is the composition of a later writer who is drawing upon the endings of St Matthew and St Luke, both of which are before him as he writes. This is a gratuitous assumption; it is at least as likely that the author is preserving a section of the παράδοσις of which St Matthew's and St Luke's endings contain somewhat elaborate literary versions. The passage records an appearance of the Risen Lord to Mary Magdalene, whose report was disbelieved by the disciples; an appearance to two disciples 'on their way into the country', who also were not believed (contrast Luke 24.34), and finally an appearance to the Eleven as they sat at meat, when Jesus upbraided them for their unbelief and commanded them to go into the whole κόσμος and proclaim the good news to the whole creation. There seems to be no reason whatever why we should doubt that there was an original παράδοσις of this kind, which was handed on by the Church's teachers from apostolic

[1] See *supra*, 24f.

times until the reading of the Gospels, which came eventually to be accepted as canonical, supplanted altogether the handing on of an oral tradition.

Within this παράδοσις, or general framework, it is possible to discern particular *pericopae* which must have been handed down by the Church's teachers from the earliest days. C. H. Dodd has recently called attention to the existence in the resurrection narratives of the Gospels of *pericopae* of the Paradigm (Apophthegm, Pronouncement-story) type.[1] He cites as examples Matt. 28.8-10, Matt. 28.16-20 and John 20.19-21. They are *pericopae* which bear all the characteristics of folk-tradition, 'in which an oft-repeated story is rubbed down and polished, like a water-worn pebble, until nothing but the essential remains, in its most arresting and memorable form'.[2] They have a common pattern: A. The Situation: Christ's followers bereft of their Lord; B. The Appearance of the Lord; C. The Greeting; D. The Recognition, and E. The Word of Command. In fact, all the elements are present by which in other contexts the form-critics would adjudge *pericopae* to be primitive. They are starkly factual, neither symbolical nor allusive; they are clearly not mythological inventions designed to bring out the significance of the historical. Contrasted with the stories of (for example) the Baptism and the Transfiguration, they contain no elaborate theological *motifs*, no apocalyptic or eschatological symbolism. They witness (on the strictest form-critical principles) to the facticity of the resurrection as an historical event, as historical as any other event of which we have knowledge through the paradigms of the Synoptic Gospels.

In addition to this paradigmatic element, there is also amongst the resurrection-narratives of the Gospels a markedly didactic element, in which profound theological truth is conveyed through the telling of stories. We must not, however, think of them as nothing more than good specimens of the story-teller's art; they are indeed works of literary craftsmanship of a high order, but their aim is didactic; they are not merely 'good stories', such as the form-critics considered their somewhat imaginary class of *Novellen* to be (e.g. the Gadarene Swine or the Epileptic Boy). Good instances of these more literary, didactic elements would be the Walk to Emmaus (Luke 24.13-35) or the Appearance to Peter and the six other disciples at the Sea of Galilee (John 21.1-14). They are doubtless founded upon fact, but the stories as we have them have been made into such superb parables, charged with

[1] In his 'Essay in the Form-Criticism of the Gospels' in *Studies in the Gospels*, ed. D. E. Nineham, 9-35.
[2] *Op. cit.*, 10.

profound theological teaching, that we cannot tell what could have been their original form. Perhaps St Luke elaborated an ancient element in the common παράδοσις about the journey of the two disciples into the country (Mark 16.12f.), so that it became a wonderful parable of the Risen Christ as the Opener of the Scriptures (*testimonium Spiritus sancti internum*) and as the Host at the Eucharist: the breaking of bread accompanied by the exposition of the (OT) Scriptures in the apostolic Church. Perhaps St John has likewise elaborated a primitive element in the tradition which is given in another form in Luke 5.1-11 (the Miraculous Draught of Fishes), and made it into a beautiful parable of the Church's missionary triumph as she obeys the command of her Risen Master. We cannot tell; but it is certain that both these stories, though they are profound theological parables, contain in its deepest sense the truth of history: the apostolic Church's experience of the reality and power of Christ's resurrection.

Finally it should be noted that there appears also in the literary tradition of the resurrection still another *motif*, viz. the apologetic. Perhaps the clearest example of it is to be seen in St Matthew's story of the Sealing of the Sepulchre and the Setting of the Guard (Matt. 27.62-66), which is designed to counter the slander of 'the Jews' that the disciples had stolen the body of Jesus (Matt. 28.11-15). Similarly an apologetic against docetic interpretations, which made Christ's resurrection purely 'spiritual', is also found. Thus, in Luke 24.41-43 the Risen Lord eats a piece of broiled fish, and in Luke 24.39 he says, 'Handle me and see, for a πνεῦμα hath not flesh and bones, as ye behold me having.' Similarly in John 20.26-29 Thomas is invited to put his hand into Christ's side.[1] St Luke tells how Peter corroborated the truth of the women's story of the Empty Tomb, having run to the tomb and seen 'the linen cloths by themselves' (24.12); St John elaborates this apologetic, supplying many more circumstantial details, and adding as an additional witness 'the other disciple whom Jesus loved' (20.1-10).

Only two NT writers claim that they have themselves seen the Risen Lord. St Paul makes the claim in I Cor. 9.1 and 15.8 (but it is St Luke who gives us the accounts of the matter in Acts 9.3-8; 22.6-11; 26.12-18; cf. 18.9); and St John in the Apocalypse describes his vision of the 'one like unto the Son of Man' in Rev. 1.10-18. It is noteworthy, however, that by comparison with this apocalyptic figure the Risen Christ of the

---

[1] The 'Touch me not' to Mary in John 20.17 is not inconsistent with this, because in the Johannine view Mary sees Christ having come out of the tomb *before* his Ascension to the Father; the appearance of Christ to the disciples 'when the doors were shut' takes place *after* Christ has ascended, and has now returned in his glorious body to impart the Spirit to the disciples. See *supra*, 116.

Gospel appearances is an essentially human and historical person. The resurrection stories of the Gospels are remarkably free from all apocalyptic imagery and symbolism, and in this respect may be strongly contrasted with the transfiguration stories; the latter are *per contra* devoid of those kerugmatic and paradigmatic elements which, as we have noted, are found in the resurrection tradition.

THE EMPTY TOMB

The fact that the tomb was found to be empty on Easter Sunday morning appears to be a part of the original παράδοσις of the resurrection, and not just a later addition designed for apologetic purposes (as perhaps Matthew's story of the Guard may be; Matt. 27.62-66; 28.11-15). The oldest MSS. of St Mark end with the finding of the tomb empty by the women who had gone 'very early on the first day of the week' to anoint the body of the crucified Master (Mark 16.1-8; cf. Matt. 28.1-7; Luke 24.1-12; John 20.1-10). The notion that the resurrection of Christ was a purely 'spiritual' affair, while his corpse remained in the tomb, is a very modern one, which rests upon theories of the impossibility of miracle drawn from nineteenth-century physics. Supporters of this view have claimed that there is no reference to the Empty Tomb in the παράδοσις which St Paul received (I Cor. 15.3-8) and that it could not therefore have been a part of the primitive tradition. Against this argument it may be replied that St Paul and others may have omitted the story of the visit of the women to the tomb because they did not wish it to be thought that the case for the resurrection of Christ was dependent upon the evidence of hysterical women. But more important is the consideration that to St Paul, as to any other Jew of the time, a merely 'spiritual' resurrection would have appeared unintelligible. Unlike the Greeks, the Jews did not think of a man as being made up of a body and a soul; a man was a living body. If Christ was raised from the dead, he must have been raised in the body. Thus, Paul cannot conceive of those who are risen in Christ as existing in a disembodied state: they have a 'spiritual body' (I Cor. 15.44). Spiritual realities, celestial or terrestrial, divine or human, are embodied in their own appropriate embodiments (I Cor. 15.35-41). When the earthly house of our tabernacle is dissolved, we shall be clothed upon with our habitation from heaven, so that we shall not be found naked (II Cor. 5.1-3), i.e. with the kind of nakedness which disembodied spirits endure. The notion of a disembodied person is repugnant to the Hebrew mind; a πνεῦμα is something unnatural, monstrous and evil, and the idea that the Risen Christ is such a πνεῦμα is rejected with horror (Luke 24.37). It is exceedingly unlikely that St Paul would have countenanced any notion of Christ's resurrection other than that of a physical resurrection in the sense of the narratives of the Empty Tomb.

Yet the body of the Risen Lord in the Gospel accounts is a glorified body (cf. Phil. 3.21); it is clearly set free from the limitations of our mortal bodies. In Pauline language it has 'put on incorruption' and 'immortality' (I Cor. 15.53f.). Barred doors do not exclude it (John 20.19), although it is a real body which can be handled as well as seen (Luke 24.39; John 20.27). No attempt is made by the NT writers to explain these things. If they could be explained by us, the mystery and miracle of the resurrection would be quite other than it is, and the Christian faith would be a different thing from what it has been throughout its history. Christianity is a religion of miracle, and the miracle of Christ's resurrection is the living centre and object of Christian faith: 'blessed are they that have not seen, and yet have believed' (John 20.29; cf. II Cor. 5.7; I Pet. 1.8). The resurrection of Christ is an act of God; and it is a postulate of biblical thinking that the acts of God are beyond the scrutiny of mortal eyes.

The bodily resurrection of Christ is important theologically because it attests the cosmic significance of God's act in raising Christ from the dead. The 'whole creation' (Rom. 8.22; cf. Mark 16.15) awaits the redemption, which includes the redemption of the body (cf. Rom. 8.23); the resurrection of Christ in the body guarantees the resurrection of Christians with their 'spiritual bodies'—this is the argument of I Cor. 15 as a whole. Thus, the resurrection of Christ is not a case of spiritualistic survival, such as might be the subject of psychical research; it is not the survival of a man, such as might be asserted at a spiritualistic seance; it is the resurrection of humanity, the new Adam. It is the beginning of the new creation of the latter days: Christ is 'the firstfruits of them that are asleep' (I Cor. 15.20-23). It is not a 'natural' event at all; and no scientific account of it may be given for the adequate reason that it is not a process or event in the natural order, even though it has all-important consequences for that order. Scientific explanations cannot be given for events in the eschatological order. It is the exodus event in the salvation-history of the New Israel, the mysterious and supernatural act by which God has brought his people out of the land of bondage into the realm of promise, over which his beloved Son reigns for evermore (cf. Col. 1.13). The power of Christ's resurrection was the very source of the life of the apostolic Church (Phil. 3.10; Eph. 1.19f.; Col. 2.12; Rom. 6.5; I Pet. 1.3; 3.21, etc.). The resurrection of Christ is the sign vouchsafed to those who believe that Christ is indeed 'the Son of God with power' (Rom. 1.4; cf. Acts 2.36; 13.33, etc.). It belongs to the sphere of eschatology and faith, not to that of the natural order and scientific verification. To the primitive Christian greeting, 'The Lord is risen', there is only one response: 'Alleluia.'

THE ASCENSION OF CHRIST

It would appear that the primitive apostolic teaching did not separate the ascension from the resurrection of Christ so thoroughly as did the later Church tradition, which was moulded upon the restyled version of the resurrection-ascension sequence found in the Lucan writings. As we have noted above,[1] the Fourth Gospel, which dates the gift of the Spirit (John 20.22) on the evening of Easter Sunday (John 20.19), after Jesus had already ascended to the Father (John 20.17) and had returned in his glorified body, probably preserves the more primitive understanding of the matter. St Matthew does not mention the ascension, nor does the shorter ending of St Mark; the longer ending merely says that 'the Lord Jesus, after he had spoken unto them, was received up into heaven, and sat down at the right hand of God' (Mark 16.19). The primitive tradition regarded the resurrection and the ascension as two episodes in the same process. Thus, it has often been commented upon as a curious matter that the Epistle to the Hebrews has scarcely any reference to the resurrection of Christ; but it is only the word which is lacking, since the exaltation of the ascended Lord is the principal theme of the book.[2] The resurrection, ascension and present status of Christ at God's 'right hand' are all results of a single action of God in vindicating[3] Christ after his humiliation on the cross (Rom. 8.34; Phil. 2.9, etc.). In several passages the resurrection is not treated as an event separate from the ascension (e.g. Acts 2.32f.; Eph. 1.20; 4.9f.; I Tim. 3.16; I Pet. 3.21f.).

Yet the truth of the resurrection is not the same truth as that of the ascension. As A. M. Ramsey has written: 'There is a clear distinction between them in theological meaning. It was one thing to assert that

---

[1] *Supra*, 116 and footnote on p. 195 *supra*.

[2] The word ἀνάστασις in the NT usually refers to the general resurrection of the dead, and in this sense is found in Heb. 6.2 and 11.35. Except in Acts it is rarely used of the resurrection of Christ (Phil. 3.10; I Pet. 1.3; 3.21; cf. John 11.25). The more usual affirmation is that Jesus (Christ) was raised from the dead or that God raised him from the dead. It may be noted that a 'credal' passage like Phil. 2.5-11 does not specifically mention the resurrection, but includes it implicitly under the heading of 'exaltation' (ὑπερυψόω in 2.9 is a *hapax legomenon* in NT). The only clear reference to Christ's resurrection in Ep. Heb. occurs in 13.20.

[3] The vindication-theme is common in OT (Joseph; Job; the Servant in Isa. 53; the nation or remnant of Israel in Zech. 3 or Dan. 7; Pss. 2, 22, 110, etc.), but in NT the words ἐκδικέω and ἐκδίκησις are never used of the vindication of Christ. (Christ is said to be the one who avenges in II Thess. 1.8; cf. Rev. 6.10.) The sense of ἐκδικέω as meaning 'vindicate' (RV, 'avenge'; RV mg. 'do justice of') can be studied in the parable of the Importunate Widow (Luke 18.1-8), where the word occurs four times. See also *supra*, 188f.

Jesus had been raised from death; it was another thing (however closely connected) to assert that he now shared in the sovereignty of God over heaven and earth.'[1] The symbol (i.e. doctrine, dogma) of the ascension, we might say, is a pictorial way of expressing the significance of the historical event of the resurrection of Christ. We have spoken above of the resurrection as being an eschatological event, a phrase which does not in the least imply that it is not an historical event: the significance of the NT proclamation is that the end-things have entered into history, and the resurrection event is the supreme, dramatic eschatological event within history. The resurrection is not (as Bultmann would have it) a mythological means of expressing the significance of the historical event of the crucifixion; it is itself an historical event, even though it cannot be explained 'scientifically', i.e. as an event in the natural order. It is a unique event, and therefore cannot be subsumed under any scientific class; but then, the difference between historical events in the full complexity of their historical 'once-ness' and events in the order of nature is precisely that the former are unrepeatable. The whole proclamation of the NT depends upon the historical fact of the resurrection of Christ. The original apostolic preaching was not the promulgation of a theology or of an ethic, still less of an existentialist philosophy; it was the assertion of a fact which had happened.[2] The resurrection of Christ is a particular historical event, not a general truth of reason; belief in it involves the acceptance of the testimony of witnesses, not the arguments of dialecticians. The apostles were 'witnesses of the resurrection' (Luke 24.48; Acts 1.8, 22; 2.32; 3.15; 4.33; 5.32; 10.39, 41; 13.31; cf. John 15.27; I Cor. 15.15; I Pet. 5.1), and they were even 'chosen beforehand by God' to bear this witness (Acts 10.41). To accept the Christian faith is to accept the apostles' testimony that Christ was raised from the dead. The NT itself is the written-down apostolic testimony, the apostles' witnessing to us today in our own generation. The Church in history exists to be the bearer of the apostolic witness to the resurrection of Christ; every Eucharist which the Church celebrates is still the testimony of chosen witnesses, 'who did eat and drink with him after he rose from the dead' (Acts 10.41).

It is this historical event of which the significance is brought out by means of the doctrine of the ascension. The ascension need not be thought of as an historical event, unless it be that of the last resurrection-appearance to the disciples.[3] The vivid account of a literal going up into heaven in Acts 1.9-11 is a graphic way of expressing what the early Church believed about the exaltation of the historical Jesus: 'a cloud

[1] *TWBB*, 22f.   [2] See *supra*, 25.   [3] Cf. A. M. Ramsey, *op. cit.*

received him out of their sight'—the traditional symbol of the *shekhinah*-presence (δόξα) of God, into which the Lord had been received to share for ever the power, the glory and the reign of God. The NT *doctrine* of the ascension of Christ teaches three fundamental truths concerning the Risen Lord: that he is our Prophet, Priest and King. Let us consider these truths in the reverse order.

First, Christ is King. That is to say, he shares the throne of God and all authority is given to him in heaven and on earth (Matt. 28.18; Mark 16.19; Acts 2.33; Rom. 8.34; I Cor. 15.25; Eph. 1.20; Heb. 1.3, 13; I Pet. 3.22; Rev. 3.21—and many other passages). He already reigns in glory, though this truth is known only to those who believe in him; its full manifestation must await the parousia. The picture-language by which this truth is expressed is drawn ultimately from the arrangement of an oriental royal court, where the Grand Vizier sits in the place of honour on the monarch's right hand; the NT usage is probably based upon Ps. 110.1, a widely quoted *testimonium* in the apostolic Church.[1] Christ sits in the unique position of dignity and honour at the right hand of God, exercising the kingly authority which the Father has given to him. But he does not sit there alone. He is the Representative Man, the new humanity of the redeemed, and already Christians share his throne, since they have been 'raised together with him' (Col. 3.1; cf. 2.12). Already they reign, as it were eschatologically, with him (I Cor. 4.8); they are even now made a kingdom (I Pet. 2.9; Rev. 1.6; 5.10; 20.6). The baptism of the individual Christian is the eschatological sacrament not only of his resurrection but of his ascension.

Secondly, Christ is Priest. At God's right hand he makes intercession for us (Rom. 8.34; Heb. 7.25; 9.24; I John 2.1; cf. John 14.16; perhaps Acts 7.56). It is the Epistle to the Hebrews which most fully expounds the idea of Christ's priesthood, although, of course, it is present in other parts of the NT. In John 17 ('the high-priestly prayer') Jesus solemnly consecrates himself, as a priest is consecrated, for the sake of his disciples. It is through Christ alone that we have *access* to God, and this is the point of calling Christ ἡ ὁδός (John 14.6, with the significant explanation, 'no one cometh unto the Father but by me'); so in Heb. 10.20 we read that we may now enter the holy place by a new and *living way* (ὁδός) through the veil of Christ's flesh; indeed, the earliest Christians had referred to themselves as those of the Way (Acts 9.2; 19.9; 22.4). A parallel conception is that of 'access' (προσαγωγή, an

---

[1] See *supra*, 154. In Acts 7.56, exceptionally, the dying Stephen sees Christ *standing* on the right hand of God. This would denote an attitude of intercession; if pressed, Christ would be represented as a suppliant, not as a co-ruler. St Chrysostom's suggestion that Christ has risen to greet his first martyr is beautiful but improbable.

'introduction' into someone's presence). The word προσαγωγή occurs three times in NT (all in the Paulines) and it implies the office of a priest: Rom. 5.2, 'through whom we have had our access (introduction) into this grace wherein we stand'; Eph. 2.18, 'through him we both (i.e. Jew and Gentile) have our access in one Spirit to the Father'; Eph. 3.12, 'in whom we have boldness and access. . . .' We might also note I Pet. 3.18, 'Christ also suffered . . . that he might bring (προσαγάγη) us to God.' Finally, we may also recall that in Rev. 1.13 the figure of 'one like unto a Son of Man' (Christ) is arrayed in a priestly garb; and, of course, Christ's priestly work is emphasized in other places in the Apocalypse (e.g. Rev. 1.5f.).

The writer to the Hebrews thinks of Christ as our high priest, who has passed through the heavens (4.14), opening for us the way to the holy presence of God (10.19f.), having made the once-for-all offering for sin, and having now sat down on the right hand of God (10.12). Taking his stand upon Ps. 110.4 ('Thou art a priest for ever, after the order of Melchizedek'), which he cites four times (5.6; 6.20; 7.17 and 21), he argues that this scripture is a prophecy of Christ (as the whole primitive Church understood Ps. 110 to be)[1] and that therefore Christ's priesthood is superior to Aaron's, since Aaron's ancestor, Abraham, received Melchizedek's blessing and paid tithes to him (Gen. 14). Outside Gen. 14 the name of Melchizedek is mentioned in the OT only at Ps. 110.4; the argument about the superiority of Melchizedek's priesthood over Aaron's had presumably been pressed into the service of the Hasmonaean dynasty, and the writer to the Hebrews finds it useful for his own purpose. Christ's priesthood is superior to Aaron's because it is a royal priesthood (7.2) and also because it is everlasting. From the fact that nothing is said in Gen. 14 about either the ancestry or fate of Melchizedek, *Auct. Heb.* concludes that he fittingly foreshadows the endless priesthood of Christ (7.3), 'after the power of an endless life' (7.16). Christ thus abolishes all further human priesthood. In the past, relays of priests were ordained because they were mortal and had to be replaced, but Christ's priesthood does not pass on to any successor, since he ever liveth to make intercession for men (7.23-25).

Thus, Christ has an inviolable, everlasting priesthood (7.24), but this does not mean that he is everlastingly re-offering himself at a heavenly altar; still less does it mean that the sacrifice of Calvary is only a manifestation in time of an eternal truth. Whatever ideas or language *Auct. Heb.* may have borrowed from Platonic sources, he has not lost the biblical awareness of the importance of what is done in history. The sacrifice which Christ offered was the offering of his body (i.e.

[1] Cf. C. H. Dodd, *Acc. Scrip.*, 34f.

himself) (10.10) upon Calvary; it was once only and once for all
(ἐφάπαξ, 7.27; 9.12, 28; 10.10); it was one offering, not many (9.26;
10.14). It is thus utterly different from the oft-repeated, multitudinous
daily sacrifices of the Aaronic priests, which can never take away sin
(10.11). The view that *Auct. Heb.* teaches that Christ in heaven is continually offering himself (or his blood) to God is based on a falsely
Platonizing interpretation which ignores the κεφάλαιον—the 'chief
point' (8.1)—which the writer himself wishes to make: because of the
one, perfect, unrepeatable sacrifice of Calvary, 'we have a high priest
who sat down on the right hand of the throne of the Majesty in the
heavens' (8.1). Christ is seated in the seat of the Vizier, not standing in
the posture and place of the suppliant. He intercedes for us, but with
the effective power of the co-ruler seated on the right hand of the Sovereign God. Because of what he has done in history, there is no more
offering for sin (10.18). The supreme miracle of grace is that he to whom
all power and all judgment is given should be our high priest, who has
carried away our sins, and who lives to make intercession for us. We
may therefore 'go on' (6.1), 'draw near' (10.22), and 'have boldness to
enter the holy place' (10.19). Through him we may offer up our sacrifice
of praise (13.15) and our good works (13.16), for with such sacrifices
God is well pleased (13.16). Christ is our altar, where we may bring our
gifts and whence we may partake of our heavenly nourishment (13.10).

The writer to the Hebrews represents Jesus as fulfilling the pattern
foreshadowed by the ritual of the Day of Atonement (Lev. 16). The
animal victim is slain 'without the camp' (cf. 13.11f.) and then the high
priest enters the holy place bearing its blood as an offering for sin
(13.11). The ascension of Christ into heaven is thought of as the
moment of entry of our high priest into the holy place of God's presence
(i.e. heaven). The true tabernacle (ἡ σκηνὴ ἀληθινή), pitched by God
and not by men, is that in heaven (8.2). The earthly tabernacle which
Moses made is only a 'copy' and 'shadow' (ὑπόδειγμα, σκιά) of the
heavenly (8.5). This is not so much a Platonic conception, as is so often
said, as one drawn from Jewish apocalyptic thought, and the outlook
of Hebrews is thoroughly eschatological.[1] Christ, as every priest must,
when he enters the holy place, carried something to offer (8.3); he
presented his own blood, not that of bullocks and goats (cf. 9.13; 10.4).
This constituted the one true offering, beside which no other was
possible. When at the ascension Christ had once for all completed the
work of high priest, he sat down at the right hand of God, and now

[1] See C. K. Barrett, 'The Eschatology of the Epistle to the Hebrews' in *The
Background of the New Testament and its Eschatology*, ed. W. D. Davies and D.
Daube, esp. 383-93.

intercedes for us. For the writer of Hebrews, the ascension is the moment of the completion of Christ's atoning work, the presenting of his blood in the heavenly tabernacle; it is in order that the typological fulfilment of the Day of Atonement ritual may be worked out in this way that *Auct. Heb.* omits specific reference to the resurrection as a separate event; there is no place for it in his typological scheme. As the high priest of our confession Christ offered himself as the sacrificial victim on Calvary; at his ascension into heaven he presented the offering, his own blood, in 'the true tabernacle'. Christ's ascension is the Christian Day of Atonement.

Thirdly, Christ is Prophet. The characteristic of the OT prophets was that they were *sent* from God (II Chron. 36.15f.; Jer. 25.4; 26.5; 29.19, etc.; Matt. 23.34; Luke 11.49; Mark 12.2-5); in the customary language of the NT they are 'apostled' (i.e. 'sent') on a special mission or with a special message from God. Thus the NT regards Christ as the Prophet *par excellence*—'the prophet that cometh into the world' (John 6.14; cf. John 1.21; 7.40; Matt. 21.11), i.e. the fulfilment of the prophecy of Deut. 18.15, 18, the prophet like unto Moses.[1] But Moses left a commandment which those who remained after his 'assumption' had no power to fulfil, and a better covenant was necessary (Heb. 7.22; 8.6f., etc.); Christ, however, had made a covenant which, after his ascension, his followers were empowered to fulfil. Unlike Moses, Christ could give what he commanded. From heaven he poured down the gifts of his grace, or, alternatively, the gift of the Spirit, upon the Church below (Eph. 4.8, misquoting Ps. 68.18: 'When he ascended on high, he led captivity captive, and gave gifts unto men';[2] Acts 2.33; John 16.7). Herein lay the necessity of the ascension; as a person localized in time and place, the power and influence of Christ was severely restricted (Luke 12.50); it was 'expedient' that he should 'go away' (John 16.7), in order that he might return as the Universal Spirit who would be with his disciples at every place and time (John 14.16, 26; 15.26; 16.7, 13, 16), even unto 'the consummation of the age' (Matt. 28.20). He is the one who has himself been *sent* by the Father, and who now sends his disciples upon their mission to the world (John 20.21). It is, however, only in Heb. 3.1 that Christ is actually called 'apostle'—'the apostle and high priest of our confession, even Jesus'.

CHRIST THE CONQUEROR

The NT represents the resurrection-ascension of Christ in pictorial, even mythological, figures as a divine victory over the hostile powers of evil. In so doing it makes use of primitive symbols akin to those which

---

[1] See *supra*, 167.   [2] See *supra*, 63.

figured in the ancient myths of the divine Conqueror who slew the dragon of chaos. The editors of the OT, because the concept had been thoroughly 'demythologized' by the prophets of Israel, were content to allow the ancient mythological language to remain in several places (e.g. Pss. 74.12-14; 89.8-10; Job 9.13; 26.12f.); the historical deliverance of Israel from Egyptian bondage could be expressed in the language of the ancient myth (e.g. Ex. 14.21; 15.1-21), and likewise also the deliverance from Babylonian captivity (Isa. 51.9-11; Ezek. 29.3f.). It is not, therefore, surprising if we find that the NT writers make use of the same kind of imagery, which, after all, is the basic material with which unsophisticated man does his thinking. He does not use philosophical concepts; he thinks in images. Because the Bible uses picture-thinking rather than philosophical concepts, it never goes out of date. Had it tried to express the truth about God and man in philosophical categories, it would have been out of date long ago. It speaks to every generation in the basic image-language of humanity, the language which all men understand, except when in their sophistication they have lost touch with the living sources of reality-thinking which lie deep at the roots of personality itself. It is a mistake to suppose (with Bultmann[1]) that we can explain to modern men the real meaning of the Gospel by explaining away its mythological symbolism. There is no reason to think, as Bultmann apparently does, that the NT writers were not as conscious as he is of the fact that they were using symbolical language when they spoke of (e.g.) Jesus's ascending into heaven or descending into hell. They could express their meaning only in such symbolic forms, and it is possible for men (except the sophisticated) in every generation to understand quite clearly what they meant. It is incredible that, for example, St Luke in telling the story of Jesus's ascension meant the parable to be taken literally; he knew better than we do that religious truth, ultimate truth, which passes the frontiers of intellectual understanding, can be grasped only by the faith-inspired human imagination, so that through it men can hear, each in his own language, the proclamation of the mighty works of God.

In his widely influential book *Christus Victor*[2] Gustaf Aulén attempted to show that there was an older view of the atonement wrought by Christ than either of the two views which have dominated Western theology for a long time—the so-called 'objective' type of view associated with St Anselm's 'satisfaction theory', and the so-called 'subjective' view, often called 'the moral theory', associated with the name of Abelard and with recent 'liberal' theology from Schleiermacher to

---

[1] Cf. his famous essay in *Kerygma and Myth*, ed. H. W. Bartsch, ET, 1953.
[2] ET by A. G. Hebert, 1931.

Rashdall. The dominant view of the NT and of the Fathers of the ancient Church, which Aulén calls 'the classic view', takes the form of a dramatic or mythological representation of the atonement as a victory won by Christ over the evil 'powers' to which man has become enslaved, especially the Devil, Sin and Death. This *Christus-Victor* conception has been greatly elaborated, especially in Scandinavia, by scholars like the late Anton Fridrichsen of Uppsala.[1] They have rendered valuable service in calling attention to this dramatic or mythological element in the NT presentation of the truth of our salvation, although it is perhaps hardly correct to speak of it as in any sense constituting a view (still less a theory) of the *atonement*. The fundamental meaning of the atonement in the NT teaching is, as we shall see, incorporation into the redeemed humanity of Jesus Christ, through baptism into Christ's 'spiritual body', the Church or Israel of God. The truth contained in the so-called 'classic view' is that this atonement 'in Christ' is made possible only by what Christ has done, which is represented mythologically by the picture of his defeat of the powers of evil. The 'classic view' is a presentation of the fact of *salvation* rather than of atonement, as indeed was its counterpart in the ancient Semitic mythology: 'God is my King of old, working salvation in the midst of the earth. Thou didst break up the sea by thy strength: thou breakest the heads of the dragons in the waters. Thou breakest the heads of Leviathan in pieces, thou gavest him to be meat to the people inhabiting the wilderness' (Ps. 74.12-14). The act of new creation in Christ is an act of salvation like the action of the first creation, when the chaos-dragon of the deep (*Tiamat*) was slain by the divine King. Since the salvation wrought by God at the exodus was thought of as an act of new creation (e.g. Isa. 43.15-19; Wisd. 19.6-8),[2] involving again a deliverance from the power of the deep, it is not surprising that we find in the NT the representation of salvation in Christ as alike an act of new creation and of the defeat of the powers of evil. The Sea-Miracles of the Gospels, in particular, should be read against this background (Mark 4.35-41; 6.45-52).[3] However closely connected with atonement doctrine these conceptions may be, they are not the same thing; it would be better to say that the idea of *Christus Victor* is concerned with the creation-salvation concept rather than with that of atonement for sin; or we might say that it is concerned with the defeat and destruction of the alien (non-human) 'powers' rather than with the reconciliation of rebellious and sinful men to the holy God. Christ's victorious death is, of course, the link between

[1] See esp. Ragnar Leivestad, *Christ the Conqueror*, 1954.
[2] And see further Strack-Bill., I, 69f., 594-6.
[3] Cf. *supra*, 100.

the two conceptions: Christ triumphed over the 'principalities and powers' which he had defeated in battle (Col. 2.15), and hence he could blot out the charge against us (Col. 2.14), thus securing the forgiveness of all our trespasses (Col. 2.13); as individuals we appropriate to ourselves these benefits when we are buried with Christ in baptism and raised with him to resurrection life (Col. 2.12).

The NT teaches that Christ has gained a victory over (the evil powers that rule) the world (κόσμος) (John 16.33) and that by faith in him Christians too may overcome (the evil powers that rule) the world (I John 5.4f.). The verb νικάω as applied to Christ is in the NT an almost exclusively Johannine word.[1] In I John it is taught that Christians overcome ὁ πονηρός (2.13f.), or unbelieving spirits and the spirit of antichrist (4.4), or the world (5.4f.), through faith that Jesus is the Son of God. The Apocalypse likewise thinks of Christians as sharing in Christ's victory and dwells upon the rewards which ὁ νικῶν shall receive (2.7, 11, 17, 26; 3.5, 12, 21; 21.7), including that of sitting with Christ in his Father's throne (3.21). The victory metaphor is a curious one, at first sight, for a Jew like the Apocalyptist: it is that of the *victor ludorum*. But it can be explained readily enough. The Greek games were, of course, pagan rites in honour of the gods ('the Olympics') and of the divine Emperor ('the Beast'); they are part of the whole diabolical counter-reign of Satan, the blasphemous caricature of the reign of God; *per contra* the Christian life is a contest in which ὁ νικῶν will receive the victor's wreath or crown (στέφανος, Rev. 2.10; 3.11, etc.; cf. I Cor. 9.25).[2] But other usages of νικάω imply a military metaphor: twice the saints are overcome in the struggle against the beast from the abyss (Rev. 11.7; 13.7). In two other passages the saints overcome through the power of Christ: when the Dragon (Satan, the Devil) is cast out of heaven by Michael, the saints 'overcame him because of the blood of the Lamb' (12.11); and the seer in his vision of the 'glassy sea' sees 'those that come victorious from the beast' (15.2). The Apocalyptist is not afraid to use the ancient mythological conception of the divine warfare against the Dragon in order to represent the cosmic

---

[1] There is, however, the very significant Luke 11.22, ἐπὰν δὲ ἰσχυρότερος αὐτοῦ ἐπελθὼν νικήσῃ αὐτόν: Jesus is the Stronger-than-Satan who binds him and divides his spoils, as the exorcisms prove (see *supra*, 98). Apart from Rom. 3.4 (quoting Ps. 50.6, LXX (EVV, 51.4)) and 12.21 all the other occurrences are in John (once), I John (six times) and Rev. (16 times). The noun νίκη is found only at I John 5.4, ἡ νίκη ἡ νικήσασα τὸν κόσμον. The late form (mid first century) τὸ νῖκος appears in OT quotations in Matt. 12.20 (Isa. 42.3) and I Cor. 15.54f. (Hos. 13.14), and in I Cor. 15.57, 'Thanks be to God who giveth us τὸ νῖκος through our Lord Jesus Christ'.

[2] A brilliant and imaginative account of the influence of the Imperial Games upon the mind of the author of the Apocalypse will be found in E. Stauffer, *Christ and the Caesars*, 179-91.

significance of what took place through the crucifixion and resurrection of Christ; it is all highly poetical and dramatic, and must be read with a poet's eye. It is a commonplace of Jewish apocalyptic that the last things will be like the first: the new creation will re-enact and restore the original 'genesis' of heaven and earth. Thus, the λόγος which in the beginning conquered chaos (*tohu wa-bhohu*, Gen. 1.2; cf. Isa. 45.18) and the deep (*tehom*, cf. Bab. *Tiamat*), the λόγος-light which preceded the light of the sun and which the darkness could not overcome (John 1.5), shall in the end-time conquer the beast from the abyss, and the chaos-dragon and his armies from Hades: the λόγος Θεοῦ appears in the seer's vision as the rider on the white horse who was given a στέφανος, going forth 'conquering and to conquer' (Rev. 6.2; 19.11-16). The forces of the beast 'shall war against the Lamb, and the Lamb shall overcome them, for he is Lord of lords and King of kings' (17.14). 'The Lion that is of the tribe of Judah, the Root of David, hath overcome' (5.5). The powers of darkness, which have held sway over this world-age, are destroyed by the Conqueror at the new creation, and henceforth there is to be everlasting, sunless Day (Rev. 21.23; 22.5; cf. Isa. 60.19f.; Enoch 45.4f.).[1]

The NT view of the κόσμος differs from Gnostic and Hellenistic views in that it does not conceive the material world to be evil.[2] The κόσμος is created by God (Matt. 24.21; Mark 13.19; John 1.10; Acts 17.24; Rom. 1.20, etc.), and therefore fundamentally good (cf. Gen. 1.31).[3] But it has fallen under the power of the evil one (cf. I John 5.19, ὁ κόσμος ὅλος ἐν τῷ πονηρῷ κεῖται), and hence there arises the distinctive NT sense of κόσμος as the world over against God, in opposition to God, rebelling against God. In this sense the κόσμος is ignorant of God (John 1.10; 14.17) and is preoccupied with its own foolish wisdom (I Cor. 1.20f.; 3.19). It hates Christ, because its works are evil (John 7.7); it is opposed to Christ because he and his kingship are not of

---

[1] N. A. Dahl (in *The Background of the New Testament and its Eschatology*, ed. W. D. Davies and D. Daube, 428), remarks that the view that the new creation will bring the *elimination* of the powers of darkness is most clearly stated in the Dead Sea Manual of Discipline and is also predominant in rabbinic sources. (See Gaster, *SDSS*, 55f.).

[2] The word κόσμος is of wide application and ranges in the NT from meaning a 'hair-do' (I Pet. 3.3) to 'the created universe'. The basic signification in cl. Gk. is 'harmonious arrangement' or 'order', hence 'ornament', 'decoration' (so LXX, Gen. 2.1; Deut. 4.19, etc.). Then it came to mean 'the universe' (but not thus used in LXX; earliest use in this sense, Wisd. and II Macc.), e.g. John 21.25; Acts 17.24; Rom. 4.13; I Cor. 3.22; 8.4; Phil. 2.15. Finally it comes to mean 'the inhabitants of the world', 'the human race', and tends to replace the γῆ or οἰκουμένη of LXX; it can merely mean 'the world and his wife', e.g. 'The κόσμος is gone after him' (John 12.19), though it is probable that St John as usual intends a deep double meaning.

[3] A common early Christian expression (ἀπὸ) καταβολῆς κόσμου (Matt. 25.34; Luke 11.50; John 17.24; Eph. 1.4; I Pet. 1.20; Heb. 4.3; 9.26; Rev. 13.8; 17.8) refers, of course, to the creation of the world by God.

this world (John 8.23; 18.36); likewise Christ's disciples are hated because they are not of the world (John 15.19; 17.14), and they must therefore go out of the world (I Cor. 5.10; 11.32). Christians must not love the world (I John 2.15-17; James 1.27; 4.4; II Pet. 2.20, etc.). The same deprecatory sense is associated with the word αἰών when it is used of ὁ αἰὼν οὗτος as contrasted with ὁ αἰὼν ὁ ἐρχόμενος, with which it is strongly contrasted (e.g. Matt. 12.32; Mark 10.30); cf. Gal. 1.4, Christ 'gave himself up for our sins, that he might deliver us out of this present evil αἰών'. In EVV αἰών is often rendered by 'world', and in the sense of 'this age' it is indistinguishable in meaning from the NT use of κόσμος as the world standing in opposition to the purpose of God (e.g. Matt. 13.22; Mark 4.19; Luke 16.8; 20.34; Rom. 12.2; I Cor. 1.20; 2.6; 3.18). In I Cor. 1.20 and Eph. 2.2f. κόσμος and αἰών are clearly synonymous terms.

The world has been subjected to Satan, and is under the domination of his demoniacal servants. The parable of the Strong Man Armed, as a commentary by Jesus himself upon the Beelzebub charge, clearly sets forth the view that Christ's power over the evil spirits proves that Satan is defeated and that the end of his kingship is at hand (Matt. 12.24-29; Luke 11.15-22; Mark 3.22-27).[1] Jesus proleptically proclaims his victory, 'I beheld Satan fallen as lightning from heaven,' when the Seventy return and report that even the demons were subject in Christ's name (Luke 10.18). A similar idea appears in Rev. 12.7-17, where it is suggested that the demonic fury of the enemies of the Church is due to the fact that Satan has been cast down out of heaven to work his wrath upon the earth and the sea, 'knowing that he hath but a short time'.[2] That 'things will get worse before they get better' is a commonplace of apocalyptic; the Lord himself had warned his disciples of 'tribulation such as there hath not been the like from the beginning of the creation' (Mark 13.19). Now that he has been defeated and his days are numbered, Satan, like a mad beast that is cornered, will work as much destruction as he can before his end finally comes. In the Apocalypse he is finally, with his false prophet, 'cast alive into the lake of fire that burneth with brimstone', after his conflict with the Rider on the White Horse (Rev. 19.20f.). A variant version of this prophecy is found in Rev. 20.1-3, 7-10, but the meaning is the same.

[1] See *supra*, 98f.

[2] In this graphic parable 'the woman' doubtless represents the faithful remnant of the old Israel, the man child is Christ, and the seed of the woman is the Christian Church. Rev. 12.5 refers to the birth and ascension of Christ and 12.6 may possibly allude to the flight of the Christians to the desert at the outbreak of the Jewish War (A.D. 66). The Church is miraculously preserved despite the fierceness of the Satanic persecutions. See *supra*, 176.

Satan has, so to speak, deteriorated in character since his first appearance in the OT as a respectable member of the heavenly council in Job 1 and 2 (cf. Zech. 3.1f.), who held the office of public prosecutor.[1] Not until after OT times is he identified with the Serpent of Gen. 3 (the earliest ref. is Wisd. 2.24, 'By envy of the devil death entered into the world'), a view common amongst the rabbis, accepted by St Paul (Rom. 16.20, 'The God of peace shall bruise Satan under your feet shortly'; cf. Gen. 3.15; II Cor. 11.2f.), and emphatically proclaimed by the Seer (Rev. 12.9; 20.2). Satan and his minions, the demons, are stirred to frenzied apprehension by the encounter with their Conqueror, the Christ (Mark 1.24, etc.). In Enoch 90.20-27 it is held that the Messiah will judge the demons; some such belief seems to underlie the plaint of the demons in Matt. 8.29, 'Art thou come here to torment us *before the time*?'—i.e. before the last judgment. St John, who records no exorcisms in his Gospel, nevertheless makes the point in his own way: 'The prince of this world hath been judged' (John 16.11; cf. 16.33).[2] St Paul believes that 'the saints' will share in the Messianic judgment not only of the world but also of angels (I Cor. 6.2f.). In his view angels are a kind of demon (there are no good angels in St Paul; cf. I Cor. 11.10; II Cor. 12.7), as they are in Enoch 1–36, where the demons are disembodied spirits (cf. Matt. 12.43-45; Luke 11.24-26) and are identified with the fallen angels of Gen. 6.1-4 (cf. also Jude 6; II Pet. 2.4, 'the angels which kept not their first estate'). These are the creatures with whom St Paul thinks that the worshippers in the mystery-religions have κοινωνία and to whom the Gentile εἰδωλόθυτα are offered (I Cor. 10.20f.); for (as in the Apocalypse) the Kingdom of God has its blasphemous caricature in the kingdom of Satan (Matt. 12.26); it, too, has its 'cup' and its 'table' (I Cor. 10.21)—a reference doubtless to the 'sacramental' meals of the mystery-cults. It is not at all improbable that the difficult

---

[1] The Heb. word *satan* means 'adversary', 'accuser', in an ordinary everyday sense (e.g. II Sam. 19.22; I Kings 5.4; 11.25; cf. Num. 22.22). Satan became the angelic tempter by slow stages (in I Chron. 21.1 he moves David to the sin of numbering Israel, whereas in II Sam. 24.1 Yahweh himself does it). In the NT the proper name Satan is often used (Mark 3.26; 4.15; Luke 10.18, etc.) and also it is translated into Greek as ὁ Διάβολος, the slanderer, accuser, calumniator (the legal opposite of ὁ παράκλητος); the adjective διάβολος, slanderous, appears in I Tim. 3.11; II Tim. 3.3; Titus 2.3. In Matt. 12.24-27 (cf. 10.25); Mark 3.22; Luke 11.14-23 he is identified with Beelzebub, a word of uncertain spelling and derivation, which may be a mocking identification with the god (demon) of Ekron (cf. II Kings 1.2), dubbed 'the lord of flies'. He is often regarded as a sky-being (cf. Eph. 2.2; Luke 10.18, etc.) but in current Jewish thought his habitat and that of his demons is held to be the underworld (cf. II Pet. 2.4; Jude 6). This ambiguity about his habitat is one of the many indications that thoughtful Jews knew that they were using pictorial symbols which they did not themselves take literally.

[2] St John, of course, takes demon-possession at least as seriously as the Synoptists. He reports the accusation that Jesus has a demon (John 7.20; 8.48f., 52; cf. Mark 3.22) and he regards Judas as demon-possessed (6.70f.; 13.2, 27) and perhaps also the unbelieving 'Jews' (8.44).

saying in Matt. 11.12 (cf. Luke 16.16) is to be explained by reference to the current belief in the struggle of the two kingdoms,[1] that of God and that of Satan, which reaches its decisive battle in the onslaught of Jesus upon the fortress of the 'Strong Man': 'From the days of John the Baptist until now the Kingdom of Heaven suffereth violence (βιάζεται) and men of violence (βιασταί) take it by force' (RV). If we translate βιασταί thus, the saying is almost unintelligible; but if the βιασταί are not *men* of violence at all, but demons, then the meaning is clear: John the Baptist is the calendar-sign in world history for the outbreak of the last, decisive battle between the two kingdoms, in which the divine kingdom, though victorious, receives many grievous blows through the violent fury of the cornered Dragon.[2] As St John puts the matter in his own way, 'To this end was the Son of God manifested, that he might destroy the works of the Devil' (I John 3.8; cf. Heb. 2.14). In this age, the eve of the final παρουσία of Antichrist, there are already many antichrists in the world, and it is by their presence that we know that this is 'the last hour' (I John 2.18, 22; 4.1, 3; cf. 3.8, 10; John 8.44).

THE DESCENT OF CHRIST INTO HELL

There has been much discussion about the identity of the 'disobedient spirits' to whom after his death Jesus is declared to have preached (I Pet. 3.18-22).[3] Selwyn and others have held that the πνεύματα ἐν φυλακῇ are the fallen angels, as II Pet. 2.4f. would suggest. But nowhere else in Jewish or Christian apocalyptic is any interest displayed in the salvation of these creatures; and such a passage as Heb. 2.14-16 might be held to deny the possibility of it.[4] It is more likely that the words 'seen of angels' in the credal formula of I Tim. 3.16 refer not to any seeing of Christ by the imprisoned angels in Hades but to the fact that the angelic hosts of heaven were spectators of the drama of human salvation (cf. Ignatius, *Trall.* 9). Reicke thinks that the 'spirits in prison' are the fallen angels of Gen. 6, which play a large part in apocalyptic speculation, together with the wicked generation (the most wicked that ever lived, Gen. 6.5, 11, 13) of the days of Noah, who alone with his household was saved in the ark (Gen. 7.1; I Pet. 3.20;

---

[1] Cf. Gaster, *SDSS*, 53-6, 261-84.

[2] Cf. A. Fridrichsen, 'Jesu kamp mot de urene ander' in *Svensk teologisk kvartalskrift*, 1929 (ET, 'The Conflict of Jesus with the Unclean Spirits', *Theology*, XXII, No. 129, March, 1931).

[3] See B. Reicke, *The Disobedient Spirits and Christian Baptism*, Copenhagen, 1946; R. Leivestad, *Christ the Conqueror*, 172-7; E. G. Selwyn, *The First Epistle of St Peter*, *ad loc.* and 318-36.

[4] On the other hand, Col. 1.20 probably implies the 'reconciliation' of the spiritual world-rulers; see *infra*, 213.

II Pet. 2.5). Leivestad thinks that they are the peculiarly wicked generation of Noah's day, and the meaning is that if even these can be saved, then truly the salvation wrought by Christ is universal. In favour of Leivestad's view is I Pet. 4.6: 'For unto this end was the gospel preached to the dead. . . .' It seems reasonable to suppose that this verse explains 3.18; κηρύσσειν is explained by εὐαγγελίζειν and τὰ πνεύματα by οἱ νεκροί. The earliest Christians must often have wondered, as we do today, what would happen to those who had died without having heard the preaching of Christ and without being given the opportunity to repent and believe. The answer, which is given in mythological form in the legend of Christ's preaching in Hades, and which is proclaimed every time the Church repeats the Apostles' Creed ('he descended into hell'), is that Christ's salvation is indeed for *all*; it extends to every person who has ever lived at any time, and it is available even for the very wicked, even for the sinful generation of Noah. Some such teaching as this is implicit in the great illustration of justification by faith which is embodied in Christ's word to the Penitent Thief: 'Today thou shalt be with me in paradise' (Luke 23.43). It is open for us to believe, if we wish to do so, that even Judas, after he had cast down his thirty pieces of silver in the sanctuary and gone to his place, was numbered among those who heard the voice of the Son of God and lived. Surely St John, in his own allusive fashion, is setting forth the doctrine of the preaching to the dead: 'The hour cometh, and now is, when the dead shall hear the voice of the Son of God, and they that hear shall live' (John 5.25; cf. 11.43). There is also one more passage in the NT which attests the doctrine of the descent into hell, viz. Eph. 4.9f.: 'Now this, he ascended, what is it but that he also descended into the lower parts of the earth (εἰς τὰ κατώτερα μέρη τῆς γῆς)? he that descended is the same also that ascended far above all the heavens, that he might fill all things.' If the meaning had been simply that Christ descended from heaven to earth, the words 'the lower parts of the earth' would not have been used. If we recall the customary NT view of the universe as existing in three storeys (e.g. Phil. 2.10; Rev. 5.13), it is clear that τὰ κατώτερα μέρη τῆς γῆς must mean the underworld.

CHRIST'S VICTORY OVER THE WORLD-POWERS

In the Hellenistic world the Christian preachers encountered the belief in a great variety of λεγόμενοι θεοί, so-called gods, which Paul, as we have noted, regards as δαιμόνια (I Cor. 8.5; 10.19-21). But apart from the δαιμόνια worshipped in the pagan cults, there are also the elemental spirits, rather like personified natural forces, which are the actual rulers of the κόσμος,[1] and which are collectively called τὰ στοιχεῖα τοῦ κόσμου (Col. 2.8, 20; Gal. 4.3, 9), 'the rudiments (elements, RV mg.) of the world'. They have many titles, such as ἀρχαί, ἐξουσίαι, δυνάμεις, κύριοι, κυριότητες, ἄρχοντες, θρόνοι, ἄγγελοι, etc.; and it is impossible to distinguish shades of meaning among them. We gather the impression from his letters that Paul would not have treated these semi-metaphysical notions very seriously if he had not found that his converts, particularly amongst the Galatians and the Colossians, were doing so. He is more concerned with man's enslavement to sin, death and law than with his bondage to such 'weak and beggarly elements', which by nature are not divine at all, and from which Christians have been liberated by Christ (Gal. 4.8f.). Paul's own interest is evangelical and religious, not at all speculative and philosophical. But his converts are still fascinated by such 'astrological' superstition with its calendar of 'days and months and seasons and years' (Gal. 4.10) and its prohibitions, 'handle not, touch not, taste not' (Col. 2.20). If Christians have died with Christ from the στοιχεῖα τοῦ κόσμου, why should they still subject themselves to ordinances of this kind (*ibid.*)? 'Now that ye have come to know God, or rather to be known by God, how turn ye back to the weak and beggarly elemental forces, whereunto ye desire to be in bondage over again?' (Gal. 4.9). The cardinal matter is that Christians have been delivered from *sin*; they belong to the new αἰών, and are no longer subject to the rulers of this age, which were *de jure* dethroned at Christ's triumphant death, although *de facto* they still wield the semblance of their authority while the Two Ages run side by side. Indeed, they still have their rôle to play in the ordering of the universe, until the day when Christ shall have abolished 'all rule and all authority and power' (I Cor. 15.24).

These elemental forces or 'world-rulers' were created by God and hence are fundamentally good: for 'in him (Christ) were all things created, in the heavens and upon the earth, things visible and things invisible, whether thrones or dominions or principalities or powers (εἴτε θρόνοι εἴτε κυριότητες εἴτε ἀρχαὶ εἴτε ἐξουσίαι); all things have been created through him and unto him' (Col. 1.16). They have thus an important place in the providential ordering of the created universe; but they are not independent deities and do not need to be worshipped or propitiated. They rule over certain domains of the created order, but they are themselves still creatures, perishable, subordinated and finite, and hence to worship them is idolatrous. Christ alone is to be worshipped, because he is πρωτότοκος πάσης κτίσεως (Col. 1.15), i.e.

---

[1] The word κοσμοκράτωρ is found only in Eph. 6.12 and not elsewhere in bib. lit. or indeed in cl. Gk. lit. Nevertheless it usefully describes the character and function of the host of 'principalities', 'powers', etc.

(as the context makes quite clear) *not* the first of all created things
(Arianism) but *the one who takes precedence*, like a first-born son, over
all the rest of creation, which was made by him and for him. It would
seem, however, that in St Paul's thought, these world-rulers had fallen
from grace and had rebelled against God and become corrupted; the
'Fall' was a cosmic event, and was not simply the Fall of Man; the
whole world-order was thus brought into subjection to corruption and
death. But the death of Christ had reconciled to God the hostile, fallen
powers, and had set free from bondage not only humanity but the world-
powers as well; redemption also had been upon a cosmic scale. Thus,
when in II Cor. 5.19 Paul says that God was in Christ reconciling
(καταλλάσσων) the κόσμος to himself, the word κόσμος here does not
mean merely the world of men, but the world as including its στοιχεῖα,
its elemental ruling powers. In Col. 1.19f. St Paul explicitly says that
the reconciliation wrought by Christ's death was total, cosmic, world-
inclusive; this was because God the Father willed that God himself in
the totality or fulness (τὸ πλήρωμα) of his being should be present in
Christ, so that Christ's death ('the blood of his cross') should effect
total reconciliation, should reconcile all things to himself, 'whether
things upon the earth or things in the heavens'. The fact that a reconciliation took place implies previous hostility, and in I Cor. 2.6-8 it is
taught that it was the rebellious world-rulers who were responsible for
the crucifixion of Jesus: Paul is saying that, had 'the rulers of this
age' known the mystery of the person of Christ, they would not have
crucified the Lord of glory. The expression ἄρχοντες τοῦ αἰῶνος τούτου
can mean only the spiritual world-rulers in their corruption and blindness—not human ἄρχοντες like Pilate and Herod (despite Acts 3.17,
where Peter says that the rulers killed the Prince of life in ignorance:
perhaps it was held that Pilate and the rest were mere cats-paws in the
hands of the world-powers). A similar conception appears in Col. 2.14f.,
where it is said that, in the act by which Christ cancelled the bond of
debt which was against us, nailing it to the cross, he also put off from
himself (the domination of) the ἀρχαί and ἐξουσίαι, and made a show of
them, as a conquering Caesar exhibited the princes and generals, whom
he had defeated in battle and taken prisoner, in the triumphal procession through his capital city. Two very vivid metaphors are here placed
(somewhat incongruously) side by side: a bill of servitude or of debt
(often a man was sold into slavery for debt) is nailed up for all to see
that it has been cancelled, and that therefore the slave or debtor is free:
the hostile powers, who formerly held the slave or debtor in bondage,
are now themselves made (perhaps willingly, if they have been reconciled) prisoners in the triumphal progress of Christ the conqueror.

But here, as elsewhere, the polarity of the 'even now' and the 'not yet' must be borne in mind. Christ has conquered, even reconciled, the hostile powers, and yet their hostility still continues in this age. Still we have to wage the unrelenting struggle against the rulers of this world-age. 'Our wrestling is not against flesh and blood, but against the principalities, against the powers, against the world-rulers of this dark-ness, against the spiritual hosts of wickedness in the heavenlies' (Eph. 6.12). The decisive battle of the war has been won, but the cells of resistance behind the enemy-lines must continue the struggle until the defeated foe at last lays down his arms. Until that day dawns, Christians know that none of the elemental forces—'neither death, nor life, nor angels, nor principalities, nor things present, nor things to come, nor powers, nor height, nor depth, nor any other creature'—can cut them off from the divine love mediated to them through Jesus Christ (Rom. 8.38f.). Thus, Christians share in Christ's victory and are 'more than conquerors through him that loved us' (8.37). The prophecy of Isa. 25.8 is fulfilled: 'Death is swallowed up in victory' (I Cor. 15.54); 'thanks be to God who giveth us the victory through our Lord Jesus Christ' (15.57). Christ sits at God's right hand in heaven, far above all rule and authority and power and dominion; he is thus Lord of all creation; and the prophecy is fulfilled that all things should be put in subjection under his feet (Ps. 8.6; cf. I Cor. 15.27; Heb. 2.8, etc.) (Eph. 1.21f.). But he is not only supreme in the order of creation; he is also supreme in the sphere of redemption. He is the head of the Church, which is his body (Eph. 1.22f.), πρωτότοκος in the order of redemption ('firstborn from the dead', Col. 1.18) as in that of creation (Col. 1.15). Therefore as the Lord of creation and as κεφαλή and ἀρχή of the Church (Col. 1.18), he is the πλήρωμα of the divine being, the fulness of God in all his creative and redemptive power (Eph. 1.23; Col. 1.19). He has conquered the κόσμος (John 16.33), reconciled to God the rulers of this world-age (Col. 1.20; cf. II Cor. 5.19), and through his death he has brought to nought him that had the power of death, that is, the Devil, and delivered all those who through fear of death were subject to bondage (Heb. 2.14f.; cf. I John 3.8). The hostile and rebellious world is reconciled to God and delivered from the power of the Evil One, and thus Christ is both the Conqueror (Rev. 6.2; 17.14, etc.) and the Saviour of the world (John 4.42; I John 4.14; cf. John 3.17; 12.47).

THE ATONEMENT WROUGHT BY CHRIST

THE word 'atonement' is scarcely a NT word at all. It is not found in the RV of the NT and occurs in AV only at Rom. 5.11 (RV 'reconciliation'). The verb 'to atone' is found in EVV of the OT, being used chiefly in connection with Heb. *kipper*. It means that by which God's wrath is propitiated or averted, or alternatively that by which sin is expiated or 'covered' (e.g. Ex. 30.15f.; 32.30; Lev. 1.4; 4.26, 31, 35; Num. 25.13; cf. 'appease' in Gen. 32.20).[1] The word 'atonement' (lit. at-one-ment) implies a reconciliation after a period of estrangement, and in the EVV of the NT the words 'reconcile' and 'reconciliation' are used (except AV of Rom. 5.11) to translate καταλλάσσω and καταλλαγή. In general theological usage, however, the word 'atonement' has come to denote, not so much the state of reconciliation with God into which Christians have been brought by Christ, as Christ's reconciling act itself, viz. his death and rising again. This usage is entirely in harmony with the use of 'atonement' in the OT as meaning that by which expiation is made; it may therefore be said to be biblical, although it is not a NT use.

RECONCILIATION

The words καταλλάσσω and καταλλαγή are found in the NT only in Paul. Indeed, apart from I Cor. 7.11 (the wife being reconciled to her husband) they occur only in the two passages Rom. 5.10f. and II Cor. 5.18-20. The metaphor is that of making peace after war, or (more probably in the context of Pauline thought) being readmitted to the presence and favour of our rightful Sovereign, after we have rebelled against him. The idea of reconciliation, however, is present also in Eph. 2.12-17, when it is affirmed that Christ, 'who is our peace', has broken down the middle wall of partition—a metaphor drawn from the Jerusalem Temple—between Jew and Gentile, and out of the two has created 'one new man', and has reconciled them both 'in one body unto

---

[1] For a brief but valuable exposition of this OT theme see art. 'Atonement' by A. G. Hebert in *TWBB*, 25f.

God through the cross, having slain the enmity thereby'. Reconciliation between man and man, even abolishing that most bitter of all racial hostilities, the Jewish-Gentile division, is a consequence of the reconciliation of man to God. The whole conception of 'peace' (εἰρήνη), very prominent in St Paul, belongs to this cycle of ideas; Christ by his death has brought to us the peace of God (e.g. Rom. 5.1; I Cor. 7.15; Gal. 5.22; Eph. 4.3; Phil. 4.7; Col. 3.15; II Thess. 3.16, etc.) and hence we are enabled to live at peace with all men (Rom. 12.18; cf. Mark 9.50). We have noted in the previous chapter that St Paul thinks of Christ's death as having effected reconciliation with God not only on behalf of men: he has reconciled all things, on earth and in the heavens, through 'the blood of his cross' (i.e. through his death)—including the spiritual 'powers' or 'world-rulers' (Col. 1.20; cf. II Cor. 5.19). (The word used for 'reconcile' in Eph. 2.16 and Col. 1.20f. is ἀποκαταλλάσσω which occurs in NT only in these passages, and indeed is found nowhere in the LXX or other Greek versions of the OT or in classical authors.)

St Paul considers the work of reconciliation to have been performed on a cosmic scale (II Cor. 5.19), but he is specially concerned to emphasize that Christians are reconciled to God. It is as though they, too, who once were enemies, have, like the conquered 'powers', been overcome by Christ's victorious cross and surrendered themselves willingly to the obedience of their rightful King. The conquering death of Christ is the supreme manifestation of the love of God: 'God commendeth his own love towards us, in that, while we were yet sinners, Christ died for us' (Rom. 5.8). The King, who could have annihilated his enemies, did not do so, but actually reconciled them by the death of his Son (5.10f.). Paul stresses the fact that it is the actual *death* of Christ which effects the reconciliation (Rom. 5.6-10; Eph. 2.13; Col. 1.20); and he equally emphatically stresses that Christ's death is an act of God on man's behalf and is in no sense a human act of propitiation offered by man to God. God 'reconciled us to himself' (II Cor. 5.18); the rebels were obviously in no position to effect the reconciliation. 'God was in Christ reconciling the κόσμος to himself, not reckoning unto them (i.e. the 'all things' of v. 18) their trespasses, and having committed unto us (i.e. those baptized into Christ's Church) the word of reconciliation' (5.19). The Christian Church is a 'ministry of reconciliation' in the world, because it has received from God, as ambassadors receive an authorization from their governments, the reconciling word, i.e. the command and the power to be at peace with God. When the Church preaches the word of reconciliation (cf. 'the gospel of peace', Rom. 10.15; Eph. 6.15), it is as though God were pleading with men, entreating them through the preachers' words, to be reconciled to him (II Cor. 5.20). The whole preaching-mission of Jesus is described in Eph. 2.17 as a preaching of peace to all men, near and far.

Thus, reconciliation is God's work, not man's. At this point we encounter a very striking difference between the OT and the NT. In the OT men are frequently said to make atonement for sin (e.g. the examples cited above from the OT). In the NT such an idea is unthinkable. All the sacrifices of the Old Covenant could not expiate sins; all they could do was to make remembrance (ἀνάμνησις) of them—i.e. make them become present and potent again: 'it is impossible that the blood of bulls and of goats should take away sins' (Heb. 10.3f.). The whole OT sacrificial system was only a shadow of the good things to come; it merely adumbrated, but could not effect, the perfecting of those who would draw nigh to God (Heb. 10.1). It was therefore only a temporary arrangement, since it could not make the worshippers perfect, being imposed only 'until a time of reformation' (Heb. 9.10). This is the verdict of the NT upon the claim that men could make atonement for themselves, a verdict which, of course, had already been anticipated by the OT prophets (e.g. Isa. 1.11-17; Micah 6.6-8, etc.). It is God alone, God in Christ, who makes reconciliation. Perhaps because of the tendency to regard the OT as equally 'inspired' with the NT, certain types of medieval and Reformation atonement-theories have tended to obscure the truth that reconciliation is a divine and not a human work. The NT does not and could not (as St Anselm and some Reformation theologians did) set forth the death of Christ as an offering or *satisfaction* rendered by Christ as man on behalf of man to make restitution for the outraged honour or majesty of the infinite God. 'Satisfaction' is a concept which has figured prominently in discussions of the Atonement in Western theology, but the word does not occur in the NT. Most of the distortions and dissensions which have vexed the Church, where these have touched theological understanding, have arisen through the insistence of sects or sections of the Christian community upon using words which are not found in the NT; and this is nowhere more true than in the matter of atonement-theories. The NT does not say that God demands satisfaction (in terms either of honour or of debt) or that man (even the God-man) renders it to him. It does not say that God needs to be reconciled to man; St Paul speaks only of man's having to be reconciled to God. What it does positively affirm is that God has reconciled rebellious man, who was unable by anything that he could do to establish 'peace' or a right relationship with God.

REDEMPTION

The metaphor of redemption (loosing from a bond, setting free from captivity or slavery, buying back something lost or sold, ransoming) is not easily understood by the modern mind, which has no experience of the sacrificial systems of Hebrew or Greek religion, or of the institution of the slave-market, or indeed of that of the pawn-shop, now almost vanished from the social scene in the Welfare age. But since religious images are frequently drawn from the social systems of the days in which they took their origin, it is inevitable that the Bible should develop redemption-metaphors which had their origins in the social customs of ancient societies. Their obscurity soon vanishes if we make the necessary effort of historical imagination. The verb λυτρόω meant originally to deliver captives (e.g. if they had been taken prisoner in war or by robber-bands) by payment of a ransom, or to liberate or manumit a slave from his bond (cf. λύω, loose, loosen, e.g. Mark 1.7, of a shoe-latchet; John 5.18, ἔλυε τὸ σάββατον). The λύτρον (in LXX usually plural λύτρα) was the ransom-price paid for the effecting of such a ransoming or liberation (λύτρωσις, ἀπολύτρωσις) and could mean the sacrifice or offering by which expiation was effected. The idea of actual purchase-money, though it was the basic meaning of the word in its original use, later tends to fall away, and in NT usage seems largely to have disappeared.[1]

In the OT it was the duty of a man's *go'el* (redeemer), usually his next-of-kin, to buy back the freedom which he might have lost (e.g. through debt). In this sense Yahweh is called Israel's *go'el*, especially in Deutero-Isaiah, where 'redemption' is a key metaphor (see e.g. Isa. 41.14; 43.1; 44.6; 47.4; cf. 60.16; 63.4, 9). God's signal act of deliverance was that of the redemption of Israel from Egyptian bondage (Deut. 7.8; Isa. 51.11; 52.3f., 12). The Creator-Saviour, who defeated Chaos and established the world, by a new act of creation redeemed his people from Egypt at the Red Sea, and is redeeming them again by a new act of creation-salvation in which 'the ransomed of the LORD shall return (from Babylon) and come with singing unto Zion' (Isa. 51.11). Thus, the concept of redemption had become a prominent metaphor of God's deliverance of his people, having a primary reference to the historical deliverance of Israel from the power of Egypt at the Red Sea. Already the notion of a transaction, of an actual payment of a cash

[1] According to ancient Hebrew ideas a firstborn (man or animal) is 'devoted' to God, and, if not sacrificed, must be redeemed by the offering of such equivalent (life or sum of money) as is prescribed by the Law (Ex. 13.2, 11-16, where the custom is aetiologically explained as a memorial of the slaying of the firstborn in Egypt; cf. 12.29; Lev. 12.6-8; Luke 2.23). This notion seems to have left little trace upon NT theology, though the ideas of Christ as 'our Passover' and as 'the Lamb of God' are distantly related to it.

λύτρον, has fallen away, so that it becomes meaningless to ask the question, to whom did Yahweh pay the ransom-price of Israel's redemption from Egypt? A good deal of speculation and controversy might have been saved if in the Christian era the early Fathers had noticed this truth and refrained from asking the utterly unbiblical question, to whom was the λύτρον of Christ's life (ψυχή) paid? (Matt. 20.28; Mark 10.45). They might, if they had required a biblical text, have pondered Isa. 52.3: 'Ye shall be redeemed without money' (cf. I Pet. 1.18f.).

By NT times the conception of redemption had become thoroughly eschatological. The redemption of Israel from Egypt was but the foreshadowing in history of the great act of creation by which history would be brought to an end. In rabbinic expectation the Messiah would be ὁ μέλλων λυτροῦσθαι τὸν Ἰσραήλ (Luke 24.21), and the great day of the Lord would be for Israel the day of redemption. Devout Jews everywhere were looking for 'the redemption of Jerusalem' (Luke 2.38). It may be because of the nationalistic sense which attached to the conception of a coming Messiah-redeemer that Jesus is never called redeemer in the NT; the word λυτρωτής occurs only at Acts 7.35, where it is used of Moses. It may also be because he thinks of Christ as a universal Saviour that St John avoids the vocabulary of redemption altogether. Other NT writers, especially St Paul (but also Heb., I Pet. and Rev.), make considerable use of the redemption metaphor. They think in terms of Christian eschatology: Christ's work in history is finished, the act of redemption foretold by the prophets has been performed (Luke 1.68; cf. Pss. 111.9; 130.7f.; Isa. 43.1; 59.20, etc.); God has through the death of Christ redeemed 'a people for his own possession' (Titus 2.14; cf. Eph. 1.14; Ex. 19.5), a new Israel, as once he had redeemed the Israel of old. But the 'day of redemption', i.e. of the full fruition of God's redeeming act in Christ, is the parousia of Christ. In this age Christians were sealed (in their baptism) with the Holy Spirit of promise, and the Spirit is the 'earnest' (ἀρραβών) of what they shall ultimately inherit, namely the eschatological redemption of God's κληρονομία (Eph. 1.14). Possessing here and now the 'firstfruits' (ἀπαρχή) of the Spirit, the evidences of the ultimate salvation, we await the redemption of our body (i.e. our whole being) (Rom. 8.23). In the passage Rom. 8.18-25 the final redemption of the whole created order is envisaged, but only we Christians who 'groan within ourselves' (i.e. through the operation of the Spirit within us, cf. 8.26) have knowledge of these things, even though the travailing creation unconsciously awaits this revelation of the parousia (8.19, 22). During this age of waiting and hoping before the coming of Christ, Christians are exhorted not to grieve the Holy Spirit, in which they were sealed (i.e. baptized) εἰς ἡμέραν ἀπολυτρώσεως (Eph. 4.30).

There is no reason to doubt that Jesus himself had taught such a doctrine of redemption to his disciples. He conceives of 'the redemption' as the Messianic salvation which he promises to those who shall faithfully endure to the end (Mark 13.13). In the Lucan version of his eschatological discourse, after describing the signs of the end (the 'Messianic woes'), he adds, 'When these things begin to come to pass, look up and lift up your heads, because your redemption draweth nigh' (διότι ἐγγίζει ἡ ἀπολύτρωσις ὑμῶν, Luke 21.28). In contexts such as this ἀπολύτρωσις is synonymous with 'salvation', which is likewise, as we have seen, an eschatological conception: cf. Rom. 13.11, 'Now is salvation nearer than when we (first) believed'—νῦν γὰρ ἐγγύτερον ἡμῶν ἡ σωτηρία. . . . The suggestion of a ransom-payment has virtually disappeared from the conception of ἀπολύτρωσις. On the other hand, Jesus taught his disciples that the offering of his ψυχή was 'a ransom for many'—λύτρον ἀντὶ πολλῶν (Mark 10.45; Matt. 20.28; these are the only occurrences of λύτρον in the NT). It used to be held (e.g. by Wellhausen, J. Weiss, Rashdall) that these words were not spoken by Jesus, but represent a Marcan insertion of Pauline theology into the teaching of Jesus: but all such contentions reflect the theological outlook of their exponents rather than that of the NT. It would indeed be remarkable that St Mark should have thus brilliantly summarized in a word the theology of St Paul, in order to attribute it to Jesus, especially when we note that that word (λύτρον) is never used in the extant writings of the Apostle. A simpler explanation lies to hand. Jesus, as we have seen above, had interpreted his own mission in terms of the Servant-Messiah of Isa. 53, to whom he gives the title of 'Son of Man'. In Mark 10.45 he is alluding to Isa. 53.10f. Perhaps in the teaching (in Aramaic) of his disciples he was wont to quote this passage; and it may be only St Mark's summary (in Greek) of his teaching which appears to be imprecise. However that may be, the reference to Isa. 53.10f. is clear enough. In that passage it is said that Yahweh afflicted the Servant of the Lord and made his ψυχή a guilt offering, i.e. an expiatory sacrifice, and that by his knowledge (i.e. obedience) God's righteous Servant should justify many (or make many righteous) and bear their iniquities. It is surely indicative of the Master's supreme insight into the redemptive purpose of God as revealed in the Scriptures that he should have gone unerringly to the one passage in the OT which clearly points to God himself as initiating the act of redemptive self-offering that is performed by the Servant-Messiah. Jesus thinks of the passage as prophetic of his own mission, and accordingly he goes up to Jerusalem to give his life a ransom for many. Such is the appointed lot of the Servant of the Lord: 'the Son of Man goeth even as it is written of him' (Mark 14.21). If this interpretation of Mark 10.45 is on the right lines, then it is a rough equivalent of the Heb. *'asham*, a guilt-offering, an expiatory sacrifice, the technical object of which in post-exilic Judaism was to make expiation for dues withheld from God (Lev. 5.14-19) or from man (Lev. 6.1-7). But the technicalities are irrelevant in imagery of such deeply poetical and symbolical meaning. Jesus regards his death as the proper work of the Messiah, which is to make expiation for the sins of 'many' (cf. Isa. 53.11f., 'justify *many*', 'he bare the sin of *many*'). The use here of 'many' must not be taken to imply a limited salvation, i.e. not for 'all'; 'many' in Semitic usage is often contrasted not with 'all' but with 'one' (cf. Rom. 5.15, 19) and in such a context virtually means 'all'. The preposition ἀντί in the expression λύτρον ἀντὶ πολλῶν occurs only here in St Mark, but its usual meaning in the papyri is 'for' in the sense of 'instead of'.[1] Thus, to say that Jesus gave his life λύτρον ἀντὶ πολλῶν means in the light of Isa. 53.10-12 that his death was a voluntary expiatory sacrifice for the sins of those who could not make expiation for themselves. The idea of ransom-money, paid to a third party, is hardly present even as an overtone. Such passages as Ps. 49.7f., I Macc. 6.44 and II Macc. 7.37f. do not seem relevant.

But the metaphor of money-payment is found in several NT passages. Twice St Paul tells the Corinthian Christians, 'Ye are bought with a price' (I Cor. 6.20; 7.23). As the context of the second of these passages makes clear, the metaphor is primarily that of the slave-market; Christ has purchased the freedom of his disciples, who now are his δοῦλοι, owing obedience to none but Christ. In the address which St Luke puts into the mouth of St Paul on the occasion of his farewell to the elders of Ephesus at Miletus, St Paul charges them: 'Take heed unto yourselves . . . to feed the ἐκκλησία of God, which he acquired (περιεποιήσατο, 'made his own') with his own blood' (Acts 20.28). Grammatically this passage refers to the blood of God, and thus is unique in Scripture; but what is intended is clearly the blood (i.e. death) of Christ; and we have here a profoundly Pauline conception (cf. Eph. 1.7, ἀπολύτρωσις διὰ τοῦ αἵματος, which however does not necessarily retain the sense of a purchase-price or ransom). In I Tim. 2.6 it is said that Christ 'gave himself a ransom for all' (ἀντίλυτρον ὑπὲρ πάντων), where the metaphor could be that of the slave-market or that of the sacrificial system; probably both meanings would be present in the mind of the first-century Christians. In either case it is affirmed that Christ gave himself *on behalf of* (ὑπέρ, a weaker preposition than the ἀντί of Mark 10.45)

[1] Cf. V. Taylor, *The Gospel according to St Mark*, 444.

all mankind. In Titus 2.14 it is said that 'Christ gave himself for us, that he might redeem us from all iniquity' (ἔδωκεν ἑαυτὸν ὑπὲρ ἡμῶν, ἵνα λυτρώσηται ἡμᾶς ἀπὸ πάσης ἀνομίας); here the metaphor is taken from the sacrificial system, and it is being affirmed that Christ's self-oblation was an expiatory sacrifice on behalf of sinners. The same idea of the death of Christ as an expiatory sacrifice effecting redemption is powerfully asserted in Heb. 9.11-28 in terms of the peculiar ascension-atonement conception of *Auct. Heb.* Christ's ascension to heaven was the final Day of Atonement, which brought the whole system of man-offered sacrifices to an end. It achieved for us αἰώνιος λύτρωσις, the true or eschatological redemption of the world to come (Heb. 9.12; cf. 9.15). In I Pet. 1.18f. we read, 'Ye were redeemed, not with corruptible things, with silver or gold (cf. Isa. 52.3) . . . but with precious blood, as of a lamb without blemish and without spot, Christ's.' The metaphor here involves a denial that Christ's death is to be likened to the payment of a sum of money, however large. Man's redemption could not be achieved by any material sacrifices, however costly. It could be achieved only by Christ's personal offering of himself as an expiatory sacrifice, as *the* lamb without blemish or spot, i.e. as the perfect, final, unrepeatable and sufficient oblation on behalf of mankind. The metaphor is based upon the idea of the Passover lamb (see esp. Ex. 12.5), which however was not regarded by the Jews as expiatory. As in so many NT passages, it is impossible to distinguish between the two strands of metaphor which go to make up the conception of redemption, viz. the sacrificial and the ransom (e.g. from slavery). In the Apocalypse the triumph song of those who have been 'loosed from their sins in his blood' (Rev. 1.5, though some MSS. read λούσαντι, 'washed', for λύσαντι, 'loosed') runs: 'Worthy art thou . . . for thou wast slain and didst purchase unto God with thy blood men of every tribe and tongue . . .' (Rev. 5.9). In Rev. 14.3f. the 144,000 who 'had been purchased out of the earth' were 'purchased from among men to be the firstfruits unto God and unto the Lamb'.

The idea of purchase certainly emphasizes the cost of our redemption, but the metaphor is not pressed in the NT and does not offer any kind of key for the solution of a so-called 'problem' of the atonement. The atonement in the NT is a mystery, not a problem. One can construct theories and offer them as solutions of problems, but one cannot theorize about the deep mystery of our redemption. The NT does not do so; it offers to us not theories but vivid metaphors, which can, if we will let them operate in our imagination, make real to us the saving truth of our redemption by Christ's self-offering on our behalf. The desire to rationalize these metaphors into theories of the atonement has created much division and rigidity amongst Christian bodies; the curious combination of Renaissance rationalism and evangelical zeal, which has characterized much Reformed and sect-type Christianity in recent centuries, has resulted in an unfortunate kind of sophistication which believes that the only thing to do with metaphors is to turn them into theories.

PROPITIATION

Although the word 'propitiation' occurs four times in the RV of the Bible (Rom. 3.25; Heb. 2.17; I John 2.2; 4.10), it is true to say that propitiation in the usual meaning of the word is hardly a biblical idea at all. We are here made aware of one of the main differences between biblical and pagan religion. In classical Greek the verb ἱλάσκομαι means primarily to propitiate, placate or appease an angry person or god, with the object of averting vengeance; it can also mean to expiate or atone for some offence (e.g. by offering sacrifice or making reparation). In Heb. 2.17 it is used in the latter sense: 'Wherefore it behoved him in all things to be made like unto his brethren, that he might be a merciful and faithful high priest pertaining to God, to make propitiation for the sins of the people' (RV) (εἰς τὸ ἱλάσκεσθαι τὰς ἁμαρτίας τοῦ λαοῦ). 'To make expiation' would have been a better translation (AV, 'to make reconciliation').[1] The idea of placating an irascible deity is almost totally absent from the Bible, although it forms a large part of pagan religion and cultus. The reason for this is not because the Bible does not consistently maintain a strong doctrine of the wrath of God, but because of the biblical conception of the covenant-mercy of God and his consequent loving-kindness towards his people. In the OT already God is known as one who has 'found a ransom' for the souls of those who are faithful to him (e.g. Job 33.24, 28, 30); as St John gives final expression to the truth of the matter, the divine love casts out all fear of the divine wrath, the φόβος which is such terrible κόλασις ('punishment') (I John 4.18). There is no fear in love, for love, as it is understood by Christians, means simply this: that God 'loved us and sent his Son to be the propitiation (ἱλασμός) for our sins' (I John 4.10). In pagan religion ἱλασμός would doubtless represent man's propitiation of an angry god. In biblical religion such an idea is impossible: the incredible, miraculous truth is the opposite of this. If there is a propitiation at all, it is God who provides it, not man: God offering his own Son as a sacrifice for man's sins! But so it is, and St John is affirming (with the rest of the NT) that Christ's death is a sacrifice which makes expiation for the sins of the

---

[1] In the passive ἱλάσκομαι means 'have mercy on', 'forgive'. The only other use of the verb in NT (besides Heb. 2.17) is Luke 18.13, ʻΟ Θεός, ἱλάσθητί μοι τῷ ἁμαρτωλῷ.

world: cf. I John 2.2, 'he (Christ) is the propitiation (ἱλασμός) for our sins, and not for ours only, but also for the whole world (κόσμος).'[1] If we retain the word 'propitiation' as a translation of ἱλασμός, we must make sure that it is understood that there is no suggestion that man can propitiate God or that God needs propitiating before he can forgive: it is God, not man, who propitiates and makes forgiveness possible.[2] In its biblical meaning 'propitiation' must be thought of as more or less synonymous with 'expiation'.[3]

It is thus that we must interpret such a statement as that in Rom. 5.9, 'we shall be saved from the wrath through him' (i.e. Christ). Such language does not imply that Christ's death propitiates an angry deity, and we must be careful to understand such phrases against the background of rabbinic thought. 'The wrath' is, as we have seen above,[4] an eschatological term denoting one aspect of the Day of the Lord, namely, the destruction of those who resist God's sovereign purpose; cf. I Thess. 1.10, 'Jesus, who delivereth us from the wrath to come'. This eschatological wrath works already in history (I Thess. 2.16), and Christians are delivered from it by Christ both now and at the final Day of the Lord. Though the word, of course, implies God's righteous and implacable condemnation of sin in every form, it does not imply that God can be appeased like an angry man; it is a technical word in the vocabulary of eschatology, not the description of a mood or state of mind in God. These considerations must be steadily borne in mind when we turn to Rom. 3.25, where St Paul says that God sent Christ to be a propitiation (so RV; RV mg. 'to be propitiatory') through faith by his blood. The thought here has nothing to do with the notion of propitiating God. The word used by St Paul is ἱλαστήριον, which is either an adjective meaning 'pertaining to ἱλασμός', and therefore to be translated 'expiatory', or else a noun derived from it, τὸ ἱλαστήριον, meaning 'an expiation', 'an expiatory sacrifice or action'. In either case St Paul would be saying (in the whole context of vv. 23-26) that, though

[1] I John 2.2 and 4.10 provide the only two instances of the use of ἱλασμός in the NT.

[2] Cf. A. E. Brooke, *The Johannine Epistles* (ICC), 1912, 28: 'The object of propitiation in Jewish thought, as shown in their Scriptures, is not God, as in Greek thought, but man, who has estranged himself from God, or the sins which have intervened between him and his God. They must be "covered" before right relations can be restored. . . . This is the dominant thought in the sacrificial system of the priestly code.'

[3] See further, C. H. Dodd's art. in *JTS*, Vol. XXXII, 1931, 352-60, where every occurrence of ἱλάσκομαι in LXX is examined. Dodd concludes that the biblical meaning of the verb is 'to perform an act whereby guilt or defilement is removed' and that therefore 'to make expiation' would be a better translation than 'to make propitiation'. Cf. also his *Romans*, 54. In point of fact the word 'expiation' occurs in EVV only at Num. 35.33.

[4] *Supra*, 76.

we, like all other men, Jew or Gentile, have sinned and fallen short of the δόξα for which mankind was created, we have nevertheless been justified at no cost to ourselves (δωρεάν) by his grace through the redemption (ἀπολύτρωσις) that is in Christ Jesus, whom God set forth (purposed) to be (for us who believe that he died for us) the expiatory sacrifice for all our sins: thus God has now demonstrated his righteousness, even though he had passed over sins done before the coming of Christ, in the great and final demonstration of the divine righteousness in the new era now begun (ἐν τῷ νῦν καιρῷ): with the result that God is not only seen to be righteous but is also known as the justifier of those who believe in Jesus.

This is broadly what Rom. 3.23-26 must be understood to mean; the word ἱλαστήριον in this context will signify Christ's death as an atoning sacrifice. But perhaps something can be said about why St Paul used the word here: it is in fact his only use of it in his extant epistles. A clue is provided by Heb. 9.5, the only other use of ἱλαστήριον in the NT. Here it is translated 'the mercy-seat' in RV and ARSV. *Auct. Heb.* is describing the Day of Atonement ritual; the ἱλαστήριον (more fully ἱλαστήριον ἐπίθεμα, Ex. 25.17) is the 'lid of expiation' or 'the propitiatory', i.e. the cover of the ark within the holy of holies, which was sprinkled with the blood of the victim on the Day of Atonement (Ex. 25.18-22; Lev. 16.2, 13f.). The Hebrew word translated ἱλαστήριον (ἐπίθεμα) in LXX and 'mercy-seat' in RV (Ex. 25.17, etc.) is *kapporeth*, a covering (from the word 'to cover', i.e. to pardon, sins). Nygren translates ἱλαστήριον at Rom. 3.25 as 'mercy-seat', following Luther's translation of it as *Gnadenstuhl* (Vulg., *propitiatorium*). There is much to be said for retaining this translation.[1] The mention of the δόξα Θεοῦ (which, of course, is present over the ark) in Rom. 3.23; the expiatory blood; the use of the word ἱλαστήριον itself, all indicate that St Paul is putting forward the view that Calvary is the Christian 'mercy-seat' and that Good Friday is the Christian Day of Atonement. Or, to put the matter in another way, Christ, sprinkled with his own blood, is the true propitiatory of which the 'mercy-seat' in the holy of holies was the antitype and foreshadowing. This would be the meaning both of St Paul and *Auct. Heb.*

THE LAMB OF GOD

In the OT the figure of a lamb is used to symbolize many things, e.g. guilelessness (Jer. 11.19; Ecclus. 13.17; cf. Isa. 11.6); uncomplaining suffering (Isa. 53.7); the burnt-offering given as a present to God (e.g. Gen. 22.8); the memorial of the deliverance from Egypt (Ex.

[1] See A. Nygren, *Commentary on Romans*, ET, 1952, Philadelphia, 1949, 156f.

12.3f., 11, 14); and expiatory sacrifice (Heb. *kebhes*, LXX ἀμνός, 87 times in Ex., Lev. and Num. in passages belonging to P, in connection with the ritual of the various sacrifices). Lambs were offered daily in the Temple at the morning and evening sacrifice. Still another metaphorical use is found in the apocalyptic tradition (e.g. Enoch 89ff.), that of the bell-wether which leads the flock and defends it against predatory animals. Thus, in the mind of Jews in NT days a multiple image would be found, and it is hardly possible to determine which of its components would be dominant in any particular NT passage in which Jesus is spoken of as a lamb or as the 'Lamb of God'. In all such cases, where a rich variety of images has contributed to NT usage, it is unwise to ask which of them is in the mind of the writer in any particular passage. They are probably all present, consciously or subconsciously.

In John 1.29 and 36 the Baptist salutes Jesus as 'the Lamb (ἀμνός) of God, which taketh away the sin of the world'. C. H. Dodd argues that ὁ ἀμνὸς τοῦ Θεοῦ is here primarily a Messianic title, virtually equivalent to ὁ βασιλεὺς τοῦ Ἰσραήλ (John 1.49), being based (like the use of τὸ ἀρνίον in Revelation) on the apocalyptic figure of the ram as a military leader.[1] He suggests that the Fourth Evangelist does not think of the Passover as the 'type' of the death of Christ, and that John 19.36 ('No bone of him shall be broken') is a fulfilment of Ps. 34.20 ('He keepeth all his bones: not one of them is broken') and not of the regulation concerning the bones of the paschal victim in Ex. 12.46 and Num. 9.12. Furthermore he holds that the Johannine alteration of the Synoptic dating of the crucifixion, so as to synchronize the death of Jesus with the hour of the killing of the paschal victims on the afternoon of Nisan 14, is likely to represent an independent historical tradition, perhaps a correct one, rather than an attempt to symbolize Jesus as the Christian paschal lamb (cf. I Cor. 5.7). Nor is Dodd convinced by the suggestion that there could have been a confusion between the Aramaic words 'servant' and 'lamb' and that consequently the expression 'lamb of God' really signifies 'Servant of the Lord'.[2] On this last point Dodd is doubtless correct, but he is unlikely to be right in thinking that the paschal lamb and the lamb of Isa. 53.7 are not in the mind of St John. Christ is the Lamb of God who takes away the sin of the κόσμος, as an expiatory sacrifice does. Now it is true that the daily burnt offerings, the passover lamb and the ἀμνὸς ἄφωνος of

[1] See C. H. Dodd, *IFG*, 230-8.
[2] So C. F. Burney, *The Aramaic Origin of the Fourth Gospel*, 104-8; J. Jeremias in *TWNT*, I, 343; Jeremias, *The Servant of God*, ET, 1957, 82f.; and cf. Barrett, *GSJ*, 147.

Isa. 53.7 are none of them expiatory sacrifices (the lamb of Isa. 53.7 is being sheared, not sacrificed). But the lamb-image in the mind of the NT writers would be an amalgam of all the OT metaphors, and Christ would be at one and the same time the paschal lamb and the expiatory sacrifice (as in I Pet. 1.18f., 'Ye were redeemed . . . with precious blood, as of a lamb without blemish and without spot, Christ's'). As C. K. Barrett says, 'The two propositions (*a*) Christ was the passover lamb; (*b*) Christ bore, or took away sins, though originally unconnected, are combined.'[1] The Isaianic lamb, moreover, though not a lamb of sacrifice, is mentioned in a context which is wholly concerned with the vicarious sacrifice of the Servant of the Lord. Since the Johannine interpretation of the Eucharist is undoubtedly paschal (cf. John 6.51-57), it is improbable that St John did not intend his careful dating of the crucifixion to be understood in terms of Christ as the Christian passover lamb (cf. John 19.14, 'Now it was the Preparation of the passover; it was about the sixth hour', i.e. the time when the passover lambs were killed). It is surely arbitrary to say that John 19.36 is intended to fulfil Ps. 34.20 but not Ex. 12.46 or Num. 9.12. St John is affirming with St Paul that Christ is the Christian πάσχα, i.e. passover lamb (as in Mark 14.12; Luke 22.7): 'For our πάσχα also has been sacrificed, Christ: wherefore let us keep festival, not with the old leaven . . .' (I Cor. 5.7f.). Paul's allusion is all the more significant because it is purely incidental to his exhortation, which is that, just as the Jews regarded the putting away of the old leaven at passover-time as symbolic of moral cleansing, so Christians should continually put away all evil, for they live always in a season of high festival; the Christian life is a perpetual Easter life, risen with Christ, dead to sins.

Whatever may be the connection between the Fourth Gospel and the Apocalypse, it is not without significance that they are the only NT books in which Christ is explicitly referred to as the Lamb (of God). But, of course, there remains the unaccountable difference in the words used: the Gospel has ὁ ἀμνός (1.29, 36); the Apocalypse has τὸ ἀρνίον (no less than 27 times). In the Apocalypse the Lamb has a two-fold character. He is, first, the sacrificial lamb: the Lamb slain from the foundation of the world, who purchased unto God with his blood men of every tribe and tongue and people and nation (Rev. 5.9; cf. John 1.29, ὁ αἴρων τὴν ἁμαρτίαν τοῦ κόσμου: both passages stress the universality of Christ's atoning work; cf. Rev. 7.14, 'they washed their robes and made them white in the blood of the Lamb'; also 1.5, 'loosed us from our sins in his blood'). But, secondly, he is also the military, conquering lamb, the ram which goes forth to fight against the enemies of the flock

[1] *GSJ*, 147.

at the head of all the fighting rams (cf. Enoch 89ff.): e.g. Rev. 17.14, 'These shall war against the Lamb, and the Lamb shall overcome them, for he is Lord of lords and King of kings, and they (shall also over-come) that are with him, called and chosen and faithful.' In the Apoca-lypse the concept of the victorious Lamb that was slain, now receiving at the throne of God the blessing and honour and glory and dominion from all ranks of angels, of saints, and of the elemental forces of nature ('the four living creatures'), is the dominating image of Christ, by which the seer in his own distinctive way sets forth the truth of Christ crucified, risen and ascended (Rev. 5.6-14).

There is one more OT text (which Dodd does not mention in con-nection with his discussion of the Lamb of God) which doubtless was present in the Fourth Evangelist's mind when he made the Baptist speak of Christ as the Lamb of God, viz. Gen. 22.8: 'God will provide him-self [Heb. 'see for himself'] the lamb for a burnt offering.' Jewish thought increasingly came to hold that the covenant-relationship with God was founded upon Abraham's offering of Isaac: St John is assert-ing that the new relationship of God and man in Christ (the new covenant) is based upon the fulfilment of the promise contained in Gen. 22.8, that God would provide the Lamb which would make atonement for universal sin. The offering of Abraham's only son (Gen. 22.12, LXX: $\tauο\hat{υ}$ $υἱο\hat{υ}$ $σου$ $\tauο\hat{υ}$ $ἀγαπητο\hat{υ}$—cf. Mark 1.11, the words of the *Bath-qol* at the Baptism of Jesus) is the type of the offering of the only son of God ($ὁ$ $μονογενὴς$ $υἱός$, John 1.18; 3.16). Possibly Rom. 8.32 ('He that spared not his own Son') is an oblique reference to the Isaac-Christ typology, but this must remain uncertain. St John would seem (as is his way) to have caught the subtle allusion to the sacrifice of Isaac implicit in the (Synoptic) tradition of the Baptism of Jesus, and he is emphasizing the truth in his own way: Christ is the Lamb of sacrifice promised by God to Abraham, the father of many nations, and thus he is the God-given universal Sin Bearer ($ὁ$ $αἴρων$ $τὴν$ $ἁμαρτίαν$ $\tauο\hat{υ}$ $κόσμου$). It is very significant that the phrase 'Lamb of God' occurs in the Fourth Gospel only at the encounter of Jesus with the Baptist. St John is underlining in his own way the truth implicit in the tradition of Christ's baptism, namely, that the baptism of the sinless one with a baptism of repentance unto the remission of sins is a fore-shadowing of that subsequent baptism of the Messiah in the waters of death by which the sins of the world were taken away. Thus Christ is the true high priest (cf. Christ's consecration of himself in John 17.19) of whom it was said that 'in his priesthood shall sin come to an end' and that 'the heavens shall be opened, and from the temple of glory shall come upon him sanctification with the Father's (or father's) voice

as from Abraham to Isaac' (Test. XII Pat. Levi, 18.6, 9). If the suggestion is correct that this passage, or some such tradition as that contained in it, has influenced the παράδοσις of Christ's baptism, then it is
pertinent to recall that the only recorded words 'as from Abraham to
Isaac' were those of Gen. 22.8: 'The LORD will provide the lamb.'

THE MEDIATOR OF THE NEW COVENANT

'There is one God and one mediator between God and men, Man
Christ Jesus (εἷς γὰρ Θεός, εἷς καὶ μεσίτης Θεοῦ καὶ ἀνθρώπων ἄνθρωπος
Χριστὸς Ἰησοῦς), who gave himself a ransom (ἀντίλυτρον) for all'
(I Tim. 2.5f.). Christ is the new Moses, because he has fulfilled the
promise contained in Moses's work. In Jewish thought Moses was 'the
mediator', a common title for him in Jewish literature. Thus, Paul in
Gal. 3.19f. says that the Torah was 'ordained through angels by the
hand of a mediator', i.e. Moses; he seems to imply that there is now
no need of a human mediator, since we have direct access to God in
Christ. Christ is nowhere called 'mediator' in the ten Paulines. Indeed,
the only other passages in the NT (besides I Tim. 2.5) in which Christ is
called ὁ μεσίτης are Heb. 8.6; 9.15; 12.24. In each of these places
he is called the mediator of a new (or 'better', 8.6) covenant. As God
through Moses had established the covenant of Sinai, so now through
Christ he has established the new covenant which Jeremiah had
prophesied. Indeed, the only place in the NT in which Jer. 31.31-34 is
expressly quoted is Heb. 8.8-12, where the author is arguing that the
covenant of Sinai has been replaced by a 'better covenant' in the
blood of Jesus Messiah. The idea of Christ as 'mediator' fits con-
veniently into the argument of Hebrews, because in Jewish thought 'the
mediator' (after the death of Moses) was the high priest, and Hebrews
is the only NT book which explicitly calls Christ 'priest' or 'high
priest'.

But if Jer. 31.31-34 is explicitly quoted only in Hebrews, nevertheless
the prophecy of the establishment of a new covenant which it contains
was influential in the development of NT theology as a whole.[1] Indeed,
the very title by which the Christian Scriptures have come to be universally known bears testimony to the importance of this passage, from
which it is ultimately derived (LXX, Jer. 38.31: διαθήσομαι τῷ οἴκῳ
Ἰσραὴλ καὶ τῷ οἴκῳ Ἰούδα διαθήκην καινήν).[2] Already in II Cor. 3.14

---

[1] Cf. C. H. Dodd, *Acc. Scrip.*, 46.

[2] The English title 'New Testament' is derived from the Latin; in Vulg. διαθήκη is
always rendered *testamentum* even where the meaning is obviously 'covenant'
(e.g. Luke 1.72; Acts 7.8). In RV of Heb. 9.15-20 διαθήκη is three times translated
'covenant' and twice 'testament'; the marg. note explains that the Gk. word signifies
both meanings. In cl. Gk. διαθήκη usually means a 'will' or 'testament', while
συνθήκη is a covenant or agreement. Because συνθήκη implies an equality between the

St Paul can refer to 'the reading of the παλαιὰ διαθήκη' in the Synagogue; so that for a later generation there was already in being the convenient distinction between (the Scriptures of) ἡ παλαιὰ διαθήκη and (the Scriptures of) ἡ καινὴ διαθήκη. The fulfilment of Jeremiah's prophecy was certainly in the mind of St Paul when he wrote this chapter; and it underlies his description of the Christian laity as διάκονοι καινῆς διαθήκης (II Cor. 3.6), an expression suggestive of the NT conception of the priesthood of the laity, since the ministers of the old covenant were, of course, the Jewish priesthood.[1] In his account of the institution of the Eucharist St Paul describes the cup as ἡ καινὴ διαθήκη in the blood of Christ (I Cor. 11.25); the adjective καινή is not found in the Synoptic accounts of the Last Supper (except in the longer Lucan version, Luke 22.20).[2] But the Synoptic accounts (like the Pauline) bear clear witness to the fact that Jesus thought of his death as being the sacrificial act by which a covenant was ratified between God and a new Israel, just as the old covenant was ratified in the blood of the sacrificed animals on Sinai. At the covenant-making on Sinai we read that Moses took the blood of the animal victims and sprinkled it upon the people and said, 'Behold the blood of the covenant, which the LORD hath made with you' (Ex. 24.8). Repulsive though the whole proceeding is to our more delicate sensibilities, this was in fact the way in which covenants were ratified in sacrificial blood in those far-off days. The words of Jesus at the Last Supper, as recorded by St Mark, are a clear reference to Ex. 24.8. Jesus took the cup of wine and declared it to be τὸ αἷμά μου τῆς διαθήκης τὸ ὑπὲρ πολλῶν ἐκχυννόμενον (Mark 14.24). It matters little whether we regard this as the more original form of Christ's words, or St Paul's version, τοῦτο τὸ ποτήριον ἡ καινὴ διαθήκη ἐστὶν ἐν τῷ ἐμῷ αἵματι (I Cor. 11.25): the meaning of Jesus is perfectly clear, and it has nothing whatever to do with the question which so preoccupied the minds of later medieval and reformation theologians. He was not making any kind of mystical or metaphysical statement about the *esse* of the wine in the cup; he was saying, in the typically

contracting parties, LXX does not use it for Heb. *berith* ('covenant') but uses διαθήκη instead: a covenant between God and man is not made between two equal partners but represents rather a divine testament or bequeathing. But since in English we have no word meaning both 'covenant' and 'testament', we should (with RV) prefer 'covenant' as nearer to the NT meaning of διαθήκη, except in Heb. 9.16f. where the sense is clearly 'testament' (ARSV here has 'will'). In the text of RV the Eng. word 'testament' appears nowhere except at Heb. 9.16f.; in Gal. 3.15 the ambiguity of the Greek word is untranslatable into English in a word. In LXX διαθήκη is used even of covenants between men, which indicates its regular biblical meaning.

[1] It may be noted that the reference in II Cor. 3.3 to writing on 'hearts of flesh' recalls Jer. 31.33, 'In their heart will I write it.'

[2] The clause in Matt. 26.28 εἰς ἄφεσιν ἁμαρτιῶν recalls Jer. 31.34, 'I will forgive their iniquity, and their sin will I remember no more'. Cf. Dodd, *Acc. Scrip.*, 45.

allusive biblical fashion, that his death, now imminent, was the sacrificial act by which God was making a covenant with a new people, replacing the old, broken covenant of Sinai. According to St Paul's account, he bade his disciples whenever they should meet, as in the past they had so often met in the fellowship (*ḥaburah*) of the disciples, to 'do this' in ἀνάμνησις of him (I Cor. 11.24f.).[1]

It is not surprising that Jesus should have regarded the shedding of his blood as a necessary condition of the making of the new covenant between God and man, which he understood to be the purpose of his own mission and work. As we have already seen, he had come to think of himself as the Messianic Son of Man of OT prophecy, which he interpreted by means of the Isaianic conception of the Servant of Yahweh. He thought of his self-oblation as the pouring out of his ψυχή in redemptive sacrifice on behalf of the 'many' (Mark 10.45; Isa. 53.10f.). Now Isaiah (or what we would speak of as Deutero-Isaiah) interprets the whole redemption wrought by the Servant of Yahweh as a second deliverance and exodus from Egypt, in which the Servant is a new Moses, who is given for the purpose of establishing a (new) covenant with the people (of God); cf. Isa. 42.6, 'I will give thee for a covenant of the people, for a light of the Gentiles'; also Isa. 49.8, 'In a day of salvation have I helped thee, and I will preserve thee, and give thee for a covenant of the people . . .' (cf. also Isa. 59.20f.). It is clear that, if our Lord understood his own mission in terms of the prophecy of Isaiah, as the evidence undoubtedly shews that he did, he would inevitably think of his death as necessary, as expiatory, and as establishing a new covenant between God and a new people, which would include the 'enlightened' Gentiles. Thus, modern biblical scholarship enables us to sweep aside the tortuous misunderstandings of medieval unbiblical speculation, and also those of more recent 'liberal' theories, such as the theory that the words attributed to Jesus at the

---

[1] We have argued from the words spoken by Christ over the cup, because there can be little doubt about their interpretation. But probably the words spoken over the bread at the Supper should be understood as having the same force. Much scholarly opinion today supports the view that when Jesus said τοῦτό ἐστι τὸ σῶμά μου (Mark 14.22; cf. I Cor. 11.24) in his mother-tongue, he used for σῶμα the Aramaic *bisri* (flesh; cf. Heb. *basar*); he was comparing himself with the paschal lamb. See esp. J. Jeremias, *The Eucharistic Words of Jesus*, ET, 1955, 142-52; also A. J. B. Higgins, *The Lord's Supper in the New Testament*, 1952, 49-55. Jeremias says: 'By comparing himself with the paschal lamb, Jesus describes his death as redemptive. Certainly the passover of later times was not regarded as expiatory but as an ordinary sacrifice, and its blood worked no expiation. But this is not true of the paschal lambs which were killed at the exodus from Egypt. Their blood had a redemptive effect . . . because of the passover blood God revoked the death sentence passed on Israel. . . . In the same way will the people of God of the last days be redeemed by the merits of the passover blood. Jesus, therefore, describes his death as the eschatological passover sacrifice: his vicarious (ὑπέρ) death brings the final deliverance into operation' (*op. cit.*, 146-8). See further *infra*, 370f.

Last Supper were in fact but a reading back into his life of the sacramental gnosticism of Hellenistic 'catholicism'. Jesus steadfastly set his
face to go to Jerusalem (Luke 9.51) with the deliberate intention of
giving his body and pouring out his blood on behalf of 'the covenant
of the people'. For more than nineteen centuries the 'people of God',
which his death did in actual fact bring into being, has made solemn
ἀνάμνησις of his atoning self-sacrifice. The name, ὁ λαὸς τοῦ Θεοῦ, which
had been distinctive of the ancient covenant-people of Israel (e.g.
Heb. 11.25), was now appropriated to the Church of Jesus Christ, who
had been given by God for 'a covenant of the people' (e.g. I Pet. 2.10;
Titus 2.14). The apostolic Church regards Christ's death, as he himself
had regarded it, as the means whereby a new people of God is 'redeemed' or delivered from bondage to sin, just as in ancient times
Israel had been 'ransomed' from Egyptian bondage; and thus there is
constituted again a people for God's own possession, the people of the
new covenant (Acts 20.28; Eph. 1.14; I Pet. 2.10; Titus 2.14).

JUSTIFICATION

Another NT metaphor of atonement is that of the justification of
sinners by the grace of God through baptism into the Church of Christ.
The noun δικαίωσις (justification) occurs in NT only at Rom. 4.25 and
5.18. The great majority of uses of δικαιοῦν (to justify, acquit, reckon or
make δίκαιος) occurs in Romans (fifteen times) and Galatians (eight
times). Outside the Paulines the verb is found in NT only eleven times
in all, and most of these occurrences are irrelevant to the theological
issue. St James is the only NT writer besides St Paul who explicitly
discusses justification, and he has clearly not grasped what St Paul
meant by it. Thus, the justification theme is virtually peculiar to St
Paul, although the basic idea which Paul is expounding by means of it
is fundamental to the whole NT and was first enunciated by Jesus
himself.[1] The metaphor of justification, as St Paul develops it, is one
drawn from the law court: a legal process culminates in a verdict of
acquittal. The whole doctrine of justification in St Paul is, as we have
seen already,[2] the development of the OT prophetic conception of
God's righteousness, to which the clearest expression is given by
Deutero-Isaiah. As W. D. Davies has said, it is a mistake to think of the
Pauline doctrine of justification by faith as having been developed
solely in opposition to a Jewish doctrine of works.[3] It is conceived in
relation to the whole prophetic (esp. Isaianic) doctrine of the saving
δικαιοσύνη Θεοῦ. Later Judaism had indeed failed to assimilate the
prophetic doctrine of justification by the righteousness of God alone

---

[1] See *supra*, 81f.　　　　　[2] *Supra*, 82f.　　　　　[3] *PRJ*, 221f.

and not by our own righteousness; and St Paul reaffirmed the prophetic insight as against the rabbinic conception of salvation by works of merit. In this, as we have seen, Paul was truly defending and expounding Jesus's own conception of his person and work, for Jesus had already interpreted his own mission in terms of the Isaianic Servant who poured out his life for the justification of 'many' (Isa. 53.10f.). The Pauline doctrine of justification is simply a way of expressing the truth, which Jesus himself had taught, that salvation is the result, not of our own meritorious works, but of the outgoing righteousness of God, which brings salvation to sinners who could not have attained it for themselves.

The background of the forensic justification-metaphor is to be found in the OT, which sometimes depicts Yahweh's 'controversy' with his rebellious people in terms of a lawsuit in a court of justice (Isa. 1.18; 43.26; cf. also Hos. 4.1; 12.2; Mic. 6.2) and speaks of God's justification of his people (Isa. 43.26; 45.25; cf. Pss. 51.4; 143.2). In fact, Paul's use of δικαιοῦν is taken over from the LXX, where (like the Heb. words which it translates) it is a forensic term, meaning 'acquit', 'vindicate', 'justify'. St Paul strongly reasserts the deep insight of the OT that 'in thy sight shall no man living be justified' (Ps. 143.2; cf. Ps. 130.3f.; I Kings 8.46; Job 9.2f.; 15.14-16; 25.4; Eccles. 7.20; Isa. 64.6). His doctrine of justification is that contained (e.g.) in Isa. 59, with the exception that whereas Isa. 59 looks forward in hope to the coming of a redeemer to Zion, wearing a breastplate of righteousness and a helmet of salvation, St Paul proclaims the gospel which even now is the power of God unto salvation, namely, that the righteousness of God has been revealed in Jesus Christ (Rom. 1.16f.; 3.25f.), in whom the promised salvation is come. Those who even now are in process of being saved (οἱ σωζόμενοι) are those who have accepted God's offer of salvation conveyed by the preaching of 'the word of the cross' (I Cor. 1.18), i.e., those who have believed the good news (εὐαγγέλιον).

There can be no compromise between this gospel of salvation by the free grace of God and the boastful, humanistic conceit that men can save themselves by their own efforts, if they try hard enough. 'All have sinned and fall short of the glory of God' (Rom. 3.23; cf. 3.9f.). 'By works of law shall no flesh be justified in his sight' (Rom. 3.20; cf. Gal. 3.22). If men can indeed save themselves by works of law, the whole Christian preaching is superfluous: 'if righteousness is through law, then Christ died for nought' (Gal. 2.21; cf. 5.2-4). This does not mean that law, whether the Torah of Moses or the law of conscience which the Gentiles possess (Rom. 2.14f.), is not a good thing in itself (cf. Rom. 7.12, 'the law is holy, and the commandment holy and righteous and good'); the law is instituted by God and has its part to play in God's providential ordering of the economy of salvation. The age of world-history from Adam to Moses was the age of innocence, the infancy of the human race. Then, as the divine education of mankind continued, the Torah was given through Moses at Sinai. Law was a stage on the road to salvation, but it could not itself confer salvation. It taught God's people in what righteousness consisted, but it contained no power that enabled men to attain it. Indeed, its primary gift to mankind was a consciousness of guilt: 'I had not known sin except through law' (Rom. 7.7); the very fact that I know a thing is forbidden makes it all the more attractive (7.8). Through law comes awareness of sin (Rom. 3.20), and therefore its effect is to 'multiply' sin (5.20). Though it is itself 'spiritual', it gives occasion to sin and death, because I am not spiritual but 'carnal' (7.14); though I know the right and may even desire to do it, I nevertheless do what is wrong (7.19f.). Only Christ can deliver me from this 'body of death' (7.24f.). But the law has now performed its appointed office, that of the παιδαγωγός (the household slave who took the children to school); it has brought us to Christ, and we are now no longer under its tutelage (Gal. 3.24f.). We are now sons, fully come of age, no longer children under law. Christ indeed is for the believer the τέλος νόμου (Rom. 10.4), both the goal and the abolition of the law. He has set us free from bondage to law by taking upon himself the curse of the law, as written in Deut. 21.23, 'Cursed is everyone that hangeth on a tree' (Gal. 3.13). Those who are still trying to justify themselves by works of law are still under the curse of the law, as written in Deut. 27.26, 'Cursed is everyone who continueth not in all things that are written in the Book of the Law to do them' (Gal. 3.10). St James quotes with approval the rabbinic saying, 'Whosoever shall keep the whole law, and yet stumble in one point, he is become guilty of all' (James 2.10). In seeking to establish one's own righteousness, one remains ignorant of the righteousness of God (Rom. 10.3). That righteousness, now manifested in Christ, was witnessed to in times past by the law and by the prophets (Rom. 3.21); neither Torah nor prophecy possessed righteousness, but they pointed forward to its realization in the coming of the Christ (Rom. 10.4f.). Righteousness and salvation were not attained in the old dispensation, save eschatologically through the Christ who has now revealed them in this, the final age of history (ὁ νῦν καιρός, Rom. 3.26). It was in fact Christ who all along was leading and sustaining the Israel of old in her pilgrimage towards the land of promise (I Cor. 10.3f.; cf. John 6.31-35). Christ was the righteousness through which the faithful in Israel had lived throughout times past.

St Paul illustrates this truth by taking the crucial case of Abraham, which must have figured largely in controversy with Jewish rabbis or Judaizing Christians (Rom. 4.1-25; Gal. 3.6-18). Abraham himself, the revered forefather of Israel κατὰ σάρκα, was not saved by his works of righteousness, but by his trust in God's promise; as the Scripture says, 'Abraham believed God, and it was reckoned unto him for δικαιοσύνη' (Rom. 4.3, 9, 22; Gal. 3.6; James 2.23, citing Gen. 15.6). It was Abraham's faith in the promise concerning his 'seed' (i.e. Christ, Gal. 3.16) which made him righteous and thus secured his salvation. At the time when he was accounted righteous, Abraham was uncircumcised, and the 'seal' of circumcision was given as a sign of his new status before God (Rom. 4.10f.). Circumcision is thus the seal and sign of Israel's justification not by works but by faith. But Abraham is the spiritual father of all who believe, Gentile as well as Jew (4.16); it was written of him that he should be the father of *many* nations (4.17, citing Gen. 17.5). Thus, as Isaac was brought alive from the dead out of the barren womb of the aged Sarah, so countless spiritual children of Abraham—the Gentile Christians as well as the Jewish—have been brought alive from the dead through the power of him who raised up Jesus our Lord from the dead (Rom. 4.19-25; cf. Gal. 4.28, 'Now we, brethren, as Isaac was, are children of promise').

Another OT text is used by St Paul in order to prove his contention that Christ was the very δικαιοσύνη Θεοῦ by which faithful Israelites had lived and been saved under the old dispensation. He quotes Hab. 2.4 in a version of his own: ὁ δίκαιος ἐκ πίστεως ζήσεται (Rom. 1.17; Gal. 3.11). The LXX reads, ὁ δὲ δίκαιος ἐκ πίστεώς μου ζήσεται, the righteous man will live (i.e. be saved) by God's faithfulness. This, of course, is akin to the prophetic conception of the justification of his people by God's fidelity to his covenant and promise; God will in fact save not only the δίκαιοι, but even sinful Israel, not because of their merits, but 'for his holy name'. The Heb. original of Hab. 2.4 would seem to mean that the righteous man, as distinct from the proud and wicked, would be preserved from death by his own fidelity or steadfastness—a meaning very different from that which Paul finds in his version.[1]

When the prophetic and Pauline doctrine of justification by the righteousness of God is isolated from the rest of the biblical teaching, it becomes a fruitful source of error. It should be noted that the formula 'justification by faith' is not an adequate statement of the biblical

---

[1] A still different version is found in Heb. 10.37f., ὁ δὲ δίκαιός μου ἐκ πίστεως ζήσεται, in a passage which is quoting Hab. 2.3f. somewhat freely with the purpose of strengthening the exhortation to endurance under affliction on the ground that the parousia is at hand.

doctrine. We are not justified by our faith, as if faith itself were one of the works of merit about which we can boast (Rom. 3.27; I Cor. 1.29-31; Eph. 2.8f.); Paul can indeed write δικαιοῦσθαι πίστει (Rom. 3.28), but the meaning is σεσωσμένοι διὰ πίστεως, καὶ τοῦτο οὐκ ἐξ ὑμῶν· Θεοῦ τὸ δῶρον (Eph. 2.8). 'Justification by faith' must be understood to mean justification by the gracious and saving righteousness of God through baptism and incorporation into Jesus Christ, because 'faith' is not a subjective emotion on our part, but an active decision concerning Christ. This decision expresses itself in the act of obedience and self-denial which is made when we are baptized into his body. Luther's *sola fide* could not have meant for Luther what it has meant in much subsequent Protestant sectarianism, viz. that if we have possessed the 'experience' of justification, it matters little whether we have complied with any merely formal ceremonies or have been made members of any visible church. Luther could not have anticipated such a misinterpretation of his formula in an age when everyone was baptized in infancy by order of the government and in which the conception of baptism as an 'optional extra' had not yet been put forward. Justification was not for him a subjective experience in the consciousness of believers, but an objective act on the part of God. Neither Luther nor Paul is speaking of our 'experience' in the post-Reformation sense of that word. Subjective experiences, religious feelings, and the like, occupy little place in the theology of the NT. 'Justification' is God's objective act of conferring upon us a new status, metaphorically described by the forensic metaphor of acquittal. If we separate this objective act of God's from the doctrines of baptism and the Church (as much post-Reformation theology has done), we lay ourselves open to the objections which have often been brought against the idea of justification. Thus, it is said that the Christian life begins with a 'legal fiction': God treats us 'as if' we were righteous, although we are still in fact sinners. Apart from the doctrines of baptism and the Church there is no answer to this objection, but it is not an objection which can be sustained against St Paul. It is by our baptism into Christ's body (i.e. corporate personality) that we possess righteousness—'a righteousness not our own . . . that which is through faith in Christ (διὰ πίστεως Χριστοῦ), the righteousness which is from God by (ἐπί) faith' (Phil. 3.9). God's faithfulness (πίστις) is what matters, not man's fickleness (Rom. 3.3): it is God's πίστις, not ours, which saves us. He has kept his covenant-promise and realized his saving purpose in spite of our disobedience and lack of faith; his very righteousness itself has saved sinners. No 'legal fiction' is involved.

When we are brought into that relationship with God which St

Paul designates by the term ἐν Χριστῷ, we actually partake of Christ's character of righteousness; it is our incorporation into Christ which is our title to righteousness and therefore to acquittal.[1] God treats us as righteous, because we are righteous in so far as we are 'in Christ'. It is not that God treats us 'as if' we were righteous. In Christ we *are* righteous even now. But this righteousness must be understood in the light of the whole NT conception of eschatology: the righteousness of God is something which belongs to the end of history, but is revealed to faith and laid hold of by faith 'even now'—ἐν τῷ νῦν καιρῷ—so that it is really ours *now*. But we are now living 'between the times', between the first and the last comings of Christ, and we partake of the character of both ages. By faith, eschatologically, we are righteous: as men still living in 'this age' the powers of sin and death still reign in our mortal bodies, and we are still sinners. It is in this eschatological sense that we are to understand Luther's formula, *simul justus ac peccator*. Our righteousness (like our entering into the Kingdom of God or like any other eschatological reality) is at once something which we now have and also something for which we still wait (Gal. 5.5; cf. Phil. 1.6, 11; 3.9, 12–16, etc.). It is through the Spirit that we have the earnest of our righteousness; we do not possess it yet, as we shall hereafter. The 'saint' of NT theology is not a perfected being but a forgiven sinner, and sanctification (ἁγιωσύνη, the state of holiness), like δικαιοσύνη, is an eschatological reality, not a simple possibility for Christians who are still subject to the 'powers' of this age, even though in principle those powers are defeated. Christians are indeed οἱ ἅγιοι, because they are the new people of God, just as they are δίκαιοι; nevertheless it is only by prayer and striving and by the power of the Spirit that the eschatological ἁγιότης (II Cor. 1.12; Heb. 12.10) and δικαιοσύνη and δόξα Θεοῦ can be manifested even to the eyes of faith in this mortal life (II Cor. 4.7-18). Holiness and righteousness are τὰ μὴ βλεπόμενα which are αἰώνια, i.e. which belong not to this age (πρόσκαιρα) but to the Age to Come; they cannot become visible except to the eye of faith in this age (II Cor. 4.18). Yet Christians must constantly strive to make them visible, to shew forth the invisible qualities of the Age to Come, to which they indeed belong, since their πολίτευμα (commonwealth) is in heaven (Phil. 3.20f.). This is the paradox of the Christian life, the 'impossible-possibility' of Christian ethics. Christian ethics is supernatural ethics, a putting into action of the laws of the kingdom of heaven, through the power of the eschatological Spirit working in us. This is the Spirit which we received in our baptism, when we died to sin and rose to

[1] For the exposition of the Pauline ἐν Χριστῷ see the next chapter, esp. 260 in relation to justification.

righteousness: 'Ye are not in the flesh but in the Spirit, if so be that the Spirit of God dwelleth in you. But if any man hath not the Spirit of Christ, he is none of his. And if Christ is in you, the body is dead because of sin; but the Spirit is life because of righteousness' (Rom. 8.9f.; see also vv. 11-17, where the baptismal implications are very clear). As circumcision was given to Abraham as 'a seal of the righteousness of faith' (Rom. 4.11), so baptism is given to the Church as the seal of the righteousness of faith which is theirs in Jesus Christ (II Cor. 1.22; Eph. 1.13; 4.30; Rev. 7.3f.; cf. Col. 2.11f.). Baptism is the sacrament of justification (cf. I Cor. 6.11, 'Ye were washed, ye were sanctified, ye were justified, in the name of the Lord Jesus Christ and in the Spirit of God'); it is the occasion of a man's justification and sanctification, i.e. of his obtaining a new status before God.[1] In order to guard against misunderstanding it would be better not to speak of 'justification by faith' but (if we want a formula) of 'justification by faith and baptism', or, more simply, 'baptismal justification', for there is no Christian baptism where there is no faith in Christ, and there is no justification apart from baptism into Christ's body. This is only another way of saying that the Church is the eschatological community of the Messiah, which by faith participates even now in the divine δικαιοσύνη, σωτηρία, δόξα, βασιλεία, ζωή, ἀγάπη and φῶς, which shall be revealed in their unveiled reality in the 'day' of Jesus Christ.

The prophetic and Pauline conception of salvation by the active δικαιοσύνη Θεοῦ, properly understood, prevents us from imagining that there can be any conflict between God's justice and his mercy. It is because God is righteous—i.e. πιστός in respect of his own covenant-promise of salvation—that man is saved despite his sinfulness. The δικαιοσύνη Θεοῦ is the fundamental ground of God's act of salvation in Christ. There was a passing over (πάρεσις, Rom. 3.25 only) of sins in the past, which did not mean that God was indifferent to man's sinfulness, for he had all along prepared his salvation from times everlasting (Luke 2.31; Ps. 98.2) and was neither surprised nor defeated by man's disobedience. His act of redemption in Christ proves that he is δίκαιος (Rom. 3.26) in the Isaianic sense of 'a just God and a Saviour'

---

[1] Sometimes theologians distinguish between justification and sanctification by speaking of justification as an act that is completed at the moment of God's acceptance of the penitent and believing sinner and of sanctification as a continuing process of growth in holiness that goes on through the life of the Christian. This is a clear and intelligible use of terms and is quite unexceptionable, once the terms have been defined. It is, however, doubtful whether the NT concept of ἁγιασμός (the process of making or becoming ἅγιος, from ἁγιάζειν, to sanctify, to make or treat as holy) is patient of such a distinction. Christ is our ἁγιασμός as he is our δικαιοσύνη (I Cor. 1.30), and baptism is the moment of ἁγιασμός as of δικαίωσις (I Cor. 6.11; I Pet. 1.2; cf. Rom. 1.7; I Cor. 1.2; I Thess. 4.7); Christians are ἅγιοι in precisely the same eschatological sense that they are δίκαιοι (II Thess. 2.13; I Tim. 2.15; Heb. 12.14).

(Isa. 45.21). There is no suggestion here or elsewhere that the death of Christ has made it possible for God to forgive sins and yet to remain 'just', 'satisfaction' having been rendered to his 'honour' or 'majesty'. As we have noted above, the metaphors of redemption and ransom are not intended by the NT writers to suggest that a price has been paid either to God or to the Devil; the metaphor emphasizes the length to which God is prepared to go for man's salvation, the sacrifice which Christ was willing to make. Medieval conceptions of God as a kind of feudal overlord who requires satisfaction for his outraged honour have no place in a genuinely biblical theology; and post-Reformation notions of Christ's bearing a penalty or punishment instead of us, in order that God might forgive us and yet remain just, have no basis in the teaching of the NT. When a NT writer says that Christ suffered for sins once, δίκαιος ὑπὲρ ἀδίκων (I Pet. 3.18), or quotes Isa. 53.5, 'by whose stripes ye were healed' (I Pet. 2.24), he is enunciating (as the context makes clear) the Isaianic doctrine of the saving righteousness of God, made visible and effective in the vicarious suffering of his Messianic Servant. The NT writers certainly regard Isa. 53, as Jesus had done before them, as predicting the sacrificial death of Christ, but they do not use it to teach a 'substitutionary' or a 'satisfaction' theory of the atonement.[1] The curious notion that God's 'justice', which demands the punishment of sinners, could be saved by inflicting the death-penalty upon the one sinless being who had ever lived on earth is not found in the NT and it should find no place in Christian theology. Such notions began when δικαιοσύνη was translated by *justitia* and legalistic conceptions began to drive out moral ones. 'Merit' and 'satisfaction' found their way into Christian theology as early as the time of Tertullian and gradually came to dominate it to the exclusion of the NT doctrine of justification by God's free grace, until at last Luther arose to proclaim again the gospel of *sola gratia*. Even after the Reformation, medieval notions of 'merit' and 'satisfaction' continued to distort the NT teaching. Merit is a notion which the NT entirely discards. St Paul does not speak of Christ's merits as being attributed ('imputed') to us, but of his righteousness (Rom. 4.11; cf. 4.22-25), and the idea that we can supplement our own scanty merits by drawing upon the bank of Christ's superabundant merits is only another version of the rabbinic doctrine of 'the merits of the fathers', with Christ

---

[1] See G. W. H. Lampe, *Reconciliation in Christ*, 1956, 42: 'Although the Servant poems are freely employed in the primitive Church to prove that death was not incompatible with Messiahship, . . . the particular texts which, at least as we read the Hebrew version as distinct from LXX, seem to favour a 'substitutionary' interpretation of his death as a punishment inflicted on him by God in place of sinners, or as a satisfaction made to God's justice, are not in fact quoted.'

instead of Abraham, Isaac and Jacob and the Maccabean warrior-saints. It goes properly with medieval conceptions of the saints as possessing superabundant merits rather than with thè NT conception of them as justified sinners.[1] It should be noted that the words 'substitution', 'satisfaction' and 'merit' do not occur in EVV of the NT and that there are no equivalents for them in NT Greek.

ST JAMES ON FAITH AND WORKS

At first sight James 2.14-26 would seem to contradict St Paul's teaching about justification.[2] Closer study, however, shews that the opposition is more apparent than real, because James and Paul clearly do not mean the same thing by 'faith' and 'works'. What James means by 'faith' can be seen from 2.19, 'The demons also believe, and shudder.' James understands by 'faith' only a cold and barren orthodoxy, mere intellectual assent to such a proposition as that 'God is one'. The demons clearly do not have faith in the Pauline sense of complete trust in and obedience towards Jesus Christ; otherwise they would not be demoniacal! Moreover, James and Paul mean different things by 'works'; James means acts of mercy and kindness to those in distress, Christian charity in action (James 2.15f.); Paul means 'the works of the law', i.e. outward acts of conformity to a ritual and moral code done for the sake of acquiring merit. Paul does not wish to belittle works of charity any more than James wishes to deny that God is one. James says that 'faith without works is dead' (2.26); for Paul, faith without works is impossible. Paul cites Gen. 15.6 (Rom. 4.3; Gal. 3.6) to shew that Abraham, while still a Gentile (i.e. uncircumcised) was accounted righteous because of his faith in God's promise; James (2.23) cites the same verse to prove that Abraham's faith was not like that of the demons who believe but do not obey, because his obedience in the offering of

[1] See further G. W. H. Lampe, *op. cit.*, 53-75, for a lucid and penetrating exposition of the NT teaching, in contrast with much medieval and post-Reformation misunderstanding.

[2] Four views of the relation between James and Paul are possible. (1) James is a Judaizer, deliberately attacking the Pauline doctrine. The difficulty about this view is that it is not the *Pauline* doctrine of justification which he attacks. (2) James has heard only a garbled version of Paul's teaching and attacks it as antinomian; we know from Paul himself that there had at one time been misunderstanding with St Peter and St James (Gal. 2.1-14, esp. v. 12), and that he had been accused of antinomianism (Rom. 3.8). (3) There was an antinomian party in the Church to which both Paul and James are opposed; James is supporting St Paul's attack on antinomianism (Rom. 3.5-8; 6.1; 6.15-7.6), not attacking Paul. (4) There is no connection at all between James and Paul beyond the fact that both are trained in rabbinic theology and are familiar with the same rabbinic arguments and proof-texts (so G. Schrenk, 'Righteousness', *TWNT*, ET, 66). Schrenk rightly says that Ep. James is as far removed from the Jewish idea of earning merit as it is from Greek ethics. 'James simply demands, in a direct untheological way, that faith shall not be distorted into a substitute for work' (*op. cit.*, 39). See further E. C. Blackman, *The Epistle of James* (Torch Commentaries), 1957, 97-101.

Isaac shewed that his faith was τέλειος, perfected: justification is by faith that is demonstrated in action ('works'). Thus, in James's language it may be said that Abraham was justified by works without contradicting Paul's assertion that no one is justified by works of law in the sense of the meritorious observance of a legal code. We may state the difference between James and Paul in this way: for James it would have been of no avail if Abraham had believed God, but had not been willing to put his faith into action by obeying God's command; on Paul's view, for Abraham to have refused obedience would have been the same thing as to have disbelieved. There is not a great difference of meaning between ἡ πίστις συνήργει τοῖς ἔργοις (James 2.22) and πίστις δι᾽ ἀγάπης ἐνεργουμένη (Gal. 5.6). The real contrast between James and Paul lies not so much in anything that they affirm or deny as in the different levels at which their minds are working. James is still at the comparatively shallow level of rabbinic moralism; faith for him is intellectual orthodoxy, and the righteousness of God is simply traditional ethical orthodoxy (1.20). He has no inkling of the problem with which St Paul is struggling; the blacks and whites of conventional morality, of rewards and punishments, are all that he can see. His simple tract for simple Christians, who are not tormented with existential problems of sin and its forgiveness, will appear only as an epistle of straw if it is placed in the theological balances over against the solid weight of the Epistle to the Romans.

II

THE WHOLE CHRIST

THE NT presents God's purpose as that of gathering up all things in Christ. This actual expression (ἀνακεφαλαιώσασθαι τὰ πάντα ἐν τῷ Χριστῷ) occurs only at Eph. 1.10[1] but the idea is expressed in many different metaphors in the NT. The original unity or harmony of things, which was disrupted on a cosmic scale by man's fall into sin, is now being restored by Christ's redeeming work; and what had hitherto existed in a state of separation or even enmity is now being unified in the new-created wholeness of Christ. Christ's saving work consists of effecting a unity of God and man, not by converting the Godhead into humanity, but by taking up manhood into God.[2] In Christ we are united to God in such a way that we partake of the character of God himself; a NT writer actually dares to say that Christians become 'partakers of divine nature' (II Pet. 1.4, θείας κοινωνοὶ φύσεως). The theologians of the patristic period dwell lovingly on the thought that in Christ God became what we are in order that we might become what he is.[3] Thus the Church on earth in this age is the 'earnest' or 'firstfruits' of the New Humanity of Jesus Christ, the New Creation of the latter days.

THE NEW MAN

St Paul represents the work of Christ as that of the creation of a new humanity, one which Christians 'put on' like a robe in their baptism, when they 'put away' their old, fallen, corrupt human nature. Though in their baptism this putting on of the new humanity has taken place eschatologically, Christians still need exhorting to be what (eschatologically or by faith) they already are: 'Put away . . . the old man, which waxeth corrupt . . . be ye renewed in the spirit of your mind, and

---

[1] The verb ἀνακεφαλαιόομαι properly means 'to summarize' in a literary sense (from κεφάλαιον, capitulum, chapter), as in Rom. 13.9, ἐν τῷ λόγῳ τούτῳ ἀνακεφαλαιοῦνται. This is the only other appearance of the verb in the NT. The noun ἀνακεφαλαίωσις (recapitulatio) does not appear in the NT.

[2] Cf. the Quicunque Vult: 'Unus autem non conversione Divinitatis in carnem, sed assumptione Humanitatis in Deum.'

[3] E.g. Irenaeus, Adv. Haer., preface of Bk. V: 'Verbum Dei, Jesum Christum Dominum nostrum, qui propter immensam suam dilectionem factus est quod sumus nos, uti nos perficeret esse quod et ipse.'

put on the new man, which after God has been created in righteousness and holiness of truth' (Eph. 4.22-24). Δικαιοσύνη is not a property of our fallen human nature ('the old man', Rom. 6.6; Eph. 4.22; Col. 3.9), but is a quality of the new creation in Christ (τὸν καινὸν ἄνθρωπον τὸν κατὰ Θεὸν κτισθέντα ἐν δικαιοσύνῃ, Eph. 4.24). The new humanity of Christ, being now at peace with God, reconciles even the bitterest of human enemies; out of Jew and Gentile Christ has created 'one new man' (ἵνα τοὺς δύο κτίσῃ ἐν αὐτῷ εἰς ἕνα καινὸν ἄνθρωπον, Eph. 2.15). Here again we note the use of the verb κτίζειν (to create): the new humanity is the new creation of God in Jesus Christ. The point is made even more explicitly in Col. 3.10f., where there is a deliberate parallel drawn with the first creation, in which man was made in the image of God (Gen. 1.26f.): 'having put on the new man, which is being renewed unto knowledge after the image of him that created him (κατ᾽ εἰκόνα τοῦ κτίσαντος αὐτόν), where there cannot be Greek and Jew, circumcision and uncircumcision, barbarian, Scythian, slave, freeman: but Christ is all and in all' (ἀλλὰ τὰ πάντα καὶ ἐν πᾶσι Χριστός). Baptism into Christ is the re-creation of mankind in the image of God, which was impaired by man's sin. 'As many of you as were baptized into Christ did put on Christ: there can be neither Jew nor Greek, bond nor free, nor male and female, for ye are all one (new man) in Christ Jesus' (Gal. 3.27f.). In the new humanity of Christ the deepest religious, political and social divisions are done away. The Book of Genesis tells the story of how these divisions within the original unity of mankind grew up: a new Genesis has taken place in Jesus Christ, the incarnate Word by which the new creation is called into being, and the divisions created by the sin of mankind are abolished. Even the opposition of male and female is done away in the new unity of humanity in Christ. 'Neither is circumcision anything, nor uncircumcision, but a new creation' (Gal. 6.15, ἀλλὰ καινὴ κτίσις). 'If any man is in Christ, there is a new creation (εἴ τις ἐν Χριστῷ, καινὴ κτίσις); the old things are passed away; behold, they are become new' (II Cor. 5.17).

This Pauline conception of the Church as a new-created humanity in Christ is a thoroughly eschatological conception: it was a commonplace of later Judaism that the end-time would be like the perfection of the original creation. God would bring in new heavens and a new earth by an act of new creation (Isa. 65.17f.; 66.22; II Pet. 3.13; Rev. 21.1).[1] In this age the Church of Jesus Christ is the 'earnest' and 'firstfruits' of the new creation of the latter days. Even now there may be discerned the καινὴ κτίσις, foretold by the prophets, made visible to faith in those who are 'in Christ'. Every member of Christ is created

---

[1] See *supra*, 80, 207.

such by an act of new creation at his baptism into Christ. The Church in its present paradoxical existence of 'even now' and 'not yet' is the eschatological reality of the end-time. But this truth is known only to faith, that is, to the Church, and not to those outside it. St Paul does not say so explicitly in any extant epistle, but he seems to hold that God in Christ took our human nature, new-created in its primal perfection, and thereby the new creation came into being.[1] His being born as man was only a necessary first stage in the process of his baptism by death into the new humanity, the risen and glorified body of his resurrection, into which Christians are baptized and through which even now they are glorified. A not dissimilar doctrine of the new-created humanity in Christ is found, of course, in John 1.1-14, where σάρξ represents both our fallen human nature (1.13) and also the perfect human nature of the new creation of Jesus Christ (John 1.14, ὁ λόγος σὰρξ ἐγένετο); and John, like Paul, teaches the truth of our participation in the new humanity of Christ (e.g. 14.23; 15.1-10; 17.23f., τετελειωμένοι εἰς ἕν). If there is a difference between Paul and John, it is that Paul seems to think of the moment of the creation of the new humanity as that of the resurrection of Christ from the dead, while John thinks of it as the entry of the Word into history. But then, John's way of telling the Gospel-story is designed to reflect the eschatological δόξα of Christ in all the events of his human life.

The *newness* of the new creation is emphasized in the Pauline teaching by the use of καινός—καινὴ κτίσις (II Cor. 5.17; Gal. 6.15), καινὸς ἄνθρωπος (Eph. 2.15; 4.24). Old things (τὰ ἀρχαῖα) are passed away: ἰδοὺ γέγονεν καινά (II Cor. 5.17; cf. Rev. 21.5). In Col. 3.10 νέος is used and not καινός, but this is doubtless because of ἀνακαινούμενον, which follows immediately. In the papyri there is not much difference between νέος and καινός; νέος means *recent*, new in the sense of new in time, while καινός means new in quality. The καινὸς ἄνθρωπος of St Paul is qualitatively new, not something merely later in time; he is a *new* creation. Thus the adjective καινός becomes in the NT almost a technical eschatological term. This is implied in two phrases of St Paul's,

---

[1] It would be upon this aspect of NT teaching that the later doctrine of *Anhypostasia* (or the impersonal humanity of Christ), as taught by St Cyril of Alexandria and the Chalcedonian theology, would find, if anywhere, its scriptural foundation. The NT doctrine, however, is not that the Logos unites with himself the Platonic universal (form) of humanity, but that in becoming man he creates mankind over again, since redemption is in the Bible necessarily an act of new creation. What the Logos assumes is not abstract humanity, or the class-concept 'man', but the manhood of every individual man who has ever lived. That is to say, he has potentially taken each individual man to himself; it is in his own baptism that each individual man is actually united with God through Christ. It is in real, suffering individual men that we encounter Christ, not in ideas and abstractions (Matt. 25.34-46). Christ's union with mankind is personal, not a union of impersonal 'substances'.

καινότης ζωῆς (Rom. 6.4) and καινότης πνεύματος (Rom. 7.6), newness of life and newness of the Spirit. Life and Spirit, as we have seen, are eschatological conceptions; even now in this age we possess them by faith in Christ, and they become distinguishing features of the Messianic community. What has happened in the Christ-event is no mere evolution from Israel's past history: it is a breaking into history of the qualitatively new, τὰ ἔσχατα. Hence the peculiar significance of the word καινός in the NT, where we read of Christ's καινὴ διδαχή (Mark 1.27; cf. Acts 17.19), his καινὴ ἐντολή (John 13.34; I John 2.7f.; II John 5); the καινὴ διαθήκη (I Cor. 11.25; Heb. 8.13; 9.15); the καινὸν ὄνομα of Christians (Rev. 2.17; 3.12); the καινὴ Ἰερουσαλήμ (Rev. 3.12; 21.2); the καινὴ ᾠδή which is sung before the throne in heaven (Rev. 5.9; 14.3), and, of course, the καινοὶ οὐρανοὶ καὶ καινὴ γῆ (II Pet. 3.13; Rev. 21.1). The last book of the NT contains the Christian seer's proclamation of the nearness of the day of new creation in which the Alpha and the Omega declares, ἰδού, καινὰ ποιῶ πάντα (Rev. 21.5).[1]

THE LAST ADAM

Closely connected with the conception of the new man is Paul's teaching that Christ is 'the Last Adam' (I Cor. 15.45). The Adam-typology (cf. Rom. 5.14, Ἀδάμ, ὅς ἐστι τύπος τοῦ μέλλοντος) plays a considerable part in Paul's thinking, and it is present to his mind when he is writing passages in which the name of Adam is not mentioned. For instance, in Phil. 2.5-11 he is thinking of the contrast between Christ and Adam, who being made in the image of God, thought that equality with God was something to snatch at: he puffed himself up and imagined himself in the fashion of a god, thus being disobedient to the life-giving tree (cf. Gen. 3.5, 24): wherefore God abased him and gave him a name lower than the angels', that at the name of man ('Adam') no knee should bow, and that every tongue should confess that man is servant, to the glory of God the Father. St Paul thus conceives of Christ as 'Adam in reverse'; Christ repairs the damage wrought by Adam and restores mankind to its original paradisal state of blessedness and peace with God. 'As in Adam all die, so also in the Christ shall all be made alive' (I Cor. 15.22).

In Rom. 5.12-21 St Paul is seeking to explain how it is that the death of one can effect the salvation of all. He takes the rabbinic

---

[1] It was doubtless Jesus himself who first taught the *newness* of the work which he was accomplishing. The sayings about New Patches on Old Garments and New Wine in Old Wine-skins (Mark 2.21f.; Matt. 9.16f.; Luke 5.36-38) contain in themselves the germ of the whole NT conception of the new order. The new-made (νέος) wine is to be put into fresh (καινός) wine-skins; Christian truth cannot be preserved under the old forms of Jewish religion (cf. John 2.1-11, 19; 14.21; Mark 11.14). St Paul has thoroughly grasped this teaching (e.g. Rom. 7.6).

conception of Adam as the representative man and proceeds to shew that Christ is the representative 'Adam in reverse'. (It will, of course, be borne in mind that the Heb. word 'Adam' means 'mankind' and is properly a collective noun, as in the P Creation story, Gen. 1.1–2.4a). In the rabbinic teaching Adam stood for the solidarity of mankind, since all men were created 'in' him.[1] There were rabbinic legends of how dust from all over the earth's surface was collected to form his body. Play was made on the letters of his name, which was made to represent the four quarters of the world: Ἀνατολή (East), Δύσις (West), Ἄρκτος (North), Μεσημβρία (South). The rabbis had no very consistent ideas about the mechanism of the transmission of Adam's guilt to his posterity. St Paul simply accepts the rabbinic view that sin and death were so transmitted, but he displays little interest in the mode of the transmission; he is concerned to make his important point, namely, that it was through one man (δι' ἑνὸς ἀνθρώπου), Adam, that sin and death entered the world. He speaks of Adam's παράβασις (transgression, Rom. 5.14) or of his παράπτωμα ('a side-slip', almost 'Fall', Rom. 5.15) and stresses the fact that it was the lapse of one man: 'By the παράπτωμα of the one many died' (5.15); 'by the παράπτωμα of the one death reigned' (5.17); 'the one man's disobedience' (παρακοή, 5.19), etc. Equally strongly he stresses the reversal of Adam's sin through the work of 'the one man, Jesus Christ' (διὰ τοῦ ἑνὸς Ἰησοῦ Χριστοῦ, 5.17), through whose δικαίωμα—act of justifying righteousness—'the many' freely received the gift of δικαιοσύνη (5.17) and δικαίωσις ζωῆς (5.18). The heavily emphasized contrast between 'the one man' Adam and 'the one man' Christ makes it impossible to draw any other conclusion than that Christ is a corporate personality in the same sense as is Adam. As we fell 'in Adam', so we are restored 'in Christ'. St Paul is presenting the doctrine of the new humanity of Jesus Christ in a slightly different form (cf. the expression ἕνα καινὸν ἄνθρωπον in Eph. 2.15). Though in Gal. 3.28 the name of Adam is not mentioned, the Adam-typology is not far beneath the surface: 'There can be neither Jew nor Greek (as Adam was neither), bond nor free (Adam was God's free man), male nor female ('Adam' is common gender): πάντες γὰρ ὑμεῖς εἷς ἐστε ἐν Χριστῷ Ἰησοῦ.'

In I Cor. 15.45-49 St Paul returns to his Adamic typology. Again he contrasts the first Adam with the last.[2] The first man is ἐκ γῆς, χοϊκός—

---

[1] For a full account of rabbinic thinking about Adam see W. D. Davies, *PRJ*, 52-7.

[2] We may note that the expression 'the Second Adam' does not occur in the NT. On the other hand, St Paul does call Christ ὁ δεύτερος ἄνθρωπος (I Cor. 15.47), so that Cardinal Newman's 'Second Adam' may be said to be justified. Paul's own expression for Christ is ὁ ἔσχατος Ἀδάμ (15.45), 'the Adam of the end-time'.

earthy (15.47); the second man is ἐξ οὐρανοῦ (*ibid.*). Paul is reproducing the teaching of Genesis (which he quotes explicitly in 15.45; Gen. 2.7) and of Judaism in general: Adam was made of the dust of earth. This in itself should be sufficient to disprove the notion that Paul's 'first man' has any connection with the Primal Man of Gnostic speculation, if such had gained popularity in St Paul's time;[1] for the fallen man of the so-called Gnostic myth was in fact a 'heavenly man'. When Paul says that ὁ δεύτερος ἄνθρωπος (i.e. Christ) is ἐξ οὐρανοῦ he means to contrast as strongly as possible the earthly origin of created man with the heavenly origin of him who assumed our manhood for the sake of our salvation. Since I Cor. 15.45-47 seems to be almost the only evidence which the supporters of the theory of the Gnostic myth can bring forward in support of its existence in the first century A.D., it is a fatal weakness of the theory that it turns out not to be evidence for it at all. St Paul would strongly deny any suggestion that the primal Adam was a 'heavenly Man', for he was 'of the earth, earthy'; and he would equally strongly deny that the pre-existent Son of God was a heavenly *man* before his ascension into heaven, after he had descended to the 'lower parts of the earth' (Eph. 4.9). There is nothing in his writings to suggest that St Paul held Christ to be *man* at all before he became poor for our sakes (II Cor. 8.9). All the evidence that there is points to an opposite view: he was originally in the form of God, not of man, till he emptied himself and took the form of a slave (Phil. 2.6f.). Thus, neither 'the first Adam' nor 'the last Adam' (I Cor. 15.45) fulfils the rôle of the Gnostic 'heavenly man'. The view that a supernatural heavenly Ἄνθρωπος came to earth to redeem a fallen fellow 'light-man' is totally different from the view that God assumed our humanity, or was made man, flesh of our flesh, in order to unite our manhood with himself. It is clear that St Paul, like St John and the other NT writers, held the latter view. He is not dealing with the mythology of two supernatural, heavenly beings, one of whom fell from the high estate of heaven and was redeemed by the other, who had not fallen. He knows of no Archetypal Man; he knows only of Christ, the pre-existent Son of God, through whom and for whom all things were created: certainly Adam, made of dust, into whom God breathed the breath of life (I Cor. 15.45, quoting Gen. 2.7), was no such Archetypal Man. Christ, the Son of God, is prior to Adam in time, but as man he is δεύτερος: he became man when he was born of a woman, born under the dispensation of the Mosaic Law (Gal. 4.4). Compared with 'dusty Adam' Christ is the πνεῦμα ζωοποιοῦν of the end-time, foretold by the prophets (I Cor. 15.45). The Age of the Spirit succeeds in time the Natural Order

---

[1] See *supra*, 142f.

(15.46), and those who have borne the image of the earthly Adam now, after their baptism into Christ, bear the image of the heavenly Adam, that is, the image and likeness of God in which humanity was originally created (15.49; cf. Gen. 1.26f.).

Paul undoubtedly thought of Adam as an historical individual who existed at a certain period of time in the eastern land; at least it presumably never occurred to him to question this inherited belief. But he writes as if Adam were not an individual man at all: for his theological purpose 'Adam' is still a collective noun. Adam for Paul is 'mankind', 'everyman', Paul himself. Adam typifies the relation of all sinful men to the God who created them and loves them. The fact that we today no longer think of Adam as an historical individual in no way lessens for us the value of the Adam-concept as a theological symbol. He represents for us (as for Paul) the unity or solidarity of the human race, as created in God's image, yet rebelling against God and asserting its independence of God; as still the object of the love and fatherly discipline of the Creator. The fact that 'Adam' is both a collective noun (Gen. 1.26f.) and a proper name (Gen. 3, though translated 'the man' several times in RV, but see 3.17,21) is profoundly symbolical and teaches deep truth about the biblical conception of personality. This is much more profound than such childish rabbinic rationalizations as that all men sinned because all were in Adam's loins at the time of his Fall. Adam represents all men, because all men have the character of Adam. The Creation and Fall stories are true of man as such, and this truth can be stated in biblical language by saying that all men are 'in Adam' (as Paul states it in I Cor. 15.22).

The expression 'in Adam' does not involve any theory of corporate personality such as modern social psychologists might formulate ('the group mind', 'the instincts of the herd', 'racial behaviour', etc.), and if we use the expression 'corporate personality' at all, we must be on our guard against confusing it with any modern theories. Perhaps it would be better to speak of 'representative man', provided that we understand the expression to mean more than a metaphor (like 'John Bull' or 'Uncle Sam'), as when we think of an individual (Churchill, Gandhi, Lincoln) as representative of his nation, or of the human race. But such analogies are not at all adequate to the biblical conception of Adam or the patriarchs as representatives of their descendants. Adam *is* mankind; Israel (or for that matter Isaac, e.g. Amos 7. 9, 16) is the name of the patriarch *and* of the nation (cf. Esau, Mal. 1.2f.; Rom. 9.13). The Jews in the Middle Ages pleaded the sacrifice of Isaac as Christians did that of Christ; in Isaac the whole Jewish race had made its act of submission to God; through Abraham's faithful obedience the whole race had been received into a covenant-relation with God. The deeds of the patriarchs, of Moses, of David and even of the Maccabean heroes, were not just dead-and-gone incidents in the past; they lived on into the present, determining it, giving it its character. A man lives on in his sons, and his name continues as long as descendants remain on earth. Hence the covenant-making of Abraham, the sacrifice of Isaac, the choice of Jacob instead of Esau, the Egyptian redemption —all these things and many more are a part of the personality, the very self, of every Jew, because he is an Israelite, because Israel lives again in him. The history of Adam, of Abraham, of Jacob and Isaac, of Joseph and Moses and David, is his history; he was, as it were, a participant in the events of ancient time, which were constitutive of the history of creation and of redemption, because he is 'in Adam', 'in Abraham', 'in Israel', and so on. 'Hearken to me, ye that follow after righteousness, ye that seek Yahweh: Look unto the rock whence ye were hewn, and to the hole of the pit whence ye were digged. Look unto Abraham your father, and unto Sarah that bare you: for when he was but one (individual) I called him, and I blessed him, and made him many' (Isa. 51.1f.). Abraham is one, and he is many, just as Adam is an individual *and* the whole human race—in fact, just as Christ is, according to St Paul, the new humanity, the Adam of the end-time, the one man and the many (cf. the use of οἱ πολλοί in Rom. 5.15, 19). 'Many' in biblical language means 'many-in-one' and it can stand for all (cf. Rom. 5.12; I Cor. 15.22).[1] Christ, like Adam, or Abraham, or Israel, is the 'many-in-one' and the 'one-in-many'; the work of the Adam of the last days (ὁ ἔσχατος Ἀδάμ) is to gather into the unity of the one the fragmented many, to heal the schisms of the fallen Adam through the perfect obedience of the Last Adam. 'Now hath Christ been raised from the dead, the firstfruits of them that are asleep. For since by man (Adam) came death, by man (Adam) came also the resurrection of the dead. For as in Adam all die, so also in Christ shall all be made alive' (I Cor. 15.20-22).

'IN CHRIST'

We are now in a position to understand the meaning of the expression ἐν Χριστῷ which occurs very frequently in St Paul in varying forms: the full form seems to be ἐν Χριστῷ Ἰησοῦ (Rom. 6.11). The expression is peculiarly Pauline, although it (or near approximations to it) is found in other NT writers and in the Apostolic Fathers (Acts 4.2; 13.39; I Pet. 3.16; 5.10, 14; I Clem. 32.4; 38.1; Ign. *Eph.* 1.1;

---

[1] See *supra*, 221, on πολλῶν in Mark 10.45. On the whole subject see A. R. Johnson, *The One and the Many in the Israelite Conception of God*, 1942.

Trall. 9.2; *Rom.* 1.1; 2.2), especially in the Johannine literature (ἐν ἐμοί, John 6.56; 14.20, 30; 15.2-7; 16.33; 17.21; ἐν αὐτῷ, ἐν τῷ υἱῷ, I John 2.6, 8, 24, 27f.; 3.6, 24; 5.11, 20; ἐν Ἰησοῦ, Rev. 1.9; ἐν Κυρίῳ, Rev. 14.13). We may also compare the Johannine expression ἔχειν τὸν υἱόν (I John 5.12). It would seem that the conception of ἐν Χριστῷ is not narrowly Pauline, but that it represents a method of speaking of our relationship to the risen Lord which was generally understood in the apostolic Church.

We may at once dismiss the notion that the expression ἐν Χριστῷ has to do with something called 'the mysticism of St Paul'. He uses it once in an autobiographical passage (οἶδα ἄνθρωπον ἐν Χριστῷ πρὸ ἐτῶν δεκατεσσάρων, II Cor. 12.2) in relation to a mystical experience in which he was 'caught up to the third heaven'; but this is exceptional. He can lay claim to having enjoyed mystical 'revelations', but he will not boast of these (12.5-7), and he does not exhort his converts to practise mystical exercises. The relation of Christians to Christ is one of faith, not of mystical absorption. The NT writers set no store at all by religious feelings or emotions, and it is impossible to translate 'religious experience' into NT Greek. We are united with Christ in faith through baptism, and whether or not we enjoy an 'experience' is irrelevant. Neither Paul nor John, when they speak of being in Christ or of Christ's being in us, is saying anything at all about an experience of mystical identification. They are simply using the familiar language in which the Hebrews had for centuries expressed their awareness of the solidarity of the human race, of the relatedness of persons with persons within a social or national whole, and of the living reality of historical events and personages at the present time. Israel may be represented as a person—as God's son, or as the Servant of Yahweh, or by the figure of 'one like unto a son of man'. The many can be—indeed are—one. Mankind is Adam; it will be Christ. The Church, the community of those baptized into Christ, *is* Christ, that is, *is* God's Son, *is* the Servant of the Lord, *is* the Son of Man. If we ask where this conception first came from, and whether it was St Paul who first invented it, we already know the answer.[1] It was Jesus himself who taught his disciples to think of him in this way. It was he who first brought them to the realization that he was in his own person the Son, the new Israel of God; that he was the Servant in whose sufferings and martyrdom his disciples must participate; that he was *Ben Adam*, the corporate Son of Man, the redeemed humanity of the new creation. The expression ἐν Χριστῷ and its equivalents (ἐν ἐμοί, etc.) are means by which St Paul, St John and other NT writers indicate that those who have believed in Christ and

[1] See *supra*, 138, 145.

have been baptized into him are now a part of the new-created humanity of the end-time which constitutes the corporate personality of Christ, the 'human nature' which at his ascension he has carried to his Father's throne in heaven.

In a similar way we must understand what the NT means by such expressions as 'Christ in you' (Rom. 8.10; II Cor. 13.5; Col. 1.27), Christ's dwelling in his disciples (Eph. 3.17; cf. Col. 3.16), or being in or abiding in them (John 14.20; 15.4, 7; 17.23, 26; I John 3.24). Here again no doctrine of 'Christ-mysticism', as that phrase is usually understood, is intended. The biblical doctrine of representative men is again the key to the truth. Adam lives again in every individual man; the patriarchs live their lives representatively in the whole dispersion-wide community of Israel; the people of the saints of the Most High make up the person of one like a son of man, to whom the glorious kingdom of the latter days will be given. So Jesus himself in his character of *Ben Adam* describes himself as present in and to his *sheluchim* in every place, suffering individual men and women and children; persons who collectively make up the *persona* of Adam: 'I was hungry . . . I was thirsty . . . I was a refugee . . . naked . . . sick . . . in prison. . . . Inasmuch as ye did it not unto one of the least of these ye did it not unto me' (Matt. 25.35-45). 'The Son of Man must suffer.' Christ is present in and to suffering humanity beyond all frontiers of Israel or of Church, because his human nature is all-inclusive, universal. But he is especially present to his disciples, who are suffering for his sake (Matt. 10.40-42; Luke 10.16; John 13.20; cf. Gal. 4.14; Philem. 17; Isa. 63.9). Paul had learnt this truth when he understood what the Lord had said to him on the Damascus road, 'Saul, Saul, why persecutest thou *me*?' (Acts 9.4).[1] Christ is most real to us in our sufferings, and Paul knew this as well as anyone (II Cor. 12.7-10). It is in our weakness and suffering that the δύναμις of Christ is made known to us. 'I have been crucified with Christ, and it is no longer I that live, but Christ liveth in me' (Gal. 2.20). In this same verse Paul emphasizes the fact that in this

---

[1] St Augustine, whose favourite expression *totus Christus* we have taken as the title of this chapter, ceaselessly taught the doctrine that 'the whole Christ' is made up of the Head and the Members of the Body. He clearly saw the implications of 'Why persecutest thou *me*?' Out of many relevant quotations perhaps the following most tellingly illustrates his teaching: 'The whole Christ is the head and the body: the head, that Saviour of the body, has already ascended into heaven, but the body is the Church which toils on earth. Now unless this body did cleave to its head in the bond of love, so that the head and the body are made one, he could not say in reproving from heaven a certain persecutor, Saul, Saul, why persecutest thou me? Since no man was touching him as he sat in heaven, how did Saul by his violence against Christians upon earth, inflict injury in any way upon him? He does not say, Why persecutest thou my saints or my servants? but, Why persecutest thou me? that is, my members. The head cried out for the members, and the head transfigured the members into himself' (*Comm. on Psalms*, XXXI (XXX), Enarrat. ii, Serm. 1).

life ('the life which I now live in the flesh') our relationship with Christ is a faith-relationship made possible by belief in the Son of God. The utterly personal quality of this faith is in this same verse brought out uniquely in the NT, for only here is it stated that Christ died *for me*: 'the Son of God who loved me and gave himself up for me.'

THE FULNESS OF CHRIST

The NT writers conceive of the history of redemption as a gathering of the redeemed into Christ. Metaphors of ingathering, or of harvest, had been used by Jesus himself, and are developed in the παράδοσις of his parables and teaching (e.g. Mark 4.26-29; Matt. 13.24-30, 36-43; John 4.35-38; cf. John 11.52). From this it is a straightforward development to the idea of the completion of the predetermined number of the elect (Rev. 7.4-8; 14.1), a notion which had perhaps already figured in Jewish apocalyptic imagery.[1] St Paul, who was not at all of a speculative turn of mind, makes no suggestion about a fixed number of the elect, but he does seem to have thought of the completed humanity, when gathered into Christ, as a kind of perfect whole, a full complement. He thinks of a process of the ingathering into Christ of Jew and Gentile, which in God's good time will be completed; the πλήρωμα of the Gentiles will come in, and 'all Israel' also shall be saved (Rom. 11.25f.). He does not mean that every individual Jew and every individual Gentile will be converted and saved: τὸ πλήρωμα τῶν ἐθνῶν means the 'full complement', the completed number, of the nations of the world, i.e. the Gentile world as a whole (cf. the conception of the πλήρωμα of the Jews in Rom. 11.12). Similarly πᾶς Ἰσραήλ means 'Israel as a whole' (cf. Dan. 9.11). St Paul's mind, being thoroughly Jewish, thinks in terms of *wholes*, which are not merely the sum of their parts and which do not lose their wholeness if individuals fall out of them. A whole in biblical thinking is not a mechanical unity but a diversified unity in which individuals are enriched by participation. This biblical idea of wholeness is present in St Paul's use of the expression τὸ πλήρωμα, the full complement, wholeness, perfected unity. It is a complement which does not gain anything if more individuals are added to it, nor does it lose anything if individuals are defective and fall from it. It takes its character from itself rather than from the individuals who compose it. Thus we may say that 'Adam', 'Israel', 'the Servant of Yahweh', 'the Son of Man' may be thought of in their corporative aspect under the category of πλήρωμα. 'The fulness of the Gentiles' (or

---

[1] In I Tim. 5.21 we read of 'the elect angels', i.e. the angels who did not fall from their first estate. It is not easy to determine at what date the view was developed that 'the number of the elect' was to be made up by filling the places of the fallen angels with 'saints' chosen from amongst men.

of Israel) is not simply a matter of the numerical addition of Gentiles (or Jews) until no individual has been left outside the total, for it is a qualitative rather than a quantitative conception. It is doubtless this quality of wholeness or completedness that St John is symbolizing when he says that the number of the redeemed Israelites is 144,000 (Rev. 7.4; 14.1); he is not expressing an exact mathematical number.

St Paul thinks of the whole company of the redeemed, in heaven and on earth, as a πλήρωμα in this sense. It is in Ephesians that the conception is most clearly developed, and if we take the view that Ephesians is non-Pauline, then we must think of a disciple of St Paul who succeeded in expressing what St Paul meant better than the Apostle himself had ever done. It is not our purpose to discuss the question of authorship here, and we will add only that the conception in Ephesians of the corporative 'new man' as constituting a πλήρωμα Χριστοῦ, in which Jew and Gentile, bond and free, male and female, find their unity, is one which is implicit in the genuine letters of St Paul. Christ's new humanity, the new creation, is a whole which embraces all the other wholes, such as the πλήρωμα τῶν ἐθνῶν and πᾶς Ἰσραήλ. It is the widest complement, the most embracing unity that it is possible to conceive (Gal. 3.28, etc.). Nothing in the old creation is excluded from the perfection of the new man in Christ. Redemption is achieved by ingathering into Christ. Out of divided and estranged humanity 'one new man' is created (Eph. 2.15), a 'full-grown man', ἀνὴρ τέλειος (Eph. 4.13), i.e. whole or perfected humanity, the perfection of which is in fact the measure of the πλήρωμα Χριστοῦ (*ibid.*). Ministry in the Church, whether of apostles, prophets, evangelists, pastors or teachers, is designed for this one purpose only, viz. καταρτισμὸς τῶν ἁγίων, 'the perfecting of the saints' or building up of the corporative personality of Christ (οἰκοδομὴ τοῦ σώματος τοῦ Χριστοῦ) (4.12). In Eph. 1.22f. the Church is explicitly defined as Christ's body, 'the πλήρωμα of him that filleth all in all'. In Eph. 3.17-19 the complementary conception to that of being in Christ, viz. that of Christ's indwelling of the hearts of his disciples, is set forth; the consequence of Christ's indwelling is that his disciples are 'filled unto all the πλήρωμα of God'. The πλήρωμα Χριστοῦ is the ingathered Church; the Church is indwelt by the πλήρωμα τοῦ Θεοῦ. St John expresses the same truth in his own language: 'I in them, and thou in me, that they may be perfected into one' (John 17.23).

Like other NT realities the πλήρωμα Χριστοῦ is in this age subject to the 'even now' and the 'not yet' of eschatological tension. Even now the Church by faith participates in the perfection and wholeness of Christ, but the Church in the world is not yet whole or perfect. It cannot exhibit its perfection to the world, because eschatological reality is apprehended in this age only by faith. The Church's treasure, her γνῶσις Θεοῦ, is in earthen vessels—a fact which at least has the advantage of making us realize that it is not her own power which is of any avail but the exceeding greatness of God's δύναμις (II Cor. 4.7), the δύναμις made perfect in human weakness. The Church, if it has sufficient faith, never needs to be anxious about its weakness as a human organization; indeed, it should rather glory in its weaknesses, for then the power of Christ will be seen to cover it (II Cor. 12.9). 'Wherefore I take pleasure in weaknesses, in injuries, in necessities, in persecutions, in distresses, for Christ's sake: for when I am weak, then am I strong' (12.10). Until the ingathering of the elect is completed, the wholeness or πλήρωμα of Christ's recreated humanity suffers loss, and the missionary labours of the Church are needed in order to fill up what is lacking of the afflictions (θλίψεις) of Christ 'for his body's sake, which is the Church' (Col. 1.24). It is in this sense that the Church in this age partakes in the sufferings (παθήματα) of Christ (Phil. 3.10; II Cor. 1.5-7; cf. Rom. 8.18, etc.). This is not at all to imply that Christ's sufferings on the cross are not indeed a 'finished work', nor is it to suggest that the Church can add anything whatever to the redemption wrought by Christ, however much it suffers. It means that, though the wholeness of Christ is something already perfect and complete, in the sense of the eschatological 'even now', the 'good fight of faith', which the Church wages in this age, is a real fight, not a sham battle in a mock contest where the issue is already decided: it means that every act of Christian self-sacrifice, of vicarious suffering and of loving service is something gained for the πλήρωμα τοῦ Χριστοῦ, for the building up and perfecting of his body, which is the Church.

THE BODY OF CHRIST

The meaning of the expression σῶμα Χριστοῦ as used of the Church should now be apparent. Christ is a 'one' who includes within his resurrection-body 'the many', i.e. a corporate personality, if that term is understood theologically rather than psychologically. In Hebraic thought 'body' means 'self', almost what we mean by 'personality'; thus, for instance, Paul writes, 'I beseech you, brethren . . . to present your bodies (τὰ σώματα ὑμῶν) a living sacrifice' (Rom. 12.1), meaning, of course, 'present your whole selves'. We may think of the σῶμα Χριστοῦ as the 'person' of Christ, provided that we do not think of 'person' as a bodiless spirit (cf. Luke 24.37, 39). It is this Hebraic conception of the one and the many, the Hebraic view of what we call 'personality', which lies behind the conception of the Church as the body of Christ. The individual Israelite was a member of Israel: the individual Christian is a member of Christ. The individual Israelite achieved his status by circumcision, the Christian by means of 'a circumcision not made with hands', i.e. baptism into Christ (Col. 2.11f.). The conception of the Church as Christ's body is emphasized and elaborated by St Paul, and it may be that it was he who first used the phrase; but the fundamental idea behind it, as we have seen, comes from Jesus's own teaching about his Messiahship and his character of *Ben Adam*.[1] His mission was to gather 'Israel' to himself (Matt. 23.37; Luke 13.34; John 11.52). St Paul is not the only NT writer to employ the conception, for it appears clearly in John 2.21, where Christ speaks of raising the Church, the temple of his resurrection-body, into the place within the purpose of God which Judaism and its Temple now no longer can hold.

St Paul's own relation with Christ, especially as determined by his experience on the Damascus road, leads him to his own distinctive emphasis upon the doctrine of the Church as the resurrection-body of Christ. He came to realize that in persecuting the Church he was persecuting Christ himself (Acts 9.4f.; 22.7f.; 26.14f.),[2] and he impresses the same truth on his converts: 'Sinning against the brethren, and wounding their conscience when it is weak, ye sin against Christ' (I Cor. 8.12). As we have noted above, Jesus had originally given this teaching to his disciples in an even stronger form (e.g. Matt. 25.40, 45); St Paul is loyally applying it to the life-situation of the Gentile churches. It is in I Cor. 12.12-30 that he most fully develops the implications of the doctrine for the life and ministry of the churches. All the members

[1] Too often the question of the origin of the *idea* of the Church as σῶμα Χριστοῦ is discussed as if St Paul and not Jesus were the originator of it. It is unnecessary for our purpose here to pursue all the suggestions that have been put forward concerning the origin of the *phrase*. See esp. W. D. Davies, *PRJ*, 57, and J. A. T. Robinson, *The Body*, 55-58; E. Best, *One Body in Christ*, 1955, 83-95. Davies holds that Paul derived the idea primarily from the rabbinic conception of the unity of mankind in Adam. Others, as W. L. Knox, *St Paul and the Church of the Gentiles* and G. Johnston, *The Doctrine of the Church in the New Testament*, 1943, think it is taken over by Paul from the Stoic analogy of a commonwealth as *like* a human body, in which the parts render varied and complementary services. A. E. J. Rawlinson in his essay 'Corpus Christi' in *Mysterium Christi*, ed. G. K. A. Bell and A. Deissmann, 1930, 228, suggested that the idea was derived from the word of Jesus over the bread at the Last Supper; cf. I Cor. 10.17, 'Because there is one loaf, we that are many are one body, for we all partake of the one loaf.' E. Käsemann (*Leib und Leib Christi*, Tübingen, 1933, 176) would *per contra* see Pauline influence behind Mark 14.22.

[2] J. A. T. Robinson, *op. cit.*, 59, points out that Acts 26.14 is the only occurrence in NT of the Aramaic spelling Σαούλ and is 'some evidence that we have here an indelible personal reminiscence'. He roundly declares that 'the appearance on which Paul's whole faith and apostleship was founded was the revelation of the resurrection body of Christ, not as an individual, but as the Christian Community'; and he quotes E. Mersch, *The Whole Christ*, ET, 1948, 104, 'Since that day, when he saw Christ in the Church he was persecuting, it seems that he can no longer look into the eyes of a Christian without meeting there the gaze of Christ.' Cf. also C. H. Dodd, *New Testament Studies*, 62. See also note on p. 251, *supra*.

of a body, though many, are one body: Christ likewise, though many, is one body. Into Christ's one body Christians were baptized, Jews and Greeks, slaves and freemen, and they all drank of the one Spirit. Thus they are now the various members (or as we would say, organs) of Christ's body, having different functions, yet all equally honourable and necessary to the efficient working of the body as a whole. The Church is thus the means of Christ's work in the world; it is his hands and feet, his mouth and voice. As in his incarnate life, Christ had to have a body to proclaim his Gospel and to do his work, so in his resurrection life in this age he still needs a body to be the instrument of his gospel and of his work in the world. This is what is meant by the assertion, sometimes made, that the Church, is 'the extension of the Incarnation'. The phrase is, of course, misleading if it is taken to mean that the actual Church in the world today is already Christ's perfected humanity; not till the 'day of Christ' will the Church of redeemed sinners be in actuality what it is now eschatologically, the perfect manhood of Christ.

Thus it is, in St Paul's view, that Christians find unity and fellowship. They enjoy ἡ κοινωνία τοῦ ἁγίου πνεύματος (II Cor. 13.14) because they are one body in Christ (I Cor. 12.13), although the functions of the body are as diversified as are the Spirit's gifts (I Cor. 12.4-11). 'We, the many, are one body in Christ, and individually we are one anothers' members' (Rom. 12.5; cf. I Cor. 10.17). In Eph. and Col. the metaphor is slightly varied, and Christ is said to be the head of the body: 'he is the head of the body, the Church' (Col. 1.18); 'he put all things in subjection under his feet, and gave him to be the head over all things to the Church, which is his body . . .' (Eph. 1.22; cf. Eph. 4.15; 5.23; also I Cor. 11.3). Christ, in this metaphor, is the Head of that body of which Christians are members; while the Head is perfect, the body is incomplete and is being built up by the apostolic, pastoral and teaching ministry of the Church into 'a fullgrown man' (Eph. 4.11-16), the whole Christ—*totus Christus, membra cum capite.*

THE BRIDE OF CHRIST

It is right to speak of the Church as the resurrection body of Christ, i.e. the manhood which Christ carried into heaven at his ascension to the Father (Eph. 2.6), even though we recognize that such language is metaphorical. Yet it is true metaphor, expressing a reality which cannot be expressed in any other way.[1] The body-metaphor is pressed

[1] Several recent expositors would apparently deny that the Pauline language is metaphor at all. 'We are members of that body which was nailed to the cross, laid in the tomb and raised to life on the third day' (L. S. Thornton, *The Common Life in the Body of Christ*, 1944, 298; cf. also E. L. Mascall, *Christ, the Christian and the*

to its most extreme point in the NT representation of the Church as having become 'one flesh' with Christ in marriage-union with him. Nothing could more vividly illustrate the fact of the wholeness of our redemption in Christ than this declaration that our union with him is no merely 'spiritual' thing, but is as physical as the union of man and wife; Christ redeems our bodies as well as our 'souls': 'The husband is head of the wife, as Christ also is head of the Church, being himself the saviour of the body' (Eph. 5.23). The metaphor of the husband-wife relationship, it would seem, was accepted teaching in the early Church, because in Eph. 5.22-33 the author uses this great theological truth, almost incidentally, to reinforce his teaching about the mutual relationships of Christian husbands and wives (cf. also II Cor. 11.2). It is, moreover, found in non-Pauline parts of the NT, particularly in the Apocalypse (Rev. 19.7-9; 21.2, 9); and it may perhaps have been suggested by Jesus himself in sayings and parables which represent his parousia as the coming of the Bridegroom (Matt. 25.6; Luke 12.35-40) and the blessedness of the redeemed as a marriage feast in the Age to Come (Matt. 22.1-14).

The metaphor of Christ as Bridegroom and the Church as his bride is, of course, based upon the OT prophetic image of Israel as the spouse of Yahweh: 'Thy Maker is thine husband, Yahweh Sabaoth is his name: and the Holy One of Israel is thy redeemer. . . . For Yahweh hath called thee as a wife forsaken . . . but with great mercies will I gather thee' (Isa. 54.5-7). 'As the bridegroom rejoiceth over the bride, so shall God rejoice over thee' (Isa. 62.4f.; cf. also Hos. 2.7; Amos 3.2). Israel's lapses into idolatry are frequently spoken of as whoredom or as adulterous union with strangers (e.g. Ezek. 16.15-43; Hos. 4.10-15). Moreover, the days of covenant-making in the wilderness of Sinai are spoken of as the time of Israel's 'espousals' (Jer. 2.2; Ezek. 16.8, 43, 60); and it is promised that, despite her sins, God would make with Israel, forgiven and restored, a new and everlasting marriage-covenant (Ezek. 16.60-63). The NT writers think of this prophecy as having been fulfilled in the marriage-covenant between Christ and his Church. The Last Supper of Jesus with his disciples was the solemnization of the marriage in a sacramental rite.[1] The metaphor involves an affirmation

Church, 1946, 161f.; J. A. T. Robinson, *op. cit.*, 49-55). On the other hand, others would say that the Pauline language is to be understood metaphorically (e.g. E. Best, *One Body in Christ*, 112, who says that the phrase 'body of Christ' is 'not used realistically and ontologically but metaphorically'). Much depends on our understanding of the necessarily symbolical character of all theological language. It would surely be wiser to say that such a phrase as 'the body of Christ' (meaning the Church) is used realistically, ontologically and *therefore* metaphorically or symbolically or analogically.

[1] See C. L. Chavasse, *The Bride of Christ* (London, 1940), who points out that the Passover was nuptial and was the ratification of the marriage-covenant between Yahweh and his people (p. 60).

of the closest possible unification of Christ with the Church as his body, in view of the biblical doctrine of marriage, stated in Gen. 2.24 (quoted by St Paul in Eph. 5.31), that man and wife become 'one flesh' (cf. also I Cor. 6.15-20, where a strong application of this theological principle is made in the sphere of the ethics of sex). Christians are 'joined to the Lord' as husband and wife are joined, and are therefore 'one spirit' with him (I Cor. 6.17). Indeed, we have in the marriage-metaphor an excellent illustration of the meaning of the doctrine of the 'one body', 'one flesh', 'one spirit', of the Pauline teaching. For the marriage-relationship is the deepest, richest and most satisfying personal human relationship of which we have experience; it is an experience of surrender without absorption, of service without compulsion, of love without conditions. In it are illustrated, as far as such divine realities can be illustrated by analogies within human experience, all the truths of God's love and grace in the lives of Christian disciples. To say that the Church is 'one flesh' with Christ is to describe a structure of personal relationships in which the Christian disciple remains completely and utterly himself, yet finds himself developed into a 'new man' through participation in the common life of Christ's body, the Church.

THE TRUE VINE

The Johannine allegory of the Vine and the Branches (John 15.1-8, 16) teaches the same truth as the metaphors of the Body and of the Bride of Christ. In the OT Israel is frequently represented by the figure of a vine, olive or fig-tree; and in Rom. 11.16-24 St Paul likens Israel to an olive tree, whose roots are the patriarchs and whose branches are the children of Israel, while the Gentiles are a wild olive that has been grafted into the 'good olive tree'. J. H. Bernard says that wherever in the OT Israel is represented by a vine, her degeneracy is being lamented or her destruction foretold (Ps. 80.8-16; Isa. 5.1-7; Jer. 2.21; Ezek. 15.1-8; 19.10; Hos. 10.1f.; II (4) Esd. 5.23; cf. Rev. 14.18f.).[1] Jesus in the Synoptic Gospels is recorded as having used this OT symbolism of vines and vineyards (Mark 12.1-12 and par.; Matt. 20.1-16; 21.28-32; Luke 13.6-9; the Barren Fig-tree episode belongs to the same cycle of ideas, Mark 11.12-14, 20-25). Indeed, the representation of Israel as a vine was familiar to everyone in his day; Israel was represented as a vine on the coins of the Maccabean rulers. The general weight of Jesus's teaching would seem to be that Israel was a vine (or vineyard) which yielded a poor grape-harvest in spite of the loving care which God had lavished upon it. St John is familiar with this tradition of his teaching, and he develops it by the words which he puts into the mouth

[1] J. H. Bernard, *St John* (ICC), 1928, II, 478.

of Jesus: 'I am the true vine, and my Father is the husbandman' (15.1). In the sentence ἐγώ εἰμι ἡ ἄμπελος ἡ ἀληθινή two words have special emphasis, the first and the last. *Christ*, not Israel, is the vine of God's planting; the vineyard of Israel has been rejected as worthless; compared with the old, barren vine, Christ is the *true* vine. The implication of the saying is that Christ is the new Israel, the true Israel of God. But, like the old Israel, he is a corporative person: 'Ye are the branches' (15.5). The vine in the allegory is a figure of *totus Christus, caput et membra*. The branches yield fruit only because their life is drawn from the vine: a branch that is broken off is fit only for burning (15.6; cf. Ezek. 15.1-8). St John intends the allegory to teach the doctrine of the essential unity of the Church, through participation in which the individual disciple receives the very life-blood of Christ himself. The allegory of the Vine was doubtless suggested by the first celebration of the Eucharist (as St John would regard the Last Supper), at which it was spoken. The symbolism of the allegory is 'at least in part eucharistic, and the union of believers with Christ which it represents is a union in his death'.[1]

The allegory of the Vine passes into a discourse of Jesus on the theme of ἀγάπη (John 15.9-17), which develops naturally from it, because in the whole NT view the Christian experience of ἀγάπη is the result of man's being taken up into the unity of the Godhead through incorporation into Christ. 'Even as the Father hath loved me, I also have loved you: abide ye in my love' (15.9). Abiding in Christ's love is defined in the next verse as obedience to Christ's commandment, which in turn is defined as the command to love one another even to the extent of Christ's love, even to the length of laying down one's life (15.12f.). Love is obedience, not the coerced obedience of a slave but the willing obedience of a friend: 'No longer do I call you δοῦλοι . . . but I have called you φίλοι' (15.15). Obedience to Christ's commandment of love is now a possibility because of the new relationship which has been created by Christ's schooling and appointing of his disciples (15.16). This new relationship is a taking up of the disciples into the unity of the divine life; in the High Priestly Prayer Jesus prays that 'they may all be one, even as thou, Father, art in me and I in thee, that they also may be in us' (17.21; cf. 17.23, 26). The ἀγάπη with which the Father loved the Son even before the foundation of the world (17.24) is the ground of the Christian's new relationship not only with God but also with his fellow Christians. Thus, as elsewhere in the NT, ἀγάπη is not a natural virtue, which men can develop within themselves if they try hard enough: it is a 'fruit' of 'abiding in' Christ, the Vine which gives

[1] C. K. Barrett, *GSJ*, 393.

life to its branches (15.16). Ἀγάπη, like δικαιοσύνη, is a real quality of life in Christ, not an 'as if'. Our love and righteousness are, of course, not our but Christ's achievement; yet they are our possession, even now, by faith, because even now we are in Christ. Because we are incorporated into Christ or 'abide in' him, we *are* Christ: not individually, but corporatively, we make up the *persona* of Christ. In Christ we are enfolded in the Father's love for the Son, who now includes us. God the Father treats us now as his Son, who in fact we are. Hence we are justified, assumed righteous, made acceptable to God, in virtue of the new relationship to him which our incorporation into Christ has set up. Hence justification is never a matter of the individual's own private relation to God; we are justified together in Christ, not as separate individuals who appear at the bar of a court of justice, each one answering for his own crimes. It is as the new Israel, the body of Christ, that we are found in the possession of ἀγάπη, which is πλήρωμα νόμου (Rom. 13.10; cf. 13.8), and which is therefore δικαιοσύνη and the ground of our δικαίωσις. No legal fiction is involved; God treats us as he treats his Son because we *are* the body, crucified and risen, of his Son: οἱ πολλοὶ ἓν σῶμά ἐσμεν ἐν Χριστῷ (Rom. 12.5).[1]

THE SPIRITUAL HOUSE

Jesus conceived of his mission as that of gathering a new Israel of God. There is a passage in Isaiah in which the gathering in of 'strangers' and of 'the outcasts of Israel' is closely associated with the house of God (i.e. the Temple at Jerusalem) in the day of the drawing nigh of God's salvation and of the revelation of his righteousness (Isa. 56.1-8). God will make the 'strangers' joyful in his house of prayer: 'their burnt offerings and their sacrifices shall be accepted upon mine altar: for mine house shall be called an house of prayer for all peoples. The Lord God which gathereth the outcasts of Israel saith, Yet will I gather [others] to him, beside his own that are gathered' (56.7f.). Jesus meditated upon the tragedy of the Temple, which in the prophetic vision was

---

[1] Quotations from three writers who approach the matter from somewhat different viewpoints will perhaps illustrate the convergence of scholarly opinion upon this conclusion: 'Justification by faith is never a solitary relationship. . . . Faith and justification are inseparable from initiation into the one body' (A. M. Ramsey, *The Gospel and the Catholic Church*, 2nd ed., 1956, 37). 'It is *in Christ* that the sinner is justified. He is placed in a right relationship, that is, restored to the condition of being within the covenant with the Father, and he is given the status of a son because he is *in* Christ. . . . We are "justified in Christ", as the Apostle says explicitly in Gal. 2.17' (G. W. H. Lampe, *Reconciliation in Christ*, 63). 'Paul . . . has in mind always God's action in justifying the individual, and not only the community. Actually, he does not think of the individual as existing by himself; when a man is justified, he becomes forthwith a member of the body of Christ, as formerly he belonged to Israel, or the Gentiles, or the human race' (G. Schrenk, *TWNT*, ET, *Righteousness*, 47).

to have become the gathering place and house of prayer of all nations (Mark 11.17; Matt. 21.13; Luke 19.46), but was in fact a den of robbers (Jer. 7.11). God was saying again, as he had spoken by the word that came to Jeremiah, 'I will do unto the house which is called by my name, wherein ye trust, and unto the place which I gave to you and to your fathers, as I have done to Shiloh' (Jer. 7.14; cf. I Sam. 4.3-12; Ps. 78.60; Mark 13.2). One of the few scraps of evidence that could be mustered against Jesus at his trial was that he had spoken against the Temple: 'We heard him say, I will destroy this Temple (ναός) that is made with hands, and in three days I will build another made without hands' (Mark 14.58). Clearly Jesus had spoken of his own work as replacing the Jerusalem Temple in the purpose of God, for the Temple had become a place of abominations (Jer. 7.10). The Temple, as the living centre of the worship of God, would be replaced by a new Temple, which Jesus was building—a Temple made not of stones (ἀχειροποίητος), but of the gathered members of the new Israel which he was incorporating into himself. In another context he had spoken of 'building his ἐκκλησία' on St Peter as a foundation rock (Matt. 16.18).

St John in his own subtle and allusive style brings out the significance of the Temple-metaphor, re-interpreting the saying preserved in the Synoptic tradition in such a way as to shew its meaning for the doctrine of the Church. After his account of the Cleansing of the Temple (John 2.13-17) he records the reply of Jesus to the request of the Jews for a sign: 'Destroy this Temple (ναός), and in three days I will raise it up.' The Jews object that even the re-building begun by Herod the Great has already taken forty-six years. The Evangelist adds the explanatory gloss, 'But he spoke of the Temple of his body' (περὶ τοῦ ναοῦ τοῦ σώματος αὐτοῦ), and notes that the disciples recalled this teaching only after Christ's resurrection (2.18-22). It is, of course, incredible that the Fourth Evangelist (especially if he wrote in or near Ephesus) should have been unaware of the meaning of σῶμα Χριστοῦ as expounded by St Paul and doubtless many others, and it is certain that we have here a typical Johannine *double entendre*: ὁ ναὸς τοῦ σώματος αὐτοῦ refers, on the one hand, to Christ's bodily resurrection, but also, on the other hand, to the raising up of Christ's body, the Church. The meaning of John 2.1-22 as a whole is that the Church of Jesus Christ replaces Judaism and its Temple in the purpose of God (cf. John 4.21-23). St John is conveying in his own style the truth that the Church is the resurrection-body of Christ.

Other passages in the NT shew clearly that the apostolic Church had assimilated Jesus's teaching about the building of a new ἐκκλησία Θεοῦ, that is, the gathering of a new Israel into his own σῶμα or *persona*. The most striking is I Pet. 2.4f. The writer thinks of Christ as a corner-stone (Isa. 28.16 and Ps. 118.22, quoted in I Pet. 2.6f.) and of Christians as built on it or around it: 'Ye also as living stones (λίθοι ζῶντες) are built up a spiritual house (οἶκος πνευματικός),[1] unto (εἰς) a holy priest-hood, to offer up spiritual sacrifices acceptable to God through Jesus Christ.' Here we have the conception of the ναὸς ἀχειροποίητος (here called πνευματικός) built out of the members of the Church who formerly had been 'no people' (I Pet. 2.10; Hos. 1.9f.; 2.23) but now are λαὸς Θεοῦ. In short, the Scripture upon which Jesus meditated is ful-filled: the strangers and outcasts are gathered into the new Temple, and in it they offer their sacrifices which are accepted on God's altar (Isa. 56.7f.). In the Christian ναός our sacrifices are acceptable to God through Jesus Christ. Exactly the same teaching appears in Eph. 2.19-22 (whatever may be the connection between Eph. and I Pet.): 'Now therefore ye are no more strangers and foreigners, but fellow-citizens with the saints and members of God's household, and are built upon the foundation of apostles and prophets, Jesus Christ himself being the chief corner-stone, in whom all that is builded (πᾶσα οἰκοδομή), fitly framed together, grows into a holy ναός in the Lord: in whom ye also are builded together for an habitation (κατοικητήριον) of God in the Spirit.' In I Cor. 3.16f. St Paul speaks of Christians as forming the ναὸς Θεοῦ, in which the Spirit of God dwells (cf. also I Cor. 6.16f.). The individual Christian is a microcosm of the Church as the habitation of God in (his activity of) Spirit (I Cor. 6.19). In II Cor. 5.1f. St Paul seems to be arguing that, as the Jerusalem Temple was 'dissolved' and replaced by a house not made with hands (οἰκία ἀχειροποίητος), i.e. the Church of Christ, so it is necessary that our earthly tabernacle (or body) should be dissolved in order that we might be 'clothed upon with our habitation (οἰκητήριον) from heaven'. At least, this interpreta-tion is suggested by the use of the rare word ἀχειροποίητος—used in the Synoptic tradition of Christ's word about the Temple that he would build, made without hands (Mark 14.58). The word occurs neither in LXX nor in classical literature, and is found only three times in NT and nowhere outside it. The third NT reference is Col. 2.11: 'in whom (Christ) ye were circumcised with a circumcision not made with hands (περιτομῇ ἀχειροποιήτῳ), in the putting off of the body of the flesh, in the circumcision of Christ.' The phrase ἡ περιτομὴ τοῦ Χριστοῦ clearly means the new Israel, and the 'circumcision made without hands'

---

[1] The Temple is frequently called οἶκος in LXX (e.g. Ps. 69 (68).9, quoted in John 2.17, ὁ ζῆλος τοῦ οἴκου σου).

refers both to Christian baptism ('the putting off of the fleshly person') and also to the Church as the ναὸς ἀχειροποίητος.

THE HOUSEHOLD OF GOD

In some NT passages οἶκος means 'household', 'family', and not the building (Temple). For instance, we read in Acts 16.15 that Lydia was baptized καὶ ὁ οἶκος αὐτῆς (cf. Acts 10.2; 11.14; 16.31-34; 18.8). An ancient household, of course, included a man's slaves, hired servants and dependent relatives, as well as children; it might be quite a large establishment. But the word οἶκος had important OT associations, and appears in such Hebraic usages as οἶκος Ἰσραήλ (Heb. 8.8), οἶκος Δαυείδ, etc. Thus, a title for the Church, the new οἶκος Ἰσραήλ, is οἶκος τοῦ Θεοῦ (Heb. 10.21; I Pet. 4.17), and in I Tim. 3.15 οἶκος Θεοῦ is defined as ἐκκλησία Θεοῦ ζῶντος. The solidarity of the ancient household as a social unit is significant here; it had its own 'economy' in which there was differentiation of function and status. Thus, in Heb. 3.1-6 the distinction between Moses, who was a θεράπων, a 'retainer' (Num. 12.7; Josh. 1.2; 8.31, 33; cf. Wisd. 10.16), and Christ, who is υἱὸς ἐπὶ τὸν οἶκον αὐτοῦ, is strongly affirmed; the passage is especially interesting because in it οἶκος is used in its two senses of 'building' and 'household'. Starting from Num. 12.7, 'My servant (θεράπων) Moses . . . is faithful in all my house (οἶκος)', *Auct. Heb.* thinks of the house that God *built*, returns to the idea of Christ as a son over God's house(hold), and concludes by saying that *we are* God's building *and* God's household. The οἰκονομία (lit. management of a household, stewardship, cf. Luke 16.2-4) of God's household the Church is the responsibility of those to whom it is specifically entrusted; in an ancient household the οἰκονόμος (steward) was a superior kind of slave who bore great responsibility for the day-to-day management of the household affairs, accounts, etc. Thus, St Paul speaks of himself and his fellow-workers as ὑπηρέται Χριστοῦ, Christ's assistants or servants, and οἰκονόμοι μυστηρίων Θεοῦ, stewards of the revelation of God in Christ (I Cor. 4.1f.); and he speaks of the οἰκονομία of this revelation which has been entrusted to himself as a responsible steward of the divine household (I Cor. 9.17; Eph. 3.2f.; Col. 1.25). All the members of God's household have their own household tasks, whether they are οἰκονόμοι or οἰκέται, the humbler household slaves (cf. Luke 16.13; I Pet. 2.18).

The conception of the Church as God's household or family logically involves the conception of the Fatherhood of God, not as the father of all men (cf. Acts 17.28f.), or even of certain very remarkable men, heroes, kings, etc. God is Father of Jesus Christ and he is 'our Father' only because we are 'in Christ', because of our new relationship to God in Christ.[1] This truth is expressed in the Pauline conception of 'adoption' (υἱοθεσία, a word found five times in Paul and nowhere else in NT: Rom. 8.15, 23; 9.4; Gal. 4.5; Eph. 1.5). In the OT Israel becomes God's son (Ex. 4.22f.; Hos. 11.1), and is not in the pagan sense 'God's offspring'; but the adoption-metaphor is not found in the OT, because adoption as a legal process was unknown amongst the Hebrews. In Roman law, however, adoption was effected on payment of money in the presence of witnesses, several of whom were required because, in an age when legal documents were not used as they are today, it was essential to have proof of the transaction; thus in Rom. 8.15f. it is said that we received the spirit of adoption, whereby we are legally entitled to address God as 'Abba', father, and the Holy Spirit is the witness-at-law of the validity of the transaction: 'the Spirit himself beareth witness with our spirit that we are children of God.' The mention of the Spirit in this way suggests that Paul thought of baptism as the ceremony of adoption. In the ancient king-making festivals of the Semites God had declared the king to be his son; since the legal institution of adoption was unknown, the ceremony was not thought of as an adoption but as a re-begetting; e.g. Ps. 2.7, 'Yahweh said unto me, Thou art my son; this day have I begotten thee.' The omission of the second half of this divine declaration by the Voice from Heaven at the baptism of our Lord (Mark 1.11 and pars.)[2] indicates that Christ's sonship is different from ours: he is a Son by right, whereas we are sons by grace. He is the unique Son (cf. Mark 1.11, 'beloved Son'), and we are sons only as we are found in him. The adoption-metaphor thus teaches profound truth concerning the nature of our sonship. We are sons because Christ is Son; God is Father, not because of his adopted sons, for then he would be Father only in a secondary sense; he is Father because he is 'the God and Father of our Lord Jesus Christ' (Rom. 15.6; II Cor. 1.3; Eph. 1.3; I Pet. 1.3). Thus, God is really and essentially Father, and his character of Father is not dependent upon our sonship, but on Christ's; therefore he is the archetypal Father, the source of Fatherhood, the Father from whom all πατριά ('fatherhood', 'ancestry', 'family', 'house'—cf. Luke 2.4, ἐξ οἴκου καὶ πατριᾶς Δαυείδ) in heaven and earth is named (Eph. 3.15). Thus, in virtue of our being ἐν Χριστῷ God is really and essentially our Father; but we must never for one moment forget that we have no claim upon God such as have the children of the human fathers who brought them into the world. There is no moral or legal obligation upon anyone to adopt children who are not his own; yet this is the true

---

[1] Cf. *supra*, 149. [2] See *supra*, 179.

analogy of what God has done for us. Through his free grace and love he has adopted us into his household at our baptism into Christ, not as slaves but as sons: 'children of God', 'heirs of God', 'joint-heirs with Christ' (Rom. 8.17). 'Thou art no longer a δοῦλος but a son; and if a son, then an heir through God' (Gal. 4.7; cf. 3.29).

12

THE ISRAEL OF GOD

THE expression 'new Israel' does not occur in the NT, but the idea of the Christian community as having now become 'the Israel of God' (Gal. 6.16; cf. 3.7, 9, 29) is expressed in many ways. The Church of Jesus Christ inherits the privileges and responsibilities which had formerly belonged to Israel. The true heir of God's vineyard, Israel, is Jesus, God's beloved Son (Mark 12.6f.), and the Wicked Husbandmen had not achieved their purpose of appropriating the vineyard: the Lord of the vineyard had given it to others (Mark 12.9). These 'others' now included Gentile Christians, who, being made children of God, were now also 'joint-heirs' (συνκληρονόμοι) with Christ (Rom. 8.17; Gal. 3.29; 4.7; Titus 3.7; and esp. Eph. 3.6, 'The Gentiles are fellow-heirs and fellow-members of the body and fellow-partakers of the promise in Jesus Christ'). Israel was formerly the sole possessor of 'the adoption' (as God's son); but 'they are not all Israel which are of Israel', and there were other children of the promise to Abraham (Rom. 9.4, 6, 8). The tragedy of God's rejection of Israel κατὰ σάρκα, or of Israel's rejection of God's Messiah, is a matter over which the NT evinces the deepest concern; it is one which the Lord himself had deeply pondered (Mark 11.20-25) and with which St Paul had earnestly wrestled (Rom. 9-11). Jesus affirmed that the 'mountain' of Jewish unbelief would eventually be cast into the sea (Mark 11.23); and St Paul concluded that the hardening of Israel's heart was part of the mystery of the divine election, according to which, by ways at present inscrutable to us, God's purpose of 'mercy to all' should be finally realized: the fulness of the Gentiles should come in, and all Israel should be saved (Rom. 11.25-32).

THE INHERITANCE
In the OT Israel is frequently spoken of as Yahweh's κλῆρος:[1]

---

[1] The word κλῆρος can mean one's 'portion' or 'inheritance' (e.g. Acts 26.18, the inheritance of the Gentiles amongst those sanctified in Christ; Col. 1.12, 'partakers of the κλῆρος of the saints in light'), but originally it meant a 'lot' (e.g. the κλῆρος which the soldiers cast for the garments of Jesus, Mark 15.24; Matt. 27.35; Luke 23.34; John 19.24; cf. Ps. 22.18; or the κλῆρος which fell on Matthias, Acts 1.26). In Acts 1.17 St Peter says that 'Judas was numbered among us and received his

'Yahweh hath taken you and brought you forth out of the iron furnace, out of Egypt, to be unto him a people of inheritance . . .' (Deut. 4.20); 'they are thy λαός and thy κλῆρος, which thou broughtest out by thy power and by thy stretched out arm' (Deut. 9.29; cf. I Kings 8.51, etc.). God's gift of the land of Canaan to Abraham and his seed (Gen. 17.8) is often described in LXX as Israel's κληρονομία or inheritance (e.g. Ps. 105 (104).11; cf. Ps. 78 (77).55); and similarly Israel herself is described as Yahweh's κληρονομία (Ex. 15.17; Ps. 74 (73).2; Isa. 63.17; Jer. 10.16). In view of such language the description by Jesus in Mark 12.7 of Israel as the κληρονομία to which he is himself ὁ κληρονόμος (heir) is highly significant.

In the NT, generally speaking, the κληρονομία which Christians shall inherit, since they are now made sons of God and therefore συνκληρο-νόμοι with Christ, is the Reign of God or (what comes to the same thing) the life of the Age to Come (Matt. 19.29; 25.34; Mark 10.17; I Cor. 6.9f.; 15.50; Gal. 5.21; Eph. 5.5; James 2.5; cf. I Pet. 3.9; Rev. 21.7). Thus, the Christian's inheritance is strictly eschatological. It is an inheritance with the saints in light (i.e. the light of the Age to Come) (Col. 1.12; cf. Acts 26.18; Wisd. 5.5). As with other eschatological realities, our inheritance is something of which we have even now the earnest, since the Holy Spirit which we now possess is the ἀρραβὼν τῆς κληρονομίας ἡμῶν (Eph. 1.14). Thus, while we even now possess the ἀπαρχὴ τοῦ πνεύματος, there is a sense in which it can be said that we are still waiting for *the* adoption, i.e. the day of redemption (Rom. 8.23). While we must wait until then to enter into the full possession of our inheritance, there is nevertheless a sense in which we possess it even now, a sense in which the Israel of old had never enjoyed it. For Israel, though the heir, was still a child, not yet come of age, and therefore of the same legal status as the household slaves; indeed, Israel was in slavery to the Torah, just as the Gentiles were enslaved to the elemental world-powers. The human race attained its majority, so to speak, when in the fulness of time God sent forth his Son and we received the adoption of sons, becoming the heirs of God's promises (Gal. 4.1-7). The very word 'heir' expresses in itself the heart of the paradox of the NT eschatology, for an heir is one who already is in possession of something, but who does not yet possess it in its fulness.

κλῆρος in this διακονία', and in Acts 8.21 he tells Simon Magus that he has 'neither part (μερίς) nor κλῆρος in this λόγος' (RV 'matter'). In I Pet. 5.3 the presbyters are exhorted not to lord it over their κλῆροι, i.e. their pastoral charges, the pastoral spheres allotted to them individually within the whole κληρονομία of Christ in his Church. From this latter usage the words, *clericus*, clergy, etc., are derived, though not found in this sense before Tertullian (see E. G. Selwyn, *The First Epistle of Peter, ad. loc.*).

THE PEOPLE OF GOD

The NT re-interpretation of the OT theology is nowhere more strikingly displayed than in its claim that the mixed Christian community of Jews and Gentiles is become the new 'people of God'. In the LXX λαός, people, is used over 1,500 times in the sense of an ethnic group of the *same* stock and language, particularly Israel herself; and the expression λαὸς Θεοῦ becomes a technical term for Israel as the chosen people of God (cf. Heb. 11.25). In the NT this use is taken over as a title for the Christian community, though the word λαός is often employed quite untechnically (e.g. Luke 1.21; 3.15; 7.1, 29, etc.) in the sense of the population in general or the assembled company.[1]

A dominant theme of the OT is God's purpose for Israel *vis-à-vis* the other nations. In Gen. 1-12 there is carefully traced the process by which the nations come into being and the manner in which God's purpose is narrowed down through the true line of Seth and Noah to the election and call of Abraham. The prophetic interpretation of history is already in evidence, for it is taught that God chose Abraham in order that all the families of the earth (LXX, πᾶσαι αἱ φυλαὶ τῆς γῆς) may be blessed (Gen. 12.3). *El Shaddai* bade Abraham to 'walk before him and be perfect' (Gen. 17.1) in order that his universal purpose should be fulfilled. But even within the covenant-group of Abraham's descendants through Isaac the process of the divine election—choice, selection—continues. Jacob (=Israel) and not Esau (=Edom) is chosen; and, though typically strong language is used ('I loved Jacob, but Esau I hated', Mal. 1.2f.; Rom. 9.13), it must be borne in mind that the whole purpose of election in the biblical-prophetic view is the ultimate salvation of all the nations of mankind, including those whose 'rejection' is dramatized by the use of the anthropomorphism 'hated'.

The OT history relates how God succoured his people in order that they might be the instrument of his universal purposes. At the lowest ebb of their fortunes, degraded to the indignity of a slave-caste in Egypt, Jacob's descendants are 'redeemed' by Yahweh, who 'with a strong arm' delivers them from Pharaoh at the Red Sea. This deliverance is the supreme manifestation alike of Yahweh's power and of his favour (grace). It is emphasized that God did not choose the enslaved Israelites because of their own qualities and virtues (Deut. 9.4f.; cf. 7.7). God's act of redemption was for 'his name's sake'; the reason for his choice and deliverance of Israel is to be found in God alone. This is the mystery of election, the miracle of grace. God loved Israel (Deut.

---

[1] In NT δῆμος is found only in Acts 12.22; 17.5; 19.30, 33, always in the sense of 'the electorate' of the Greek city-state as it still survived in Roman times. The LXX usage of λαός appears clearly in Rev. 5.9; 7.9; 10.11; 11.9, etc., in such a list as γλῶσσα, φυλή, λαός, ἔθνος.

10.15; 23.5; Hos. 11.1), and the ground of his love lies solely in his own good pleasure, not in the lovableness of those whom he loved: throughout the Bible God's love is ἀγάπη, not ἔρως.[1] After the deliverance at the Red Sea, God, mindful of his covenant with Abraham (Ex. 2.24), makes a covenant with Israel through Moses at Sinai, his purpose (in the view of the prophets of Israel) being still that of the salvation of 'all the earth'. In other words, Israel is elected not to privilege but to service, to further God's purpose for the nations. This is made quite explicit in Ex. 19.4-6, a passage which embodies the prophetic understanding of the nature of God's covenant with Israel and which is crucial for the whole biblical doctrine of the Church: 'Ye have seen what I did unto the Egyptians, and how I bare you on eagles' wings and brought you unto myself. Now, therefore, if ye will obey my voice indeed, and keep my covenant, then ye shall be a peculiar treasure unto me from among all peoples (LXX, ἔσεσθέ μοι λαὸς περιούσιος ἀπὸ πάντων τῶν ἐθνῶν): for all the earth is mine: and ye shall be unto me a kingdom of priests, and a holy nation' (LXX, ὑμεῖς δὲ ἔσεσθέ μοι βασίλειον ἱεράτευμα καὶ ἔθνος ἅγιον). Here we find the classical statement of the prophetic teaching concerning the purpose of God's call of Israel and of his covenant with her. God has elected Israel, not because he has no interest in the rest of the nations, but because he has a concern for 'all the earth'. Israel is therefore appointed to be 'a kingdom of priests', i.e. a kingdom of those set apart to represent God to the world and the needs of the world to God; Israel is to be a dedicated nation, the light of the Gentiles (cf. Isa. 42.6, 'for a covenant of the λαός, for a light of the Gentiles'). As the Levites were set apart as a priesthood within Israel, so Israel as a nation is set apart as a priesthood

---

[1] It is sometimes said that the NT writers had to invent a new word, ἀγάπη, for a new quality of life which came into the world with Christ. It is true that the noun hardly occurs in pre-biblical Gk. lit., but this does not mean much. The important point is that the LXX translators had adopted the colourless verb ἀγαπᾶν to translate the Heb. for 'love' (root 'ahebh), a very frequent OT conception found in many forms. There were obvious objections to the use of ἐρᾶν and even to φιλεῖν, since these words had been spoilt by Greek mythology and pagan 'erotic' religion. The verb ἀγαπᾶν is frequent in OT: God loves Israel (Deut. 10.15; Hos. 11.1, etc.) and it is the Israelite's duty to love God (Deut. 6.4f., the *Shema*'; 11.1, etc.) and his neighbour (Lev. 19.18), including even 'the stranger' (Deut. 10.19). The noun ἀγάπη (or ἀγάπησις, a form not found in the NT) occurs some 30 times in LXX. The difference between the OT and the NT teaching about ἀγάπη is that whereas the former develops an attempt to organize ἀγάπη into codes of law, and so loses spontaneity, the latter regards ἀγάπη as an eschatological reality, a quality of life in the Age to Come, but one which is nevertheless even now 'shed abroad in our hearts through the Holy Spirit' (Rom. 5.5). But in OT and NT alike ἀγάπη differs from ἔρως in that the latter is brought into action by the attractiveness of the object loved, whereas ἀγάπη loves even the unlovable, the repellent and those who have nothing to offer in return. It is thus a word which exactly describes God's attitude of free and utter grace in his dealings with Israel, old and new. The words ἐρᾶν and ἔρως do not occur in NT.

to the world.[1] We are reminded of the vision of Zech. 8.23, which looks forward to the day when this covenant-promise shall be realized: 'Thus saith the LORD of hosts, In those days it shall come to pass, that ten men shall take hold, out of all the languages of the nations, shall even take hold of the skirt of him that is a Jew, saying, We will go with you, for we have heard that God is with you.' The biblical doctrine of 'the priesthood of the laity' (λαός) is written into the covenant of Sinai, to which the people of Israel had bound themselves and which Moses had ratified in sacrificial blood (Ex. 24.3, 8).

It is unnecessary to enlarge upon the lament of the prophets of Israel over the melancholy fact that Israel had broken the covenant of Sinai (cf. Jer. 31.32, 'which my covenant they brake') and had failed to be the light of the Gentiles (cf. Jonah 4.1-11). As Jeremiah perceived, the old covenant was a dead letter by reason of Israel's disobedience; and nothing less than a new covenant, by which God gave the righteousness that he demanded, could avail; he prophesied that God would in fact make such a covenant by which a new people of God would be created: καὶ ἔσομαι αὐτοῖς εἰς Θεόν, καὶ αὐτοὶ ἔσονταί μοι εἰς λαόν (LXX, Jer. 38.33). The NT claims that by the making of this new covenant through the pouring out of the blood of Jesus Christ the new λαὸς Θεοῦ has in fact been created.[2] The long expected Shepherd of 'my people Israel' has come forth from Bethlehem of Judaea (Matt. 2.6; Micah 5.2). 'Blessed be the Lord, the God of Israel, for he has visited and wrought redemption for his λαός' (Luke 1.68; cf. 7.16). Through the preaching of the name of Christ, 'God did visit the Gentiles to take out of them a people for his name' (Acts 15.14; cf. also Acts 18.10; Heb. 4.9; Rev. 18.4). St Paul, reflecting deeply upon the election of the Gentiles to salvation, recalls the prophecy of Hosea, which he now perceives to have been fulfilled: '. . . even us, whom he also called, not from the Jews only, but also from the Gentiles, as he saith also in Hosea, I will call that my people which was not my people, and her beloved which was not beloved. And it shall be, that in the place where it was said unto them, Ye are not my people, there shall they be called the sons of the living God' (Rom. 9.24-26; Hos. 2.23; cf. I Pet. 2.10; Hos. 1.10). In accordance with the prophecy of Hosea God had raised up a new Israel and made with her a new covenant, because the old Israel had failed to keep the promise, solemnly made, to be obedient to all that Yahweh had commanded (Ex. 24.3). Now therefore God had acted through 'our Saviour Jesus Christ, who gave himself for us, that he might redeem us from all iniquity, and purify unto himself a people

[1] See G. A. Danell, *The Root of the Vine* (ed. A. Fridrichsen), 28.
[2] For the idea of 'the covenant of the λαός' (Isa. 42.6; 49.8) see *supra*, 231.

for his own possession' (λαὸς περιούσιος, Titus 2.14; cf. Ex. 19.5, LXX). The most striking affirmation in the NT that the Christian community is now the true λαὸς Θεοῦ is to be found in I Pet. 2.9f., where the author somewhat freely quotes Ex. 19.4-6 and applies what was there said of Israel to the Christian Church: 'Ye are an elect race (γένος ἐκλεκτόν), a royal priesthood (βασίλειον ἱεράτευμα), a holy nation (ἔθνος ἅγιον), a people of possession (λαὸς εἰς περιποίησιν instead of λαὸς περιούσιος in Ex. 19.5), that ye may shew forth the excellencies of him who called you out of darkness into his marvellous light; which in time past were no λαός (cf. Hos. 2.23), but now are λαὸς Θεοῦ.' The passage affirms that the Christian community is commissioned and enabled to perform the task of being the light of the nations, which the old Israel had failed to become. Likewise the Church of Jesus Christ was in fact a royal priesthood (cf. Rev. 1.6; 5.10; 20.6), a consecrated nation, representing God to all the nations of the world and the needs of all the world to God. The missionary implication of God's call to Israel was now being realized through the witness of the Church to the ἀρεταί ('moral excellences' in pagan ethics: here perhaps 'acts of power'; cf. II Pet. 1.3) of the God who had called his new people out of heathen darkness into the light of his wonderful self-revelation.

THE ELECT OF GOD

In the OT the idea of election is met with in two connections, that of Israel and that of Yahweh's Anointed. Election in the Bible is a social conception, since it is comparatively rarely that we meet with the idea of the election of an individual, such as a prophet, for a special task (e.g. Jer. 1.4f.; contrast Isa. 44.2, 24; 49.1; Pss. 22.9f.; 71.6). In the NT St Paul after his conversion came to think of himself as having been separated from his mother's womb and called through God's grace to evangelize the Gentiles (Gal. 1.15f.). The primary biblical doctrine of election, however, is that of the election of Israel and of Israel's Messiah-King. These two conceptions flow into one another, because Israel as a whole is involved in the *persona* of the King or of the Messiah. The OT standpoint is carried over into the NT and determines the meaning of the concept of election in the NT.

As pointed out in the last section, the Torah itself embodies the prophetic conception of Israel's election for the service of God's universal purpose. 'Thou art an holy people unto Yahweh thy God: Yahweh thy God hath chosen thee to be a peculiar people (λαὸς περιούσιος[1])

---

[1] The word 'peculiar' in EVV of this great passage is most unfortunate in view of its changed meaning; 'personal' might be better. The word περιούσιος of LXX means 'of one's own special or personal possession'; it occurs in NT only at Titus 2.14, which is based on OT passages where the phrase occurs, e.g. Ex. 19.5; Deut. 7.6; 14.2, etc.

unto himself out of all peoples. . . . Yahweh did not set his love upon
you nor choose you because ye were more in number than any people,
for ye were the fewest of all peoples: but because Yahweh loveth
(ἀγαπᾶν, LXX) you . . .' (Deut. 7.6-8; cf. Ps. 135.4; Isa. 41.8f. and a
great number of other passages). In the prophetic conception Israel is
not elected for privilege, i.e. to be served by other nations, but in order
to serve them (cf. Mark 10.45); she was redeemed from Egypt and
made λαὸς ἅγιος Κυρίῳ (Deut. 7.6) in order that she might serve God
(7.11) and his purpose for the nations (e.g. Isa. 45.4-6). We may note
that two modern objections to the idea of election at once disappear.
First, the election of Israel does not involve the rejection of any other
nation; Israel is chosen for the sake of the world's salvation. We might
ask (though the Bible does not) how God could have shown his character and purpose otherwise than by taking a weak and uncouth nation
and demonstrating his grace and power through it. A second objection
falls to the ground when it is recognized that election in the OT is to the
service of God in this world and has nothing at all to do with salvation
in the world to come. God's choice of Israel and 'hatred' (i.e. non-
choice) of Edom has nothing whatever to do with the exclusion of the
Edomites from the blessedness of the Age to Come.

This prophetic conception of election had, however, been completely
obscured in the rabbinic Judaism of our Lord's day. Israel, it was held,
was holy and would therefore always enjoy the favour of God (e.g.
Pss. Sol. 9.17f.; 14.3), whereas sinners (i.e. Gentiles) were to be
destroyed from before his face (12.7f.). So far were the rabbis from
holding that Israel existed for the service of the nations that they now
taught that the world was created for the sake of Israel (II (4) Esd. 6.55;
7.11; 9.13), and the question of the salvation of the Gentiles did not
arise: 'O Lord, . . . for our sakes thou madest this world. As for the
other nations, which also come of Adam, thou hast said that they are
nothing, and are like unto spittle . . . And now, O Lord, behold, these
nations, which are reputed as nothing, be lords over us and devour us.
If the world be made for our sakes, why do we not possess for an
inheritance our world? how long shall this endure?' (II (4) Esd. 6.55-59).
The Jews of our Lord's day believed that their covenant with God
implied that they and they alone were the centre and object of all
God's activity in creation and redemption and that they had no responsibility for the 'sinners of the Gentiles'.

Against this religion of pride and merit, the teaching of Jesus and his
disciples, notably St Paul, represents a vigorous 'protestant' reformation, a reformation based upon a return to the *sola gratia* of Israel's
prophets and to their parallel doctrine of election for service. Indeed,

the NT as a whole affirms the continued operation of the principle of election as embodied in the biblical history since the days of Jacob, Abraham, Noah and Seth; for now the most astounding instance of that principle's working has recently occurred. God has rejected the elect, Israel herself, and chosen a new covenant-people out of all the nations of the earth. St Paul in Rom. 9-11 seeks to explain this astonishing paradox: God has not reversed the principle which has all along operated in biblical history; indeed, he has given a signal demonstration of it in the coming of Christ and his Church. In times past God has chosen between the different descendants of Abraham. He chose the Israelites and rejected the Edomites, Ishmaelites, etc.; so now he rejects Israel κατὰ σάρκα and chooses those other spiritual descendants of Abraham, who is the father of *many* nations (Gen. 17.5; Rom. 4.17f.; 9.6-13), for these other descendants 'walk in the steps of that faith of our father Abraham which he had in uncircumcision' (Rom. 4.12). This operation of the principle of election (or, to use Paul's own phrase, ἡ κατ' ἐκλογὴν πρόθεσις, 'the purpose of God according to election', Rom. 9.11) is the very heart of the mystery that has been hidden from the foundation of the world but has now been revealed (Rom. 16.26; Eph. 3.1-12), viz. that the Gentiles are now being included in God's saving purpose, while the rejection of Israel is only for a season (Rom. 11.25-32). It is God who 'hardens' the heart, whether of Pharaoh, or of Israel, or of Gentile nations (Rom. 9.14-18), but he 'shuts up all unto disobedience' only in order that he might have mercy upon all (Rom. 11.32).

The clue to Rom. 9-11 and to what is sometimes (not very happily) called St Paul's philosophy of history is to be found in the phrase ἡ κατ' ἐκλογὴν πρόθεσις τοῦ Θεοῦ (Rom. 9.11). It means 'God's purpose in history which operates by means of the principle of selection'.[1] In the later Paulines and in the Pastorals the word πρόθεσις has become a technical term for the purpose that had existed in the mind of God since before the creation of the world, though the word is used occasionally in a non-technical sense in other parts of the NT (e.g. Acts 11.23; 27.13; the phrase ἄρτοι τῆς προθέσεως is a technical term for the 'shewbread', Mark 2.26 and pars.; Heb. 9.2). The idea of divine purpose in this sense is expressed by βουλή in the Lucan writings (Luke 7.30; Acts 2.23; 4.28; 13.36; 20.27; cf. also Eph. 1.11; Heb. 6.17); the word means the foreordained counsel and purpose of God through the ages. So far

---

[1] The word ἐκλογή appears late in Jewish lit., its earliest use being in the Psalms of Solomon (e.g. 18.6). In NT it is found at Acts 9.15; Rom. 9.11; 11.5, 7, 28; I Thess. 1.4; II Pet. 1.10. It means 'election' in the sense of the 'principle of selection' and is thus a new word for a well-known OT idea. It can also be used as an abstract noun standing for a concrete one, ἐκλεκτοί, 'the chosen', as at Rom. 11.7.

as is known, no one before St Paul had used πρόθεσις in this deep sense. The Christians are 'called according to God's πρόθεσις' (Rom. 8.28), which was the operative principle of selection in the history of salvation (Rom. 9.11), and so they are now 'in Christ', in whom they have been made a κλῆρος or inheritance for God, 'having been foreordained according to the purpose (προορισθέντες κατὰ πρόθεσιν) of him who worketh all things after the βουλή of his will (θέλημα)' (Eph. 1.11; cf. the verb προτίθεμαι, uniquely in this sense in Eph. 1.9: κατὰ τὴν εὐδοκίαν αὐτοῦ, ἣν προέθετο ἐν αὐτῷ; cf. Rom. 3.25). In Eph. 3.11 we read of God's 'purpose of the ages' (πρόθεσις τῶν αἰώνων) in Christ Jesus. In II Tim. 1.9 we read that God 'saved us and called us with a holy calling, not according to our works, but according to his own πρόθεσις and grace, which was given us in Christ Jesus before times everlasting' (πρὸ χρόνων αἰωνίων).

The conception of God's calling (κλῆσις) and of Christians as 'called' is largely Pauline, but not quite exclusively so (see Matt. 22.14; Heb. 3.1; Jude 1; II Pet. 1.10; Rev. 17.14). The idea is based, of course, on God's call to Israel (cf. Hos. 11.1; Ps. 95.7; Heb. 3.15f.): Christians are called into a covenant-relation with God, as Israel of old had been called. The word κλῆσις in the NT always means our 'calling' in this sense—never 'vocation' in the Reformation sense of one's calling in the world, even at I Cor. 7.20.[1] In this sense all Christians are κλητοί ('called'), a word which is thus in the NT virtually synonomous with ἐκλεκτοί or ἅγιοι (Rom. 1.6f.; I Cor. 1.2; Rev. 17.14; cf. II Pet. 1.10). St Paul seems to think of himself as having been specially or personally called to the status or office of an apostle (Rom. 1.1; I Cor. 1.1); perhaps a tendency developed to think of all the apostles as having been 'chosen before by God' (Acts 10.41; cf. the choice of Matthias by lot, Acts 1.24: 'Shew of these two the one whom thou hast chosen'). But broadly speaking there is no emphasis at all in the NT upon the individual's call, and certainly no suggestion that he ought to hear voices or undergo emotional experiences. The fact is that κλῆσις is a social conception: it is significant that except in the special case of Paul in Rom. 1.1 and I Cor. 1.1 the word κλητός is never found in the singular. Christians are corporately 'the called' and corporately 'the elect', and they are these things, as we shall see, because they are one body in Christ, the Elect One.

A proper understanding of the NT doctrine of election in Christ will dispel the sombre and frightening mists of post-Reformation theories about predestination, double predestination, reprobation and the rest of the lingering errors of medievalism, from which the rise of

[1] See Alan Richardson, *The Biblical Doctrine of Work*, 36.

biblical science has happily set us free. We must note that in Rom. 9-11 St Paul is still speaking about groups and nations, not about individuals. God is still Lord of the nations, and it is still entirely of God's will and grace that this nation or that is elected as the servant of his universal purpose: it is solely to achieve this purpose that 'he has mercy on whom he will and whom he will he hardeneth' (Rom. 9.15-18). Election refers to God's purpose in this world. It is true that the elected ones, if they do not fall away, will be saved in the world to come, but that is not the primary meaning of election. In the NT, as in the OT, election is a matter of service, not of privilege. Nothing is said or implied by the phrase ἡ κατ᾽ ἐκλογὴν πρόθεσις (Rom. 9.11) about election to life in the Age to Come, and Calvin's gloss *dum alios ad salutem praedestinat, alios ad aeternam damnationem* is nowhere implied in the text.[1] Furthermore, nothing is implied about the rejection of any individuals whatsoever. Even if corporately or as a nation 'the Jews' are rejected by the principle of ἐκλογή, this does not imply that individual Jews are not being numbered by thousands amongst the κλητοί, ἅγιοι, ἐκλεκτοί or σωζόμενοι (I Cor. 1.24, τοῖς κλητοῖς, Ἰουδαίοις τε καὶ Ἕλλησι). The NT does not teach that any human beings whatsoever have been created for reprobation, or that they are now irredeemably predestined to damnation. Indeed, it was against precisely such a view—the rabbinic notion of the rejection of the 'other nations'—that the Christian movement was a protest.

In the NT it is Jesus Christ who is the predestined one, the Elect of God (cf. the Lucan form of the utterance at the Transfiguration, οὗτός ἐστιν ὁ υἱός μου ὁ ἐκλελεγμένος, Luke 9.35; and cf. 23.35; I Pet. 2.4, παρὰ δὲ Θεῷ ἐκλεκτόν; 2.6, citing Isa. 28.16; and John 1.34, WH text, οὗτός ἐστιν ὁ ἐκλεκτὸς τοῦ Θεοῦ, which is, if not original, at least of great antiquity: cf. Isa. 42.1, Ἰσραὴλ ὁ ἐκλεκτός μου). The early Church believed that everything that had occurred in the story of the life, death and resurrection of Christ had happened according to 'the determinate counsel and foreknowledge of God' (Acts 2.23; cf. Luke 22.22; Acts 3.18; 13.27). Herod and Pilate, Gentiles and Jews, had done precisely that which God's counsel (βουλή) had foreordained to come to pass (Acts 4.27f.). The Fourth Evangelist, indeed, goes so far as to make Jesus himself fully cognizant of this whole pre-determined βουλὴ Θεοῦ and thus able to foresee the course of the Passion in advance (John 12.32f.; 13.19, 27f.; 18.32); but this tendency is already well developed in the Synoptists. This insistence upon the pre-established plan of events is a characteristically biblical and Hebraic way of stressing

---

[1] So Sanday and Headlam, *Romans* (ICC), 245, on Rom. 9.11, where an illuminating note will be found.

the divine initiative in the whole Christ-event; though at first sight it might seem that the disaster which overwhelmed Christ was unforeseen by God and entirely beyond his control, the glorious, saving truth of the Gospel was that God himself had actually planned what had happened: God sent his Son to die for man's salvation. Hence Christ is ὁ ὡρισμένος ὑπὸ τοῦ Θεοῦ (Acts 10.42; 17.31; Rom. 1.4), and all who have to do with him in his Passion are drawn, as it were, into the fatal, pre-determined course of salvation-history—Herod, Pilate, Judas, Gentiles, Jews. But this does not mean that Herod and Pilate and Judas were mere puppets in the hand of God, with no personal choice or responsibility in the drama; the NT does not teach that anyone is pre-determined to commit a crime, chosen to be a murderer or a traitor. It means that, since human nature is what it is, it was inevitable that the Son of God, having taken flesh, should suffer at the hands of wicked men, and therefore that, if God willed the incarnation of his Son, he must also have willed his death: this is what the ὡρισμένη βουλὴ καὶ πρόγνωσις τοῦ Θεοῦ (Acts 2.23) means in relation to the Passion story. It is a characteristically Hebraic way of stating this truth to assert that God foreordained all the details of the drama in advance, like a playwright working out the fate of his *dramatis personae*.

The NT writers never raise questions about the compatibility of divine foreknowledge with human free will. Such problems are therefore not within the scope of our discussion, but we may perhaps assert the necessity of maintaining the reality both of divine foreknowledge and of human freedom. Jesus must have known well enough, as the Gospels assert that he did, that Judas was going to betray him: does this mean that Judas was predestined to the betrayal and had no choice in the matter? Of course not; the fact that my friend, who knows me well, can predict what I am likely to do in a given situation does not in the least mean that I am not free or am not fully responsible for my action. It was inevitable, in the circumstances of Christ's incarnate life, that he should have been rejected, betrayed, set at nought and put to death: it was not inevitable that any particular individual—Caiaphas, Judas, Herod, Pilate—should have been the instrument of the inevitable. Each participant in the action did what he did consciously and deliberately, knowing that he could have done otherwise. 'Pilate answered and said, What I have written I have written' (John 19.22). 'All the people answered and said, His blood be on us and on our children' (Matt. 27.25). 'Then Judas . . . repented . . . saying, I have sinned in that I have betrayed innocent blood' (Matt. 27.3f.). The mystery of determinism and freedom in human life is indeed beyond our comprehension, but we must acknowledge it as a fact. Statisticians can compute with astonishing accuracy how many people will commit suicide in London or New York next year: it would seem to be mysteriously predetermined that these unhappy events shall happen. But no one can predict *which* individuals will kill themselves; the categories of predestination, foreknowledge, and so on, are valid, as we have suggested, for the behaviour of groups, but do not apply to this or that individual person. Caiaphas, Judas, Herod and Pilate were in their actions free and uncoerced; and yet, such is the mystery of our corporate involvement in human relationships in their totality, each became a representative man, acting on behalf of fallen humanity at large. I cannot boast my moral superiority to them, because I know that 'in Adam' they were *my* representatives, they were myself rejecting, betraying and condemning the Christ. And yet, in the overruling providence of God's almighty love, their very rejection, betrayal and condemnation of Christ became the means of the salvation of 'Adam', who was recreated in God's image in the person of the crucified Son of God. Caiaphas had declared it expedient that one man should die for the people, that the whole nation perish not (John 11.49f.). He did not know what he was saying, but those words in the mouth of the Jewish high priest bore an unintended prophetic truth: 'he prophesied,' says St John, 'that Jesus should die for the nation, and not for the nation only, but that he might also gather together into one the children of God that are scattered abroad.' From that day forth they took counsel that they might put Jesus to death (John 11.51-53). The ὡρισμένη βουλὴ καὶ πρόγνωσις τοῦ Θεοῦ means this also, that man's sinfulness cannot frustrate God's plan of salvation, because even in exercising his freedom to choose evil man is still effecting the foredetermined purpose of God. In this sense even the crimes of Pilate and the rest were committed for the accomplishing of whatever God's hand and βουλή had foreordained should come to pass (Acts 4.28).

Because Christ is the Elect of God, we who are 'in Christ' are therefore ἐκλεκτοί. It is probable that this conception of the Messiah as Elect and of Christians as elect in him owes its origin to Jewish apocalyptic thought. From ancient times the king was regarded as having been 'chosen' by God; indeed, the *anointing* of the king expresses God's choice (cf. I Sam. 16.1-13; I Kings 8.16; Ps. 89. 3, 19f., etc.). The Servant of Yahweh in Deutero-Isaiah is anointed with God's Spirit and is therefore 'the elect one' (Isa. 42.1, etc.). In apocalyptic circles the heavenly eschatological deliverer, the Anointed, was styled 'the Elect One' or 'My Elect One' (Enoch 39.6; 40.5; 45.3f.; 49.2, 4; 51.3, 5; 52.6, 9; 55.4; 61.4f., 8, 10). Here, as in the OT generally, the elect one

is the one whom Yahweh favours and cherishes and whom he uses as
the instrument of his purpose. He is the leader of all the rest of the
elect, a great company in heaven, consisting of the patriarchs of old
and of all faithful and righteous Jews of former generations, the righteous and holy ones, existing already in the presence of the Lord of
Spirits (i.e. God). The Messiah in the Similitudes of Enoch is the king
of this community of the elect. Indeed, in a sense the Messiah, the
Elect One, represented in his own person the whole company of heaven,
though the extent to which he may be said to be identified with them as
their own corporate personality is a question upon which differences of
opinion are possible.[1] In such apocalyptic views the elect are regarded
as divine, or at least superhuman beings; they are the 'holy ones'
(Enoch 38.4; 39.4, etc.), a name which means divine or angelic beings
in the OT (Deut. 33.2f.; Ps. 89.6; Job 5.1; 15.15; Zech. 14.5; Dan. 8.13).
It is from such patterns of apocalyptic thought that the NT sayings
about the Messiah and his holy ones are drawn (Matt. 24.30f.; 25.31;
Mark 8.38; John 1.51; I Thess. 3.13, where ἁγίων means 'holy ones' in
the OT sense; 4.16; Jude 14). Three times in the Marcan Apocalypse
Jesus refers to 'the elect': the days of the tribulations (Messianic woes)
are to be shortened for the sake of 'the elect, whom he chose' (Mark
13.20): false Christs and prophets may deceive, if possible, the elect
(13.22): the Son of Man shall 'send forth the angels and shall gather
together his elect from the four winds, from the uttermost part of the
earth to the uttermost part of heaven' (13.27). Jesus thinks of his
apostles as sent out into all the world preaching the gospel of the
Kingdom of God, issuing the invitation to the Messianic Supper, calling 'many' (i.e. all), preaching the gospel to 'all the nations' (13.10).
The number of the 'called' is great; in ideal, at least, it is all mankind;
but the response is only partial. He himself summed up the situation
in the words πολλοὶ γάρ εἰσιν κλητοί, ὀλίγοι δὲ ἐκλεκτοί (Matt. 24.22).
But God would vindicate his oppressed elect (Luke 18.7), and it was
the purpose of God that the elect should be gathered to the Christ at
the harvest which the angel-reapers were about to begin (Mark 13.27).
This is a metaphorical way of speaking of the missionary labours of the
apostolic Church as it set out to preach the Gospel to all the nations.[2]

ELECTION AND GRACE

The NT conception of 'the elect' is thus thoroughly eschatological.

[1] See N. A. Dahl, *Das Volk Gottes*: *eine Untersuchung zum Kirchenbewusstsein
des Urchristentums*, Oslo, 1941; S. Mowinckel, *He that Cometh*, esp. 381, n. 2, where
he criticizes Dahl's view. On the whole subject see Mowinckel, *op. cit.*, 36-8, 63-7,
365f., 379-83.

[2] See *supra*, 26-9.

The Anointed One is 'the Elect': cf. Luke 23.35, ὁ Χριστὸς τοῦ Θεοῦ ὁ ἐκλεκτός. Christ, as the Elect, is even now in the latter days gathering together his elect into his body the Church. If Christians are 'the elect', it is because they are 'in Christ', because they are baptized into the person of him who alone may with complete propriety be called the Elect of God. In him their salvation is assured, and nothing can be laid to the charge of God's elect (Rom. 8.33). The divine purpose from the foundation of the world was to re-create a new humanity in Christ. Thus, in Rom. 8.28-30 St Paul says that the whole Church corporately was in this sense 'foreknown' of God, who ordained beforehand that it should be conformed to the image of his Son: God's 'foreordaining' came first, that is, his determination of the plan to create a new humanity who responded and were justified in Christ: those who are justified in Christ shall be 'glorified' in him at the parousia. If we read this passage as if it related to atomic individuals, we shall create difficulties which are wholly of our imagining; we will then have to ask why it was that God picked out some individuals, and not others, and 'predestined' them to salvation since the foundation of the world. Paul, of course, does not think of the Church as made up of a collection of individuals, but as a body: it is *the body* which is foreknown, foreordained, called, justified and is to be glorified. There is no suggestion here or elsewhere in the NT that some individuals are predestined to a mechanical salvation irrespectively of their own decision for Christ. It is stressed that, though God calls us, we must respond. There are no elect automatons in the Kingdom of God. God works in us, but we have our 'work' to do (Phil. 2.12f.). The mystery and paradox of grace is that grace does not do away with our free will or our responsibility for our own decisions; our will is never more truly free and never more completely *our* will than when it is wholly surrendered to God (I Cor. 15.10).[1]

The fact of election shews, on the one hand, the absolute sovereignty of God in the unconditional exercise of his freedom. Man has no 'rights' as over against the Creator, any more than an earthenware vessel has the right to dictate to the potter the use to which it shall be put (Rom. 9.20f., alluding to a frequent scriptural analogy: Isa. 29.16; 45.9; 64.8; Jer. 18.6; Wisd. 15.7; Ecclus. 33.13). The potter makes his vessels for his own purposes, one for this use, another for that: so God chooses Moses as an instrument of his mercy or raises up Pharaoh as an instrument by means of which his name might be made known in all the earth (Rom. 9.15-18). God uses Moses, but he also uses Pharaoh, for the accomplishment of his purposes; the biblical way of putting this

[1] See D. M. Baillie, *God Was in Christ*, 114-18.

is to say that God himself 'hardens' Pharaoh's heart (Rom. 9.18; cf. Ex. 4.21; 7.3; 9.12, etc.). In the same way God has 'raised up' the Chaldaeans (Hab. 1.6) and other nations or their rulers (e.g. Zech. 11.16; Jer. 27.41: the word ἐξεγείρειν is virtually a technical expression: cf. Rom. 9.17; Ex. 9.16). God rules all history, so that even the deeds of the Assyrians ('the rod of mine anger', Isa. 10.5) or the Chaldaeans are themselves instrumental to his purpose. St Paul rejects the view that this means, since righteous Israel and wicked Assyria are both doing the will of God, that they are both on the same footing with God in respect of righteousness, and that God should therefore not find fault with either (Rom. 9.19-24). It means only that God's sovereign will is done, though unintentionally, even by wicked nations. God endures 'vessels of wrath' (such as imperialistic Assyria or Pharaoh) because they are, in spite of themselves, instruments by which his larger purpose of mercy will be achieved (Rom. 9.22-24). Again we may note that in this passage (Rom. 9.14-24) 'election' is set forth in terms of nations or their representative rulers (like Pharaoh) considered as the agents of God's purpose in history; the passage is not saying anything at all about ultimate salvation in the world to come, and the phrase 'vessels of wrath' does not refer to individuals predestined from the creation of the world to everlasting damnation; it means nations (or their rulers in their representative capacity) who are 'raised' up to execute God's righteous ὀργή in this present age. St Paul, of course, certainly holds that individual Christians who were once numbered among the ἐκλεκτοί can fall from this state of grace. He knows that only by ἄσκησις (cf. ἀσκέω, Acts 24.16), by spiritual discipline, can he himself keep his place in the race so that in the end he is not ἀδόκιμος, 'reprobate' (I Cor. 9.23-27; cf. II Cor. 13.5-8; cf. Heb. 6.4-8; I John 5.16).[1] There are indeed reprobates (II Tim. 3.8; Titus 1.16; cf. Jer. 6.30), but there are none who have been 'elected' for reprobation.

The fact of election shews also, on the other hand, the utter sovereignty of God's grace. Election may be defined as the action of God's grace in history; cf. Rom. 11.5, κατ' ἐκλογὴν χάριτος. All election is the result of the operation of God's grace, by which we are saved (Acts 15.11; Eph. 2.5, 8; II Tim. 1.9; Titus 2.11; 3.7; cf. Rom. 3.24). Election is not the result of the divine ὀργή (cf. I Thess. 5.9), but only of the divine χάρις, which works in history to accomplish God's ultimate purpose of salvation: God 'saved us, and called us with a holy calling, not according to our works, but according to his own purpose and

---

[1] The word ἀδόκιμος means 'rejected after testing'; cf. δοκιμάζω, to test (e.g. I Cor. 3.13), to approve after testing (Rom. 1.28; 2.18; 14.22). The word reminds us that Christians, though justified, still await the last judgment; see *infra*, 341-4.

grace' (κατ' ἰδίαν πρόθεσιν καὶ χάριν) (II Tim. 1.9). Paul points to an actual, visible effect of the operation of the divine grace, working according to the principle of selection, in the existence of Jewish Christians in the Church now (ἐν τῷ νῦν καιρῷ): they constitute a λεῖμμα[1] or 'remnant', a token and pledge that Israel has not been finally rejected, but is still within the scope of God's ultimate saving purpose (Rom. 11.1-6). They correspond to the 7,000 in Israel who in Elijah's day had not bowed the knee to Baal (I Kings 19.18), and they were thus the pledge of Israel's future recovery and restoration to God's favour. Thus, in one of its principal NT meanings, χάρις is simply the power or activity of God at work in history for the salvation of mankind; this saving grace in history operates by the method of the selection of instruments (or, to use the Pauline word, 'vessels') by means of which—whether by obedience ('vessels of mercy') or by disobedience ('vessels of wrath')—God's universal design is accomplished. The special significance of the word χάρις, as thus used almost synonymously with 'the purpose of God according to election' (Rom. 9.11), is that it implies that God's choice of instruments has nothing to do with their merits, their ἔργα (II Tim. 1.9; Rom. 11.5f.; cf. Rom. 4.4), but rests solely in his unconditioned freedom. God's salvation itself is unearned, a free gift; so also is the privilege of serving God's purpose as an elected vessel of his design. As St Augustine insists, *Gratia nisi gratis sit gratia non est.*

THE GRACE OF GOD

The word 'grace' (χάρις) in the Bible, though it can be used of human relationships (Esth. 2.17, LXX; Acts 2.47; 7.10), is used almost entirely of God (or in NT of Christ). It thus bears a quite different meaning from that which it usually carries in classical Greek, viz. the essentially human qualities of charm, sweetness and attractiveness (none the less human even when attributed to the gods; cf. the three Graces, αἱ Χάριτες, of mythology, who confer all grace, even the favour of victory in the games). The OT speaks of God as gracious towards helpless humanity and often at the same time declares that he is merciful (e.g. Ex. 33.19; 34.6; II Chron. 30.9; Neh. 9.17; Pss. 77.9; 86.15; 103.8; Joel 2.13; Jonah 4.2: God is a gracious God, full of compassion, slow to anger, plenteous in mercy, and he will abundantly pardon). There is a verbal difference between the usage of the LXX and that of the NT, because while LXX generally uses τὸ ἔλεος (mercy) as the translation of ḥesedh, the NT uses χάρις much more frequently to

---

[1] Only at Rom. 11.5 in NT; not used in OT in the technical sense of 'remnant' (τὸ καταλειφθέν, not in NT, but cf. Rom. 11.4, κατέλιπον ἐμαυτῷ ἑπτακισχιλίους ἄνδρας . . .).

express the same idea. Thus, *ḥesedh* or ἔλεος (loving-kindness, mercy) bears the meaning of 'grace' or 'unmerited favour'; it also represents the idea of God's loyalty to the covenant, and may indeed be translated as 'covenant-love'. In the LXX χάρις is used especially of men's finding favour in God's sight (e.g. Gen. 6.8; 18.3, etc.). There is a tendency in the later prophets to regard the realities represented by *ḥesedh* as eschatological gifts which will be plentifully outpoured in the last days; cf. Zech. 12.10, 'I will pour out upon the house of David and upon the inhabitants of Jerusalem the spirit of grace and mercy' (πνεῦμα χάριτος καὶ οἰκτιρμοῦ, LXX). In the NT ἔλεος is not frequent; of its 27 occurrences nine are found in OT allusions and seven in salutations; its place is taken by χάρις. The words χάρις and ἔλεος are associated in I Tim. 1.2; II Tim. 1.2 and II John 3. In the LXX ἔλεος especially represents God's pitying regard for man as weak and helpless, while in the NT χάρις means primarily God's forgiving love towards man as sinful and gone astray.

In the NT Christians are frequently bidden to emulate the divine mercy and compassion; Jesus said, 'Blessed are the merciful' (Matt. 5.7), and 'Be ye merciful, even as your Father is merciful' (Luke 6.36); and twelve times in the Synoptics he is himself said to have been moved to mercy, or 'moved with compassion'.[1] Works of charity (ἐλεημοσύνη), almsgiving and the like, forgiveness of injuries, mutual aid, and so on, are the proper response of the Christian to the grace and mercy which he himself has received but not earned (cf. Eph. 4.32; Col. 3.12f.; James 3.17; I Pet. 3.8, etc.). The gratitude elicited by a gracious act can itself be called χάρις (Luke 6.32-34, ποία ὑμῖν χάρις ἐστίν; Matt. 5.46 has μισθόν: cf. I Cor. 10.30), and the word χάρις can be used quite simply for an act done by a Christian that is pleasing to God, as in I Pet. 2.19f., where it is said that to suffer wrongfully for conscience' sake is χάρις. This does not mean that we can earn χάρις or favour with God, but that our works are pleasing to God because they are motivated by our thankfulness for what God has done for us. In this sense either χάρις or εὐχαριστία (gratitude, thanksgiving) may be used as meaning the motive of Christian service in gratitude for God's gift to us (cf. Heb. 12.28, 'Let us have χάρις whereby we may offer service well-pleasing to God'; II Cor. 4.15: the χάρις of God causes εὐχαριστία to abound to the glory of God; II Cor. 9.11f.). Thanksgiving to God for his inexpressible gift in Christ (II Cor. 9.15) is the mainspring of Christian conduct and the key-category of Christian ethics. The whole Christian life is response to the gift of God (Rom. 5.15-17; Eph. 2.8; 3.7; 4.7; I Pet. 4.10); it is response to the grace of our Lord Jesus Christ, by

---

[1] Cf. Alan Richardson, *Miracle Stories of the Gospels*, 29-34.

which he became poor, though he was rich (II Cor. 8.1-9). Christians give themselves in thanksgiving to God (II Cor. 8.5); they live in a state of grace, empowered by the grace of thanksgiving to perform their good works (cf. Acts 6.8; 13.43; Rom. 5.2; Col. 3.16f.; II Tim. 2.1; Heb. 13.9, etc.). The Spirit, who is the Spirit of grace (Heb. 10.29), gives to each Christian his peculiar grace-gift (χάρισμα, a word found only in the Paulines and Pastorals, but cf. I Pet. 4.10) and so enables him to perform his allotted ministry within the Church (Rom. 12.6; I Cor. 12.4-11; Gal. 2.9; Eph. 4.7). It is sometimes said[1] that the later technical use (esp. of the Latin *gratia*) for the divine prompting and help which precedes and accompanies right action does not correspond exactly to the usage of the NT; but we are surely very near to such a conception in such passages—not all Pauline—as, e.g., Acts 11.23; 14.26; 20.32; Rom. 12.3; I Cor. 15.10; II Cor. 1.12; 6.1; 9.14; 12.9; I Tim. 1.14; Heb. 4.16; I Pet. 5.5, 10; II Pet. 3.18; Jude 4.

There is sufficient evidence to shew that 'grace' was a word and conception in general use beyond the Pauline churches, but it is, of course, St Paul who most thoroughly develops the theme of grace. He is doubtless led to do this by the necessity of preserving the Gospel, which is for him 'the gospel of the grace of God' (Acts 20.24; Gal. 1.6), from being perverted by the Judaism of the rabbis. Hence for St Paul the primary contrasts develop: on the one hand, grace and works, on the other hand, grace and law. He sees very clearly that the idea of *gift*, absolutely free and unearned, is essential to the innermost meaning of χάρις (Eph. 2.8f.), and that the merest hint of a salvation by works destroys that gospel of grace of which God had made him the appointed preacher to the Gentiles: his own case proves that God's election and grace are utterly undeserved (I Tim. 1.12-16, surely a Pauline 'fragment'). There can be no righteousness of one's own (Rom. 10.3; Phil. 3.9); it must be a free gift from God (Rom. 5.17f., etc.). Thus, for St Paul, grace and faith may be said to represent complementary processes in the whole act of salvation: grace is the objective, saving activity of God in Jesus Christ through the Holy Spirit, while faith is the subjective aspect of the process in us; it is, however, not something that we do, but is itself a χάρισμα πνεύματος (I Cor. 12.9). Christians are no longer under law but under grace, and therefore sin has no more dominion over them (Rom. 6.14-23; Gal. 2.21, etc.). It is probable that Pauline influence lies behind John 1.14-17, where the incarnate Word is said to be 'full of grace and truth' and is contrasted with the Torah: 'The law was given by Moses; grace and truth came by Jesus Christ' (1.17). Jesus Christ is the fulness (πλήρωμα—perhaps

[1] E.g. by Sanday and Headlam, *Romans* (ICC), 11.

'fulfilment of the law'; cf. Rom. 13.10, πλήρωμα νόμου ἡ ἀγάπη) of grace (1.16); 'of his fulness we all received, and grace for grace'. The meaning of this phrase, χάριν ἀντὶ χάριτος, is (according to C. K. Barrett[1]) that Christian life is based at all points upon grace; as it proceeds, one grace is exchanged for another. These verses contain the only uses of χάρις in the Johannine literature, apart from the salutations in II John 3, Rev. 1.4 and 22.21, and apart from a doubtful reading in III John 4, where χαράν (joy) should probably be read (with RV) for χάριν.[2]

THE CHURCH OF GOD

'Church' (ἐκκλησία) is one of those words (cf. 'atonement', 'forgiveness', 'dispensation', 'providence') which have come to carry an inclusive meaning which in the NT they do not possess.[3] In the NT it is only one of a considerable number of expressions which are used to signify the new people of God; and there are several NT books in which it does not appear at all (viz. Mark, Luke, John, II Tim., Titus, I and II Pet., I and II John). In Ep. Heb. it occurs only twice; in 2.12, quoting Ps. 22.22, and in 12.23, where the reference is to 'the heavenly Jerusalem': 'the πανήγυρις ('festival assembly') and ἐκκλησία of the firstborn', i.e. the company of those who are even now enjoying the blessings promised to the faithful. This is the only NT passage in which the word ἐκκλησία apparently refers to the church in heaven.

In secular Greek ἐκκλησία had no religious associations whatever and was therefore suitable for use by the LXX translators to render the technical term *qahal Yahweh*, 'the congregation of the LORD'. They well knew that the congregation of God's people was unique and that it could not be represented by any word which was used for a Greek religious society or pagan cultus. So they used ἐκκλησία, which was a political term, meaning the δῆμος (electorate) of a Greek city state. Indeed, we find ἐκκλησία used in this secular Greek sense in Acts 19.32,

---

[1] *GSJ*, 140.

[2] Many of the NT epistles begin with the salutation χάρις ὑμῖν καὶ εἰρήνη ἀπὸ Θεοῦ πατρός and end with the benediction ἡ χάρις [τοῦ Κυρίου Ἰησοῦ Χριστοῦ] μεθ' ὑμῶν. 'Peace' is the old Hebrew greeting *shalom*. 'Grace' ('may you enjoy God's favour or help') takes the place of the usual Greek salutation χαῖρε, χαίρετε (from χαίρειν, to rejoice; cf. Mark 15.18; Luke 1.28; Acts 15.23; II John 10). St Paul christianizes the Gk. salutation in Phil. 3.1 and 4.4 by adding ἐν Κυρίῳ. Joy (ἡ χαρά) is next to ἀγάπη on St Paul's list of the fruit of the Spirit (Gal. 5.22) as one of the eschatological-Christian virtues (cf. I Pet. 1.8; Heb. 10.34; 12.2; I Thess. 1.6; Acts 13.52; Col. 1.11; Phil. 3.1; 4.4; etc.).

[3] The English word 'church' (cf. *Kirche, kerk, kirk*) is probably derived from κυριακός, 'pertaining to the Κύριος', and may originally have meant 'the Lord's house' in the sense of the building. It is used in EVV to translate those Heb. words ('*edhah*, *qahal*) which LXX renders by ἐκκλησία. It is not easy to explain why ἐκκλησία was not translated into Latin (e.g. *convocatio*) but merely transliterated, *ecclesia* (cf. French *église*, etc.). The Gk. ἐκκλησία cannot mean a building.

39f. K. L. Schmidt says that the derivation of ἐκκλησία is significant, since the assembled citizens (the δῆμος) are the ἔκκλητοι (called out), those who have been summoned by the κῆρυξ (herald): 'this naturally suggests that in the Bible the reference is to God in Christ calling men out of the world.'[1] The Heb. *qahal* also has the same ultimate derivation of 'call out' (cf. Heb. *qol*, voice), but in itself (like ἐκκλησία) it has no religious connotation and simply means a 'gathering'. It receives its religious significance from its use in the sense of the *qahal Yahweh*, the congregation of the Lord, i.e. Israel as assembled before God. The LXX uses ἐκκλησία to translate *qahal* some hundred times; RV consistently uses 'assembly'. The LXX also uses συναγωγή to translate *qahal* in many places—often in the Pentateuch (except Deuteronomy). The word συναγωγή is not in itself a word of religious significance and can be used of any kind of gathering; e.g. Ps. 22.16 (LXX, 21.17), 'assembly of evil-doers'; Ps. 68.30 (LXX, 67.31), 'multitude of the bulls'.[2] The other OT word for the nation of Israel in its religious aspect, beside *qahal*, is *'edhah*, which comes from a root meaning 'to appoint', and thus means the properly constituted congregation of the Lord. In the LXX it is translated by συναγωγή, and in the RV it is consistently rendered by 'congregation'. In general use *qahal* and *'edhah*, like ἐκκλησία and συναγωγή, are synonyms. AV uses 'assembly' and 'congregation' for *qahal* and *'edhah* entirely at random.

K. L. Schmidt is doubtless right in suggesting that it was Greek-speaking Jewish Christians who, even before St Paul's time, first began to use ἐκκλησία. They chose it because they wished to distinguish their communities from the Jewish συναγωγαί in every city; the latter were not called ἐκκλησίαι in everyday speech; yet it was a word which the Christians found in their (Greek) Bibles and it supplied exactly what

---

[1] *TWNT*, ET, *The Church*, 1950, 28f. In point of fact the words ἐκκαλεῖν and ἔκκλητος (as distinct from ἐκλεκτός, chosen out, elect) do not occur in NT, but the parallel could hardly have escaped notice. K. L. Schmidt, however, advises caution in the matter (*ibid.*, 57). Yet he remarks that the LXX translators were probably influenced in selecting ἐκκλησία to translate *qahal* by the similarity of sound between the two words, since the Jewish ear is fond of assonance (*ibid.*, 31), as well as by the similarity of meaning between ἐκκλησία and *qahal*.

[2] The use of συναγωγή as a *place* of meeting is peculiar to the NT, and is frequent in the Synoptists and Acts (cf. also John 6.59; 18.20; cf. Rev. 2.9; 3.9 'synagogue of Satan'). James 2.2 is the only NT use of συναγωγή as a Christian place of meeting (but cf. Heb. 10.25); it was, however, the worship and constitution of the synagogue rather than those of the Temple, which became the model for the Christian congregations. The institution of the synagogue probably originated in Babylon in the period of the Exile, but by NT times it was believed that it dated from Moses' own day (cf. Acts 15.21; Josephus, *c. Apion.* 2.17); the synagogues of the Dispersion performed a vital rôle in the *praeparatio evangelica*. Though amongst Ebionites, Marcionites, etc., Christian congregations were called 'synagogues', it seems that from a fairly early date the assemblies of Jews and of Christians were generally called by the distinctive titles of συναγωγαί and ἐκκλησίαι respectively and the two words ceased to be synonymous.

they needed—a word which suggested that the true *qahal Yahweh* was now the Church of Jesus Christ. The congregations (ἐκκλησίαι) of Christ in every place were the local manifestations of the new Israel of God, the one true ἐκκλησία Θεοῦ.

ONE, HOLY, CATHOLIC CHURCH

Even when no genitive follows ἐκκλησία, one must always be understood (cf. *qahal Yahweh*): Θεοῦ, Κυρίου or Χριστοῦ. The Church is the Church of God in Christ Jesus (cf. I Thess. 2.14). It is God's Church, not ours, something which God creates, not we. Men did not found the Church, nor can they found a new Church (cf. I Cor. 3.11). There is only one Church of God, the one of which Christ's original apostles were the foundation members. There can be only one Church because there is only one Christ (Eph. 4.5), one body of Christ, one Spirit (I Cor. 12.13; Eph. 4.4). Christ is not divided (I Cor. 1.13) and therefore he cannot have two or more bodies; there cannot be two or more Churches. The plural ἐκκλησίαι occurs very frequently in the NT, but it is always a plural of distribution, i.e. it refers to the several local churches of Corinth, Philippi, Ephesus, etc.; it never means denominations, as in the phrase 'World Council of Churches'. Paul recoils with horror from the news that denominations have sprung up in Corinth— a Paul-party, an Apollos-'church', a Cephas (Peter)-denomination, even a Christ-party! (I Cor. 1.12; cf. 3.5). 'Is Christ divided? Was Paul crucified for you? Were ye baptized into the name of Paul?' (1.13). If the Church of the baptized is the *persona* of Christ, it is a body with many and varied organs, but it cannot be two bodies (cf. Rom. 12.4-8; I Cor. 12.12-30). Christians were 'called in one body' (Col. 3.15; cf. Eph. 2.16). Whether they recognize the truth or not, they are members of Christ's body (Eph. 5.30) and they are therefore members one of another (Eph. 4.25). The only words by which 'denominations' or 'churches' (in the sense of 'the confessions') could be translated into NT Greek would be σχίσματα and αἱρέσεις; if we used words in their biblical meaning only, we would have to speak of the 'World Council of Schisms and Heresies', a truth which the leaders of the ecumenical movement and the officers of the World Council of Churches have themselves emphasized again and again. In I Cor. 1.10 Paul appeals to the Corinthians that there be no σχίσματα ('divisions', from σχίζειν, to divide); and later in the epistle he again insists that there should be no σχίσμα in the body of Christ (12.25). In I Cor. 11.18f. he associates αἱρέσεις ('sects', 'self-chosen opinions', from αἱρεῖσθαι, 'to choose for oneself') with σχίσματα, and in Gal. 5.20 he reckons αἱρέσεις ('church-parties') as one of the works of the flesh (cf. II Pet. 2.1). The word αἵρεσις is used in a neutral sense of the sects of the Sadducees and Pharisees (e.g. Acts 5.17; 15.5), but the word is never used neutrally of the Christian community; there is to be neither sect nor sectarianism in the body of Christ.

There can be no Christians who are not 'members' of the one body of Christ and therefore of one another (I Cor. 12.25-27), so that to be out of communion with other Christians is to be out of communion with Christ. The test of whether we are 'in Christ' is whether we are in communion with other Christians: Church unity, which St John calls ἀγάπη, is the only test of whether a church is the Church. The ἀγάπη about which St John speaks in I John 3 and 4 is not, of course, good will in a general sense, but is precisely obedience to the divine commandment to exhibit in church-relations, in actual brotherly love (φιλαδελφία, Rom. 12.10; Heb. 13.1; I Pet. 1.22, and esp. II Pet. 1.7), the very ἀγάπη with which the Father loves the Son and the Son the Father (John 17.26; I John 4.16). 'Αγάπη is essentially the divine love of Christ and the Father manifested in terms of Church unity (I John 3.14-24; 4.7-11). Disunity is disobedience to the commandment of love, and is the same thing as unbelief (I John 5.1-3). Church unity is not a 'desirable feature' in the life of the Church; it is the condition of the Church's existence, the test of whether the Church is the Church. A divided Church is a contradiction of its own nature as Church; it is witnessing to a falsehood. Its evangelism cannot be effective. Jesus prayed 'that they all may be one, even as thou, Father, art in me and I in thee, that they also may be in us: that the world may believe that thou didst send me' (John 17.21; cf. 17.23). If we took the NT point of view seriously, we should expect to find that the single most serious obstacle to the evangelization of the world is the disunity of 'the churches'.

In Acts and the Paulines, except Eph. and Col., the word ἐκκλησία (often in the plural) usually means the local community of Christians. But it is a mistake to think with K. L. Schmidt and others that Eph. and Col. must be non-Pauline because they develop the conception of the ἐκκλησία as a 'mystery', the consummation of God's purpose of the ages (Eph. 3.9-11; 5.32), the body and bride of Christ (Eph. 1.22; 5.23-32; Col. 1.18, 24). The references to the Church in Eph.-Col. develop ideas which have all along been present in Paul's conception of the body of Christ, even though he has not used the word ἐκκλησία in this connection. As a matter of fact, however, it is hardly true to say that he has not used ἐκκλησία in the sense of Eph.-Col., but only in the sense of 'local congregation', as a glance at I Cor. 12.28 in its context will prove: St Paul cannot be saying that God has 'set' apostles in the local congregation! To imagine that Eph.-Col. derives its conception of the Church as a 'mystery' from Gnostic fancies about the 'heavenly man' is to miss the whole meaning of the NT doctrine of the Church as the corporative person of the risen Christ—a truth taught throughout the NT, and not only by St Paul, in such metaphors and images as those of the Messiah-Servant, the Son of Man, the Kingdom of God, the body or bride of Christ, the true vine, the spiritual house, the inheritance, the Israel of God and other symbols. There is nothing in Eph.-Col. which is not already implied in these metaphors.

The unity of the Church in the NT is not to be conceived of arithmetically: the Church is not simply the sum of the local congregations (ἐκκλησίαι). The unity of the Church derives from her 'one Lord' (Eph. 4.4f.), from the fact that all the local ἐκκλησίαι are 'in Christ'. They are united with one another, not as a federation of congregations, not by 'federal union', but through their common participation in Christ. And, since the Church is an organic and not an arithmetical unity, the whole Christ is present in every local congregation and at every meeting of the local church, however few it may be numerically: 'Where two or three are gathered together in my name, there am I in the midst of them' (Matt. 18.20; cf. 28.20). The Church is the κοινωνία of Christ (I Cor. 1.9; I John 1.3), and the local churches are one Church because Christ is fully present in the whole and in the parts. This union of Christ and his Church is indeed a great mystery (Eph. 5.32), but that does not mean that the Church is an 'invisible unity'. There are those who speak as if the invisible unity of the Church is all that matters and as if the outward and visible forms of unity are unimportant. This is certainly not the NT view. It implies a kind of 'Christian Science' view of the wounds (σχίσματα) of the body of Christ, treating them (as Paul did not) as if they were only figments of the imagination. The Church exists to make manifest in her own life that unity which exists between Christ and the Father, so that men may know that Christ is come forth from the Father. The new commandment of love concerns the actual visible relations of the disciples of Christ with one another: 'by this shall all men know that ye are my disciples, if ye have love one to another' (John 13.34f.; cf. 17.21, 23).

The Church, then, according to the NT, is neither an invisible entity ('known only to God') nor a Platonic 'idea', but is an actual, bodily existence. An 'invisible Church' would be as repugnant to Hebraic thought as a disembodied spirit. The Church is bodily, visible, tangible; it has a definite structure with differentiated parts or 'members'; it is actual, local. The fact of locality is a very important feature of the NT doctrine of the Church. The Church is not like a school of Stoic or Epicurean philosophers, whose existence in a given place is quite accidental. The 'catholic' Church is always a local Church, the Church of some city or country—ἡ ἐκκλησία καθ' ὅλης τῆς Ἰουδαίας καὶ Γαλιλαίας καὶ Σαμαρείας (Acts 9.31), ἡ ἐκκλησία τοῦ Θεοῦ ἡ οὖσα ἐν Κορίνθῳ (I Cor. 1.2; II Cor. 1.1), ἡ ἐκκλησία Θεσσαλονικέων (I Thess. 1.1).[1] By the fact that it is *the* Church *of* this city or country, and not a denomination of somebody's followers (Apollos' or Cephas' or Paul's), it may be known to be the Church of Jesus Christ in that place. Locality, nationality, particularity are essential marks of the universal Church; the local congregation is the embodiment at a given place and time of the Church of all the world and of all the ages. The contradiction of universality is not locality but denominationalism.

Thus, the Church is set in the world and is bound up with the world in all its particularity and in all the complexity of human relationships, racial, national, social and individual. Yet the Church is not 'of the world' (John 17.6, 11, 14-16). Christ's disciples are, like Christ, 'sanctified' (ἡγιασμένοι), made holy, set apart from the world (John 17.17, 19). The Church is holy; it is the fulfilment of the ancient command to Israel to be a 'holy nation' (Ex. 19.6; I Pet. 2.9; cf. Lev. 20.26, 'Ye shall be holy unto me: for I the LORD am holy, and have separated you from the peoples, that ye should be mine'; also Deut. 7.6; 26.19; 28.9; Isa. 62.12). The Christian congregations are 'the churches of the saints' (I Cor. 14.33); they are made up of those who are ἡγιασμένοι ἐν Χριστῷ Ἰησοῦ, κλητοὶ ἅγιοι (I Cor. 1.2). The word ἅγιοι is very common in the NT, especially in Paul; it is the word which the NT uses where we would speak of 'Christians'. The saints are those who through

---

[1] The phrase in Acts 9.31, ἡ ἐκκλησία καθ' ὅλης τῆς Ἰουδαίας, κτλ., is the nearest that the NT comes to speaking of 'the Catholic Church'. (The expression καθ' ὅλης, 'throughout all', is found in NT only in the Lucan writings, and Acts 9.31 is its only occurrence in connection with the Church; the other refs. are Luke 4.14; 23.5; Acts 9.42; 10.37 and 13.49.) But here it is significant because it implies that there is one and the same ἐκκλησία throughout the local ἐκκλησίαι of Judaea, etc.: this would be the fundamental NT idea behind the phrase 'the Catholic Church'. The one Church of Jesus Christ in all its many congregations is the Church of Judaea, Samaria, etc., or the Church of England, the Church of Scotland, the Church of Norway, and so on. The root idea of *place* as found in the expression καθ' ὅλης must never be eliminated from the conception of Catholicity; a church which is not *the* Church *of* Somewhere is not in the full sense the Catholic Church; it is one which is denominational rather than catholic, broken off from the original stem. The adjective καθολικός, -ή, -όν, 'general', 'universal', is occasionally found in cl. authors and is frequent in eccl. writings from the second cent. A.D. The first occurrence of the expression ἡ καθολικὴ ἐκκλησία is Ignatius, *Smyrn*.8. Eventually the adjective became the means of distinguishing the true, original and universal ἐκκλησία (or doctrine) from various schismatic or heretical denominations (or doctrines). But it did not originally mean 'orthodox' as opposed to 'heretical'. The seven 'Catholic Epistles' (i.e. those of James, Peter, John and Jude), commonly so called in the ancient Church (Eusebius, *Hist. Eccl.*, 2.23, 25), received their title probably because they were not addressed to a particular church but were 'general' or encyclical in character; Eusebius (ibid., 4.23) can still use the word in this sense and speak of a heretical Epistle of Themison, a disciple of Montanus, as 'catholic' (i.e. encyclical).

Christ's work and God's calling participate in the divine holiness; they are the individual members of the holy people of God (I Pet. 2.5, 9).

The holiness of the Church is, like its unity, something which God gives and which we cannot make for ourselves. We cannot sanctify ourselves, for instance, by redoubling our efforts at righteousness and good works. In the Bible holiness is not strictly a moral quality, though it is very closely connected with the commandment of obedience involved in the covenant relationship; it is a category *sui generis*, which cannot be reduced to any other thing than itself, such as morals or feelings. The Church can shew forth the divine holiness, or it can obscure it; but it cannot either create or destroy it. The same is true of the unity of the Church. The Church's unity is not something which we can create, or arrange for, or decide upon in conferences about reunion: it is the gift of God. Men cannot create Church unity, and (let us thank God for it) they cannot destroy it. If men could destroy it, they would be able to destroy the Church itself, for a Church whose unity is destroyed is no longer the *Church*. But men can obscure the unity of Christ's Church, and this is what they have done. In deep repentance and in faith in God's power to overrule human self-will and pride the Church prays that God will give that unity which is in accordance with his will, so that it may be seen by all men to be indeed the Church of God, and thus all men may come to know that Christ was sent by God to be the Saviour of the world.

13

THE APOSTOLIC AND PRIESTLY MINISTRY

THE ministry of the Church is the continuation of the apostolic and priestly ministry of Christ himself. In this present age, between Christ's resurrection and his parousia, his ministry to the world is fulfilled through the instrumentality of his resurrection body, the Church. All true ministerial acts of the Church are *gesta Christi*, the acts of Christ, the Head of the body. Christ is still the one who commissions and sends the pastors of his flock; he is the celebrant at every Eucharist, the minister of every act of loving service that his disciples perform in his name. To put this truth in another way, because Christ is the Apostle, the Church is apostolic; because he is the High Priest, the Church is sacerdotal; because he is Servant, the Church is ministerial. The historic threefold ministry of the Church, represented by the words 'apostolate', 'priesthood' and 'diaconate', is derived from the threefold ministry of Christ. Christ himself is our Apostle, Priest and Deacon, and the missionary, priestly and ministerial functions of the Church are the ways in which he works through his body in the world.

THE APOSTOLIC CHURCH

The character of the Church as apostolic is made abundantly clear in the NT, even if the precise status and function of 'the apostles' remains uncertain.[1] The whole Church is apostolic, not merely a particular order within it, just as the whole Church is priestly and is ministerial. Throughout the Bible God is a God of *sending*, of *mission*. His characteristic approach to men is by sending someone to speak to them for him: he sends Moses to Pharaoh, Nathan to David, Elijah to Ahab, Amos to Bethel, Isaiah to Hezekiah, and so on almost indefinitely. 'Since the day that your fathers came forth out of the land of Egypt unto this day, I have sent unto you all my servants the prophets, daily rising up early and sending them' (Jer. 7.25; cf. 26.5; 29.19; 35.15; 44.4). In the NT 'apostles' are closely associated with 'prophets' in their character of having been *sent* from God; e.g. Luke 11.49,

---

[1] See *infra*, 319-25.

'Therefore also the wisdom of God said, I will send unto them prophets and apostles, and some of them they shall kill . . . ' (contrast Matt. 23.34). In Eph. 2.20 God's household is said to be built upon the foundation of the apostles and prophets, Christ Jesus himself, as the chief apostle-prophet, being the chief corner stone. Again, apostles and prophets are virtually synonymous terms, or at least of equal rank and importance as the receivers of the revelation of the Spirit, in Eph. 3.5 (cf. also Rev. 18.20). The only place in the NT where Christ is actually called 'Apostle' is Heb. 3.1, but the sense of having been sent from God is clearly expressed by Jesus himself, especially in the parables (Mark 12.1-12; Luke 15.3-10; Matt. 23.37). The Fourth Evangelist, though he never uses the word 'apostle', stresses very strongly the truth that Jesus is the one sent by God (John 3.17; 5.30, 36f.; 6.29, 38-40, 44; 7.16, 18, 28f.; 8.16, 18, 26, 29, 42; 9.4; 10.36; 11.42; 12.45, 49; 14.24; 15.21; 16.5; 17.3, 18, 21, 23, 25; 20.21; cf. I John 4.14). Because Christ is thus 'apostled', therefore the Church is apostolic: καθὼς ἐμὲ ἀπέστειλας εἰς τὸν κόσμον, κἀγὼ ἀπέστειλα αὐτοὺς εἰς τὸν κόσμον (John 17.18); καθὼς ἀπέσταλκέ με ὁ πατήρ, κἀγὼ πέμπω ὑμᾶς (John 20.21).

The metaphor of the Shepherd and the sheep is another characteristically biblical way of presenting the apostolic character of the Church of God. In the OT the metaphor of Israel as the flock of which Yahweh is the Shepherd-Ruler is frequent (e.g. Pss. 23; 78.52; 80.1; 95.7; 100.3), and the Messiah-King (of whom David is the ideal 'type') is set up by Yahweh as the chosen shepherd of his flock (I Sam. 17.34-36; Ps. 78.70-72). A nation's rulers were spoken of as 'shepherds' (e.g. Jer. 23.1-4; Ezek. 34 *passim*; Zech. 11 *passim*), and the element of government is an essential constituent of the NT conception of the 'pastor' (Lat. *pastor*, a shepherd, from *pasco*, to drive to pasture, to feed) or shepherd (ποιμήν). Ezekiel prophesies that, in contrast with the wicked shepherds (rulers) of Israel whom he denounces, God will raise up a Davidic prince who will cherish his flock: 'I will set up one shepherd over them, and he shall feed them, even my servant David; he shall feed them, and he shall be their shepherd' (34.23; cf. Jer. 23.4f.). Likewise the Isaianic redeemer, upon whose mission Jesus meditated profoundly, is represented as the Messianic Shepherd: 'He shall feed his flock like a shepherd; he shall gather the lambs in his arm . . . and shall gently lead those that give suck' (Isa. 40.11; cf. also Micah 5.2; 7.14; Isa. 63.11; Ezek. 34.15f.; and esp. II Esd. 2.34: 'O ye nations, that hear and understand, look for your shepherd, he shall give you everlasting rest; for he is nigh at hand that shall come in the end of the world').

It is, then, hardly surprising that Jesus should think of his own mission as that of the Shepherd sent to gather again the Israel of God, the Messianic Shepherd-Ruler of scriptural prophecy. St John in characteristic fashion sums up the traditional Gospel-material on the theme of Jesus as Shepherd (e.g. Matt. 18.12-14; Luke 15.3-7; Luke 12.32; cf. Matt. 7.15; 10.16; 26.31) in his meditation upon the Good Shepherd (John 10.1-18). The parable of John 10.1-6 and its subsequent interpretation present Jesus as both 'the door of the sheep' (cf. 14.6, ἡ ὁδός) and as the shepherd himself. The passage again stresses the unity of the Church of God and portrays the mission of the Church to the Gentiles as an activity of Christ himself: 'Other sheep I have which are not of this fold (αὐλή, the courtyard of a house where the sheep are kept, hence 'fold'); them also I must bring, and they shall hear my voice, and they shall become one flock, one shepherd' (μία ποίμνη, εἷς ποιμήν). The reference, of course, is not to denominations within the Church, but to the mission to the Gentiles, which could not begin until after the death of Christ, the Good Shepherd who laid down his life for the sheep (10.11, 17f.; cf. Matt. 26.31; Zech. 13.7). Because of Christ's voluntary self-oblation, Jew and Gentile are now one flock; the 'Greeks', who did not 'see' Jesus in his earthly lifetime (John 12.20f.), are now drawn into the flock of God by the 'lifting up' (i.e. crucifixion) of the Son of Man (12.32). St John teaches that Jesus died not for the nation (of the Jews) only, but that he might gather into one the children of God that are scattered abroad (John 11.51f.).

The NT, following the Lord's own teaching concerning his person and mission, represents Christ as the Messianic Shepherd-King of God's flock: he is 'the Great Shepherd of the sheep' (Heb. 13.20), 'the Good Shepherd' (John 10.11), 'the Shepherd and Bishop of your souls' (I Pet. 2.25) and 'the Chief Shepherd' (I Pet. 5.4; ἀρχιποίμην, a *hapax legomenon* in NT). Thus, while the whole Church is apostolic, i.e. sent by God to bear witness to Christ in the world, there is within the wider apostolic body a particular apostolic ministry consisting of those chosen to bear rule over the churches and to exercise pastoral oversight or ἐπισκοπή.[1] The very conception of Israel or the Church as a flock involves the institution of pastoral rule and oversight; the flock must have shepherds who rule it and feed it under the ultimate supervision of the Chief Shepherd himself. The very word ἀρχιποίμην (I Pet. 5.4) implies a pastoral ministry of under-shepherds who are commissioned

---

[1] The word ἐπισκοπή is found four times in NT. At I Tim. 3.1 it means 'pastoral oversight', the office of an ἐπίσκοπος; perhaps this is implied in Acts 1.20, but the passage is quoting Ps. 108.8 (LXX; EVV, 109.8) as a proof-text with the object of shewing that Judas's defection was foretold in the Scriptures. The other two occurrences (Luke 19.44; I Pet. 2.12) of ἐπισκοπή are in the sense of 'visitation', 'the day of visitation'.

to exercise within the flock of Christ a particular pastoral office. This, in fact, is precisely the conception of the ἐπισκοπή which is enjoined upon the presbyters in the preceding verses: 'Tend (ποιμάνατε) the flock (ποίμνιον) of God which is among you, exercising the oversight (ἐπισκοποῦντες[1]), not of constraint but willingly, according unto God; nor yet for filthy lucre, but of a ready mind; neither as lording it over the-charge-allotted-to-you (μηδ' ὡς κατακυριεύοντες τῶν κλήρων), but making yourselves examples (τύποι) to the flock' (I Pet. 5.1-3). The passage clearly attests the existence of a pastoral ministry, which is an instrument of the ministry of Christ himself as Chief Shepherd, within the Church or flock of God. Certain office-holders in the Church, here called presbyters (5.1), have been assigned a κλῆρος[2] or share in the ministry of Christ in his Church. It is the office of oversight or pastoral rule (ἐπισκοπή); and the faithful discharge of it will bring its due reward at the parousia of the Chief Shepherd (5.4). It is nothing less than a participation in the ministry of Christ, who is himself the true ποίμην and ἐπίσκοπος of the flock (I Pet. 2.25). The shepherd presbyter-bishop feeds that portion of the flock which is committed to his care; he bears the shepherd's staff, the symbol of his pastoral rule; the 'rod and staff' (Ps. 23.4) in the hand of the shepherd are for the disciplining as well as for the protecting and guiding of the flock (cf. I Tim. 3.4f.).

The Fourth Gospel (or the appendix to it) bears witness to the fact that, in some parts of the Church at least, it was believed that the Risen Lord had given a special commission to St Peter to institute the pastoral ministry of the Church ('Feed my lambs', 'Tend my sheep'; John 21.15-17); and it is therefore especially interesting to find St Peter (or, what is equally significant, someone writing in his name) urging his 'fellow-presbyters' to 'tend the flock of God . . . exercising the oversight'. The fact that St Peter calls (or is made to call) himself a presbyter (I Pet. 5.1) is sufficient indication of the high seriousness with which the episcopal office of the presbyters was regarded in the apostolic Church. To this testimony we need add only the words addressed by St Paul to the presbyters of the Ephesian Church at Miletus (Acts 20.17): 'Take heed unto yourselves, and to all the flock, in which the Holy Spirit has made you ἐπίσκοποι, to feed the Church of God, which he purchased with his own blood' (Acts 20.28). It is clear that the pastoral and episcopal ministry of the presbyters was an essential character of the apostolic Church.

---

[1] The only other occurrence of the verb ἐπισκοπέω in NT is Heb. 12.15, where the usage is less technical. We may note that I Peter dates from a time when the function of ἐπισκοπή, or the office of ἐπίσκοπος, was not distinguished from the duty of the πρεσβύτεροι: cf. Acts 20.17 with Acts 20.28; and see *infra*, 325-9. Some MSS, however, omit ἐπισκοποῦντες at I Pet. 5.2.

[2] See *supra*, 266n.

THE ROYAL PRIESTHOOD

Because Christ is the High Priest, the Christian Church is priestly. It fulfils the task assigned to the Old Israel at Sinai, that of being a priest-nation to the Gentiles, the 'kingdom of priests' of Ex. 19.6 (LXX, ὑμεῖς δὲ ἔσεσθέ μοι βασίλειον ἱεράτευμα), the 'light to lighten the Gentiles' of the prophetic vision.[1] The NT claims that the Church of Jesus Christ is this divinely consecrated 'royal priesthood' (βασίλειον ἱεράτευμα) (I Pet. 2.9). It presents the ἀρεταί (saving acts) of God to the Gentiles (I Pet. 2.10) and the offerings of the whole human race to God. Mankind is unworthy to bring to God any offering at all, but now through Jesus Christ a 'way' has been opened to God's presence and the sacrifices of the human race may be laid upon God's altar. The Christian Church is the sacrificing priesthood instituted by God himself, so that mankind should have access to him and might bring before him acceptable offerings. Besides I Pet. 2.9 the only other use of ἱεράτευμα (priesthood in the sense of a body of priests[2]) in the NT is found in I Pet. 2.5: 'Ye also, as living stones, are built up a spiritual house, to be a holy priesthood (ἱεράτευμα ἅγιον), to offer up spiritual sacrifices acceptable to God through Jesus Christ' (ἀνενέγκαι πνευματικὰς θυσίας εὐπροσδέκτους Θεῷ διὰ Ἰησοῦ Χριστοῦ). Corporately, therefore, the Christian community constitutes a sacrificing priesthood which offers up spiritual sacrifices, i.e. presumably, not material sacrifices like those of sheep and bullocks and goats under the old dispensation (cf. Rom. 12.1). The emphasis is placed upon the corporate character of the Christian priesthood; but individual Christians are to look upon themselves as 'priests unto God', just as in the prophetic vision every Israelite was to be a priest to ten Gentiles (Zech. 8.23): cf. Rev. 1.6; 5.10, 'made to be a kingdom and priests unto God'; also Rev. 20.6, 'They shall be priests of God and of Christ, and shall reign with him a thousand years.' In each of these three passages from the Apocalypse the influence of the 'kingdom of priests' of Ex. 19.6 is apparent. There is to be a Christian theocracy, but it is a theocracy of the whole Christian body.[3]

The prophets of the OT had come to question the propriety of bringing material sacrifices to God. What need had the God of all the earth of such presents? In rationalistic vein they had even ridiculed the

[1] See *supra*, 269f.

[2] The word for 'priesthood' in the sense of 'priest's orders' is ἱερωσύνη (Heb. 7.11f., 24 only).

[3] These passages in the Apocalypse are the only places in the NT in which the word ἱερεύς is applied to Christians; all the other uses of the word are either of Christ (Heb. 7.15, 17; 10.21), or (most frequently) of the Jewish priesthood (Mark 1.44; Luke 1.5; John 1.19; Acts 6.7, etc.), or of a pagan priest (Acts 14.13).

cultus: 'If I were hungry, I would not tell thee, for the world is mine and the fulness thereof' (Ps. 50.12; cf. vv. 8-14). God did not want calves or rams or oil; he required justice, mercy and humble obedience (Micah 6.6-8; I Sam. 15.22); he would be pleased not with expensive gifts but with the sacrifice of thanksgiving (Ps. 50.14) and penitence (Ps. 51.17). They had learnt the truth that sinful man cannot bring an acceptable sacrifice to God, precisely because, being sinful, he has no access to God. How then was he to come before the Lord? How might his offerings be made acceptable to the holy God? This problem the OT leaves unsolved. The NT answers it decisively: through Christ man has access to God and his sacrifices are made acceptable. We must take note of the great διά of the NT vocabulary—*through* Jesus Christ (e.g. I Pet. 2.5, θυσίας εὐπροσδέκτους Θεῷ διὰ Ἰησοῦ Χριστοῦ: Heb. 13.15, δι' αὐτοῦ ἀναφέρωμεν θυσίαν αἰνέσεως). Through Christ 'the Way' we have access to God, and through him alone our oblations are acceptable.

The question of the acceptability or otherwise of sacrifices has a history as old as Cain and Abel (Gen. 4.4f.), and the matter is often raised in the OT (e.g. Isa. 1.11-14; Amos 5.21f.). Hence the importance of such NT words as δεκτός ('acceptable') in connection with sacrifice (Phil. 4.18), or εὐπρόσδεκτος (a near synonym) (Rom. 15.16; I Pet. 2.5), or εὐάρεστος ('well-pleasing') (Rom. 12.1; Phil. 4.18). The good works and almsgiving of Christians have become acceptable to God through Christ; and Christian sacrificial living is a genuine offering which God accepts. In this connection St Paul uses the OT expression 'an odour of a sweet smell' (ὀσμὴ εὐωδίας), which referred to the sweet-smelling savour of the sacrifices (or of the burning incense) and remained in Jewish religious language as a synonym for an acceptable sacrifice long after the idea that God actually *smelt* the savour had been outgrown (cf. Amos 5.21, RV mg.). He speaks in Phil. 4.18 of the gifts of the Philippians, which he had received by the hand of Epaphroditus, as ὀσμὴν εὐωδίας, θυσίαν δεκτήν, εὐάρεστον τῷ Θεῷ. In Eph. 5.2 he exhorts Christians to 'walk in love, even as Christ also loved you, and gave himself up for us, an offering (προσφορά) and sacrifice (θυσία) to God for an odour of a sweet smell' (εἰς ὀσμὴν εὐωδίας). The suggestion of the whole passage in which this exhortation occurs is that the Christian life of self-oblation is an *imitatio Christi* and an offering that is acceptable to God: cf. 5.10, 'proving what is εὐάρεστον to the Lord'. In II Cor. 2.15 he says that Christians are themselves a sweet savour of Christ unto God (Χριστοῦ εὐωδία ἐσμὲν τῷ Θεῷ); the word ὀσμή is found in the verse preceding and in the verse following this statement: Christians are themselves an offering of Christ to God, and the sweet fragrance of the knowledge of God is spread abroad by the Christian community in every place (2.14).

THE CHRISTIAN SACRIFICES

The NT is rich in sacrificial language, though this is not always apparent in our EVV. For instance, the verbs λατρεύειν and λειτουργεῖν, which both mean 'to serve', and the nouns λατρεία and λειτουργία, which mean 'service', carry a strong biblical and therefore sacrificial flavour because of their use in the Greek OT in connection with the ministrations of the priests at the sacrificial offerings in the Temple. In classical Greek λατρεύειν means 'to serve for hire' (cf. λάτρις, a hired servant; λάτρον, hire); in the LXX it *always* refers to the service of God (or of a heathen deity), and it includes the service of the whole nation of Israel as well as that of the priests (cf. Matt. 4.10, citing Deut. 6.13; Luke 1.74; 2.37; Acts 26.7; Rom. 9.4, etc.). In Rom. 12.1 and Heb 9.14 and other passages we should doubtless keep before our minds the sense of the priestly oblations in the Temple, which is clearly intended in (e.g.) Heb. 9.9 and 10.2. In classical Greek λειτουργεῖν means to render public service to the State at one's own expense; in the LXX it can be used of the service of men (e.g. Josh. 1.1; I Kings 1.4; 10.5; 19.21, etc.), as λατρεύειν never is; but its principal meaning relates to the ministrations and offerings of the priests and Levites in the Tabernacle or the Temple.[1] Even at Rom. 13.6, where the classical sense might be thought to be uppermost, the LXX sacrificial ('liturgical') associations cannot be entirely dissociated from its use; while such associations are obviously in mind at Rom. 15.16 (cf. Acts 13.2: does this mean 'While they celebrated the eucharistic liturgy'? II Cor. 9.12: does this in its context refer to the gifts or offertory at the Eucharist? Phil. 2.17; Heb. 8.6). It is not without significance that at the end of the NT period St Clement of Rome can speak of the ministry of the presbyters and of 'those who have offered the gifts of the ἐπισκοπή' as their λειτουργία (I Clem. Rom. 44); and we must give due weight to the fact that, after the close of the NT period (unless Acts 13.2 is sufficient evidence of its use in apostolic times), the word λειτουργία, which in the LXX had meant the sacrificial ministrations of the priests and Levites in the Temple, came to be regularly used as a title of the Eucharist.

The words used for 'presenting an offering' or 'making a sacrifice' are worthy of careful study. In Rom. 12.1 St Paul exhorts Christians to offer up themselves as a living sacrifice, a rational priestly action

[1] In the LXX λειτουργός is used technically of a priest (cf. II Esd. 20.36, LXX [EVV, Neh. 10.36]: τοῖς ἱερεῦσι τοῖς λειτουργοῦσιν ἐν οἴκῳ Θεοῦ ἡμῶν) and particularly of a Levite (cf. II Esd. 20.39, LXX [EVV, Neh. 10.39]: καὶ οἱ ἱερεῖς καὶ οἱ λειτουργοί). Thus, in Heb. 8.1f. Christ is called ἀρχιερεύς and τῶν ἁγίων λειτουργός. See esp. Rom. 15.16 (*infra*, 299).

(παραστῆσαι τὰ σώματα ὑμῶν θυσίαν ζῶσαν . . . τὴν λογικὴν λατρείαν ὑμῶν). The verb παριστάνω or παρίστημι is a technical term for presenting a sacrifice (cf. Luke 2.22; I Cor. 8.8; II Cor. 4.14; Col. 1.28; Eph. 5.27). The idea reappears elsewhere in Paul; for instance, in Rom. 6.13-16, where Christians are urged to present themselves or their 'members' unto God and not unto sin. The idea of being 'without blemish', of the sacrifice as being the best that we can offer, is taken over from the OT legislation on this theme and used as an argument for moral purity (Phil. 2.15). Thus, the word ἄμωμος is not infrequent in the NT Epistles. Etymologically it means 'blameless', but it ought to be translated 'without blemish', since in the Greek OT it is the technical Levitical term for offerings that are not defective in any way and so are fit for sacrifice (cf. Ex. 12.5; Lev. 22.19-21; Deut. 17.1; Mal. 1.8, 14; Heb. 9.14; I Pet. 1.19, etc.). The sacrifices of Christians are acceptable to God, not because Christians or their gifts are ἄμωμοι in themselves, but because they are sanctified and thus rendered acceptable by the Holy Spirit (Rom. 8.8f.; 15.16; cf. Heb. 9.14). Christ has cleansed and sanctified the Church by the washing of water (in baptism) with the word (of preaching), in order that he might present (παραστήσῃ) to himself a glorious Church, ἁγία καὶ ἄμωμος (Eph. 5.27). It is Christ who has reconciled Christians to God by his death, to present (παραστῆσαι) them ἁγίους καὶ ἀμώμους καὶ ἀνεγκλήτους before him (Col. 1.22). Christ is thought of as a high priest offering the Church to God in the sacrificed body of his own flesh (*ibid.*); Christ offers the Church, cleansed and ἄμωμος, to God (cf. Eph. 1.4; Jude 24). In Rev. 14.5 the 144,000 redeemed in heaven are declared to be ἄμωμοι. 'These are they which follow the Lamb whithersoever he goeth. These were purchased from among men, the firstfruits (ἀπαρχή) unto God and unto the Lamb' (14.4). They are the firstfruits of the harvest of the world (cf. Rom. 16.5, ἀπαρχὴ τῆς ᾿Ασίας εἰς Χριστόν: I Cor. 16.15, ἀπαρχὴ τῆς ᾿Αχαίας: II Thess. 2.13, RV mg.). The conception of ἀπαρχή in this sense is drawn from the OT sacrificial system, for the firstfruits are offered and consecrated to God (Deut. 26.1-11; Lev. 2.12; Ezek. 45.1, LXX; 48.9, LXX).

The verb ἀναφέρειν, to carry or lead up (e.g. Mark 9.2), also means to offer up on an altar as a sacrifice (e.g. Heb. 7.27); it is used of the sacrifices of Christians at Heb. 13.15 (the sacrifice of praise) and at I Pet. 2.5 ('spiritual sacrifices'). In Heb. 7.27; 9.28 and I Pet. 2.24 it is used of Christ's self-oblation; and in James 2.21 it is used of Abraham's offering up of Isaac. The word ἀναφορά, an oblation, which is derived from it, is not found in the NT; it came later to be used for the eucharistic liturgy as a whole, and eventually for the central part of it, viz.

the Prayer of Consecration. The word προσφορά, an offering, gift, sacrifice, is derived from προσφέρειν, to bring to or lead to; the verb is used frequently in LXX of people offering gifts, prayers and sacrifices to God and is used more than a score of times in the NT of the offering of a δῶρον, θυσίαν, λατρείαν or προσφοράν (e.g. Matt. 2.11; 5.23f.; Mark 1.44; John 16.2; Acts 7.42; 21.26; Heb. 5.1, 3, 7, etc.). The verb is used more than twenty times in Hebrews, but is found nowhere in the Paulines. But the noun προσφορά is twice used in the latter in a most significant context. In Rom. 15.16 St Paul describes himself as 'a λειτουργός ('sacrificing priest', RV mg.) of Christ Jesus in respect of the Gentiles, ministering-in-sacrifice (ἱερουργοῦντα) the Gospel of God, that the προσφορά of the Gentiles might be made acceptable (εὐπρόσδεκτος), being sanctified in Holy Spirit'. Here we have a striking example of the royal priesthood in action, shewing forth to the Gentiles the ἀρεταί of him who called us into his marvellous light: St Paul thinks of himself as an evangelizing priest-apostle, bringing his converts and laying them as an offering upon God's altar; they are now no longer 'unclean' Gentiles, because, having been sanctified in Holy Spirit (i.e. baptized), they are 'acceptable' in the technical sense as a προσφορά (sacrifice) (cf. the conception of the ἀπαρχή, mentioned above, and cf. also Rom. 11.13, 'As apostle of the Gentiles, I glorify my διακονία'—i.e. liturgical service: II Cor. 9.12). In Eph. 5.2, the other use of προσφορά in the Paulines, the writer is commending to Christians for their imitation the example of Christ, who gave himself up for us, a προσφορά and θυσία to God, for an acceptable oblation (εἰς ὀσμὴν εὐωδίας). The suggestion of the passage, as we have already noted, is that the Christian life of loving service of others is, through Christ's sacrifice, an acceptable (v. 10, εὐάρεστον) oblation to God. Of the nine occurrences of προσφορά in the NT, the only others which are significant for our present purpose are two of the five that occur in Heb. 10, viz. 10.10, 14, in which Christians are said to have been sanctified through the one προσφορά of the body of Christ. The NT teaches that because of the one, perfect προσφορά made by Christ, Christians may approach God's altar with their sacrifices and oblations, confident that they will not be rejected by him.

Let us now attempt to summarize the different kinds of offerings which the NT specifically mentions as Christian sacrifices or oblations. (1) First, Christians must offer themselves, their souls and bodies, for that is what σώματα means in Rom. 12.1. They are to offer themselves as living sacrifices, acceptable by virtue of their baptismal cleansing in Holy Spirit. The bodies of Christians are to be μέλη Χριστοῦ (I Cor. 6.15), temples of the Holy Spirit (6.19). Because he is at every moment being presented to God in Christ, the Christian (in the state of eschatological tension in which he finds himself in this age) must endeavour to be what he already by faith is—holy, pure, chaste, without blemish. The Christian sacrifice differs from Jewish and heathen sacrifices in being θυσία ζῶσα, not a sacrifice of dead animals: Christ having died unto sin once, and the Christian having in his baptism died with him and been raised to new life, there is henceforward no more offering of dead things but an on-going living sacrifice. In the death of Christ Christians have already been presented in sacrifice to God; the Christian life is the working out in daily living of this oblation of Christ's: 'present (παριστάνετε) yourselves unto God, as alive from the dead (i.e. as a θυσία ζῶσα), and your members as weapons of righteousness unto God' (Rom. 6.13, which should be studied in its whole baptismal context, 6.1-14). Christian sacrificial living is achieved through the power of Christ's resurrection (cf. I Cor. 5.7f.—the Christian life as continuous Easter festival). The Christian life is liturgy; and morality and cultus are (as the OT prophets longed to see them) at one. There is no longer a divorce between living and worshipping, for Christian living is λογικὴ λατρεία (Rom. 12.1)—a rational divine service, contrasted with the divine service of the Temple priests. For the offering of irrational animals there has been substituted the self-oblation of rational and spiritual beings who give themselves in thanksgiving to the service of God (cf. I Pet. 2.5).

(2) It would follow from this conception of the Christian life as sacrificial service—with the word 'sacrificial' as no mere metaphor—and as an oblation acceptable to God, that the deeds of charity and fellowship performed by Christians are particular sacrifices which God delights in.[1] This truth is explicitly stated in Heb. 13.16: 'Do not forget εὐποιΐα and κοινωνία (well-doing and sympathetic giving), for with such θυσίαι God is well-pleased (εὐαρεστεῖται).' (Cf. also Heb. 13.21.)

(3) Next, as we would expect, their material gifts and the offerings of their wealth are acceptable oblations which Christians bring to God. Thus, St Paul can speak of the material gifts which he has received from the Philippians by the hand of Epaphroditus as 'a sacrifice acceptable, well-pleasing to God' and as 'an odour of a sweet smell' (ὀσμὴν εὐωδίας, θυσίαν δεκτήν, εὐάρεστον τῷ Θεῷ) (Phil. 4.18).

(4) Then, also, the sacrifices of Christians include their praises and confession of his name, and their prayers. 'Through him let us offer up a sacrifice of praise (ἀναφέρωμεν θυσίαν αἰνέσεως) to God continually, that is, the fruit of lips which make confession to his name' (Heb. 13.15). Thus, Christian corporate worship was regarded as the offering of

---

[1] Cf. the OT expression 'the sacrifice of righteousness' (Pss. 4.5; 51.19; Mal. 3.3).

sacrifice by the priestly body; and since the only corporate act of worship in the apostolic Church (apart from services of baptism) was the meeting for the celebration of the Lord's Supper, the expression 'the eucharistic sacrifice', used in this sense, would be entirely justified. The Eucharist was the weekly oblation offered by the royal priesthood. Perhaps it is right to conclude that the prayers of the Church were regarded as a sacrificial offering from the metaphor of Rev. 8.3f., where the seer in his vision sees the angel standing by the altar in heaven, with his golden censer and much incense, which was to be added 'to the prayers of all the saints upon the golden altar which was before the throne'. The idea of prayer itself as an oblation is familiar from the OT (Ps. 141.2; cf. Luke 1.10); and elsewhere in the Apocalypse it would seem that prayer is the oblation of the saints at the heavenly altar (Rev. 5.8).

(5) Lastly, the converts made by the missionary efforts of the Church are regarded as oblations that are offered up to God (Rom. 15.16; I Cor. 16.15; Col. 1.28; Rev. 14.4f.). The converted Gentiles in the apostolic Church were looked upon as the 'firstfruits' of the harvest of the world which was now being gathered in at the Messianic reaping.

THE PRIESTHOOD OF THE LAITY

The priesthood about which the NT speaks is a corporate priesthood of the whole Christian community, and the word ἱερεύς (*sacerdos*, priest) is never used in respect of any priestly order or caste within the priestly community. All the members of the Church, men and women, are ἱερεῖς τῷ Θεῷ (Rev. 1.6; 5.10; 20.6); their priesthood is in relation to the world outside the Church (I Pet. 2.9). Their corporate priesthood is exercised in their gathering every Lord's Day to offer their due λατρεία or λειτουργία to God, which is their θυσία αἰνέσεως, i.e. the eucharistic sacrifice. This liturgical or sacramental offering is the expression in worship of the continuing sacrificial διακονία of the Christian life, which the ἱερεῖς τῷ Θεῷ offer every day and at every moment of the day. It was at their baptism, when hands were laid upon them and they received the Holy Spirit, that they obtained their part and lot, their individual ministry, within the total priesthood of the Church of God. Baptism is, as it were, the ordination of a new member of the royal priesthood; it is the making of a layman in the Church of Christ. A layman in the NT sense, i.e. a member of the λαὸς Θεοῦ, is certainly not (as he tends to be in modern usage) a church-member who has no ministerial responsibility, one who has handed over his functions of evangelism and pastoral care to certain professional Christians who are paid to perform them. All the laity (members of the λαὸς Θεοῦ), if we use the word in a biblical way, are priests and ministers of the Church of Jesus Christ; and all the 'ministers' are equally 'laymen'.

Thus, the priesthood of the laity means that all the members of the Church of Christ have both an individual and a corporate responsibility. Individually, in their lives of Christian witness and service, whatever their secular profession or trade, they perform their λειτουργία or διακονία: even the work of slaves (δοῦλοι) can be an adornment of and an advertisement for Christian doctrine (Titus 2.10; I Tim. 6.1), and the Christian worker (δοῦλος) does his work not for earthly praise or reward but 'as unto the Lord' (Eph. 6.5-7, etc.). Such patient service in the tasks and tribulations of the workaday world is χάρις παρὰ Θεῷ (I Pet. 2.20).[1] Corporately, the laity of the Church, i.e. the whole membership of the people of God, exercise their priesthood in the offering up of their priestly oblation, the θυσία αἰνέσεως or eucharistic worship.

The doctrine of the priesthood of the laity is in the fullest sense a biblical doctrine (Ex. 19.4-6; I Pet. 2.9f., etc.); but its content is far richer than that which is generally understood by the phrase 'the priesthood of all believers'. It was, indeed, necessary at the Reformation to stress that every individual Christian man or woman had through Christ direct access to God, apart entirely from the offices of any human intermediary: there is one Mediator only (I Tim. 2.5). This basic truth of the Gospel had been obscured by medieval sacerdotalism. The expression 'priesthood of all believers' represents a truth that must always be reasserted in face of the pretensions of all forms of priestcraft. But the expression is usually taken to mean simply that every man is his own priest; whereas the biblical conception of the priesthood of the laity is much more profound than this. It means that the Church is the appointed priest-nation to the 'Gentile' world, i.e. to all that is not-Church; that the Church is responsible before God for 'the world' and all its concerns, and that every individual Christian should strive to be a priest to ten 'Gentiles'. The problem of evangelism in the secular world would lose much of its intractability if the 'layfolk' of the churches would take seriously the biblical teaching concerning their calling and office as laymen in the Church of God.

The priesthood of the Church is not something which exists apart from Christ; it is not something that men may seize and manipulate for their own ends. Our offerings have no magical efficacy; and however costly they may be they have no value in themselves. No merit is earned by them, nor is salvation bought by them. God's favour is not obtained by bringing presents to him; on the contrary, it is because

[1] See further on this theme Alan Richardson, *The Biblical Doctrine of Work*, 35-9

it has already been freely given that we are able to bring offerings which are acceptable to him. Our sacrifices are not propitiations, for nothing that we could do could have turned away his wrath. It is solely because of what God has done that we are able to approach him and bring offerings in which he will take pleasure. It is because of Christ's one, true, effective sacrifice, offered once for all, that our unworthy oblation is possible. In the language of *Auct. Heb.*, it is because Christ has cleansed our conscience from dead works—from all legalist preoccupation with 'merit'—that we are set free to serve (λατρεύειν) the living God (Heb. 9.14; cf. Ps. 51.19). God remains the holy God, but our approach to him is no longer as to a burning mountain of blackness, darkness and tempest; we come now not to the fearful Sinai, but to Mount Zion, the heavenly Jerusalem, through the mediation of a new covenant in the blood of which we have been sprinkled; and thus, having received an unshakeable kingship, we have 'grace whereby we may offer service well-pleasing to God' (χάριν, δι' ἧς λατρεύωμεν εὐαρέστως τῷ Θεῷ). But still we approach with reverence and awe, because our God is still holy, still a consuming fire that burns up everything that is not cleansed and rendered worthy of his acceptance (Heb. 12.18-29; cf. 13.21). Christ is himself the altar to which our offerings may be brought; and the new priesthood of Jesus Christ is fed from that altar, just as under the old dispensation those who ministered to the altar ate their portion from the altar (Heb. 13.10; cf. I Cor. 9.13; 10.18). Christ is both the altar to which our gifts are brought and the high priest by whom they are presented to God (cf. Heb. 3.1). In the beautiful phrase of St Clement of Rome, Jesus Christ is 'the high priest of our offerings, the guardian and helper of our weakness' (I Clem. Rom. 36). If the λαὸς Θεοῦ is indeed the true βασίλειον ἱεράτευμα, this is solely because of 'Ιησοῦς Χριστὸς ὁ ἀρχιερεὺς τῶν προσφορῶν ἡμῶν. It is hardly surprising that the language of sacrifice, in which the NT is so rich, should have passed gradually and almost imperceptibly into liturgical use, thus acquiring new shades of meaning,[1] or that it should have been at once gathered in the post-apostolic age into a rich and wonderful vocabulary by which the Church could interpret to itself the meaning of its own characteristic act of communion and worship, the eucharistic offering.

THE MINISTERING CHURCH

The Church is ministerial because Christ is Servant. The Church as Christ's body, the instrument of his purpose, continues his apostolic and priestly ministry to the world. Jesus himself conceived of his mission in terms of service: 'the Son of Man came not to be deaconed

---

[1] Cf. Sanday and Headlam, *Romans* (ICC), 353.

unto, but to deacon' (Mark 10.45); 'I am in the midst of you as ὁ διακονῶν' (Luke 22.27). We have seen reason to think that Jesus used his self-designation of 'Son of Man' in the sense of the Isaianic conception of the Servant of Yahweh, and there can be no doubt that his characterization of himself as ὁ διακονῶν is derived, humanly speaking, from the Servant Songs (Isa. 42.1-4; 49.1-6; 50.4-9 and esp. 52.13-53.12). In these passages the Servant of the Lord[1] fulfils a divine mission to the world, not merely to Israel: 'I will also give thee for a light to the Gentiles, that thou mayest be my salvation unto the end of the earth' (Isa. 49.6). This mission is accomplished through suffering vicariously borne for the sins of others; and the suffering Servant is then raised up and vindicated by God, so that those who rejected him are constrained to recognize that he has suffered for their sins and for their salvation. Jesus taught his disciples quite specifically that they also were to be servants; in the story of the Foot Washing (John 13.1-11), which vividly illustrates the truth that Jesus is ὁ διακονῶν, he says to his disciples: 'If I then, the κύριος and the rabbi, have washed your feet, ye also ought to wash one another's feet. For I have given you an example, that ye also should do as I have done to you' (John 13.14f.). He contrasts the overbearing pride of the great ones of the secular order with the humility of the leaders in his own community: 'Whosoever would become great among you shall be your διάκονος, and whosoever would be first among you shall be δοῦλος of all' (Mark 10.43f.).

It is not surprising therefore that the conception of Christian disciples as *ministers, servants*, should have received great emphasis in the early Church, or that baptism into the Church should have been regarded as an ordination to the ministry of the Church (I Cor. 12.13 in its context). There are no 'lay' members of the Church who are without a ministry in it; the Church is a ministerial priesthood of the laity or people of God. We must not allow the development of a special order of διάκονοι to obscure the truth that the whole community and every individual member of it were a ministry which participated in the one ministry of Christ. There are 'diversities of ministrations' (διαιρέσεις διακονιῶν) in the Church, but all are performed to and through 'the same Lord' (I Cor. 12.5). Every member of the Church receives his own φανέρωσις τοῦ Πνεύματος (12.7) to enable him to perform his own particular God-given ministry: the Holy Spirit of God distributes his various χαρίσματα 'as he will' (12.11). The whole passage I Cor. 12.4-30

---

[1] Heb.: '*ebed Yahweh*, rendered by the Greek translators by παῖς, which properly means 'son', but secondarily 'servant'. They would doubtless avoid δοῦλος because a δοῦλος is a born slave. Hence the παῖς Θεοῦ of Acts 3.13, 26; 4.27, 30; cf. Matt. 12.18. In Phil. 2.7 St Paul possibly has Isa. 53 in mind when he says that Christ took the form of a δοῦλος. Jesus is never called δοῦλος in NT.

makes it very clear that διακονία is not a function merely of certain 'orders' in the Church, but that every layman has his part in the total ministry of the body of Christ, which corporately through the empowering of the Spirit constitutes an organic ministry that renders service (whether λειτουργία or δουλεία) to God. All Christian ministry is the service of God and of Christ; even the daily toil of a household slave (δοῦλος or οἰκέτης) is service rendered to the Κύριος in heaven and not merely to an earthly κύριος (Eph. 6.5-7). The Church's ministry to the starving, the refugees, the necessitous, the sick or the imprisoned is service rendered unto Christ (Matt. 25.35-45; cf. Mark 9.37).

The primary meaning of διακονεῖν, like the Latin *ministrare*, is 'to wait upon', especially 'to wait at table' (cf. Luke 17.8; Acts 6.2). It indicates a menial office; and we should always remember that διακονία (Lat. *ministerium*) is the office of a slave. Christ is pre-eminently the Servant of God, and Christians are servants of the Servant of God. In the OT, however, 'servant of God' was an honourable title (e.g. Gen. 26.24, Abraham; Ex. 14.31, Moses; II Sam. 3.18, David; etc.), and similarly in the NT St Paul delights to call himself δοῦλος Χριστοῦ (Phil. 1.1; cf. Rev. 1.1), and Christians are called δοῦλοι τοῦ Θεοῦ (Rev. 7.3; cf. Rom. 6.22; I Cor. 7.22; I Pet. 2.16). Christ is κύριος in the sense of the 'master' or 'owner' of his slaves (Eph. 6.6, 9; John 13.13), as well as in the sense of cultic 'Lord'. The use of δοῦλος in this connection is significant because it rules out any suggestion of merit or reward in the 'work' of Christians; the δοῦλος is one who by definition receives no wages (contrast μίσθιος, a hired worker, Mark 1.20; Matt. 20.1-16; Luke 15.17, 19). Christians are not justified by their διακονία, however strenuous or successful it may be. Jesus himself actually uses the κύριος—δοῦλος metaphor to make this truth quite clear: 'Who is there of you having a δοῦλος ploughing . . . when he is come in from the field . . . that will not say unto him, Make ready . . . and serve (διακονεῖν) me. . . ? Doth he thank the δοῦλος because he did all the things that were commanded? Even so ye also, when you have done all the things that were commanded you, say, We are unprofitable δοῦλοι: we have done that which it was our duty to do' (Luke 17.7-10). All our διακονία must be inspired by gratitude for the free mercy and gift of God; it is not the earning of a reward but the utterly inadequate acknowledgment of a debt that can never be paid. It is our privilege that we are made συνεργοὶ Θεοῦ (I Cor. 3.9; cf. III John 8).

But this participation in the διακονία of Christ himself necessarily involves suffering: 'A δοῦλος is not greater than his κύριος. If they persecuted me, they will also persecute you' (John 15.20). 'I rejoice in my sufferings for your sake, and fill up on my part that which is lacking of the afflictions of Christ in my flesh for his body's sake, which is the Church, whereof I was made a διάκονος (Col. 1.24f.); cf. Phil. 3.10, ἡ κοινωνία τῶν παθημάτων αὐτοῦ; Gal. 6.17, 'I bear branded (i.e. like a δοῦλος) on my body the marks of Jesus'; II Cor. 4.10, etc. Jesus himself had taught that discipleship involved taking up one's cross (Mark 8.34; cf. Luke 9.57f.). The privilege of Christians is that of suffering with their Master, and this suffering with Christ is the means by which the knowledge of Christ is deepened and assured. St John, as so often, puts the truth in his own distinctive way: 'No longer do I call you δοῦλοι, for the δοῦλος knoweth not what his κύριος doeth: but I have called you φίλοι' (John 15.15). The way of obedience is the means to the intimate, personal knowledge of God in Christ, which is the reward of discipleship; but obedience, though it is necessarily the first word in the vocabulary of discipleship, is not the last word. Friendship (φιλία),[1] or as the conception is more usually expressed, ἀγάπη, is the final word in the dialogue between God and man, because God's ultimate word to mankind is Christ.

Closely connected with the concept of διακονία is the new and distinctively Christian virtue of humility or lowliness (ταπεινοφροσύνη); cf. Acts 20.19, δουλεύων τῷ Κυρίῳ μετὰ ταπεινοφροσύνης; Eph. 4.2; Phil. 2.3; Col. 3.12; I Pet. 5.5. We might define humility as the quality of mind and heart which makes a man content with the privilege of serving another; it is the antithesis of pride and self-exaltation. The ancient world had hardly recognized humility as a virtue before the Christian ethic was taught; Josephus and Epictetus had used ταπεινοφροσύνη, but only in a bad sense as denoting pusillanimity.[2] In Eph. 4.2 and Col. 3.12 humility is associated with meekness (πραΰτης), a conjunction of virtues which sends us at once back to Jesus's own description of himself: 'I am meek and lowly in heart' (πραΰς εἰμι καὶ ταπεινὸς τῇ καρδίᾳ) (Matt. 11.29; cf. 21.5), and to his Beatitude upon the meek (οἱ πραεῖς) (Matt. 5.5; cf. Ps. 37.11). It was Jesus who taught that humility was a characteristic of the members of the divine realm: 'Whosoever shall humble himself (ταπεινώσει ἑαυτόν) as this little child, the same is the greater in the kingdom of heaven' (Matt. 18.4): 'He that is greater among you shall be your διάκονος. And whosoever shall exalt himself shall be humbled; and whosoever shall humble himself shall be exalted' (Matt. 23.11f.). In illustration of the value of humility he told the vivid parables of the Scramble for the

---

[1] The word φιλία in fact occurs in NT only at James 4.4: ἡ φιλία τοῦ κόσμου ἔχθρα τοῦ Θεοῦ ἐστιν. Perhaps φίλοι became a technical term for Christians (cf. III John 14; John 11.11). In later Judaism Abraham was called φίλος Θεοῦ (James 2.23; II Chron. 20.7; Isa. 41.8), and in Wisd. 7.27 Wisdom is said to make 'holy souls' φίλοι Θεοῦ.

[2] The word is not found in LXX.

Chief Seats at the Marriage Feast (Luke 14.7-11) and of the Pharisee and the Publican (Luke 18.9-14).

JESUS AND THE CHURCH

It is not long since it was widely held that Jesus himself had no intention at all of founding a Church. The reason given (e.g. by A. Schweitzer) was that he expected the parousia to follow immediately upon his death. Eschatology and a doctrine of the Church were incompatible. Today we see clearly that the biblical eschatology always involved a doctrine of the Church as the Messianic community of the last times, the gathering together by the Shepherd-Messiah of the scattered, elect people of God, the corporate Son of Man which constitutes the *persona* of the Christ, or the body of which he is the Head. The NT indicates clearly enough that Jesus conceived of his divinely appointed mission as that of creating the Church, the new people of God, and that from the beginning he intended that there should be a definite ministry within it, that is, an appointed order of ministers who should serve it in the capacity of 'shepherd-rulers': the 'greater' were to be the servants (διάκονοι) of all.

In two passages only in the Gospels is Jesus recorded as having used the term ἐκκλησία (or its Aramaic equivalent, whatever that might be). One of them is easily dealt with, for it raises no difficulty: 'If he refuse to hear them (i.e. the two or three witnesses), tell it to the ἐκκλησία, and if he refuse to hear the ἐκκλησία also, let him be unto thee as the Gentile and the publican' (Matt. 18.17). The difficulty which this passage raises does not concern the word ἐκκλησία, but the phrase 'Gentile and publican': did Jesus really use the term 'Gentile' in such a disparaging way, as the Jews did, and did the 'friend of publicans' refer to them in the harsh tones of the rabbis? We may reasonably conjecture that the verse as it stands is coloured by the Jewish-Christian environment in which this part of the Matthaean tradition of the words of the Lord was developed. But if Jesus said anything of this kind at all, about reporting an offender to the ἐκκλησία, he meant by whatever term he may have used nothing more than the local congregation (so RV mg.), a particular gathering of his followers. The word therefore is untechnical and carries no great significance for the doctrine of the Church.

The other passage is Matt. 16.18, which contains part of the Lord's reply to St Peter's confession of his Messiahship: σὺ εἶ Πέτρος, καὶ ἐπὶ ταύτῃ τῇ πέτρᾳ οἰκοδομήσω μου τὴν ἐκκλησίαν. Recent scholarship no longer rejects the saying out of hand.[1] The integrity of the text cannot

---

[1] Cf. esp. K. L. Schmidt, *TWNT*, ET, *The Church*, 35-50; O. Cullmann, *Peter: Disciple, Apostle, Martyr*, ET, 1953, 158-212.

be impugned; the passage is cited from Justin Martyr onwards. The fact that Matt. alone contains the passage is no argument against it, for the verses 16.17-19 are thoroughly Semitic in character and must have originated in the early Palestinian community. Nor is the fact very significant that we do not know what Aramaic word for ἐκκλησία Jesus might have used; K. L. Schmidt suggests *kenishta'*, which is used both for ἐκκλησία and συναγωγή in Syriac versions—a language closely akin to the Palestinian Aramaic of the time of our Lord. The saying, if genuine, indicates that Jesus thought that the future community of his disciples was going to become the true ἐκκλησία Θεοῦ instead of the old Israel; we may note the future tense, οἰκοδομήσω. The conception is entirely congruous with what we have already on other grounds dis-covered to be Jesus's view of his own person and mission: the true ἐκκλησία Θεοῦ would come into existence when he, the Son-of-Man-Servant-Messiah, had ratified the new covenant in his own blood. Jesus is saying that St Peter will be the foundation-stone of the spiritual house (cf. I Pet. 2.5) which through the making of a new covenant was to take the place of the old Israel and its Temple, an idea which has been preserved in another form in the Fourth Gospel (John 2.19-21; cf. 4.20-24).

The Gospel tradition contains sufficient evidence that Jesus addressed a special charge to St Peter and gave to him a special commission. In Matt. 16.17-19 Jesus declares him to be the rock on which the Church will be built, and built so securely that the demonic powers ('gates of Hades') will not prevail against it. The keys of the Kingdom of heaven, representing the power to bind and loose in heaven as well as in the Church on earth, are promised to St Peter, though this power of bind-ing in heaven is later promised to all the disciples (Matt. 18.18; cf. John 20.23).[1] In Luke 22.28-34, a solemn saying of Christ before his passion, Jesus covenants (διατίθεμαι) the βασιλεία, which his Father had coven-anted to him, to his disciples, making them participants of his royal table and viceregents on his behalf in the New Israel; Peter is singled out, as if to receive some kind of pastoral primacy: 'Simon, Simon, behold, Satan obtained thee for the asking, that he might sift thee as wheat: but I made supplication for thee, that thy faith fail not: and do thou, when once thou hast turned again, stablish (στηρίζειν) thy brethren.' This passage is peculiar to St Luke, though Matthew gives the saying about sitting on thrones judging the twelve tribes of Israel in another context (Matt. 19.28). In the appendix to the Fourth Gospel a special commission is given to St Peter to feed the flock of Christ John 21.15-17) and a veiled prophecy is put into the mouth of Jesus

[1] See *infra*, 317-9.

concerning Peter's death as a martyr (21.18f.). It would seem, therefore, that the Gospel tradition attests a certain primacy of St Peter in the apostolic group to which Jesus committed the pastoral oversight of his flock. At least there is no need whatever to doubt the authenticity of the word of the Lord concerning Peter as the rock upon which he would build his Church. Cullmann conjectures that the rock-saying, which St Matthew has interpolated into the Marcan narrative of Peter's Confession, properly belongs to the passion sayings of the Lord and is of the same cycle of tradition as the Lucan 'Stablish thy brethren'.[1] The suggestion is plausible: Jesus, about to offer his life-blood for the making of a new covenant on behalf of the Israel that he has come to gather, declares that he will build his new people of God upon St Peter as the foundation-rock.

It should be noted that Jesus says he will build his Church, not on the Messiahship that Peter confessed, not on the faith that Peter held, not on the revelation that Peter received (Matt. 16.17), but quite simply on St Peter himself. Elsewhere in the NT the apostles and prophets are collectively said to be the foundation upon which is built the household of God, and Christ is the corner-stone (Eph. 2.20; cf. I Pet. 2.6f.; Rev. 21.14); or again in another place Christ is declared to be the only foundation of the Church (I Cor. 3.11; cf. Isa. 28.16). But here St Peter is declared by Jesus to be the foundation-rock. He explains the title Πέτρος by saying that his ἐκκλησία was to be built upon this πέτρα. In the Greek πέτρος (masc.) means a 'stone' and πέτρα (fem.) means a rock (cf. Rom. 9.33; I Cor. 10.4; I Pet. 2.8); in Aramaic the word would be the same in each case: 'You are *Kepha*' and upon this *kepha*' I will build my Church.'[2] The words of Jesus are best understood as a prophecy, and one which came true: upon Simon Peter and his labours the existence of the Church in its early days seems to have quite literally depended, if the matter is viewed from a purely human point of view. Had Peter failed, there would have been no Church. But to say 'had Peter failed' takes no account of the operation of the divine election. St Peter perfectly illustrates the NT teaching concerning election.[3] Jesus knows Peter better than he knows himself and tells him what he will do in the crisis that has overtaken him. Peter is free to do otherwise, but he does not in fact do otherwise; he denies his Master, as Jesus predicted. Yet that he knows himself to have been free, though in a sense predetermined by his own character, is evidenced by his repentance: 'When he thought thereon, he wept' (Mark 14.72). Jesus prophesied that Peter, despite his weakness and denial, would be the strong and sure foundation for the Church of the New Covenant.

---

[1] *Op. cit.*, 182f. [2] Cullmann, *op. cit.*, 185. [3] See K. L. Schmidt, *op. cit.*, 44.

That Peter was regarded as the Chief Pastor of the early Church is attested by John 21.15-17, which by the time it was written was a prophecy after the event, although there is no reason to suppose that the verses do not preserve a genuinely historical tradition of the Lord's commissioning of St Peter. Christ's choice of Peter as the foundation-stone of his Church is as mysterious and as real as God's election of Israel: Peter is chosen, is disobedient, but remains the chosen instrument of God's will; despite his failings and failures he fulfils the purpose for which he and his fellow-witnesses were 'chosen before of God' (Acts 10.41). It should perhaps be added, in view of later developments in the history of the Church, that neither Matt. 16.17-19 nor any other part of the NT contains a hint of any 'successors' of St Peter. Indeed, in Matt. 16.18 St Peter is assigned a unique position in the divine economy of salvation; the entire significance of the saying of Jesus depends upon the once-only character of a foundation-stone. The stones that are laid upon it are not foundation-stones at all. Nothing is said in John 21.15-17 about any successor of St Peter, although at the time the words were written the question would have been a real one, if the primitive Church had thought in terms of a literal succession in the primacy. The significance of St Peter in the NT is determined by his own unique relationship to his Lord and by the part which he played in history as the foundation-stone of the new building by which Judaism and its Temple were now replaced in the saving purpose of God.

We must conclude that Jesus intended to 'found' the Church. The expression 'the Founder of the Church' (to say nothing of 'the Founder of Christianity'!) is inadequate in its modern connotation to express the full NT truth about the relation of Jesus to his Church. To modern ears it suggests merely the setting up of an association of like-minded people who are eager to promote a good cause, as one might 'found' a charitable organization or a religious society; the metaphor of *building* in its biblical sense has almost entirely disappeared from the phrase. Christ is not so much the 'Founder' of the Church as he *is* himself the Church, since the Church is not a company of like-minded people, but the body of those who have been incorporated into the *persona* of Christ, *totus Christus*, the head and the members. Thus, the future tense (οἰκοδομήσω) used by the historical Jesus is significant: there could be no Church of the New Covenant until Christ had died and was risen. The Church was not constituted by a number of admiring disciples who had gathered around the personality of the historical Jesus (cf. II Cor. 5.16); it was not the *ḥaburah* of an individual rabbi, even if that rabbi was Jesus Messiah. The Church came into being with the pouring out of the Holy Spirit by the risen and ascended Lord upon the disciples who awaited the fulfilment of his promise (Mark 9.1; John 20.22; Acts 1.8; 2.1-4). This is another way of saying that the Church is the resurrection-body of Jesus Christ: 'even though we have known Christ after the flesh, yet now we know him so no more. If any man be in Christ, there is a new creation' (II Cor. 5.16f.).

14

MINISTRIES WITHIN THE CHURCH

THE whole Church constitutes an apostolic and priestly ministry, in which every individual member has a share. But within the total ministry of the Church in NT times there was a variety of 'ministrations' and 'operations' (ἐνεργήματα, found only at I Cor. 12.6, 10), for which the individual ministrants were empowered by appropriate endowments of the Holy Spirit (I Cor. 12.4-11). Unfortunately we can obtain from the NT only a very indistinct picture of these ministries and operations. We cannot even tell which of them were regarded as distinct 'orders' within the Church and which were only functions or offices. Nothing could more pointedly illustrate the casual nature of the NT literature; not even the Acts of the Apostles gives us a coherent account of the ministry of the early Church. St Luke, like the writers of the Epistles, mentions bishops, presbyters, prophets, and so on, and assumes that his readers will know precisely what is meant. Unfortunately for the most part we can only guess. Even if all the denominations of the World Council of Churches agreed tomorrow to set up a common ministry on the NT pattern, their scholars would not be able to tell them what that pattern was. The true or 'apostolic' ministry of the Church cannot be determined archaeologically. It is hardly surprising that the post-Reformation sectarians, who sought to reconstruct the ministry of the primitive Church from the evidence of the NT, could not agree amongst themselves about how that ministry was constituted. They laboured under the disadvantage of living some centuries before the revolution in historical method, which was the achievement of the nineteenth century, and they consequently could have no conception of the relation of the NT documents to the living growth of the primitive Christian communities. Today we know that the NT Scriptures were not given to us as divinely inspired blueprints of ecclesiastical polity, upon which every detail of church organization must be modelled. The NT writings must be understood historically, that is, in relation to a development which emerges into clearer daylight in the time of St Clement of Rome or St Ignatius of Antioch: the living tradition of developing church order is 'inspired' by the Holy Spirit as well as the writings that were later collected in the NT canon. The writings are to be interpreted by the organic development of the Church's life, not received as divine oracles that have miraculously dropped down from heaven, to be interpreted unhistorically without any reference to the Church as it came to exist in the second century. The question that should be asked about any particular branch of the Church Catholic, or any particular denomination or Christian sect, is not whether it conforms archaeologically to an assumed NT pattern of ministry, but whether it manifests the threefold character of the NT church—its apostolic, priestly and ministerial character. It should be asked in what ways ἐπισκοπή, ἱερωσύνη and διακονία, which we have seen to be essential forms of the life of the apostolic Church, are manifested or obscured both in the total laity and in the particular ministerial organization. This is the only rational question to ask, in view of the fact that, as we shall see, it is impossible to draw a picture of the ministries within the apostolic Church, save in the most general terms. The NT evidence is at many points so embarrassingly ambiguous that it is almost impossible to avoid the danger of interpreting it in terms of the particular church polity which we happen to admire. But if we ask about the manifestation of ἐπισκοπή, ἱερωσύνη and διακονία in our church life and order, none of the churches or denominations of the world Christian community today would find occasion for complacency or for pointing to the mote in their brother's eye.

'THE TWELVE'

We begin with the twelve disciples of the historical Jesus, rather than with 'the apostles' as such, because several NT passages suggest that 'the apostles' were a wider company than the original 'disciples'. 'The disciples' (οἱ μαθηταί) are mentioned several times by St Mark before he tells how Jesus 'made twelve (ἐποίησε δώδεκα), that they might be with him, and that he might send (ἀποστέλλῃ) them to preach (the εὐαγγέλιον), and to have authority to cast out demons' (Mark 3.14f.). The clause which some MSS. insert after 'he made twelve', viz. 'whom also he named apostles', cannot be regarded as original and is transferred to the margin by RV. The parallel Lucan text runs, 'He called his disciples, and he chose from them twelve, whom also he named apostles' (Luke 6.13). St Matthew has no account of the choice of the Twelve; they simply appear as an existing group at 10.1. St Mark's setting for the solemn calling of the Twelve—the great company from all over Palestine (3.7f.), the confession of Christ's Sonship by the unclean spirits, the high mountain—makes it clear that a new Israel is being fashioned on a new Sinai, a truth which is further underlined by the choice of *twelve*. The apostles are, as it were, the twelve patriarchs of the new people of God.[1] 'Ye shall sit upon twelve thrones, judging the twelve tribes of Israel' (Matt. 19.28; cf. Luke 22.30). There is no reason whatever to doubt that Jesus did in fact appoint twelve special disciples out of the wider circle of his followers, in order to emphasize the truth of his teaching that he was come to build a new house of Israel, a new ἐκκλησία Θεοῦ. Moreover, it is improbable, as some have suggested, that his appointment of the Twelve was intended to be merely temporary, as though they were 'apostled' only for the duration of the mission recorded in Mark 6.7-13, Matt. 10.1-15 and Luke 9.1-6.[2] It is true that St Mark and St Matthew each use ἀπόστολος only once, and that each uses it only in connection with the mission of the Twelve (Mark 6.30; Matt. 10.2; cf. Luke 9.10); but there is no reason to suppose that they did not share the general belief of the NT Church that the Lord had appointed twelve apostles.[3] Indeed, Matthew's casual introduction of the group with the phrase 'the twelve apostles' (10.2) suggests that he expected all his readers to understand what he meant. There are, however, certain passages in the Gospels which represent Christ as giving a solemn and continuing commission to the twelve disciples. Perhaps the most remarkable of these is the Lucan account of the Last Supper and of the words spoken by our Lord on the

[1] It is quite probable that the early Church speculated about which apostle represented which tribe of Israel (or patriarch), e.g. Simon Peter for Simeon, and so on. Dr Farrer has drawn attention to the remarkable fact that, as in the OT there are really twelve tribes of Israel plus Levi, the priest-tribe, so in St Mark's Gospel there are twelve apostles plus Levi, who is 'called' as Peter and Andrew, James and John have been called (Mark 2.13f.), but who is not enumerated as one of the twelve (3.16-19). St Paul, as one 'born out of due time' (I Cor. 15.8), would fit into this scheme as the Benjamin of the New Israel (cf. Rom. 11.1; Phil. 3.5). See Austin Farrer, *A Study in St Mark*, esp. Chap. XIV. The title 'the Twelve' has become a technical term in the Gospels, where it occurs more than a score of times, ten of them in Mark.

[2] St Luke (alone of the evangelists) knows of a mission of the Seventy, a symbolic number (Gen. 10) representing all the nations of the earth (Luke 10.1-20). Mark is not thinking of a mission to Jews only: the number twelve is representative for him of the fulness of the New Israel, which is drawn from all the nations. But Matthew records a tradition which insists that the mission of Jesus is to Israel only (Matt. 10.5f.). St Luke is naturally anxious to counteract the Jewish-Christian interpretation of the episode of the sending out of the Twelve, which was a symbolic or prophetic gesture on the part of the Lord. He does this by reporting a mission of the Seventy, about whom nothing further is heard after they have reported their success (Luke 10.17-20). None of the three Synoptists says anything at all about the success or failure of the mission of the Twelve: that was not significant—its significance lies solely in the fact that it was undertaken as a 'prophetic sign' (in the OT sense) that the Messianic reign of God was at hand. St Luke does not call the Seventy ἀπόστολοι, but he uses the verb ἀποστέλλειν in connection with their mission at 10.1 and 10.3 (cf. also 10.16).

[3] Cf. Luke 6.13; 9.10; 17.5; 22.14; 24.10. The expression 'the apostles' has become synonymous with 'the disciples', but it is still fluid in its meaning for St Luke, who can use it of the OT prophets (11.49, προφήτας καὶ ἀποστόλους, instead of the 'prophets and wise men and scribes' of Matt. 23.34).

occasion of it (Luke 22.14-38). The whole passage should be studied as a unity, for it combines the making of the New Covenant with the institution of the Eucharist in the Church (the drinking of the fruit of the vine in the days of God's βασιλεία, 22.18) and with the commissioning of the apostles in respect of ἐπισκοπή, ἱερωσύνη and διακονία. Critics of the Gospels have for so long been absorbed with the question about the sources from which St Luke derived the components of his narrative that they have almost forgotten to ask what truth he intended to teach by his somewhat bold and novel rearrangement of the traditional material in this form.

What we have in the Lucan story of the Last Supper is nothing less than an account of the ordination of the apostolic ministry of the Church in a eucharistic setting, doubtless reflecting the custom of the primitive Church of performing the ceremony of ordination during the liturgical worship of the congregation. Of course, St Luke knew well enough that the actual endowing of the apostles with 'power from on high' did not and could not take place until after the resurrection and ascension of Christ (Luke 24.49; Acts 1.5, 8), but he nevertheless presents the scene of the Last Supper, when 'the hour was come and Jesus was sat down and the apostles with him' (Luke 22.14), as the solemn ritual of ordination, the speaking by the Lord of the words of commission to his chosen apostles, just as the words over the bread and the cup constitute the ritual of his own self-oblation which is to follow on Calvary. The words which Jesus now speaks constitute the rite of the ordination of the royal priesthood of the New Israel. At this solemn covenant-making on behalf of the new people of God's possession Jesus covenants to his apostles βασιλεία—not 'a kingdom' (RV), but 'royal authority' or 'kingly rule'. The image of the giving of the βασιλεία to the people of the saints of the Most High (cf. Luke 12.32) is, of course, drawn from Dan. 7.14, 27, and is charged with biblical meaning;[1] here the fulfilment of Daniel's prophecy is represented as about to take place in the handing over of βασιλεία to the apostles of the new ἐκκλησία Θεοῦ. That authority within and over the ἐκκλησία itself is intended is proved by the words, known also to St Matthew (Matt. 19.28), 'Ye shall sit on thrones judging the twelve tribes of Israel' (Luke 22.30). It is, of course, the new Israel of God which is meant. That is to say, pastoral oversight and rule (ἐπισκοπή as the Church later understood it) is committed to the apostles. The symbolism of the θρόνοι is quite simply that which in later ages of the Church was developed in the symbol of the bishop's throne (*cathedra*), which was at once the sign of his authority as teacher

---

[1] See *supra*, 87.

and as ruler; it is the chair both of the learned doctor and of the magistrate.

The Lucan text (only) says also that the apostles are appointed to their kingly rule in order that (ἵνα) they might eat and drink at Christ's table in his βασιλεία (22.30). The idea of the Messianic banquet was, of course, familiar both in Judaism and in the teaching of Jesus (Matt. 8.11; Luke 13.29: 14.15; 22.18); but in this context we must understand the Church's eschatological anticipation of the Messianic banquet in the weekly Eucharist. 'The table of the Lord' had a particular meaning for primitive Christianity (cf. I Cor. 10.21), and it inevitably carried with it the suggestion of a priesthood that is fed from the table or altar which it serves (I Cor. 9.13; 10.16-21; Heb. 13.10; cf. Lev. 6.16, 26; 7.6, etc.; Num. 5.9f.; 18.8-20; Deut. 18.1; Ecclus. 45.21). The appointment of places at the table of the Lord means that Christ is consecrating a new priesthood of those who will share in his ἱερωσύνη and who will offer through his priesthood the Church's oblations. Christ is thus represented as consecrating the apostles as the ministers of the eucharistic feast, at which he himself will be present (Luke 22.18), those who are to break the bread and pour the wine, the priests of the table that is set up in his βασιλεία, of which the Church on earth is the eschatological sign. They are the λειτουργοί of the new royal priesthood which is formed by the whole ἐκκλησία Θεοῦ. Lastly in this connection it should be noted that great emphasis is placed in this passage upon διακονία, in the sense of self-effacing, humble, even menial, service, after the model of Christ himself, ὁ διακονῶν (Luke 22.24-27); it would seem that St Luke has almost gone out of his way to bring into this context of the Last Supper-Ordination elements which in Matthew and Mark are found in quite different contexts (Mark 9.34; 10.42f.; Matt. 18.1-5; 20.25-27). It is as though he is determined to stress διακονία as an essential character of the apostolic ministry.

It is, then, difficult to doubt that in this whole passage (Luke 22.14-38) St Luke is setting forth in his own individual style the significance of Jesus's appointment of the apostolic ministry to the offices of ἐπισκοπή, ἱερωσύνη and διακονία within the Church. It is St Luke's method to present his own stylized sketch of history in order to bring out its underlying truth; we have seen how he has done this in respect of his 'Elijah' typology and of his Pentecost typology; and we need not be surprised to find him here also rearranging and re-presenting the traditional Gospel material in order to communicate his own personal insight into the meaning of 'those matters which have been fulfilled among us'. If to anyone today this interpretation of Luke 22.14-38 seems far-fetched or artificial, let him ask himself what else these verses could mean in the light of the developing eucharistic worship and episcopal-presbyteral church-order of the later years of the first century, when St Luke was meditating deeply upon the significance of the Gospel tradition in the light of the expansion of the faith from its beginnings as a Jewish sect in Jerusalem to its existence as the Empire-wide community of the disciples of the Way. It should not surprise us that St Luke should seek for the origins of the remarkable consummation of 'all that Jesus began' (Acts 1.1) in the commission given by the Lord to his twelve original disciples, and that he should find in the tradition of the Lord's words the clue to the astonishing growth of the ecumenical Church of which he had made himself the historian. We may notice that his 'ordination-charge', if so we may consider Luke 22.24-38, includes a reference to the leading part to be played by St Peter in 'stablishing' his brethren (22.32), and it concludes with a reference to an implied 'sending forth' (cf. the use of the verb ἀποστέλλειν in 22.35) which was to be a sterner and more strenuous campaign than the earlier mission of the Twelve had been.

THE POWER OF THE KEYS

St Matthew's Gospel also contains a commissioning by Jesus of his disciples, but it takes a form quite different from St Luke's. It is given in two contexts, first to St Peter alone, then to the disciples in general. In Matt. 16.19 Jesus says to St Peter, 'I will give unto thee the keys of the Kingdom of Heaven, and whatsoever thou shalt bind on earth shall be bound in heaven, and whatsoever thou shalt loose on earth shall be loosed in heaven.' In Matt. 18.18 the same commission, but without mention of the keys, is addressed by Jesus to the disciples in general (cf. 18.1). The omission of the reference to the keys in the second instance is probably unimportant, because 'the keys of the Kingdom of Heaven' is only a poetic way of saying the same thing as is said by the words about binding and loosing.

The metaphor of the keys which open and shut the gates of heaven is readily understandable. The Jewish rabbis who interpreted the Torah were considered to possess the keys of the heavenly doors; but Jesus is recorded as speaking strong words about their stewardship of them: 'Woe unto you, scribes and Pharisees, hypocrites! because ye shut the Kingdom of Heaven against men: for ye enter not in yourselves, neither suffer ye them that are entering in to enter' (Matt. 23.13). Not Torah but Christ is the key of heaven: so we read in Rev. 3.7 that Christ is 'he that openeth, and none shall shut, and that shutteth, and none openeth', and also that Christ has 'the key of David' (cf. Rev. 1.18, 'I have the keys of Death and of Hades'). The expression 'the key of

David' is a reference to Isa. 22.22, where Yahweh lays the key of the house of David upon the shoulder of Eliakim the priest, 'and he shall open, and none shall shut; and he shall shut and none shall open.' The bestowal of the keys, whether those of the Davidic royal house to Eliakim or those of the Kingdom of Heaven to St Peter, means the handing over of the responsibility of stewardship, authority over the household, and the right to admit to it or to exclude from it. Christ is committing to St Peter representatively, i.e. to the Church, the power to act in his name, the dread responsibility of inclusion in or exclusion from the eschatological realities of the realm of salvation ('heaven'). This is what is involved in the saying about binding and loosing. Admission to or exclusion from the ἐκκλησία Χριστοῦ upon earth carries with it admission to or exclusion from the heavenly realm of salvation.

'Binding' and 'loosing' in rabbinic usage mean in the first place to prohibit or to allow something; then to impose penalties or excommunication upon someone or to acquit him.[1] In their Christian context, in view of the great stress laid upon the forgiveness of sins, their meaning will chiefly be that of 'retaining' or forgiving sins. To enter the βασιλεία τοῦ Θεοῦ means to be forgiven, and *vice versa*. Thus the Fourth Evangelist rightly interprets the Gospel tradition when he places in the mouth of the Risen Lord words which are virtually a paraphrase of the commissioning of the disciples in Matt. 18.18: 'Whosesoever sins ye forgive, they are forgiven unto them; whosesoever sins ye retain, they are retained' (John 20.23). The Johannine version of the words occurs in the narrative of the appearance of the Risen Lord in the evening of the day of resurrection-ascension, when he breathes on 'the disciples' and imparts the promised Holy Spirit, commissioning them to exercise his own power of forgiving and retaining sins, with all that this implies. This episode constitutes the Johannine account of the ordination of the apostolic ministry of the Church, but as at Matt. 18.18 it is not possible to determine whether the ministerial power is being conferred upon the whole Church or upon a particular group within it, vaguely called 'the disciples' and probably to be identified with the Twelve.[2] This question cannot be answered by considering these passages by themselves; but in the light of developments in the Church in the days when St Matthew's and St John's Gospels were written, it would seem more probable that the Evangelists themselves would understand the ordination of a specific order of ministry within the Church. Such an order would act representatively on behalf of the whole Church, exercising the corporate

---

[1] See further O. Cullmann, *Peter, op. cit.*, 204f.; Strack-Bill., I, 738-47.

[2] The Fourth Evangelist never speaks of 'the apostles'; 'the Twelve' occurs at 6.67-71; 20.24.

ἐπισκοπή of the body of Christ, but it would act also as the ministerial agent of the Risen Lord himself, as head of the body, deriving its authority and power from him rather than from the Church as such.

We may conclude that Jesus chose the symbolic number of twelve disciples as the nucleus of his new people of God, and that he not only appointed them to assist in his own Galilean ministry of preaching and exorcism, but also he commissioned ('apostled') them to exercise his own ministry of ruling, feeding and serving the flock of God after his earthly task was done. Indeed, the ordination of the apostolic ministry did not and could not take place until after the resurrection-ascension and the gift of the Holy Spirit. The NT is emphatic that such an ordination of the Twelve took place after Christ's resurrection, though the different accounts of this ordination in Holy Spirit, as they appear in different NT books, are widely divergent as to the manner of it (Matt. 28.18-20; Mark 16.15-18; Luke 24.48f. with Acts 2.1-4; John 20.19-23). We cannot now from these records reconstruct an 'historical' account of 'what happened', and it does not in the least matter that we cannot do so. Each of the writers of the NT accounts of the ordination of the apostolic ministry has 'stylized' the matter according to his own theological understanding of the significance of the truth that Christ set up on earth an apostolic ministry; and the revelation of the truth of the ministry of the Church has nothing to do with literalistic historicizing or archaeological reconstruction.

THE APOSTLES

By the end of the NT period usage had crystallized the word 'apostles' to mean 'the twelve apostles' (as in Matt. 10.2),[1] or the twelve apostles and St Paul. But the word is used in a wider sense than this in the NT generally, and it is virtually impossible to find a *rationale* for the word which will cover all cases. It is clearly a matter of great honour to be called an apostle, as the existence of ψευδαπόστολοι (a *hapax* in all literature), 'fashioning themselves into ἀπόστολοι Χριστοῦ' (II Cor. 11.13; cf. also Rev. 2.2), will testify. It is doubtless significant that the title is withheld from certain leading personalities in the Church, such as Apollos (I Cor. 3.5), Timothy, for whom other titles are found (II Cor. 1.1; Phil. 1.1; Col. 1.1; I Thess. 3.2; Philemon 1; I Tim. 1.2; II Tim. 1.2), and Titus (Titus 1.4). The refusal of the title to Titus is all

---

[1] Cf. Rev. 21.14, 'the twelve apostles of the Lamb', whose names are written on the foundations of the heavenly Jerusalem (cf. Eph. 2.20); we are not told that each apostle represents one of the twelve gates, on which are written the names of the twelve tribes of Israel, but the idea of the 'keys' does not seem far away. Cf. also the first footnote on p. 314 *supra*.

the more pointed when in II Cor. 8.16-24 St Paul is trying to commend Titus to the Corinthians in every way he can think of; cf. esp. v. 23: 'Whether (any enquire) about Titus, (he is) my partner and my fellow-worker to you-ward; or our brethren, (they are) ἀπόστολοι of the churches, the glory of Christ.' Obviously in the NT period the title of apostle was not bestowed lightly. The *Didache* indicates that at a later period itinerant Christian evangelists were called apostles, but there is no such usage in the NT.

There is perhaps one class of people called ἀποστόλοι in the NT, which may be left on one side as of no theological significance, although the use of the word in connection with them is in itself somewhat surprising. This is the class mentioned in II Cor. 8.23, quoted above, ἀπόστολοι ἐκκλησιῶν, which RV rightly translates 'messengers of the churches', for they are not apostles at all in the technical sense of the word. They are trusty delegates sent out by one church on an errand to another, as when in Phil. 2.25 Epaphroditus, the ἀπόστολος (RV, 'messenger') of the Church of Philippi, is sent back there after his serious illness by St Paul. Clearly delegates of the churches must be distinguished from the ἀπόστολοι Χριστοῦ of II Cor. 11.13 or I Thess. 2.6 (cf. Jude 17). Perhaps the recognition of a class of ἀπόστολοι ἐκκλησιῶν, distinct altogether from that of ἀπόστολοι Χριστοῦ, solves the problem raised by the fact that St Barnabas is called ἀπόστολος in Acts 14.4 and 14: he is an apostle of the Church of Antioch, commissioned for a special errand by that Church with the laying on of hands (Acts 13.3). Even so, it remains somewhat surprising that St Luke should use a phrase like οἱ ἀπόστολοι Βαρνάβας καὶ Παῦλος, in view of the fact that they were apostles of such very disparate orders. But the likelihood that two classes of ἀπόστολοι were recognized in the early Church is supported by St Paul's insistence that he was an apostle of the first, or divinely appointed, order: 'Paul, an apostle not from men, neither through any individual man, but through Jesus Christ . . .' (Gal. 1.1); at least this verse lends plausibility to the suggestion that there were recognized man-appointed ἀπόστολοι in the Church of Paul's time. This assumption would seem to be the only possible solution for certain otherwise insoluble problems. What otherwise could we think about Andronicus and Junias in Rom. 16.7: 'Salute Andronicus and Junias, my fellow-Jews (cf. Rom. 9.3) and fellow-prisoners (? where), who are of note among the apostles, who also have been in Christ before me'? We gather from this verse that Andronicus and Junias were Hellenistic Jews (their names are Greek), perhaps of the company of St Stephen, for they were Christians before St Paul's conversion. The expression 'of note among the apostles' could mean 'well known to the apostles', but scholarly opinion rejects this interpretation.[1] Junias (masc.) could equally well be Junia (fem.), since the text reads Ἰουνίαν (acc.), in which case Andronicus and Junia would presumably be man and wife, like Aquila and Priscilla. The circle of apostles would then include women; indeed, St Chrysostom commented on the wonderful character of Junia, since she was counted worthy of the title of apostle! On the whole, it seems that Andronicus and his partner supply corroborative evidence of the existence of recognized ἀπόστολοι ἐκκλησιῶν quite distinct from the primary order of ἀπόστολοι Χριστοῦ.[2] The only other person, apart from the Twelve and St Paul, who seems to be called an apostle is St James, the Lord's brother (Gal. 1.19: 'Other of the apostles saw I none, save James the Lord's brother'), if we may (with RV) assume that εἰ μή means 'except' and not 'but only' (RV mg.). It may well be that, in view of James's status in the Church of Jerusalem, his relationship to the Lord, and his having seen the Risen Lord (I Cor. 15.7), he was accorded the title of apostle (as would seem probable from Acts 15): but the evidence is not conclusive. On the whole it seems reasonable to conclude that in the Church of apostolic times the only men who were regarded as apostles in the full and primary sense, i.e. ἀπόστολοι Χριστοῦ, were the Twelve, including Matthias, together with St Paul and perhaps St James. In addition to these there was another and altogether inferior class of ἀπόστολοι ἐκκλησιῶν, that is, delegates who had been sent on an errand from one church to another (e.g. Epaphroditus) or upon some special commission on behalf of their local church (e.g. Barnabas). The difference was that the former received their commission (apostleship) directly from the Lord himself while the latter were commissioned by some local church.

APOSTLESHIP

The original ministry in the Church was a divinely appointed 'apostolic ministry' (for so we may translate the phrase in Acts 1.25, διακονία καὶ ἀποστολή). The word ἀποστολή is used four times in the NT (Acts 1.25; Rom. 1.5; I Cor. 9.2; Gal. 2.8) and, taken together,

[1] See Sanday and Headlam, *Romans* (ICC), *ad loc.*; C. H. Dodd, *Romans* (Moffatt), *ad loc.*; K. H. Rengstorf, *TWNT*, ET, *Apostleship*, 1952, 28; C. K. Barrett, *The Epistle to the Romans*, 283.

[2] There is a further obscurity, which can hardly be removed by the hypothesis of 'apostles of the churches', since such an order could hardly then have existed: in I Cor. 15.5 Paul mentions an appearance of the Risen Lord to the Twelve (but there were only eleven: however, 'the Twelve' has become a technical term) and then in v. 7 mentions an appearance to 'all the apostles'. This suggests that 'the apostles' was a wider group than the Twelve. But such a conclusion would be precarious. Perhaps Paul knew of the tradition that St Thomas was absent when Jesus first appeared to 'the Twelve' (and, of course, the place of Judas was unfilled); perhaps he means that at the last appearance of the Risen Lord all the apostles were present, including St Thomas and the elected Matthias. We can but conjecture.

these references emphasize the truth that apostleship is a matter entirely of divine commissioning (cf. Gal. 1.1, 11f.). At the election of Matthias it is God who must select a new apostle to fill the place left vacant by the defection of Judas, and the number of the Twelve is made up before the commissioning with 'power from on high' takes place (Acts 1.15–2.4). Our view must be that apostleship in the NT is constituted by the commissioning of particular men, called apostles, by the Risen Christ himself; their apostleship must be attested and recognized by the Church, or at least by the other apostles (Gal. 2.6-9). Apostleship is principally concerned with the stewardship and the preaching of the Gospel (Rom. 1.1; I Cor. 9.16f.; Gal. 1.1, 11; 2.2); it is a matter of being 'entrusted with the Gospel' (Gal. 2.7). It might even be thought that it involved appointment to an apostolic 'cure' in a particular field or area or ethnic group (Gal. 2.7f.), but such a conclusion could not be substantiated. In the nature of the case the apostolic ministry could be founded only once; and that is why there is only one generation of apostles and no more. The number of the Twelve must be made up before the ordination of the apostolate takes place; after it has taken place, it is not necessary to elect any further apostle when an apostle dies: St Luke records no fresh election after the execution of St James (Acts 12.1f.). The apostolic ministry which the Risen Lord has ordained will now henceforward make due provision for the continuation of ἐπισκοπή, ἱερωσύνη and διακονία in the Church of the Messiah; but the continuing ministry in the Church will not be ordained by the direct, unmediated action of the Risen Lord (John 20.21-23; Acts 2.1-4; Matt. 28.19f.; Mark 16.15), but by his action through his body, the Church, that is, by Christ's acting through the appropriate ministerial organ ('member', I Cor. 12.12) of his body. This is what ordination to the ministry of the Church of God has meant ever since the first apostles appointed in all the churches a ministry which could act in their absence (e.g. Acts 14.23). In due course the apostolate was removed by death, and in its place an appointed ministry, the ministerial agents of Christ in his body, was established in every church.

It is commonly asserted that the qualification for apostleship in the primitive Church was to have seen the Risen Lord. The evidence quoted is that of I Cor. 9.1 ('Am I not an apostle? have I not seen Jesus our Lord?'); in I Cor. 15.8f. Paul again seems to connect his apostleship with having seen the Lord, even if 'out of due time'. There is, however, a simple but quite conclusive disproof of the view that St Paul considered that having seen the Risen Lord was the qualification of an apostle, viz. the record of the appearance to 'above five hundred ἀδελφοί at once' (I Cor. 15.6). It is obvious that Paul did not consider all these ἀδελφοί to be apostles. It is not having seen the Risen Christ, but having been commissioned by him that creates an apostle. Nor is the fact of having companied with Jesus and his entourage from the days of John the Baptist a sufficient qualification for apostleship, for 'Joseph called Barsabbas surnamed Justus' had done that (Acts 1.21-23), but he is not made an apostle. Even though we cannot now be certain how the primitive Church understood the commissioning by the Risen Lord to have taken place, since the accounts of this supernatural event vary considerably, there is ample evidence from the different NT strata that the Church implicitly believed that the apostles had been commissioned by the Risen Lord (Matt. 28.18-20; Mark 16.15; Luke 24.49; John 20.21-23; Acts 2.1-4; Eph. 4.8-12). Such commissioning, moreover, was not thought of as a private or mystical revelation to individual apostles, but as in some sense a corporate and authenticated event. St Paul strives hard to shew that his own commissioning was no mere private 'revelation' such as on other occasions he had enjoyed (II Cor. 12.1-4, 7), but was an authentic commissioning of the same order as those of the older apostles (I Cor. 9.1f.; 15.7-9; II Cor. 11.5; 12.11f.; Gal. 2.7f.); and in an age when there were many false claims to apostleship, he is quick to point to the evidence of the superabundance of his labours and sufferings (I Cor. 15.10; II Cor. 11.23-33), to the solid reality of the churches he has fathered ('the seal of my ἀποστολή are ye in the Lord', I Cor. 9.2; cf. II Cor. 3.2), and to the undeniable σημεῖα or 'signs of an apostle' which he has wrought—signs, wonders and miracles (II Cor. 12.12). St Paul provides all the evidence that is needed to shew that the essential qualification of an apostle is that he should have been commissioned by the Risen Lord himself.

We probably cannot get much farther than this in the attempt to understand the NT conception of apostleship, and we must admit that there is much that eludes our grasp. The very word ἀπόστολος is something of a mystery, since we cannot tell how or why it came to be adopted in the Greek-speaking churches. In classical Greek it was chiefly associated with naval or overseas expeditions and was never commonly used for 'messenger', 'commissioned agent'. Its adoption by the Christian communities does not seem to arise from any ordinary current usage. Doubtless a word had to be adapted or coined, since the Greeks had no word for an office to which there was no parallel in Greek life; the travelling philosophical preachers, Cynics, Stoics and Epicureans, who were called κατάσκοποι, 'inspectors' of sublime truths, were not in any sense comparable figures to the Christian missionary preachers. A new word had to be found for a new institution, but we cannot tell why this word was chosen. It was not in vogue among the

Jewish communities of the Dispersion, at least so far as we know. Its use is not taken over from the Greek Bible.[1] When the new faith took roots in the west, it was not translated, but was latinized as *apostulus*.

K. H. Rengstorf has recently suggested that the NT apostolate represents a Christian development from the Jewish legal institution of the *shaliach*.[2] This word (plur. *sheluchim*), from *shalach*, to send (often ἀποστέλλειν in LXX), used as a noun, means an authorized delegate who is empowered to execute a legal or personal commission for the principal (an individual or a group, such as a synagogue) whom he represents. The Aramaic form is *shelicha'*. The evidence of II Chron. 17.7-9 is offered on behalf of the assertion that the institution of the *sheluchim* goes back to pre-exilic times, but this is not very convincing. As a developed legal institution it seems in fact to belong to post-NT times.[3] According to the developed custom, a *shaliach* acting for his principal committed him irrevocably; he could act in such matters as buying and selling, effecting a betrothal or a divorce. To honour or to slight a *shaliach* was to honour or slight the one whom he represented: 'a man's *shaliach* is as the man himself.'[4] The high priest on the Day of Atonement is the *shaliach* of the whole congregation; the reader of the prayers in the synagogue is the representative of the congregation (*shaliach zibbur*), and if he makes a slip in his office the whole congregation will incur the divine displeasure. Rengstorf claims that this rabbinic institution was well developed before A.D.70, but the only evidence which he offers is that of the Gospels themselves; he says, for instance, that 'the envoys were not sent out alone but in groups, usually two by two', and he cites in evidence Mark 6.7; Matt. 11.2 and Luke 10.1—together with a Latin inscription of the fifth or sixth century A.D.![5] It is doubtful whether the *sheluchim* throw any light at all on the NT conception of the apostolate. It is true that Jesus used language that is congruous with the later institution when he said to his disciples, 'He that receiveth you receiveth me' (Matt. 10.40; cf. Luke 10.16; John 13.20), but by the same reasoning it could be argued that he taught that little children (Matt. 18.5) or the sick, naked, prisoners, etc. (Matt. 25.40, 45) were his *sheluchim* or apostles.

The late Dom Gregory Dix and others have attempted to utilize Rengstorf's conclusions in the service of a doctrine of apostolic

---

[1] In LXX ἀπόστολος occurs only at I Kings 14.6 (Codex Alexandrinus), where it translates Heb. *shaluach*, a passive participle used as a noun, 'one sent'. Ahijah the prophet is commissioned to speak a word from God to the wife of King Jeroboam and he says ἐγώ εἰμι ἀπόστολος πρός σε σκληρός (III Regn. 14.6).

[2] In his art. Ἀπόστολος in *TWNT* (ET, *Apostleship*).

[3] A. Ehrhardt, *The Apostolic Succession*, 1953, 17, says that it cannot be proved that the word *shaliach* is used in any Jewish source before A.D.140.

[4] Strack-Bill., III, 2.   [5] *Op. cit.*, 13, 19.

succession.[1] The apostles were *sheluchim* of Christ, empowered to act on his behalf, and to bind him as the *sheluchim* of rabbinic Judaism could commit their principals; they handed on their commission to their successors, the bishops of the Church, who are thus, like the apostles themselves, 'plenipotentiaries of God'. This argument, however, fails over the fact that a *shaliach* did not have any power to appoint a successor, if for any reason, such as sickness, he could not himself execute his commission; a new *shaliach* could be appointed only by the Court of Magistrates (*beth din*).[2] Nor can the argument be sustained that the practice of ordination by the laying on of the hands of the apostles and their successors was taken over from the *shaliach* institution. The view that the *sheluchim* were ordained by the laying on of hands and thus commissioned for their task is based on a mistranslation of the verb χειροτονεῖν in Justin Martyr (*Dial. Tryph.* 108): Justin is saying that certain Jewish delegates were appointed—not that they received the laying on of hands.[3] It seems that we cannot explain the existence of the NT apostolate as a Christian adaptation of an already existing Jewish legal institution. The apostolate is *sui generis*; it cannot be accounted for in terms either of Jewish or of pagan institutions: a new situation has created a new form of organization: 'no man putteth new wine into old wine-skins . . . but they put new wine into fresh wine-skins' (Mark 2.22).

PRESBYTERS AND BISHOPS

In the absence of an apostle the local churches were placed under the pastoral rule of πρεσβύτεροι (lit. 'elders') or ἐπίσκοποι ('overseers', 'bishops'). In apostolic days these words appear to have been two names for the same office-bearers. At Acts 20.28 St Paul addresses the πρεσβύτεροι of Ephesus (see Acts 20.17) as ἐπίσκοποι. In I Pet. 5.2 the πρεσβύτεροι are bidden to tend the flock of God, exercising the oversight (ἐπισκοποῦντες). In Titus 1.5 Titus is bidden to appoint elders in every city of Crete (καταστήσῃς κατὰ πόλιν πρεσβυτέρους), and immediately a list of the qualifications of an ἐπίσκοπος is appended (1.7-9). Apparently it was not until after the decease of the apostles themselves that it was found necessary to distinguish a presiding officer (the ἐπίσκοπος) from the πρεσβύτεροι, but by the middle of the second century A.D. such an arrangement (often called 'monepiscopacy') had become universal;

[1] In *The Apostolic Ministry*, ed. K. E. Kirk, 1946. The view there put forward is effectively criticized in T. W. Manson, *The Church's Ministry*, 1948.

[2] See Manson, *op. cit.*, 36f.

[3] The verb χειροτονεῖν meant originally 'to vote by stretching out the hand', and so 'to appoint by vote'; it lost entirely the sense of stretching out the hand and came simply to mean 'appoint'. It is used twice in the NT (Acts 14.23; II Cor. 8.19), where it means nothing more than 'appoint'.

according to the letters of St Ignatius it was already the rule in Asia
Minor early in the second century. It remained the universal form of
Church government until the time of the Reformation. The process of
evolution from the order of presbyter-bishops to that of monepiscopacy
in the latter half of the first century A.D. is somewhat obscure, but it is
not quite as obscure as it is sometimes made out to be. Once we have
shaken ourselves free from the old ideological inhibitions and realized
that Jesus did in fact intend to build an ἐκκλησία and to establish a
pastoral ministry over the new Israel of God, we shall not be surprised
to find that this is in truth just what his apostles did, and that the
ministry of the universal church is the outcome of their obedience to
the teaching of their Master under the power and guidance of his
Spirit.

In Acts 14.23 we glimpse the first step in the setting up of a pastoral
ministry in a missionary church. Passing through Lystra and Iconium,
Paul and Barnabas 'appointed for them presbyters in every church'
(χειροτονήσαντες δὲ αὐτοῖς πρεσβυτέρους κατ' ἐκκλησίαν). It seems probable that the local ἐκκλησίαι were thus modelled upon the pattern of the
Jewish synagogues throughout the world: a body of elders managed
the affairs and charities of the local Jewish community, represented it
in its dealings with the civil power, and exercised oversight in matters
of discipline and of the observance of the Law. They did not, however,
as the Christian elders unquestionably did, conduct the worship of the
assembled community or exercise pastoral responsibility. The choice
of the actual word πρεσβύτερος probably indicates the influence of
Palestinian Judaism, since in the Dispersion the Jewish elders were
called *archontes* or *gerontes* and were not called presbyters until the
end of the second century A.D.; for what it is worth the point may be
noted that Barnabas, who came from the Church of Jerusalem, is with
St Paul at the appointment of the presbyters of Lystra and Iconium
(Acts 14.23); the word πρεσβύτερος is never found in the ten Paulines;
St Paul refers instead to ἐπίσκοποι (Phil. 1.1 only; cf. Acts 20.28).

It is natural that the influence of the Church of Jerusalem over the
Gentile churches should have been strong, and it is probable that
the organization of the Jerusalem Church was a principal factor in the
evolution of monepiscopacy.[1] It provided a model which the other
churches could copy, indeed the kind of model which met their need
after the apostle whom they had regarded as their spiritual father in

---

[1] Sectarian Jewish communities had an official called the 'superintendent' (*mebaqqer*) who is mentioned in I QS and CD (see Gaster, *SDSS*, 45, 60, 107). Although
the Heb. *mebaqqer* is the precise equivalent of ἐπίσκοπος, Bo Reicke is right when he
says that 'there is little reason to assume that the Church got its episcopal office
from the Essenes and their *mebaqqer*' (Stendahl, *SNT*, 154).

the Lord (I Cor. 4.15) had passed from the scene. The picture of the Church of Jerusalem as found in Acts 15 suggests strongly that the government of that Church was modelled upon the Jewish Sanhedrin, with its chief priests and elders (cf. οἱ ἀρχιερεῖς καὶ οἱ πρεσβύτεροι, Matt. 27.20; Acts 4.23, etc.). James the Lord's brother appears in Acts 15 as the high priest who presides over the Sanhedrin of the New Israel. Although St Peter is present, St James nevertheless presides over the council of 'apostles and presbyters'—a phrase which occurs at 15.2, 4, 6, 22, and cf. 23.[1] The council of the Jerusalem Church, as we meet it in Acts 15, is clearly a Christian Sanhedrin: a high priest presides over the chief priests and presbyters. This becomes the model on which the Gentile churches are shaped after the disappearance from the scene of St Paul and the other apostles: a bishop (ἐπίσκοπος) presides over his elders and deacons—this is the normal pattern of church government in the second century. When we recognize the importance of the Sanhedrin-model in the constitution of the local Christian ἐκκλησίαι, we can see why it is that even an apostle like St Peter can be fittingly described as ὁ συμπρεσβύτερος (I Pet. 5.1) or the writer of the Johannine Epistles, who apparently exercises a kind of metropolitical authority, can describe himself simply as ὁ πρεσβύτερος (II John 1; III John 1). The title is one of very great distinction, and as yet it has not come to stand for an order subordinate to that of the ἐπίσκοπος. An apostle was, of course, in virtue of his unique commissioning, a figure apart from all other ranks of ministers in the Church, but he was essentially πρεσβύτερος, with all that the word implied in the days of the presbyter-bishops; the fulness of the ministry of the Church of Christ was given to him.[2] The apostle differed from the presbyter-bishop in that his presbyteral ministry was derived directly from Christ himself while the presbyter's was derived from Christ through the instrumentality of the apostle who commissioned him. Since the days of the first apostles there have been no presbyters (or presbyter-bishops) who have not been ordained by the commissioning of the 'presbytery' (in the sense of I Tim. 4.14). To claim that one has received a commission to minister directly from Christ himself without the instrumentality of the appropriate organ of his body the Church, is to claim to be an apostle, to be another St Paul; it is, in fact, to proclaim 'another gospel', for the apostolic Gospel declares that, after the commissioning of the first apostles, the functions of ἐπισκοπή, ἱερωσύνη and διακονία are to be exercised only by those to whom they are duly and solemnly committed

---

[1] Cf. also Acts 21.18: 'Paul went in with us unto James, and all the presbyters were present'; also Gal. 1.19; 2.9, 12.

[2] Cf. St Ignatius, *Philad.* 5, '. . . the apostles as the presbytery of the Church' (τοῖς ἀποστόλοις ὡς πρεσβυτερίῳ ἐκκλησίας).

by Christ acting through the appropriate ministerial organs of his body the Church.

From the close of the NT period onwards the minister of ordination in the Church became the ἐπίσκοπος (though the presbyters were doubtless associated with him in the ordination of presbyters). There is little point in asking whether the bishop evolved 'upwards' from the ranks of the presbyters (J. B. Lightfoot; B. H. Streeter) or devolved 'downwards' from the apostolate by way of 'apostolic men' like Timothy, Titus or the Elder John (C. Gore; C. H. Turner). The original presbyters exercised ἐπισκοπή, and they too derived their ministry by 'devolution' from the apostles. The historical truth is that monepiscopacy was an urgent practical necessity. Doubtless different presbyters could have taken it in turns to celebrate the Eucharist or to preside at the church-meeting; but nothing short of the setting up of one representative man, an ἀρχιποίμην of the flock, who should be the visible, personal guarantee of the unity and continuity of the apostolic fellowship and doctrine, could meet the need of the Church in an age in which schismatics and heretics of every kind threatened the very continuance of the Church and the Church's Gospel. The bishop became in his person—in what he was as well as what he did—the embodiment of the Gospel of God, by which the Church itself was called into being. The existence of the Church is bound up with the Church's unity and cannot be separated from it: this is the truth which brought the episcopate into being, as distinct from the presbyterate, and which monepiscopacy enshrines and defends. Thus St Ignatius of Antioch early in the second century saw the matter: 'Shun division and wrong doctrines; where the shepherd is, there follow ye. . . . For as many as are of God and of Jesus Christ, they are with the bishop. . . . If any man followeth one that maketh a schism, he doth not inherit the Kingdom of God; if any man walketh in strange doctrine, he hath no fellowship with the passion. Be ye careful therefore to observe one Eucharist, for there is one flesh of our Lord Jesus Christ and one cup unto union in his blood; there is one altar, as there is one bishop, together with the presbytery and the deacons my fellow-servants. . . . He in whom I am bound is my witness that I learned it not from flesh of man; it was the preaching of the Spirit, who spake on this wise: Do nothing without the bishop. . . .' (*Philad.* 2.4, 7). But before Ignatius wrote his letters, somewhere about the time when three of our canonical Gospels were being written, St Clement of Rome was writing thus: 'The apostles received the Gospel for us from the Lord Jesus Christ. . . . Having received a charge (παραγγελία), and having been fully assured through the resurrection of our Lord Jesus Christ and confirmed in the word of God with full assurance of the

Holy Spirit, they went forth with the glad tidings that the Kingdom of God should come. So preaching everywhere in country and town, they appointed their firstfruits, when they had proved them by the Spirit, to be bishops and deacons to them that should believe. . . . And our apostles knew through our Lord Jesus Christ that there would be strife over the name of the bishop's office (ἐπισκοπή). For this cause therefore, having received complete foreknowledge, they appointed (κατέστησαν) the aforesaid persons, and afterwards they provided a continuance (ἐπιμονή), so that if these should fall asleep, other approved men should succeed to their ministry' (διαδέξωνται τὴν λειτουργίαν αὐτῶν) (I Clem. Rom. 42, 44). This is the teaching of the Church concerning ministerial appointment and succession before the close of the NT period, and it is right to interpret the NT documents in the light of what we know of the development of the Church's ministry in NT times. The biblicism which since the Reformation has regarded the written words of Scripture as alone 'inspired', as if the NT had fallen down from heaven and bore no relation to the living παράδοσις of the Church in which it was written, has always been the source of the sectarianism which, denying the truth of the Gospel in favour of a modern theory of 'inspiration', is today one of the principal hindrances to the union of Christendom.

THE LAYING ON OF HANDS

In the NT the laying on of hands is connected with healing (Mark 5.23; 6.5; 7.32; 8.23, 25; 16.18; Acts 9.12, 17; 28.8), baptizing (Mark 10.16; Acts 8.17-19; 19.5f.; possibly Heb. 6.2) and ordaining or commissioning (Acts 6.6; 13.3; I Tim. 4.14, probably 5.22; II Tim. 1.6). In the OT it is connected with blessing (e.g. Gen. 48.14-18), sacrificing (leaning or pressing the hands on the head of the victim to be sacrificed, e.g. Lev. 16.21; cf. Lev. 24.14) and ordaining or commissioning (Moses thus ordains Joshua, Num. 27.18, 23; cf. Deut. 34.9, 'Joshua was full of the spirit of wisdom, for Moses had leaned his hands on him'). Perhaps the ordination of the Levites, upon whom the children of Israel laid their hands (Num. 8.10), is midway between sacrificing and commissioning, for they are offered to and accepted by Yahweh instead of the firstborn of Israel, who should properly have been 'devoted' to him (8.16-18). An ordained ministry is thus consecrated to God's service and so is 'holy' and is at the same time commissioned to act representatively by those who have laid (leaned, Heb. *samakh*) on hands. The laying (leaning) of hands, as distinct from 'placing' as in blessing (Heb. *sim*, *shith*), transfers a part of the personality from the person who leans to the person or animal upon whom he leans his hands.[1] Thus, Israel's guilt is transferred to the scapegoat; Moses's 'spirit' is transferred to Joshua, who thus becomes a new Moses (cf. Elijah and Elisha, II Kings 2.9, 15; Ecclus. 48.12); and the children of Israel impart their essential character to the Levites, so that in all that they do the whole people of Israel will be doing it through them. In rabbinic Judaism apart from the sacrificial use, there seems to have been no laying on of hands except at the ordination of a rabbi: the *shaliach*, whether of an individual or of a synagogue or of the Court (*beth din*), did not have hands laid upon him.[2] Any rabbi could ordain one of his disciples and thus confer his own authority upon him; the laying on of hands is here a *leaning*, not a mere placing of the hands, on the head of the ordinand, and 'its object is the pouring of the ordaining scholar's personality into the scholar to be ordained'.[3] There was, of course, no suggestion of an imparting of the Holy Spirit or of any sort of 'grace of ordination'.

Thus, while there is precedent for ordination by the laying on of hands both in the OT and in contemporary rabbinic practice, it is difficult to say what precisely led the Christian Church to adopt the ceremony. Jesus had not laid hands on his apostles; they had in fact received their unique commissioning with 'power from on high'. The ordination of the Seven in Acts 6.6 in the plain meaning of the Greek text (which Codex Bezae thinks it necessary to correct) was by the laying on of the hands of the congregation, not those of the apostles; the congregation is empowering the Seven to act in the distribution of charity on its behalf. Perhaps St Luke has the ordination of the Levites in mind. There is certainly here no hint of an 'order' of deacons—a word which is not found in Acts. The commissioning of Paul and Barnabas by the laying on of the hands of the other 'prophets and teachers' of the Church of Antioch (Acts 13.3) is likewise not a conferring upon them of an 'order' which they did not previously possess; it seems to be a commissioning of them as church-delegates (ἀπόστολοι ἐκκλησιῶν). We are left with the references in I and II Timothy. Here we are confronted by an apparent contradiction. In I Tim. 4.14 we read 'Neglect not the gift (χάρισμα) that is in thee, which was given thee by prophecy, with the laying on of the hands of the presbytery'. We cannot determine what is meant by the πρεσβυτέριον, because this is the only NT use of the word in respect of a Christian presbytery (cf. Luke 22.66; Acts 22.5, where it refers to the Jewish Sanhedrin). A commissioning

---

[1] LXX translates the Heb. words (whether meaning 'lean', 'press', or simply 'lay', 'place') by ἐπιτίθημι and thus the important distinction between the two ideas is obscured. See the suggestive and instructive art. 'The Laying on of Hands' in D. Daube, *The New Testament and Rabbinic Judaism*, 224-46.

[2] D. Daube, *op. cit.*, 229f.   [3] *Ibid.*, 231.

after a prophetic utterance reminds us of Acts 13.3, but here a χάρισμα of ordination is implied, whereas there the laying on of hands seems merely to signify the appointment of ἀπόστολοι ἐκκλησίας. A grace of ordination is also implied in II Tim. 1.6: 'I put thee in remembrance that thou stir into flame the χάρισμα τοῦ Θεοῦ which is in thee through the laying on of my hands.' The passage unambiguously affirms that a spiritual gift has been received by Timothy through the laying on of St Paul's hands. Many explanations have been suggested to account for the apparent contradiction between these two passages, which are the only NT passages that refer to a χάρισμα of ordination. The traditional one is that apostles and presbyters both laid on hands at the ordination of presbyters. Another is that the presbytery commissioned Timothy as their ἀπόστολος ἐκκλησίας for a special task, while Paul conferred his 'episcopal' status upon him. Or, again, the presbytery ordained Timothy a presbyter, St Paul an ἐπίσκοπος. D. Daube has suggested that the phrase ἐπίθεσις τῶν χειρῶν τοῦ πρεσβυτερίου is a rendering of the technical rabbinic term *semikhath zeqenim* (e.g. Bab. San. 13b), literally 'the leaning on of presbyters', i.e. ordination by presbyters to the office of rabbi; the proper translation of I Tim. 4.14 would then be something like, 'Neglect not the gift which was given thee by prophecy with due ordination to the rank of presbyter'.[1] In view of our uncertainty in the whole matter we can infer nothing from these passages except that ordination by a council of presbyters (πρεσβυτέριον) was known in the sub-apostolic Church and that it was believed that St Paul ordained by the laying on of hands. It was also believed that a grace-gift was received as a result of such ordinations. Perhaps we can add that it was believed that St Paul expected Timothy to ordain others to the ministry, if I Tim. 5.22 ('Lay hands hastily on no man') refers, as it probably does, to ordination and not to baptism; it would be reasonable to suppose in the light of I Tim. 3.1-13 that Timothy was held to have been authorized by St Paul to ordain or appoint bishops and deacons in the Church over which he presided. In the light of the development of the universal practice of ordination by the laying on of hands in the Church of the second century it would seem probable that the ordination of a pastoral ministry was undertaken by the original apostles in the local ἐκκλησίαι Θεοῦ. In the light, moreover, of the practice of the laying on of hands in the OT and in rabbinic Judaism, it becomes reasonable to hold that the apostles themselves practised the laying on of hands at the institution of local ministries; nor should we be surprised to find that the new thing about Christian ordination was that it conveyed a χάρισμα Θεοῦ, a gift of the Holy Spirit. This is

[1] *Op. cit.*, 244f.

what ordination to the ministry of the Church of God has meant ever since NT days. Christ, the head of the Church, acts through the appropriate members of his body at the ordination of a minister or at the making of a layman in baptism, and both these acts of Christ in his Church are signified by the laying on of hands and both are accompanied by the gift of the Holy Spirit.

The NT teaches that the different members and ministries of Christ's body have their own proper functions to fulfil and must neither usurp nor disparage those of others. In this sense it is entirely congruous with NT doctrine to regard the function of ordination as one which belongs solely to the ministry to which it is committed, whether the presbyter-bishops or later the bishops; no one else can exercise this function of the body of Christ. Nothing but the strictest adherence to this principle in the second and following centuries could have preserved the NT Gospel amidst all the heresies and schisms of that age of the conflict of religions. Succession from the apostles by an authentic ordination was valued in those years because it was the guarantee of apostolic doctrine as against the novelties of the Gnostics; thus St Irenaeus in his *Adversus Haereses* claims to be able to give the names of the bishops appointed by the apostles in the different churches with the list of their successors down to his own day (i.e. *c.* A.D. 180).[1] The NT itself, however, says nothing about succession from the apostles; indeed, the technical term διαδοχή (succession) is not found in the NT. The only διάδοχος of whom we read is Festus, the 'successor' of Felix (Acts 24.27); the verb διαδέχομαι is found only at Acts 7.45, a passage which has no bearing on the question. Succession by the laying on of hands is a fact, but it is one which should be accepted with humble thanksgiving and not as a matter that needs explanation or argument. Much theological disputation and obfuscation has resulted from the attempt to define what the Bible itself does not define. The impressive thing about the chain of laying on of hands, down all the centuries and across all the continents, is that it is a *fact*, not a problem that requires explaining by a theory. It is a fact which testifies to the Gospel of Jesus Christ, that he is come in the flesh, and that he has gathered the elect into one Church, one body. The Gospel is not a series of 'spiritual' truths; it is the proclamation of a redemption in history, in the flesh of Jesus Christ, in his actual, visible tangible body (I John 1.1; 4.2), his body which

[1] *Adv. Haer.* III, iii. 1-4. On the succession lists in the ancient Church see A. Ehrhardt, *The Apostolic Succession.* The early succession lists all derive from St James, not from St Peter; Ehrhardt suggests that II Tim. 1.6 is an attempt to prove a succession from St Paul and I Tim. 4.14 a succession from a certain presbytery, the innovation being justified διὰ προφητείας (32f.). Such speculations are ingenious but unconvincing.

is still actual, visible and tangible, upon which hands have been literally, even materialistically, laid. The succession by the laying on of hands
is the sign and instrument of the unity of the Church, which is not an
'ideal' Church, a 'spiritual' body merely, but a real body that can be
seen in the bodies of those on whom hands have been laid. The laying
on of hands in baptism and in ordination is the Church's witness in
every century that Jesus Christ is come in the flesh. Docetism in every
age seeks a 'spiritual' Gospel, because it cannot believe that God can
or will tabernacle in humanity, in real, flesh-and-blood men and women
with bodies as well as souls to be saved.

OTHER MINISTRIES

The NT gives us only a rough and partial outline of the Church's
ministry in the first century, and the task of filling in the details of the
picture is inevitably precarious. In the early second century the order
of deacons was already well developed in the time of St Ignatius, who
constantly refers to the bishop, the presbytery and the deacons. This
development must have been taking place in the first century, but the
NT contains only one (or at most two) clear reference(s) to an order of
deacons, viz. I Tim. 3.8-13: 'Deacons must be grave, not double-
tongued. . . .' Unfortunately, from the point of view of our knowledge,
this passage speaks only of their moral character and gives no hint of
their functions. After NT times deacons became an order of great
importance and honour; they were the personal assistants of the
bishops both in the liturgy and in the administration of church affairs
and discipline. The other *possible* reference in the NT to an order of
deacons is Phil. 1.1: 'Paul and Timothy, δοῦλοι of Jesus Christ, to all
the saints in Christ Jesus which are at Philippi, σὺν ἐπισκόποις καὶ
διακόνοις.' It is natural to take this as referring to two orders, those of
presbyter-bishops and of deacons. But there is a doubt in the matter,
since nowhere else does St Paul refer to an order of deacons, whereas
he uses the word διάκονος in a general sense, even applying it to himself (e.g. I Cor. 3.5; Eph. 3.7; Col. 1.23, 25; cf. Col. 4.17).[1] Thus, it
may well be that the phrase in Phil. 1.1 should be translated, 'bishops
and other ministers'. There is no mention at all in the NT of an order of
deaconesses. In Rom. 16.1 Phoebe is called the διάκονος of the Church
at Cenchreae, but the word is in all probability used in its general sense;
therefore RV 'servant' is to be preferred to RV mg. 'deaconess'. In
I Tim. 3.11, where a sentence about women is inserted in the list of the
requirements of deacons ('Women in like manner must be grave . . .'),

[1] In secular Greek the word had no religious significance whatever and it is often
found in the NT in its non-technical meaning (e.g. Mark 10.43; John 2.5, 9; Rom.
13.4).

the reference is clearly to the wives of the deacons; γυναῖκες should be translated 'wives'.

By the end of the NT period there had emerged three orders in the Church's ministry, those of bishops, presbyters and deacons; admission to these orders was conferred by the solemn laying on of hands. But beyond this special or ordained ministry, the work of ministry (ἔργον διακονίας, Eph. 4.12) in its wider sense was carried on by every member of the Church according to the personal χάρισμα of the Holy Spirit which he had received at his baptism. The whole Church was a ministry in this wider sense, as we have already seen.[1] It is to this ministry of the whole people of God, rather than to any 'ordained' ministry within the body, that St Paul is referring in three passages in which he lists different kinds of ministrations. In I Cor. 12.28 he writes: 'God hath set (ἔθετο) some in the Church, first apostles, secondly prophets, thirdly teachers, then δυνάμεις (presumably 'workers of miracles'), then gifts of healings, helps (ἀντιλήμψεις), governments (κυβερνήσεις), kinds of tongues.' It is difficult to say precisely what can be the significance of the very definite 'first', 'secondly', 'thirdly', 'then': it looks as if some sort of order of importance is being asserted. Speaking with tongues comes at the bottom of the list, which seems its right place in view of Paul's mild deprecation of it in I Cor. 14. But what are we to say of 'governments'? Is this the office of Paul's ἐπίσκοποι, and are 'helps' the order of deacons? The answer must be that we do not know, and it is not very profitable to guess. In Eph. 4.11f. we find another list, which begins in the same way, i.e. with apostles and prophets, but then diverges: 'And he gave (ἔδωκε) some apostles, and some prophets, and some evangelists, and some pastors (ποιμένες) and teachers, for the perfecting of the saints, unto the work of διακονία, unto the building up of the body of Christ.' The pastoral ministry (presumably the ἐπίσκοποι) seems now to be accorded much fuller recognition, while other ministries are not mentioned. Lastly, there is Rom. 12.6-8: 'Having χαρίσματα differing according to the grace that was given to us, whether prophecy, according to the proportion of the faith; or διακονία, in deaconing; or the teacher, in the teaching; or an exhorter, in the exhortation; the giver, in singleness (of motive); the ruler (ὁ προϊστάμενος), in diligence; the charitable worker (ὁ ἐλεῶν), in cheerfulness.' These are surely not all intended to be 'orders' of ministry—there could hardly be an order of 'givers'!—but rather the same people at different times. The three lists together hardly give us a coherent picture of the ministry of the apostolic Church. They were not intended to do so; each was written in the course of a practical instruction in the duties of churchmanship

[1] *Supra*, 303-7.

as these were to be performed by the laity. But if that be so, what is 'the ruler' doing in such lists? Does ὁ προϊστάμενος mean the bishop? Again we must confess that we do not know.

The striking thing about all three lists is the place of honour which they give to the prophets, next to the apostles themselves. Prophets enjoyed great authority and prestige, because they were the agents by which the Holy Spirit declared God's will or revealed coming events to the churches. It was they through whom the Holy Spirit separated Barnabas and Saul for the work to which he had called them (Acts 13.1-3); they foretold coming events such as the famine in the days of Claudius (Acts 11.27f.) or the tribulations that awaited St Paul (Acts 21.10f.). They were principally concerned with shewing the things which should be hereafter, especially in the sense of foretelling the catastrophes which would shortly precede the end of the world and the parousia of Christ. This is the activity which the author of the Fourth Gospel has in mind when he makes Jesus say that when the Spirit of truth is come, he shall guide the disciples into all truth: 'he shall declare unto you the things that are to come' (John 16.13). In the days of waiting for the Lord's return, the prophets speak 'edification and comfort and consolation' (I Cor. 14.3). They are associated with the Church's teachers and their task is edificatory (Acts 13.1; I Cor. 12.28; 14.31). They clearly took a prominent part at the gatherings of the local church, if we may regard I Cor. 14 as evidence of congregational activity in apostolic days; and it would seem that all the members of the congregation are regarded as potential prophets, liable to prophesy at any time. From I Cor. 11.5 it might be concluded that there were women prophets (cf. also Acts 21.9), but from 14.34f. it would seem that their utterance was much restricted. If we want to know the content of a prophetic utterance in the early Church, we should turn to the Apocalypse of St John, which is a book of the deliverances of a particular prophet (cf. the phrase 'the words of the prophecy of this book', Rev. 22.7, 10, 18f.; cf. 1.3). The prophets doubtless often spoke in the symbolic language of dreams and visions, which is probably why St Paul says that prophesying is for a sign not to the unbelieving, but to those who believe (I Cor. 14.22). Whereas (we may conjecture) the teachers taught the παράδοσις of the faith, the prophets were concerned with τὰ μυστήρια πάντα καὶ πᾶσα ἡ γνῶσις (I Cor. 13.2), i.e. apocalyptic secrets concerning things to come. Prophecy would vanish away when the day of revelation dawned (I Cor. 13.8f.).

Prophecy, however, vanished away in another sense, along with certain other ministries of the apostolic church, such as miracles, healings and tongues. At least, they vanished as normal Sunday activities of the congregations of the Church, though doubtless they have at different times and in differing forms been renewed during the centuries that have passed since the days of the apostles. We have heard a good deal in recent times about the Church's 'prophetic ministry', but those who use that phrase today would be surprised to discover that the NT interpretation of it would be so very different from their own. Today it is taken to justify pronouncements by clergymen or conferences of churchfolk upon social and industrial questions, or to sanction sermons about the atom bomb. If there is any biblical justification for a prophetic ministry of the Church in this sense, it would perhaps be wiser to look for it in the OT and to appeal to Amos rather than to St Paul. There is certainly nothing in the NT to suggest that prophecy in the apostolic Church could be taken as a model for the so-called 'prophetic' function of the Church as liberal theology has conceived it in recent times. The apostolic Church, following the example of the Lord, did not look upon itself as 'a judge or a divider' over social and political questions (Luke 12.13f.). The concern of the Church for the social order must be justified on more solidly theological grounds than these. The ministry of the Church is still essentially the ministry of Christ in the service of the world, acting through the appropriate members of his body the Church.

Many problems concerning the Church's ministry in NT times are likely to remain unsolved, but the reality of the ministry of Christ in and through his Church is, happily for us, not bound up with our ability to solve historical and archaeological problems. The danger is that we shall become so fascinated by the problems that we shall lose the sense of the mystery. We may not solve the problems, but we may by the grace of God understand the mystery—that the ministry, like the Church itself, is not something that men create but something that Christ gave and still gives, 'for the perfecting of the saints, unto the work of ministering, unto the building up of the body of Christ' (Eph. 4.11f.).

15

THE THEOLOGY OF BAPTISM

IN the Church of NT times the ceremony of baptism was the only and the indispensable means of becoming a member of the Christian ἐκκλησία. A Christian was not a follower of the teachings of Jesus in the sense that a Platonist is a follower of Plato; such a usage of the word 'Christian' could have arisen only after the Enlightenment. In his baptism the individual was anointed with Holy Spirit, and hence baptism was at once his ordination and his coronation, whereby he was made priest and king within the Israel of God. It was his incorporation into the body of Christ, with whose death and resurrection he was now identified. Decisive proof of the universality of the practice of baptism in the apostolic Church is to be seen in the fact that St Paul can write to the Christians of Rome, a church which he had not founded and had not yet visited, 'Are ye ignorant that all we who were baptized into Christ Jesus were baptized into his death?' (Rom. 6.3). The Apostle can assume without question that the Roman Christians are all baptized. Before their baptism catechumens were given careful instruction in the faith (cf. Gal. 6.6, ὁ κατηχούμενος τὸν λόγον, cf. also Luke 1.4; Acts 18.25) and at their baptism were required to make public profession of it in the presence of the congregation (cf. Rom. 10.9f.; I Cor. 12.3; Phil. 2.11, and esp. I Tim. 6.12, ὡμολόγησας τὴν καλὴν ὁμολογίαν ἐνώπιον πολλῶν μαρτύρων).[1] Baptism accomplished not merely the washing away of sin and of all the stain and filth of heathendom (cf. John 13.8-10; Acts 22.16; I Cor. 6.11; Eph. 5.26; Titus 3.5; Heb. 10.22; cf. Ps. 51.2, 7, 10; Isa. 1.16; Jer. 4.14), but also the driving out of the unclean spirits which were in a man. It must be admitted that direct NT evidence for this latter statement is lacking, but it is reasonably

[1] Of course, I Tim. 6.12 *may* refer to Timothy's appearance in court, before the Roman magistrate and to his affirmation Κύριος Ἰησοῦς when he was required to make the political confession Κύριος Καῖσαρ (so O. Cullmann, *The Earliest Christian Confessions*, 25-30). Even if this were so, the baptismal reference is still implicit; the next verse (6.13) speaks of Christ's 'good confession' before Pontius Pilate: Christ himself made his baptismal profession—his witness to himself—before Pilate at his baptism of death (cf. Luke 12.50). Christians who confess Christ in their baptism or in the magistrate's court are making the 'good confession' in the presence of witnesses, as Christ himself had done. On the whole subject of baptismal confessions, see Cullmann, *op. cit.*; also *supra*, Chap. 1, *ad fin.*

certain that the ancient practice of baptismal exorcism goes back to apostolic days.[1] Indirect NT evidence is perhaps to be found in the story of the Epileptic Boy (Mark 9.14-29), which may have been intended by the Evangelist for use by the catechists in their teaching about baptism[2] (cf. also Mark 16.15-17; Acts 8.7, 16; 16.18, etc.). Baptism was the moment at which the individual passed out of the kingdom of darkness into the realm of light, and hence the baptized were spoken of as 'the enlightened' (φωτισθέντες, Heb. 6.4; 10.32; cf. Eph. 1.18) and baptism is conceived of as a φωτισμός, an act of illumination (cf. Justin Martyr, *Apol.* 1.16), although this word is not directly applied to baptism in the NT (it occurs only at II Cor. 4.4 and 6).

THE CHRISTIAN MEANING OF 'BAPTIZE'

In cl. Greek βάπτω means 'to dip'. Its intensive form βαπτίζω also means 'dip', 'immerse', and can be used figuratively, as when Josephus says that the city is flooded with refugees (*Jewish War*, 4.3.3). In LXX βάπτω is often used in a literal sense (e.g. Ps. 67.23), while βαπτίζω is less frequent and carries a rather more intransitive sense—'to dip (oneself)', 'to wash (oneself)', e.g. II Kings 5.14; Ecclus. 34.25; Judith 12.7.[3] On the other hand τὸ βάπτισμα and ὁ βαπτισμός seem to be technical terms invented for use in connection with the baptism of John and adopted by the Christians for their baptism; they do not occur in LXX or in cl. lit., except that βαπτισμός is used by Josephus in connection with John's baptism (*Antiquities*, 18.5.2). In the same passage Josephus uses ὁ βαπτιστής of John 'the Baptist'; this is the only known use of this word outside the NT. The word βαπτισμός is found in the NT only three times; twice it refers to ceremonial washings (Mark 7.4, 'washings of cups and pots . . .' and Heb. 9.10, 'meats and drinks and divers washings'); the remaining usage is the difficult passage Heb. 6.2, 'teachings of βαπτισμοί', where the context suggests baptismal instruction (but why the plural?). The usual NT noun for baptism (both John's and the Church's) is βάπτισμα, and this (like the English word 'baptism') appears to be a *terminus technicus* coined specially to denote a new religious ceremony.

There has been a lengthy and exhaustive discussion of the origins of

[1] Cranmer's first Prayer Book of 1549 still retained the Exorcism in the Administration of Public Baptism: 'Then let the Priest looking upon the children say, I command thee, unclean spirit, in the name of the Father, of the Son, and of the Holy Ghost, that thou come out and depart from these infants. . . .' In the ancient Church the chief exorcist was the bishop.

[2] See *infra*, 359f.

[3] Cf. Acts 9.18: are we to translate the passage as in secular Greek, 'he arose and washed, and he took food and was strengthened', or as in Christian technical terms, 'he arose and was baptized, and he received the (sacramental) food and was confirmed (with Holy Spirit)'? See also *infra*, 356, footnote.

John's and of Christian baptism.[1] This investigation does not concern our present task, until it is shewn that the question of origins has an important bearing on the theological meaning of baptism as understood in the apostolic Church. We would remark only that, whatever outward ceremonial similarities may have existed between the practice of Christian baptism and the washings of Jewish sects of the Qumran type, the *doctrine* of baptism in the NT is quite unique, and there is no parallel in any known religious movement to the conception of baptism into the death and resurrection of the Servant-Messiah. The word βάπτισμα, which is virtually the only noun used in the NT for Christian baptism (since, as we have seen, βαπτισμός hardly qualifies), is a new word for a new thing—the great new reality of baptism into Christ's body, of which the baptism of John was the prophetic foreshadowing. An entirely new teaching, itself a notable feature of the brilliant re-interpretation of OT theology which is found in the NT, is proclaimed to be the significance of the act of baptism, whatever affinities that ceremony as practised in the primitive Church may or may not have had with Jewish (or for that matter pagan) antecedents. The important question to ask is not what precedents there were for Christian baptism in the lustrations of the Essenes or in the proselyte baptisms of rabbinic Judaism, but what is the origin of the wholly new conception of baptism as the act of incorporation into the resurrection-body of the crucified Messiah. To this question there can be only one answer: it was Jesus himself who first taught that his own death was a baptism that could and must be shared by all who would participate in the Messianic salvation.[2] The only satisfactory answer to the question why baptism was the universal and unquestioned method of initiation in the apostolic Church from the days before the conversion of St Paul is that Jesus himself had taught his disciples the necessity of baptism into his death and resurrection, the great act of Messianic salvation by which the New Age was inaugurated and the outpouring of the Spirit begun.

We must therefore abandon the view that, when Jesus referred to his forthcoming baptism (of death), he was only using a metaphor, common enough in the OT and indeed in human speech everywhere, and that the evangelists were responsible for the introduction of the Christian technical word βάπτισμα into the context. On the contrary, we shall take very seriously the sayings of Jesus about 'the βάπτισμα that I am baptized with' (Mark 10.38) or 'I have a βάπτισμα to be

[1] See W. F. Flemington, *The New Testament Doctrine of Baptism*, 1948; H. G. Marsh, *Origin and Significance of the New Testament Baptism*, 1941; F. J. Leenhardt, *Le Baptême Chrétien*, Neuchâtel, 1945.
[2] See *supra*, 179-81.

baptized with' (Luke 12.50). We do not, of course, know what Aramaic word Jesus may have used, but there is no reason whatever to think that St Mark and St Luke were in like perplexity: they are conveying to us what they, as teachers of the Church in their day, understood to be the thought of the Lord on the subject of baptism into the death of the Messiah. If they had understood that Jesus was merely speaking metaphorically about being 'overwhelmed' by the approaching catastrophe (cf. Ps. 42.7, 'All thy waves and billows are gone over me'), they would not have used the technical term $\beta\acute{a}\pi\tau\iota\sigma\mu a$; if they were mistaken about what Jesus meant, then there is no point whatever in our trying to guess either what Jesus meant or even what he said. But there is no reason to suppose that St Mark and St Luke were mistaken, since their evidence that Jesus taught the central importance of baptism into the death of the Messiah is attested by the place given to baptism in the practice and in the theology of the apostolic Church. St Paul is merely giving his own expression to the teaching of Jesus and of the whole Church when he writes, 'All we who were baptized into Christ Jesus were baptized into his death; we were buried therefore with him through baptism into death, that like as Christ was raised from the dead through the glory of the Father, so we also might walk in newness of life' (Rom. 6.3f., and cf. vv. 5-11; also Col. 2.12). The Messiah had come and had brought the divine judgment, the judgment of death; but the judgment had fallen upon the Messiah himself; the pouring out of the Spirit in the Messianic Age was now being fulfilled, and the baptism of the individual was the moment at which he personally underwent the divine judgment of death, and also the moment at which he received his individual endowment ($\chi\acute{a}\rho\iota\sigma\mu a$) of the Messianic Spirit. The $\beta\acute{a}\pi\tau\iota\sigma\mu a$ in Holy Spirit and with the fire of judgment which John the Baptist had prophesied was now a reality in the life of the Church of Jesus Messiah. 'In one Spirit were we all baptized into one body, whether Jews or Greeks, slave or free; and were all made to drink of one Spirit' (I Cor. 12.13).

For St Paul almost the whole meaning of baptism is contained in the conception of dying and rising with Christ; other ideas, such as cleansing, hardly appear at all, though washing is mentioned in I Cor. 6.11 ('But ye were washed . . . sanctified . . . justified in the name of the Lord Jesus Christ, and in the Spirit of our God'), where the reference is obviously to the baptism of the Corinthians. 'Baptized into one body' (I Cor. 12.13) indicates clearly the character of baptism as the act by which the convert is incorporated into the *persona* of Christ. In 'Adam', that is, in their solidarity with unredeemed humanity in its sinfulness, all must die; but in Christ, that is, through incorporation into the

redeemed humanity of the body (*persona*) of Christ, all are made alive
(Rom. 5.12–6.11, a passage in which the doctrine of baptism is completely integrated with the doctrines of redemption and of the Church).
In Christ's death on Calvary the whole human race died, because Christ
is the representative Man ('one died for all, therefore all died', II Cor.
5.14); in Christ's resurrection the New Man is created (Eph. 2.15;
Col. 3.9f.). The individual appropriates to himself the salvation thus
procured by Christ through his baptism into Christ. He dies—and
this is no mere metaphor in NT thought—and a new man is born;
hence the practice, begun perhaps in NT times, of giving the baptized
a new name, a baptismal name. What Christ has done for all humanity
on Calvary is appropriated by each individual Christian in his baptism.
In his baptism the Christian dies with Christ, is crucified with Christ
(Rom. 6.6, 8; Col. 3.3); his death frees him from sin, just as the death
of a debtor cancels the debt (Rom. 6.7, 18; cf. I Pet. 4.1). He begins a
new life, risen with Christ (Rom. 6.11-13; 7.4-6; Col. 3.1, etc.). Of
course, the life of the baptized is in this age lived under the eschatological tension of the 'even now' and the 'not yet'; the Christian has
died, yet he must still 'die daily' (I Cor. 15.31); he must still 'mortify
his members which are upon the earth' (Col. 3.5). Eschatologically the
Christian has died already; he is already 'raised with Christ'. The crisis
of death, that is, the judgment, has already passed; but this truth is as
yet known only to faith. 'Ye died, and your life is hid with Christ in
God' (Col. 3.3). The process of physical death has still to take place as
an event in the natural order; the life of the Age to Come is possessed
in this age only by faith. Not until Christ, who is our inner, hidden life,
shall appear at his parousia, shall the full glory of the new life, possessed
even now by faith, be made manifest to sight (Col. 3.4).

BAPTISM AND JUDGMENT

Baptism involves judgment. God's judgment upon sin was executed
in the baptism of death which Christ underwent. To be baptized is to
accept God's verdict of guilty, and so to be brought past the great
assize and the final judgment of the last day into the life of the Age to
Come.[1] Does this mean that, so far as the individual Christian is concerned, there is only 'realized eschatology' and that there is no judgment
after death? The NT forbids us to answer this question in the affirmative. It is true that the Christian believer 'has the life of the Age to
Come and does not come into judgment, but has passed out of death
into life' (John 5.24), and that 'there is now no condemnation

---

[1] So C. F. D. Moule in his essay, 'The Judgment Theme in the Sacraments' in
The Background of the New Testament and its Eschatology, ed. W. D. Davies and
D. Daube, 467.

($\kappa a \tau \acute{a} \kappa \rho \iota \mu a$) to those that are in Christ Jesus' (Rom. 8.1). That is to say, in his baptism the Christian receives assurance that he will not be judged or condemned with 'the world' and its demonic 'rulers'; God's verdict of acquittal has already delivered him from that court of world-judgment. Those who have made their baptismal confession that 'Jesus is the Son of God' are indwelt by God and consequently know that God, who is love, exercises his love in their case; thus, love is perfected with them, so that they may have boldness in the day of judgment (I John 4.15-17). All this is true; it is an integral part of the good news of our salvation. But it does not mean that there is to be no judgment at all. On the contrary, the NT contains the most solemn warnings concerning the judgment of Christian believers by Christ himself. This would appear to be a different judgment from the judgment of 'the world', from which the members of Christ's body have been delivered already. But it is none the less a reality to be seriously faced. St Paul, who has asserted with all his vigour the gospel of baptismal justification, asserts also in the same Epistle to the Romans that 'we shall all stand before the judgment-seat of God. . . . Each one of us shall give account of himself to God' (Rom. 14.10, 12). In II Cor. 5.10 he asserts again, 'We must all be made manifest before the judgment-seat of Christ'— Christ's or God's, it is all the same judgment, since it is a tenet of NT faith that God has committed all judgment to the Son (John 5.22, 27; 17.2; Acts 10.42; 17.31; 24.25; Matt. 16.27; Rev. 2.27)—'that each one may receive the things done in the body, according to what he hath done, whether it be good or bad'.

This doctrine of a judgment of Christians according to their works is no mere relic of Paul's Pharisaic ideology; it is no unconscious clinging to a doctrine of works. It is an assertion of the seriousness of the moral struggle in the Christian life, a struggle which begins only after baptismal justification has been freely received. So far is Paul removed from the charges of antinomianism which were brought against him (cf. Rom. 3.8; 6.1) that he considers that the use which the Christian makes of the grace ($\chi \acute{a} \rho \iota \sigma \mu a$) which he has received in his baptism is a matter of a solemn divine judgment at the resurrection from the dead (cf. Jesus's parable of the Talents, Matt. 25.14-30; also Luke 19.11-27). He does not hold that baptismal justification confers an automatic salvation, which cannot be forfeited (I Cor. 9.27; cf. Heb. 2.1-4; 3.12; 4.1f., 11). Having received God's grace, each man must work out his own salvation in fear and trembling (Phil. 2.12f.); the obedient disciple of the Lord will have something of which he can be proud in the (judg-ment-) day of Christ (Phil. 2.16). The analogy between baptismal faith-justification and the life of faith and good works which should follow after it, is already foreshadowed in the salvation-history of Israel, whose story is written in the Scriptures for the admonition of those upon whom the ends of the ages have come: those who were delivered at the baptism of the Red Sea, and were nourished in the wilderness by the eucharistic food and drink, nevertheless displeased God and perished without reaching the promised land (I Cor. 10.1-13). They had experienced God's righteousness and salvation, but they did not escape his judgment. So also Christians, who in their baptism have participated in Christ's justifying, redemptive baptism of death, must live all their life in this world under the judgment of Christ and finally at the resurrection of the dead appear before his judgment seat.

It must be acknowledged that it is very difficult to fit all the NT passages which speak of judgment into a single unified conception. We have suggested that the apostolic view was that Christians who had remained faithful to their baptismal confession would not come into the general judgment of 'the nations' (the Great Assize, e.g. Matt. 25.31f.; II Thess. 1.7-10), since they have been already acquitted ('baptismal justification', cf., e.g., Luke 21.36; John 5.24; Rom. 8.1; I John 4.17; Rev. 6.17). The judgment that even the faithful Christians would undergo (Rom. 14.10, 12; II Cor. 5.10, etc.) is quite different from the judgment of 'the world'; it is the personal meeting with the beloved Master, whose verdict of praise or blame is itself the fulness of reward or punishment (cf. Matt. 25.21, 23; Luke 19.17; 22.61f.). But it must be acknowledged that there are passages which seem to speak of only one judgment for Christians and non-Christians alike (e.g. II Tim. 4.1, 'Christ Jesus, who shall judge the quick and the dead'; Heb. 9.27, 'it is laid up for men once to die, and after this judgment') or of a judgment of *all* men according to their works (Matt. 16.27; John 5.29; Rom. 2.6; I Pet. 1.17; Rev. 2.23; 22.12; cf. Dan. 12.2). In Rev. 20.4-6 the martyrs and confessors arise from the dead at 'the first resurrection'; *perhaps* the seer means this to include *all* Christians, since he seems to think that all Christians will be martyred or at least persecuted. Then, after the thousand-year reign of the saints, and after the final casting of the devil into the lake of fire and brimstone (20.10), there takes place the general resurrection, when all (except those raised at the first resurrection) are judged according to their works as they appear before the Great White Throne (20.11-15). Perhaps the judgment at the general resurrection does not involve any Christians at all (except apostate ones). We can hardly determine the question, and we are left to conjecture how far these pictures were meant to be regarded as literal prediction at all. Perhaps, after all, it is an error to try to find coherent and tidy theories where the NT is concerned with a mystery so profound that it can be spoken of only in the language of poetry and imagination, which cannot be rationalized without being falsified.

'PUTTING ON' CHRIST

Baptism is an eschatological sacrament which anticipates the day of judgment. The Christian life, which arises out of it, is therefore necessarily a matter of the 'even now' and the 'not yet'. Already in our baptism we have 'put on' Christ: 'as many of you as were baptized into Christ did put on Christ' (Gal. 3.27); 'ye have put off the old man with his doings, and have put on the new man' (Col. 3.9f.). Yet the baptized are still exhorted to 'put on the Lord Jesus Christ' (Rom. 13.14), or to 'put on the new man' (Eph. 4.24), because the 'clothing' which they have received in baptism is the earnest (ἀρραβών, II Cor. 1.22; 5.5) of the Spirit (cf. Luke 24.49, 'until ye be clothed with δύναμις from on high', i.e. the Spirit); it is not yet the complete σῶμα πνευματικόν which they will receive at the general resurrection (I Cor. 15.44). But the baptized need have no anxiety about their state of 'nakedness' before that consummation, for even now the Spirit is at work in them to renew their 'inward man' day by day (II Cor. 4.16; Eph. 3.16). The Spirit within us is the guarantee of our resurrection in the new creation of the end-time: 'If the Spirit of him that raised up Jesus from the dead dwelleth in you, he that raised up Christ Jesus from the dead shall quicken also your mortal bodies through his Spirit that dwelleth in you' (Rom. 8.11). Even now, eschatologically, our *bodies* are incorporated into the resurrection-body of Christ; they are strictly no longer ours, but are members of Christ (I Cor. 6.15; Eph. 5.30); this fact has very important consequences for our bodies in this earthly life.[1] It also has important ethical implications in such spheres as those of sex relations (I Cor. 6.12-20).

But while our 'inward man' is thus being renewed by the Spirit, our bodies are dying. In this age, before the ultimate eschatological 'redemption of our body' (Rom. 8.23), death and sin, though conquered, will still effect the dissolution of our bodies. Our body is still τὸ σῶμα τῆς σαρκός (Col. 2.11), our human nature in its opposition to God; σάρξ, in the sense of our sin-affected human nature, cannot inherit the Kingdom of God, because corruption does not inherit incorruption (I Cor. 15.50). But even while our earthly dwelling-tent is passing into dissolution, we, the baptized, the members of Christ's resurrection body, have a building from God, a mansion of the Age to Come in the heavenly places (II Cor. 5.1). Even now we long to be clothed upon

---

[1] On this whole subject see O. Cullmann's essay, 'The Proleptic Deliverance of the Body', in his book *The Early Church*, 1956, 165-73.

with our habitation from heaven (5.2-4): Paul's metaphor becomes very mixed, because while he is speaking of our heavenly dwelling he perceives the relevance of the baptismal language about putting on clothing. We shall not be left naked in God's sight at the judgment, as Adam and Eve knew that they were naked before God (Gen. 3.10); God has provided us with a baptismal robe of righteousness (cf. Gen. 3.21; Job. 29.14; Ps. 132.9), our baptismal justification, which is the guarantee of our heavenly domicile: 'he that wrought for us this very thing is God, who gave unto us (in our baptism, of course) the earnest of the Spirit' (II Cor. 5.5). There is no need for anxiety or groaning over the possibility that we may die before the parousia and so be left γυμνοί (naked), i.e. without any bodies at all: God will provide us with our resurrection body (I Cor. 15.35-38; II Cor. 5.3f.). We may be of good courage, for we know that to be absent from our physical bodies means to be present with the Lord (II Cor. 5.8). It is possible that St Paul in II Cor. 5.1-10 means that during our earthly life our spiritual bodies are growing in heaven, in readiness for us to put them on at the general resurrection; perhaps he means even that our good works in this life are the means by which our heavenly οἰκητήρια are developed. We cannot be sure about such matters, since his words are open to more than one interpretation.[1] But it is clear that St Paul holds that those who have died already in the Lord will be at no disadvantage as compared with those who are still alive at the parousia; they will come with the Lord at his return, and we with them shall be 'for ever with the Lord' (I Thess. 4.13-18).

The apostolic Church seems to have held that we do not receive our resurrection bodies immediately after we die, but that we 'sleep' in Christ until the parousia (I Cor. 15.18; I Thess. 4.13-15; Rev. 14.13; cf. Mark 5.39). The baptized dead, being in Christ, are not 'naked' (i.e. bodiless) spirits because of their incorporation into Christ's body. Heb. 12.1 ('we are compassed about with so great a cloud of witnesses') can hardly alone justify the view that the dead (i.e. the OT heroes) are fully conscious observers of the Church's struggle against the world; the words are surely a graphic and poetic way of encouraging Christians to emulate the valour of the saints of old, pictured as a great applauding crowd of spectators who urge the athletes to even mightier efforts in the race.[2]

[1] See R. P. C. Hanson, *II Corinthians* (Torch Commentary), 1954, 47f., 55-9. For a different interpretation see J. A. T. Robinson, *The Body*.

[2] In the NT μάρτυς means an eye-witness (or ear-witness). Perhaps in Acts 22.20 and Rev. 2.13 we are approaching the later sense of 'martyr'—one who bears testimony to Christ before the magistrate's court and consequently suffers the penalty of death. It is conceivable, but not perhaps likely, that this sense is being applied to the OT 'martyrs' in Heb. 12.1, in which case the notion of their being spectators of the struggles of the Christians would not be present at all.

Nor can Luke 23.43 ('Today shalt thou be with me in paradise') be
held to contradict the general NT view, since the words are again
poetical and imply nothing more than being 'with' Christ, a condition
which was deemed to confer the utmost blessedness on those who had
fallen asleep (cf. Phil. 1.21, 23; 'to die is gain . . . to depart and be with
Christ, for it is very far better'; also John 12.24-26; II Cor. 5.8). Nor
should we take literally Rev. 6.9-11, where the souls of the slain (in
their place of nearness to God) underneath the altar are said to cry
'How long?' Even in this passage they are spoken of as 'resting' (cf.
14.13). The idea of the saints as even now interceding at the altar in
heaven appears in Rev. 5.8 and 8.3f., but such passages are highly
poetical and would provide but a precarious biblical basis for the practice of praying to the saints. On the whole it may be concluded that the
beautiful metaphor of sleep most adequately expresses the deepest conviction of the apostolic Church concerning those of the baptized who
had already died (cf. the later use of 'cemetery', from the Greek
κοιμητήριον, a sleeping-place). It may be added that no entirely satisfactory explanation has ever been found for the reference to baptizing
for the dead in I Cor. 15.29—apparently a practice of baptizing by
proxy on behalf of someone who had died. Perhaps, in view of the NT
evidence that the faith of a sponsor was considered to avail for a
person—an infant or an epileptic—who could not answer for himself,
it was the custom to baptize by proxy on behalf of a catechumen,
who had died before he could be baptized. This is conjectural,
of course, but at least it makes sense of an otherwise inexplicable
verse.

We may ask what it was that first suggested the language of 'putting
on' (ἐνδύω, ἔνδυσις, ἐπενδύομαι), which is found in connection with
baptism. Of course, there is the OT language about putting on righteousness (Job 29.14) or about the priests being clothed with righteousness (Ps. 132.9)—language which might naturally suggest baptismal
justification to a mind like that of St Paul as he read the Scriptures.
But this kind of literary explanation seems more like an after-thought
than the starting point of a vivid metaphor. It is altogether more
probable that it arose from the practice of the putting on of the white
baptismal robe by the candidates for baptism. Older commentators,
such as J. B. Lightfoot,[1] thought that this practice could hardly have
begun in St Paul's day and that therefore the metaphor must have arisen
from the very common parallel usages of the LXX. But there is no
reason why the practice should be less likely to have arisen in A.D. 50
than in 150: Justin Martyr (*Dial. c. Tr.* 116) attests its prevalence in the

[1] *St Paul's Epistle to the Galatians*, 1865, *ad* 3.27, 8th ed., 1884, 149f.

second century. After all, some such practice must have been necessary from the very beginning, since baptism was by total immersion in running water (cf. *Didache* 7.1-3; Heb. 10.22), and the earliest Christians doubtless shared in full the very un-Greek aversion of the Jews from the state of γυμνότης. What is more likely than that the putting on of the white robe should from the beginning have represented to the mind of the Church the putting on of Christ, just as the actual immersion in the river represented the burial of the Christian with Christ in his death, and as the rising from the water symbolized his resurrection from the dead (cf. Rom. 6.3f.)? It was this latter symbolism which led the Church in post-NT times to hold the baptismal ceremony at or near the Pascha (Eastertide), as soon as the calendar of the Christian year came to be generally observed. It is probable also that the picture of the white robe (στολὴ λευκή) given to the saints in Rev. 6.11 (cf. 3.4 and 7.9) is derived from the image vividly present to the seer's mind of the great company, composed of people of many nationalities and languages, who were gathered together at a great service of Christian baptism, where the catechumens with palms in their hands acclaimed the Lamb upon the throne. The seer's conception of the robes of the saints washed in the blood of the Lamb (Rev. 7.14; 22.14) is his way of expressing the great truth which the whole NT affirms, namely, baptismal justification.

BAPTISM, FAITH AND FORGIVENESS

We have already seen in Chapter 10 that justification in the NT means justification by the gracious and saving righteousness of God through baptismal incorporation into the corporate personality of Christ.[1] That which saves is no mere negative renunciation of sins of the flesh, but the positive acquisition of an actively good conscience through our being made part of the resurrection-life of Christ himself (cf. I Pet. 3.21). Thus, faith in Christ is inseparable from baptism, and this faith is itself the result of the operation of God's prevenient grace, or of the Holy Spirit, before ever the candidate can come to baptism at all (cf. I Cor. 12.3). Baptism apart from faith, as an *ex opere operato* initiatory ceremony, would have been incomprehensible to the mind of the apostolic Church. The NT has no answer at all to the question about the standing of a person who has been baptized, perhaps as a matter of social or family custom, but who possesses no real personal faith, because in a missionary situation such a case does not arise; the apostolic Church would not have regarded anyone who had gone through the ceremony of being baptized without making a genuine response of faith

[1] *Supra*, 236.

as having been effectively baptized at all. But equally the NT mind could not have contemplated the possibility of saving faith apart from baptism; again it would have been unthinkable that there should have been sincere believers who were not baptized, except for those who were awaiting the opportunity of baptism. Again, too, the NT gives us no answer to the question of the standing of believers who are not baptized. We must not try to answer questions which the NT leaves unanswered.

In the Church of the NT, faith and baptism belong together, like soul and body in biblical thought: the one cannot exist without the other. To regard sincere faith as adequate to salvation apart from baptismal incorporation into Christ's body is sheer 'Christian Science' by the standards of NT theology; by ignoring the reality of the body it makes salvation a subjective affair, a disembodied soul-salvation of individuals who have 'enjoyed' a certain 'experience'. The profession of faith without the bodily action of submission in baptism is not the obedience of the whole man; a mental act which has no outward embodiment is a mere phantom of the full-blooded, full-bodied wholeness of biblical thinking. Believing while dispensing with the act of obedience, with the act of baptism, is a kind of docetism, and is thus not belief in the NT sense at all. The action—or, rather, the passion—of being baptized, is itself part of the act of believing, since to believe means to obey. So often we hear it said that the thing which matters is the inward attitude of mind and heart and will, and that outward conformity to a 'mere' ceremony is formalism, externalism, or institutionalism. Thus, baptism ceases to be a necessity and becomes an optional extra for those who like pretty-pretty ceremonies; and those who insist on baptism are accused of exalting the letter above the spirit. Such reasoning develops from the post-Renaissance breaking up of the biblical unity of body and soul, of faith and obedience, of inner truth and outward expression. It is not surprising that it did not emerge in Christian thought until after the Reformation; but it belongs to the Renaissance rather than to the Reformation. The parallel to the view that baptism is a dispensable extra is the docetic view that the historical question about whether Christ really suffered and died is unimportant: all that matters was his own inner self-dedication. The actual historical baptism of the individual Christian is important precisely in the sense in which the actual historical death of Christ is important. Both are ἐφάπαξ, unrepeatable. In Heb. 6.4-8 *Auct. Heb.* is not saying that the forgiveness of post-baptismal sin is impossible; he is saying that those who were once enlightened (ἅπαξ φωτισθέντας)—a technical term for 'baptized'—and tasted of the heavenly gift (i.e. the Holy Spirit in baptism), and were made μέτοχοι of the Holy Spirit, etc., and then fell away, cannot be renewed unto repentance (πάλιν ἀνακαινίζειν εἰς μετάνοιαν), i.e. be re-baptized. The NT doctrine of the cross of Christ as a baptism is not far from the writer's mind, for he says that to fall away after baptism is to 'crucify to themselves the Son of God afresh and put him to an open shame' (6.6). To receive baptism is to accept the cross, to die with Christ, as St Paul would have said; apostasy after baptism is to throw in one's lot with the world that rejected and still rejects Christ. It is with this sin, rather than with post-baptismal sin in general, that *Auct. Heb.* is here concerned; and apostasy is mortal sin precisely because it is the negation of the fundamental act of baptism. In the view of *Auct. Heb.*, and probably of other NT writers also, apostasy is, like baptism, ἐφάπαξ, an act that can be performed only once.[1] This is because baptism itself is the indispensable, effective symbol of salvation, the sealing or ratification of the believing act of obedience by which the individual disciple is made one with Christ in his death and resurrection and is endowed with the gift of the Spirit, whereby even now he tastes the powers of the Age to Come.

In the preaching of Jesus faith and repentance were conditions of entering into the reign of God (Mark 1.15, etc.).[2] The baptism of John had been a 'baptism of repentance unto remission of sins' (ἄφεσις ἁμαρτιῶν) (Mark 1.4; Luke 3.3). Remission of sins was in Jewish expectation one of the benefits that would be conferred in the Messianic Age (cf. Isa. 43.25; Jer. 31.34b; 33.8; 50.20; Micah 7.18f.), and hence it was entirely appropriate that Christian baptism, which was the eschatological sacrament of the outpouring of the Spirit in the latter days, should be closely associated with the declaration of the forgiveness of sins: cf. Acts 2.38, 'Repent ye, and be baptized in the name of Jesus Christ unto the remission of your sins; and ye shall receive the gift of the Holy Spirit' (cf. also Luke 24.47; Acts 5.31; 10.43; 13.38; 26.18; Eph. 1.7; Col. 1.14; I John 1.9; 2.12). Baptism, with its accompanying repentance and faith, was the divinely appointed way by which the individual entered into the sphere of the Messianic ἄφεσις ἁμαρτιῶν and of the outpouring of the Spirit; there was no other way of entering upon the life of the Age to Come. The Messiah is the bringer of ἄφεσις (forgiveness), which is a consequence of his coming and is available to all upon whom the Spirit of the latter times is bestowed. There is no suggestion in the NT that God could not forgive sins until Christ had by his self-sacrifice made it possible. In the NT 'forgiveness is not directly connected with the death of Christ; it is nowhere said that he

---

[1] Cf. *supra*, 107-9.   [2] See *supra*, 20-2.

died that men might be forgiven.'[1] Forgiveness, in its NT sense of ἄφεσις ἁμαρτιῶν, is one of the blessings brought by the Messiah (cf. I Tim. 1.15) and it must characterize the lives of those who have been baptized into the Spirit of God and of Christ (cf. Matt. 6.12, 14f.; 18.21-35; Mark 11.25; Luke 11.4; Acts 7.60; Eph. 4.32, etc.). In the Gospels Jesus is powerfully represented as the Messianic bringer of forgiveness: 'The Son of Man hath power on earth to forgive sins' (Mark 2.10). He says to those whom he will cure, 'Thy sins are forgiven thee'. There is a subtle connection between the healing miracles of Jesus and baptism and the Eucharist in the apostolic Church; the sacraments are looked upon as 'greater works than these'—greater even than the σημεῖα of healing which Jesus in his earthly ministry had wrought.[2] 'He that believeth on me, the works that I do shall he do also; and greater works than these shall he do, because I go to my Father (and will then send the Spirit)' (John 14.12). The work of baptism is the continuance of the healing ministry of Jesus, who by means of it demonstrated the reality of the Messianic ἄφεσις ἁμαρτιῶν (Mark 2.10-12). To this end were the disciples endowed with Holy Spirit and commissioned with the power of binding and loosing: 'Receive ye the Holy Spirit: whosesoever sins ye forgive, they are forgiven unto them; whosesoever sins ye retain, they are retained' (John 20.22f.; cf. Matt. 16.19; 18.18). 'Go ye and make disciples of all the nations, baptizing them . . .' (Matt. 28.19).

THE SEAL OF THE SPIRIT

There is only one baptism in the Church of Christ, just as there is one Lord, one faith, one Father, one Spirit and one body (Eph. 4.4). Baptism is therefore the symbol of the universality of Christ: all nations and classes drink of the one Spirit; Jew and Gentile, master and slave, are baptized together (I Cor. 12.13; Gal. 3.27f.). All Christian baptism is baptism in Holy Spirit, the outpoured δύναμις from on high of the Messianic Age; indeed, this is what distinguishes it from the baptism of John, which was baptism only in water (Mark 1.8; Matt. 3.11; Luke 3.16; John 1.33; Acts 1.5; 11.16; 19.1-7). In his baptism the individual Christian was ordained to the ministry of Christ's Church and given his personal χάρισμα of the Spirit to enable him to fulfil his God-given

[1] Vincent Taylor, *Forgiveness and Reconciliation*, 1946, 3. In Chap. I of this work Dr Taylor has given us a valuable study of forgiveness (ἄφεσις, ἀφίημι, χαρίζομαι), in which he shews that 'forgiveness' in the NT is a narrower conception than it has become in modern theological usage, where it is virtually the equivalent of reconciliation in the widest sense. This modern usage is largely based on the parable of the Prodigal Son (Luke 15.11-32), although the 'forgiveness' words do not occur in it. In the NT forgiveness means the removal of the barriers to reconciliation rather than reconciliation itself. Forgiveness is always remission of sins (never of penalties).

[2] Cf. O. Cullmann, *Early Christian Worship*, ET, 1953, 87, 118.

διακονία (I Cor. 12.4-13; Eph. 4.7);[1] he was 'sealed' with the Holy Spirit, and he was anointed king and priest in the new Israel of God.

The idea of baptism as the seal of the Spirit appears in II Cor. 1.22; Eph. 1.13 and 4.30, and probably in Rev. 7.3-8. St Paul teaches that God has firmly established us in Christ and has anointed us (with Holy Spirit in baptism) and sealed us and given us in our hearts the earnest (ἀρραβών) of the Spirit as our means of inner assurance (II Cor. 1.22). Baptismal sealing with the promised Holy Spirit is the ἀρραβών of our inheritance in the day when God redeems his own possession (Eph. 1.13f.); Christians were sealed in the Holy Spirit of God until the dawning of redemption-day (Eph. 4.30). The verb used in these passages is σφραγίζειν, which means 'to mark with a sign', 'to brand' (as of cattle or slaves), 'to set one's seal upon', and hence 'to ratify', 'confirm', 'attest'.[2] A similar notion is found in Gal. 6.17, where St Paul says that he bears branded on his body the marks (στίγματα) of Jesus, as a slave bears his owner's mark (cf. Phil. 1.1, δοῦλοι Χριστοῦ); but he is probably thinking here of the marks left by his sufferings rather than of the baptismal sign. What St Paul means by 'branding' or 'sealing' with Holy Spirit is that Christians in their baptism receive the internal mark or sign of the Holy Spirit; this 'mark' is not accessible to human inspection in this age, but it is nevertheless the sign by which those who belong to God will be recognized in the day of judgment (cf. II Tim. 2.19).

The idea that God sets his mark upon his own is a familiar one in the Bible. Thus, God set his mark upon Cain (Gen. 4.15), the man who was his brother's murderer, and here is seen as in a parable the mystery and miracle of grace: God will not let man go or abandon him to his justly merited fate. Cain in his wanderings, even when far from the presence of God, nevertheless stands under the protection of God. It was upon the lintels of the dwellings of the Israelites that the mark was set, not upon their persons, on the first passover-night in Egypt (Ex. 12.13, 22). But the most important OT passage in this connection is Ezek. 9.4-6, where the prophet in his vision sees the mark *taw* (i.e. a cross) set upon the foreheads of the faithful Jews who had resisted the heathen abominations; in the day of vengeance all who are marked with the cross are spared. This passage is taken up by the author of the Apocalypse (Rev. 7.3; 9.4; cf. 14.1), who sees in his vision the sealing (both σφραγίζειν and σφραγίς are used) of the δοῦλοι τοῦ Θεοῦ on their foreheads before the avenging angels are allowed to begin their hurtful work. One hundred and forty and four thousand (i.e. the complete

---

[1] See *supra*, 110, 304f.

[2] The noun σφραγίς (a seal) is never directly applied to baptism; it is found in NT at Rom. 4.11, I Cor. 9.2, II Tim. 2.19 and some thirteen times in Rev.; of these occurrences Rom. 4.11 and Rev. 9.4 are important for our purpose.

number of the saved) of the tribes of the New Israel are sealed before the judgment begins: the seer is thinking of the present age as the age of baptism, the time of the sealing of the redeemed, which will shortly be completed before the onset of the avenging powers in the day of judgment. The brand-mark of Christ's δοῦλοι (cf. Phil. 1.1; Gal. 6.17), the σφραγίς on their foreheads, is, of course, as in Ezek. 9.4, the sign of the cross, now received in baptism. It is, of course, just as likely that the use of the sign of the cross in baptism should have arisen before the end of the first century A.D. as that it should have originated at a later date; the Ezekiel passage would hardly have been overlooked by those Christian rabbis who first searched the Scriptures for their testimony to Christ, and the evidence of the Apocalypse proves that the passage was noticed at least before the close of the first century. Ezek. 9.4-6 would be regarded, as it seems to be in the Apocalypse, as a prophecy of Christian baptism which was now fulfilled in the Church of the Messiah.

The evidence of the Apocalypse shews us that the idea of the baptized as the slaves of Christ, branded with their owner's seal, is not only a Pauline idea, or at least that, if it was originally Pauline, it had been adopted into the thought of the Church at large a generation or so after St Paul's time. There is, however, one other passage in the Johannine writings which suggests that the conception of baptism as a sealing was known outside the more narrowly Pauline circle. In John 6.27 we read, 'Work not for the meat which perishes, but for the meat which endures into the life of the (new) Age, which the Son of Man shall give unto you: for him the Father has sealed, even God himself.' According to the rabbis the Messiah when he came would bring again the manna from heaven: Jesus gives the bread of life, the bread from heaven, which, unlike the manna given by Moses, does not perish: this he does because he is the Son of Man or Messiah, i.e. the one who is anointed in Holy Spirit or the one who is 'sealed' in the Spirit.[1]

But thus far we have hardly as yet touched upon the essential meaning of the conception of baptism as a sealing; we have dealt, indeed, with important matters, but we have not mentioned what must surely be held to be the real origin and significance of the NT use of σφραγίς in connection with baptism. This, of course, is to be found in the fact that the rabbis spoke of circumcision as a seal, the divinely appointed sign or seal of the individual's standing within the Covenant. In the OT itself circumcision is not actually called a seal, but at its institution it is

[1] Cf. C. K. Barrett, *GSJ*, 238: 'In view of the aorist (ἐσφράγισεν) it is natural to look to a particular act of sealing; this should probably be found in the baptism of Jesus, or rather, since John does not record the baptism itself, in the descent of the Spirit upon Jesus. See especially 1.33f.'

said to be ἐν σημείῳ διαθήκης (Gen. 17.11). In Jewish usage, however, the term 'seal' was regularly applied to circumcision,[1] and St Paul is adopting rabbinic terminology in Rom. 4.11: 'He (Abraham) received the sign of circumcision (σημεῖον περιτομῆς), a seal (σφραγίς) of the righteousness of the faith which he had while he was still in uncircumcision.' Paul is arguing that Abraham was justified by his faith while still a Gentile; circumcision was given to him after his faith had been credited to him for righteousness; it was like the seal on a document which authenticates a transaction already completed: thus Abraham is the father of believing Gentiles as well as of those Jews who share his faith in God's promise. Paul thus comes to think of baptism as a seal of the New Covenant in the sense in which circumcision was the sign and seal of the Old Covenant. But whereas circumcision was a physical mark, visible in the flesh, baptism was a seal of the Spirit, an invisible, inward sealing. A similar thought is expressed in Rom. 2.28f.: 'He is not a Jew who is one outwardly; neither is that circumcision which is outward in the flesh: but he is a Jew who is one inwardly: and circumcision is that of the heart, in the Spirit, not in the letter; whose praise is not from men but from God.' This 'circumcision of the heart' corresponds to the 'circumcision not made with hands' of Col. 2.11, which the context clearly proves to be Christian baptism: '(Christ) in whom ye were also circumcised with a circumcision not made with hands, in the putting off of the body of the flesh (i.e. the unredeemed carnal self), in the circumcision of Christ, having been buried with him in baptism, wherein ye were also raised with him through faith in the working of God, who raised him from the dead.' From this passage, unique in the NT, we learn that baptism is the Christian circumcision, the means by which the individual is made a member of the Covenant people, and as a result of which he bears the Spirit's seal in his heart. It is not surprising in view of this teaching of St Paul's to find that the term σφραγίς was at an early date transferred from Jewish circumcision to Christian baptism and indeed becomes a technical term for the latter; for instance, in II Clement there is great stress laid on 'keeping baptism pure and undefiled' (6.9) which is apparently synonymous with 'keeping the seal' (7.6) or 'keeping the seal unstained' (8.6).[2]

To regard baptism as the Christian circumcision is an inevitable corollary of the recognition of the Christian Church as 'the Israel of

---

[1] Sanday and Headlam (*Romans*, ICC, 107), cite the prayer pronounced at the circumcision of a child: 'Blessed be he who sanctified his beloved from the womb, and put his ordinance upon his flesh, and sealed his offspring with the sign of a holy Covenant'; also *Targum Cant.* iii.8, 'The seal of circumcision is in your flesh as it was sealed in the flesh of Abraham'; *Shemoth R.* 19, 'Ye shall not eat of the passover unless the seal of Abraham be in your flesh.'

[2] See also J. B. Lightfoot, *Apostolic Fathers*, Part I, Vol. 2, 1890, 226.

God' (Gal. 6.16; cf. 3.7, 9, 29). Thus, St Paul in Phil. 3.2f. explicitly denies the title of 'the circumcision' to Israel κατὰ σάρκα (but cf. Gal. 2.7-9) and uses instead the scornful title 'the concision' (ἡ κατατομή— a word not found elsewhere in NT or in cl. Gk. lit. or in LXX): the expression means 'mutilation' (Lat. *concisio*; cf. the play on the verb ἀποκόπτω, 'to amputate', in Gal. 5.12). The Jewish circumcision is a mere physical mutilation, unworthy of being placed alongside the Christian circumcision of the heart, which is the seal of the Spirit: St Paul's words in Phil. 3.2f. are, 'Beware of the concision, for we are the circumcision (ἡ περιτομή), who worship by the Spirit of God' (οἱ Πνεύματι Θεοῦ λατρεύοντες, cf. the rational worship of Rom. 12.1 and the spiritual sacrifices of I Pet. 2.5). Thus, St Paul regards the Christian Church as the true circumcision, i.e. the New Israel, and baptism is the Christian σημεῖον περιτομῆς and σφραγίς τῆς δικαιοσύνης τῆς πίστεως (cf. Rom. 4.11). But the character of the Christian σημεῖον and σφραγίς is qualitatively different from that of circumcision as practised in Judaism. Not merely is it inward and invisible instead of outward and physical; it is also universal. It is universal not merely in that baptism is not the badge of a single race, but is for 'all nations'; it is universal in a sense in which the Jewish circumcision could not be: it included male and female. 'There can be no male and female: for ye are all one in Christ Jesus' (Gal. 3.28; note v. 27). The truth of this deep insight was doubtless acted upon in the Church's life and worship long before it was formulated by St Paul or anyone else; from the earliest days women as well as men were baptized into the body of Christ without discrimination. We are apt to take this for granted and we hardly pause to consider what a revolutionary change had been made, so important in its consequences for the subsequent history of the human race. But reflection will convince us that nothing else that has happened in history has been quite so important in establishing the true status of women as the fact that the Christian Church from the beginning baptized alike both men and women.[1] The distinctions that had seemed important in the old order now no longer mattered: race, social status, sex counted for nothing in the new order (Gal. 3.28), not even circumcision or uncircumcision, but only new creation (Gal. 6.15). It is through baptism that the new creation of the end-time comes into being. As in the beginning the Spirit 'brooded' over the waters of the old creation (Gen. 1.2): as the dove, the symbol of the divine mercy, returned to the ark at the saving-baptism of Noah, which foreshadowed Christian baptism (cf. I Pet. 3.20f.): so the Spirit as a dove brooded again over the waters at the baptism of Christ (Mark 1.10; Matt. 3.16; Luke 3.22;

[1] For a specific instance of the baptism of a woman see Acts 16.15 (Lydia).

John 1.32f.): now in Christian baptism the Spirit broods over the waters and breathes life into the new creation, the life of the Age to Come. The dove which is so often found over the font in the churches of Christendom is a profound symbol of the meaning of Christian baptism.

THE LAYING ON OF HANDS

The likelihood that the laying on of hands was a regular feature of baptism in the apostolic Church is attested rather by the universal and continuous tradition of the Church in post-NT times than by direct NT evidence. Only two passages, both in Acts, refer explicitly to the matter: from the obscure reference to the laying on of hands in Heb. 6.2 nothing more may be inferred than that catechetical instruction upon the subject was given in the apostolic Church, but whether the reference is to the use of the ceremony at baptism or at ordination it is impossible to determine.[1] It is reasonable to suppose, though it cannot be proved, that the laying on of hands at baptism was intended to symbolize both 'ordination' to the ministerial priesthood of the laity and also 'coronation' in the kingly office of those appointed to share the βασιλεία of Christ (cf. I Pet. 2.9; Rev. 1.6; 5.10; 20.6). In each case the idea of *anointing* would be the primary meaning of the act, since both kings and priests were anointed in Israel;[2] the aspect of baptism as an anointing in Holy Spirit would be symbolized by the laying on of hands. This does not mean, however, that the moment of the laying on of hands was thought of as the moment of the imparting of the Holy Spirit.[3] In the NT the whole baptismal action is a unity which cannot be analysed into its component parts, and it is in the whole action that the Spirit is bestowed. If we had to assign a moment for the imparting of the Spirit, it could on the evidence of the NT only be the moment of the coming up out of the water, as it was at this moment that the Spirit came upon Jesus (Mark 1.10). But such attempts to define what the Scriptures leave undefined are rationalistic intrusions into the mystery of revelation and are almost always the cause of disunity amongst Christians.

St Luke at least has no theory about the laying on of hands as the necessary condition or as the moment of the Spirit's descent; and

---

[1] On the general theme of the laying on of hands in the Bible see *supra*, 329.

[2] See *supra*, 178.

[3] Still less does it mean that the apostolic Church considered that baptism in water was not baptism in Holy Spirit at all and that it was the ceremony of the laying on of hands which was thought of as baptism in Holy Spirit—a position which has been maintained in A. J. Mason, *The Relation of Confirmation to Baptism*, 1890, G. Dix, *The Theology of Confirmation in relation to Baptism*, 1946, etc. All attempts to exalt confirmation as 'the seal of the Spirit' as over against 'mere' water-baptism fail for lack of scriptural warrant. On the whole subject see G. W. H. Lampe, *The Seal of the Spirit: a Study in the Doctrine of Baptism and Confirmation in the New Testament and the Fathers*, 1951.

he is the only NT writer to give us any information upon the subject. In the former of his two passages which mention the laying on of hands (Acts 8.14-18) the Holy Spirit indeed descends upon the Samaritans, whom Philip had previously baptized, when the apostles Peter and John lay their hands on them. The point of the story is that Philip had taken the unprecedented step of baptizing non-Jews, Samaritans; Peter and John come down from Jerusalem to investigate the matter; they signify their approval of Philip's action and *confirm* the baptism of the Samaritans by the laying on of hands, and the Samaritans immediately receive the Holy Spirit. Philip's action, that is to say, is confirmed not only by the apostles but by God himself, who sends the Spirit. In this passage the laying on of hands has little to do with 'confirmation' in the modern church sense; what is being 'confirmed' is the unprecedented action of baptizing Samaritans. A similar unprecedented step is taken by St Peter himself in the baptism of the household of Cornelius, 'the Pentecost of the Gentiles' (Acts 10). Now, for the first time, Gentiles—not Jewish half-cousins, like the Samaritans—are baptized; again the Holy Spirit descends, but this time the gift occurs *before* the baptism has taken place (10.44-48): God 'confirms' the action before Peter had even mentioned baptism in his preaching. There is now no reference to the laying on of apostolic hands, because no apostolic confirmation is necessary; as St Peter remarks, 'Who can forbid the water, that these should not be baptized, who have received the Holy Spirit as we did?' (10.47).

The second passage in Acts which deals with the laying on of hands is Acts 19.5f.: Paul baptizes the twelve disciples of John in Ephesus, 'and when Paul had laid his hands upon them, the Holy Spirit came on them, and they spake with tongues and prophesied'. The point of the story is that the Baptist's sect of disciples, numerous in many parts of the world as the story suggests, were still awaiting the Messianic outpouring of the Spirit, which John had prophesied: they did not know that the prediction had been fulfilled in Christian baptism; Paul's proclamation that John's prediction was fulfilled in Jesus was demonstrated at the baptism of the men by the descent of the Spirit. It would indeed be precarious to base on this single passage a doctrine of 'the relation of baptism to confirmation', in view of the silence of St Paul and the rest of the NT upon the whole subject of the laying on of hands in baptism.[1]

---

[1] It would also be precarious to conclude anything from Acts 9.17f.; the laying on of hands by Ananias seems to be connected with the healing of Paul's blindness rather than with the baptism which follows, but the whole complex is doubtless closely connected in St Luke's thought: the laying on of hands, the restoration of sight (cf. baptismal φωτισμός; see p. 338 *supra*), the baptism, the taking of food (? Eucharist), 'strengthening'. In post-NT times the catechumens after they had been baptized were given the τροφή of milk and honey to symbolize their entry even now by faith into the Promised Land. See also note 3 on p. 338 *supra*.

We must conclude that the baptismal act as a whole is regarded in the NT as the anointing of the members of the New Israel with Holy Spirit, which is not to be identified with any particular moment or action (such as the laying on of hands) within it. Baptism is a being born anew of water *and* of the Spirit (John 3.3-8), and the NT knows no Christian baptism which is baptism in water only and is a mere preliminary to some other ceremony of the imparting of the Holy Spirit which follows upon it. There is nothing in the NT to suggest that any physical anointing with oil (chrismation) took place in baptism in the apostolic Church, though in James 5.14 we read of the anointing of *the sick* with oil (contrast Mark 16.18). The baptized are anointed with water, which symbolizes the outpoured Holy Spirit; at least, nothing more than this can be inferred from the few passages which specifically allude to baptismal anointing: in II Cor. 1.21f. St Paul writes, 'He that stablishes us (ὁ δὲ βεβαιῶν ἡμᾶς) with you in (εἰς) Christ, and anointed us (καὶ χρίσας ἡμᾶς), is God, who also sealed us and gave us the ἀρραβών of the Spirit in our hearts'; and in I John 2.20 and 27 it is claimed that because of their 'anointing (χρίσμα) from the Holy One' Christians know all the truth (cf. John 14.26; 16.13).[1] It has been usual amongst commentators on Acts 11.26 to repeat from one another the remark that the dubbing of the disciples 'Christians' (Χριστιανοί, cf. Acts 26.28; I Pet. 4.16) was a witticism of the Antiochenes, who had noticed that they were always talking about Christ; it is much more likely that the Greek-speaking disciples of Antioch adopted the word because they regarded themselves as those who were anointed, as Jesus had been, with the Holy Spirit in the latter days. Baptism is always baptism in Holy Spirit; the laying on of hands (whether performed, as in the Orthodox and Lutheran churches, at the baptism of infants or at 'years of discretion') is an integral part of the action, and there are no scriptural grounds for elaborating a 'theology' of the one in relation to the other. The unity of the Church (whether the separated 'churches' will recognize the truth or not) is something which is already given by God in the great fact of the 'one baptism' (Eph. 4.4): all the baptized have drunk of the 'one Spirit' (I Cor. 12.13; Eph. 4.4)—a truth which is acknowledged when 'the churches' disallow the re-baptism of those who have already been baptized in other denominations. The unity of baptism, and therefore of the Church itself, should not be obscured by insistence

---

[1] The noun χρίσμα occurs in NT only at I John 2.20 and 27; the verb χρίω is used of Christians only at II Cor. 1.21, and of Christ as having been anointed at Luke 4.18 (cf. Isa. 61.1); Acts 4.27; 10.38; Heb. 1.9 (citing Ps. 45.7). At James 5.14, the only reference in the epistles to a physical anointing with oil, the verb used is significantly not χρίω but ἀλείφω (used also eight times in the Gospels of physical anointing with oil).

upon theories of 'confirmation' which clearly cannot be 'proved by most certain warrants of Holy Scripture'.

INFANT BAPTISM IN THE NEW TESTAMENT

Recent NT scholarship has emphasized the organic connection that exists between the worship and practice of the earliest Christian communities and the actual words of the NT records, particularly those of the various *pericopae* of the Gospels. The records, that is to say, arise out of the inner life and faith of the apostolic Church. In the light of recent NT scholarship there can be no reasonable doubt that the practice of baptizing in infancy the children of Christian parents goes back to the days of the apostles themselves. Furthermore, in the light of our present understanding of the theology of the apostolic Church it would seem that the practice of such infant baptism is a natural and indeed inevitable expression of the faith of the church of NT days. The recovery in our own times of the full biblical theology of the NT has helped us to understand more clearly that objections to the practice of baptizing the infant children of Christian parents arise rather from the rationalistic and individualistic attitudes of renaissance humanism than from a right understanding of the NT teaching about faith and justification.

In the missionary situation of the apostolic Church, as on the mission-field today, baptism would be for the most part adult. But the solidarity of the family, or more accurately the household, would mean, in baptism as in all other matters, that when the head of the household took a decisive step, he committed every member of his 'house' (οἶκος); he was a 'representative man', a kind of inclusive personality, and what happened to him happened to all. Thus, we read that 'so-and-so was baptized and all his house' (Acts 16.15, 33; I Cor. 1.16; cf. Acts 10.48). Whether this means that the slaves and children were all baptized individually we have no means of knowing: in any case the NT principle of representative faith is established. There is no place for our modern individualism in biblical thinking; we do not live unto ourselves; the faith of one is available for those who are unable as yet to express their own faith. This is clearly brought out in the story of the conversion of the Philippian gaoler (Acts 16.19-34). 'Believe on the Lord Jesus, and thou shalt be saved, thou and thy house; . . . he was baptized, he and all his, immediately' (παραχρῆμα) (16.31, 33). What has happened to the gaoler happens also to 'all his': is not this still an essential truth of family relationships? When the head of the family, or the parents of the children, are baptized, something happens to the children: they are no longer pagans, outside the fellowship of the Spirit. Thus St Paul appeals to a universally acknowledged principle—the fact that the children of believing parents are ἅγια, holy: 'The unbelieving husband is sanctified in the wife, the unbelieving wife is sanctified in the brother: else were your children unclean; but now are they holy' (I Cor. 7.14). Cullmann takes this passage to imply that the children of Christian parents did not need to be baptized because they would belong automatically to the body of Christ by reason of their birth, and he says that in this respect the situation was parallel to the practice of proselyte baptism in Judaism, where the children of proselytes were baptized along with their parents, while the children born to such parents after their reception into Judaism did not need to be baptized.[1] If Cullmann were right, Christian baptism would presumably have been limited to the baptism of proselytes, like Jewish baptism; but clearly the post-apostolic Church did not share Cullmann's view of St Paul's teaching: the children of believing parents were, as a matter of historical fact, always baptized. Paul means, of course, that because of the parents' faith, their children have been baptized; hence they too have become ἅγια, whereas the unbelieving husband or wife, being unbaptized, is only 'sanctified' (ἡγίασται). The fact is that the true analogy to Christian baptism in Judaism is not proselyte baptism but circumcision. As circumcision was the seal of the old Covenant, so baptism is the seal of the new Covenant, the seal of the Spirit. Now in Judaism the male children were 'circumcised the eighth day' (i.e. a week after birth) (cf. Luke 1.59; 2.21; Phil. 3.5) and were given their names; the idea of the imparting of the seal to the infant children of believing parents would be taken over quite naturally by the Christian Church from normal Jewish practice. The story of the circumcision of the infant Saviour, and the naming of him 'Jesus' (Luke 2.21), would have a direct meaning for those who took their children to be sealed and named in Christian baptism. We may agree with Cullmann, however, when he says that the one thing for which there is no evidence or justification in the NT is the practice of baptizing the children of Christian parents only after they have grown up.[2] If the children are already ἅγια though unbaptized, it is clear that their baptism, since it does not *make* them 'saints', is not what is meant by baptism in the NT.

The NT principle that the faith of one person may avail for another is illustrated in the miracle-story of the Epileptic Boy (Mark 9.14-29), where the father's faith is accepted on behalf of the helpless lad. The connection between the healing-saving work of the historical Jesus and

[1] *Baptism in the New Testament*, 26, 44f.
[2] *Op. cit.*, 26: 'Adult baptism for sons and daughters born of Christian parents . . . is even worse attested by the NT than infant baptism (for which certain possible traces are discoverable) and indeed lacks any kind of proof.'

Christian baptism is also illustrated in this *pericope*, which St Mark probably meant to be a story that could be used by his catechists in their instruction upon baptism. An exorcism takes place, as was held to take place in every baptism. The faith of a sponsor is necessary before the saving action can begin. The disciples have no power of themselves to effect the work; Jesus alone is the true minister of baptism. A death and a rising again take place: 'the child became as one dead, insomuch that the more part said, He is dead. But Jesus took him by the hand and raised him up; and he arose' (ἀνέστη): Jesus is the resurrection and the life. Finally the importance of prayer at baptism is stressed (and a later age adds fasting). Perhaps the miracle-stories of the Paralytic (Mark 2.1-12) and the Johannine Lame Man at the Pool (John 5.2-9) had a similar baptismal reference. The healing and saving ministry which Jesus began in Galilee and Judaea is continued through the sacraments of his Church (cf. John 14.12).

The sayings of Jesus upon the subject of 'little children' (παιδία) are relevant, because they make it clear that in his view they are, as it were, by nature at home in that βασιλεία of God to which baptism is the gateway: 'of such is the Kingdom of God' (Mark 10.14). 'Unless ye turn and become as little children, ye shall in no wise enter into the Kingdom of heaven' (Matt. 18.3). St John certainly understands the teaching of the Lord about the παιδία to have a bearing upon the question of baptism; this is his interpretation of it: 'Except a man be born anew (or from above), he cannot see the Kingdom of God. . . . Except a man be born of water and the Spirit, he cannot enter into the Kingdom of God' (John 3.3, 5). Jesus in Mark 9.36f. (cf. 10.16) makes the παιδία his *sheluchim*:[1] he takes a (representative) child, sets him in the midst and takes him in his arms (ἐναγκαλίζομαι, only here and at 10.16 in NT; from ἀγκάλη, the crooked arm) and says, 'Whosoever shall receive one of such little children in my name receiveth me; and whosoever receiveth me, receiveth not me but him that sent me.' In receiving the little children the Church receives Christ himself: the real, living Christ is present in the sacrament of holy baptism, for this is where the παιδία are 'received' into it. The meaning of the passage is made clearer in Mark 10.13-16. Most of the *pericopae* which St Mark included in his Gospel were selected because they had an important bearing upon some urgent question of faith or discipline in the apostolic Church, and it is likely that this *pericope* is included because it gives a word of the Lord which the Church understands to represent his mind upon the question of the baptism of infants. Jesus is indignant with those who would prevent the little children from coming to him: 'Suffer the

[1] See *supra*, 137f.

little children to come unto me and forbid them not, for of such is the Kingdom of God.' Cullmann has collected sufficient evidence to suggest that the phrase 'forbid them not' (μὴ κωλύετε αὐτά) is a deliberate allusion to the baptismal rite of the early Church, where the question 'What hinders?' (τί κωλύει;) was asked liturgically before the candidates were baptized (cf. esp. Acts 8.38; 10.47; also Matt. 3.14, διεκώλυεν, and Acts 11.17, κωλῦσαι).[1] The concluding verse of the *pericope* (10.16), 'he took them in his arms (ἐναγκαλισάμενος) and blessed them, laying his hands upon them', is, of course, the literal description of the minister's action at the baptism of infants, then as now. It should be noted that the verse supplies evidence that the laying on of hands was an essential part of the baptismal action of the apostolic Church even when παιδία were being baptized. St Mark clearly expected his catechists to use this story as a lesson-illustration when instructing the catechumens upon the meaning of baptism. His intention was well understood by the Church of later centuries; this passage has been read as a baptismal lection from medieval times.[2]

The important question, however, is whether the practice of infant baptism is in accord, not with possible interpretations of certain passages in the Gospels, but with the principles of NT theology as a whole. Since the rise of post-renaissance individualism, when men no longer profess their creed by family or region, and are aware of themselves as atomic, isolated self-existents, it is understandable that insistence should have been laid upon personal faith and upon the responsibility of the baptized for their own decision. Furthermore, in ages when baptism had become a mere social convention and everyone was automatically baptized in infancy by order of the State, or at least as a result of strong social pressure, a protest was necessary on behalf of personal faith and decision.[3] The witness of a 'Baptist' sect to the essential element of personal decision in the total act of Christian initiation is doubtless a necessary contribution to the full understanding of baptism

---

[1] See *Baptism in the New Testament*, 71-80.

[2] So the BCP (1549 onwards) reads it from St Mark; the Sarum Rite read it from St Matthew's version.

[3] Karl Barth in his *The Teaching of the Church regarding Baptism*, ET by E. A Payne, 1948, protests against the convention of infant baptism. The pamphle (originally written in 1943) echoes the struggle of the Confessional Church under the Nazis against the 'German Christians', who, though baptized in infancy, were not in any real sense Christian. Barth's prophetic insight and courage were indeed God's gift to the Church in perilous times, and it is probable that, despite the massive 'Dogmatics', he will be remembered as a prophet rather than as a theologian. Like all the great heresiarchs, he tries to turn a valuable prophetic insight into a dogmatic theological position and thus denies a larger truth for the sake of the aspect of th truth which he sees so vividly. See also M. Barth, *Die Taufe—eine Sakrament? Eine exegetischer Beitrag zum Gespräch über die kirklicher Taufe*, Zürich, 1951; and J. Schneider, *Baptism and Church in the New Testament*, ET by E. A. Payne, 1957.

within Christendom as a whole. Yet this witness can never become the faith of the Church as such, nor can it set aside the wisdom of the Church of the ages, because in emphasizing one truth it obscures another, one even more central to the Gospel and even less likely to be understood in our modern individualistic and rationalistic civilization. The central truth of the Gospel which infant baptism enshrines is that faith is the response to God's saving act, not the condition of it. I am not baptized because I have decided to believe; I believe because I have come to know that I have already been admitted to the sphere of Christ's redemption. My decision to believe follows from the saving fact; it is not the saving fact itself—a truth which distinguishes the NT doctrine of faith from all forms of existentialism, Barth's as well as Bultmann's. That is to say, I am not saved by any decision which I have taken; on the contrary, while I was weak and helpless, God took me and placed me within the sphere of the redemption wrought by Christ. I did not choose to be born into a Christian family or to be taken to the font; I could no more have done this than the paralysed man borne of four could have walked to Christ where he was thronged by the crowd, or the impotent man at Bethesda's pool could have lifted himself into the waters. I did not earn the grace which was freely given to me; God's election of *me* remains a mystery, something of which I can give no rational explanation at all. I did not choose Christ; it was Christ who chose me (cf. John 15.16); I love, because he first loved me (cf. I John 4.19). This is the NT doctrine of baptismal justification: I am not justified by my faith: I believe because I have been justified. This doctrine, which is the heart of the apostolic faith, is perfectly symbolized in the baptism of infants: the important thing that happens in baptism is what God does, not what we do. Our faith is not the condition of our baptism but the response to it, made possible by our having already received the Holy Spirit (cf. I Cor. 12.3). Of course, there should be some form of public profession of belief on the part of those who were baptized in infancy, when they have reached 'years of discretion' and are able to assent personally in faith to the promises made on their behalf by their sponsors in baptism;[1] this, indeed, should be regarded as a part of the act of Christian initiation itself, however many years

[1] This is the standpoint of the BCP of 1662. In baptism a child is made 'a member of Christ, a child of God, and an inheritor of the Kingdom of Heaven'. Cf. G. W. H. Lampe, *The Seal of the Spirit*, 315: 'The concept of sealing is absent from the Anglican Confirmation service. The seal of the Spirit is implicitly associated with baptism, and the outward seal of the cross, the mark, as Aquinas expressed it, of the Christian soldier, has already been received at baptism. The only seal in our Confirmation rite is the candidate's ratification of his baptismal profession and the sealing to him of God's promises. That the bishop should be its minister is obviously highly fitting and appropriate, although, as the history of Confirmation compels us to believe, it is in no way essential.'

may have separated the first part of the action from its completion. And when we are asked about the standing with God of one who was baptized in infancy, but never came to personal faith, we will reply that we do not know; we will not guess at what the NT does not tell us. We may confidently leave the fate of all, baptized or unbaptized, in the hands of that God for the sake of whose family our Lord Jesus Christ was contented to be betrayed, and given up into the hands of wicked men, and to suffer death upon the cross. The whole medieval mumbo-jumbo of hell and purgatory and limbo must go the way of astrology and alchemy and the rest of the pre-scientific gropings of self-tortured mankind. Christ's death upon the cross avails for all; it was the baptism of the *whole* human race; Christ is the Saviour, not only of the Church, but of *the world*. In some way unrevealed to us his death avails for men without faith, as in another way, which has been revealed to us, it avails for those who respond in faith. But Christ's death upon the cross, the baptism of the human race, was not the result of men's believing. It created our faith; it did not result from it. So, too, the baptism of the individual, by which he appropriates to himself the benefits of Christ's death and resurrection, theologically precedes the awakening of faith and is not the consequence of it. Baptism is the sacrament and effective symbol of justification and, especially at the baptism of infants, it powerfully proclaims the antecedent love of God by whose prevenient grace all the virtues, including that of faith, are imparted through the gift of his Holy Spirit.

16

THE EUCHARISTIC THEOLOGY OF
THE NEW TESTAMENT

APART from the 'occasional' office of baptism the only form of corporate worship in the primitive church was the offering of the eucharistic oblation. The word εὐχαριστία is not directly applied to such worship in the NT.[1] The two names found in the NT are 'the breaking of the bread' (ἡ κλάσις τοῦ ἄρτου, Acts 2.42, 46; cf. 20.7; Luke 24.35) and 'the Lord's Supper' (κυριακὸν δεῖπνον, I Cor. 11.20). The NT tells us little about the actual celebration of the Eucharist. Had not certain abuses at Corinth elicited further instruction from St Paul (I Cor. 10.14-22; 11.17-34), we would have gathered almost nothing beyond the fact that in some places at least the breaking of bread took place on the first day of the week (Acts 20.7). A discreet use of the tradition and practice of the second century is therefore necessary, if we are to obtain any kind of picture of eucharistic worship in NT times; and hence there will always be room for differences of opinion amongst scholars. In the light of our present-day understanding of the Gospels certain questions, which only a few years ago were thought to be of utmost importance, now seem quite unreal, for instance the question whether Jesus instituted the Eucharist. Today it is widely held that the NT accounts[2] of the words and actions of Jesus at the Last Supper are not eye-witness reports of the scene in the upper room, although their content enshrines the apostolic tradition of what there took place; they are rather a quotation from the liturgical recitation of the events of the Last Supper, familiar to the writers through its stereotyped use Sunday by Sunday. Thus St Mark's tradition may well be based upon the liturgical recital of the days when the original apostles themselves presided at the eucharists of the churches.[3] A generation ago, the

---

[1] 'Saying amen to thy eucharist' in I Cor. 14.16 can hardly be a technical use for the Eucharist. The title 'Eucharist' is found as early as Ignatius (*Philad.* 4; *Smyrn.* 6; 8) and the *Didache* (9); Justin Martyr calls the consecrated elements 'eucharist' (*Apol.* 1.66).

[2] Matt. 26.26-30; Mark 14.22-25; Luke 22.15-19a (19b-20 is probably an interpolation, om. WH); I Cor. 11.23-26.

[3] J. Jeremias in *The Eucharistic Words of Jesus*, 106-35, argues that Mark 14.22-25 preserves a liturgical formula which had already long been fixed through its use in the cult; Mark's usual plain style gives place to a solemn, stylized speech; 14.22a

fact that only St Paul records Jesus as saying 'Do this' (I Cor. 11.24 and 25) was commonly held to cast grave doubt upon the intention of Jesus to establish the Eucharist. But today it is apparent that, since the Gospel accounts are primarily evidence of the first century rite rather than the reminiscences of the apostles as such, the doubt arose from a misunderstanding of what a Gospel is; and it may be dismissed on the principle that '*on ne recite pas une rubrique, on l'execute*'.[1]

THE WITNESS OF THE EUCHARIST TO HISTORY

The fact that from apostolic days the Church has met to break the bread and drink the cup is a continuing testimony to the truth of Jesus's interpretation of the significance of his own death as the means of ratifying a new covenant between God and man. The eucharistic action, the fact that it has been performed numberless times by every generation of Christians since the first, is more impressive testimony than any documentary evidence: 'as often as ye eat this bread and drink the cup, ye proclaim the Lord's death till he come' (I Cor. 11.26). St Paul means, of course, 'proclaim the Lord's *saving* death', for the eucharistic action implies an interpretation of the fact of Christ's death, the interpretation which, we have suggested, had been first perceived and taught by Jesus himself. No other interpretation of the eucharistic action in the Church is at all convincing, and we must not make the mistake of the older NT critics who thought that what was to be interpreted was a number of ancient documents, which could be more objectively judged if they were isolated from the paradosis of the Church. Actually the documents are themselves primarily witnesses to the existence of the paradosis and cultus of the earliest Christian communities and are misjudged if they are not seen in the light of the Church's faith and worship. The Eucharist, every time it is offered, bears witness not only to history, but also to an interpretation of history. It is the proclamation of the saving death of Christ. 'Every Eucharist proclaims the beginning of the time of God's salvation.'[2]

Thus, though the Eucharist proclaims an eschatological truth about history, it none the less witnesses to things which actually happened in real flesh-and-blood human history. This is what was meant by writers like St John or St Ignatius of Antioch when they emphasized, as against

appears almost a liturgical rubric (69). Similarly he holds that in I Cor. 11.23-25 Paul is handing on the formula in use at Antioch about A.D. 40 (131). But see Nigel Turner, 'The Style of St Mark's Eucharistic Words', *JTS*, NS, Vol. VIII, Pt. 1, April 1957, 108-11, where Jeremias's argument is criticized. Of course, the view which we have suggested concerning the NT accounts of the Last Supper is not dependent on the details of Jeremias's argument.

[1] P. Benoit, *Revue Biblique*, 48, 1939, 386; cited by J. Jeremias, *op. cit.*, 159

[2] J. Jeremias, *op. cit.*, 164.

all docetic tendencies, that Jesus Christ was come in the flesh (I John 4.2; II John 7). The Holy Spirit testifies in baptism and in the Eucharist that Jesus Christ has come in human history, not in pagan theophany or in docetic play-acting, but in real human life; the three witnesses, the Spirit, the water (of baptism) and the blood (of the Eucharist), testify to the historicity of the Gospel (I John 5.6-8). 'Be ye careful to observe one Eucharist', writes St Ignatius, 'for there is one flesh of our Lord Jesus Christ and one cup unto union in his blood; there is one altar, as there is one bishop . . .' (*Philad.*, 4); he goes on to speak of 'taking refuge in the Gospel as the flesh of Jesus' (*ibid.*, 5). Elsewhere he says that those who hold strange doctrine abstain from eucharist and prayer, 'because they allow not that the Eucharist is the flesh of our Saviour Jesus Christ, which suffered for our sins and which the Father of his goodness raised up' (*Smyrn.*, 6). That is to say, docetists, who do not believe that Christ is come in the flesh, do not understand the Eucharist, because in it testimony is given to the fact that ὁ λόγος σάρξ ἐγένετο (John 1.14), that the Gospel of the Incarnation concerns real historical happening.

In the simplest and most straightforward sense of the word the Eucharist is ἀνάμνησις ('remembrance') of Christ. It recalls the days in Galilee when, as head of the *haburah*[1] or fellowship of the disciples, Jesus broke bread for the group. It recalls the Lakeside meals when Jesus broke the bread for the hungry multitudes on those memorable 'guest-nights' of the *haburah*, when he spoke about the bread from heaven. Like the fish which appear in the frescoes representing the Eucharist in the catacombs in Rome, the breaking of the bread is a reminder of Galilee and of the original fellowship of the fishermen-disciples. The Eucharist is rooted in time and place; it is recognizable as the *Lord's* Supper because the same Jesus is host at the Church's Eucharist as was host in the *haburah* of the disciples: 'he was known of them in the breaking of the bread' (Luke 24.35). It is therefore for ever a witness—a memorial or ἀνάμνησις in another sense—that Jesus Christ is come in the flesh, in all the stark, unalterable actuality of history. It is a proclamation, above all, of the death of Jesus, of his body broken and his life outpoured, in all its grim and bloody reality— no play-acting, no appearance—at a determinate moment of history under Pontius Pilate. Small wonder that those who prefer a 'spiritual' gospel, today as in the days of St Ignatius, 'abstain from eucharist'.

[1] See W. O. E. Oesterley, *The Jewish Background of the Christian Liturgy*, 1925, 167; F. L. Cirlot, *The Early Eucharist*, 1939, 14f.; G. Dix, *The Shape of the Liturgy*, 1944, 50-4. We are putting forward no view about whether the Last Supper was a passover-meal or only a solemn *haburah* meal; in either case it certainly carried paschal significance for the early Church.

But if the Eucharist is a memorial of the passion of our Lord, it is also the abiding witness of his resurrection: only a Church which possessed a living experience of the Risen Christ in her midst could have celebrated week by week the memory of how on that dreadful night on which he was betrayed the Lord Jesus took bread and made eucharist. It was no sad, funerary commemoration which the apostles kept: 'breaking bread at home, they did take their food with gladness and singleness of heart, praising God' (Acts 2.46f.). This brings us to the essential meaning of the Eucharist as an action performed as Christ's ἀνάμνησις.

THE REAL PRESENCE OF CHRIST IN THE EUCHARIST

There is a great difference between modern psychological conceptions of memory and the biblical notion of 'remembering'. The phenomenon of memory constitutes one of the most baffling of all the problems of philosophy. *Ex hypothesi* a past event is something which no longer exists, for if it still existed it would not be past. Yet the historian does not believe that he is talking about things that do not exist; if he were, it would be just as true to say that Caesar murdered Brutus as to say that Brutus murdered Caesar. In what sense, then, does the past exist? What precisely happens when I remember something which happened some years ago? Most unreflective folk today would say that I have an 'idea' of that something in my mind, but that it is only an idea, not the thing itself. The Bible takes a more realistic view of memory.[1] When we remember something from the past, we do not merely entertain a pale idea of it; we actually make it present again, make it once more potent in our lives for good or evil. Thus, in the OT a man who is dead lives on in his sons (II Sam. 18.18), or wherever his 'name' is remembered. When his name is remembered no more, then he is dead indeed; this is why men of substance call lands after their own names (Ps. 49.11). The horror of Sheol is precisely that it is 'the land of forgetfulness' (Ps. 88.12) and that in Sheol the dead are no more remembered, even by Yahweh (Ps. 88.5). Non-existence means not being 'remembered' by God. This is especially the fate of the wicked (Ex. 17.14; Deut. 25.19; 32.26; Job 18.17; Pss. 34.16; 109.15, etc.); but the joy of the righteous is that they are remembered both by God and by men (Ps. 112.6; Prov. 10.7). The good works which men have done are made present and active for good when God remembers them; this is particularly true of the sacrifices which they have offered (Ps. 20.3). When God 'remembers' a sacrifice or a work of

[1] On the biblical view of memory, see J. Pedersen, *Israel*, I-II, ET, 1926, 245-59; relevant to our subject also is *Israel*, III-IV, ET, 1940, 401ff.

mercy he acts with favour towards the doer of it, as when in Acts 10.4 the angel says to the devout Cornelius, 'Thy prayers and thine alms are gone up for a memorial (εἰς μνημόσυνον) before God' (cf. Ps. 141.2, prayer as incense and as a sacrifice). When Jesus in Mark 14.9 says that the 'good work' wrought by the unnamed woman who anointed his body for burial would be spoken of εἰς μνημόσυνον αὐτῆς wherever the Gospel is preached, he means that the continual remembrance of her by the Church would avail like a memorial-sacrifice and be effective for her in the day of judgment. God's remembrance of someone is always active for mercy or for judgment; it is never a neutral memory, like a mere idea in the mind. To remember someone, in biblical language, means to be gracious unto him (cf. Luke 23.42, 'Jesus, remember me when thou comest in thy Kingdom'; Ps. 74.2; etc.), unless it is his misdeeds which are remembered, in which case the consequences are dire (e.g. Pss. 25.7; 79.8, etc.). Indeed, Jeremias says that εἰς ἀνάμνησιν and εἰς μνημόσυνον, like their Aramaic equivalents, normally in LXX and in pre-Christian Judaism refer to God's remembering in this sense, and not to man's; hence he concludes that εἰς τὴν ἐμὴν ἀνάμνησιν in I Cor. 11.24f. and Luke 22.19 must mean that, when the community comes together for the breaking of bread, God is being besought to 'remember his Messiah', just as in an old Passover prayer which beseeches God for 'the remembrance of the Messiah'.[1] God is, as it were, being 'memorialized' to remember his Messiah by bringing about his Kingdom in the parousia; the Eucharist, we may say, is a kind of dramatization of the prayer, 'Thy Kingdom come'.

This interpretation of εἰς τὴν ἐμὴν ἀνάμνησιν is doubtless correct as far as it goes; and it is important. The eucharistic ἀνάμνησις is primarily a divine and not a human remembering. But its meaning is by no means exhausted here; as with so many biblical words and phrases, the obvious presence of one particular meaning must not be taken to exclude other shades of meaning, *nuances* and overtones. What does the fact of the divine ἀνάμνησις of the Paschal sacrifice of Christ mean for our eucharists? What does it mean that we who today receive the created things of bread and wine in remembrance of Christ's death and passion are made partakers of his most blessed body and blood? The biblical answer to such a question arises from the fact that when we remember the past, we make it present. It is no longer the dead-and-gone

---

[1] Jeremias, *op. cit.*, 161-3. This conclusion is criticized by Douglas Jones in his art. '*Anamnesis* in the LXX' in *JTS*, NS, Vol. VI, Pt. 2, October 1955, 183-91, where a valuable account of the evidence will be found. It is perhaps a pity that the author does not entertain the possibility that a phrase such as εἰς τὴν ἐμὴν ἀνάμνησιν may contain not merely one meaning but several meanings and several reminiscences and overtones of different biblical themes and passages.

past, but it is the past which is even now present again and active for our salvation. This is still more true, of course, when God remembers something. In God's presence, or in the presence of his holy representative, all our past sins come crowding into the present to our hurt. Thus, as A. G. Hebert has emphasized in this connection,[1] the widow of Zarephath says to Elijah, 'Art thou come hither to bring my sin to remembrance and to slay my son?' (I Kings 17.18), although the prophet has said no word to her about her sins. 'She means that the coming of the holy man has set in motion spiritual forces, so that the guilt of the sins, which would otherwise have lain dormant (covered, as it were, in layers of dust), now awakes to activity and pounces on the life of her child.' Another instance is found in Num. 5.11-31, where the law of trial by ordeal is set forth as it was to be applied to a suspected adulteress; here the oblation that is offered, the meal offering, is described as 'a meal offering of memorial, bringing iniquity to remembrance' (5.15). Probably all sacrifices were 'memorials' in this sense and not only the '*azkarah*, the sacrificial memorial (meal offering) which was τὸ μνημόσυνον and θυσία and ὀσμὴ εὐωδίας τῷ Κυρίῳ (Lev. 2.2). They brought past sins into the present and rendered them harmless. At any rate, as Fr Hebert suggests, when Jesus is recorded as saying 'Do this in ἀνάμνησις of me', what is intended is a concrete remembering, not of sins, but of the once-for-all sacrifice of the Lamb of God, the Christian πάσχα, which takes away the sins of the world. When the congregation met to make eucharist in ἀνάμνησις of the crucified Lord, the Risen Christ, in the power of his accepted sacrifice, would be present in the midst in his living reality. Where a handful of Christians, however few, met for eucharist, there was Christ in the midst of them (Matt. 18.20); the Eucharist in the Church is the abiding witness to Christ's resurrection, for in it his real presence in his Church is made known (Luke 24.35). In every eucharist of the local congregation are made present again the Lakeside meals and the ḥaburah meetings of Jesus and his apostles, the Maundy scene in the Upper Room, as well as Golgotha and the Garden of Resurrection: the whole Gospel, in fact, is represented, is made present, in all its saving power. Christ's once-for-all full, perfect and sufficient sacrifice and oblation is held in perpetual ἀνάμνησις and becomes newly present. While it would be unjustifiable to build a doctrine of the eucharistic sacrifice solely upon the use of the word ἀνάμνησις in I Cor. 11.24f. and Luke 22.19, we cannot overlook the close connection that exists between μνημόσυνον or ἀνάμνησις and sacrifice in the OT (e.g. Lev. 24.7; Num. 10.10; cf. Heb. 10.3) and it is important to notice the implication of the fact that Christ is described

[1] See his art. 'Memory' in *TWBB*, 142f.

as our passover-lamb which has been sacrificed (I Cor. 5.7), for this brings out another very clear implication of the Eucharist as ἀνάμνησις.

Unquestionably the primary meaning of εἰς τὴν ἐμὴν ἀνάμνησιν is to be found in the conception of the Eucharist as the Christian pass-over-feast. The passover of the Jews was above all things a memorial of the deliverance of Israel from Egypt at the exodus: 'This day shall be unto you for a memorial (LXX, μνημόσυνον), and ye shall keep it a feast (ἑορτή) to Yahweh; throughout your generations ye shall keep it a feast by an ordinance for ever' (Ex. 12.14). The next verse goes on to speak of the feast of Unleavened Bread, which is later said also to be for a memorial of 'what Yahweh did for me when I came forth out of Egypt' (Ex. 13.8f.). It is clear, therefore, what St Paul has in mind when he writes, 'Purge out the old leaven, that ye may be a new lump, even as ye are unleavened. For our πάσχα also has been sacrificed, namely Christ: wherefore let us keep the feast (ἑορτάζωμεν), not with old leaven . . .' It must follow that, when in I Cor. 11.24f. St Paul records Jesus as bidding his disciples to 'do this' as his ἀνάμνησις, he under-stands Jesus to be instituting a new passover-memorial which com-memorates the deliverance of the new Israel from sin and death.[1] The 'this' which Jesus commanded in the words τοῦτο ποιεῖτε must be understood to mean the whole act of eucharistic worship, including the recital of what the Lord Jesus had done and said on the night on which he was betrayed: it must include the *taking* of bread and of wine, the *blessing* (or giving of thanks), the *breaking* of the bread and the *giving* of these elements to be eaten and drunk—the fourfold 'shape' of the liturgy. The symbolism is quite straightforward. The bread of the Christian passover is, like the unleavened bread of the Jews, itself a σημεῖον and μνημόσυνον of what God has done for us (Ex. 13.8f.); it is also the paschal lamb of the Christian passover-feast, the body or σάρξ of Jesus, who is himself the Lamb of God which takes away the sins of the world.[2] But the Lamb is slain: the blood is already separated from the body. The wine is already mixed in a cup by itself, and there is no outpouring of it during the eucharistic action; the wine is already ἐκχυνόμενον (cf. Mark 14.24), for the enacted parable of the Last Supper proleptically sets forth the redemptive death of Christ. The Eucharist is not a re-enactment of his dying, but a parable of the significance of his death. The symbolism of the bread and the wine come directly

---

[1] In the LXX ποιεῖν is used in the sense of 'to sacrifice' at least sixty times (e.g. Ex. 29.38-41; and cf. perhaps Luke 2.27); but it would be rash to translate τοῦτο ποιεῖτε as 'sacrifice this'. Nevertheless there remains in the expression an echo of biblical sacrificial language. Probably Matt. 26.18 (ποιῶ τὸ πάσχα) is the nearest parallel.

[2] See *supra*, 230f.

from the Jewish passover ceremony, whether the Last Supper itself was or was not a passover meal; the important point to notice is that, as it occurred about passover-time, the early Church interpreted its meaning in terms of OT passover-theology. Jesus had died at passover-time; what could be more significant to a Jewish Christian in the early days of the Church? There is no reason whatever to doubt that Jesus himself had taught this interpretation of his own death or indeed that he had deliberately gone to Jerusalem for the feast of the Passover because he had come to think of himself as 'the Lamb' which God had provided for sacrifice. Hence when he said 'This is my body', 'This is my blood', he meant: 'I am the Lamb of God, which taketh away the sins of the world.' But we must be on our guard against interpreting either the Last Supper or the Christian Eucharist exclusively in terms of the Passover; we have already seen that the passover lamb is identified with the expiatory sacrifices, and that the cup is interpreted in terms of the 'blood of sprinkling' of Ex. 24.8 by which Moses ratified the covenant of Sinai, and also in terms of the making of the new covenant of Jer. 31.31.[1] Here again we have an obvious illustration of how fatal for our understanding of the Scriptures is the assumption that any particular passage will have only one interpretation. Jesus regarded his death as the sacrifice by which a new and better covenant was ratified between God and a new Israel, and this is the truth he taught to his disciples when on the night on which he was betrayed he took bread and wine.

One further circumstance in particular reinforces the view that we ought not to give the Eucharist in the early Church an exclusively paschal interpretation. If the apostolic Church had thought of the breaking of the bread as the Christian Passover and as nothing else, the Eucharist would have been observed annually instead of weekly (cf. Acts 20.7), at the season of the paschal moon. In fact, it seems probable that the observance of a special Easter festival did not begin in the Church until after NT times, whereas the weekly 'Easter', the commemoration of the Lord's resurrection on the first day of the week, was observed from the days of the apostles themselves. This can be only because the Eucharist in the Church took the place of *all* the Jewish sacrifices and feasts, and not only the place of the Passover and Unleavened Bread. The Eucharist was in fact the celebration of the New Year, of creation and harvest, of the Day of Atonement and of every sacred occasion; and it was each of these every Lord's day. In the Eucharist every partial insight of the OT into the character of the worship that is due to the God of our creation, preservation, redemption and ultimate triumph, is perfected and fulfilled.

[1] See *supra*, 225-32.

THE ESCHATOLOGICAL CHARACTER OF THE EUCHARIST

The Eucharist, as we have noted, was not only the memorial of an historical deliverance; it was also, and perhaps primarily, a looking forward to the forthcoming deliverance of the parousia. It makes not only the past but also the future a present reality. That is to say, it is not a mere looking forward to something which shall be, any more than it is a mere looking back to events of long ago. It is the holding of past and future in the 'now' of faith. It is an anticipation, an ἀρραβών in the sense in which the Holy Spirit is an ἀρραβών, of that which shall be. The Eucharist is, of course, closely connected with the activity of the Holy Spirit, although there are no texts in the NT which make the connection clear; perhaps John 6.63 in its context is the most relevant: 'It is the Spirit that quickeneth; the flesh profiteth nothing; the words that I have spoken unto you are spirit (i.e. the vehicles of the communication of the Spirit) and are life.' The essential character of the Spirit is to give life, the life of the Age to Come. The Spirit is the agent of the new birth (John 3.5f., 8) and of the new creation (John 20.22; cf. Ezek. 37.1-14; Gen. 1.2). In the Eucharist, St John is saying, the life-giving Spirit of Christ is received; that is why the Eucharist is necessary to salvation: 'Except ye eat the flesh of the Son of Man and drink his blood, ye have not life in yourselves. He that eateth my flesh and drinketh my blood hath the life of the Age to Come, and I will raise him up at the last day. For my flesh is true meat and my blood is true drink. He that eateth my flesh and drinketh my blood abideth in me, and I in him' (John 6.53-56). But St John does not wish to be misunderstood, and he is aware that many would-be disciples, doubtless the 'spiritualizers' of the higher paganism, were repelled by the materialistic crudity of the Eucharist (John 6.60f.). He reassures them: the Eucharist is not magic. It is not σάρξ itself which avails, but Spirit. The whole completed work of Christ, including the ascension and gift of the Spirit, must be taken into account (6.62). Jesus is the bearer of the Spirit, and it is thus that he comes to us in the Eucharist (cf. John 14.18 in its context): the Eucharist is not cannibalism, the eating of literal flesh and blood, a notion which would have been utterly intolerable to any Jew.[1] It is the receiving of the life-giving Spirit of the Risen Christ, so that the closest personal union and communion exists between the worshipper and Christ: 'He that eateth my flesh and drinketh my blood abideth in me and I in him' (6.56). The worshipper has received the Spirit, the life-giver: 'He that eateth me, he also shall live because of me' (6.57). The life-giving Spirit is the Spirit of Christ himself. It is the gift of Christ's own life through

[1] See Jeremias, *The Eucharistic Words of Jesus*, 145, for references.

personal union with Christ that we receive in the Eucharist. It is here and now in this present age the ἀρραβών of that perfect union with Christ and God which will be the reward of the faithful at the parousia: 'I will raise him up at the last day' (6.54). 'The flesh of Jesus is (for John, *ex hypothesi*) the vehicle of the Spirit and therefore gives life.'[1] The Eucharist is supremely the means by which those who have received the Spirit in their baptism are renewed in the Spirit on their pilgrimage through this world. Just as those who under the old dispensation were baptized into Moses in the Red Sea and all ate the same spiritual meat and drank the same spiritual drink, which was Christ, so now in the new dispensation those who are baptized in one Spirit into one body of Christ also participate in the heavenly refreshment which Christ provides (I Cor. 10.1-4; 12.13). The sacraments of the old order have given place to those of the Age of the Spirit; they typified the Christian sacraments, but were only shadows of that which was to come: 'Your fathers did eat manna in the wilderness, and they died. This is the bread which cometh down out of heaven, that a man may eat thereof and not die. I am the living bread, which came down out of heaven: if any man eat of this bread he shall live for ever: yea and the bread which I will give is my flesh, for the life of the world' (John 6.49-51). The dispensation of 'the flesh' has given place to the Age of the Spirit. Hence it is not surprising that only those who were baptized were allowed to be present at the Church's eucharists; the catechumens were dismissed when the Synaxis, or synagogue-type of introduction to the Eucharist proper, was over.[2] For this there was, of course, precedent in the Jewish passover, since no uncircumcised person was allowed to partake of it (Ex. 12.48).[3] The Eucharist—so the NT implies rather than states—is the means whereby those who once received the Spirit in baptism are constantly renewed in the Spirit until their life's end.[4]

The Eucharist, then, was the anticipation in this age of the final

---

[1] C. K. Barrett, *GSJ*, 251.   [2] G. Dix, *Shape of the Liturgy*, 41.

[3] In the Qumran community novices were not admitted to the fellowship meal until after their second year, according to the *Manual of Discipline* (Gaster, *SDSS*, 61).

[4] G. Dix (*op. cit.*, 266f.) notes that in both East and West the Church in post-NT times developed the view that the Holy Spirit was received at the Eucharist. 'There is a whole class of liturgical and patristic passages from the first four centuries or so . . . which do speak precisely as though what was received in Holy Communion was accession of spirit.' One of the examples which he cites from the East is the *Liturgy of St James*: 'He took the cup . . . and gave thanks and hallowed and blessed it and filled it with the Holy Spirit and gave . . .' For early Western usage he cites the petition from the *Apostolic Tradition* of St Hippolytus: 'that thou wouldest grant to all who partake to be made one, that they may be filled with Holy Spirit.' In the East there developed the practice of *epiclesis* or Invocation of the Holy Spirit upon the elements of bread and wine (as upon the water of baptism), as distinct from the invocation of the Spirit upon the communicants. On the whole subject see Dix, *op. cit.*, esp. 281-302; also J. E. L. Oulton, *Holy Communion and Holy Spirit*, 1951, esp. Chap. VII.

blessedness of the Age to Come. The eucharistic bread is even now the manna which the rabbinic doctrine declared would be given from heaven to the true Israel in the days of the Messiah.[1] It is, even now, that covenanted eating and drinking at the Lord's table in his Kingdom which Jesus had appointed to his apostles (Luke 22.29f.). Jesus had himself made use of the common Jewish imagery of the Messianic banquet, at which the faithful would sit down with Abraham, Isaac and Jacob in the Kingdom of heaven (Matt. 8.11; Luke 13.28f.); and the Eucharist is the banquet of the Messiah in which even now the elect take part. In St Mark's account of the Last Supper, immediately after the words over the cup about the blood of the covenant, Jesus continues: 'Verily I say unto you, I will no more drink of the fruit of the vine, until that day when I drink it new ($\kappa\alpha\iota\nu\acute{o}\nu$) in the Kingdom of God' (Mark 14.25). Another version of the saying is placed by St Luke before the supper: 'With desire I have desired (a Semitism for 'I have earnestly longed') to eat this passover with you before I suffer; for I say unto you, I will not eat it until it be fulfilled in the Kingdom of God' (Luke 22.15f.). These words could have been understood in the Church for which St Mark and St Luke were writing only in one way: Jesus is declaring that this is the last fellowship meal of which he would partake with his disciples before his death, but that he would nevertheless be present when the apostles met to drink the new ($\kappa\alpha\iota\nu\acute{o}s$) wine of the Messianic Age in their fellowship meals in the future: that is to say, Christ, the host at the Messianic banquet in the Kingdom of God, was also the host at the Church's Eucharist, in which the heavenly bread and the new wine of the Age to Come were already received by the faithful, and in which the passover was 'fulfilled'.

Thus, though the eucharists of the Church were celebrated in somebody's drawing-room (Acts 2.46; I Cor. 16.19; Col. 4.15; Philemon 2), they were nevertheless a participation in the worship which is for ever offered at the golden altar that stands before the throne of God in heaven, where the angels with their golden censers add their incense to the prayers of all the saints (Rev. 8.3; cf. 6.9; 9.13). Of course, the seer is here using pictorial language, but only the poet's tongue can speak of the things which eye hath not seen nor ear heard. It may be that St John draws his imagery from the worship of the local congregations in which he has participated on the Lord's day, for every mystic uses language drawn from his familiar earthly surroundings, since he has no other language. Thus, St Bernard and the medieval hymn-writers drew their pictures of heaven, 'Jerusalem the golden', from the familiar

---

[1] Cf. the 'hidden manna' of Rev. 2.17 and R. H. Charles's note *ad loc.* (ICC). See also *supra*, 101.

scenes of the Church's worship here below—a great abbey, perhaps, on a feast day, decked with colourful banners, illuminated with scores of candles and 'conjubilant with song'. Nevertheless it would be somewhat precarious to reconstruct the eucharistic worship of the apostolic Church from St John's word-pictures: the twenty-four elders round the throne (the bishop's *cathedra*), the angelic acolytes with their censers, the ministrants (deacons) with their robes of white, and so on. (Many of the details of the seer's imagery are clearly drawn from the worship of the Temple, not as he has known it in Jerusalem before A.D. 70, but as he has read about it in the OT.) But it is still true that the worship in which St John took part in the Church on earth is a counterpart and a real analogy of the worship of 'angels and archangels and of all the company of heaven', and that in our worship on earth we are at one with angels, humans and 'beasts'—with the supernatural, the human and the elemental forces—who praise the name of him that sitteth upon the throne (Rev. 5.6-14; 14.1-5). The saints who 'even now' sing a new song before the throne (14.3) are but the 'firstfruits ($\dot{\alpha}\pi\alpha\rho\chi\dot{\eta}$) unto God and unto the Lamb' of that great Church which shall be gathered in heaven. The Church's Eucharist is at once the eschatological anticipation of the worship of heaven, and also a participation in it. The 'even now' and the 'not yet' of the biblical eschatology are applicable to the Church's worship, as they are to every other form of her existence in this age. Time is transcended altogether, not by some philosophical analysis of its nature, but by the eschatology of faith, which makes the past and the future contemporary. The worshipper at the Eucharist is himself present in the Upper Room, on Golgotha, in the Garden of Resurrection, at the Golden Altar before the heavenly Throne. The eucharistic action shews forth the Lord's death, but also his future coming (I Cor. 11.26); the Eucharist belongs wholly to the age between the resurrection of Christ and his parousia, pointing backwards to the one and forwards to the other. It is the viaticum of the Christian pilgrim, the 'iron ration' of the soldier of Christ, as he passes through this world; it will sustain him until he comes at length to that city in which there is no temple (Rev. 21.22) and where sacraments are no more.

Thus, while the Eucharist was on the one hand the memorial of an historical deliverance, it was also on the other hand the anticipation of the future deliverance of the parousia and the inauguration of the new creation. This double reference, whereby the historical becomes the sign or type of that which is to come, is peculiarly biblical; a parallel double reference may be discerned within the OT itself in its conception of the exodus from Egypt as the sign and type of a deliverance that still lay in the future. Devout Jews, who in the days of our

Lord fervently kept the passover, were not, of course, thinking only or perhaps even primarily of the historical deliverance in the far-away times of Moses; they were earnestly awaiting and praying for 'the consolation of Israel' (Luke 2.25), the expected great new deliverance both from foreign oppression and from national infidelity, of which the historical deliverance at the Red Sea was the promise and pledge. The main scriptural foundation of this eschatological point of view was to be found in the Book of Isaiah (or what we call Deutero-Isaiah). As we have already seen, the original outline of the NT re-interpretation of OT theology is to be found in (Deutero-) Isaiah,[1] who thinks of the redemption to be wrought by the Servant of the Lord as a kind of second deliverance and exodus from Egypt, in which the Servant is a new Moses who shall establish a new covenant (Isa. 42.6; 49.8; cf. 59.20f.; etc.). To devout Jews, searching the Scriptures and looking for the fulfilment of the Isaianic prophecies, the passover must have been indeed an ἀνάμνησις, a memorial, in the sense of a solemn holding up before the Lord of the pledge which he himself had given when he instituted the passover in Egypt long ago (Ex. 12.1-28). In just the same profoundly eschatological sense the Christian Eucharist was an ἀνάμνησις, a solemn holding up before the Lord of the pledge that was given by Christ when he instituted the Eucharist on the night on which he was betrayed. The Eucharist, given to us by Christ himself, is thus 'a perpetual memory (ἀνάμνησις) of that his precious death, until his coming again'.[2] It is a 'memory', 'memorial' or 'remembering' in the biblical, paradoxical sense of memory, whereby we can 'remember' things which are to come because their essential content is already given in what has been. In this sense the eucharistic remembrance of Christ's death and passion may properly be said to be eschatological.

THE EUCHARISTIC FELLOWSHIP

The title 'Holy Communion' probably arises from I Cor. 10.16f.: 'The cup of blessing which we bless, is it not a communion (κοινωνία, RV mg. 'participation in') of the blood of Christ? The bread (τὸν ἄρτον, more correctly with RV mg., 'the loaf') which we break, is it not a κοινωνία of the body of Christ? seeing that we who are many are εἷς ἄρτος, ἓν σῶμα: for we all partake (μετέχομεν) from the one loaf.' Whatever else it may be, participation in the Eucharist implies a corporate sharing of a common salvation. The passage suggests that the one loaf and common cup of the Eucharist, being communion in the body and blood—in the person and life—of Christ, are the means of sustaining unity and not merely the expression of the unity which

---

[1] *Supra*, 79-83.   [2] BCP, Prayer of Consecration in the Holy Communion.

Christians have already obtained through baptism in Holy Spirit (I Cor. 12.12f.). St Paul is perhaps thinking here (as is entirely natural in view of the practical purpose of his epistle) of the fellowship of Christians with one another in Christ through the Eucharist, whereas St John in his eucharistic teaching (John 6.26-65) is thinking primarily of the communion of the believers with God (cf. esp. 6.56). But for St Paul and St John, as for the whole Church, both aspects of communion are inseparable. The Eucharist is given to the Church to be the sacrament of unity; it is that by which the Church becomes what it is, namely, one body in Christ. The Johannine symbolism of the true vine is relevant here: the blood of the vine sustains the branches which 'abide' in it (John 15.1-6). Since the Eucharist is the divinely appointed means of communion with God and with our fellow-members in the body of Christ, it is the indispensable means of salvation (John 6.53; 15.4f.). It is constitutive of the Christian community itself, and where there is no Eucharist there is no Church of Christ.

When the Word of God became incarnate, he assumed our humanity so completely that it has always been possible for men to imagine that he is merely one of themselves and nothing more (cf. Mark 6.3). It is wholly in keeping with the religion of Incarnation that its worship should gather up into itself, and express in final form, the inarticulate and half-comprehending religious aspirations of all men everywhere. It is only to be expected that those who have not understood the uniqueness of Christ should think of Christianity as one 'religion' amongst many, that they should include it as one element in the subject matter of 'comparative religion' or *religionsgeschichtliche* studies, and that they should subsume the Eucharist under the general class of pagan and Jewish sacrificial fellowship meals.[1] The NT writers, however, do not think of the Christian 'way' as 'religion' at all—or, if they were to think of it in terms of religion, they would say that it was the religion to end all religion.[2] The faith of Christ is not presented as one—even the

[1] For a balanced comparison and contrast of the Christian Eucharist with the sacred meals of the Essenes see the essay 'The Lord's Supper and the Communal Meal at Qumran' by K. G. Kuhn in Stendahl, *SNT*, 65-93. Jewish parallels to the Eucharist, though still theologically remote, are closer than those of Hellenistic sacramentalism.

[2] Like a number of other words which also have figured prominently in theological discussion (e.g. 'providence', 'dispensation', 'inspiration') the word 'religion' is hardly a biblical word at all. It does not occur in EVV of the OT. In James 1.26f., where θρησκεία is used, the author is echoing the old prophetic teaching that good works are the only form of *cultus* or religious observance that God desires; and in Acts 26.5 St Paul asserts that he had lived a Pharisee, 'after the strictest sect of our θρησκεία'. Elsewhere he uses the word Ἰουδαϊσμός of the Jewish religion (Gal. 1.13f.). The only other use of θρησκεία in the NT is Col. 2.18, which refers to some cult of angel-worship at Colossae. The word δεισιδαιμονία ('fear of the gods'), a general word for religion or superstition (cf. Acts 25.19; also 17.22), is not applied by Christians to either Jewish or Christian faith. See arts. 'Religion', 'Superstition', in *TWBB*, 188 and 253.

highest—in the series of the 'religions of the world', but as the unique and final truth with which no 'other gospel' may be compared (Gal. 1.6-9). The sacraments of the Gospel are not put forward as illustrations of general religious truths which are also perceived, though perhaps less clearly, in other religions: they are the unique and necessary saving acts of Christ in his Church, 'the works which none other did' (John 15.24). Just as the Lord Jesus looked like other men and the words which he used were words which other men, including other religious teachers, used, so also baptism and the Eucharist look from the outside like the lustrations and the fellowship meals of other religions. If the *Religions-geschichte* school had been able to point to the sacred banquet of a mystery religion which was a hundred times more closely parallel to the eucharists of the early Church than anything which it has in fact discovered, there would still be an infinite distinction between it and the Church's Eucharist. If fresh evidence from the Dead Sea were to appear, shewing some real parallel between the washings of the Jewish sects and Christian baptism, the difference between the two actions would still be that it is the latter which is the saving activity of God in the world.

This fundamental difference between the Christian sacraments and all Jewish or pagan θρησκεία was understood by St Paul and the apostolic Church perfectly well. This is why St Paul can speak so confidently to his pagan converts in the language of their old religion; they will recognize that the difference between the Lord's Supper and the fellowship meals of the pagan mystery religions is the difference between communion with Christ and communion with demons. Look, he says to them (I Cor. 10.18), at the sacrifices of the Jews who are still living under their old Torah: they believe—and St Paul does not say they are wrong—that they have fellowship with (the God of) the altar of sacrifice. Here St Paul states succinctly the view which all down the ages has underlain the sacred meals at the altars both of Jews and of pagans, where the worshippers believe that they have communion with their God. He goes on to consider the case of the sacrifices of the Gentiles. They do not sacrifice to God at all, but to the demons; and to participate in the idolatrous sacrificial meals of the Gentiles means entering into communion with the demons of their altars (10.19f.). A Christian cannot join the pagan banquets, because one cannot enjoy communion with demons and with Christ at the same time: 'ye cannot drink the cup of the Lord and the cup of demons; ye cannot partake of the table of the Lord and of the table of demons' (10.21). The pagan 'mysteries' belong to that underworld of 'religion' which Christ has abolished.

The NT nowhere calls the Lord's table (τράπεζα Κυρίου, I Cor. 10.21; cf. Luke 22.30) an altar; this verse is the nearest that it comes to doing so. The one, true and sufficient sacrifice for the sins of the whole world was made once for all on Calvary; it is not repeated, it is not even re-enacted, on the Lord's table at the Eucharist. If the Lord's table is by ancient Christian custom called an altar, that is because it is the place where the ἀνάμνησις of Christ's sacrifice is made, and also because it is the place to which Christians, who now through Christ have access with their oblations to the holy God, bring their offerings.[1] The very expression 'Lord's table', however, would have sacrificial associations for St Paul and his Corinthian disciples, since it had been a sacrificial expression in Greek religion for some hundreds of years; indeed, we need feel no surprise that a missionary faith should adopt words from the vocabulary of those whom it sought to convert and edify, while at the same time it radically altered their connotation. For at least two centuries before Christ the word εὐχαριστία had been used as a technical term in Greek religion to describe an elaborate act of thanksgiving culminating in a sacrifice (θυσία), though we have no clear evidence that it was adopted by the Church in NT times; similarly language about 'the table of the god' and τὸ ἱερὸν δεῖπνον was in widespread use in connection with Greek sacrifices long before the time of Christ.[2] Thus, the very phrases 'the table of the Lord' and 'the Lord's Supper' would from the beginning have borne sacrificial associations for the Church of the Gentiles; but this does not in the least imply that Pauline Christianity was just one mystery religion amongst a variety of similar mystery religions. St Paul probably thought of the sacrifices of Greek religion as a kind of debased parody of Jewish sacrifice; they achieved communion not with God but with the demons. The Jewish sacrifices were the true type and foreshadowing of the sacrifice of Christ and of its eucharistic ἀνάμνησις. A portion of the meal offering (*minḥah*), called 'azkarah (often rendered ἀνάμνησις), was burnt on the altar; the remainder was eaten by the priest. It is thus quite possible, but in no way demonstrable, that St Paul thought of the Eucharist as a kind of 'azkarah or ἀνάμνησις which was partaken of by the Christian priesthood, that is, the whole λαός assembled for eucharistic worship. At least, such an interpretation is rendered plausible by the statement which he regards as an axiom: 'they who eat the θυσίαι have communion with the (God of the) altar' (I Cor. 10.18). Those who eat the eucharistic bread and wine have communion with God through the sacrificial death of Christ.

If this interpretation be allowed, it does not, of course, imply that

[1] See *supra*, 297-301.

[2] See R. K. Yerkes, *Sacrifice in Greek and Roman Religions and Early Judaism*, New York, 1952, 108, 213f.

the Eucharist is a sacrifice newly offered, but rather that it is the ἀνάμνησις of Christ's 'one oblation of himself once offered', in which and through which we enjoy communion with God. The Eucharist is a kind of extended sacrificial meal, at which the worshippers are gathered for the banquet (δεῖπνον) round the Lord's table 'till he come'; the sacrificial oblation has been offered once for all by Christ on Calvary, and now the fellowship meal continues and the royal priesthood, the partakers of the altar, have communion in the body and blood of Christ with the one true God of the altar upon which Christ offered himself. A similar conception appears in Heb. 13.10: 'We have an altar, whereof they have no right to eat who serve the tabernacle' (i.e. the Jewish priesthood). Here there is no explicit reference to the Eucharist, but the Eucharist is not far removed from the thought of the passage. The writer goes on to speak of the sacrificial oblation of Christ (13.12) and of the identification of Christians with it (13.13). He then immediately speaks of the Christian sacrifices which may now be offered 'through him'—the sacrifice of praise (*perhaps* the Eucharist), good works and almsgiving; and he concludes, 'for with such sacrifices God is well pleased' (13.15f.). The conception of the Christian laity as a priesthood which in the Eucharist is fed from the altar of Christ's sacrifice on the sacred body and blood of the holy offering is the fundamental NT idea of 'communion'. This is the underlying meaning of St Paul's: 'The cup of blessing which we bless, is it not a communion of the blood of Christ? The loaf which we break, is it not a communion of the body of Christ?' (I Cor. 10.16). Under the old dispensation every sacrifice, whether a victim was slain or not, effected reconciliation with God (cf. Ezek. 45.15, 17) and thus established communion between God and his worshippers; in Christ's self-oblation every kind of sacrifice enjoined in the scriptures of the old covenant is fulfilled, and therefore through him is established perfect communion between God and his new people.

THE EUCHARISTIC SACRIFICE

In the Church of the Apostolic Fathers and of the Ante-Nicene and Nicene Fathers the Eucharist is everywhere spoken of as a sacrifice. Sacrificial phraseology is habitually employed in connection with it.[1] There are no exceptions to these statements, and it cannot be seriously denied that the Fathers of the ancient Church understood the apostolic tradition of the Eucharist in this way. The burden of proving that their unanimous interpretation of the scriptural evidence was wrong

[1] For the detailed evidence in support of the contention of this paragraph see Darwell Stone, *History of the Doctrine of the Holy Eucharist*, 1909, 42-54, 109-23; many citations are given in full.

rests upon those who would deny any form of doctrine of the Eucharistic sacrifice. If they were wrong, then we are faced with the quite incredible proposition that all the teachers of the Church from the time of St Clement of Rome or St Ignatius of Antioch were in error until the true doctrine was revealed to the Protestant reformers. If they were mistaken about such a matter as this, it would surely be impossible to believe that the Holy Spirit guides the Church into all truth; and indeed it would cast grave doubt upon the claim that there is such a thing as divine revelation at all. Scripture, tradition and reason are inseparably bound together in the formulation of Christian belief; if one is set aside, the others become incredible. That the Eucharist is the Christian sacrifice, that the oblations of the royal priesthood are offered in it, and that Christ himself is the high priest of our offerings—these doctrines are clearly taught in St Clement of Rome, St Ignatius of Antioch, St Justin Martyr, the *Didache*, St Irenaeus, Tertullian, St Clement of Alexandria, Origen, St Athanasius—where shall we stop? It is remarkable how frequently and how unanimously the words of Malachi are treated by patristic writers as a prophecy that has been fulfilled in the institution of the Eucharist: 'From the rising of the sun even unto the going down of the same my name shall be great among the Gentiles; and in every place incense and a pure oblation are offered' (Mal. 1.11). It is unlikely that the unanimous tradition of the post-apostolic Church has misrepresented the teaching of the apostles or that there could be any other valid interpretation of the somewhat scanty and obscure evidence of the NT concerning the apostolic doctrine of the Eucharist.

Nevertheless the doctrine of the eucharistic sacrifice has been widely repudiated in post-Reformation theology and is still today vigorously denied by some eminent Protestant theologians. Luther objected to the sacrifice of the Mass because it was conceived as an offering from man to God; he asserted that the sacrament is a gift from God to man, not an oblation of man to God.[1] The Lutheran reformers rejected the doctrine of the eucharistic oblation and abolished the offertory from the liturgy. Now it is possible for us to understand why the reformers adopted these extreme measures: they were resiling from late medieval

[1] Cf. Professor Ragnar Bring in *World Lutheranism Today* (Lund, 1950), 55: 'If there is the slightest thought that communion is an offering to God . . . then the Gospel is rendered null and void at once.' Cf. also Bishop Anders Nygren, *The Gospel of God*, ET, 1951, 67: 'The sacramental is what God does, the sacrificial that which we do. Luther's principal objection against the Roman service (of the Mass) is that it changes the sacrament into an act of ours. It changes God's sacrament into an offering which we make, a sacrifice which we offer. . . . These two, a gift which is received and a sacrificial offering which is given, are mutually exclusive'; also Nygren's *Agape and Eros*, 1953, 696f., where citations from Luther's works are made. See further, Alan Richardson, *The Biblical Doctrine of Work*, 67f.

corruptions of eucharistic doctrine and in particular from the utterly unbiblical (and unpatristic) notion of the Mass as a re-enactment or even a repetition of the sacrifice of Calvary, in which the priest offers afresh the body and blood of Christ as a sacrifice on behalf of the living and the dead.[1] Of course, in rejecting such corruptions the reformers were entirely right; but they were betrayed by their uncompromising biblicism into rejecting also that patristic tradition by which alone the Bible may be adequately interpreted in those matters in which its teaching is not entirely clear and full. Four hundred years after the Reformation we may perhaps today raise the question whether it is still necessary to maintain a denial which, though aimed at the recovery of the central truth of the Gospel, nevertheless obliterates an essential insight of the primitive Christian faith and liturgy.[2]

Let us then briefly attempt to outline the apostolic theology of the Eucharist as it was received and understood by the Fathers of the ancient Church. The patristic tradition is unanimous in stressing the truth that the Christian sacrifices are not carnal but spiritual (cf. Rom. 12.1; I Pet. 2.5; Heb. 10.1-10). The one true God (unlike the demons of the pagans) needs nothing; even the institution of sacrifice in the Law of Moses, it is often claimed, is only a concession to the hardness of heart of the Jews (cf. I Sam. 15.22; Pss. 40.6-8; 50.8-14; 51.16f.; Prov. 21.3; Isa. 1.11-13; Jer. 7.22f.; Micah 6.6-8; Heb. 10.6-9). On the other hand, though their sacrifices are not carnal, Christians must necessarily offer oblations to God, because they are a priesthood, and a priest is by definition one who offers sacrifice. The Christian priesthood is derived from the priesthood of Christ; because Christ is priest, therefore Christians are a priesthood. Because he has offered the one true sacrifice once for all, therefore the Church in the Eucharist makes memorial of the self-oblation of Christ, offering bread and wine sacramentally or symbolically as a sacrificial ἀνάμνησις of his saving death. The bread and wine are symbolic of the Christians' offering of themselves, their good works, their alms and material gifts, and of their praises. At the oblation of the bread and wine in the liturgy the Church offers itself, or rather, Christ offers himself, his body, to the Father. This is what is meant by saying that Christ is the high priest of the Church's offering; he offers to God his own obedience, his own body,

---

[1] The Anglican reformers rejected all such notions as 'blasphemous fables and dangerous deceits' (*The Thirty-nine Articles of Religion*, XXXI), and in 1552 Cranmer abolished the offertory (other than alms and money 'oblations'); the offertory of the bread and wine was restored at the revision of the BCP in 1662.

[2] The late Professor D. M. Baillie's fine essay on 'The Eucharistic Offering' in his posthumous work *The Theology of the Sacraments*, 1957, 108-24, betokens the new attitude now developing in Protestant thought as a direct result of participation in ecumenical discussion in recent years.

and in the Eucharist we offer ourselves to God as we are found 'in Christ'.[1] The Church's offering is the offering of the whole Christ; it is therefore the offering of Christians as found in Christ; that is why the bread and wine, the outward and visible tokens of the offering, 'are' the body and blood of Christ, the person and life of Christ, who is both offered to God and given to the Church in the Eucharist.

Thus, the Eucharist is not a sacrifice that the Church offers in addition to the sacrifice of Christ, or apart from the sacrifice of Christ; it is not a repetition or re-enactment of Christ's sacrifice, but a *memorial* of it, in the full biblical (and not the modern attenuated) sense of that word. It is the means by which the Church on earth takes part in Christ's offering in heaven, where even now he appears before the face of God for us ($\dot{v}\pi\grave{\epsilon}\rho$ $\dot{\eta}\mu\hat{\omega}\nu$) (Heb. 9.24) and where the smoke of incense with the prayers of the saints goes up before God from the golden censer of the angel who stands over the heavenly altar (Rev. 8.3f.). The language is, of course, metaphorical, but the patristic writers stress in many different ways the truth that the reality of which the Eucharist is the sacrament has its centre and meaning in heaven, and not upon the earth. The oblation of the Church on earth is made one with Christ's self-offering in heaven, and the worship of the Church below is a participation in the worship of him that sitteth upon the throne in heaven: 'with angels and archangels, and with all the company of heaven, we laud and magnify thy glorious name.' Already the Church is eschatologically present in heaven, and her eucharistic worship is a participation even now in the worship of heaven; even now we are present at the marriage-feast of the Lamb. The Fathers regard this as one of the chief differences between the worship of the old covenant and that of the new; it illustrates better than anything else could the infinite difference between the inadequacy of the sacrifices under the old covenant and the complete efficacy of the one true sacrifice of Christ. For under the old covenant, when the high priest entered into the holy of holies, he entered alone,

---

[1] Cf. the opening lines of a fine eucharistic hymn written by a patristic scholar who became Regius Professor of Ecclesiastical History at Oxford in 1868, William Bright:

'And now, O Father, mindful of the love
   That bought us, once for all, on Calvary's tree,
And having with us him who pleads above,
   We here present, we here spread forth to thee,
That only offering perfect in thine eyes,
   The one, true, pure, immortal sacrifice.

'Look, Father, look on his anointed face,
   And only look on us as found in him;
Look not on our misusings of thy grace,
   Our prayer so languid and our faith so dim:
For lo! between our sins and their reward
   We set the passion of thy Son, our Lord.'

and the people stood outside the veil; but now, under the new covenant, the worshippers no longer stand outside, for the veil has been done away, and Christ has brought us into the presence of God; he has taken us with him into heaven, for we are his manhood, his person, his ascended body. In his offering of himself, we are offered; the new and living way is consecrated for us, through the veil, and this way is his own flesh (Heb. 10.20). The way into the holy place, which was not manifested under the old covenant, is now manifested for us, so that we may henceforward acceptably offer gifts and sacrifices to the Lord (Heb. 9.8f.). Thus it is that the eucharistic offering is always one and the same offering; though there are many eucharists, there is only one offering. The truth is well taught by St Chrysostom: 'We ever offer the same person, not today one lamb and tomorrow another, but the same offering. Therefore the sacrifice is one. By this reasoning then, since the offering is made in many places, does it follow that there are many Christs? By no means. For Christ is everywhere one, complete here and complete there, one body. Just as when he is offered in many places he is one body and not many bodies, so also there is one sacrifice. Our high priest is he who offered the sacrifice which cleanses us. We offer also now that which was then offered, which cannot be exhausted. This is done for a memorial of that which was then done. "Do this," he said, "for my memorial." We do not offer another sacrifice, as did the high priests of old, but we ever offer the same; or rather we make memorial of the sacrifice.'[1]

In view of the patristic teaching it is not surprising that the offertory of the bread and wine held a prominent place in the liturgy of the ancient Church. Without an offering of bread and wine there can be no eucharist; unless someone, ceremonially or unceremoniously, places bread and wine upon the table, there will be no communion. If there is no human offering, there will be no divine gift. The miracle of the Eucharist is that the oblation which we offer becomes for us the bread which comes down from heaven. It is St John who is profoundly aware of this mystery and who confronts us with it. He knows that if there had been no oblation of the 'elements', of the bread and the fishes, there would have been no Desert Feedings by the Lakeside. He notes the significance of the fact that Jesus accepts the offerings, takes them and gives thanks over them. St John's account differs significantly from those of the Synoptists in that in John it is not the apostles who bring the offering of bread and fish but a lad ($\pi\alpha\iota\delta\acute{\alpha}\rho\iota\sigma\nu$) in the 'congregation' (John 6.9). The loaves and fishes are thus in St John's view 'the people's

---

[1] *In Heb. Hom.* 17.3; Darwell Stone, *History of the Doctrine of the Holy Eucharist*, 117.

offering', not the apostles'; and it was doubtless the liturgical practice, even as early as St John's own day, that the offertory should be presented not by the presbyter-bishops (*vice* the apostles) but by the deacon on behalf of the people. The word παιδάριον means either 'boy' or 'slave', 'waiter' (cf. French, *garçon*). May it not be that St John is deliberately emphasizing the importance of the people's offering in the sacrament of the Bread from Heaven? Has any more probable explanation of the appearance of the παιδάριον ever been suggested? Without the offering of the worshippers there is no divine gift. There is not any suggestion here that man's part in the work of salvation is of the same order as the divine work; such a notion would be utterly unbiblical and false. Yet men have a part to play; they are not passive recipients of salvation; they have a response to make, an offering to bring. Unlike the bread from heaven given by Moses, which fell as manna from the skies, the bread of the Eucharist is the product of the labour of men's hands.

The ancient Church did not lay much stress upon the fact that the elements in the sacrament of the Eucharist (unlike the water of baptism) are manufactured articles, the work of men's hands. This is doubtless because of the danger of a relapse into idolatry of converts from paganism, who would be only too familiar with the practice of laying upon heathen altars offerings of meat and drink for the sustenance of the gods.[1] But the idea of the offering of the fruits of creation was nevertheless prominent. The Eucharist in the ancient Church was a sacrament of creation as well as of redemption; the tradition of the Jewish *Berakah*, which begins with a thanksgiving to God for his bounty in the creation, was continued. 'The earliest references to the Eucharist outside the NT,' writes J. H. Srawley, 'present it in the light of a Christian "thank-offering" (*eucharistia*), in which the gifts of bread and wine, the first-fruits of the creatures, are offered in thanksgiving to God.'[2] In the early Church every Lord's Day was not only an Easter Sunday, but a Rogation Sunday and Harvest Festival as well. It is only because the primitive wholeness of life and worship has been lost that it has been necessary to institute particular days and seasons when God's blessings in the creation and providential ordering of the world are to be specially emphasized. As Dr Srawley notes, 'this association with the Eucharist of the offering of the gifts of bread and wine, as an act of thanksgiving for God's creation, was a fine Christian instinct, which brought the commemoration of Christ's redeeming activity into relation with his creative activity as the Word, and so

---

[1] Cf. Père de la Taille, *Mystery of Faith*, II, ET, 1950, 80.
[2] *Early History of the Liturgy*, 2nd ed., 1947, 214.

gathered up in one act of worship the whole conception of God's providence and dealing with men.'[1]

Not until the nineteenth and twentieth centuries did the Church perceive certain deeply significant aspects of the fact that the elements in the Eucharist are manufactured articles. One reason for the fact that this significance was hardly noted at all in the ancient Church would undoubtedly be the sinister connotation of the expression 'the work of men's hands' in the Bible (e.g. Deut. 4.28; II Kings 19.18; Ps. 115.4; Isa. 37.19; 44.10-20; Jer. 10.3-5; Acts 19.26), even though the expression is used in a quite different sense in relation to the eucharistic offering. More important still, it was probably not until a certain stage of social evolution had been reached, when men could see their daily work in relation to the needs of the community as a whole, that such an insight into the meaning of the eucharistic oblation could have been truly attained. Many of the social implications of the Christian gospel remained unperceived for centuries; for instance, many devout Christians in the eighteenth century saw nothing wrong in the institution of slavery as such. In every age God has more light to break forth from the Holy Scriptures, and there is no reason to suppose that we today have discovered all the truth which they contain. It is only in quite recent times that Christian congregations have become aware that in presenting the eucharistic oblation they are offering to God all the work of farm and factory, of home and school and office, and asking for his blessing upon it. They have become conscious of themselves as a royal priesthood in a new way, for it is not only their own work, but that of the whole workaday world around them, that they bring to God. Those who took part, however remotely, in the making of the bread and the wine—not only farmers and millers and bakers and vintners, but ship-builders and steel-workers and miners and office workers—have all in an important sense taken part in the Church's Eucharist, although it was the Church which presented their offering for them. The new priesthood reigns in Salem and presents the fruits of men's labours to the Lord: 'Melchizedek, King of Salem brought forth bread and wine, and he was priest of God Most High' (Gen. 14.18).[2]

Thus, the Eucharist gathers up and focusses in a single act of worship all the aspirations of men's natural religion as well as the whole meaning of the revelation in Jesus Christ through which it is fulfilled. It is the sacrament of our creation and preservation, as well as of our

---

[1] *Op. cit.*, 215. See also the quotations from St Irenaeus made by Darwell Stone, *op. cit.*, 47.

[2] See further on this whole theme Alan Richardson, *The Biblical Doctrine of Work*.

redemption and final salvation. The Eucharist satisfies the deep longing of the human heart to bring our costliest treasures to God in sacrifice by providing the Way by which sinners may come before his presence, cleansed and sanctified, with their acceptable offerings. In the Eucharist the three great themes of human religious aspiration in all times and cultures are finally and satisfyingly fulfilled: reconciliation, offering and communion. Hence it is only in the eucharistic worship of the Church that the theology of the New Testament can be truly understood; this understanding arises at the point at which theology and worship meet and are no longer two separate activities, but one action of believing adoration. When everything has been written and rewritten, it still remains true that the best introduction to the theology of the New Testament is participation in the continuing, living tradition of the Church's eucharistic worship week by week and day by day.

INDEX OF REFERENCES

OLD TESTAMENT

THE APOCRYPHA

SEPTUAGINT

THE PSEUDEPIGRAPHA OF THE OLD TESTAMENT

NEW TESTAMENT

THE APOSTOLIC FATHERS, ETC.

INDEX OF AUTHORS

INDEX OF SUBJECTS

(Principal references only are given)

INDEX OF HEBREW AND ARAMAIC WORDS

(All Hebrew and Aramaic words in this book are transliterated into English characters. As there is no satisfactory system of transliteration in general use, we have in certain instances adopted the form which will be more easily recognized or the form more familiar to English readers, even at the cost of a measure of consistency. For example, *ben adam* is more recognizable than *ben 'adham* and *shaliach* seems to be more widely used by English writers than *shaliah*. The student of Hebrew will not be misled if he notices certain inconsistencies.)

INDEX OF GREEK WORDS

(Only the principal words and references are given.)